In memory of my parents,
Mary and Michael McKenna

BUSINESS PSYCHOLOGY AND ORGANISATIONAL BEHAVIOUR

Eugene McKenna

 LAWRENCE ERLBAUM ASSOCIATES, PUBLISHERS
Hove (UK)   Hillsdale (USA)

Lawrence Erlbaum Associates Ltd., Publishers
27 Palmeira Mansions
Church Road
Hove
East Sussex, BN3 2FA
U.K.

British Library Cataloguing in Publication Data

McKenna, Eugene F.
    Business Psychology and Organisational Behaviour:
    Student's Handbook. - 2Rev.ed
    I. Title
    150.24658

ISBN 0-86377-304-4 (Hbk)
ISBN 0-86377-305-2 (Pbk)

Cartoons and cover illustration by Sanz
Cover design by Joyce Chester
Indices by Sue Ramsey
Printed and bound by BPC Wheatons Ltd., Exeter

Contents

Acknowledgements

This book owes its existence to a number of beneficial influences originating from many sources. In particular my thanks to the publisher and those mentioned below who reviewed the draft manuscript and made valuable comments and suggestions which were acted on.

Professor Chris Brotherton, University of Ulster
James Clinton, Regional Technical College, Dundalk
David McHugh, University of Central Lancashire

Preface

The main emphasis in the first edition of this book was the study of the individual and the group. In response to reviewers' comments on the first edition, together with the author's own ideas for improvement, not only have additions (for example, about intelligence and team-building) been made in the original chapters, but also new chapters have been added.

The latter are mostly concerned with various facets of organisation and human resource practices. The psychological perspective is still the primary focus, though some sociological explanations and contributions from organisation theory have been introduced, particularly in the last part of the book devoted to analysis at the organisational level.

The revised edition of *Psychology in Business* is retitled *Business Psychology and Organisational Behaviour: A Student's Handbook* in order to reflect the new format and contents, and it is the author's belief that the book is now better placed to serve the needs of business and management students at the undergraduate and postgraduate levels pursuing programmes of study in organisational psychology and organisational behaviour. The book, which requires no previous study of psychology, is likely to engage the interest of the reader and pays a lot of attention to a firm conceptual or theoretical base upon which actual or potential applications can be built. The original approach of providing numerous relevant examples from business and work organisations to illustrate the text is retained.

Introduction:
Perspectives and Enquiry

The study of psychology provides valuable knowledge and insights that help us to understand the behaviour of people in business organisations and settings. As a consequence, the manager is equipped with pertinent information about human behaviour when faced with human problems in a business and management context.

The contribution that psychology has made to the solution of many human problems encountered in business is significant. It has resulted in better management of human resources, improved methods of personnel selection, appraisal and training, improved morale and efficiency of operations, a reduction in accident rates, and better working conditions.

Despite these claims to success, it should be stated that psychology is not a panacea for all the human problems associated with business. For example, there are occasions when the outcome of the application of personnel selection techniques is less than perfect. Likewise, a programme to raise the level of morale in a company may, for a variety of reasons, fail to meet the expectations of the management, even though the results provide grounds for optimism.

In the study of human behaviour the psychologist is concerned with a repertoire of behaviour that is both observable (e.g. walking and talking) and unobservable (e.g. feeling and thinking). Animal behaviour has also captured the interest of the psychologist.

DIFFERENT PERSPECTIVES IN PSYCHOLOGY

The development of psychological thought has been influenced by the different traditions associated with the study of behaviour. These traditions are often referred to as "perspectives" or "models of man". The major perspectives can be classified as:

- the psychoanalytical approach;
- the behaviourist approach; and
- the phenomenological approach.

Psychoanalytical

The psychoanalytical approach, initiated by Freud, ignores or shows little interest in certain areas of contemporary psychology (e.g. attitudes, perception, learning) because of a prime preoccupation with providing help for neurotic patients. This approach, which is discussed in Chapter 1, gave a major impetus to the early development of modern psychology.

In psychoanalysis, the therapist takes note of what the patient has to say, and perceives emotional reactions and signs of resistance to the treatment. In a discussion with the patient the therapist interprets the information emanating from the analysis session. The central thrust of this approach is that people's behaviour can be investigated in a non-experimental way, that behaviour is determined by some unconscious force, and that behavioural difficulties or abnormalities in adult life spring from childhood.

Behaviourism

Behaviourism is the approach to psychology that is confined to what is objective, observable, and measurable. This approach, which featured prominently in psychology until the 1950s, advocated a scientific means of studying behaviour in carefully controlled conditions. The use of animals in many behaviourist experiments may be influenced partly by the fact that they are less complicated than humans, with a lower propensity to rely on previous experience when faced with a stimulus. Behaviourism, which is discussed in Chapter 4, provided psychology with a number of valuable experimental methods.

However, the preoccupation with behaviour that can be observed and measured objectively has obvious weaknesses. These are primarily associated with the neglect of the processing capacity of the human brain. Factors such as subjective feelings, expectations, plans, and thought processes are ruled out because they do not lend themselves to scientific analysis in the same way that observable behaviour does. In a sense, behaviourism may be viewed as a mechanistic view of people, with the emphasis on the inputs and outputs from the "machine" but with little regard to the functioning of the internal mechanics.

Phenomenology

The final approach, phenomenology, amounts to a humanistic reaction to behaviourism. In this approach the emphasis is essentially on people's experience rather than their behaviour. For instance, even though on occasions we all share common experiences, each person perceives the world in his or her own distinctive way. Our unique perceptions, and action strategies based on them, tend to determine what we are and how we react. In the process the individual utilises previous experience, needs, expectations, and attitudes. This approach to psychology is adopted throughout the book where a cognitive view of man is acknowledged.

Although organisational behaviour relies heavily on a psychological perspective, other disciplines have a part to play as well. Therefore, the book has been extended to incorporate topics and areas of study found in textbooks on organisational behaviour but not dealt with in the first edition (which took a narrower view). For example, when the spotlight falls on the organisation as the unit of analysis, a socio- logical perspective related to organisation theory is used; anthropological principles apply when examining the meaning and influence of culture; and insights from political studies are relevant when the analysis is concerned with the distribution and use of power in organisations. Also, it was recognised that certain areas of applied psychology that were given only cursory treatment or ignored in the first edition warranted serious examination. These included certain aspects of ergonomics, psychometrics, selection, appraisal, training, team-work, and organisational and management development.

The primary emphasis in Part I (Chapters 1 to 6) is on the individual, and in Part II (Chapters 7 to 9) it is on the group. Part III (Chapters 10 to 15) focuses on the organisation broadly conceived.

Among the main issues discussed in the book are the following:

- personality and intelligence testing;
- job satisfaction and motivation;
- perception and communication;
- learning and training;
- decision making and creativity;
- employee attitudes and morale;
- social interactions of people in groups and team-work;
- supervision and leadership;
- power, politics, and conflict;
- organisational design and change;
- selection and appraisal;
- the impact of modern technology; and
- pressures and hazards at work.

Explanations of these and other issues dealt with in the book come from the different perspectives identified earlier. As the various chapters draw heavily on empirical or research evidence in psychology, it seems appropriate to acknowledge the methods used in psychological enquiry.

METHODS OF PSYCHOLOGICAL ENQUIRY

Knowledge about human behaviour can be obtained in part through experience, and it is possible to derive some useful insights by this means. However, insight into human behaviour derived from experience has its limitations, simply because our perceptions of the behaviour of others are not always reliable, partly due to the influence exerted by our attitudes and values. In addition, our observations may be based on a limited and possibly unrepresentative sample which does not provide an adequate basis for generalisation about human behaviour.

By contrast, research provides an approach for obtaining information about many dimensions of behaviour that cannot be acquired through experience alone. When psychologists conduct research into various aspects of behaviour they try to apply the scientific method. Scientific enquiry is based on the assumption that events and phenomena are *caused*. So a major objective of psychological research is to determine what factors cause people to behave in a particular way. However, achieving this objective is extraordinarily difficult because psychologists, unlike physical scientists, have to deal with unpredictable material. Subjects lie, lack self-insight, give socially approved responses, and try to satisfy the needs of the experimenter as they see them.

In reality, a great deal of psychological research at the empirical level is concerned with identifying relationships between events and phenomena, and the question of why people behave in a given manner often remains unanswered. However, identification of relationships can be productive in increasing our knowledge and insight. For instance, a strong relationship between management style and a low level of morale among subordinates might not tell us what particular aspects of management style cause the problems, but it does allow us to focus more clearly on the source of the difficulties.

Research psychologists in the course of their work evaluate claims, impressions, ideas, and theories, and search for real and valid evidence to test and generate ideas about relationships between circumstances and behaviour. As more empirical information about behaviour is accumulated, hypotheses or speculations about certain aspects of behaviour are developed. This can be done in a systematic and controlled way, and the aim is to discover general explanations or theories. In building theories the researcher is engaged in explaining, understanding, predicting, and controlling phenomena.

As research data accumulates and theories are confirmed, laws and principles are put forward. Although in certain areas of psychology it has been possible to create an impressive collection of empirical evidence that has some theoretical credibility (or a resemblance to the ingredients of a cause-and-effect relationship), much of the research in business psychology is at the empirical stage with modest developments in the theoretical sphere.

Characteristics of the Scientific Method

In order to ensure that the findings of psychological research are as objective, reliable, and quantifiable as possible, the characteristics of the scientific method are adopted. These include:

- definition and control of the variables used in the research study;
- data analysis;
- replication; and
- hypothesis testing.

Variables used in research are referred to as "independent" and "dependent" variables. The independent variable is the factor that is varied—e.g. the level of illumination in a particular task is physically controlled by the experimenter. This could then be related to a measurable dependent variable, such as the number of units of production. In other circumstances the dependent variable could be classified rather than measured. For example, the subject's behaviour (dependent variable) in response to a variation in experimental conditions to stress (independent variable) might be classified as belonging to one of the following categories: (1) remains calm; (2) loses composure; (3) loses self-control. Such classifications should be made in a reliable manner, sometimes by more than one observer.

Apart from control of the independent variable by the experimenter, it is also necessary to control extraneous variables to prevent a contaminating effect. For instance, in assessing the significance of training techniques to employee performance, it would be necessary to ensure that factors other than training methods did not significantly influence the results.

Contaminating factors in this case could be educational background, intelligence, age, and experience. In some cases extraneous variables cannot be foreseen, but it must be recognised that they can have a contaminating effect on results, leading to incorrect conclusions.

The requirement to come forward with operational definitions of variables or phenomena that can be subjected to empirical testing is prompted by the desire to bring precision into the meaning of concepts used in research. Ambiguities could otherwise arise. In experimental conditions raw data, often in quantitative form, are collected and summarised, and usually subjected to statistical analysis. Descriptive statistics, as the term implies, are concerned with describing phenomena in statistical terms—e.g. a key characteristic of a sample of managers, such as the average weekly hours spent at work. Inferential statistics are concerned with drawing inferences from the analysis of the data. In measuring the strength of the association between two variables, the question of statistical significance arises. Is the relationship significant or not significant, or is it due to chance? The psychologist uses inferential statistics to make inferences about general events or populations from observations of samples, and to convey to us some idea of the confidence we should have in those inferences.

Replication arises when an experiment is repeated. We expect to come up with the same result if the study is repeated, otherwise our explanations and descriptions are unreliable. The notion of reliability and validity is discussed in the Attitude Measurement section in Chapter 6, and in connection with human resource practices in Chapter 13.

A final characteristic of the scientific method is hypothesis testing. The research starts with the formulation of hypotheses, which are predictions or "hunches", preceded by a search of the literature. Research evidence is then related to the hypotheses, resulting in their acceptance or rejection—Karl Popper is of the view that science proceeds by refuting hypotheses. The researcher then comes up with new observations that challenge new hypotheses.

Techniques and Settings

Different branches of psychology use different techniques when applying the scientific method. For instance, in certain branches of social psychology (e.g. attitudes) questionnaires are used. Reinforcement schedules, referred to in Chapter 4, can be used in operant conditioning (part of learning theory). Electrodes that stimulate the brain are the preserve of physiological psychology. The important thing to bear in mind is that the technique used should be appropriate to the research problem in hand.

Different settings are used to carry out psychological research. An experiment can be carried out under controlled conditions in a laboratory or work situation where the independent variable is under the control of the experimenter. For example, in Chapter 4 there is an account of the systematic manipulation of the independent variable to demonstrate a causal effect on the dependent variable in the discussion of operant conditioning. Here the frequency of dispensation of food pellets to the pigeon in Skinner's experiment is varied because the experimenter thinks this will cause changes in behaviour. In another case, the experimenter may introduce different types of incentive schemes and assess the impact they make on the individual's performance.

Another approach is the study of human behaviour in real life settings. For example, the researcher collects data on identical groups of workers engaged in the same task but working under different styles of supervision. Their job performance under different supervisory conditions could then be compared. However, it might prove difficult to create groups that are identical in terms of age, sex, skill, length of service, etc.

Survey research methods, using both interviews and questionnaires, are frequently used in real life settings. When various attributes of a particular population are collected, this is referred to as a "descriptive" survey. When causal relationships or associations (e.g. the relationship between systems of executive reward and motivation) are explored, surveys are "explanatory" in nature. The two types of survey can be interrelated. In the section on Attitude Measurement in Chapter 6 there is a discussion of scales used in attitude surveys. A derivative of this method is the survey feedback technique in organisational development discussed in Chapter 12.

The major advantage of surveys is that comparable data from a number of respondents can be obtained, and patterns in the data can be explored. The major disadvantages are that we may oversimplify behaviour and that, by placing such a heavy reliance on the subjects' verbal reports, the research is exposed to certain weaknesses. These could include shortcomings in the memory of the subject as well as biased viewpoints. In addition, the subject is free to withhold critical information.

Memories, thoughts, and feelings (non-observable data) can be inferred from observing behaviour and from self-reporting by the individual. Sometimes the psychologist uses observation to corroborate the evidence in a self-report. For example, the subject's statements about his or her active involvement in the life of the organisation could be validated by observing the nature and extent of that involvement.

Observation, as a method of investigation, can be used in a variety of ways. It lends itself to the development of insights which could subsequently lead to hypothesis formation, and it may facilitate the interpretation of data obtained by other techniques. It can be used where subjects (e.g. infants or animals) cannot provide verbal reports. Likewise, it could be suitable where people do not like being interviewed or having to fill in questionnaire forms, or where they might distort the answers.

The psychologist engaged in observation can record the behaviour of individuals and groups as it occurs, although the recording of observations during the actual process of observation can prove difficult. If keeping a record follows the act of observation, the question to ask is how soon after the event does one make the record. Without the benefit of an action playback facility, it is difficult to check the accuracy of one's perceptions. Not all behaviour can be observed, because of the subject's need for privacy in certain circumstances, and it is important to acknowledge the possibility that people may alter their behaviour if they know they are being watched. The observer has to guard against bias stemming from personal prejudice, and must try to maintain objectivity when relationships develop between the observer and other members of the group.

In the light of these considerations it is imperative that an observation episode is planned and executed in a systematic and rigorous way. Observation can be structured or unstructured, and it is helpful if there are two or more observers so that they can compare notes and check bias.

Unstructured observation often takes the form of participant observation and is often used in exploratory investigations. A participant observer could be knowingly a member of the group he or she is observing. Participant observation can also be carried out in secret—e.g. an experimenter may pose as a convert in a religious sect. A participant observer involved in the life of a group is better placed strategically to understand the complexities and subtleties of behaviour and its meaning than the psychologist who applies standardised questionnaires or creates artificial and restrictive laboratory situations.

However, field work is a time-consuming exercise. In structured observation, the observer knows in advance what behaviour is relevant to the research objectives. A specific plan can be devised to collect and record observations with the opportunity to exercise more precision and control. Although the well-trained observer may produce very reliable results, some of the subtleties detected in unstructured observation may be lost in structured observation.

Ethical Issues

Finally, those who conduct research in organisations ought to be sensitive to potential ethical issues. In this respect the following matters should be considered. A person's right to privacy should be respected. Violation of this principle is evident when subjects are observed without their knowledge, when highly personal questions are asked of them or, without their knowledge, their colleagues, or when a participant observer parades himself or herself as, for example, a worker, thereby concealing his or her true identity.

In addition, subjects should be free to decide whether or not to participate in a research study, and should be given the opportunity to obtain detailed information about the study prior to a commitment to take part. The anonymity of the respondent should be respected, particulary when a statement to this effect is a made by the researchers prior to the collection of the data.

A copy of the recent British Psychological Society approved *Ethical Principles for Conducting Research With Human Participants*, to which chartered psychologists are required to adhere, appeared in the January 1993 issue of *The Psychologist*.

PART I

The Individual

1

Personality and Intelligence

Personality, a complex topic comprising a number of perspectives, has been studied by psychologists from many different angles. Definitions of the concept of personality reflect this state of affairs. This chapter opens with a definition of personality, followed by an examination of the approaches used by researchers to study the subject. Next, there is a review of the psychoanalytical perspective, and a brief description of projective tests. The latter, which have an indirect relationship with psychoanalysis, are used in consumer motivation research and are complementary to role playing and visualisation. There follows a discussion of a number of other perspectives on personality, some more important than others. These perspectives can be classified as follows: traits (and their measurement by personality tests); types; interpersonal; behavioural; social; and cognitive. Psychographics is an approach used in consumer behaviour research.

All of the perspectives mentioned in the previous paragraph provide valuable insights that illuminate our understanding of the personality factor. There is a link between personality and intelligence. At the end of the chapter we examine the nature of intelligence and its measurement. The discussion is illustrated, where appropriate, with examples relevant to the business context

This chapter provides a firm conceptual basis for the study of issues connected in particular with culture (Chapter 11), human resource practices (Chapter 13), and organisational change and development (Chapter 12).

DEFINITION

Repeatedly, we evaluate the people we meet in everyday life. We make subjective assessments of their behaviour. We note their personal appearance and their mannerisms. We listen to what they have to say and watch what they do in different settings. We use this information to make a subjective judgement of the "personality" of the person concerned. This process elicits descriptions of personality traits such as boring, cautious, rigid, uninspiring; or alternatively, lively, innovative, imaginative, and so on. The definitions that follow capture what is generally meant by personality.

Personality consists of the physical, mental, moral, and social qualities of the individual. These qualities are dynamic and integrated: they can be observed by other people in everyday life. Personality comprises the individual's natural and acquired impulses, habits, interests, sentiments, ideals, opinions, and beliefs as they are projected to the outside world. Personality consists of "those relatively stable and enduring aspects of the individual which distinguish him from other people and at the same time form the basis of our predictions concerning his future behaviour" (Wright et al., 1970).

Just as there are many definitions of personality, so there are also many theories of personality.

RESEARCH APPROACHES

There are two fundamental approaches to the study of personality. One is the idiographic approach, and the other, the nomothetic.

Idiographic Approach

The researcher adopting this approach operates in the belief that the individual is not just a collection of separate traits, but is a well-integrated organism. The individual reacts as a system to various situations, with past experiences and future intentions contributing to present behaviour.

Allport (1965) constructed an idiographic portrait of a woman named Jenny, by using the 301 letters she had written over a period of 11 years, and by examining them from a number of different perspectives.

This emphasis on a very intensive study of individual cases is said to capture the wholeness and the uniqueness of the personality as it functions in the many and diverse situations found in day-to-day life. The approach tries to capture the essence of the total personality, but it is often criticised because it does not lend itself easily to scientific measurement, and because there are difficulties in extrapolating from the particular—the single or few cases—to people in general. This problem could be overcome by studying many more individual cases, but it would prove very costly.

Nomothetic Approach

The main objective of the nomothetic approach is the isolation of one or more of the variables of personality. This is done by measuring the variables scientifically under controlled conditions, using a sufficiently large test sample. It is hoped that the relationship between traits and behaviour is generalisable and repeatable in other samples of people at other times. This approach is fundamentally opposed to the idiographic approach.

There follows an example of a nomothetically based empirical study from Hetherington and Wray (1964). In the study, subjects were asked to state their feelings about aggression and social approval using questionnaires. Each subject was presented with photocopied cartoons expressing aggression, and was asked to evaluate what they saw on a scale ranging from extremely funny to extremely unfunny. Their responses were then classified according to the four criteria set out in Table 1.1. The researchers assumed that if the cartoons were viewed as funny the subject found little difficulty in condoning aggression. If the opposite was the case, they assumed that aggression was disapproved of, or perhaps was considered a delicate subject.

In an attempt to evaluate the disinhibiting effect of alcohol on the acceptance and expression of aggression following exposure to the cartoons, half the subjects were given alcoholic drink. Those subjects who did not take alcoholic drink, and who were classified

TABLE 1.1

Variables in Hetherington and Wray's (1964) Nomothetic Study

Criterion No	Aggression	Desire for Social Approval
I	High	High
II	High	Low
III	Low	High
IV	Low	Low

in accordance with Criterion I in Table 1.1, were more disturbed by the cartoons and rated them "much less funny" than those subjects who fitted into Criterion II. The subjects who took alcoholic drink, and who were also classified in accordance with Criterion I, perceived the cartoons as being funny. They had a high need for social approval, but it appears that the alcohol diluted this strong desire and permitted them enjoyment of the aggressive humour that would otherwise have been disturbing. Those subjects who took alcoholic drink and were classified in accordance with Criterion II acted in a similar way to their counterparts who did not take alcoholic drink.

The researchers contend that subjects classified as low in aggression did not have much of an impulse to express aggression, whether or not they had taken alcoholic drink. Subjects classified in accordance with Criterion I—high in aggression and high in desire for social approval—have strong aggressive impulses, but they repress these impulses because of their strong desire for social approval. It would be interesting to know whether social approval diminishes in importance under the influence of alcohol, or whether alcohol reduces the fear of social disapproval of an aggressive act.

The final comment on the weaknesses of the idiographic and nomothetic approaches to personality must be reserved for somebody who has made a close study of personality: Lazarus (1971) makes the point that the idiographic approach is too global and does not possess valued scientific features, such as controlled observation, precision of measurement or repeatability. Neither does he believe that the nomothetic approach is the correct one, because distortions arise in any analysis when component parts are studied in isolation and when there is a failure to examine the full range of reactions to the variety of life's circumstances.

PSYCHOANALYTICAL PERSPECTIVE

Freud's greatest contribution to our understanding of human behaviour was probably his recognition of the power the unconscious has in directing that behaviour (Freud, 1938).

Levels of Awareness

Freud classified awareness into three levels—the conscious, the preconscious, and the unconscious.

Conscious. That of which one is aware, is in the *conscious* mind. As I write this section, I am fully aware of what I am doing.

Preconscious. But I am not aware of a great deal of information which, if required, could be brought to the level of awareness. For example, once I had put my mind to it, I could recall the broad details of the way I spent each day of my holiday last year. All such material is said to be *preconscious* in the sense that it is not currently in awareness but, with some effort, can be recalled.

Unconscious Concerns. The third level of awareness—the *unconscious* mind—concerns that of which we are totally unaware, and therefore cannot normally be brought into awareness. The material in the unconscious mind comprises drives, desires, urges, some memories and deep-rooted moral standards.

Unconscious motivation. It follows that the individual can be motivated by forces in the unconscious mind of which he or she is unaware, called *unconscious motivation.* For example, one may hear reference to an individual's behaviour as being "entirely out of character" and difficult to explain, or we recognise a person's behaviour as being due to a strange impulse. These are examples of a lack of insight into forces that are motivating the individual. Psychotherapy or hypnosis could be used to gain a clearer understanding of the unconscious factors that motivate behaviour.

Structure of Personality

Freud conceived the structure of personality as comprising three parts, each with different functions: the id, the ego, and the super-ego.

Id

The id is the biological basis of personality. It consists of the inherited characteristics of the individual and can be viewed as a collection of instinctive desires, urges or needs, all demanding immediate gratification. It is concerned with trying to maintain a balance between forces within the person, which produce conflict and tension. The id finds these conflicts difficult to accept and is therefore keen to reduce them.

The id tends to be irrational and impulsive; it adheres to the pleasure principle. That is, it invites and accepts pleasure and tries to avoid displeasure. It has no values, no sense of right or wrong, no moral standards, and no consideration for other people. The id is cut off from the external world and, because it is frequently kept in check by the ego, it is forced to fantasise in order to relieve tension.

The main force energising the id is the libido. The libido, which is sexual in nature, is also concerned with self-preservation. Sex is interpreted widely by Freud. Pleasurable sensations applied to any bodily function, as well as feelings such as tenderness, friendship, and satisfaction at work, could fall within the definition of sex. After analysing the dreams of battle-shocked soldiers, Freud concluded that, as well as sex, aggression might be an important instinct separate from the libido. This was called the *death instinct*, and if put into action could, in extreme cases, result in masochism, self-injury, and suicide.

Ego

The new-born child has no ego. Exposed to grim realities—cold, thirst, noise, etc—which can produce anxiety, and powerless to be rid of these disturbing situations, help is only forthcoming from those close to the child. It is the confluence of forces in the environment acting on the surface of the id that contributes to the formation of a separate mental process called the ego. The internal part of the id will still remain latent as its external part is transformed into the preconscious ego. The infantile ego is only dimly aware of the external world and tends to be narcissistic—as its needs are met, so it is happy. Objects responsible for the gratification of its needs come from outside. Hunger, for instance, is satisfied by its mother's milk or a substitute. When the infant is free from such discomforts as pressure in the bowels and bladder, irritation of the skin, and extremes of temperature, it falls asleep.

As the child grows up he or she becomes less narcissistic and begins to recognise the omnipotence of the outer world that satisfies his or her needs. There are times when external reality may be perceived as overwhelming and results in fantasies. The ego gradually becomes able to protect the growing child from the internal threats from the id, as well as external threats; in fact, it is the main mental force controlling behaviour in the well-adjusted adult. The ego pursues pleasure; it seeks to avoid unpleasant situations.

Unlike the id, which is intent on the immediate gratification of instinctual urges, the ego is capable of logical reasoning and learning by experience. It clings to the task of self-preservation and postpones or suppresses demands made by the instincts when it feels that meeting these demands would be to the disadvantage of the organism. But there are times when it considers it appropriate to meet these instinctual demands. It is rational in its perspective in the sense that it weighs up situations realistically, taking into consideration such factors as special abilities, aptitudes, temperament, limitations and the prevailing circumstances.

There are times when the ego is caught off balance, and impulses from the id reach the level of consciousness in disguised forms. The psychotherapist is then offered scope to place interpretations on behaviour such as slips of the tongue, jokes and so on. In sleep the ego severs contact with the external world permitting the id to express itself. This should not have any adverse repercussions because the ego controls the movement of the organism. Wishes that are warded off when awake now take the stage and reveal themselves in dreams, often in symbolic form. The interpretation of dreams is a well-known approach in psychoanalysis. Anxiety is said to develop when the ego is experiencing difficulty facing the demands of the id.

Super-ego
The super-ego is a new mental process that develops as a result of the weakness of the infantile ego. Eventually it represents the standards and ethical values acquired from parents and society in general. Initially, however, it represents the "voice of the parents" and their moral standards, as perceived by the child. It may be childish and irrational, imposing rigid restrictions that persist into adulthood without much consideration for the changed circumstances. The super-ego is mostly unconscious—thus, if the ego does not live up to its expectations, then conflict develops. When there is conflict, the aggressive forces stored in the super-ego turn against the ego with accusations, creating feelings of depression and guilt.

Depression is said to be self-directed aggression. The manic depressive oscillates between the joy and happiness resulting from the approving super-ego, and the tortures resulting from the feelings of guilt and depression when the super-ego becomes sadistic. At a less severe level, the disapproval of the super-ego is evident when the individual claims to feel bad about something he or she has or has not done, and is troubled by his or her conscience. When somebody feels proud of something they have done, self-congratulation comes into play, no doubt with the approval of the super-ego.

As the individual gets older, the super-ego gradually draws away from the infantile images of the parent; it becomes more impersonal and more related to the objective social and ethical standards to which the individual subscribes. In the course of its development, an individual's super-ego takes over from parent substitutes, such as teachers, admired figures in public life, or high social ideals.

Defence Mechanisms

The interaction of the three aspects of personality structure produces constant strife. "Id, the psychic powerhouse, a lawless mob of instinctual urges, demands release; super-ego, the harsh unbending moralist, demands total inhibition of these urges; ego, the rational decision maker, has to try to keep the peace between these two forces and to take into account the demands of external reality" (Mackay, 1973). It is argued that the ego needs reinforcements to function adequately. These are called *ego defence mechanisms* and they shed light on our understanding of the behaviour of people.

Consisting of at least five major strategies, they are designed to protect the ego from the excessive demands of the id and the super-ego, and to cope with external reality. Each strategy is illustrated by simple examples.

Repression
This is the mechanism whereby the ego protects itself from damage or discomfort by denying the existence of a potential threat from within. Distressing felings and memories are unconsciously removed from the level of awareness. The individual may repress sexual or aggressive desires that would adversely affect the stability of the self. Likewise, the individual may repress painful memories which, if recalled, would make him or her feel bad. Repression can create problems when the repressed desire or memory becomes so strong that it makes its way into the level of consciousness, perhaps through dreams or some form of anxiety.

Suppression

As a contrast to repression, *suppression* amounts to the conscious control of desires, fantasies, wishes or memories. Suppression appears to be a healthier form of defence, for in suppressing a desire a conscious decision is made that, for the time being at least, it will not find expression in its present form.

Projection

This is a mechanism whereby feelings that create acute discomfort are projected onto an object or another person. In this case, the disturbing emotions can be blamed on the other person.

The manager who continually interprets other employees' behaviour as conspiratorial or politically inspired might have such tendencies. A student who has a strong desire to cheat in an examination, but somehow cannot go through with it, might become suspicious of other students and unjustifiably accuse them of cheating.

Fixation

This is the mechanism whereby the ego is protected by not proceeding from a particular stage of personality development. So if a child experiences a lot of anxiety about asserting its independence and moving away from being dependent on its parents, the ego refuses to accept the challenge to develop. As far as this characteristic is concerned, it tends to become fixated at an immature level.

Regression

This is the mechanism whereby the ego reverts to an earlier form of behaviour when confronted by a threat. For example, an employee facing a frustrating situation at work may burst into tears or sulk. This form of coping behaviour may well have been successful when dealing with threats of a lower magnitude earlier in life. The child experiencing major difficulties at school may play truant, and as an adult may adopt similar behaviour when confronting significant problems at work.

Reaction Formation

This is the mechanism whereby the ego copes with undesirable impulses or desires by developing a pattern of behaviour that is the

"SO....ERM....WE'LL JUST PUT YOU DOWN AS A...UM... 'DONT KNOW' SHALL WE,... P.J.?..P.J?..."

direct opposite of those impulses or desires. An employee who harbours deep antisocial feelings towards people may develop pleasant mannerisms and good social skills in dealings with colleagues at work as a means of keeping his or her feelings in check. If an occasion arises when this mechanism fails to function properly, colleagues will be shocked by this individual's outburst of hostility.

Defence mechanisms are entirely unconscious and the person is unaware of using them. When used successfully, they become a normal feature of coping behaviour whereby the individual can resolve personal conflicts. They also play a crucial part in the development of characteristics of personality. If used unsuccessfully, the ego cannot cope and neurosis or psychosis may result.

Personality Development

Freud subscribed to the view that there are three stages of sexual development during infancy. The stages are associated with libidinous satisfaction derived from a preoccupation with different parts of the body.

The infant derives pleasure at first from its mouth (sucking its mother's breast or an inferior substitute such as sucking its thumb) followed by pleasure from the anus, and finally pleasure from the genitals. If conflicts are not resolved at any one of these stages, the person may become fixated at that stage, producing a profound effect on character.

Oral Stage

The first stage is the oral stage and it lasts for a year. During this period in which the infant is highly dependent upon others for its survival, the libido manifests itself through sucking and chewing. Early oral pleasures are perpetuated when the adult indulges in, for example, excessive smoking, eating, kissing, and the chewing of gum. If a person fails to negotiate this stage successfully, and develops an oral fixation, this could lead to adult behaviour such as dependency (as in the original feeding situation), immaturity, optimism or pessimism, sadism, oral aggression (the need to bite), or a suspicious nature.

Anal Stage

In the second year of life the anus becomes the focal point for libidinous satisfaction. The infant is intensely interested in the bowel movements and obtains satisfaction from this process. The child establishes that the control of the bowel movements is something with which the parents are obviously concerned. During the anal stage, toilet training takes place, and the way this is handled can have significant effects on later developments. If the person becomes fixated at this stage, this can affect adult behaviour and is reflected in such characteristics as stinginess, obstinacy, obsessionality, sadism, and orderliness. These characteristics are said to be associated with the early pleasure derived from the excretion and the retention of faeces.

Phallic Stage

Around the age of three the child's interest moves towards a preoccupation with the genitals. The main focus is the exploration and manipulation of the genitals, and this is known as the phallic stage. The little boy develops feelings of sexual attraction towards his mother and at the same time feelings of jealousy or resentment are directed against his father who he looks upon as a rival for the mother's affection.

This phenomenon is known as the *Oedipus complex*. In Greek mythology Oedipus Rex, a character from a play by Sophocles, killed his father and married his mother without knowing the identity of either. The Oedipus complex comes to an end in the fourth or fifth year as a result of the boy's fear that his illicit desires might be punished by the father with castration.

The position of the little girl is unclear, although penis envy is attributed to her. This comes about when the little girl recognises the alleged inferior nature of her sexual organ in relation to the masculine one. She develops an envious desire to be like the boy and turns her attention towards her father. Her attachment to her father is crystallised in the *Electra complex*. In Greek mythology, Electra connives at the death of her mother, Clytemnestra, who murdered her father, Agamemnon.

The boy resolves the Oedipal conflict by modelling himself on his father and repressing his incestuous urges; the girl, on the other hand, resolves the Electra conflict by the recognition that she might lose the love of her mother if she realised her illicit desires. Unsuccessful resolution of these conflicts for both sexes can lead to major problems in adulthood, particularly problems of sexual identification and neurotic tendencies. Those fixated at this stage of development are said to display characteristics such as extreme self-love, excessive ambition, exhibitionism, and bragging.

After the phallic stage comes the latency period which lasts until adolescence, during which time sexual impulses are inhibited and satisfying relationships are developed.

Freud has been criticised for the prime emphasis he placed on sexual desires. Lazarus (1971) puts an interesting interpretation on the Oedipus complex. He maintains that the Oedipus complex could be better understood in terms of social relations within the family. "The boy might come to fear the father not because he literally expects castration, or because of sexual urges toward the mother, but because the father controls power within the family, particularly in the Viennese society of the late-1800s. Also the girl might envy the boy, not literally for his penis, but because in most societies girls are usually considered subordinate to boys."

Psychoanalytical theory sees the origin of personality in the conflicts between the id, ego and super-ego and in the way in which the conflicts are resolved at each stage of development. Adult behaviour is said to be related to the success, or otherwise, of negotiating the various stages of development.

Other Explanations

Some of Freud's followers, notably Jung and Adler, felt that it was unsatisfactory to emphasise persistently the sexual roots of neurosis to the exclusion of other factors.

Adler was of the view that human behaviour can be explained in terms of a struggle for power in order to overcome feelings of mental or physical inferiority (Brown, 1961). This contribution was of significant benefit to psychoanalysis because it recognised that non-sexual factors could also lead to conflict, and that neurosis is a disorder of the total personality.

In modern developments in the mainstream of psychoanalysis, the ego receives increasing attention, and the influence people have on each other receives a high priority. The quality of the mother–child relationship is a critical interpersonal influence because it is the base of subsequent personal relationships (Peck & Whitlow, 1975).

Freud's greatest contribution is not the detail of his theory of personality but his systematic approach to the study of personality and the emphasis on the part played in behaviour by unconscious forces and previous experience (Robertson & Cooper, 1983).

Applications

If one were to apply Freudian analysis to the behaviour of consumers, one might conclude that the marketeer must recognise that products and advertisements appeal to unconscious as well as conscious motives, and that the symbolism inherent in the design of products and advertisements, especially if it contains sexual implications, can have an effect opposite to that intended. For example, if an advertisement is sexually explicit, it could offend the super-ego and therefore lose its impact. In the promotion of an aftershave lotion for men, an explicit sexual theme may be projected through packaging and advertising with the intention of appealing to the id. The product could be made acceptable to the super-ego by projecting a subsequent image of the consumer in a more sober social setting. The ego could very well be satisfied with this outcome (Williams, 1981).

Other applications of the psychoanalytical perspective have focused on the behaviour of managers in work organisations. Kets de Vries and Miller (1984) identified five neurotic styles among managers:

- *Paranoid*. They tend to be suspicious of others, and are exceptionally vigilant for hidden threats.
- *Compulsive*. They tend to be perfectionist in what they do and are concerned with the right way of doing things.
- *Dramatic*. They frequently draw attention to themselves, and show a desire for activity and excitement.
- *Depressive*. They display feelings of guilt, inadequacy and hopelessness.
- *Schizoid*. They show symptoms of withdrawal, lack of involvement, lack of excitement or enthusiasm.

Where these neuroses are reflected by senior managers, the organisation could be considered sick and action should be taken to treat this condition.

Psychoanalytical theories of personality, such as Freud's, are often criticised by other psychologists for the lack of a satisfactory definition of their key concepts, for their lack of scientific rigour, and the fact that the theories either do not generate testable predictions about human behaviour or, when predictions are made, that they do not work out in practice.

PROJECTIVE TESTS

An appropriate way to assess personality based on unconscious processes is to use assessment methods that include face-to-face analysis and projective techniques. These methods are expensive and time-consuming to administer and they do not lead to quantifiable results. However, they are used as a framework for motivational research in studies of consumer behaviour. The ideas of Freud were the inspiration behind projective techniques, but the relationship between psychoanalytic theory and projective techniques is merely indirect.

Projective techniques require a person to respond to ambiguous or unstructured situations as a means of exploring unconscious impulses and motives. Subjects are unaware of the purpose of the test; consequently the ego's defences are off guard, and unconscious forces emerge in disguised form. It is the job of the assessor to interpret these responses. Two well-known projective tests are examined in the following sections.

Rorschach Test

The Rorschach test consists of a series of ten ink-blots or formless shapes in which one half is the mirror image of the other. An ink-blot, similar to the one used in the test, is shown in Fig. 1.1.

The subject is asked to say what the blot resembles. The abnormal personality is likely to perceive gruesome or horrific images in the blots, and this may be indicative of serious conflicts which are still unresolved. The

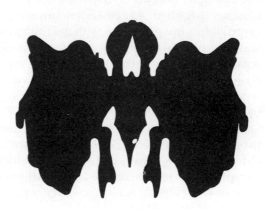

FIG. 1.1. An ink blot

normal personality sees more tranquil images.

Thematic Apperception Test

The thematic apperception test (TAT) consists of 20 pictures of varying degrees of clarity. An example of a straightforward scene would be a boy reading at a desk. The subject examines each picture and then tells a story about the scene portrayed, including what led up to the scene, the current situation, and what is likely to happen in the future. The responses are analysed and recurrent themes mentioned in the stories are particularly noted. A subject who harbours intense hostility may read hostility in one form or another, such as severe conflict or death, into the stories.

In motivation research in the field of marketing, a similar test to the one described was used (Anastasi, 1979). In a cigar survey a cartoon was used portraying a man coming home from work who announces to his wife, "I've decided to take up smoking cigars, dear". The respondent is asked to fill in the wife's response.

Tests of this type are carried out in the belief that a person may attribute to another person an opinion that he or she holds but is unwilling to express. In order to get around the expression of a direct personal view, a question may be worded in the third person. For example, instead of "What are the health hazards attached to cigarette smoking?", respondents are presented with the following statement: "Some people who smoke cigarettes may suffer from ill-health at some stage in their life." They are then asked, "I wonder if you can guess what adverse effects of cigarette smoking they are referring to?"

Whereas some psychologists find projective tests useful in providing initial clinical insights, others are sceptical of their value in assessing unconscious processes and believe that subjects can quite easily fake the tests (Holmes, 1974).

ROLE PLAYING OR VISUALISATION

Apart from the use of projective tests in consumer motivation research, role playing or visualisation techniques have been used to create personality descriptions of consumers.

Stereotyping

A study was conducted in the USA into the consumption of instant coffee at a time when instant coffee was not widely used (Haire, 1950). Direct questioning of housewives revealed that they did not like its flavour.

Subsequently, the housewives were given two shopping lists covering a number of items and asked to describe the personality of the woman who bought the groceries. The main distinguishing feature between the two lists was that one shopping list—"list A"—contained *Nescafé* instant coffee and the other—"list B"—included ground coffee. The results showed that 48% of the women shown list A said the shopper was lazy and did not plan well, but less than 12% of the women shown list B arrived at that conclusion. The shopper was perceived as a spendthrift by 12% of the women shown list A, but none of the women shown list B expressed that view. Again, 16% of the women shown list A said the shopper was not a good wife, but none of the women shown list B expressed that view.

By the addition of a pie-mix to the two shopping lists, and by using two new samples of housewives, the personality descriptions of the shopper using the B list became closer to those of the shopper using the A list. Was it the inclusion of a prepared food item (the pie-mix) that evoked a stereotyped personality description?

The original sample was divided into users and non-users of instant coffee, as the result of a pantry check. Significant differences were found between the two groups of housewives, as illustrated in Table 1.2.

The shopping list study was repeated 18 years later. No significant differences were found between the characteristics attributed

TABLE 1.2

Haire's Analysis of Shopper Profiles (1950)

Descriptions of Shoppers	Instant Coffee Users %	Instant Coffee Non-users %
Shopper is economical	70	18
Shopper is a good housewife (plans well and cares for the family)	29	0
Shopper cannot cook/does not like cooking	16	55
Shopper is lazy	19	39

by the subjects to the ground coffee *vs* the instant coffee user. However, a fairly large number of subjects felt that the instant coffee shopper was a busy, active person in contrast to the shopper preferring ground coffee, who was seen as dull, unadventurous, and not very elegant (Webster & Von Pechmann, 1970). A Canadian replication of the original shopping list study concluded with the assertion that the original findings still hold true with a sample of French-Canadians in a middle class suburb of Montreal (Lane & Watson, 1975).

These studies highlight role playing or visualisation and, although the association between personality stereotypes and consumer behaviour is interesting, it cannot be conclusive. People might find it difficult or impossible to come up with an authentic personality description from a shopping list and, in order not to disappoint the interviewer or to give what is expected, they co-operate. We never know the depth or strength of the personality stereotype (Anastasi, 1979).

Brand Personality

In recent years the emphasis has switched to brand personality. Apart from a brand's physical and functional attributes, the images and symbolism portrayed by the product is considered very important. But the images and symbolism must have meaning and significance in the minds of consumers. The "Poison" brand of fragrance could evoke a perception of danger, and the "Obsession" brand may be perceived as erotic by some consumers but not by others (Engel, Blackwell, & Miniard, 1990).

The Cooper Research and Marketing Agency in the United Kingdom claim to use creative and projective techniques in qualitative and motivational research for clients, by trying to get beneath consumers' conscious rationalisations about a brand, so as to enter their inner world of feelings about the particular personality of the brand being studied. This organisation conducted research in the 1980s into the deeper meaning of the brand of stout known as "Guinness" (Broadbent & Cooper, 1987). The findings indicated that Guinness supplies satisfying, nourishing values which, at the inner level, relate to fertility and archetypal myths of power and energy. The outward character of Guinness—rich, creamy, black, fascinating to pour and drink—reinforces these images.

Guinness was also perceived at the outer level as bitter, black, and strong, with a social reputation for manliness, mature experience, and wit. This type of thinking led to the creation of a model called the "Guinness Egg" that subsequently resulted in the successful *Pure Genius* advertising campaign. The inner part (the yolk) of the egg was symbolic of the wholesome, natural, mysterious, and poetic characteristics of the brand, and the key symbols used in the advertisement were mist, barley, fire, earth, and sun. The outer part (the shell) was people-centred with manifestations of play, humour, and confident, independent individuals who are in control and proud to be associated with the brand in an appropriate setting (pubs, etc).

The qualitative researchers stress brand personality and product symbolism, as shown by this example. Some might consider their techniques—for example, role playing, psycho-drama, and clay modelling—to be controversial, but they certainly generate challenging hypotheses.

TRAIT PERSPECTIVE

An important means of studying personality is the trait perspective. A trait is an individual characteristic in thought, feeling, and action, either inherited or acquired, and refers to tendencies to act or react in certain ways (Drever, 1964). The possession of a particular trait—for example, anxiety—does not imply that the person will always be anxious; rather, it suggests that the person is disposed to react with anxiety in given situations.

Traits can be placed in particular categories as follows:

- *Motive traits*. These refer to goals that guide the behaviour of the individual; for example, a person may possess a recognisable trait related to achievement.
- *Ability traits*. These refer to the individual's general and specific capability and skill; for example, this category would include cognitive traits such as knowing, perceiving, and reasoning.
- *Temperament traits*. These would include optimism, depression, and various energetic tendencies.
- *Stylistic traits*. These refer to gestures and styles of behaving unrelated to specific tactics to achieve a particular goal.

Traits contain two basic dimensions. One is the manner in which the trait manifests itself at the surface—for example, the display of aggressive behaviour—and the other is where the trait exists below the surface, and the observer has to infer the nature of the quality. Such a quality could be a belief held by the individual or, again, his or her power of self-control. In distinguishing between people, the use of a rich vocabulary of traits can help enormously. Each individual's traits may be considered unique. For example, one person's loyalty, and the way he or she expresses it, will differ from another person's loyalty. Likewise the way traits are organised in the individual's total personality can be considered distinctive (Allport, 1961).

Allport's Trait Categories

Allport puts traits into three categories:

- *Cardinal trait*. These refer to some predominant characteristic; for example, a determined stance taken by a politician on a number of issues.
- *Central trait*. One can have five to ten central traits which distinguish one individual from another; for example, intelligence, a sense of humour, compassion, sensitivity, and honesty.
- *Secondary trait*. These are weak or peripheral and are relatively unimportant in characterising a person or their life-style.

Allport emphasises that traits are not independent entities within a person; they are an interdependent set of attributes which come together to produce an effect on behaviour. The following example illustrates this point.

Many traits contribute to the total performance of a person telling a joke or a story at a party. Motive traits (such as entertaining others or showing off) are evident, and stylistic traits (such as being bashful, boring, or delightfully entertaining) are also reflected. In essence, the entertainer's traits combine to form a coherent cluster. This leads to Allport's concept of the self (*proprium*)—a concept which embraces distinctive and important personal characteristics, such as self-image, self-esteem, rational thinker or, alternatively, irrational, impetuous, and so on.

Cattell's 16 PF Test

Cattell (1965) is another influential trait theorist. His approach was to reduce systematically the list of personality traits to a small manageable number by using a statistical method called factor analysis. The attraction of this method is that it enables complex data to be quantified and reduced to a more manageable form, though the total research process in which factor analysis is used does contain some intuitive judgement.

Source Traits and Surface Traits
The following example illustrates Cattell's approach. We are concerned with measuring the ability of a group of students in relation to four activities: using calculus; understanding physics; playing football; and skating on ice. We would expect those who do well in mathematics also to do well in physics, but not necessarily to do well in sport. Though we are unlikely to use factor analysis in this situation, if it were used it would reveal two factors, or *source traits*, underlying the activities in question—namely mathematical and scientific ability and ability in sport. The source traits affect the pattern of behaviour that is visible to the observer.

The observable behavioural patterns are called *surface traits*. At work or college a cluster of surface traits—e.g. possession of a large vocabulary, an understanding of accounting and quantitative methods, and a knowledge of business history—may be observed in the behaviour of the individual.

The surface traits could be underpinned by at least three independent source traits—education, intelligence, and a studious temperament. Through various forms of tests, inter-correlations of personality variables, and the use of observational data, Cattell

chose 16 personality factors that are said to represent source traits (see Table 1.3).

The source traits are the backbone of the enduring aspects of behaviour, and it is through their interaction that the more readily observed surface traits of an individual are determined. These surface traits happen to coincide with descriptions of personality in everyday use. The factors on the 16 personality factor ("PF") questionnaire used to measure personality are relatively independent, and are not correlated significantly among themselves. So a person's score on any one of these factors should not influence their score on another, though there may be some weak correlations.

After further analysis, Cattell arrived at *second-order factors*, of which anxiety is one. The second-order factors are said to influence behaviour only through the source traits or primary factors. The source traits are considered to be more accurate than the second-order factors in describing and predicting behaviour.

Though source traits are said to be enduring aspects of personality, there are circumstances in one's life when predictions of behaviour on the basis of traits alone can be misleading. For example, a person who is suffering from fatigue or who is frightened or under the influence of drugs may indulge in unexpected behaviour.

Cattell recognises that environmental and hereditary factors interact with and influence the source traits to different degrees. The validity of the 16 PF test has been questioned (Howarth & Browne, 1971), but a more recent version of the questionnaire was considered by Cattell to be an improvement on earlier versions (Cattell, 1974). The major criticism of Cattell's theory centres on the proposition that the assumptions governing factor analysis force us to oversimplify personality (Peck & Whitlow, 1975).

Nevertheless, a number of researchers have used the 16 PF questionnaire with managers. The 16 PF instrument comprises 187 questions presented in a forced choice

TABLE 1.3

Factors in Cattell's 16 PF Questionnaire

Low-score Description	Factor	High-score Description
Reserved, detatched, critical	A	Outgoing, warm-hearted
Less intelligent, concrete thinking	B	More intelligent, abstract thinking
Affected by feelings, easily upset	C	Emotionally stable, faces reality
Humble, mild, accommodating	E	Assertive, aggressive, stubborn
Sober, prudent, serious	F	Happy-go-lucky, impulsive, lively
Expedient, disregards rules	G	Conscientious, persevering
Shy, restrained, timid	H	Venturesome, socially bold
Tough-minded, self-reliant	I	Tender-minded, clinging
Trusting, adaptable	L	Suspicious, self-opinionated
Practical, careful	M	Imaginative
Forthright, natural	N	Shrewd, calculating
Self-assured, confident	O	Apprehensive, self-reproaching
Conservative	Q1	Experimenting, liberal
Group-dependent	Q2	Self-sufficient
Undisciplined, self-conflict	Q3	Controlled, socially precise
Relaxed, tranquil	Q4	Tense, frustrated

Source: Cattell, R.B. (1974). How good is the modern questionnaire? General principles for evaluation. *Journal of Personality Assessment*, 38, 115–129. Reproduced by permission.

format. For each question, three possible answers are provided—"Agree", "Uncertain" and "Disagree". The instructions discourage the excessive use of the "Uncertain" response. In this type of process there is always a danger that respondents may distort their true position on various issues by unwittingly giving an inaccurate or a socially acceptable response. However, this danger may be minimised in a supportive climate where questionnaires are completed anonymously.

PERSONALITY TESTING

It is often recognised that a number of job failures result from personality deficiencies. Being endowed with the necessary intellectual attributes, knowledge, and skills does not guarantee that the individual will be an effective or satisfied worker, or a well-liked colleague. Personality characteristics could be influential in determining success or failure in a job, particularly where substantial interpersonal contacts are involved, as required in selling and managerial or supervisory work. These are areas where the application of personality tests to personnel selection has been explored to a greater extent than elsewhere. Often, the motivation to use the tests is to improve the personnel selection process by cutting down the cost of making errors in selecting people. Methods of personnel selection will be discussed fully in Chapter 13.

Personality tests, along with interest tests, could also be used in vocational guidance and counselling, with the emphasis on placing people in jobs compatible with their personal characteristics. Interest tests measure vocational interests or preferences. The person whose interests are being tested indicates the strength of his or her interests in such matters as various jobs, hobbies, and recreational activities.

Most of the personality tests used are pencil and paper tests with multiple-choice elements. In practice, they are not tests in the sense that correct and incorrect answers are possible to the various questions. They are really questionnaires in which the job applicant or employee seeking advancement in the organisation is requested to state how he or she feels about certain issues, or how he or she would react in certain specified situations.

Personality Questionnaire

The first personality questionnaire used as a placement or selection tool operated as a screening device on soldiers in World War I. It was used to identify soldiers who it was felt were unable to face the challenge of combat, and it enabled the prompt testing of thousands of candidates. Handling so many people using interviews would be impracticable. The personality questionnaire was called the "Personal Data Sheet".

A personality questionnaire can have "Yes" or "No" answers, although some questionnaires have an intermediate category such as "Don't know" or "Cannot say". A typical item in a personality questionnaire might read, "I feel comfortable with other people":

1. Yes.
2. Don't know.
3. No.

There are other ways of making assessments of personality. In daily life we are constantly making subjective assessments of the personality of others. In a formal sense we use the interview as a method to assess personality. Other ways of assessing personality are described elsewhere in this chapter; for example, there are sections devoted to the use of projective tests and on the repertory grid.

The answers provided by respondents to questions on the personality questionnaire could be distorted for a number of reasons, such as the following:

- Subjects may not have sufficient self-awareness to give a response that reflects their true feelings.
- The questions may be misread for a multitude of reasons.
- Subjects deliberately sabotage the process by giving random, meaningless responses.
- Subjects may deliberately set out to create a false impression. Unlike tests of intelligence and aptitude (discussed later) which are almost impossible to fake—i.e. the candidate comes up with either the right or wrong answer—tests of personality are open to faking.

If a person applying for a job takes a personality test, the motivation to secure the job may lead that person to generate responses that he or she thinks will make them an attractive candidate in the eyes of the employing organisation. There was some evidence in one study to suggest that applicants for the position of salesman faked some of the responses on a personality test (the Cattell 16 PF) because of the high scores they received on two particular dimensions—extraversion and low anxiety. These dimensions are considered to be desirable qualities in a salesman (Poppleton, 1975).

It seems that where a personality test is taken for the purposes of vocational guidance, people are motivated to give relatively truthful answers to the questions because it is in their interest to discover all they can about themselves in order to make sound vocational choices. However, one cannot rule out faking to create a good impression even in these circumstances (Tiffin & McCormick, 1969).

The tester can use forced-choice techniques specifically designed to minimise faking. With a forced-choice item the respondent must choose between answers that appear equally acceptable (or unacceptable), but that differ in validity for a specific criterion. The following is an example of a test item from a personality test (the Gordon Personal Profile) using the forced-choice technique:

- a good mixer socially;
- lacking in self-confidence;
- thorough in any work undertaken;
- tends to be somewhat emotional.

The respondent is asked to examine this set of descriptions of personal characteristics, and select one description that is most like, and one description that is least like, him or her. It should be noted, however, that the forced-choice technique reduces but does not eliminate faking, especially by the applicant for a specific job (Anastasi, 1979).

Other measures to neutralise faking are disguising the test so that it appears to be something quite different from what it really is, and introducing "lie scales". The latter is a set of questions designed to detect distortion by the person being tested. One approach is to introduce a number of statements depicting ultra perfect qualities that, bar a few, the normal person could not conceivably possess. If the respondent scored too highly on these items, then the tester could challenge the credibility of all the other responses and disregard the test score. Another approach is to repeat individual test items, sometimes slightly disguised, and then see whether the respondent gives the same answers to both sets of questions.

Serious consideration has been given to the issue of faking by subjects completing personality questionnaires or tests used in personnel selection. In one study the results, which were in line with previous findings, indicated that the questionnaires used were all highly susceptible to faking. Though recognising certain caveats, the researcher found that subjects were able to fake in a selective way by projecting desirable profiles compatible with their perception of the occupation in question (Furnham, 1990).

Features of Tests

Personality tests, just like psychological tests generally, possess a number of features (Toplis, Dulewicz, & Fletcher, 1987).

With the odd exception they tend to be objective, standardised measures with well-controlled and uniform procedures governing the way the test is conducted and scored. Therefore, the test items, instructions, and time allowed (where a time limit exists), should be the same for every candidate. Also, every candidate should be exposed to the same physical test conditions, such as adequate illumination, appropriate temperature, a distraction-free environment, and adequate space.

Scoring, whether operated manually, or computerised, must be objective to ensure that the tester's or scorer's judgement does not lead to variations in the score. Therefore, the tester has a "key" that contains a value allocated to a given answer. The raw scores derived from values placed on the responses are only significant when they are compared with *norms* for the particular occupational group in question. The norms are the range of scores obtained from a large representative sample of people for whom the test was designed. The sample could, for example, consist of a group of sales representatives in the UK, and the norms relate to the normal or average performance of this group, with degrees of deviation above and below the average. To ensure standardisation and objectivity, a normative score is read from a norms table. Also, this ensures that the subjective interpretation of the data by the tester is removed from the process.

A percentile score is taken from the conversion tables, and this represents the proportion of the reference group (the occupational group with which the individual tested is compared) that has a lower score than the person tested. For example, if a sales representative scored at the 75th percentile on a particular dimension of a test using UK norms, his or her score would be better than 75% of UK sales representatives. Only 25% of UK sales representatives would have a better score.

The manual supporting the test should contain scientific data to show the "quality" of the test and what it is supposed to do. In this context two factors are crucial—reliability and validity. A personality test is reliable if it gives the same profile on a repeated basis in the same conditions. In other words, the measure must be consistent. A personality test is valid if it measures what it is supposed to be measuring. A more detailed explanation of these concepts appears in Chapters 6 and 13

in connection with attitude measurement and selection methods.

Finally, it should be noted that training those responsible for the administration and interpretation of tests is very important: as is restricted access, for example, preventing candidates getting hold of tests before selection, and therefore reducing the chances of tests being misused.

Personality Profiles

A study of 400 managers and accountants attending different courses at a UK management college was undertaken using the 16 PF test (Barden, 1970). Their personality profiles appear in Fig. 1.2.

The researcher makes the point that the profiles in Fig. 1.2 refer to the people who participated in the study, and that there is no

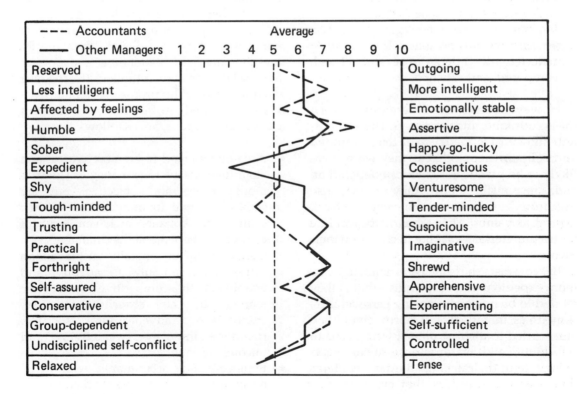

FIG. 1.2. Personality profiles of accountants and managers using Cattell's 16 PF test.

implication that accountants or managers in general should be like this, or that this constitutes the profile of successful accountants or managers (although one cannot rule out this possibility). The following characteristics were shared by both accountants and managers:

- *Tendency towards assertiveness and shrewdness.* This would be reflected in an inclination to be self-assured, dominant, independent-minded, bold in approach, hard, stern, hostile, solemn, tough-minded, and authoritarian. Also, there would be a tendency to be polished and experienced.
- *Tendency towards experimentation.* This would be reflected in a tendency to be interested in intellectual matters and fundamental issues. There was also a tendency to take issue with old or new ideas, to be better informed with less of an inclination to moralise but more of an inclination to experiment generally in life.
- *Tendency towards relaxation.* This would be reflected in a tendency to be calm, relaxed, composed, and satisfied.

However, there were differences between the accountants and managers. The accountants showed a tendency to be tough-minded and self-sufficient—that is they were more likely to be practical, realistic, independent, and responsible—but they were also uncultured, sometimes phlegmatic, hard, cynical, and smug. They tended to be resolute with a preference for taking decisions on their own.

By contrast, the managers tended to be more expedient and suspicious—that is they tended to be unsteady, lacking perseverance, sometimes impatient and obstructive. They also tended to distrust others, were prone to self-doubt, and were self-opinionated and deliberate in their actions. Barden maintains that it is not surprising that managers and accountants have problems with communication.

The two groups display different approaches to solving problems. The managers would like to solve problems quickly, are prepared to bend the rules to achieve their objectives, and are also more prepared to take risks. The accountants, who offer services to the managers, are quite prepared to take time over problems, but are not prepared to bend the rules and, in any case, prefer to go it alone. As both are assertive, conflict is likely to develop. Barden feels that certain personality types choose accounting as a career, and she is of the view that anybody who proposes to study and qualify in accounting needs to be able to pay great attention to detail, and have patience, good concentration, a good memory, and an ability to handle figures. These characteristics are said to be compatible with the qualities identified in the profile of the accountant's personality, as illustrated in Fig. 1.2.

In another study, a sample of 603 middle managers representing a wide range of managerial jobs completed the 16 PF questionnaire when attending a course at another UK management college (Hartston & Mottram, 1976). The profiles emerging from this exercise, and attributable to the different occupational groups, are as follows:

- Accountants tend to be more critical and aloof than the average manager. They are more precise and objective, but are somewhat rigid in their attitudes. They share with bankers a lower level of competitiveness than other managers.
- Sales managers generally displayed an extravert nature—outgoing, adaptive, and attentive, with a competitive nature. They tended to be cheerful, talkative, enthusiastic, adventurous, sociable, friendly, impulsive, carefree, and unconventional.
- Engineers, like accountants, tend to be more critical and aloof than other managers. They also tend to be introspective and less communicative than

other managers, and show a tendency towards slowness and caution. They are more tough-minded than other managers, unsentimental, self-reliant, responsible and capable of keeping to the point. They tend to be conventional and are concerned with objectivity and immediate practicalities, rather than indulging in far-fetched imaginative ideas.

- Production managers, like engineers, are tough-minded and conventional, but are more assertive and feel free to participate in and to criticise group behaviour.
- Research and development managers, like accountants and engineers, tend to be critical, aloof, and tough-minded. They are brighter and more alert than other managers, but are more restrained and socially inhibited. As a result, they are likely to minimise personal contact with others. Though they may have feelings of inferiority and experience threats from the environment, they are more radical in their thinking than other managers. They tend to be well informed and inclined to experiment with solutions to problems. Likewise, they are receptive to change and new ideas, and are inclined towards analytical thought.
- Personnel managers tend to be more outgoing and adaptable than other managers and prefer occupations that deal with people. They are more sensitive and tender-minded, less realistic and tolerant of the rougher aspects of life, and more cultured. They tend to fuss more in group or committee meetings, slowing down the process of decision taking. They tend to be more imaginative than other managers and are more concerned with introspection and the inner life—an important characteristic for anyone involved in planning and looking beyond immediate needs. Though they may be somewhat impractical, careless, and, to a limited extent, lacking in self-control, they display a romantic liking for travel and new experiences.

A group of researchers in Australia created a profile of the Australian manager after using the 16 PF instrument with 475 managers. Having engaged in international comparisons they arrived at the following tentative conclusions (Barry & Dowling, 1984):

- Australian and British managers are less extravert than US managers.
- Australian and US managers have lower scores on intelligence than British managers.
- Australian managers tend to be more dominating and assertive than British or US managers.
- Australian managers appear more imaginative and less practical than British or US managers.
- Australian and British managers are more forthright and less shrewd than US managers.
- Australian managers are more self-sufficient than British or US managers.

These studies are illustrative of a research process designed to identify personality traits. The results could profitably be used by a psychologist, particularly in a counselling situation. In this sense, profiles could be used in management development to foster self-awareness and assist in planning self-development, but it would appear unwise to use them for selection purposes because of the possibility that a respondent may distort the results. This matter was discussed earlier in the chapter.

Other Tests

Examples of other tests used to measure personality traits are the Thurstone and Edwards schedules, and Saville and Holdsworth's Occupational Personality Questionnaire (OPQ) developed in the UK The latter consists of some 11 questionnaires for use in selection, development, counselling, and team-building. The OPQ is based on 30 traits listed in Table 1.4 (Saville & Holdsworth, 1984).

TABLE 1.4

Traits in Saville and Holdsworth's (1984) Occupational Personality Questionnaire

Trait	*Characteristics*
Relationships with people	
Persuasive	Enjoys selling, changes opinions of others, convincing with arguments, negotiates.
Controlling	Takes charge, directs, manages, organises, supervises others.
Independent	Has strong views on things, difficult to manage, speaks up, argues, dislikes ties.
Outgoing	Fun loving, humorous, sociable, vibrant, talkative, jovial.
Affiliative	Has many friends, enjoys being in groups, likes companionship, shares things with friends.
Socially confident	Puts people at ease, knows what to say, good with words.
Modest	Reserved about achievements, avoids talking about self, accepts others, avoids trappings of status.
Democratic	Encourages others to contribute, consults, listens and refers to others.
Caring	Considerate to others, helps those in need, sympathetic, tolerant.
Thinking style	
Practical	Down-to-earth, likes repairing and mending things, better with the concrete.
Data rational	Good with data, operates on facts, enjoys assessing and measuring.
Artistic	Appreciates culture, shows artistic flair, sensitive to visual arts and music.
Behavioural	Analyses thoughts and behaviour, psychologically minded, likes to understand people.
Traditional	Preserves well proven methods, prefers the orthodox, disciplined, conventional.
Change-orientated	Enjoys doing new things, seeks variety, prefers novelty to routine, accepts changes.
Conceptual	Theoretical, intellectually curious, enjoys the complex and abstract.
Innovative	Generates ideas, shows ingenuity, thinks up solutions.
Forward planning	Prepares well in advance, enjoys target setting, forecasts trends, plans projects.
Detail conscious	Methodical, keeps things neat and tidy, precise, accurate.
Conscientious	Sticks to deadlines, completes jobs, perserveres with routine, likes fixed schedules.
Feelings and emotions	
Relaxed	Calm, relaxed, cool under pressure, free from anxiety, can switch off.
Worrying	Worries when things go wrong, keyed up before important events, anxious to do well.
Tough-minded	Difficult to hurt or upset, can brush off insults, unaffected by unfair remarks.
Emotional control	Restrained in showing emotions, keeps feelings back, avoids outbursts.
Optimistic	Cheerful, happy, keeps spirits up despite setbacks.
Critical	Good at probing the facts, sees the disadvantages, challenges assumptions.
Active	Has energy, moves quickly, enjoys physical exercise, doesn't sit still.
Competitive	Plays to win, determined to beat others, poor loser.
Achieving	Ambitious, sets sights high, career-centred, results orientated.
Decisive	Quick at conclusions, weighs things up rapidly, may be hasty, takes risks.

Jackson and Rothstein (1993) say of the OPQ: "It has not yet been the subject of the peer review process nor the focus of independent research that is necessary for all scientific achievements." Robertson and Kinder (1993) carried out a major meta-analysis looking at the criterion-related validity of OPQ personality measures and reported supportive findings. The results show that OPQ fares well in relation to other predictors of performance, such as assessment centres, cognitive ability tests, and work samples. These predictors are examined in Chapter 13.

The Thurstone Temperament Schedule attempts to measure personality traits on seven dimensions. A high score on a particular dimension would reflect the characteristics set out in Table 1.5. Using the Thurstone Temperament Schedule, Westfall (1962) concluded that the traits "active" and "impulsive" were associated with the ownership of convertible cars, whereas the traits "stable" and "sociable" applied to owners of standard and compact cars.

Another test, the Edwards Personal Preference Schedule, was used to measure the relative strength of 15 needs (such as achievement, affiliation, dominance, sex, deference, or compliance) in relation to particular purchases (Koponen, 1960). Personality profiles varied between groups on the basis of demographic factors such as age, sex, income, size of town or city, and region. When the profiles were related to purchases of various products (e.g. cars, cigarettes, cosmetics, and paper towels) certain relationships emerged.

An illustrative finding was the relationship between personality and cigarette smoking. Heavy smokers scored high on sex, aggression, and achievement, and low on order, deference, and compliance. Smokers of filter cigarettes scored high on dominance,

TABLE 1.5

Personality Traits on the Thurstone Temperament Schedule

Trait Dimension	Characteristics
Active	The person is likely to be in a rush, probably speaking, walking, driving, working, and eating at a fast rate when it is not necessary to do so.
Vigorous	The person usually enjoys physical activity requiring a lot of energy, is active in sport and outdoor occupations, and engages in work requiring the use of hands or tools.
Impulsive	The person is usually happy-go-lucky, likes to take chances, and makes quick decisions.
Dominant	The person has the capacity for taking the initiative and assuming responsibility, and probably takes satisfaction from organising social activities, persuading others, and promoting new ventures.
Stable	The person is likely to remain calm in a crisis, is able to disregard distractions while stuying or working, and is not irritated if interrupted when concentrating.
Sociable	The person enjoys the company of others, makes friends easily, and is sympathetic, co-operative, and agreeable in relations with others.
Reflective	The person indulges in meditative thinking, enjoys dealing with theoretical rather than practical problems, and prefers to work alone with material requiring accuracy and fine detail.

change, and achievement, and low on aggression, autonomy, and need for independence.

If one were to take this type of study seriously, it would be natural to attempt to direct an appropriate sales message to the most prominent needs. In one study, a mail order advertisement written around an appeal for change brought in twice as many returns from the group scoring high on the need for change than from the group scoring low on this need (Anastasi, 1979).

Another study (Landon, 1972) singled out the role of achievement as a personality trait. Subjects scoring high on the need for achievement appeared to favour products that might be referred to as virile and masculine—e.g. boating equipment, skis, and lawn mowers. On the other hand, male subjects scoring low on the need for achievement tended to favour products that might be thought of as meticulous or fastidious—e.g. automatic dishwashers, headache remedies, mouthwashes, electric toothbrushes, and deodorants (Landon, 1972).

The trait approach to personality has been used extensively in research into consumer behaviour but the results have been generally disappointing. In the 1970s Proctor and Gamble decided to discontinue the use of personality measures, because the results obtained were not good enough for brand and advertising managers to develop marketing strategies more effectively than they could with alternative approaches. Some would argue that this was not surprising because the standardised personality measures used at that time were more appropriate to clinical settings than to marketing (Engel et al., 1990). They would then go on to say that personality measures designed for a specific purpose to profile consumers have greater potential to predict the behaviour of consumers with respect to specific products. But, of course, the generalisability of such an exercise is questionable. Notwithstanding what has been said, the trait approach has contributed to the development of psychographics, a topic that will be discussed later.

Criticisms

Having reviewed the criticisms levelled at the trait approach, Chell (1987) concludes that "trait theory has suffered a rough ride over the past decade or so. Criticisms have been so incisive that there is really no turning back." However, this is a view that would certainly be challenged by Buss (1989), who concludes that if there is to be a distinct field of study called "personality", its central and defining characteristic must be traits.

Recently, Deary and Matthews (1993) have provided a comprehensive review of advances in personality research, and from their evaluation of this area they make a very strong case for the potency and vitality of trait psychology. They argue that there is broad agreement about personality traits and their biological determinants, and that traits can be called on to explain and predict behaviour. Reflecting on the Deary and Matthews review, Bentall (1993), a clinical psychologist, raises the following objections that may be shared by some psychologists:

It is not yet clear whether personality research can contribute to the greater good. Certainly, a greater sensitivity to the ethical and political implications of personality research seems necessary. Personality research as it stands at present is unlikely to be of use to those of us who wish to apply psychology to help solve pressing human problems. It may be that these objections are not fatal. I look forward to a science of personality which is value-free, and which makes specific and useful predictions about how particular individuals will respond in particular circumstances.

As a postscript to this discussion of personality testing, it seems appropriate to dwell momentarily on Ghiselli's (1973) general conclusion from two decades ago that personality tests have some modest value when used to assist with the personnel selection process. In contrast, a comparatively recent study by Blinkhorn and Johnson (1990) in the UK casts doubts on the use of personality tests for recruitment and promotion purposes. The researchers looked at the three most widely used and respected tests (including the 16 PF and the OPQ) and concluded that there is little evidence of enduring relationships between personality test scores and measures of successful performance at work.

Jackson and Rothstein (1993), in a balanced and helpful analysis of the use of personality tests for personnel selection, take issue with Blinkhorn and Johnson on their conclusions. They maintain that "the criticisms do not accurately or fairly characterise *all* personality measurement in personnel selection research".

Despite their reservations, however, Blinkhorn and Johnson do acknowledge that personality testing may be invaluable for counselling purposes, or in other situations where self-perception is as important as the truth.

Graphology

Parallel to the scientific assessment of personality is the growth in non-scientific methods such as astrology and graphology (handwriting analysis). In the words of two exponents of handwriting analysis, "handwriting holds the key to one of life's most fascinating and tantalising mysteries—the true personality of another human being" (Greene & Lewis, 1988). Adopting an allegedly "scientific" approach to graphology, called graphonomy, a profile (shown in Fig. 1.3) was produced from an inspection of a person's handwriting. The person profiled was a 27-year-old man occupying a managerial position in the buying department of a London department store. Married with one young daughter, he was promoted from the position of sales clerk having spent 10 years

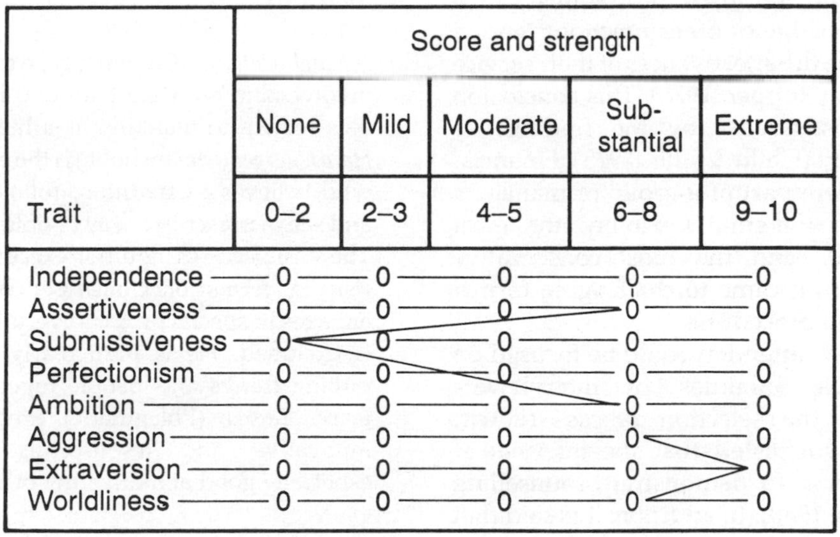

	Score and strength				
	None	Mild	Moderate	Sub-stantial	Extreme
Trait	0–2	2–3	4–5	6–8	9–10
Independence	0	0	0	0	0
Assertiveness	0	0	0	0	0
Submissiveness	0	0	0	0	0
Perfectionism	0	0	0	0	0
Ambition	0	0	0	0	0
Aggression	0	0	0	0	0
Extraversion	0	0	0	0	0
Worldliness	0	0	0	0	0

FIG. 1.3. A personality profile created by a graphologist. Source: Greene, J. and Lewis, D. (1988). *The hidden language of your handwriting.* London: Macdonald & Co. Reproduced by permission of Souvenir Press Ltd.

with the same firm. He wields considerable authority in his job and carries significant responsibilities. He is said to be an attractive, outward-going person with many friends.

The results of a study of personnel selection techniques used for managers in the mid-1980s showed that 2.6% of the top 1000 UK companies always used graphology in the assessment of managers (Robertson & Makin, 1986). However, drawing inferences about the personal qualities of the person from an analysis of his or her handwriting is challenged as a reliable form of assessment (Klimoski & Rafael, 1983).

Further observations

Other observations of personal characteristics of accountants, which are not based on personality inventories or tests, indicate that the accountant is cold or impersonal, and conservative (De Coster & Rhode, 1971). This is said to be particularly so for accountants with a professional accounting background (Lawler & Rhode, 1976). In a study of the role of management accountants it was concluded that caution, risk aversion, conservatism, preference for well-tried procedures and a lack of knowledge of other functions tended to undermine the effectiveness of their service to managers (Hopper, 1978). This conclusion can be substantiated by the findings of another study (Child & Ellis, 1973). Financial managers were part of a group of managers with the least mental flexibility, the most closed minds and the most conservative attitude when it came to challenging formal authority and procedures.

By contrast, attention could be focused on the desirable qualities of interviewers involved in the selection process (Lewis, 1984). It is suggested that the interviewer should be able to demonstrate counselling skills (Lewis, 1980). In addition, it is said that capable interviewers possess characteristics that are not highly valued in a social sense—timidity, anxiety, and insecurity—and that people with these qualities feel the most

need to subject others to assessment (Bayne & Fletcher, 1983).

TYPE PERSPECTIVE

When a person shares a pattern of traits with a large group of people, he or she is said to belong to a personality type.

The Four Humours

The best known typology in ancient Greece was that of Hippocrates in the 5th century BC He theorised that the body contained four fluids or humours—yellow bile, black bile, high blood pressure, and phlegm. In AD 180, Galen allocated temperaments to the four humours to show how physical conditions in the form of internal abnormalities could affect patterns of behaviour. These relationships are depicted in Table 1.6.

An American consultant (Leigh, 1985) generalised on the basis of his experience of personality testing and came to the conclusion that personality types in business roughly correspond with the classical temperaments as follows:

A *People Catalyst* (Choleric) type thrives on involvement with those around him, and sees service to mankind as a life goal. A *Hard Charger* (Melancholic) is the executive who believes in tradition, follows rules, and sees a prescribed way of doing things. The *Fast Track* (Sanguine) executive sees risk in terms of challenge. When he engages in special projects everything else is excluded. He is particularly good at pulling things and people together. The *Power Broker* (Phlegmatic) executive is innovative and resourceful, and is especially good at motivating others.

Sheldon's Typology

Probably the best known modern physical typology is that of Sheldon (1954).

TABLE 1.6

The Four Humours

Humours	Temperaments	Behaviour
Yellow bile	Choleric	Active but changeable mood; rapid thinking; highly strung; easily provoked; strong emotions.
Black bile	Melancholic	Pessimistic; tendency towards ill-founded fears; resistance to provocation; strong emotions once aroused.
High Blood Pressure	Sanguine	Cheerful; easy going and supremely confident; weak emotions though easily aroused.
Excess Phlegm	Phlegmatic	Sluggish; supremely calm; slow thinking; resistant to provocation; weak emotions even when aroused.

Working from the photographs of 4000 college students he defined physical types similar to those that appear in Fig. 1.4.

Eysenck's Typology

A prominent type theorist is Eysenck (1953). In his work he stresses the second-order factors or types, as opposed to traits, in the personality of the individual. Take, for example, the personality type known as *extraversion*. It is expressed in the form of a hierarchical organisation in Fig. 1.5.

Eysenck shares Cattell's view that biological factors are involved in the determination of personality, but unlike Cattell, much of Eysenck's early work grew out of his interest in abnormal psychology and psychiatry. Eysenck related his own research to the ancient typology referred to in Table 1.6 and found a fairly good relationship with the original theory, as shown in Fig. 1.6.

It was in his original study of 700 neurotic soldiers that Eysenck found that factor analysis of 39 items of personal data, including personality ratings, resulted in the establishment of two basic dimensions of personality—extraversion/introversion and neuroticism/stability (Eysenck, 1947).

This structure of personality was substantiated by further research with a large number of subjects. In a later investigation with psychiatric patients, Eysenck established a third dimension of personality, unrelated to extraversion and neuroticism, which he called psychoticism. It should be noted that these dimensions of personality relate to the extreme ends of a continuum, and only very few people would fall into these categories. With regard to extraversion, for example, most people would fall somewhere in between—they would be neither very extraverted nor very introverted.

Extravert
According to Eysenck, the typical extravert is sociable, likes parties, has many friends, needs people to converse with, but does not like reading or studying alone. Extraverts need excitement, take chances, are often adventurous, act on the spur of the moment, and are generally impulsive individuals. They are fond of practical jokes, always have a ready answer and generally like change. They are carefree, optimistic and like to laugh and be merry. They prefer to keep moving and remain active, tend to be aggressive and lose their temper quickly. Altogether their feelings are not kept under tight control and they are not always reliable (Eysenck, 1965).

(a)

(b)

(c)

FIG. 1.4. Sheldon's physical typology.
(a) Endomorphic: Soft round body, stocky but not exactly fat. Large trunk, thick neck and relatively short legs. Generally relaxed in temperament, loves comfort, sociable and affectionate. (b) Mesomorphic: Well rounded with bone and muscle - the Greek God type of body build. The temperament is assertive, noisy, aggressive, and energetic. (c) Ectomorphic: A fragile body build, with a temperament that is inhibited in actions, over-restrained, and socially withdrawn, with an inferiority complex.

Introvert

The typical introvert is a quiet, retiring person, introspective, and fond of books rather than people. Introverts are reserved and distant except with intimate friends. They tend to plan ahead, take precautions, and distrust any impulse of the moment. They do not like excitement, take matters of everyday life with proper seriousness, and like a well-ordered approach to life. They keep their feelings under close control, seldom behave in an aggressive way, and do not lose their temper easily. They are reliable, somewhat pessimistic, and place great value on ethical standards (Eysenck, 1965).

Neurotic

The neuroticism dimension is akin to the idea of emotional instability. Individuals who fall into the extreme end of the neuroticism dimension tend to be more prone to worries and anxieties, and more easily upset. They are also likely to complain of headaches, and experience sleeping or eating difficulties. Although they may be more likely to develop neurotic disorders under stressful conditions, in practice the frequency of such events is low and most individuals function adequately in their family, work, and social life. Most of Eysenck's research and theory has been concerned with the extraversion and neuroticism dimensions and, until recently, the psychoticism dimension received less attention.

Psychotic

The psychoticism dimension in its extreme form would be concerned with states such as obsessions, phobias, hysteria, acute depression, and schizophrenia.

Eysenck's Concept of Personality

It embraces the view that an individual *inherits* a particular type of nervous system that predisposes him or her to develop in a particular way. However, the final form personality takes will be determined by the biological basis of personality as well as by the

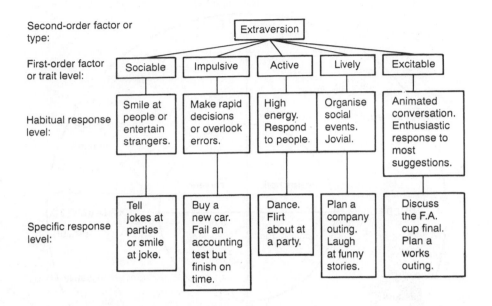

FIG. 1.5. Eysenck's structure of personality as related to extraversion. Adapted from Eysenck, H.J. (1967). *The biological basis of personality*. Courtesy of Charles C. Thomas, Publisher, Springfield, Illinois.

various socialising influences the individual encounters in everyday life (Eysenck,1967).

The Eysenck Personality Inventory (EPI)

This is a device used to measure the dimensions of personality, and lie scale items are included to screen out respondents making socially desirable responses. In evaluating the model of personality postulated by Eysenck, two clinical psychologists (Peck & Whitlow, 1975) have made the following observations:

At present there seems to be little justification for Eysenck's suggestions that psychiatrists, educationalists, or parole boards should base their recommendations for treatment, teaching or probation on measures of extraversion, neuroticism or psychoticism. The questionnaires which Eysenck has developed may continue to be useful tools for personality investigators but their practical value in relation to groups or individuals remains to be demonstrated. Despite these reservations, the main body of Eysenck's theory seems certain to prove a fruitful source of ideas for investigation in the field of personality for many years to come.

Kline (1987) analysed a large amount of data from personality questionnaires (i.e. the EPI) and endorsed Eysenck's three dimensions—extraversion, neuroticism and psychoticism. He also identified an additional two dimensions, described as sensation seeking and obsessionality. A person scoring high on sensation seeking tends to get involved in activities likely to satisfy his or her need for sensation, such as rally driving or mountain climbing. The person endowed with a significant level of obsessionality displays obsessive behaviour exemplified by almost an unnatural adherence to rules and regulations, often accompanied by a strong

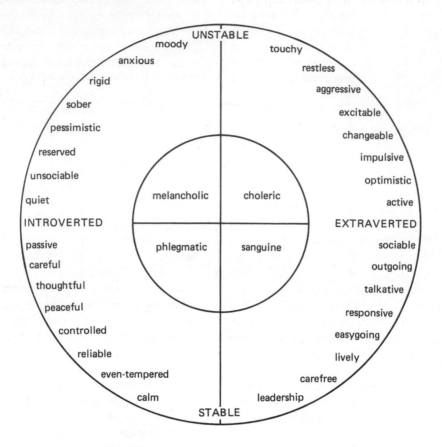

FIG. 1.6. Eysenck's typology of personality. Source: Eysenck, H.J. (1947). *Dimensions of personality*. London: Routledge and Kegan Paul. Reproduced by permission of Curtis Brown Ltd. Copyright H. J. Eysenck.

preoccupation with tidiness, and sometimes stinginess. Another manifestation of obsessionality is authoritarianism, and should a manager possess this trait there is a likelihood that he or she could adopt an autocratic style of management.

As a postscript, the "Big Five" factor theory dominates current personality research (McAdams, 1992; Bayne, 1994). The five basic dimensions of personality according to this theory are Extraversion, Agreeableness, Conscientiousness, Neuroticism, and Openness. Sometimes, a sixth—Intellect—is added, but this is considered problematic.

Personality Types and Accidents

As long ago as 1926 researchers were particularly interested in the relationship between personality and accident-proneness, and accident rates (Farmer & Chambers, 1926). Accident-proneness was defined as a personal idiosyncrasy predisposing the individual who possesses it to a relatively high accident rate.

Although aware of the weaknesses of the tests used, the researchers concluded that variations in accident liability are not solely determined by external factors or by chance, but are due in a significant way to measurable individual differences. A relationship was found between accidents and aesthetokinetic co-ordination; the latter refers to the way the individual uses the hand and arm in response to stimuli recorded and interpreted by the sense organs. Poor integration and nervous instability could lead to accidents. There was a slight indication that the accident-prone are industrially inefficient and more liable to report sick, and consequently react unfavourably to their work environment, but this needed to be confirmed.

In more recent studies the concept of accident-proneness appears to be elusive. It is suggested that the accident-prone personality can be described variously as aggressive, hostile or overactive, but no permanent or stable personality trait of the accident-prone person can be identified (Haddon, Suchman, & Klein, 1964). It is also suggested that the propensity to accidental injury increases at certain times—e.g. in conditions of poor vision, fatigue, alcoholic use, and where certain hazards or stressors exist in the environment. But these conditions may be of a temporary nature (Hirschfield & Behan,

1963). The young and inexperienced could also be vulnerable to accidents, but likewise this could be a temporary state, just as it could be for a person going through a bad patch of ill-health or stress. Sometimes people are defined as accident-prone if they are not as good as their peers at recognising hazardous situations. It may be more sensible to suggest that it is only at certain times that a person's accident liability increases.

An H.M. Principal Inspector of Factories (Accident Prevention Advisory Unit) in the UK, had this to say about accident-proneness:

> Accident-proneness as a concept has little use in practical accident prevention. The concept itself is ill-defined, no stable personality characteristics that can be identified with accident-proneness have been discovered. So therefore, nothing can be done to identify individuals who may be accident-prone in order to treat them or to remove them from areas of greatest risk. Alternative explanations must be found for persons experiencing multiple accidents.... Rather than focusing on

" IT SAYS 'ERE, YOU'VE GOT A DODGY SAFETY RECORD...."

accident-proneness we should concentrate on the elimination of risk and provide education to assist employees to cope with unforeseen hazard situations.

Notwithstanding this, a study conducted in South Africa concluded that accident-prone pilots were more neurotic (emotionally unstable) and more extraverted (impulsive) than those who were less accident-prone. In Canada, taxi drivers with a high frequency of accidents were said to have had more disturbed childhoods, to have been more frequently absent without leave while in the forces, and to have displayed more aggression than those who had a low frequency of accidents (Feldman, 1971). Studies conducted among male workers in British industry suggest a highly significant relationship between accidents and extraversion, but no direct relationship between accidents and neuroticism (Craske, 1968).

In recent years, psychologists have been reluctant to stress a fine dividing line between personal factors (e.g. accident-proneness) and environmental factors (e.g. a slippery floor, poor visibility, etc.) when trying to establish the cause of an accident. As a result, the tendency is now to accept the term "accident liability", for by doing so one is acknowledging the involvement of a number of factors, both personal and environmental, in the determination of accident rates (Glendon & McKenna, 1994).

Let's now move on to a brief examination of other typologies of personality.

Jung's Typology

Jung, a prominent psychologist whose work preceded that of Eysenck, identifies two broad categories—extravert and introvert. An extravert is outward-looking, responds better to facts and is more scientific than philosophical. An introvert is subjective, philosophical, a day-dreamer, and an artistic type.

Jung entered the domain of traits when he classified personality using primary characteristics. Because a simple introversion–extraversion dichotomy is unlikely to be descriptive enough, due to the tremendous variability among people, Jung introduced four so-called *functions:*

1. Sensing: the person is aware of things and processes information through the senses.
2. Thinking: the person understands what a thing is and puts a name to what is sensed.
3. Feeling: the person reacts to things emotionally and defines them as acceptable or unacceptable.
4. *Intuition*: the person has hunches about past or future events in the absence of real information.

This approach concentrates on the information-processing characteristics of the individual (Jung, 1965). These characteristics can be viewed as being located at the ends of the orthogonal axes shown in Fig. 1.7:

- A type 1 person (sensation–thinking) is cold, analytic, lives for the present, is interested primarily in facts, and is extremely practical.
- A type 4 person (intuition–feeling) is the opposite of type 1, and is emotional, sociable, takes a broad view, and is more prone than others to hypothesising.
- A type 2 person is rational, analytic, takes a broad view, and is sociable.
- A type 3 person is the opposite of type 2, and is factual, wishes to grasp tangible things, but is emotional.

Myers–Briggs Type Indicator
This indicator, or an abridged version of it, is used to identify managerial decision styles based on Jung's personality typology (Myers, 1962).

In a study of simulated investment decisions, sensing–feeling executives were more venturesome when undertaking innovative projects than executives falling into the other categories (Henderson & Nutt, 1980). When the focus of attention shifted to

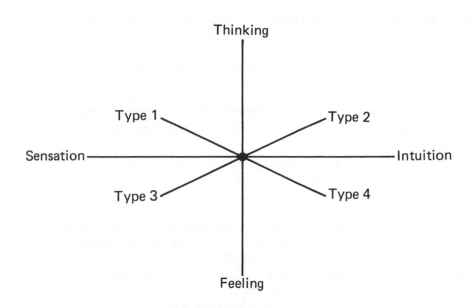

FIG. 1.7. A graphic representation of Jung's functions of personality

the implementation of management science techniques, managers who exhibited sensation–thinking characteristics were said to be more willing to construct and accept management science techniques—e.g. linear programming—than were managers who were predominantly endowed with intuition–feeling characteristics. Yet many top-level executives are of the latter type. The manager with the intuition–feeling characteristics is said to be more able to implement change and innovation within an organisation if he or she is convinced of the usefulness of the management science techniques (Mitroff et al., 1974).

In a comparatively recent study of personality types and success in business of small retailers, there was no convincing support for any purposeful link between the Jung typology and the performance of small businessmen, apart from a cautious conclusion that the thinking extrovert did best as a small retailer (Rice & Lindecamp, 1989).

Allport's Typology

A typology propounded by Allport, Vernon and Lindzey (1960) has the following characteristics:

- *Theoretical*—pursuit of knowledge;
- *Aesthetic*—striving towards art and natural beauty;
- *Social*—pursuit of humanitarian goals;
- *Political*—pursuit of power;
- *Religious*—spiritual pursuits;
- *Economic*—pursuit of material possessions.

The characteristic that features most prominently in an individual is the determining factor of personality. In a study of managers in diverse cultures and countries, a questionnaire was used bearing some similarities to the typology mentioned here. The results of the study indicate that different values and cultures pose different problems with respect to interaction between people (England & Lee, 1974).

Personality Types and Career Choice

Over a number of years, Holland (1985) has developed a theory of career choice rooted in personality. It is maintained that people in each personality type (listed in Table 1.7) gravitate towards a small set of jobs. The reason they do so is because they are seeking

TABLE 1.7

Personality Types and Career Choice

Personality	Occupational Type
Realistic - Tends to like, and has proficiency in, activities requiring physical strength and co-ordination	Farming, carpentry, architecture
Investigative - Tends to get involved in observing, organising, and understanding data, and generally enjoys and is adept at abstract thought. But dislikes social activities and situations where persuasive powers are expected to be used	Mathematics, engineering, dentistry
Social - Enjoys the company of others more than being engaged in intellectual or physical activity. Tends to be warm and caring and enjoys the process of informing, training and enlightening others	Religion, social work, diplomatic service, teaching
Conventional - Likes rules, regulations, structure and order and is prepared to sub-ordinate personal needs to situations where personal or organisational power and status exists. Is usually well organised but generally is not very imaginative	Accounting, finance, military, clerical work
Enterprising - Enjoys activity rather than observation and reflection. Likes to use verbal communication skills to persuade others and gain power and status	Publishing, industrial relations, sales management
Artistic - Dislikes ordered and repetitive situations. Likes to express feelings and ideas, and be expressive and imaginative. Enjoys drama, music and art	Advertising, interior design, drama, art

From J.L. Holland *Making Vocational Choices* (2nd Ed.). Copyright © 1985 by Allyn and Bacon. Adapted by permission.

work which is compatible with their likes and dislikes.

There is research evidence to suggest that when people choose a career that matches their personality they are more likely to be satisfied with their choice and less likely to change professions (Feldman & Arnold, 1985). Holland's model has obvious appeal but it is well to bear in mind that, in reality, choices are remade over time and that many significant developments can occur between the initial choice and subsequent modifications to choices (Arnold, Robertson, & Cooper., 1991).

PSYCHOGRAPHICS

Given the weak predictive relationship between personality variables and buyer behaviour, researchers in consumer behaviour have investigated alternative approaches.

Psychographics, which incorporates life-styles or patterns of behaviour adopted by consumers, is one such approach. To gather psychographic data a distinctive technique is used by which consumers are classified by activity, interest, and opinion (AIO). Researchers assemble a large number of items similar to those found in standardised personality and interest inventories. The responses derived from the administration of these inventories are correlated with the buying of products or exposure to the advertising media.

This type of technique measures activities in terms of how people spend their time at work and leisure, their interests expressed as what they consider important in their immediate surroundings, their opinions on social issues, on institutions, and on themselves. Finally, demographic data—such as their age, income, and where they live—may be added. Colonel Sander's Kentucky Fried Chicken was originally advertised in a folksy, homely, small town way. Then it was established that it was consumed heavily by young housewives with an AIO profile that reflected a more contemporary image. The advertising and packaging of the product were changed to reflect these findings (Wells & Tigert, 1971).

General Foods identified a health- conscious segment of consumers through psychographics. The new market segment for a brand of decaffeinated coffee was active achievers of all ages, as opposed to the previous conception of consumers as elderly people. As a result, the advertisements for the decaffeinated coffee were aimed at consumers interested in adventurous life-styles (Engel et al., 1990).

Since the main purpose of psychographic analysis is to understand the life-styles of core consumers in order to communicate more effectively with their particular market segment, it has assumed importance in a commercial world where change is ever present. The importance of trends in life-styles is shown in the following examples:

There is growing awareness of the effects of physical fitness and dietary habits on health. People are more conscious of the need to control the intake of such ingredients as salt, sugar, and caffeine, and to reduce or cease the consumption of cigarettes and alcohol. Therefore, it is in the interests of manufacturers to adapt or develop products that appeal to people's desire for a healthier life-style.

For example, exercise equipment, nutritional and natural food, decaffeinated tea and coffee, and non-alcoholic wines and beers would fall into this category. The advertising of Alka Seltzer has been influenced by movements to healthier life-styles—the emphasis is on a product which can relief the stress symptoms that accompany success, rather than being an antidote for over-indulgence (Assael, 1987). Equally the advertising of established products, such as the condom, reminds people of the value of the product in protecting them against a potent health hazard as opposed to the primary contraception message of earlier years.

In the 1980s the self-centred life-style was reflected in the advertisers' emphasis on individualism, pointing to products and services that portray a sense of personal achievement.

A relatively new system to combine life-styles and values (VALS) has been developed. Conceptually, it represents a linkage between the personality angle of psychographics and the activities emphasis of life-style research. Although psychographics provides quantitative measures that can be used with large samples (in contrast to the soft or qualitative research associated with the psychoanalytical perspective and consumer motivation research), it should be borne in mind that much psychographic research lacks a solid grounding in personality theory and should be interpreted cautiously (Wilkie, 1986).

INTERPERSONAL PERSPECTIVE

Psychoanalysis, trait, and type theories attempt to analyse personality in terms of dimensions or insights previously developed by researchers in the field. Interpersonal approaches focus instead on how individuals perceive themselves and their environment, and how a subjective view is matched against objective reality. In effect, individuals try to make sense out of their experience.

The personality theories of Rogers and Kelly are prime examples of the interpersonal approach. Though these theories were developed from the fields of counselling and psychotherapy, they are not concerned with the hidden meanings of an individual's behaviour, as in psychoanalysis. The individual is considered to be in the best position to make statements about himself or herself, and these form the basis for therapy.

Self-concept

The important factor in Rogers' theory is the concept of the self (Rogers, 1951). The self in this context comprises the pattern of perception, feelings, attitudes, and values that individuals consider to be unique to themselves. Rogers also refers to the "ideal self", which is the individual as he or she would like to be. In the well-adjusted individual, the difference between the self and the ideal self would not be significant. But where there is a discrepancy between the self and actual experience, imbalance arises and this can result in tension and maladjustment.

However, when individuals are aware of the state of imbalance, they may change their behaviour to bring it into line with their self-concept, or alternatively modify that self-concept. When experiences are clearly perceived as too threatening to the individual's self-concept, they may be repressed. Rogers speaks of defence mechanisms—e.g. repression—in much the same way as Freud, as a means of maintaining the integrity of the self. He also emphasises the importance of different forms of positive gestures in the shaping of the self-concept (Rogers, 1959). These would include approval, sympathy, and love and respect from others, though the conditions to be satisfied before acquiring these benefits could put a lot of pressure on the individual and may elicit defence mechanisms.

For example, if the parents value scholastic success, the child is likely to develop a self-concept that emphasises academic achievement. But if the child's performance at school does not match this ideal, an "ego defensive strategy" may have to be used—e.g. ignoring actual experience. The problem with this is that, as more and more experiences are not allowed to reach the level of awareness, the self can sever contact with reality and the individual becomes increasingly maladjusted.

The neurotic individual is placed in a position of heavy reliance on defence mechanisms because of a significant mismatch between actual experience and self-concept.

It is important that the therapist who uses Rogers' ideas is neither directive nor disinterested, but is client-centred. Understanding clients' own view of themselves necessitates an exploration of their total experience. The desired result is constructive change to facilitate greater self-fulfilment of the client. Important conditions for the success of client-centred therapy appear to be the provision of adequate levels of empathy, genuineness, and warmth on the part of the therapist, and an environment suitable for self-exploration by the client of feelings, values, fears, and relationships. This type of approach could be valid in certain counselling situations identified in Chapters 12 and 13.

Criticisms
A particular criticism of Rogers' theory is that it focuses too much on the cognitive dimensions of personality, to the relative neglect of unconscious processes. Also, the use of self-reports can prove unreliable because the client may be unduly influenced by what the therapist expects from the encounter, and may be prone to make socially desirable responses to the therapist.

In addition, it can be argued that the client does not have perfect insight into his or her own condition (Peck & Whitlow, 1975).

Consumer Self-concept
There is some support for the self-concept in studies of consumer behaviour. It appears that consumers prefer brands that relate both to their self-perceptions and to subjective images of brands.

In one study the relationship between consumers' self-images and product images in 19 product categories (e.g. club membership, coffee, beer, and wine) was investigated. It was found that the preferences of consumers were positively related either to self-image or to ideal self-image (Landon, 1974).

In another study consumers of cars perceived themselves as having characteristics similar to owners of their particular make of car, and saw themselves as possessing a self-concept different from consumers of a competing make (Grubb & Hupp, 1968). The words used to describe the owners of the different makes of car are set out in Table 1.8. These are examples of consumers choosing products that reflect their self-image.

It is also worth noting that the products we choose can have a material influence on our self-image (Solomon, 1983). Certain products have the symbolic value of a badge and say something about ourselves.

Personal Construct Theory

According to Kelly, a psychological theory should be about understanding a person's behaviour with a view to predicting future actions. Humans are seen as scientists who are trying to make sense out of their world. They are continually testing assumptions about various things with reference to experience and evidence. There is no absolute truth or objective reality, but humans can use *constructs* to interpret situations in order to improve their understanding and ability to predict future events.

So a construct is a way of predicting future happenings, and it is only useful if predictions are fairly accurate (Kelly, 1955). If the construct "dishonest" is applied to a person, then a prediction is made about how that person is expected to behave in a position where, for example, he or she handles a lot of money or is in some other way placed in a position of trust.

When using constructs, we are concerned with opposite poles—beautiful/ugly, honest/dishonest, good/bad, warm/cold, intelligent/stupid, and so on. Constructs arise when a person construes two persons or objects as having a characteristic in common, which is different from that associated with a third person or object. Some constructs are more general than others. For example, the construct beautiful/ugly may apply to nearly everything in the world, whereas the construct intelligent/stupid may fit only humans or mammals. Each construct will have its own hierarchy, illustrated in Table 1.9 (Bannister, 1970).

In this example a person was asked whether he would prefer to see himself as well dressed or badly dressed, and replied that he

TABLE 1.8

Self-image of Car Owners

Volkswagen Owners	Pontiac GTO Owners
Thrifty	Status-conscious
Sensible	Flashy
Creative	Fashionable
Individualistic	Adventurous
Practical	Interested in opposite sex
Conservative	Sporty
Economical	Style-conscious
Quality-conscious	Pleasure-seeking

TABLE 1.9

Hierarchy of Constructs

Happier ↑	vs	Unhappier ↑
Closer personal relationships ↑	vs	Poorer personal relationships ↑
More accepted by people ↑	vs	Not so well accepted by people ↑
Makes a good first impression ↑	vs	Makes a poor first impression ↑
Well dressed	vs	Badly dressed

would like to see himself as well dressed. When asked why, he replied that it was in order to make a good first impression on people. The question "Why?" was repeatedly asked after each reply until the person reached the ceiling of the hierarchy. When asked why he wanted to be happier, he gave no direct response, other than saying it was what life was about. Some constructs are classified as superordinate (superior) and are related to a number of subordinate or peripheral constructs. The superordinate constructs, which are really stable, are considered to be core constructs and give the person a sense of identity and continuity.

If a person can only state one pole of a construct, the other pole is said to be submerged. For example, if a person uses "intelligent" to describe people, the existence of the opposite pole "stupid" is implied, even though it is not used. So if it is asserted that somebody is intelligent, this implies a contrast. To have abstracted the idea of intelligent, a person must be aware of several intelligent people, and at least one stupid person. Thus, at one moment, the person's construct is intelligent versus stupid.

Normally, people revise their constructs in the light of experience. If predictions based on a construct are continually wrong, this could give rise to a revision of the appropriate construct. Constructs, then, may change over time, particularly where they are flexible enough to accommodate new events, although others are relatively inflexible in that they rarely allow new events to be accepted. Constructs that are closely correlated with others are called "tight" constructs, and predictions do not vary; for example, "This is a library, therefore it contains books". When constructs are "loose", it is possible to make a number of predictions in similar circumstances—in the same way that, for example, a track-suit could be used for a variety of sporting activities at a given venue. Generally, constructs should not be too tightly or too loosely organised. Each individual has his or her own personal construct system, and its structure and organisation constitutes that individual's personality.

Important Factors in Personal Construct Theory
Anxiety, threat, hostility and aggression are important factors in Kelly's Personal Construct Theory:

- Anxiety is said to arise when the person is aware that perceived events cannot be construed within the construct system. An accountant who cannot decide how to write a management report may experience anxiety. The anxiety arises when the accountant recognises that the challenge with which he or she is presented lies outside the orbit of his or her construct system. The real cause of the anxiety is the realisation that the construct system is inadequate to cope with the situation.

- Threat is an awareness of an imminent major change in the person's core construct. An academic construes himself or herself to be an able scholar. However, over the years their research and scholarly achievements are patchy and the number of publications is negligible. Therefore, they have to reappraise their role and find the experience threatening.

- Hostility arises when there is a realisation of a mismatch between a construct and its prediction. A senior manager recruits an accountant to provide a management accounting service to the organisation. However, the accountant prefers to operate as a financial accountant. The hostile senior manager does not change his or her view of the accountant, but instead offers inducements and incentives so that the accountant may gravitate towards the provision of a management accounting service.

- Aggression is a response that arises when constructs are not working. A sales representative might consider him or herself to be first rate in a large group of companies, but then attends a sales convention organised by head office and encounters other sales representatives with excellent track records. The sales representative finds it difficult to keep up with them, and his or her response is aggression.

It is obvious that Kelly's definitions of anxiety, threat, hostility, and aggression are not quite the same as the conventional definitions of these terms. He has nothing to say about the development of the person, and pays little attention to how the individual comes to construe events. It is as if all that matters is how the individual sees the world at a given moment.

Role Construct Repertory Test

The Role Construct Repertory Test (Rep Test) is a method used to arrive at the basic constructs that a person uses, and the interrelationship between them. The test is based on the premise that a construct can be measured by first noting the similarities and contrasts among events.

For example, a person is asked to list a series of people or events that are regarded as important—e.g. lecturers, friends, relatives, marriage, purchase of a house. Once the list is prepared, the person is asked, in the case of people, to give the name of three individuals who can be classified as a lecturer, friend, and relative respectively. The person receives three cards, each card bearing one of the names he or she has given. The person is asked to say in what way two of them are alike but different from the third name. This procedure is repeated with different cards until an adequate number of constructs has been elicited. A simple example of the elicitation of a construct is as follows:

> Counsellor: List three people that you most admire.
> Client: My friend, my relative, and my tutor.
> Counsellor: How are two of these people alike and yet different from the third person?
> Client: My friend and my relative are outgoing, but my tutor is introverted.

Repertory Grid. A method developed from the Rep Test is called the repertory grid, and has been used in a variety of settings, including management selection and development activities (discussed in Chapters 12 and 13). This method allows the investigator to use a number of different types of element, such as the title of a job or a name. Constructs may be elicited, or alternatively provided, by the investigator. In the previous example the construct "outgoing" was elicited by the counsellor. In Table 1.10 the constructs provided may be considered critical, in terms of personality characteristics, in an industrial environment. The elements (job titles) are listed as single and paired combinations; the pair share the same constructs (i.e. innovative and optimistic).

In this process, more constructs could be elicited until constructs are either repeated or the subjects cannot give any more constructs. Other elements expressed in triad form, in the domain of executive personality characteristics, could be elicited, and this in turn would lead to the elicitation of more constructs.

The final list of elements and constructs will then be used to produce a grid with the elements along the top and the constructs down the side. The subject is then asked to grade each element on each construct using either a five or seven-point scale. The grid shown in Fig. 1.8 is a simplified representation of constructs and elements after being

TABLE 1.10

Elements and Constructs in a Repertory Grid

Elements	Constructs
Research Scientist Head of department } (pair)	Innovative Optimistic
Production manager (single)	Favours status quo, pessimistic

Scale:
- 5 = definitely yes
- 4 = yes
- 3 = uncertain
- 2 = no
- 1 = definitely no

	Manager	Workers in general	Senior union official	Person W	Top management	Person Y	Government	Person X	Person Z	Junior supervisors	Welfare	Person V	Person U	Staff in general	Managers' staff association
Powerful															
Leaders															
National															
Elected															
Takes management view															
High ranking															
Have control															
Responsible															
Take workers' view															
Employed by organisation															
Impersonal															
Co-operative															
Takes decisions															
Militant															
Communicative															
Good															

FIG. 1.8. A repertory grid. From: Smith, M. (1978). Using repertory grids to evaluate training. *Personnel Management*, February, 36–37.

reduced in number following a consensus process. The grid was the outcome of an elicitation procedure with a group of supervisors attending a short course at an educational establishment (Smith, 1978). To assist with the processing of the grid data, statistical computer software can be used as a prelude to the interpretation of the outcome of the exercise.

BEHAVIOURAL PERSPECTIVE

Though there is no single behavioural position among researchers, there is a significant view that the main source of behaviour can be found in the individual's environment, and not within the person. Though genetic inheritance is not discounted, the feeling is that reference to traits, psychoanalysis, and the physiological basis of behaviour is not particularly illuminating. It is maintained that a person's development and behaviour is primarily influenced by what happens to him or her from childhood onwards, and by the learning that takes place. Therefore, the environment is said to exert a powerful influence in terms of behavioural change. A major exponent of this view is Skinner (1974), and his views on conditioning and reinforcement are more fully reported in the discussion of learning in Chapter 4.

Reinforcement

A behavioural or social learning approach can be illustrated with reference to reinforcement in child training. When the child conforms to certain standards it may receive parental reinforcement in the form of a reward such as an expression of pleasure, a smile, praise, a pat on the head, and so on. The parent has the capacity to shape the child's response. When the child emits an inborn social response—e.g. a smile—it becomes part of the child's repertoire of responses when it is reinforced.

In the development of language, inter-mittent reinforcement may also be applied.

For example, the mother is positively encouraging the development of language when, periodically, all meaningful language sounds emitted by the child are reinforced. The reinforcer could simply be the expression of delight on the mother's face. However, if the mother does not reinforce or reward the early, crude attempts to pronounce words, this could give rise to a delay in the learning of language. But equally, understanding a child's crude utterances too readily and quickly may encourage late talking. Sometimes it is difficult to establish the reinforcers associated with the child's behaviour. For example, the motives for stealing or lying may be connected with the values of the child's peer group and this is something that lies outside the control of the parents.

Negative and non-reinforcement are also strategies at the disposal of parents:

- Negative reinforcement takes the form of punishment and may be appropriately applied in certain circumstances—for example, when a child with insufficient road sense is corrected. Punishment that inflicts pain should be avoided. It may inhibit rather than stamp out undesirable behaviour. It may also lead to delinquency, block the flow of communication, and create resentment.
- Non-reinforcement can take the form of a threat to withdraw approval, or alternatively actually withdrawing approval, and can be effective when there is a good relationship between the parent and the child. With non-reinforcement, the child's response is likely to become extinct, and further training may be needed in order to reinstate it.

Imitation

Do we always have to experience happenings personally or directly in order to learn? According to Bandura (1969), much learning takes place when we observe what other people do and note the consequences of their behaviour.

The child may imitate the mannerisms of its father, the intonation and favourite phrases of its mother, and the same accent as members of its peer group. Words that are imitated may be used without perfect understanding. Imitation is encouraged where the child observes its role model—e.g. the parent—being rewarded for engaging in a certain work or leisure activity. Likewise, the child finds imitation easy when it is specifically rewarded for copying a role model. Of course, the child could imitate a "deviant" parent but, if the parent is punished for the deviancy, then there is less likelihood of the child copying the parent.

Socialisation

The child learns the significance of a number of roles in society. There is the realisation that one has to conform to rules, but equally to learn the contradictions inherent in the complex system of rules; in fact parents may not be able to help in resolving this difficulty. There is the realisation that there are times for competition, and times for co-operation. Bending the rules may be permissible in order to win, but one expects to be penalised if one is caught cheating. One learns to control aggressive and other impulses.

The notion of right and wrong (conscience) is transmitted in a variety of ways and is often developed fortuitously. For example, a child taking money from the father's wallet is stealing, but taking a slice of cake off the table without permission is bad manners. Not very long ago it was more acceptable for the young man to "sow his wild oats"; the young girl, however, was expected to preserve her virginity. One finds here a pragmatic acceptance of prostitution but a moral rejection of it. During early socialisation, a number of values are internalised (adopted); these subsequently regulate behaviour without the need for the imposition of control in the form of punishment.

Learning to be male and female is also part of the socialisation process. Boys are often expected to be rough and tough, to play football or rugby, and not to cry. They are often also expected to be assertive and certainly not encouraged to play with dolls. The non-conformist boy is frequently called a cissy. The little boy is more likely to use his fists in an aggressive encounter. The little girl is often expected to play with dolls and be quiet, gentle and decorous, and to take up a pastime such as ballet. The non-conformist girl is called a tomboy. However, in today's society this stereotyping is being challenged, and roles are changing.

The work of Mead (1935) in primitive societies highlights the effect of child rearing practices on subsequent adult behaviour. For example, child rearing practices in the Tchambuli tribe produced males who played stereotyped female roles. The men were domesticated, looked after the children, attended to the household needs, curled their hair and adorned themselves with flowers. The women were unadorned, had their heads shaven, did the hunting, and generally engaged in masculine pursuits. However, it was the men who were the warriors. Perhaps the male is temperamentally more suited to the performance of aggressive acts, although in the animal world the female can be aggressive when protecting her young.

In an organisational setting, imitation and socialisation can also be prevalent. This is manifest when the company highlights the behaviour that members (particularly new employees) should emulate. Of course, when a fundamental culture change within the organisation is contemplated, all employees could be involved in the process. A detailed discussion of organisational culture appears in Chapter 11.

A behavioural approach to personality has been criticised because it is said to present an oversimplified view of human behaviour, but particularly because it does not pay sufficient attention to the importance of cognitive processes (Peck & Whitlow, 1975).

Situational Variables

To complement a behavioural approach, reference is made to the potency of situational variables and how they are selected and evaluated (Mischel, 1973). The same situation can elicit a different response in different individuals, and different situations can elicit similar responses in one individual. The way the person selects information and evaluates it can have a profound effect on his or her response to a particular stimulus. Of course, previous learning of an appropriate nature also has a part to play in this process. In the following example one accountant has a situational advantage over the other.

A balance sheet depicting the financial position of a company is presented to two accountants. One accountant has a particular insight into the quality of the senior management of the company and the state of its market. The other has no such knowledge apart from a superficial understanding of the internal affairs of the company. In these circumstances it is highly likely that the balance sheet will be interpreted differently by each of the two accountants. In other circumstances we would normally be confident that the two accountants would produce an identical response to a particular stimulus. If they encountered a red traffic light while driving in separate cars, for example, one would expect them to stop their cars. Finally, one must acknowledge that situations alone do not determine behaviour.

Interactionist Perspective
This perspective takes into account both the situation and the personality characteristics of the individual. People bring something of themselves to situations that they encounter in everyday life, and these personal characteristics vary from one person to another. Therefore, every situation interacts with personality and is interpreted and analysed with reference to the unique set of past experiences, learning, and the biological qualities of each individual (Phares, 1984).

It is now time to examine the main social and cognitive approaches to personality.

SOCIAL CONTEXT

Some psychoanalysts, who revised Freud's doctrine of instinctual and sexual motives in human behaviour, began to stress the role of social context in the determination of behaviour. As mentioned earlier, Adler stressed humans striving for superiority in order to compensate for feelings of inferiority (Brown, 1961). According to Fromm (1941), humans have a compelling need to belong, and seek ways of relating to others and escaping from freedom, but in the process conflict and anxiety can be encountered.

It would appear that certain advertisements contain messages that can be related to these concepts. The purchaser of a unique car is told he or she will feel superior; only distinctive and discriminating buyers purchase a particular brand of perfume! Likewise, the consumer is told that loneliness will be dispelled once membership of a particular club is obtained.

Horney (1945) felt that the way to appreciate the individual's conflicts was to understand how personality is shaped by the texture of society. In a highly competitive culture the child feels helpless, alone, and insecure because of being dependent on adults. The child develops ways of coping with the basic anxiety generated by these forces. Each way of coping involves a different strategy:

- *Compliance*. This way involves moving towards people—e.g. protecting oneself by gestures of affection, dependency, and submission. Compliant people are likely to conform to social norms, to subordinate themselves to the wishes of others, and will tend to avoid conflict. Likewise, they are unlikely to be assertive or to seek power.
- *Aggression*. This way involves moving against people—protecting oneself through aggression, hostility, and attack.

Aggressive people want to excel and manipulate others by securing power over them. They need to confirm their self-image because of uncertainty about their talents.

- *Detachment.* This way involves moving away from people—protecting oneself by isolation and withdrawal. Detached people place emotional distance between themselves and others, place a high value on freedom from obligations, like their independence and self-sufficiency, and prefer to use their intellect more than their feelings.

A measure of personality (based on Horney's model), not otherwise employed to any significant extent, has been used in connection with the behaviour of consumers. This measure, which needs refinement and development, sets out to gauge a person's interpersonal orientation (Cohen, 1967). The results indicate that people of different personality types tend to use different products and brands. The compliant types prefer well-known brand names, and are heavy users of mouthwash and toilet soaps. The aggressive types (males) tend to use a razor rather than an electric shaver, they are heavy users of cologne and after-shave lotion, and buy Old Spice deodorant and Van Heusen shirts. The detached types seem to be least aware of brands.

COGNITIVE PERSPECTIVE

In the Introduction at the beginning of this book, there was reference to the phenomenological approach to the study of psychology. A cognitive perspective is embraced by this approach, and is evident when people's unique perceptions and the action strategies based on them tend to determine who they are and how they react. In the process, they rely on previous experience and future expectations, guided by their attitudes and prominent needs.

An early behavioural theorist, Rotter (1954), developed the notion of internal–external control of reinforcement.

Internal–External Locus of Control

Because of its strong cognitive emphasis, this is considered to be a dimension of personality. Internal–external (I–E) is not a typology. Rather it is a continuum: a person can fall anywhere along that continuum from external at one end to internal at the other. Most people are clustered somewhere in the middle.

Externals and Internals

People differ in their attitude to control. Certain people (externals) feel that the outcome of their efforts is controlled by forces and events external to themselves, such as chance, fate, and powerful figures in authority; whereas others (internals) are convinced that control is an internal matter related to their own efforts and talents.

Internals will be confident that they can bring about changes in their own behaviour and environment, whereas externals feel somewhat powerless to bring about change. With regard to home security, internals are likely to take certain precautions, such as installing burglar alarms, mortice locks, and bright outside lights, if such action discourages intruders. Externals are much less likely to take such precautions if they believe that a person determined to break into the house will always find a way regardless of deterrents.

Internals and externals view reward or reinforcement differently. If internals receive positive reinforcement after a particular behavioural act, this will increase the likelihood of that behaviour occurring again; negative reinforcement will have the opposite effect. Externals are more likely to believe that positive reinforcement following a particular behavioural act was a matter of pure luck, and so there is little point in repeating that behaviour in the future. Faced with a problem, internals expect that defining the situation as one in which personal efforts will make a difference will help them to resolve the problem. On the other hand, externals will operate with the expectation that chance or other uncontrollable factors are critical, and they will behave accordingly.

The Importance of Expectations

One of the most distinctive assumptions that Rotter makes is that human behaviour is determined not just by the rewards that follow it but also by our expectations that the behaviour chosen will, in fact, bring about reinforcement. He believed that an essential human quality is our pervasive tendency to think and to anticipate (Phares, 1987).

The person builds up expectations about the relationship between behaviour and its consequences, and these expectations will be either strengthened or weakened depending upon their similarity to the actual consequences of the behaviour. In this way the person distinguishes behaviour that brings about predictable results from behaviour that does not. The executive will develop a relatively stable set of expectations regarding the control of his or her behaviour at committee meetings, in terms of results or success either due to his or her own actions, or to some other factor. A further example of expectancy manifesting itself is shown in the panel below.

Externals are likely to be compliant and conforming individuals, prone to persuasion and ready to accept information from others. Because they expect that they cannot control the consequences of their own behaviour, they are more willing to place reliance on others. Internals seem to have greater confidence in their own competence and they appear to be more independent. They prefer to be in control, and consequently resist any efforts on the part of others to manipulate them.

The most fundamental difference between internals and externals lies in the way they seek knowledge about their environment. The internals, unlike the externals, realise that they are in control of the reinforcement or reward that follows their behaviour, and they put greater effort into obtaining information about their environment (Phares, 1984). Apparently secretarial staff, who were classified as externals, were found to be more reluctant to use word-processing equipment, whereas their non-external peers displayed natural curiosity about the potential of the equipment (Arndt, Feltes, & Hanak, 1983).

Reflecting on empirical evidence relating to the personal qualities and characteristics of successful entrepreneurs, Kuratho and Hodgetts (1989) propose that successful entrepreneurs believe that they can achieve success through their own efforts, and are convinced that if they work hard and keep things under control the desired outcome is almost assured. They do not believe that the success or failure of their venture will be

---

Expecting the Best and the Worst

I consider it necessary to have an extension built to my house. Following various enquiries I approach a particular building contractor to discuss the costs of such a project. I will have certain expectations about a satisfactory outcome if the contract is given to this builder: these expectations could be based on my previous experience of doing business with him. But if I had no previous experience of his work, then my expectation that using him would result in satisfactory work could depend on other factors.

I could rely on the recommendation of somebody I know who had a similar extension constructed by the builder in question, and who was pleased with the outcome. Likewise I may be able to inspect similar projects undertaken by the builder, with the help of an expert. Of course I could be optimistic about the venture and this could be reflected in a general expectancy that the contract will work out well. If, however, I am a distrusting person, this will lower my expectancy that doing business with the builder will be a productive exercise. If I am an external in disposition, the expectancy that commissioning work on the extension will lead to a positive outcome could be dampened.

governed by fate, luck, or similar forces. These individuals exhibit an internal locus of control orientation. Their view of failure is interesting. They go ahead with a new venture despite set-backs, and freely admit that they learn more from their failures than from their successes.

In trying to increase their understanding of the effects of participation in the budgetary process, academics in the management accounting area might well turn to the concept of locus of control. Brownell (1982) examined the effects of locus of control on the relationship between participation and performance in a budgetary context. Those with an internal locus of control orientation performed best in highly participative situations where they were able to exert much influence. By contrast, those with an external locus of control orientation performed best in conditions of low participation where the potential for exercising influence was that much less. A discussion of the relationship between budgeting and participation appears in Chapter 8.

A questionnaire, referred to as the I–E scale, has been developed by Rotter (1966) and is used to measure the orientation of internals and externals. The questionnaire consists of 29 items, each of which contains two statements. The subject is asked to select the statement that is closest to his or her belief. The following statements bear some similarity to statements on the I–E scale:

1. (a) Many people can be described as victims of circumstance.
   (b) What happens to other people is pretty much of their own making.
2. (a) Much of what happens to me is probably a matter of luck.
   (b) What happens to me is my own doing.
3. (a) It is foolish to think one can really change another person's basic attitudes.
   (b) When I am right I can convince others.

The concept of the internal–external locus of control has generated a fair amount of research in recent years. The validity of the I–E scale has been questioned, particularly on the grounds that it is socially desirable to be portrayed as an internal. It is suggested that some people fake the test in order to project a favourable image (Peck & Whitlow, 1975).

Field Dependency–Independency

This concept was developed following experiments on perception. A field-dependent person tends to be strongly influenced by the background or surroundings of a particular stimulus. A field-independent person is not so influenced and can differentiate more easily between parts of the stimulus and its surroundings (Witkin, 1965). This concept was extended to embrace cognitive style, and as a consequence entered the domain of personality.

The field-independent person has the capacity to interpret events in a detailed, organised way, and has a clearer view of the constituent parts of the objects or situations encountered. He or she has a clearer view of his or her own beliefs, needs, and characteristics, and of the ways in which they differ from those of other people. To arrive at the cognitive orientation of the personality of the individual, using this concept, the person is required to identify a specific item(s) embedded in a more complex figure. For example, there are 9 items embedded in Fig. 1.9 (e.g. a pumpkin, a clock, a witch's hat, etc.).

People differ in the speed with which they identify the various items embedded in a figure. Field-independent people are fast at locating items because they take an analytical, structured approach to the study of the picture they are viewing. Field-dependent people are slow at locating the items because they are rigidly tuned into the whole picture, and are less able to look at each part of the picture independent of the other parts; generally, they tend to perceive things in a more global fashion.

In one study, subjects had their cognitive style tested prior to being set a task involving

FIG. 1.9. Embedded figures to measure field independence/field dependence. Based on: Pennington, D.C. (1986). Essential social psychology. Sevenoaks, Kent: Edward Arnold. (p.110).

the use of a computer program and a set of data to answer a series of questions. It was concluded that cognitive style was related significantly to the number of correct answers. It is interesting to note that field-independent individuals performed particularly well (Egly, 1982).

The field-dependent person tends to be susceptible to social influences and relies less on his or her own judgement. He or she cannot always see how the individual parts fit into the total picture, and finds it difficult to differentiate between them and to relate his or her own beliefs, needs, and characteristics. Likewise, he or she finds it difficult to see a clear distinction between the latter characteristics and those of a similar nature possessed by others.

INTELLIGENCE

One might well ask where intelligence fits in relation to personality. According to Phares (1987), intelligence in some ways epitomises the trait approach to personality. Although there is no generally accepted view of intelligence, a definition containing the following ingredients seems appropriate.

Intelligence is an ability to adapt to a variety of situations both old and new; an ability to learn, or the capacity for education broadly conceived; and an ability to employ abstract concepts and to use a wide range of symbols and concepts (Phares, 1987).

Models of Intelligence

The importance of intelligence is reflected in the controversy over its measurement. In particular, there have been repeated attacks on the use of intelligence tests in the USA. Spearman (1904) proposed that people possess a general factor—called *g*—in different quantities, and a person could be described as generally intelligent or stupid. According to Spearman, the *g* factor contributes significantly to performance on intelligence tests. He also mentioned other factors—called *s* factors—and these are specifically related to particular abilities. For example, an arithmetical test would be aimed at a specific *s* factor. Overall, the tested intelligence of the individual would reflect the *g* plus the various *s* factors. A diagrammatical representation of Spearman's model of intelligence appears in Fig. 1.10.

Subsequently, Thurstone took exception to the emphasis placed on general intelligence (Thurstone, 1938). He felt that intelligence could be segmented into a number of primary abilities. The seven primary abilities revealed by intelligence tests are listed in Table. 1.11.

Both Spearman and Thurstone used a statistical technique (factor analysis) to provide a better picture of the types of abilities that determine performance on intelligence

tests, and Guilford (1967) proposed a model of intelligence, called the structure of the intellect model. It categorises intelligence on three dimensions:

- operations (what the person does);
- contents (the information on which the operations are performed); and
- products (the form in which information is processed).

This model of intelligence is shown in Fig. 1.11. In the cube, each cell represents a separate ability—120 in all ($5 \times 4 \times 6 = 120$).

A drawback of the Guilford model is that it seems to be a taxonomy or classification rather than an explanation of intellectual activity (Phares, 1987).

Information Processing Models

Research on intelligence was dominated by the factorial approach used by researchers such as Thurstone and Guilford until the 1960s. Subsequently, a new approach emerged influenced by the development of cognitive psychology and its emphasis on information processing models. The basic proposition in this approach is the attempt to understand intelligence in terms of the cognitive processes that operate when individuals engage in intellectual activities, such as problem solving

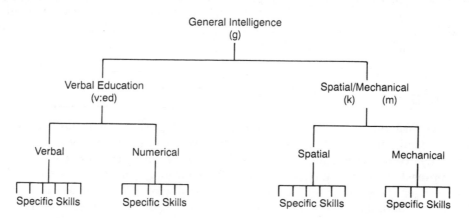

FIG. 1.10. Spearman's hierarchical model of intelligence

TABLE 1.11

Thurstone's Primary Mental Abilities

Ability	Description
Verbal comprehension	The ability to understand the meaning of words; vocabulary tests represent this factor.
Word fluency	The ability to think of words rapidly, as in solving anagrams or thinking of words that rhyme.
Number	The ability to work with numbers and perform computations.
Space	The ability to visualise space-form relationships, as in recognising the same figure presented in different orientations.
Memory	The ability to recall verbal stimuli, such as word pairs or sentences.
Perceptual speed	The ability to grasp visual details quickly and to see similarities and differences between pictured objects.
Reasoning	The ability to find a general rule on the basis of presented instances, as in determining how a number series is constructed after being presented with only a portion of that series.

Source: Thurstone, L.L. & Thurstone, T.G. (1963). *SRA primary abilities*. Chicago: Science Research Associates.

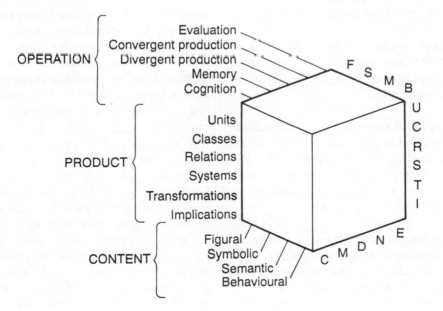

FIG. 1.11. Guilford's model of the structure of the intellect.

(Hunt, 1985). In specific terms, the information processing approach poses a number of questions, such as:

- What mental processes come into play in the various ways intelligence is tested?
- How quickly and accurately are these mental processes operationalised?
- What types of mental representations of information do the mental processes draw on?

Here the emphasis is on attempts to identify the mental processes that underlie intelligent behaviour (Atkinson et al., 1987). The information processing approach is reflected in Sternberg's (1985) work: he proposed a triarchic theory of intelligence involving the individual functioning intellectually in three ways:

1. *Componential*. This refers to analytical thinking, and is associated with success in taking tests.
2. *Experiential*. This refers to creative thinking, and characterises the person who can dissect experience into various elements, and then combine them in an insightful way.
3. *Contextual*. This refers to being "streetwise" and is reflected in the person who can play the game, and manipulate the environment.

Sternberg is of the view that the performance of the individual is governed by these three aspects of intelligence. He takes a broader view of intelligence than the more traditional approaches and his view encapsulates the following (Atkinson et al., 1987):

- ability to learn and profit from experience;
- ability to think or reason abstractly;
- ability to adapt to the vagaries of a changing and uncertain world; and
- ability to motivate oneself to complete speedily tasks one is expected to accomplish.

Another broad view of intelligence is propounded by Gardner (1983). He maintains that there is no such thing as singular intelligence. Rather there are six distinct types of intelligence independent of each other, each operating as a separate system in the brain according to its own rules. The six intelligences are:

1. linguistic;
2. logical–mathematical;
3. spatial;
4. musical;
5. bodily–kinaesthetic; and
6. personal.

The first three types are familiar and are normally measured by intelligence tests. The last three (4, 5, and 6) may appear unusual in the context of a discussion of intelligence, but Gardner feels that they should be treated similarly to the first three.

Musical intelligence, involving the ability to perceive pitch and rhythm, has been with us since the dawn of civilisation, and forms the basis for the development of musical competence. Bodily–kinaesthetic intelligence involves the control of one's body motion, and the ability to manipulate and handle objects in a skilful way. For example, the dancer exercises precise control over movement of the body, and the skilled worker or neurosurgeon is able to manipulate objects in a dexterous way. The last of the six intelligences—personal intelligence—can be divided into two parts; interpersonal and intrapersonal intelligence. The former is the ability to register and understand the needs and intentions of other people and to develop sensitivity to their moods and temperament in order to be able to predict how they will behave in new situations. Intrapersonal intelligence, by contrast, is the ability to develop awareness of one's own feelings and emotions, to discriminate between them, and to use this information as a guide to personal actions.

It is recognised that some people will develop certain intelligences to a greater extent than others, but all normal people should develop each intelligence to some extent. The intelligences interact with each other, as well as building on one another, but they still operate as semi-autonomous systems. In Western society the first three types of intelligence (linguistic; logical–mathematical; spatial) are given prominence, and of course they are open to measurement by standard intelligence tests. But historical evidence indicates that the other intelligences (musical; bodily–kinaesthetic; personal) were highly valued at earlier periods of human history, and currently in some non-Western societies (Atkinson et al., 1987). Even in Western cultures, children endowed with unusual non-traditional intelligences such as bodily–kinaesthetic intelligence, can be groomed to become, for example, a first-rate footballer, or a ballet dancer.

Measurement of Intelligence

Tests are available to measure general intellectual ability. These tests are called "intelligence tests". The first tests resembling contemporary intelligence tests were devised by Binet in France, who had been asked by the French government to create a test that would detect children who were too slow intellectually to benefit from a regular school curriculum. Binet felt that intelligence should be measured by tasks that required reasoning and problem-solving abilities, rather than perceptual–motor skills. The test required the child to execute simple commands, to name familiar objects, to think of rhymes, to explain words, etc. It was both a verbal and a performance test.

Binet joined forces with Simon and published a scale, later revised, in 1905. Binet maintained that a slow or dull child was merely a normal child who was backward in mental growth. Therefore, the slow child would produce a result on the test normally associated with a child younger than him or her. A bright child would perform at a level associated with a child older than him or her.

It followed that the bright child's mental age (MA) was higher than his or her real or chronological age (CA); a slow child's MA is below his or her CA.

The selection of items to be included in the test is of crucial importance. Normally one would expect to find both novel and familiar items. The choice of novel items is meant to ensure that the uneducated child is not at a disadvantage. In Fig. 1.12 an example of a novel item is given where the child is asked to choose figures that are alike, on the assumption that the designs are unfamiliar to all children.

When familiar items are chosen for the test, there is the assumption that all those for whom the test is designed have had the requisite previous knowledge to cope with the items. The following request and statement provides an example of an allegedly familiar item (Atkinson et al., 1987).

Circle F if the sentence is foolish; circle S if it is sensible.

S F Mrs Smith has had no children and I understand the same was true of her mother.

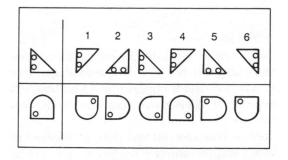

FIG. 1.12. Novel items used in intelligence tests. *The following instructions accompany the test:* Mark every card to the right that matches the sample card on the left. You can rotate the sample card but not flip it over. *(Cards 2, 3, and 6 are correct in the first line; 1, 3, and 5 are correct in the second line.)* Source: Atkinson et al., (1987). *Introduction to psychology* (ninth edition). Orlando, FL: Harcourt Brace Jovanovich.

It should be noted that recognition of the fallacy of this statement is valid as a test of intellectual ability for the child who can read and understand all the words in the sentence. The possession of general knowledge and familiarity with the language of the test is necessary to cope with many of the items on intelligence tests. It may be difficult to meet this requirement because of the variability in the educational background and experience of the child. Where the child is tested on novel items, a difficulty may also arise because the discrimination required in a perceptual sense to solve the problem may be found more readily in one culture rather than in another. Nevertheless, the items found in contemporary intelligence tests have endured the rigour of application in the practical world, but it should be noted that the validity of intelligence tests in predicting school performance is applicable only to a particular culture.

Stanford-Binet Intelligence Scale

This was developed in the US out of the earlier work of Binet, is well known and widely used, and has been revised on a number of occasions. The index of intelligence used is the intelligence quotient (IQ), and this is expressed as a ratio of mental age (MA) to chronological age (CA) as follows:

$$IQ = \frac{MA}{CA} \times 100$$

Using 100 as a multiplier means that when MA = CA, then the IQ will have a value of 100.

If MA is less than CA, the IQ will be less than 100; if MA is greater than CA, the IQ will be more than 100.

An IQ between 90 and 110 is considered to be normal, but above 130 it is considered to be very superior. The person with an IQ below 70 is judged to be retarded. As with many differences between individuals, the distribution of IQs in the population approximates the bell-shaped normal distribution curve. Most cases would fall into the mid-value of the curve, with just a few cases at the left and right extreme positions on the curve.

The Stanford-Binet scale was designed to ensure that all items contributed equally to the total IQ score. This means that an individual might perform well on a test inviting the production of geometric forms, but badly on a test of vocabulary. Although the tester might note the strengths and weaknesses, they would cancel each other out in arriving at the IQ score. Under the 1986 revised scale, standard age scores are substituted for IQ scores, and it is now possible to obtain scores for different areas of the test. In accordance with the current view of intelligence as an accumulation of different abilities, a separate score can now be obtained for each of the broad areas of intellectual ability set out in Table 1.12 (Thorndike, Hagen, & Satlet, 1986).

TABLE 1.12

IQ Test Scoring Segments

Category	*Sub-category*
Verbal reasoning	Vocabulary
	Comprehension
	Absurdities
	Verbal relations
Quantitative reasoning	Quantitative
	Number series
	Equation building
Abstract/visual reasoning	Pattern analysis
	Copying
	Matrices
	Paper folding and cutting
Short-term memory	Bead memory
	Memory for sentences
	Memory for digits
	Memory for objects

Wechsler Intelligence Scales

One of the first intelligence tests to test separate abilities, which has been widely used, was developed by Wechsler in 1939. These scales were developed because it was felt that the Stanford-Binet test relied heavily on language ability and did not cater for the needs of adults (Wechsler, 1981).

The Wechsler Adult Intelligence Scale (WAIS) has two sections: (1) a verbal scale; and (2) a performance scale. Each section generates separate scores, as well as an overall IQ score. A similar test with some modifications was also developed for children. The items in the WAIS are shown in Table 1.13.

In the performance scale section in Table 1.13 the items specify the manipulation or arrangement of blocks, pictures, or other materials. The stimuli and the responses are non-verbal in this section. The Wechsler scales allow for scores to be recorded for each of the sub-tests; therefore, the tester has a better view of the intellectual strengths and weaknesses of the individual.

It is claimed that both the Stanford-Binet and Wechsler scales satisfy the conditions for a good test—i.e. they show good reliability and validity. Also, both tests are fairly valid predictors of achievement, particularly at school (Atkinson et al., 1987).

TABLE 1.13

Tests in the WAIS

Scale item	Description
Verbal scale	
Information	Questions tap a general range of information; e.g. "How many nickels make a dime?"
Comprehension	Tests practical information and ability to evaluate past experience; e.g. "What is the advantage of keeping money in a bank?"
Arithmetic	Verbal problems testing arithmetic reasoning.
Similarities	Asks in what way certain objects or concepts (e.g. *egg* and *seed*) are similar; measures abstract thinking.
Digit span	A series of digits presented auditorily (e.g. 7-5-6-3-8) is repeated in a forward or backward direction.
Vocabulary	Tests word knowledge.
Performance scale	
Digit symbol	A timed coding task in which numbers must be associated with marks of various shapes; tests speed of learning and writing.
Picture completion	The missing part of an incompletely drawn picture must be discovered and named; tests visual alertness and memory.
Block design	Pictured designs must be copied with blocks; tests ability to perceive and analyse patterns.
Picture arrangement	A series of comic-strip pictures must be arranged in the right sequence to tell a story; tests understanding of social situations.
Object assembly	Puzzle pieces must be assembled to form a complete object; tests ability to deal with part-whole relationships.

Mediating Influences

We realise that people differ in intellectual ability, and many would agree that some aspects of intelligence are inherited. However, opinions differ as to the relative contributions made by our genetic inheritance (heredity) and environment (i.e. what happens to the individual during the course of development).

The environmental conditions likely to determine how an individual's intellectual potential will develop include nutrition, health, quality of stimulation, emotional climate of the home, and appropriate rewards for accomplishments (Bayley, 1970). Inevitably, one feels forced to take a pragmatic position on this issue. For example, heredity and environment interact. Heredity sets the scene in terms of specifying the possible limits of achievements for any person in a given situation, but the environment determines how near to these limits of achievement any individual will move in any given situation.

The debate over genetic factors in intelligence raises the possibility of inherited racial differences in intelligence—in particular the question of whether black people are innately less intelligent than white people. Black Americans as a group score 10–15 points lower on standard intelligence tests than white Americans as a group. The controversy focuses not on the difference in IQ but on the interpretation of the difference. Some argue that the two groups differ in inherited ability (Jensen, 1977), while others maintain the black-white differences in average IQ can be put down to environmental differences between the two groups (Kamin, 1976). From the available evidence it is not possible to draw firm conclusions about innate racial differences in intelligence.

If intelligence was simply an innate quality, then IQ would not be expected to alter throughout the life of the person, apart from minor changes due to the measuring instrument used. However, there is evidence to suggest that IQ scores fluctuate over time

(Anastasi, 1976). Also a person's performance on a test could be influenced by temporary states; for example, the person is affected by illness, is demotivated for some reason, or is going through an emotional upheaval. In addition, intelligence tests tend to measure different things at different ages. For example, test items that require young children to stack blocks and identify parts of the body are quite different from items that are highly verbal, abstract, and mathematical, found in tests for older children and adults.

Another factor that can influence performance on tests is age (Botwinick, 1984). A decline in performance over time can be attributable to a number of factors. There may be a general deterioration of health, or growing deficiencies of hearing and eyesight. Also, as people grow older they may become more cautious and fearful of making mistakes, and this may undermine their test performance. It is said that giving extra time to older people to do the test, or allowing them more time to familiarise themselves with the test procedures, will often lead to higher scores (Phares, 1987). In the final analysis, it would be wise to distinguish between those with a defective mental capacity because of an age-related infirmity and those who are not disadvantaged in that way.

Finally, attempts have been made to devise culture-fair tests. These tests attempt to neutralise the effects of forces that distinguish one culture or sub-culture from another. In essence what is attempted is the removal of factors that reflect cultural background rather than innate ability. These could include language handicap (i.e. lack of total familiarity with the language of the test) or speed of reaction. In the latter case, not all cultures or sub-cultures subscribe to the view that faster means better. Although sound in theory, culture-fair testing has not worked very well (Phares, 1987). Tests are being looked at closely, particularly in the USA, if it is felt that they are inappropriately used and act to the disadvantage of a particular racial or ethnic group.

Aptitude and Achievement Tests

These are essentially tests of ability, but differ in certain respects from the intelligence tests discussed earlier. Vernon (1956) drew a distinction between intelligence and achievement as follows:

Intelligence refers to the more general qualities of thinking—comprehension, level of concept development, reasoning, and grasping relations—qualities which appear largely to be acquired in the course of normal development without specific tuition. By contrast, achievement refers more to knowledge and skills which are directly trained.

The use of ability tests to stream children in schools, to admit pupils and students to schools and colleges, and to select people for jobs can arouse passions and much debate. When they were first developed they were approved of as an objective and impartial method of identifying talent in the face of subjective elements in the form of various types of favouritism (e.g. based on class, wealth, politics, and so on).

However, they have their critics who label them as narrow and restrictive. In essence this means that they do not measure those characteristics that are the most important in determining how well a person will perform in an educational setting or at work (for example, motivation, social skills, qualities of leadership) and they discriminate against minorities (Atkinson et al., 1987). It should be noted that the factors that make personality tests useful (discussed earlier in the section on personality testing) are equally applicable to ability tests.

A distinction is made between achievement and aptitude tests (Atkinson et al., 1987):

An achievement test is designed to measure developed skills and tells us what the person can do currently. An aptitude test is designed to forecast what a person can attain with training. However, the distinction between the two types of test is not neat, because the intention is to assess the current standing of those tested whether the purpose of the test is to assess what has been learned to date, or to predict future performance.

Both types of test include similar kinds of questions. The real differentiating factor seems to be the purpose of the test. For example, on completion of a course in mechanics a test of knowledge of mechanical principles is given to the participants. This amounts to a test of achievement. But similar questions might be incorporated into a battery of tests for those applying for pilot training, because knowledge of mechanical principles has been found to be a good predictor of success in flying. In this case, the test would be considered a test of aptitude.

Although the significant factor differentiating achievement and aptitude tests has been identified here as the purpose rather than the content of the test, nevertheless, the existence of relevant prior knowledge and experience is an important factor to note. An aptitude test assumes little in terms of relevant prior knowledge and experience, whereas an achievement test assumes the person tested has accumulated specific subject matter, the mastery of which is measured by the test.

In practice the possession of relevant prior knowledge or experience, though not required by the aptitude test, could nevertheless influence the test results. This arises because tests using verbal, numerical, or symbolic material are not totally unfamiliar, and obviously previous education and experience inevitably exerts an influence.

Aptitude Tests at Work

Examples of the nature of aptitude tests in the occupational field are examined in this section (Toplis et al., 1987). These tests could be used in the selection process to be discussed later in Chapter 13.

Verbal Ability.   There are a number of tests that measure lower levels of word meaning and comprehension. Some of these tests necessitate an element of reasoning with words. Also, there are verbal tests involving more complex mental operations of reasoning and critical evaluation and these are available for assessing candidates of high ability, such as graduates and managers.

Numerical Ability.   There are lower level numerical tests requiring an understanding of, and skill at, arithmetical calculations. In these tests candidates' existing accomplishments, as well as their aptitude, are being assessed. There are also numerical tests for candidates of high ability, such as graduates and potential managers, which are concerned with higher-order numerical reasoning and with critical evaluation of quantitative information.

Spatial Ability.   There are tests for lower ability and higher ability candidates requiring mental proficiency in identifying, visualising, comparing, or manipulating two or three dimensional shapes.

Diagrammatical Ability.   These tests focus on abstract symbols and diagrams ranging from superficial perceptual tasks to complex abstract logical processes. They do not include verbal or numerical items.

Manual Dexterity.   Eye-hand co-ordination features in tests falling into this category, and the emphasis is on perception and manipulation involving the fingers and hands. Some tasks require speed with little precision, whereas other tasks place the primary emphasis on precision where speed is considered to be of lesser importance. The abilities involved in manual dexterity tests are relevant to most manual jobs, and are not closely related to the other ability and intelligence tests discussed in this chapter.

Mechanical Ability.   These tests are distinct from the manual dexterity tests described in the previous section. There is an element of intelligence and reasoning ingrained in them, and they are designed to measure the capacity to succeed and learn in jobs that require mechanical ability.

The Scholastic Aptitude Test
There are certain tests—e.g. the Scholastic Aptitude Test (SAT) in the US—that measure both aptitude and achievement. SAT is used to test applicants for admission to colleges and it consists of a verbal section which measures vocabulary skills and the ability to understand what is read, and a mathematical section, which tests the ability to solve problems requiring arithmetical reasoning, algebra, and geometry. The emphasis is on the ability to apply skills acquired to date to solve problems. Questions based on knowledge of particular topics are not included.

SUMMARY: PERSONALITY AND INTELLIGENCE

- Having defined what we mean by personality, two basic approaches to the study of personality were introduced. These are referred to as the idiographic and nomothetic approaches.
- There followed an analysis of a number of perspectives on personality, starting with the psychoanalytical. This draws heavily on the contribution of Freud and was discussed with reference to levels of awareness; personality structure (id, ego and super-ego); defence mechanisms (repression, projection, fixation, regression, and reaction formation); and finally personality development.
- Projective tests, designed to assess personality based on unconscious processes, were said to be only indirectly related to psychoanalysis. Two well-known projective tests are the

Rorschach test and the thematic appercep-tion test. These tests, though subject to certain weaknesses, can be used in consumer motivation research. In addition, role playing and visualisation techniques used to create personality descriptions of consumers were explained. The notion of brand personality was acknowledged.

- The next major perspective on personality discussed was trait theory. Different categories of traits, including Allport's, were described. Cattell was identified as an influential trait theorist. He drew a distinction between source traits and surface traits. His 16 PF personality test represents source traits. The outcome of personality testing, using the 16 PF, was discussed with reference to a managerial and executive population. Other tests mentioned, which can be used to measure personality traits, were the Thurstone Temperament Schedule, the Edwards Personal Preference Schedule, and the OPQ.

- A number of observations connected with personality testing were made. It was suggested that the trait approach to personality has weaknesses, particularly in research into consumer behaviour and when used for the selection of people for jobs. There appears to be a natural tendency to refer to the desirable or undesirable personal characteristics of occupational groups, quite independent of formal personality tests. The growth of non-scientific methods—e.g. graphology—in personality assessment was mentioned.

- When a person shares a pattern of traits with a large group of people, he or she is said to belong to a personality type. Types, as a perspective on personality, were discussed initially with reference to the theory of the four humours and Sheldon's physical typology. This was followed by a brief examination of the typologies advanced by the influential psychologists, Jung and Allport. A derivative of Jung's typology is the Myers-Brigg type indicator. The major part of the discussion was devoted to the important contribution made by another influential psychologist, Eysenck. The relationship between personality types and accidents and career choice was explored, as were psychographics and life-styles as techniques in consumer research designed to compensate for the weaknesses of the trait and type approaches.

- An interpersonal perspective on personality, suitably illustrated, focused on how individuals perceived themselves and their environment, and how a subjective view is matched against objective reality. The notion of the Self-concept (Rogers) and Personal Construct Theory (Kelly) were introduced. The important factors in Personal Construct Theory were noted, and examples of the use of the repertory grid (derived from Kelly's theory) were given.

- A behavioural perspective on personality, primarily concerned with reinforcement, imitation and socialisation recognised that a person's development and behaviour is primarily influenced by happenings from childhood onwards and by the learning that takes place. The weakness of the behavioural approach was accepted, and the relevance of a situational emphasis to complement it was noted. An inter-actionist approach was said to be more realistic because it recognised both the situation and personality characteristics.

- The social context, as a determining influence on behaviour, and a cognitive perspective on personality were acknowledged. The latter consists of the internal–external locus of control and field dependency–independency.

- Finally, models of intelligence were introduced and matters to note when measuring intelligence were examined. The role of mediating influences was emphasised. Examples of aptitude tests in the occupational field were given and a distinction was made between aptitude and achievement tests.

QUESTIONS

1. What is meant by the term "personality"?
2. Distinguish between the idiographic and nomothetic approaches to the study of personality.
3. Examine the potential of Freudian analysis in any business context.
4. Identify the differences between projective tests and role playing or visualisation, and comment on the usefulness of these techniques in the field of marketing.
5. What is meant by the term "brand personality"?
6. Define a trait, giving examples of different categories of traits.
7. What significance is attached to trait and type analysis in an employment setting?
8. Consider the issues involved in personality testing.
9. Is there any scientific basis for the suggestion that certain people are accident-prone?
10. Examine the relationship between personality and career choice.
11. Why do marketeers use psychographics?
12. What is the relationship between Personal Construct Theory and the repertory grid?
13. Discuss the difference between reinforcement and socialisation in the context of a behavioural perspective on personality.
14. Define the following terms: (a) interactionist view; (b) compliant strategy; (c) internal–external locus of control; and (d) field dependency–independency.
15. Define the "models of intelligence", and comment on the debate surrounding intelligence.
16. Distinguish between achievement and aptitude tests.

REFERENCES

Allport, G.W. (1961). *Pattern and growth in personality.* New York: Holt, Rinehart & Winston.

Allport, G.W. (1965). *Letters from Jenny.* New York: Harcourt Brace & World.

Allport, G.W., Vernon, P.E., & Lindzey, G. (1960). *A study of values: A scale for measuring the dominant interests in personality.* Boston: Houghton Mifflin.

Anastasi, A. (1976). *Psychological testing* (fourth edition). New York: Macmillan.

Anastasi, A. (1979). *Fields of applied psychology.* Tokyo: McGraw-Hill.

Arndt, S., Feltes, J., & Hanak, J. (1983). Secretarial attitudes towards word-processors as a function of familiarity and locus of control. *Behaviour and Information Technology, 2,* 17–22.

Arnold, J., Robertson, I.T., & Cooper, C.L. (1991). *Work psychology. Understanding human behaviour in the workplace.* London: Pitman.

Assael, H. (1987). *Consumer behaviour and marketing action* (third edition). Belmont, CA: Wadsworth.

Atkinson, R.L., Atkinson R.C., Smith, E.E., & Hilgard, E.R. (1987). *Introduction to psychology* (ninth edition). Orlando, FL: Harcourt Brace Jovanovich.

Bandura, A. (1969). *Principles of behaviour modification.* London: Holt, Rinehart & Winston.

Bannister, D. (1970). *Perspectives in personal construct theory.* New York: Academic Press.

Barden, V. (1970). Yes, the accountants are different. (Report of a study at The Ashridge Management College.) *Accountancy Age,* 16 October, 15.

Barry, B. & Dowling, P. (1984). *Towards an Australian management style: A study of the personality characteristics and management style of Australian managers.* Victoria: The Australian Institute of Management.

Bayley, N. (1970). Development of mental abilities. In P. Mussen (Ed.), *Carmichael's manual of child psychology, Vol. 1.* New York: Wiley.

Bayne, R. (1994). The "Big Five" versus the Myers-Briggs. *The Psychologist,* January, 14–16.

Bayne, R. & Fletcher, C. (1983). Selecting the selectors. *Personnel Management,* June.

Bentall, R.P. (1993). Personality traits may be alive, they may even be well, but are they really useful? *The Psychologist,* July, 307.

Blinkhorn, S. & Johnson, C. (1990). The insignificance of personality testing. *Nature, 348,* 671–72.

Botwinick, J. (1984). *Ageing and human behaviour. A comprehensive integration of research findings* (third edition). New York: Springer.

Broadbent, K. & Cooper, P. (1987). Research is good for you. *Marketing Intelligence and Planning, 5,* 3–9.

Brown, J.A.C. (1961). *Freud and the post-Freudians.* Harmondsworth: Penguin.

Brownell, P. (1982). The effects of personality—situation congruence in a managerial context: Locus of control and budgetary participation. *Journal of Personality and Social Psychology, 42,* 753–763

Buss, A.H. (1989). Personality as traits. *American Psychologist,* November, 1378–1388.

Cattell, R.B. (1965). *The scientific analysis of personality.* Harmondsworth: Penguin.

Cattell, R.B. (1974). How good is the modern questionnaire? General principles for evaluation. *Journal of Personality Assessment, 38,* 115–129.

Chell, E. (1987). *The psychology of behaviour in organisations.* Basingstoke, UK: MacMillan Press.

Child, J. & Ellis, A. (1973). Predictors of variation in management roles. *Human Relations, 26,* 227–250.

Cohen, J.B. (1967). An interpersonal orientation to the study of consumer behaviour. *Journal of Marketing Research, 4,* 270–278.

Craske, S. (1968). A study of the relation between personality and accident history. *British Journal of Medical Psychology, 41,* 399–404.

Deary, I.J. & Matthews, G. (1993). Personality traits are alive and well. *The Psychologist,* July, 299–311.

De Coster, D.T. & Rhode, J.G. (1971). The accountant's stereotype: Real and imagined, deserved or unwarranted. *The Accounting Review, 46,* 651–662.

Drever, J. (1964). *A dictionary of psychology.* Harmondsworth, UK: Penguin.

Egly, D.G. (1982). Cognitive style, categorisation and vocational effects on performance of REL. DATABASE users. *SIGSOC Bulletin, 13,* 91–97.

Engel, J.F., Blackwell, R.D., & Miniard, P.W. (1990). *Consumer behaviour* (sixth edition). Fort Worth, TX: The Dryden Press.

England, G.W. & Lee, R. (1974). The relationship between managerial values and managerial success in the US, Japan, India, and Australia. *Journal of Applied Psychology, 59,* 411–419.

Eysenck, H.J. (1947). *Dimensions of personality.* London: Routledge & Kegan Paul.

Eysenck, H.J. (1953). *The structure of human personality.* London: Methuen.

Eysenck, H.J., (1965). *Fact and fiction in psychology.* Harmondsworth, UK: Penguin.

Eysenck, H.J. (1967). *The biological basis of behaviour.* Springfield, Ill.: C.C. Thomas.

Farmer, E. & Chambers, E.G. (1926). *A psychological study of individual differences in accident rates.* Report No. 38, Industrial Fatigue Research Board, Medical Research Council, 1–46.

Feldman, M.P. (1971). *Psychology in the industrial environment.* London: Butterworths.

Feldman, D.C. & Arnold, H.J. (1985). Personality types and career patterns: Some empirical

evidence on Holland's model. *Canadian Journal of Administrative Sciences,* June, 192–210.

Freud, S. (1938). *The basic writings of Sigmund Freud.* New York: Modem Library.

Fromm, E. (1941). *Escape from freedom.* New York: Rinehart.

Furnham, A. (1990). Faking personality questionnaires: Fabricating different profiles for different purposes. *Current Psychology: Research and Reviews,* Spring, 45–55.

Gardner, H. (1983). *Frames of mind: The theory of multiple intelligences.* New York: Basic Books.

Ghiselli, E.E. (1973). The validity of aptitude tests in personnel selection. *Personnel Psychology, 26,* 461–477.

Glendon, A.I. & McKenna, E.F. (1994). *Human safety and risk management: A psychological perspective.* London: Chapman & Hall.

Greene, J. and Lewis, D. (1988). *The hidden language of your handwriting.* London: Macdonald & Co.

Grubb, E.L. & Hupp, G. (1968). Perception of self, generalised stereotypes and brand selection. *Journal of Marketing Research, 5,* 58–63.

Guilford, J.P. (1967). *The nature of human intelligence.* New York: McGraw-Hill.

Haddon, W., Suchman, E., & Klein, D. (1964). *Accident research: Its methods and approaches.* New York: Harper & Row.

Haire, M. (1950). Projective techniques in market research. *Journal of Marketing, 14,* 649–656.

Hartston, W.R. & Mottram, R.D. (1976). *Personality profiles of managers: A study of occupational differences.* Cambridge, UK: Industrial training research unit.

Henderson, J.C. & Nutt, P.C. (1980). The influence of decision style on decision-making behaviour. *Management Science, 26,* 371–386.

Hetherington, E.M. & Wray, N.P. (1964). Aggression, need for social approval and humour preferences. *Journal of Abnormal and Social Psychology, 68,* 685–689.

Hirschfield, A. & Behan, R. (1963). Etiological considerations of industrial injuries. *Journal of the American Medical Association,* October.

Holland, J.L. (1985). *Making vocational choices* (second edition). New York: Prentice-Hall.

Holmes, D.S. (1974). The conscious control of thematic projection. *Journal of Consulting and Clinical Psychology, 42,* 323–329.

Hopper, T. (1978). *Role conflicts of management accountants in the context of their structural relationship to production.* Unpublished M.Phil. thesis. Birmingham, UK: University of Aston.

Horney, K.B. (1945). *Our inner conflicts.* New York: W.W. Norton.

Howarth, E. & Browne, A. (1971). An item factor analysis of the 16 PF. *Personality, 2,* 117–139.

Hunt, E. (1985). Verbal ability. In Sternberg, R.J. (Ed.), *Human abilities: An information-processing approach.* New York: Freeman.

Jackson, D. & Rothstein, M. (1993). Evaluating personality testing in personnel selection. *The Psychologist, 6,* January, 8–11.

Jensen, A.R. (1977). Cumulative deficit in IQ of blacks in the rural South. *Development Psychology, 13,* 184–191.

Jung, C.G. (1965). Analytical psychology. In W. Sahakian (Ed.), *Psychology of personality: Readings in theory.* Chicago: Rand McNally.

Kamin, L.J. (1976). Heredity, intelligence, politics, and psychology. In N. J. Block & G. Dworkin (Eds.), *The IQ controversy.* New York: Pantheon.

Kelly, G.A. (1955). *The psychology of personal constructs.* New York: W.W. Norton.

Kets de Vries, M.F.R. & Miller, D. (1984). *The neurotic organisation.* London: Jossey-Bass.

Klimoski, R.J. & Rafael, A. (1983). Inferring personal qualities through handwriting analysis. *Journal of Occupational Psychology, 56,* 191–202.

Kline, P. (1987). Factor analysis and personality theory. *European Journal of Personality, 1,* 21–36.

Koponen, A. (1960). Personality characteristics of purchasers. *Journal of Advertising Research, I,* 6–12.

Kuratho, D.F. & Hodgetts, R.M. (1989). *Entrepreneurship: A contemporary approach.* Fort Worth, TX: The Dryden Press.

Landon, E.L. (1972). *A sex-role explanation of purchase intention differences of consumers who are high and low in need for achievement.* Association for Consumer Research, Proceedings of Third Annual Conference (Ed. M. Venkatesan), pp. 1–8.

Landon, E.L. (1974). Self-concept, ideal self-concept and consumer purchase intentions. *Journal of Consumer Research, 1,* 44–51.

Lane, G.S. & Watson, G.L. (1975). A Canadian replication of Mason Haire's shopping list study. *Journal of the Academy of Marketing Science, 13,* Spring, 48.

Lawler, E.E. & Rhode, J.G. (1976). *Information and control in organisations.* Santa Monica, CA: Goodyear.

Lazarus, R.S. (1971). *Personality.* New York: Prentice-Hall.

Leigh, J. (1985). Executives and the personality factor. *Sky, 4,* May, 34–38.

Lewis, C. (1980). Investigating the employment interview: A consideration of counselling skills. *Journal of Occupational Psychology, 53,* 111–116.

Lewis, C. (1984). What's new in selection? *Personnel Management,* January, 14–16.

Lindsey, F. (1980). Accident-proneness: Does it exist? *Occupational Safety and Health, 10,* February, 8–9.

Mackay, K. (1973). *An introduction to psychology.* London: Macmillan.

McAdams, D.P. (1992). The Five-Factor Model in Personality: A critical appraisal. *Journal of Personality, 60,* 329–361.

Mead, M. (1935). *Sex and temperament in three primitive societies.* New York: William Morrow.

Mischel, W. (1973). Toward a cognitive social learning reconceptualisation of personality. *Psychological Review, 80,* 252–283.

Mitroff, I. et al. (1974). On managing science in the systems' age: Two schemes for the study of science as a whole systems' phenomenon. *Interfaces, 4,* 50.

Myers, I.B. (1962). *Myers-Briggs type indicator.* Palo Alto, Cal.: Consulting Psychologists Press.

Peck, D. & Whitlow, D. (1975). *Approaches to personality theory.* London: Methuen.

Pennington, D.C. (1986). *Essential psychology.* Sevenoaks, UK: Edward Arnold.

Phares, E.J. (1984). *Introduction to personality.* Columbus, Ohio: Charles E. Merrill.

Phares, E. J. (1987). *Introduction to personality* (second edition). Glenview, Ill: Scott, Foresman.

Poppleton, S.E. (1975). *Biographical and personality characteristics associated with success in life assurance salesmen.* Unpublished M.Phil. thesis. London: Birbeck College.

Rice, G.H. & Lindecamp D.P. (1989). Personality types and business success of small retailers. *Journal of Occupational Psychology, 62,* 177–182.

Robertson, I.T. & Cooper, C.L. (1983). *Human behaviour in organisations.* Plymouth: Macdonald & Evans.

Robertson, I.T. & Kinder, A. (1993). Personality and job competences: The criterion-related validity of some personality variables. *Journal of Occupational and Organisational Psychology, 66,* 225–244.

Robertson, I.T. & Makin, P.J. (1986). Management selection in Britain: A survey and critique. *Journal of Occupational Psychology, 59,* 45–58.

Rogers, C.R. (1951). *Client-centred therapy.* Boston: Houghton Mifflin.

Rogers, C.R. (1959). A theory of therapy, personality and interpersonal relationships as developed in the client-centred framework. In S. Koch (Ed.), *Psychology: A study of a science, Vol. 3.* New York: McGraw-Hill.

Rotter, J.B. (1954). *Social learning and clinical psychology.* New York: Prentice-Hall.

Rotter, J.B. (1966). Generalised expectancies for internal versus external control of reinforcement. *Psychological Monographs, 8,* (1, Whole No. 609).

Saville & Holdsworth Ltd. (1984). *The occupational personality questionnaires.* Thames Ditton, Surrey: Saville & Holdsworth Ltd.

Sheldon, W.H. (1954). *A guide for somatotyping the adult male at all ages.* New York: Harper.

Skinner, B.F. (1974). *About behavioursim.* London: Jonathan Cape.

Smith, M. (1978). Using repertory grids to evaluate training. *Personnel Management,* February, 36–37.

Solomon, M.R. (1983). The role of products as social stimuli: A symbolic interactionism perspective. *Journal of Consumer Research, 10,* 319–329.

Spearman, C. (1904). General intelligence" objectively determined and measured. *Journal of Psychology, 15,* 201–293.

Sternberg, R.J. (1985). *Beyond IQ: A triarchic theory of human intelligence.* New York: Cambridge University Press.

Thorndike, E.L., Hagen, E.P., & Satlet, J.M. (1986). *Stanford-Binet intelligence scale: Guide for administering and scoring the fourth edition.* Chicago: Riverside Publishing.

Thurstone, L.L. (1938). Primary mental abilities. *Psychometric Monographs,* No. 1. Chicago: University of Chicago Press.

Thurstone, L.L. & Thurstone, T.G. (1963). *SRA primary abilities.* Chicago: Science Research Associates.

Tiffin, J. & McCormick, E.J. (1969). *Industrial psychology* (third edition). London: George Allen & Unwin.

Toplis, J., Dulewicz, V., & Fletcher, C. (1987). *Psychological testing: A practical guide for employers.* London: Institute of Personnel Management.

Vernon, P.E. (1956). *The measurement of abilities.* London: University of London Press.

Webster, F.E. & Von Pechmann, F. (1970). A replication of the shopping list study. *Journal of Marketing, 34,* 61–77.

Wechsler, D. (1981). *Manual for Wechsler adult intelligence scale* (revised). San Antonio, TX: The Psychological Corporation.

Wells, W.D. & Tigert, D.J. (1971). Activities, interests and opinions. *Journal of Advertising Research, 11,* 27–35.

Westfall, R. (1962). Psychological factors in predicting product choice. *Journal of Marketing, 26,* 34–40.

Wilkie, W.L. (1986). *Consumer behaviour.* New York: Wiley.

Williams, K.C. (1981). *Behavioural aspects of marketing.* London: Heinemann.

Witkin, H.A. (1965). Psychological differentiation and forms of pathology. *Journal of Abnormal and Social Psychology, 70,* 317–336.

Wright, D.S., Taylor, A., Davies, D.R., Sluckin, W., Lee, S.G.M., & Reason, J.T. (1970). *Introducing psychology: An experimental approach.* London: Penguin.

2

Motivation and Job Design

The opening section of this chapter is devoted to a definition of the concept of motivation. This is followed by an analysis of factors that contribute to a state of arousal in motivated behaviour. Next is a brief description of frustration, followed by an identification of situations that may contribute to monotony and boredom at work—a condition likely to affect the motivation of employees. Rest pauses may be used to counteract the worst effects of monotony and fatigue. Need or content theories of motivation are considered at length. There follows a discussion of cognitive or process theories of motivation, with particular applications to budgeting and management control. There is a comment on the integration of motivation theories.

The final section is devoted to a discussion of job design and the role of new technology.

This chapter provides a foundation for the study of topics discussed in subsequent chapters—e.g. job satisfaction (Chapter 6), leadership (Chapter 8), culture (Chapter 11), change and development (Chapter 12), and rewards (Chapter 13).

DEFINITION

The question of motivation arises when we ask why people behave in a certain way. When people are motivated, they are responding to conditions operating within and outside themselves. Motivation is frequently studied with reference to needs, motives, drives, and goals or incentives. The emphasis on needs and motives highlights the interconnection between motivation and personality.

Needs

Needs can be classified as, for example, physiological, security or safety, social, and ego or esteem needs. It is possible to have a need and do nothing about it, but equally a pressing need can give rise to a specific pattern of behaviour.

Motives

Motives consist of inner states that energise, activate, and direct the behaviour of the individual as he or she strives to attain a goal or acquire an incentive. A single motive may produce many effects, whereas a single effect may have several motives. For example, a person's purchase of a cake mix may be influenced by a craving for sweet things, pride in his or her ability as a cook, and a need for social approval from family or guests.

Motives can act in concert or vary in intensity, and are related to needs and goals or incentives. Motives can serve as a means by which consumers evaluate competing products. This can be seen when a car buyer, motivated by convenience, is attracted to a model with electronic windows, central door locking, and electronic speed control, in preference to a similar car without these facilities.

Drives

The concept of drive is an important feature of many theories of motivation and is linked with theories of learning, such as Hull's theory (see Chapter 4).

An individual is said to be in a state of drive when he or she adopts a pattern of behaviour in order to achieve a particular goal. For example, a hungry person, who is obviously preoccupied with satisfying a physiological need, behaves (a state of drive) in such a way as to indicate that he or she is in search of food or nourishment (a goal or incentive). When the person obtains sufficient nourishment the behaviour (the drive) subsides for the time being. The stronger the drive the greater the level of arousal experienced by the individual. A raised level of arousal implies increased awareness, energy, and speed, and can be effective in the performance of well-learned mental and physical skills. On the other hand, a lower level of arousal is more suited for tasks of a really complex nature.

Arousal

The thalamus and reticular formation (both areas of the brain) exert influence on the arousal mechanism. The thalamus is the focal point of excitement and depression, pleasure and pain. The function of the reticular formation is to increase or decrease the level of arousal, and, apart from filtering information, it decides what should be passed on to the higher brain and what should be rejected. Obviously a high priority would be given to information that alerts us to a potential danger. An illustration of arousal in the motivation process is provided in the panel below.

The emotion of fear features prominently in the illustration—it activated flight. Anger is also an emotion that is considered in the context of motivation, and produces a physiological change in the form of a greater production of nor-adrenalin, resulting in a "fight" response.

Goals or Incentives

Goals or incentives satisfy or reduce the behaviour associated with the drive. For example, the eating of food by the hungry person could lead to a reduction or elimination of the hunger drive.

In the field of safety, various incentive programmes have been designed to motivate

---

Arousal and Motivation

A person suddenly realises that what appears to be a harmless cow in a field is actually an angry bull about to charge. There is a high level of motivation to escape, and information is registered in the hypothalamus (an organ with an important central control function), which directs two processes simultaneously. One process is from the reticular formation, which transmits a message electrically through the sympathetic nervous system to the various parts of the body; the other is from the pituitary gland which, under the control of the hypothalamus, transmits chemically through the adrenal medulla that secretes adrenalin.

The nervous system and chemical processes

together prepare the body for effective speedy action by increasing the blood supply to the brain and muscles and decreasing the blood supply to the digestive system; by increasing the heartbeat and rate of breathing; by alerting relevant parts of the brain to ensure that the necessary skill (to run) is properly performed; and finally, directing the movement of the body by monitoring the bull's movements, the condition of the ground, where the gate is located, and so on.

It is through the co-ordination of all these processes that the person escapes. After these processes are complete, the level of arousal drops and the person enters a state of relative calm with the help of the parasympathetic nervous system.

people to meet good safety standards. Tangible rewards, such as jewellery, gifts, and plaques, as opposed to cash, for meeting safety targets, are especially common in the United States. Something like a pin is said to provide a symbol of achievement, it is visible to others and it provides a lasting memento of the occasion that justified recognition. It is often suggested that the key to a successful safety incentive programme is to make safety a group activity, for, in so doing, peer pressure is used to reinforce safe work habits.

AROUSAL STIMULI

The stimuli which influence states of arousal are illustrated using examples drawn from marketing and accounting. Sandwiched between the wants and needs of the consumer and the product or service advertised by a company is the appeal of the product or service, the feeling tone, the colour and print type, and the sounds and imagery.

Appeal

The appeal is the message contained in, for example, an advertisement. Consumer studies conducted for a sweet manufacturer established that eating sweets was associated with completing a job that the sweet-eater considered disagreeable—a form of reward for doing an unpleasant or tough job. The company switched its advertising slogan in two test markets from "smooth, rich, creamy coated chocolates—everybody likes them" to "make that tough job easier, you deserve our chocolates", with a consequent increase in sales (Yoell, 1952).

Advertising Appeals
These can either be positive or negative. They are positive when a pleasant situation follows the use of the product, and negative when an unpleasant situation may occur if the product is not used. An example of a negative appeal is a message on the label of a garment containing an assurance that the cloth will not shrink if a particular washing detergent is used. The way a negative appeal is presented is crucial, for if the situation presented is too unpleasant, as in the case of a detailed picture of a serious accident, people could turn away completely from the advertisement. With negative appeals the emphasis is placed on the action the individual may take to avoid the unpleasant situation; it is escaping from fear that reinforces learning, rather than being confronted by fear itself.

Feeling Tone

The feeling a product generates is also worthy of note. This is referred to as a feeling tone. In a house-to-house survey of hosiery preferences in one city, four identical samples of hosiery were presented to housewives. Some of the samples contained a card that had been immersed in a faint perfume; and though awareness of the scent was not altogether evident, the perfume created a pleasant feeling towards the product, with significant results in consumer choice (Laird, 1932).

Similarly, in an advertisement for soup, pictures of the glowing health of happy children or the warmth and comfort of a hot bowl of soup on a blustery day, could generate certain feelings about the product.

Product Image
Companies deliberately change the image and appeal of a product in the hope of influencing the motivational disposition of consumers. The brand image of *Marlboro* cigarettes was originally elegant and somewhat feminine. The company adopted a strategy to change the product image by conducting an advertising campaign in which ranchers, hunters, and other sturdy outdoor types, often displaying tattoo marks, were seen smoking *Marlboro* cigarettes.

Brand names and trade marks are sometimes chosen to strengthen the desired brand image. The story of *Green Giant* peas is a good example of this strategy (Crawford,

1960). A small firm called the *Minnesota Valley Canning Company* marketed extra large peas grown from a particular seed. The company selected the brand name *Green Giant*, and pictures of a smiling green giant were used in the packaging and all product advertisements. The company extended the use of the green giant brand to some of its other canned products, such as corn. Because the symbol was both popular and effective, the company changed its name to the *Green Giant Company*.

This is an example of transforming a successful brand image into a corporate image. Usually the reverse is the case—for example, when a company such as *BP* or *ICI* uses its corporate image to promote the public acceptability of a product.

Colour and Print Type

Colours in an advertisement can capture our attention, portray realism, and may arouse feelings about an object. From common experience, red is associated with danger (fire, blood, etc.), blue with cool rivers and lakes, and orange/yellow with sunlight and comfortable warmth.

Printing types and other graphic elements also have significant motivational implications. When reading a book, poor legibility of type may decrease speed and accuracy of reading, and increase visual fatigue. In an advertisement poor legibility reduces the motivation to read further, and the ensuing frustration may become associated with the product. Various print types, and the layout of printed matter, have to be considered in order to ensure good legibility (Anastasi, 1979). Unfamiliar type and arrangement tends to slow down reading. A passage set completely in capitals rather than capitals and lower case letters, for example, can have an adverse effect on reading speed. At the same time, capitals are suitable for a message that will be read from a distance—for example, on a billboard.

The fastest reading rate and the fewest eye fixations were found to be associated with black print on a white background. Other good combinations of colour were green on white, blue on white, and black on yellow (Anastasi, 1979). Bad combinations were red on green and black on purple, which could slow down reading by more than 50%.

Because of emotional reactions and associations aroused by different types of print, brand names may use particular typefaces to convey certain qualities—old English or elaborate types, for example, might be used to create a genteel or aristocratic impression.

Sounds and Imagery

When devising brand names or selecting appropriate words for advertising copy, feeling tones aroused by different sounds should be considered. Meaningful associations in a phonetic sense should be explored when choosing a brand name. Likewise, ease of pronunciation is important because difficult pronunciation can arouse annoyance and hostility. The makers of *Suchard* chocolates printed on their wrappers the slogan "Say Soo Shard" because consumers were finding it difficult to pronounce the name. Eventually the company adopted a live trademark—an attractive little girl known as "Sue Shard"—who was featured in all advertisements and radio commercials and made personal appearances (Grube, 1947).

Imagery is evoked by language, and a factually correct statement about a product could generate imagery that is unappetising. For example, "Evaporated milk makes a fine curd in the stomach and is therefore more digestible than regular milk" (Anastasi, 1979).

Accounting Data as Stimuli

Accounting information is a stimulus to a particular pattern of behaviour in business and, to this extent, it creates a state of arousal. In effect, it triggers off a drive when it provides a decision maker with the financial information necessary to formulate and implement a strategy regarding a particular goal. Though the accounting information stimulates the drive, it is the motive behind the decision-maker's goal that provides the drive in the first place. Of interest to the accountant in his or her assessment of the relative usefulness and relevance of accounting information, is the nature of the decision maker's motives and goals, and the effect accounting information has on the drive state of the recipient. Like any other desired information, accounting information serves to alleviate a state of anxiety by increasing knowledge and minimising the uncertainty facing decision makers within the system.

How useful is financial accounting information as a stimulus or motivating force in the making and taking of investment decisions and actions? The relationship between published information with regard to earnings expectations and subsequent share price movements for selected companies was examined, in order to see which financial data confirmed or conflicted with the investor's own expectations and, in turn, influenced the price of shares through decisions to buy or sell (Benston, 1967). It was concluded that accounting data constituted a small part of the total information used by investors for this type of decision, and that there was little correlation between published data expectations and subsequent share price movements.

Certain users of financial accounting information (financial analysts, financial executives, and bankers) were asked how useful and relevant they felt current cost and price level-adjusted accounting information to be. All the groups sampled felt that both types of accounting information were useful, although the financial executives were the least enthusiastic about the relevance of the information (Estes, 1968).

In a similar survey, shareholders, bankers, and financial analysts were asked to express their views on the usefulness of current cost accounting information, and it was found to be regarded generally as a useful addition to historic cost information. But only a small number of respondents wanted current cost data to completely replace historical cost information (Brenner, 1970).

In a laboratory experiment, accounting students played the role of investment analysts in a business game (Pankoff & Virgil, 1970). The researchers tried to assess the relative usefulness of items of accounting information by measuring the demand for particular items of information that could be purchased for money, and then went on to assess the effects of these items of information on the subjects' forecasts of price movements and the investment decisions that followed. One might view this study as artificial; however, the major findings of any significance were that information relating to the industry was more widely used than individual company information, and that accounting information was considered useful in the making of investment decisions.

These studies indicate that certain types and items of accounting information have a better motivating effect than others. It is therefore necessary to highlight relevance in the provision of accounting information.

FRUSTRATION

There are occasions when the individual is in a motivated state in order to achieve a particular goal which will satisfy a deficient need—for example, the hungry person is seeking food, or the ambitious employee is seeking a more challenging job. But when an obstacle is placed in the individual's pathway to the achievement of the goal (such as being caught up in a traffic jam preventing a job applicant from attending a selection interview), this can give rise to feelings of frustration and produce either positive or negative reactions.

A positive reaction comes about when the person tries to resolve the difficulty in a constructive manner. For example, in the face of opposition to the implementation of a certain part of safety policy, the safety practitioner might decide to engage in more consultation with those who object to the scheme. It is also conceivable that the frustrating event makes the individual divert his or her energies into the achievement of alternative goals. In the lives of individuals over the centuries, frustrating events could have been responsible for significant personal accomplishments.

However, frustration can generate various forms of destructive behaviour. The individual may engage in physical or verbal aggression, or regress to an earlier form of behaviour when, for example, a display of temper achieved the desired result. There are other circumstances when the individual reacts to frustrating situations in the same way irrespective of the magnitude of the event and, as a result, the reaction may be totally inappropriate in given circumstances (e.g. shouting or making caustic remarks irrespective of the degree of magnitude of the frustrating event). Some individuals show a tendency to give up and withdraw from the situation, whereas others find the atmosphere surrounding the obstacle to the achievement of the goal unsettling and repress the experience to the unconscious mind.

MONOTONY AND BOREDOM

Monotony and boredom are associated with problems of motivation and, as such, are risk factors in safety at work. Boredom can be caused by a number of factors, and is a particular problem in mass production industries.

Lack of Variety and Challenge

Lack of variety and the absence of challenge due to a short job cycle, which is a result of keeping the number of operations to a minimum, causes boredom. A comment by an assembly line worker in a car plant a number of years ago highlights this problem: "The job gets so sickening, day in day out, plugging in ignition wires. I get through one motor, turn around and there's another staring me in the face. It is sickening" (Strauss & Sayles, 1960).

Accidents apparently occur when employees perform repetitive tasks by instinct rather than thinking about what they are doing.

Loss of Skill and Independence

Another source of boredom is the lack of opportunity to exercise skill or to act independently. This arises when the work is subdivided and simplified to such an extent that the person feels there is little scope to exercise ingenuity or initiative. As a result, the individual's contribution seems to be negligible.

For some people the challenge of the job is important, and when they experience an inadequate sense of accomplishment they feel dissatisfied. But it should be noted that others prefer to day-dream and this is more likely to be possible in a job that does not offer much of a challenge—in fact in a job that is likely to require only surface attention. However, having pride in one's work and involvement in the efficient execution of one's duties, is a good way of keeping alert and thus avoiding most accidents.

Pace of Work

Another factor contributing to boredom is the inability to control the pace of work, particularly on an assembly line where a machine determines how fast somebody will work. The relentless rhythm of the assembly line makes natural pacing difficult or impossible, although the worker may have some opportunity to vary the pace of work by "bank building". Probably most people want a varied work pace, but some prefer to be machine-paced because they find that there is no need to pay attention to how fast they work, and that in these circumstances there is little interference from the supervisor. Eventually, people accept the rhythm of movement imposed on them.

Workers try to alleviate boredom in a number of ways. Some try to make a game out of work by varying the speed of the production line and setting their own sub-targets. Some might make frequent visits to the cloakroom or, if the noise is not too loud, engage in conversation. Other outlets can be gambling or horseplay, and the ultimate tactic would be to go absent or leave the organisation altogether. There may also be attempts to change work practices, and active resistance to management initiatives could be mounted.

Repetitive Work

The safety implications of highly repetitive work, which is monotonous and boring, need restating.

The prospect of dozing close to a vat of molten lead is not a pleasant thought. Apart from lead poisoning, there is the risk of drowning. Likewise, there is the danger of the nodding heads of workers, drowsy after lunch, hitting projecting parts of machinery.

How can boredom be combatted? Canned music may be used as a means of keeping people at least partially awake. Another method is to startle workers into instant wakefulness by an occasional announcement over the loudspeakers, though this should be done with due care. The taped music could be switched off in mid-bar, followed by a 30-second pause to give the "sleeper" time to wake up, and then an announcement made in a clear-toned, urgent voice that, "In a few moments there will be a special announcement".

Items likely to scare people should be avoided, but the announcement ought to be of some interest. An item of low interest would be the dangers of smoking in the toilet, whereas an item of strong interest would be news of a works outing, or the latest score in a major football match. News related to work should be confined to relevant items such as proposed pay increases or a visit by a factory inspector. Controversial subjects should be avoided.

In recent times the advent of the industrial robot and automatic handling systems has had the effect of eliminating repetitive,

"I WANT ALL ASSEMBLY PERSONNEL IN MY OFFICE, FIRST THING MONDAY MORNING."

tedious, and often unpleasant tasks. At *Volvo*, automatic welding lines replaced manual jigs and manual welding lines, freeing people from hard and tedious work where absenteeism and labour turnover was high. Likewise, the use of paint-spraying robots can eliminate unhealthy and monotonous jobs. The automation of work processes involving asbestos, lead-based products, or intensive dust creation is welcome on health grounds. At the same time such developments amount to deskilling of jobs and, in turn, create other problems. The impact of new technology on job design is discussed later in this chapter.

Rest Pauses

The effect of a rest pause is particularly beneficial in repetitive work of a monotonous nature. Heavy muscular work, tasks which require close concentration, and operations involving a continuous standing or sitting posture are also suitable cases for the introduction of rest pauses. The speed of operations at work is another factor to be considered in relation to rest pauses. Work conditions that require a working rate in excess of the natural rhythm of the body are likely to lead to fatigue and, if they cannot be avoided, at least their effects should be alleviated by suitable rest pauses.

Because of complaints about fatigue among operators of VDU equipment, it is suggested that regular rest pauses should be provided for employees who frequently use VDUs (Manos, 1980). Ideally, continuous work at a VDU should be interrupted by occasional movement or by spells of alternative work. Otherwise it is recommended that mid-morning and mid-afternoon breaks of 10 to 15 minutes are taken, away from the equipment. The maximum continuous work period at a VDU should not exceed two hours, and there should be no more than seven hours' viewing in any one day (Anderson, 1980). Recently the Health and Safety Executive issued guidelines on the use of display screen equipment at work (HSE, 1992).

The following are examples of union agreements, concluded in the late 1970s, on rest pauses (Manos, 1980). In an agreement between APEX and *International Harvester* it was recommended that a maximum of one hour's continuous work at a VDU should be followed by a minimum break of 10 minutes. Another agreement (between the same union and *Coventry Climax*) recommended rest pauses at regular intervals to total not less than 60 minutes in a normal working day. New technology agreements seem to represent a lower priority for trade unions in the 1990s. This could be due to concern with more fundamental issues following the challenge to their power by the British government in the 1980s, and to the impact of the prevailing economic conditions.

Apart from scheduled rest pauses, the unscheduled rest pause is a feature of repetitive tasks, when the worker decides for himself or herself to have a break. At other times workers experience a lapse of attention (an involuntary rest pause) and this can give rise to mistakes and accidents. It is said that just before a rest pause, inhibition sets in—central nervous fatigue—and this undermines to some extent what has previously been learnt, leading to a lower level of performance. Several minutes after the rest pause, disinhibition and consolidation occur to restore performance to the customary level, which reflects what the employee has learnt about the job to date.

NEED THEORIES

Need theories fall into the category of content theories of motivation. They assume that individuals possess a "baggage" of motives awaiting gratification, and there is an attempt to explain motivation in terms of what arouses and energises behaviour. The theoretical perspective of content theorists will be examined in this section.

One particular view of motivation suggests that people strive towards realising their inner potential (self-actualisation) and may suffer some personal disadvantage in doing so. For example, the adolescent may feel it necessary to leave the comfort of the parental home in order to assert his or her independence. Likewise, there are occasions when a person forfeits comfort and security in order to support an unpopular principle or cause. These are examples of a person's desire to satisfy a pressing need. Maslow (1954) identified a hierarchy of needs ranging from the most primitive, which humans share with the lower forms of life, to those associated with the higher forms of life.

Hierarchy of needs

The hierarchy of needs is represented in pyramidal form in Fig. 2.1. The foot of the pyramid represents the most basic needs, and the individual strives to move upwards through the hierarchy. Maslow observed that "man is a wanting animal and rarely reaches a state of complete satisfaction except for a short time. As one desire is satisfied, another pops up to take its place." Thus, only if the lower needs are satisfied will the higher needs appear.

Physiological Needs

With respect to some physiological needs, there are certain automatic responses to internal imbalances in the human body. A self-correcting mechanism ensures that the level of sugar remains constant in the blood stream (except in diabetics). We are motivated to drink lots of liquid after eating salty foods. When our body temperature becomes too high, we perspire and are motivated to remove a garment or open a window in a room. A feature of physiological needs is that they have to be satisfied regularly. Consumption of products related to these needs is high, and apart from the emphasis in an advertising message on the convenience factor of certain foodstuffs, the nutritional value may also be acknowledged.

Safety Needs

Safety needs include physical security, emotional security, job security, a modestly comfortable and predictable routine, and a desire for fair treatment and justice at work. The need for security could motivate the car buyer to emphasise safety features, such as child-proof locks, head restraints, and a

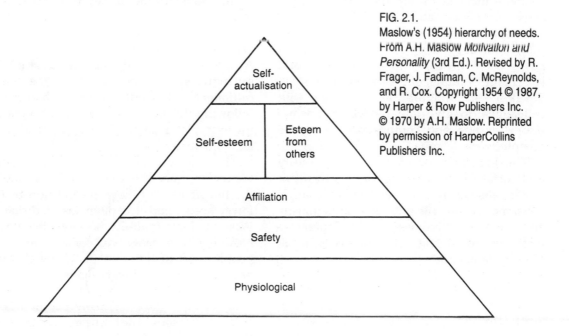

FIG. 2.1.
Maslow's (1954) hierarchy of needs. From A.H. Maslow *Motivation and Personality* (3rd Ed.). Revised by R. Frager, J. Fadiman, C. McReynolds, and R. Cox. Copyright 1954 © 1987, by Harper & Row Publishers Inc. © 1970 by A.H. Maslow. Reprinted by permission of HarperCollins Publishers Inc.

collapsible steering wheel when making a choice. The need for security could also be manifest when the individual is convinced that a signalling system is necessary for his or her future security; as a result, he or she is motivated to install a smoke detector in the house. Security needs could be aroused at work when there is uncertainty about continued employment with the company. Likewise, the threat of health and safety hazards could arouse safety needs.

Affiliation Needs

Higher than safety needs come affiliation needs. These include social contacts, belonging to a group, friendship, and love. Social motivation is also described as dependency (submissive behaviour aimed at an authority figure), dominance, personal relationships (both platonic and sexual), and aggression (Argyle, 1968). It can find expression, for example, in the following ways: in order to avoid a feeling of inferiority among others, a consumer may be attracted to the use of a mouthwash to counteract bad breath; and some people may purchase goods that meet with the social approval of others. Similarly, shoppers tend to be more inclined to rely on a friendly sales assistant for information and advice.

Social or affiliation needs act as important motivators of behaviour when the individual has a need to belong to a group at work, which, for example, offers the opportunity to develop meaningful associations with colleagues, to give and receive friendship, understanding and compassion, and to be accepted by colleagues.

The consequences of not satisfying security and social needs could be various forms of undesirable behaviour—resistance to change, resistance to budget pressures, antagonism, and an unwillingness to co-operate—intended to defeat the achievement of organisational goals.

Esteem Needs

The next level in the hierarchy deals with esteem needs, divided into self-esteem and esteem from others. Self-esteem includes the need for self-respect and self-confidence, the need to achieve something worthwhile as a result of job performance, the need to be fairly independent at work, the need to acquire technical knowledge about one's job, and to perform one's duties in a competent manner.

A message in an advertisement could stimulate the need to attain a feeling of self-esteem. In an advertisement for an Audi sports car a female engineer proclaims, "I pick the car and my husband picks the colour".

Esteem from others includes the need for recognition as a result of efficient and effective job performance, the need to be appreciated by colleagues for one's overall contribution at work, and the need to establish a reputation and status in the organisation. The desire for power would also probably belong to the category of esteem needs. Argyle (1968) recognises self-image as an essential part of esteem motivation, and there is a tendency to develop attitudes and beliefs towards the self which are consistent and integrated. The person could be motivated to get others to accept and respect the self-image, and perhaps avoid people or alternatively try to change their attitudes if they are not prepared to do so.

Self-actualisation Needs

At the apex of the pyramid are the self-actualisation needs, implying self-fulfilment derived from achievement following the successful accomplishment of, for example, a demanding and challenging assignment at work.

The sequence of events in climbing the hierarchy of needs is that the gratification of the higher needs follow gratification of the lower needs, and it is often asserted that in Western industrialised society the lower needs are reasonably well satisfied for most people most of the time. As needs that are gratified are no longer determinants of behaviour, it follows that the higher needs assume importance for many people in our culture. This should be borne in mind by those

"YOU SAID YOU LIKED A CHALLENGE, RIGHT?..."

responsible for the design of control systems in organisations.

People seem to have different priorities when it comes to specifying the most important human needs at a particular time. Maslow maintains that if a person has a history of chronic deprivation at a particular need level—e.g. an individual cannot find a job that adequately utilises his or her abilities—this person is likely to be very sensitive to that particular need. On the other hand, where people have previously experienced adequate and consistent gratification of a lower need, they can become relatively unconcerned about subsequent deprivations of that need because their focus has shifted to higher need gratification—the artists' preoccupation with their work pushes problems of subsistence to one side.

How does the accountant fit into this scheme of things? A study conducted in the United States in which the subjects were 269 Certified Public Accountants (CPAs) employed in large and small public accounting firms, provides some interesting insights (Strawser, Ivancevich, & Lyon, 1969).

Overall the accountants employed in the smaller firms reported less satisfaction of the social, security, and self-actualisation needs than those employed in the larger firms (see panel overleaf).

A sample of 1900 managers rated several needs similar to the ones identified by Maslow—security, social, esteem, autonomy, and self-actualisation—in terms of the importance and level of satisfaction associated with each need. It was found that highly satisfied needs were seen as relatively unimportant, and vice versa. There was an exception as far as self-actualisation needs were concerned; they appeared to remain constant, irrespective of how satisfied people felt about them. The self-actualisation needs lost importance only if lower level needs were deprived (Alderfer, 1972).

In a study based on the success of managerial trainees over a five-year period in the American Telephone & Telegraph Company, Maslow's concept was also subjected to an empirical test. The successful group (success being measured in terms of fifth-year income) reported the highest

---

Motivation of Accountants

For the purposes of this study physiological needs were not considered. Instead they were replaced by autonomy needs. Autonomy needs are concerned with the opportunity for independent thought and action, authority in one's position, and the opportunity to participate in setting work goals.

In addition to the size of the firm, the researchers considered the level at which the accountant operated within the firm. They found that partners and principals in the large firms felt that they experienced more opportunity for personal growth, development, self-fulfilment, and accomplishment (self-actualisation) than did their counterparts in the small firms. Partners and principals in the larger firms also indicated that the job security need is the most satisfied need, followed by self-actualisation, social, autonomy, and esteem needs, in that order.

The satisfaction enjoyed by partners and principals in the smaller firms assumed a different pattern. They perceived autonomy (opportunity for independent thought and action, authority in position, and opportunity to participate in goal-setting) as the need most satisfied, with lesser degrees of satisfaction (in descending order of importance) attached to social, security, esteem, and self-actualisation needs.

Below the level of partner and principal, the need satisfaction of managers and supervisors, employed in both the large and small firms, did not differ in any significant way, and is in line with the findings of other studies of managerial motivation which show that the higher-level needs—autonomy, esteem, and self-actualisation—are the least satisfied in practice. So partners and principals are out of step in this respect. In the larger firms their self-actualisation needs are well satisfied, and in the smaller firms their autonomy needs are well satisfied. (Strawser et al., 1969)

---

satisfaction of achievement, esteem, and self-actualisation needs (Hall & Nougaim, 1968).

If one were to accept and generalise on the basis of the findings from the CPA study reported earlier, one might suggest to the go-ahead professional accountant to seek employment in the larger firm when in need of self-actualisation—i.e. when opportunities for growth and development and feelings of self-fulfilment and accomplishment are sought. On the other hand, if the ambitious professional accountant values the opportunity to exercise a high degree of autonomy in the form of an opportunity for independent thought and action, authority in his or her position, and opportunity to participate in goal-setting, then the smaller firm is the better option.

Apart from needs that form part of the hierarchy of needs, Maslow acknowledges other needs, for example; a desire for beautiful things could be classified as an aesthetic need. Satisfaction of this need would come from beautiful or attractive surroundings. A person sitting in a room with a picture hung crookedly on the wall may go through the motions of straightening it. Maslow also acknowledges that not all behaviour is motivated, at least in the sense of need gratification—i.e. seeking what is lacking and needed. Though behaviour may not be motivated, it is certainly determined. For example, expressive behaviour could simply be an expression of personality—e.g. a smile on the face may be brought about by an association of ideas or some external stimulus.

The assumptions behind the hierarchy of needs have been criticised as mystical and value-laden, because they flirt so continuously with the evaluation of people in terms of normative judgements of high and low, advanced and primitive, good and bad (Lazarus, 1971). Nevertheless, Maslow's theory has made a significant impact on the development and application of theories of motivation based on "human needs".

ERG Theory

Alderfer (1972) proposed a hierarchical theory consisting of three need categories:

- *Existence (E).* These are needs that are related to Maslow's physiological and certain safety needs.
- *Relatedness (R).* These are needs that are related to Maslow's safety, social and some esteem needs—in particular the need for interpersonal relationships.
- *Growth (G).* These are needs that are related to Maslow's esteem and self-actualisation needs—in particular the need for personal growth and capability to exercise one's creativity.

This matching exercise highlights the fact that there is basically only a general fit between Maslow's and Alderfer's theories. Also, one should recognise that there are not strict demarcation lines between the compartments of ERG needs. An important distinction between the two need theories is that with ERG theory the person will regress to a lower-level need if frustration is encountered. For example, if the individual is unsuccessful at gratifying growth needs, the ERG theory predicts that because of the frustration encountered the person will show an increased desire for relatedness needs. Having satisfied the relatedness needs, the person will strive once again to satisfy growth needs in the hope that this time he or she will encounter a successful outcome. The pattern described could also apply if the person was intent on moving from existence needs to relatedness needs.

Another distinction between ERG theory and Maslow's hierarchy of needs is that with the former more than one need could be active at the one time. So instead of progressing up the hierarchy the person may be operating at all levels simultaneously, but obviously to different degrees. Hodgetts (1991) views ERG theory as a workable approach to motivation, with an acknowledgement of a plausible response to frustration when the individual realises it is not possible to progress from one level to the other.

Achievement Motivation

A person with a motive to achieve tends to define his or her goals in accordance with some standard of excellence. Six components of the construct *achievement motivation* have been identified by Cassidy and Lynn (1989):

1. *Work ethic.* This refers to the motivation to achieve based on the belief that performance in itself is good.
2. *Pursuit of excellence.* A desire to perform to the best of one's ability.
3. *Status aspirations.* A desire to progress up the status hierarchy and dominate others.
4. *Mastery.* This refers to competitiveness against set standards, rather than against other people when aspiring to status.
5. *Competitiveness.* A desire to compete with others and outmanoeuvre them.
6. *Acquisitiveness.* A desire to acquire money and wealth.

McClelland (1967) believes that a society's overall economic performance will be high if the average level of the need to achieve is high in the population (e.g. in the United States). He cites evidence to the effect that in any society the amount of achievement imagery in its children's literature (a reflection of the values society places on achievement) is a fairly good predictor of economic growth in that country for the following 20 years. Apparently, parental expectations and rewards are important conditioning influences on the performances of children high in the need to achieve. The need to achieve (termed *N.Ach*) can be modified through a training programme that supports the view that learning is an important agent in motivation. McClelland developed a method for measuring achievement motivation whereby unconscious projections of the individual's dominant needs were analysed. (Projective tests were examined in connection with personality in Chapter 1.)

Entrepreneurs are said to be high in N.Ach but distinguished scientists are not. Perhaps in the latter case, because of long periods without feedback on progress and working on tasks with low success probabilities, this is understandable. High achievers can flourish if the tasks given to them are challenging but feasible, where they have a sense of control over what they accomplish, and where they are receiving regular feedback on how well they are doing.

High achievers prefer to work on their own where they have control over the outcome of action; they do not like situations where there are no standards to measure their performance by, or where the task is too difficult or too easy. Money is looked upon more as a symbol of achievement rather than an intrinsic motivating factor. The desire for success appears to be the major motivating force; the fear of failure is said to depress N.Ach, causing a person to shy clear of achievement-type tasks. Women are said to feel differently about achievement and score lower than men in the tests; the assertion has been made that many women have a fear of success because high achievement is seen as being incompatible with traditional notions of femininity and female roles (Horner, 1970). This situation is likely to be different today!

McClelland has devised programmes to arouse N.Ach in executives by helping the individual to develop self-insight and cultivate the appropriate outlook. Most organisational conditions would appear not to be compatible with the needs of the high achiever, because managers, particularly in large organisations, frequently cannot act alone. However, an association between achievement motivation and budgetary control has been emphasised—"the most sophisticated budgetary system may be of little practical consequence if it fails to elicit the achievement motivations of a significant number of managers and employees" (Hopwood, 1974).

It is recognised that achievement motivation research has been of value in enlarging our understanding of the characteristics of the high achiever, and helpful to managers in trying to develop this need in subordinates (Hodgetts, 1991). A suggested drawback of the research on achievement motivation is the lack of emphasis placed on why people desire to achieve. Instead the emphasis is on identifying, or trying to develop, a desire to achieve (Stahl & Harrell, 1982). This observation could equally apply to a *need for power*, discussed in the following section.

Need for Power

A system has been devised for arriving at a need for power profile (termed *N.Pow*) in a similar manner to that adopted by McClelland with N.Ach (Veroff, 1953). McClelland, having closely studied the relationship of N.Pow to style of management and performance, concludes that for managers in large organisations, rather than for entrepreneurs, N.Pow is more important for effectiveness than N.Ach (McClelland, 1970).

N.Pow is a motive that involves other people, whereas N.Ach can exclude other people. Because managers in large organisations frequently cannot act alone, they have to depend on influencing others for their success. For this reason McClelland believes that N.Pow is related to success in the exercise of managerial leadership. For example, McClelland and Boyatzis (1982) found an empirical association between success in managerial positions and a moderately high need for power, high self-control, and a low need for affiliation manifest in a warm relationship with others and an ability to empathise with them.

This profile would not be far removed from Miner's (1978) conception of the motivational disposition necessary to manage effectively in large organisations. Miner developed a projective test (similar to the Rorschach ink-blot test described in Chapter 1) of managerial motivation, called the Miner Sentence Completion Scale. As the name implies, the test involves completing partial sentences, and is based on the notion that people will project their personalities into their responses. The test is scored in order to give measures of a person's willingness to engage in the following aspects of managerial motivated behaviour:

- Positive attitudes towards superiors.
- Competitive in the quest for scarce resources.
- Assertive, active, with a propensity to take charge of situations.
- Directs and controls subordinates, and feels comfortable administering rewards and sanctions.
- Highly visible and behaves in such a way as to invite attention, and perhaps criticism.
- Able to perform a wide variety of administrative duties that involve repetitive, detailed work.

Miner has developed a training course designed to increase managerial motivation by teaching managers and potential managers to behave in a manner consistent with the six managerial behavioural patterns listed.

People might feel uncomfortable about being told that they are high in N.Pow because of the traditional association between seeking power and suppression, exploitation, and tyranny. McClelland (1975) expresses some observations about those high in N.Pow and suggests two types of groups:

1. At the fantasy level, the first group projects itself in terms of sexual exploitation and the use of physical aggression. They tend to act as impulsive tough guys behaving in accordance with their fantasies.
2. At the fantasy level, the second group projects itself in a more conventional form, such as winning in a competitive game or election. The members of this group prefer to seek *institutionalised power* with its established environment and rules; they seek posts of responsibility in organisations and have a capacity for creating a good work climate.

Unlike the need for achievement, the need for power is a motive that involves other people in the organisation and is closely linked with management styles (discussed in Chapter 8). One group of managers high in the need for power has been identified by McClelland as being competitive, with management potential, in search of responsibility and institutional power (McClelland, 1975). Power is often associated with prestige, status, social eminence, or superiority, and it can affect an individual's self-concept. Sometimes managers who exercise control in organisations are looked up to with respect because they occupy positions of power, although they might feel uncomfortable if they were told they were high in the need for power because of the traditional link between seeking power and its negative associations referred to earlier (e.g. suppression, exploitation, and tyranny). It can be argued as a general proposition that members of an organisation may prefer to exercise influence than to be powerless, and it is conceivable that managers and workers are much more likely to feel that they have too little, rather than enough or too much, authority in their work.

Certain psychological fulfilment is likely to be derived from the exercise of power, and certain managers get enormous pleasure and satisfaction from influencing the work situation in a way that is compatible with their own interests. There is a discussion of power in Chapter 9.

In some respects, the rationale for certain organisational controls may be embedded in the psyche of the manager. But it is all too easy to become preoccupied with the rewards accompanying power and forget its more unpalatable side. Managers in their role of exercising control can suffer frustration and serious tension as a result of a number of organisational demands. Some of these have been identified as extra responsibility, commitment, loyalty, and the burdens of taking decisions (Tannenbaum, 1962). (There is a discussion of executive stress in Chapter 15.)

Dual-factor Theory   x b y

The work of Herzberg (1966) is consistent with Maslow's and McClelland's theories. His dual-factor theory is based on considerable empirical evidence and is built on the principle that people are motivated towards what makes them feel good, and away from what makes them feel bad. His research identifies motivators as factors producing good feelings in the work situation; these are listed in Table 2.1. By contrast he suggests that hygiene factors, also listed in Table 2.1, arouse bad feelings in the work situation.

Hygiene factors are clearly concerned with the work environment rather than the work itself. They differ significantly from motivators in as much as they "can only prevent illness but not bring about good health". In other words, lack of adequate "job hygiene" will cause dissatisfaction, but its presence will not of itself cause satisfaction; it is the motivators that do this. The absence of the motivators will not cause dissatisfaction, assuming the job hygiene factors are adequate, but there will be no positive motivation. It is axiomatic in Herzberg's approach that job satisfaction and job dissatisfaction are not opposites. The opposite of job satisfaction is not job dissatisfaction, it is no job satisfaction—the opposite of job dissatisfaction is lack of job dissatisfaction. This is illustrated in Table 2.2.

Empirical endorsement of Herzberg's theory is available. Hodgetts and Luthans (1991) report a number of successful international replications of Herzberg's findings. However, this evidence should be considered in the light of the criticisms voiced later in this chapter.

Adopting Herzberg's approach, a manager should build motivators into the job so as to promote job satisfaction positively; in order to minimise dissatisfaction, hygiene factors should be improved. In the motivation of sales representatives, the motivators and hygiene factors discussed in the panel overleaf might be considered.

Theory X and Theory Y

While advocating a similar position to that advanced by Herzberg, McGregor (1960) postulates two views of humans—namely, theory X and theory Y. Theory X is the belief that people are naturally lazy and unwilling to work and must be bribed, frightened, or manipulated if they are to put in any effort at all.

This is contrasted with the optimistic perspective of people—theory Y. This view is likely to be held by a manager who believes in providing "motivators" as motivational devices. A theory Y view states that work is as natural as play; the capacity to assume responsibility for directing one's own efforts is widely, not narrowly, distributed in the population, and if people are passive, indolent, and irresponsible on the job, it is because of their experiences in organisations and not generally because of some inherent human weakness. McGregor would subscribe to the theory Y view, in the belief that there are more people than is generally believed who are able and willing to make a constructive contribution towards the solution of organisational problems.

Earlier it was suggested by Herzberg that motivators are critical factors residing in the job. Towards the provision of motivators he

TABLE 2.1

Dual-Factor Theory

Motivators	Hygiene Factors
Achievement	Company policy and administration
Recognition	Supervision
Work itself	Salary
Responsibility	Interpersonal relations
Advancement	Working conditions
Growth	Status
	Security

TABLE 2.2

Herzberg's View of Factors Contributing to Job Satisfaction and Dissatisfaction

Adequate ———————————	**Motivators**	——————————— Inadequate
(Satisfaction)		(No satisfaction)
Adequate ———————————	**Hygiene factors**	——————————— Inadequate
(No dissatisfaction)		(Dissatisfaction)

prescribes various methods of job enrichment. This is an approach to job design (considered in the final section of this chapter) that attempts to make tasks more intrinsically interesting, involving, and rewarding. It comprises both vertical and horizontal loading: vertical loading entails injecting more important and challenging duties into the job, whereas horizontal loading is akin to job enlargement (increasing the number or diversity of task activities) and job rotation—i.e. moving people back and forth among different tasks.

The underlying belief in Herzberg's approach is that increased job satisfaction is an important source of motivation and will lead to better performance because of its association with increased productivity and reduced turnover, absenteeism, and tardiness. There is a discussion of a number of facets of job satisfaction in Chapter 6.

Sales Motivation

With regard to motivators, sales representatives could be given responsibility for making decisions, such as negotiating prices and terms subject to certain conditions; involved in setting their own sales targets; and given responsibility for planning their own time and journeys. The organisation could ensure that as much relevant information as possible is available to the sales-force, and that feedback of information from the sales-force is acted on and seen to be acted on.

The hygiene factors associated with material reward are likely to receive emphasis. Salary, commission, bonuses, promotions, and competitions are rewards that could be related to the achievement of sales objectives. These objectives could include sales volume, expense control, profitability of sales volume and new account development. Incentive schemes could be devised for a predetermined period aimed at, for example, the movement of old models from retailers' inventories before the launch of a new product. A system of "prize points" could be used, which would be linked to specific performance targets, allowing each representative to compete against himself or herself. This might be used to raise the level of a representative's performance. As an alternative to money, which may be swallowed up in household expenditure, merchandise incentives (such as holidays abroad) may create greater excitement, with lower tax implications.

From the organisation's point of view it is important that extra effort flows from the incentives given, and that the costs of providing the incentives are less than the extra sales revenue (Guirdham, 1972).

Other hygiene factors worthy of mention in the field of sales are an efficient administrative back-up service and good working relationships with colleagues. In a study of the motivation of sales executives in two major companies in the UK, it was concluded that those who held the most favourable attitudes derived satisfaction from the motivators—the job itself, achievement, and scope for development (Smith, 1967). However, if the motivators were in any way restricted, social relationships, security, and other "hygiene" benefits arose as factors promoting satisfaction. Particular hygiene factors (communication and budgetary control systems) aroused dissatisfaction in the more enthusiastic groups.

Criticisms of Dual-factor Theory

There is research evidence that is not entirely compatible with the findings of Herzberg. A study by Wernimont (1966) replicated Herzberg's investigations, using 50 accountants and 82 engineers, and the results suggest that either "motivators" or "hygiene" factors can cause both satisfied and dissatisfied feelings about the job. Although this result conflicts significantly with the claims of Herzberg that hygiene factors contribute most to dissatisfaction with the job, the Wernimont study agrees with him that motivators are important determinants of satisfied feelings about the job.

Another view suggests that it is dissatisfaction, rather than satisfaction—as in the Herzberg model—that is tied up with performance (March & Simon, 1958). When dissatisfied, the employee will search for alternative courses of action to alleviate this condition. He or she will take into account, and strike a balance between, the expected worth of the reward for action and his or her own level of aspiration.

The findings of a study (McDougall, 1973) on the motivation of senior business executives employed by a large public company in the UK show that financial reward assumes a position of significant importance as a motivator rather than as a hygiene factor.

A sample of 2246 executives was divided into the following six motivational groups: material reward; leadership; variety and challenge; job interest or vocation; comfortable, secure life among friends; and status and prestige.

The group of executives who displayed a strong drive for material reward was the largest of any of the six groups, accounting for 25% of the total sample. "They rated highly such rewards as money in terms of spending power, fringe benefits affording tax advantages, or opportunities to accumulate capital.... Relatively unimportant to these people, on the other hand, were opportunities for plenty of free time, having congenial colleagues, and a job with a high degree of intellectual or vocational interest."

The results of a study conducted by the Industrial Society among employees in the south of England in 1993 appear in the panel below.

The supremacy of financial reward as a motivating force has been underlined by recent developments in pay remuneration. In particular, performance-related pay often increases productivity (Bratkovich, 1989), and can result in satisfaction with this system of remuneration (Heneman, Greenberger, & Strasser, 1988). A discussion of performance-related pay appears in Chapter 13.

Besides adequate motivators and hygiene factors, the nature of the expectations that the employee brings to the work situation must be considered (Wernimont, 1966). People approach their jobs with a desire and expectation to have an interest in their work, to be recognised for their efforts, to feel a sense of achievement, to receive a particular level of remuneration, to have congenial colleagues, and so on. Lack of attainment or frustration of

---

The Industrial Society's (1993) Motivation Study

Enjoyable work, good pay, and a sense of achievement were rated more highly than job security. It was stressed by a spokesperson from the Industrial Society that job security is a concern for everyone, but not an expectation for anyone, because people know they no longer have jobs for life. A good relationship with the boss, good terms and conditions of employment, and status were given a lower priority than job security.

One third of employees were dissatisfied with their work, and only 17% of employees said that they could contribute their full potential at work. The most satisfied employees were public sector workers, and the least satisfied were those in the financial services and engineering sectors of the economy (Wood & Goodhart, 1993).

any of these needs cause people to be dissatisfied with their jobs. This is a perspective ignored by the dual-factor theory.

The relationship the individual has with work can be viewed from two angles—input and output. The individual's education, intelligence, training, status, health, appearance, etc., may be conceived as his or her input. The output can be thought of in terms of rewards that can be intrinsic or extrinsic; intrinsic in the sense of deriving satisfaction from completing the job to one's standards; extrinsic in the sense of financial reward. A mismatch of the input and output factors would therefore have significant implications for the level of satisfaction, irrespective of the distinction between motivators and hygiene factors. This view resembles *equity theory*, which is considered later.

A feature of the dual-factor theory of motivation propounded by Herzberg is the association of the motivators with job satisfaction. The prescribing of job enrichment is the logical extension to this line of thinking. But a pertinent question to ask is whether (in terms of more challenging work, etc.) every category of worker responds positively to job enrichment. There is convincing evidence to suggest that the answer is "no". For workers of one cultural background, jobs characterised as varied, complex, and demanding were associated with low job satisfaction; this is out of step with the motivator/hygiene concept. In a similar vein it is maintained that individual differences must be accepted; job enlargement as a means to enriching jobs may produce benefits for certain individuals—for example, white collar and supervisory workers and non-alienated blue collar workers.

Other workers may not welcome an opportunity to become more involved in their work and to participate more in decision making (Hulin & Blood, 1968; Turner & Lawrence, 1965). A large group of technicians in both high and low satisfaction groups mentioned hygiene factors more frequently than motivator factors as determinants of both job satisfaction and job dissatisfaction (Hinrichs & Mischkind, 1967).

At Luton in the UK, researchers found that workers sought jobs voluntarily on the assembly line, and they had previously given up jobs elsewhere offering interest, status, responsibility, and the opportunity to use their ability and skill (Goldthorpe et al., 1970). Further criticisms of Herzberg's theory have been raised and these are based on evidence derived from a review of roughly 40 studies related to Herzberg's dual-factor theory of motivation (House & Wigdor, 1967). These are:

- Methodological weaknesses. Because Herzberg asks subjects to "think of a time when you felt exceptionally good or exceptionally bad about your job" and relate what happened, people are likely to respond in such a way as to take credit for satisfactory happenings, but they will blame failure on the environment in order to protect their self-image. This accounts for the hygiene/motivator equation and therefore it is weak methodologically.
- Because the respondents' statements are evaluated and interpreted by a rater or experimenter under uncontrolled conditions, the outcome could be contaminated as a result of the evaluation method used.
- Herzberg's measure would not pick up a situation where a person dislikes a part of the job, but overall is satisfied with the job.
- The theory is not consistent with previous findings in research on satisfaction and productivity.

Methodological considerations feature prominently in serious evaluations of the dual-factor theory. Generally, studies that use the same methodology as Herzberg employed—i.e. content analysis of recalled incidents by respondents—are supportive of the theory (Pinder, 1984). Studies that use other methods for measuring satisfaction and dissatisfaction often come forward with results quite different from Herzberg's findings (Hulin & Smith, 1967). Therefore, it should be noted that if a theory is dependent on a particular research method for its substance, as appears to be the case with Herzberg's theory, its validity could be considered questionable.

Criticisms of Need Theories

In an evaluation of need theories, Arnold, Robertson, & Cooper (1991) maintain that accounts of motivation based on needs have only very limited value. Need theories offer interesting ways of thinking about human functioning, but their theoretical foundation is doubtful, and they have offered no clear guidance to managers about how to motivate individuals.

Maccoby (1988) is critical of need theories because they fail to capture the realities of today's world, characterised by the growth of automation and competitive pressures, with a consequent change in values. He postulates the importance of developing a match between dominant values held by individuals and the work situation, otherwise people will become defensive, frustrated, and resentful. Where there is a match between the work environment and human values, people will embrace opportunities for personal development and be more successful at what they are doing.

Maccoby identifies five ideal types of social character: the expert; the helper; the defender; the innovator; and the self-developer. Each character consists of a cluster of values. These clusters of values will in turn influence the nature of the work environment likely to motivate the individual.

For example, the expert needs a job where application of his or her expertise is pronounced, and where personal autonomy and control of others prevails. By contrast, the self-developer, who is likely to be under 40, constitutes the new generation of managers who have values congruent with work environments offering opportunities for expression, challenge, progression in career, equitable rewards, enlightened management, work involvement, the right balance between team and individual performance, and understanding of the total business situation. Some might argue that this work amounts to no more than a repackaging of existing theories and perspectives. However, the volatile nature of changing organisational environments in the context of motivation is worth stating.

COGNITIVE THEORIES

A cognitive perspective in psychology was explained briefly in the Introduction to this book. The cognitive approach to motivation is primarily concerned with the desire of individuals to produce an effect on their environment and in the process to develop certain skills. Early in life, we learn about visual forms, how to grasp and let go of objects, and to co-ordinate the hands and the eyes. Constancy, which is explained in Chapter 3, facilitates the stabilisation of our perception, and we develop a cognitive map to guide and structure our behaviour. Individuals in their relationship with the environment like to be active, to explore, to manipulate, to control, to create, and to accomplish things (White, 1960). Likewise, young children like to hold, rattle, and pull toys apart. Monkeys became more skilled with practice at manipulating mechanical devices placed outside their cages (Harlow, 1953).

A cognitive theory of motivation recognises that many aspects of motivation arise when people are fully aware of their motives and actions, and of the risks involved, and make plans guided by their expectations. We find a number of instances where people engage in purposeful behaviour, in which they set a course of action right at the beginning, recognise the obstacles on the way to achieving their plans, and finally overcome the obstacles and feel satisfied with their performance. It appears that the greater the sense of self-control attained, the greater the level of success in carrying out both short and long-term plans.

The most popular cognitive theories are goal-setting, expectancy theory, and equity theory. They are called *process theories*. Unlike content theories, discussed earlier in this chapter, which assume that individuals are endowed with a bundle of motives awaiting gratification and which do not acknowledge individual choice or social influence, process theories focus on how behaviour is initiated, redirected, and terminated.

Goal-setting

A goal is basically a desirable objective, the achievement of which is uppermost in the mind of a person. Goals can be used for two purposes in organisations·

- As motivational devices in the sense that employees work towards meeting these goals.
- As a control device when performance is monitored in relation to the goals set for individuals and departments.

Organisational goals might be expressed as "to reduce overhead costs by 10%" or "to increase sales revenue by 10% over the next year". Subsumed in these organisational goals would be numerous individual goals directed towards achieving the overall goal.

The starting point for a goal-setting theory of motivation is that behaviour is influenced by conscious goals and intentions. The original model of goal-setting was postulated by Locke (1968), who felt that performance was shaped by goal difficulty and goal specificity. Subsequent research has shown a close association between performance and goal difficulty and specificity (Hollenbeck & Klein, 1987).

Goal Difficulty
Goal difficulty is the extent to which a goal is challenging and demanding of effort. For a particular athlete a difficult goal could be to secure a place in the national squad for the Olympic Games. This could necessitate a lot of hard work to achieve the goal. For another athlete such a goal would be too difficult to achieve, and it could be considered unattainable. In such a case it is unlikely to have any motivating effect, so the athlete in question puts little effort into training.

Goal Specificity
Goal specificity amounts to a definition of the target to which performance will be directed. An example of a specific goal is to reduce overhead costs by 10%. You will notice the goal is expressed in quantitative terms. In areas where qualitative factors (e.g. state of morale) are considered, specificity is difficult to establish.

Latham and Locke's Model
An expanded model of goal-setting, designed to reflect the complexity of the setting of goals in organisations, was proposed by Latham and Locke (1979). This is shown in Fig. 2.2.

You will notice that goal-directed effort or behaviour in this model is influenced by four goal attributes—difficulty and specificity (as in the original model), plus acceptance and commitment.

Goal Acceptance and Goal Commitment. Goal acceptance is the extent to which a person accepts the goal as legitimate for him or her. Goal commitment is the extent to which the person is interested in attaining the goal, and this is reflected in the extent to which the person will take the necessary steps to attain the goal.

According to Latham and Steele (1983), acceptance and commitment are enhanced by factors such as participation in goal-setting, coming up with realistic and challenging goals, and accepting that goal achievement will lead to rewards that are valued by those

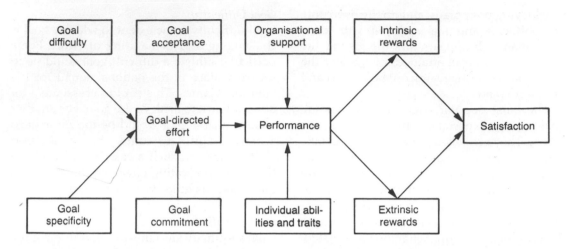

FIG. 2.2. Expanded model of goal-setting. Source: Latham, G.P. & Locke, E. (1979). Goal-setting: A motivational technique that works. *Organizational Dynamics*, Autumn, 68–80. Reprinted by permission. Copyright © 1979, American Management Association, New York. All rights reserved.

involved.

Other researchers view commitment to difficult goals as a natural precondition for effective performance (Hollenbeck & Klein, 1987). Apparently goal commitment is stronger when the goal is made public by communicating it to peers. Those people who believe they can control their fate (internal locus of control) and are high achievers, tend to have the strongest goal commitment (Hollenbeck, Williams, & Klein, 1989).

On the question of a participative style in goal-setting, the case for it is far from clear. However, Arnold et al., (1991) maintain that participation in goal-setting in laboratory experiments is an improvement on a style that amounts to simply telling people the goal assigned to them. But participation in goal-setting is not better than a style that takes the form of assigning goals to people and then offering them a rationale or justification for those goals.

Related to participation is the question of feedback. Good feedback can engender a sense of achievement, accomplishment, and recognition. It highlights present performance in relation to past performance, personal performance in relation to others' performance, and can produce improved and more creative effort (Latham & Locke, 1979).

The next step in the model shows how goal-directed effort leads to performance, but the outcome is influenced by two intervening variables—organisational support, and individual abilities and traits. An example of positive organisational support is ensuring that staffing levels and resources generally are of the required magnitude to achieve the goal. Negative organisational support could manifest itself as a failure to repair equipment essential for the execution of the tasks involved in attaining the goal.

The abilities, skills, and other personal characteristics required to do the job have also to be considered. The last but one step shows that when the person has performed the task, he or she receives various intrinsic and extrinsic rewards. The final step shows the level of satisfaction being influenced by intrinsic and extrinsic rewards.

The relationship between performance, rewards, and satisfaction in Latham and Locke's model bears some similarity to the expectancy model postulated by Porter and Lawler (1968), discussed later in this chapter.

Some scholars have expressed views about constraining influences on the effectiveness of goal-setting. Austin and Bobko (1985) maintain that goal-setting theory has not been properly tested in four areas:

- Goals that reflect quality, rather than quantity, do not feature prominently.
- Goal-setting theory could be compromised in situations where there are conflicting goals, and the person may have to select one at the expense of ignoring the other.
- Group goals and performance are neglected in favour of those relating to the individual.
- The effectiveness of goal-setting has not been satisfactorily evaluated outside of laboratory conditions.

The question of goals assigned to people can be a contentious issue. Assigned goals are meant to create a situation where performance is expected and materialises. But a question to ask is what constitutes appropriate performance in relation to a particular goal? There is the danger that the organisational conception of appropriate performance may be at odds with notions of acceptable performance as perceived by particular groups (Meyer & Gellatly, 1988).

It is suggested that goal-setting may not be helpful in conditions where novelty surrounds a task, and various strategies are available to tackle the situation. In a novel task—which was a stock market prediction exercise—subjects who were assigned difficult goals performed worse and changed their strategies more than subjects given a "do your best" goal (Earley, Connolly, & Ekegren, 1989). Perhaps too much attention is given to devising strategies to attain goals in difficult conditions, and not enough attention given to task performance!

Arnold et al. (1991) make a very interesting observation when they state that "nobody has yet satisfactorily explained why goals have motivating effects; most of the research on goal-oriented motivation is concerned with how goal-oriented motivation is harnessed". Moorhead and Griffin (1992) say that it has been argued that "goal-setting theory is not really a theory but simply an effective motivational technique" and that it takes a rigid and narrow view of behaviour with short-term rather than long-term considerations in mind. Nevertheless, they argue that it appears to be a useful approach to motivation. An approach through which goal-setting is applied in an organisational context—called management by objectives (MBO)—is discussed in Chapter 12.

Applications to Budgeting
The application of goal-setting to budgeting will be discussed with reference to aspiration level, budget standards, budget tightness, and bargaining and tactics.

Aspiration Level. In experiments connected with studying the level of aspiration (something within our reach) the setting of goals has received particular attention. We are more likely to be motivated by realistic goals where we recognise the possibility of failure (Atkinson, 1964).

Group influence can be an important factor when it comes to fixing the level of aspiration. If one's performance in an activity is better than the average for the group, this may lead to a lowering of the level of aspirations next time round. But equally, if one establishes that one's performance is worse than that of somebody whose standing in the group is low, this could give rise to an upward shift in the level of aspiration (Lewin, 1964). If achievement falls far below the aspiration level, the aspiration level may be subsequently reduced until the disparity is slight (Child & Whiting, 1954). Equilibrium is said to occur when the aspiration level exceeds achievement by a small amount.

Budget Standards. Budgets and cost standards are said to motivate employees by acting as goals or incentives, and a fair amount of research evidence focuses on the motivational effects of budget standards or targets of varying degrees of tightness (Hofestede, 1968; Stedry, 1960). Good standards of performance have been associated with high levels of aspiration (Stedry & Kay, 1964). The performance implications of different levels of budget difficulty were analysed using the following procedures.

Goals were set at a normal level (capable of being achieved 50% of the time), and at a difficult level (capable of being achieved 25% of the time). When compared with normal goals, difficult goals gave rise to either good or bad performance. When good performance followed the difficult goal, this goal had become an aspiration level. So where the difficult goal was seen as a challenge (as was the case with high achievers and younger performers), actual performance was better than target. In this situation results were in excess of the aspiration level. Where bad performance followed the difficult goal, the budgetee obviously viewed the achievement of the goal as being impossible, failed to set an aspiration level, and began to show withdrawal symptoms (Stedry & Kay, 1964).

Variation in levels of aspiration appears to be a function of success or failure. It is maintained that success raises the level of aspiration and failure lowers it, and that failure has a more varied effect on level of aspiration than has success. Movements in levels of aspiration are to some extent influenced by changes in a person's confidence in his or her ability to achieve the goal (Child & Whiting, 1954).

Apparently, past budget performance is likely to affect the level at which future budget targets are set. Managers felt it to be in their interest to agree lower rather than higher budget targets, striking a balance between present job security and increasing future income (Lowe & Shaw, 1968). These managers, whose track record may be either impressive or wanting, were quite subtle in the manner in which they tried to influence forecasts in order to win short or long-term approval or personal benefits.

Budget Tightness.   Another study tested the effect on performance of varying degrees of tightness in the budget (Hofestede, 1968). As the budget gets tighter, the employee is motivated and aspires to higher levels of aspiration with results lower than the aspiration level. At this stage the budget target is not achieved. Beyond this stage, both levels of aspiration and results fall because the budgetee no longer believes that it is possible to achieve the budget target. This can create negative motivation resulting in a deterioration in performance.

Similar findings are reported in a study conducted in the UK (Otley, 1977). As can be seen in Fig. 2.3, the budget level that motivates the best performance is unlikely to be achieved most of the time, but a budget that is usually achieved will motivate only at a lower level of performance. In other studies it was concluded that the best performance was achieved in situations where budget targets were clearly understood, and where they were tight but attainable (Kenis, 1977; Merchant, 1981).

Department meetings were found to be useful in facilitating the adoption of budget targets as the manager's personal goals. But cultural, organisational, and personality factors all affect an individual manager's reaction to a budget standard (Otley, 1977).

Bargaining and Tactics.   We have already seen how success or failure in meeting budget targets gives rise to variations in levels of aspiration, and how past performance in relation to the budget can affect future budget levels. When the budgetees were able to bargain on a budget standard, they presented biased information so as to secure the best personal advantage; this would normally manifest itself in a lower rather than higher budget standard. The budgetees (managers) tried to strike a balance between two objectives—present job security and increasing future income (Lowe & Shaw, 1968).

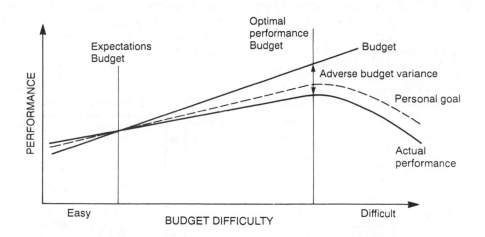

FIG. 2.3. The effect of budget difficulty on performance. Adapted from: Otley, D.T. (1977). Behavioural aspects of budgeting. *Accountants' Digest ICAEW (Institute of Chartered Accountants in England and Wales)*, 49, Summer.

For example, one manager may disappoint a superior now because of the conservative budget he or she has adopted for the coming budget period, hoping to win the superior's approval when he or she achieves the budget at the end of the budget period. Another manager may feel he or she has little reputation left because of poor past budget performance, but submits an almost unreal forecast (excessively high) so as to win approval now. At the end of the budget period he or she will have to live with the unfavourable consequences of this action. Yet another manager has a high standing with his or her superior because of good past performances, and decides to aim for an easier budget target for the coming budget period, an action that will receive acclaim later when the budget is met. His or her record can quite easily absorb the present disappointment on the part of the superior. Of course there are also circumstances when genuine over- or under-estimation occurs and this may arise when sales are subject to fluctuation. When sales are rising there is a tendency to underestimate budgeted sales (Lowe & Shaw, 1970). Tactics are discussed in greater detail in Chapter 9.

Expectancy Theory

A recognisable development within the cognitive theory of motivation was the emergence of expectancy theory. This theory expounds the view that we choose among alternative behaviours—i.e. we anticipate the possible outcome of various actions; we place a weighting or value on each possible outcome, assessing the probability that each outcome will be the result of an alternative action; and finally, the course of action that maximises our expected value will be chosen.

Vroom's Expectancy Model
Vroom (1964) put forward a well-known formulation of expectancy theory, and this is depicted in Fig. 2.4. The terms used in the theory are as follows:

Valence: strength of preference for a particular outcome—can be positive (desired) or negative (not desired).

Outcome: that which results from action.

First-level outcome: immediate effect of one's actions—e.g. a "job well done"—this is normally what the organisation is looking for.

Second-level outcome: that which results from the first-level outcome—e.g. a job well done may eventually lead to a promotion.

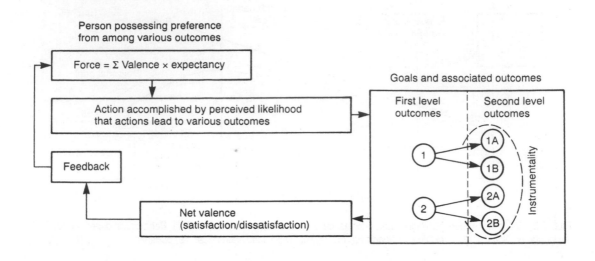

FIG. 2.4. Vroom's expectancy model. Adapted from: Vroom, V.H. (1964). *Work and motivation.* New York: John Wiley & Sons.

Expectancy: the probability that a certain piece of behaviour (i.e., certain level of effort in the job) will give rise to a particular first-level outcome (i.e. improved performance).

Instrumentality: strength of the causal relationship between the first-level outcomes and second-level outcomes (e.g. a strong causal relationship would exist if increased effort had a beneficial effect for the employee, such as a pay increase).

It is possible to quantify valence, expectancy, and instrumentality in Vroom's model. If we multiply each of the first-level outcomes by the expectancy (probability) that an outcome will follow action, and add up the results, we arrive at the strength of motivation to elect for a particular course of action. The preference for a first-level outcome depends on how effective this outcome is in bringing about a second-level outcome which is valued. We can expect the person to choose a pattern of behaviour that has a high motivational force attached to it. Expectancy theory, therefore, postulates that if this process was followed, a person's choice of behaviour would approximate the model's prediction.

Porter and Lawler's Expectancy Model
Porter and Lawler (1968) place expectancy theory firmly in an organisational context, with practical ramifications. They also put forward the view that the strength of motivation is dependent upon the person's perceived probability that the motivated behaviour will lead to a desired outcome. Their model is illustrated in Fig. 2.5.

The factors that affect the amount of effort people put into their work are the value they place on the outcome that they hope will materialise as a result of their efforts and the probability that reward will follow the effort. Porter and Lawler are in agreement with Vroom when they propose that the probability that effort will lead to acceptable performance should be multiplied by the strength of the causal relationship between first-level and second-level outcomes (instrumentality)—the good performance/reward equation.

But effort is not the only consideration; a person's abilities and traits will also have an effect on performance, as well as the person's perception of his or her organisational role. Based on research evidence, it is concluded

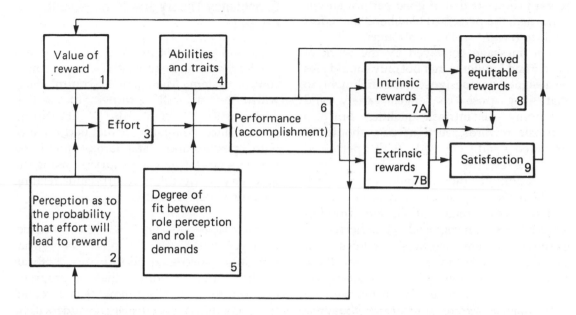

FIG. 2.5. Porter and Lawler's expectancy model. Based on data from: Porter, L.W. & Lawler, E.E. (1968). *Managerial attitudes and performance*. Homewood IL: R.D. Irwin.

that successful managers perceive their roles as requiring the display of inner-directed personality traits, such as forcefulness, imagination, independence, self-confidence, decisiveness, etc. Other things being equal, these managers are expected to perform better than managers who perceive their roles as requiring the display of other-directed traits—i.e. co-operation, adaptability, caution, agreeableness, tactfulness, etc. (Porter & Lawler, 1968). Managers with other-directed traits are considered less effective as measured by peer ratings, supervisor ratings, and promotions.

The next thing to consider is the relationship between performance and rewards. Rewards comprise two types: intrinsic (such as a sense of challenge, achievement, and success) and extrinsic (organisational rewards such as pay, promotion, and fringe benefits). Satisfaction should come about if the receipt of both intrinsic and extrinsic rewards is the consequence of performance; but the level of satisfaction depends on how near the rewards

are to what the person perceives as equitable for the services rendered. The closer the fit between actual rewards and perceived equitable rewards, the greater the level of satisfaction experienced.

The feedback loop between satisfaction and reward indicates that rewards associated with higher order needs (intrinsic rewards) assume greater importance as the individual receives more rewards for his or her effort. Apparently the more intrinsic rewards the individual receives the better this is from the point of view of higher future effort. The emphasis on intrinsic rewards reminds one of Herzberg's motivators; but unlike Herzberg's model in which satisfaction precedes performance, the Porter and Lawler model shows performance leading to satisfaction, with rewards and perceived equity serving as intervening variables. But note the weight given to extrinsic rewards, such as pay, in the Porter and Lawler model.

Reverting to Fig. 2.5, the feedback loop between intrinsic/extrinsic rewards and the perceived probability that effort will lead to reward suggests that, if good performance is rewarded, the perceived likelihood that effort leads to reward will grow stronger.

The message conveyed by the work of Porter and Lawler is that not only should jobs be designed or redesigned (job enrichment) so that they pose challenge, variety, and autonomy—i.e. intrinsic qualities—but also extrinsic rewards, such as pay, should be provided and equated with perceived equitable rewards.

In addition, there should be a match between the employees' traits and abilities and the requirements of the job. This has already been recognised elsewhere. For example, where workers' abilities and experience correspond closely to those required by their jobs, job satisfaction is said to have a high positive relationship with job performance, whereas in those situations where there is inconsistency the relationship is likely to be progressively lower (Carlson, 1969).

The Porter and Lawler model has not been extensively tested, but the authors have amassed some evidence which is consistent with the model. The message conveyed by this work is as follows:

- One should endeavour to relate employees' traits and abilities to the job and ensure that employees have accurate role perceptions. This action is likely to contribute to a high level of effort.
- Jobs should be designed so that they pose challenge, variety, and autonomy (intrinsic qualities), but make sure that extrinsic rewards, such as pay, are equated with perceived equitable rewards.

Porter and Lawler maintain that some employees with relatively low performance are dissatisfied with the rewards received, and they attribute this condition to the belief that low performers tend subjectively to overrate their performance relative to that of high performers.

Expectancy Theory and Management Control

I shall now attempt to place the Porter and Lawler model in the context of a management control system. Management control deals with the overall process of setting performance standards, measuring performance, comparing actual performance with performance standards, providing feedback (and, where appropriate, taking the necessary corrective action), and relating rewards to performance.

Standards of Performance. These reflect managements' expectations of what constitutes successful performance, with an implicit understanding that appropriate extrinsic rewards will follow. It is accepted that recognition (an intrinsic reward) will be forthcoming if actual performance reaches the standards laid down. While the individual is engaged in assessing subjectively the rewards associated with meeting standards of performance, it would be beneficial if he or she had access to knowledge or was aware of the set of rewards associated with effective performance. The subordinate's expectancy of future extrinsic satisfaction or utility associated with meeting standards can be affected by the degree to which the manager (his or her boss) has recognised past achievements. In fact it is likely that there could be revision of the expectancy that the meeting of standards gives rise to extrinsic rewards if management has been inconsistent in providing rewards related to performance.

The significance of deviations from past performance standards is important when perceiving the difficulties inherent in achieving standards, and expectations may have to be adjusted accordingly. Apart from the satisfaction derived from achieving standards, there are likely to be occasions when people derive satisfaction from having activities structured and ambiguities minimised along the path to the attainment of goals. This interpretation of an expectancy approach to control places much emphasis on the superior and subordinate relationship and the provision of extrinsic rewards, but it does not detract in any way from the potency of intrinsic rewards in this process.

Measurement of Performance. The process leading up to performance evaluation (performance measurement), for the purpose of reward, has been the subject of close scrutiny, particularly in the context of management accounting. Confidence in the measuring aspect of a control system is likely to be undermined if the individual feels that some aspects of his or her performance should be measured but are not (Porter, Lawler, & Hackman, 1975). Confidence could also be diluted if the measurement includes items that the individual feels are misleading indicators. There may, for example, be situations where accounting measures of performance are inadequate in conditions of uncertainty or ambiguity surrounding the performance of the task (Hirst, 1981).

It is also suggested that greater trust is vested in measurements where subjective elements—i.e. the superior's informal notion of what constitutes good performance—are minimised or eliminated. Also, formal objective measures should be relevant and highly focused. In a study of the information needs of managers it was found that a significant amount of control data was not used because it related to events outside the province of the manager, it was too detailed or not detailed enough, and it arrived too late (Beresford Dew & Gee, 1973).

There are other criticisms of management accountants operating in the budgeting process, due to their failure to present information in an easily understandable form relevant to the manager's responsibilities, and their reluctance to ensure accuracy and realism of the information by sufficient managerial involvement in the determination of the manager's needs (Hopper, 1978).

Because of the difficulty of measuring non-monetary aspects of performance, the accounting system usually restricts itself to reporting on financial performance. But therein lies a danger, in that managers may be motivated to emphasise things that can be measured to the neglect of those that cannot. It is of course possible to create a composite measure of performance, incorporating non-financial measures, but then the priorities and the value system of senior management may be ingrained in the weighting each dimension receives. For this very reason it may be considered unacceptable, apart from the difficulty of translating it into numerical form.

Frequently in practice attention is focused on significant deviations from standards, as opposed to the meeting of standards. In such a system it is generally the unfavourable deviation requiring corrective action that activates a response, whereas it requires exceptional success to attract management's attention and recognition. This type of system may be viewed by subordinates as negative rather than positive, with an emphasis on failure. The consequences may be defensiveness, over-cautious behaviour, and other dysfunctional effects (Sayles & Chandler, 1971).

Employees may be motivated to distort measurements used for policing purposes so as to present a favourable impression of their performance (Likert, 1961). The motivation to distort the measurements is to a large extent removed, according to Likert, if measurements are supportive and used for self-guidance rather than for policing purposes. In many situations in organisations it is difficult to measure a person's contribution to a set of results, because frequently tasks are interdependent and efforts are joint, or group-based, where an individual may have only partial control over the outcome of a group's activities. In addition, external disturbances or chance events can, to some extent, invalidate the performance of even the most skilled operator.

It is suggested that one should separate performance evaluation for the purposes of reward from control measures, otherwise there might be an inclination to distort information and set easy standards to secure personal advantage (Ross, 1957). This is particularly so when significant, valued rewards—such as enhanced promotion prospects, status and salary bonuses—are tied to the attainment of budgetary targets. In such circumstances, managers will be highly motivated to attain such targets and many will report performance at or near the target levels. This would be achieved by bargaining for easier targets in the discussions of budgets, particularly in conditions where estimates and judgements are difficult to validate. Likewise, figures could be adjusted to make short-term results look better, not to mention the falsification of reported information. Therefore, if measures of performance are imperfect, putting too much stress on the attainment of budgets that are linked to rewards can produce a range of undesirable consequences (Otley, 1982). A fuller discussion of performance appraisal and measurement appears in Chapter 13.

Rewards.   The adequacy of intrinsic rewards is a function of the role the individual occupies; these rewards originate from within the individual in the form of psychological satisfaction. However, management has some influence in the determination of intrinsic rewards because it can create organisational conditions under which opportunities exist for the exercise of self-control. This will become evident later in the chapter when discussing job design.

Perhaps management's influence is even more pronounced in the provision of extrinsic reward, e.g. pay, promotion, etc, to reinforce performance. But it is claimed, quite emphatically, that for differential extrinsic rewards to be effective in motivating performance a number of conditions must be present (Porter et al., 1975). These are:

- The organisation can offer important rewards.

- Rewards can be varied widely depending on the individual's current performance.
- Meaningful performance appraisal sessions can take place between superiors and subordinates.
- Performance can be measured objectively, including all relevant measurable items.
- It must be possible to publicise how rewards are given.
- Superiors are willing and able to explain and support the reward system in discussions with their subordinates.
- Trust is high.
- The plan will not cause negative outcomes to be tied to performance.

The condition that refers to objectivity in performance measurement could be difficult to meet, but this would hardly invalidate the effectiveness of a scheme that satisfies most of the conditions. Rewards are also discussed in connection with the concept of reinforcement and behaviour modification in Chapter 4, and in relation to pay in Chapter 13. The equitable nature of reward is important; equity theory is examined in the next section.

Finally, expectancy theory has much to offer, even if the research support for it is modest. However, it is a complicated theory and not easy to test. In reality it is questionable that people are so rational and objective in choosing options as the theory implies (Pinder, 1984).

Equity Theory

Equity theory as a social comparison theory takes a similar view to expectancy theory on the importance of the underlying cognitive processes governing an individual's decision whether or not to put effort into an activity. But the main thrust of equity theory is that people are motivated to secure what they perceive to be a fair return for their efforts.

We are all inclined, consciously or otherwise, to compare each other's inputs (e.g. education, experience, effort, and skill) and outputs (e.g. salary, increases in salary, promotion, and fringe benefits). If we perceive our input as justifying a larger output, or if, on a comparative basis, we feel we are unfairly treated, feelings of inequity can arise (Adams, 1963).

Feelings of inequity amount to a state of discomfort, and apparently this state can also arise when people feel they are over-compensated for their efforts. Feelings of inequity could motivate people to do more or less work depending on the nature of the inequity. The greater the inequity, the stronger the level of motivation. Normally one would expect people to compare themselves with others who are doing similar work or occupying similar positions.

It has been suggested that there are six methods at the disposal of people to reduce inequity (Adams, 1965):

1. Inputs may be modified. For example, if a person believes he or she is not sufficiently rewarded, personal effort (an input) may be reduced. If the person believes he or she is over-rewarded, personal effort may be increased.

2. Outputs may be modified. For example, the person may demand a better financial package or greater opportunities (an output) in return for the effort that is currently under-rewarded.

3. Perceptions of self are modified. For example, the person may alter the original perception of inequity by concluding that he or she is contributing less but receiving more than was originally believed to be the case.

4. Modification of the perceptions of others with whom comparisons are made. For example, the person who experiences inequity may conclude that the other person is working harder than originally appeared to be the case, and therefore deserves the perceived extra outputs.

5. The person with whom a comparison is made is no longer used. For example, the person may conclude that the other person used as a basis for comparison is no longer

suitable and should be replaced by someone else who is considered more appropriate.

6. Leave the situation. For example, the person believes that the only way to resolve the inequity is to get a transfer to another department, or to leave the organisation.

There is a prominent view in the research literature that equity theory has good predictive powers (Griffeth, Vecchio, & Logan, 1989) and particularly when conditions of underpayment apply (Lord & Hohenfeld, 1979). In another study the importance of social comparison in equity theory was relegated to insignificance. Apparently, there is now a view that some people are more sensitive to perceptions of inequity than others and act accordingly, so it would appear that individual differences have to be considered (Huseman et al., 1987). Finally, equity theory has a role to play in the study of motivation, and it would be ill-advised, for example, to ignore it because of one's preoccupation with job design.

INTEGRATION OF MOTIVATION THEORIES

The process theories examined under the heading of cognitive approaches handled the study of motivation in slightly different ways, just as we found with content theories (i.e. need theories) earlier in this chapter.

The difference of emphasis is apparent in process theories when expectancy theory and goal-setting theory are examined. For example, with expectancy theory individuals tend to be motivated by projects where the success rate is high. By contrast, goal-setting theory suggests that individuals are motivated by difficult assignments where success is not guaranteed. Of course there are similarities between the three process theories. They recognise individual and situational influences that are likely to affect outcomes, and all have an orientation embedded in the future in the sense that they are concerned with how people will behave.

Over a decade ago it was suggested that more attention needed to be devoted to integrating the various perspectives on motivation (Mitchell, 1982). For example, goal-setting and equity theory could be incorporated into expectancy theory. Also, given the prominence of groups in our lives, there is a need to develop a greater understanding of how group processes affect motivation (see Chapter 7 for a discussion of groups). There is scope for developing contingency models of motivation.

Landy and Becker (1987) speculate about the natural arrangement of approaches to motivation. For example, need and equity theories might be best suited to exploring the affective or emotional implications of work, whereas reinforcement models and goal-setting theory could be well suited to understanding specific work behaviour. Expectancy theory would be restricted to the prediction of choices among alternatives. Landy and Becker are adamant in admonishing motivational researchers on the need to identify specific cognitive operations (i.e. cognitive abilities) and explore the role of these operations in various motivational theories. The type of cognitive operations they refer to have been discussed in the section on intelligence in Chapter 1.

Control Theory

A control theory model of human motivation is put forward by Lord and Hanges (1987), consisting of the following features:

- A standard or goal that the system attempts to achieve.
- A sensor that measures or gathers information important to the system.
- A comparator or a discriminator that compares the sensed information to the standard.

- A decision mechanism by which the system decides what action to take in order to reduce any discrepancy between the sensed information and the standard.
- An effector or response mechanism that enables the system to interact with its environment.

Lord and Hanges believe that control theory provides a viable model for understanding the way specific goals and feedback affect people's behaviour and performance on the job. They believe the model is dynamic, flexible, and that it incorporates responses to changes in standards over time, as well as feedback from the environment. Also, it can be integrated with recent cognitive theory.

Discussion of this model creates an appropriate frame of mind in which to consider the work of another researcher wedded to the control system approach. Klein (1989) has postulated a control theory that provides a general framework within which motivational issues can be addressed. The model, based on integrated control theory, is shown in Fig. 2.6.

Control theory operates on the supposition that behaviour is regulated by a system under which an individual's current condition or state is compared with some desired condition or state. If there is a discrepancy between the current and desired conditions, behavioural strategies will be used to reduce that shortfall. Refer to Fig. 2.6 and follow the commentary below:

- Box 1: A goal or standard is a desired position which triggers behaviour and performance.
- Boxes 2 and 3: The person follows a course of behaviour and performs particular tasks.
- Boxes 4 and 5: Feedback on performance is received, and this is compared with the standard by the comparator.
- Boxes 6 and 7: Where no discrepancy or error is detected by the comparator, the

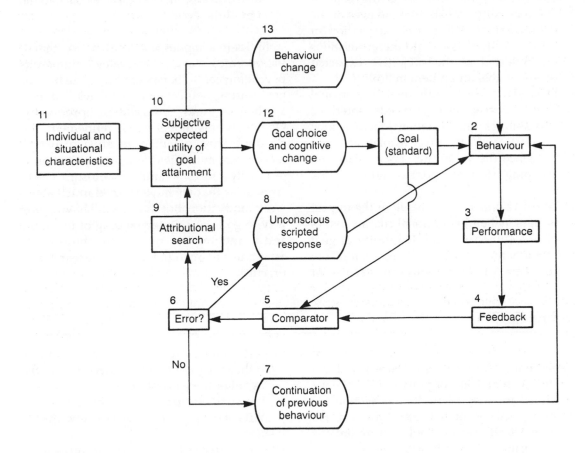

FIG. 2.6. Integrated control model of work motivation. Source: Klein, H.J. (1989). An integrated model of work motivation. *Academy of Management Review*, 14, 150–172.

person knows that he or she is on course and that the behaviour to date is acceptable.

- Boxes 8 and 9: But if there is an error or discrepancy, two courses of action are open to the person. The first course relates to the familiarity of the situation. Where the situation is familiar, the person engages in an unconscious scripted response. (The idea of a script or cognitive plan which refers to familiar sequences of events and behaviours is discussed in Chapter 4 in connection with memory.) The response in

Box 8 brings into existence more behavioural patterns previously learned to confront the error or discrepancy so that it can be reduced. The second course of action arises if the reasons for the discrepancy between actual and desired conditions are not immediately obvious. In Box 9 the person attempts to attribute a reason for the error or discrepancy. This can give rise to probing questions in an attempt to find acceptable explanations. (Attribution theory is discussed in the context of perception in Chapter 3.)

- Box 10: Out of the attributional search come questions such as, is the goal or standard still appealing in the eyes of the person, and what is the expectation of achieving it? Answers to these questions are reflected in the subjective expected utility of goal attainment in Box 10.
- Box 11: The individuals' personal characteristics, such as needs, interests, and abilities, and situational factors, such as time and resource availability, can influence the value the person places on attaining his or her goal as shown in Box 10.
- Boxes 12 and 13: As a result of the impact of personal and situational characteristics on the subjective expected utility of goal attainment, two things can happen. There could be a mental switch and change of goal (Box 12), or a change in behaviour (Box 13), or both. This takes us back to the start of the cycle.

In Klein's model you will notice that it incorporates and integrates numerous psychological perspectives, such as goal-setting, expectancy, feedback, control, attribution, and information processing. Obviously this model needs refinement, but no doubt has potential as an explanatory mechanism in the field of work motivation.

Finally, Katzell and Thompson (1990) emphasise that we have learned much about work motivation, but that we still have a long way to go in our understanding of this topic and in refining our research methods. They offer a useful agenda for future research and practice.

JOB DESIGN

Job design draws heavily on motivation theory, particularly content theories, and to a certain extent on organisational theory, discussed in Chapter 10. In this section the primary focus is on job specialisation, job rotation, job enlargement, job enrichment, the job characteristics model, and the relationship between job design and new technology. Additional issues—social information, work schedules and worker flexibility—will also be considered.

Job Specialisation

An early feature of job design was job specialisation, pioneered by Frederick W. Taylor, the main proponent of scientific management in the 1920s (Taylor, 1947). The following represents the approach he adopted:

- Study the way a job is done scientifically.
- Break down a job into its smallest component parts.
- Determine the most efficient way of performing each part of the job, in addition to the design of any tools needed and the layout of the workplace.
- Train workers to undertake the component parts of the job in the way laid down as the best.
- Use money as the primary incentive.

These principles were enshrined in the assembly line production process, with the alleged advantages of proficiency stemming from acute specialisation, less costly and shorter periods of job training, less remuneration because the job is unskilled, and greater managerial control. However, the disadvantages are that the individual's contribution is insignificant and lacks meaning; the individual does not have the opportunity to develop skills to further his or her career; and the work is repetitive and boring with negative side effects such as dissatisfaction, apathy, and carelessness.

Nevertheless, scientific management based on Taylor's principles still appears to be alive (see panel overleaf).

Scientific Management Mark 2

Professor Adler from the University of Southern California studied the work methods at a car factory in California, run by a company jointly owned by *General Motors* and *Toyota*. He attributes the company's great success to the widespread application of Taylor's principles of meticulous observation, and continuous refinement of work methods. Workers do their jobs in teams, with a high level of autonomy; for example, the stop-watches and clipboards are in the hands of the workers, not in the hands of supervisors and industrial engineers as in the original version of scientific management (Economist, 1993).

In the 1950s, Walker and Guest (1952) studied people who worked in a car assembly plant in order to establish how satisfied they were with varied aspects of their jobs. The workers stated that, by and large, they were reasonably satisfied with matters, such as pay, working conditions, and the quality of supervision. But they were extremely dissatisfied with the actual work they were doing. It should be noted that job design in the plant was influenced by the principles of scientific management. The workers reported six factors as being responsible for dissatisfaction:

1. Mechanical pacing by the assembly line, over which workers had no control.
2. Repetitive work.
3. Low level of skill required in the job.
4. Involvement with only a small part of the overall production cycle.
5. Limited social interaction with colleagues at the place of work.
6. No control over the methods and tools used in the job.

It was observations from studies such as the one conducted by Walker and Guest, that led management to reconsider the advisability of adhering religiously to the precepts of scientific management. It was recognised that application of the principles of scientific management had implications in terms of efficiency but, if carried too far, acute specialisation would generate a number of adverse side effects. As a result, there was a desire to devise ways to create less monotonous jobs.

Two alternative approaches—job rotation and job enlargement—were developed.

Job Rotation

This approach involves moving workers in a systematic way from one job to another in order to promote interest and motivation. Proponents of job specialisation would argue that job rotation may adversely affect efficiency because one is not taking full advantage of the proficiency that springs from specialisation. Those who advocate that workers should have more meaningful jobs might conclude that the fundamental problem of routine jobs still exists under job rotation. Their view is likely to be that the rotation cycle means that workers experience several routine jobs instead of one. However, proponents of the benefits of training on the job are likely to stress that job rotation is an effective training method because a worker rotated through a number of related jobs ends up with a broader set of job skills. This provides the organisation with greater flexibility.

Job Enlargement

This approach—often referred to as "horizontal job loading"—entails an expansion of the worker's job to include tasks previously performed by other workers. The rationale for the change is that the increased number of tasks creates greater variety and interest, with a reduction in the monotony and boredom associated with the previous narrowly defined, specialised task. In practice, job enlargement often failed to live up to expectations. This was particularly the case where the enlarged job was no more than a collection of simple tasks.

Job Enrichment

The disappointing results arising from the adoption of job rotation and job enlargement paved the way in the late 1950s for a more sophisticated approach to job design. This was called job enrichment and, as we saw earlier in this chapter, it was underpinned by Herzberg's dual-factor theory of motivation. He advocated *vertical job loading* to promote positive job-related experiences, such as a sense of achievement, responsibility, and recognition. Vertical loading amounts not only to adding more tasks to a job, as you find with horizontal loading, but also to granting the worker more control over the job. Herzberg (1968; 1974) viewed vertical job loading as a vehicle for enriching jobs in the following ways:

- *Accountability*. The person should be held responsible for his or her performance.
- *Achievement*. The person should feel that he or she is doing something worthy of note.
- *Feedback*. The person should receive unambiguous information about his or her performance.
- *Workpace*. The person should be able to set his or her pace at work, where this is practicable.
- *Control over resources*. The person should, where possible, have control over resources used in the job.

There have been mixed results with the application of job enrichment schemes. Early

successes were claimed by large organisations, such as AT&T in the United States and ICI in the United Kingdom, but equally one has to acknowledge that many job enrichment programmes have failed. Some organisations found them too costly to administer, and others felt that they did not live up to expectations (Griffin, 1982).

Criticisms of the theoretical basis of job enrichment—the dual-factor theory—were highlighted earlier in the chapter. Job enrichment has lost the popularity it once had, but some of its ingredients are worth preserving. In the 1970s and early 1980s a new perspective, called the job characteristics approach, occupied a prime position in thinking about job design. It drew on motivational concepts, such as autonomy and feedback, but was enlarged to give serious consideration to differences between individuals in the way they respond to jobs.

The Job Characteristics Model

A development of the earlier approach to job enrichment is propounded by Hackman and Oldham (1975). The authors focus on what they call the five core characteristics of a job (see panel overleaf and Fig. 2.7). The five characteristics are given a numerical value and are then combined into a single index called the motivating potential score (MPS) (see equation below).

The job diagnostic survey, filled out by the job holder, is used to measure the five core characteristics so as to arrive at the MPS calculation. For job enrichment to work, three factors have to be considered: (1) employee growth; (2) need strength; and (3)current job context.

The individual who desires growth will respond positively to a job that scores highly on the core dimensions (high MPS). But the individual who does not place much value on

$$MPS = \left[\frac{Skill\ variety \times Task\ identity \times Task\ significance}{3} \right] \times Autonomy \times Feedback$$

Hackman and Oldham's 5 Core Job Characteristics

1. Skill variety. This focuses on the extent to which a job requires a number of different skills and talents. The job of a personnel specialist would receive a high score on this dimension, whereas the job of an operator on a production assembly line would receive a low score.
2. Task identity. This focuses on the extent to which the job requires the performance of a whole unit, which is identifiable with a visible outcome. The job of a carpenter, who constructs a piece of furniture from raw material, would receive a high score on this dimension, whereas an operator who solders wires on to a piece of equipment would receive a low score.
3. Task significance. This focuses on the extent to which the job makes a significant impact on the lives and work of other people inside and outside the organisation. The job of a surgeon in a hospital would receive a high score on this dimension, whereas the job of a filing clerk would receive a low score.
4. Autonomy. This can be viewed as the degree of freedom, discretion, and independence that a job possesses at both the planning and execution stages. The job of a college or university lecturer would receive a high score on this dimension, whereas the job of an accounts clerk, who is closely supervised, would receive a low score.
5. Feedback from the job. This focuses on the extent to which direct and unambiguous information about the effectiveness of the job holder's performance is available while he or she is engaged in carrying out the job activities. The airline pilot receives information on the progress of the flight from the instrument panel in the cockpit and from ground control. The pilot's job would receive a high score on this dimension, whereas the job of a sales representative, who may have to wait some time to establish the effectiveness of his or her performance, would receive a low score.

personal growth or accomplishment would find a high MPS situation both uncomfortable and a source of anxiety. It is also suggested that if an employee is grossly dissatisfied with contextual job factors (pay, job security, or supervision) job enrichment will not be as effective as if the reverse was true.

Finally, the MPS is used to assess the extent to which the job is enriched. Where appropriate, the job may be enriched by redesigning it so as to increase its score on the core characteristics.

Hackman et al. (1975) developed a set of guidelines to help managers implement the job characteristics model. The implementing concepts are set out on the left-hand side of Fig 2.8

The motivating potential of jobs can be improved by the application of the following five implementing concepts:

- *Combining tasks.* Enlarge the range of tasks undertaken by an employee so as to increase the variety of the work and the individual's contribution. For example, a receptionist in a suite of offices could undertake tasks additional to his or her main duties, such as word processing and telephonist duties.

- *Forming natural work units.* Provide employees with a job which incorporates a number of steps from start to finish, rather than offering them a fragmented part of the whole job cycle. This is likely to enhance the significance of the job in the eyes of the job occupant and increase the individual's contribution.

- *Establishing client relationships.* Allow the employee to take responsibility for making personal contacts with people inside and outside the organisation on matters connected with the processing of work. This offers greater freedom, more potential for feedback, and job variety. It can be contrasted with a system whereby the employee is expected to go through a supervisor or other third party when interfacing with clients.

- *Vertical loading.* Give the employee responsibilities normally associated with supervisors, such as the scheduling of

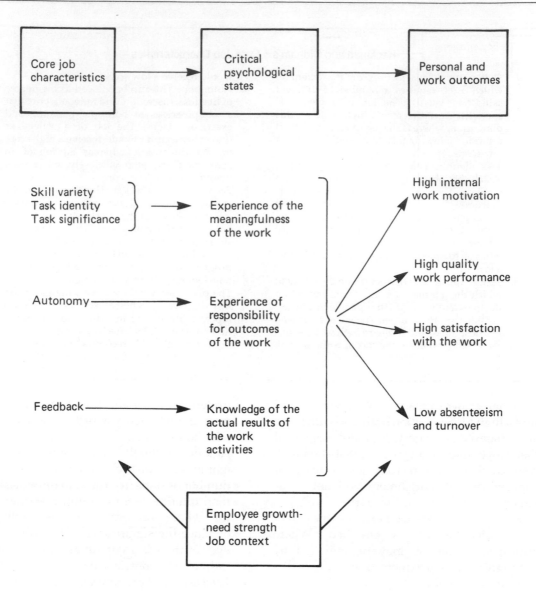

FIG. 2.7.   The job characteristics model. Source Hackman, J.R. (1977). Work Design. In J.R. Hackman and J.L. Suttle (Eds.), *Improving life at work.* Santa Monica, CA.: Scott, Foresman.

work, control of quality, determining priorities, recruiting and training, improving work practices, and so on. This offers the employee greater autonomy, with the result that the supervisory role needs adjustment (possibly a delicate situation for the remaining supervisors). Cordery and Wall (1985) argue that supervisors must receive help so as to change from an overseeing or controlling mentality to an enabling outlook.

- *Opening feedback channels.* Give the employee greater opportunities for feedback on performance. This could be achieved through analysis of performance showing how well the employee has done, and perhaps pointing to areas where performance could be improved.

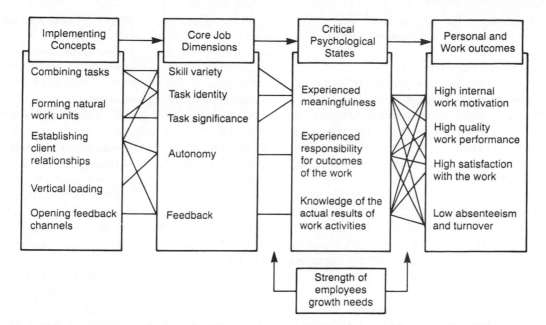

FIG. 2.8. Implementation of the job characteristics model. Source: Hackman, J.R., Oldham, G.R., Janson, R., and Purdy, K. (1975). A new stage for job enrichment. *California Management Review, 17,* 57–71. Copyright 1975 by the Regents of the University of California. By permission of the Regents.

A fair amount of research has been done in the area of job design from a "job characteristics" perspective. There is general support for the Hackman and Oldham model, particularly with reference to satisfaction, although not productivity (Umstot, Bell, & Mitchell, 1976). In a recent evaluation of the model, Moorhead and Griffin (1992) make the following observation:

> Several apparent weaknesses in the model have come to light. First, the job diagnostic survey which is used to test the model is not always as valid and reliable as it should be. Second, the role of individual differences frequently has not been supported by scientific assessment. Third, the implementation guidelines are not specific, and managers are forced to modify at least part of the model to use them.

Reflecting on the track record of the job characteristics model (JCM), Arnold et al. (1991) state:

All in all the JCM has stood empirical test reasonably well, especially considering the relatively large numbers of connections between the specific variables it proposes. However, it is not the whole story, and paradoxically it still has not often been tested in the context of job redesign. Further well-focused investigations are needed to build on the existing foundations.

Groups and Job Design

So far the focus has been primarily on job design in the context of individual jobs. But there are many situations where jobs have to be designed for groups (for a discussion of groups, see Chapter 7).

There are at least two reasons why one might consider groups in the context of job design. First, it may be more practicable and efficient to use a group to do a job, as with a maintenance crew. Second, the organisation may wish to use a group to transform the attitudes and behaviour of members, as with autonomous groups and work teams. This represents job enrichment at the group level and draws sustenance from the job characteristics model.

Autonomous Work Groups

With autonomous work groups or teams, the groups enjoy a substantial amount of self-determination in the management of their day-to-day work. This is tantamount to group control over the pace of work, the scheduling of work, the arranging of rest pauses, deciding on modes of inspection, selecting new members of the team, and performance appraisal of members. The consequence of this development could be a diminution in importance of the supervisor's role, if not its elimination. Other features of self-managed groups identified by Wall et al. (1986) are:

- A group of workers performing tasks that are interrelated, and who bear responsibility for the end product.
- A group of workers who possess a variety of skills that enable them to perform all or most of the tasks of the group.
- A group of workers who are able to evaluate the group's performance, and provide feedback.

A departure from the traditional assembly line system of production in the manufacturing of cars took place in *Volvo*'s new plant in Uddevalla in Sweden, where the *Volvo 740* model is built using teams (Kapstein, 1989). Each team consists of seven to ten workers, working in one area, with an output rate of four cars per shift. Members of the team are trained to undertake all assembly jobs; in practice this means that variety and diversity is built into the system and an average of three hours elapses before a worker repeats the same task. Each team manages itself to a great extent by scheduling work, controlling quality, selecting members, etc. In effect they undertake the duties normally the responsibility of the supervisor. As a result, the teams have no first-line supervisors. However, they appoint a spokesperson, who reports to a plant manager. The latter reports to the chief of the manufacturing unit.

A significant advantage of the way jobs are designed at the Uddevalla plant is the avoidance of the routine and boredom experienced by workers on the conventional car assembly line where the duration of work cycles is no more than one or two minutes. An absence rate of 20% is associated with *Volvo*'s conventional plants, but this rate drops to 8% in the case of the Uddevalla plant. Also, the productivity record and quality is said to be better at the Uddevalla plant than at other *Volvo* plants in Sweden. From what has been said about the nature of jobs at the plant, one could conclude that such jobs score high in motivating potential on the job characteristics model.

Another example of self-managed teams applies to *General Motors'* joint venture with *Toyota* in California (referred to earlier in connection with scientific management). The factory workers are divided into small teams, and each team is charged with defining its own jobs, monitoring the quality of output, and conducting daily quality audits; the latter is an activity once undertaken by a group of inspectors. The team is also empowered to pull the stop-line cord which activates a shutdown of the line if a problem is encountered (Robbins, 1991).

In recent years the concept of empowerment, previously used by social scientists when dealing with issues concerning the powerlessness of minority groups in the United States, has entered the domain of job design. It is also used in connection with leadership, power, new organisational forms, and teambuilding. Conger and Kanugo (1988) show a preference for empowerment as a motivational concept associated with "enabling" rather than "delegating". Enabling implies the creation of conditions by management so that people can experience enhanced motivation to achieve desired levels of performance. Apart from providing conditions, such as offering the necessary support and recognition, management is also expected to remove conditions that foster powerlessness.

Little empirical work has been done on empowerment. Conger and Kanugo mention some of its negative effects, such as the over-confidence it may create in subordinates, leading to misjudgements on their part.

At the Annual Conference of the Institute of Personnel Management, Kanter (1992) contrasted empowerment with the traditional concept of control. She maintained that powerlessness has a corrupting influence in organisations because it forces people to stick to the old rules, and extolled the virtues of empowering employees to make their own decisions in their dealings with customers in conditions where quality of service is important.

For a discussion of a recent process likely to impact on job design, refer to the discussion on process re-engineering in Chapter 8.

New Technology and Job Design

New technology refers to a set of changes produced by the development of microchips, and can be broadly classified as advanced manufacturing technology and office technology.

Advanced manufacturing technology includes a wide range of equipment used in the production process, such as industrial robots for welding and paint spraying, and computer-numerically controlled machine tools for precision cutting, drilling, or grinding of materials. Office technology places the emphasis on the storage, retrieval, presentation, and manipulation of information, as these are manifested in word-processing equipment and electronic point of sale equipment in stores. The latter uses bar codes on goods, not only to provide the customer with a record of the transaction but also to generate data for use by the organisation in ordering and stock control. Decision support systems, which are discussed in Chapter 5, fall into the category of office technology.

When commenting earlier in the section on "Repetitive Work", the effects of modern technology in displacing labour and eliminating unhealthy and monotonous jobs were briefly considered. In Chapter 10, the impact of modern technology on the organisation is examined. Here, however, we return to the former theme and continue the analysis of the relationship between technology and jobs.

Nearly three decades ago in a study of the effects of automation, Blauner (1964) concluded that, instead of increasing feelings of alienation from the task, as was generally the view at that time, automation in the chemical industry actually reduced alienation. In an attempt to explain Blauner's conclusions in more recent times it has been suggested that the subjects in his study were blue-collar workers who performed fragmented manual work. As a result of automation, they became semi-skilled white-collar workers responsible for the monitoring of complete segments of work. Therefore, the consequence of the implementation of the automation process was the creation of enriched jobs; and it was not surprising to discover that alienation assumed a position of minor significance (Crawley & Spurgeon, 1979).

A valid question to ask is whether the same outcome would arise if computers were introduced into traditional white-collar jobs. Apparently, it depends upon the type of white-collar employment that is under consideration. When clerical workers have an involvement with the computer, which amounts to keying data and the retrieval of information, then it is said that the computer system restricts the employees' personal control over their work, with predictable results (Mumford & Banks, 1967).

A similar finding was reported in a study of managerial staff in the production function, after a production and scheduling computer system was introduced into three assembly plants of an electronics company. The computer system contributed to changes in the content of the jobs of production planners and resulted in a loss of discretion, culminating in greater control of their work by the organisation. The same applied to all managers who were involved with the computer system. They all felt constrained by policies, plans, and procedures, and were more dependent on the work of others than ever before (Bjorn-Anderson & Pedersen, 1977).

In the two studies cited, there was evidence of alienation springing from white-collar employment (managerial and clerical staff) as a result of the implementation of computer systems. However, other evidence relating to white-collar employment seems to indicate that computer systems produce the opposite effect in particular circumstances. For example, specialists in computing and those in certain managerial positions are at an advantage when they can control the periods of time during which they use the computer. Also, in many cases the computer can enlarge the jobs of users (Kling & Scacchi, 1980). Other evidence showed that the introduction of computers generated more varied, interesting, responsible, and productive work (Oborne, 1994).

Some positive and negative features of computerised information systems have been identified (Strassman, 1982). The positive features are:

- Responsibility shifts to the person most suited to carry out the task. For example, the author or journalist keys in information to the computer, and corrects the script or document. This process, together with a freer flow of information between individuals, blurs somewhat the traditional organisational roles. Also, the change in direction of information flows tends to create new social groups with their own particular phraseology.
- The shifts in resources and the changing roles lead to enlarged jobs in a qualitative sense—i.e. more varied tasks when in contact with others for secretarial and support staff.
- An increase in communication results from the rapid turn-round of messages due to electronic mail systems.

The negative features are:

- The need for increased security measures can seriously disrupt working practices.
- An unhealthy identification with and a personal attachment to an electronic work station may give rise to minor behavioural disturbances (issues connected with this are discussed in Chapter 14).

Arnold et al. (1991) draw a number of general conclusions from the debate on how new technology affects job characteristics (see panel overleaf).

Wall et al. (1990) have identified a number of job characteristics that ought to be considered prior to be introduction of new manufacturing technology. These characteristics, which may have a material influence on the performance of the socio-technical system (i.e. technology and people) and on the level of job satisfaction and dissatisfaction, are as follows:

1. *Control.* This refers to control over when tasks are to be done, how they are to be done, and what happens at the boundary of the job.
2. *Cognitive demand.* This refers to maintaining acute and constant vigilance over the process of diagnosing and solving problems. Accepting this condition is almost tantamount to acknowledging that advanced manufacturing technology requires sophisticated and flexible operators.
3. *Responsibility.* The need to ensure that there is a clear line of responsibility for the technology and the output of the system.
4. *Social interaction.* The quantity and quality of interaction between people.

The debate on the impact of technology on jobs and organisational systems is likely to continue for a long time, simply because the rate of change in this field is quite significant. There is now a view that the traditional status of technology as a variable determining a

New Technology and Job Characteristics

- New technology has the effect of both enriching jobs and simplifying jobs, and this can occur within the same place of work. In this context the approach of those who introduce the new technology, and the principles underlying the job subjected to design or redesign, are crucial considerations. Therefore, poor planning and implementation of the new technology, and poorly designed jobs, are likely to produce a less than satisfactory result.

- As a general principle, simplification of jobs is probably more common than enrichment of jobs for workers in manufacturing industry who work on the shop floor.

- Where the introduction of new technology results in enriched jobs, some skilled workers may perceive no material change in terms of the quality of the job. Others may perceive a material change in the sense that new skills are now needed—e.g. abstract thinking, computer literacy, and a broader view of organisational functioning.

- Worker resistance to the introduction of new technology in itself is considered to be rare. Nevertheless, the resistance that exists is more likely to be directed at management who may be perceived as using the technology to exploit the workers.

- It is not always apparent that management has seriously considered in advance the likely impact of new technology on various job characteristics. Long (1987) attributes failures in the operation of automated systems in the office more to poor planning, poor technical skills of managers, lack of training of users of the system, and uncertainty, about the appropriate problems to tackle, than to technical failures.

number of aspects of organisational structure, which obviously includes jobs, is in question. What appears to be critical currently is the impact of decisions to select technological equipment, the capabilities of the equipment, and the way it is used. In addition, the influence of cultural and political forces within the organisation with respect to the use of the technology, and the way key staff control computerised systems, are considerations that have to be borne in mind (Child, 1984).

There is a suggestion that the human and organisational implications surrounding the adoption of computer technologies are often pushed aside or given insufficient attention, even though these are intimately tied up with the success of technical change (Buchanan and Huczynski, 1985). A further suggestion from this source is that work should be organised around the technology, and that one should recognise that the choices an organisation has to make to accommodate the new technology are often not given serious consideration. In fact, the physical layout of the workplace and organisational structures created by past decisions are too easily accepted, and insufficient attention is given to the exploration of new ways and means to build the infrastructure of work around computing technology. A more focused discussion of the impact of technology on organisations appears in Chapter 10.

Further Perspectives on Job Design

When examining other perspectives on job design, alternative approaches such as social information, work schedules, and worker flexibility come to mind (Moorhead & Griffin, 1992).

Social Information

According to Salancik and Pfeffer (1978), social information in the workplace shapes the individual's perceptions of the job and the way he or she responds to it. Information on certain facets of work (e.g. management is caring around here) is transmitted to individuals by peers or others and registered as a critical judgement about work. In the example given, the newcomer to the organisation registers the impression that management has a humane streak. Salancik and Pfeffer have constructed a rather complex model, called the social information processing model of job design, which suggests that the needs of individuals, task perceptions, and reactions to work are socially constructed realities. The social information processing model has had a mixed reception from researchers in the field of job design (Thomas & Griffin, 1983).

Work Schedules

Although not normally associated with job design, work schedules come between the employee and the job. They are aimed at improving the employee's experiences at work in the hope that the individual's attendance, motivation, and commitment will be better.

Examples of work schedules are the "compressed working week" whereby the worker works longer hours on, for instance, Monday to Thursday, so that four days constitute the working week; and "flexitime" whereby the worker is committed to core times at work during the week, but outside these times he or she can choose a flexible work schedule. Flexitime can contribute to individual autonomy because it gives employees more control over their working hours. As a consequence, it has real motivational significance.

An alternative to the traditional work schedule is job sharing whereby, for example, one employee works in the morning or for half the week, and the other works in the afternoon or for the remainder of the week. Job sharing could be desirable for people who prefer to work part-time, perhaps for family reasons. It can also be beneficial for the organisation because it is able to use the talents of people whose circumstances demand a flexible work schedule. A further example of a work schedule is the permanent part-time worker whose time allocation is expanded or contracted depending on the volume of work.

Worker Flexibility

This approach amounts to a refinement of job rotation discussed earlier. The central tenet of this approach is that it is advantageous to the organisation if employees are trained to perform a number of jobs, and can then be deployed as circumstances dictate. The system of remuneration should reflect this level of worker flexibility. The idea of the flexible worker has a certain appeal. It offers the worker a more varied and exciting range of work experiences than would apply with the normal process of job rotation and of course the worker receives a financial incentive for becoming proficient at more than one job (Dupuy, 1990).

Some final reflections on job design and redesign, attributable to Blackler and Shimmin (1984), pointing to the constraints on managers are as follows:

> Personal development and individual involvement are championed by new forms of work design. On the other hand … managers in business organisations tend to be guided by the values of economy and profitability and are concerned to design work systems that, with those values in mind, are both reliable and robust. There are limits to most managers' commitment to redesigning work. If arrangements can be made for people to co-operate more, all well and good, but businesses exist to make a profit, they have to operate in an unsympathetic and competitive world, and employees are hired to make this possible.

> Managers often point out that there are limits to the amount of control they feel they can sensibly devolve to others. This attitude is neatly summed up in the suggestion that many managers seek as much rationalisation in the organisation of work as is possible, but are prepared to allow only as much "humanisation" of work as is necessary.

SUMMARY: MOTIVATION AND JOB DESIGN

- The concept of motivation consists of needs, motives, drives, and goals or incentives. Level of arousal, which is related to a drive, is an important feature of the motivated state. Various examples of arousal stimuli in marketing and accounting were given. Frustration, which can produce either positive or negative reactions, can obstruct the attainment of the goals of the individual, and as such is an important ingredient in the motivational process.

- Monotony and boredom, brought about by conditions such as a lack of variety and challenge in the job, lack of opportunity to exercise skill and to act independently, highly repetitive work, and an inability to control the pace of work, can have a demotivating effect. The safety implications of highly repetitive work should be noted, particularly in the area of production. Various measures to mitigate the effects of boredom were suggested. Rest pauses have particular relevance when considering work of a repetitive or monotonous nature.

- Need or content theories of motivation—the hierarchy of needs, ERG theory, achievement and power motivation, dual-factor theory, and theories X and Y—were considered and their shortcomings noted. Illustrations of the motivation of sales representatives, accountants, and business executives and employees were given.

- Cognitive or process theories of motivation—goal-setting, expectancy theory, and equity theory—were discussed, with reference to budgeting in the case of goal-setting and to management control generally in the case of expectancy theory. Equity theory was considered relevant in the context of equitable rewards for efforts expended.

- It was recognised that there was a need to integrate the various perspectives on motivation, and therefore an integrated model of work motivation was examined.

- As a logical extension of the discussion of motivation theories, developments in job design, together with the impact of new technology and work groups on job design, were reviewed.

QUESTIONS

1. Illustrate what is meant by needs, motives, drives, goals, or incentives.
2. Distinguish between feeling tone and appeal when considering the motivational disposition of the consumer.
3. How important is accounting data as arousal stimuli?
4. In what circumstances is frustration likely to generate destructive behaviour?
5. What causes boredom among workers in a factory, and what steps can be taken to reduce it?
6. Why are rest pauses necessary in modern office conditions?
7. Select any cognitive theory of motivation and explore its application in an organisational setting.
8. Assess the value of equity theory.
9. Examine the main features of Klein's integrated control model of work motivation.
10. Examine the range of theories underpinning job design, noting any shortcomings.
11. Highlight significant points in the debate about the impact of new technology on job design.
12. Contrast the dual-factor theory approach to job design with that of the job characteristics model.
13. Comment on work schedules and worker flexibility in the context of job design.

REFERENCES

Adams, J.S. (1963). Towards an understanding of inequity. *Journal of Abnormal and Social Psychology*, *67*, 422–36.

Adams, J.S. (1965). Inequity in social exchange. In L. Berkowitz (Ed.), *Advances in experimental social psychology, Vol. 2*. New York: Academic Press.

Alderfer, C.P. (1972). *Existence, relatedness and growth: Human needs in organisational settings*. New York: Free Press.

Anastasi, A. (1979). *Fields of applied psychology* (second edition). Tokyo: McGraw-Hill.

Anderson, D. (1980). VDUs: Eyestrain or eyewash? *Health and Safety at Work*, August, 36–39.

Argyle, M. (1968). *The psychology of interpersonal behaviour*. Harmondsworth: Penguin.

Arnold, J., Robertson. I.T., & Cooper, C. (1991). *Work psychology. Understanding human behaviour in the workplace*. London: Pitman Publishing.

Atkinson, J.W. (1964). *An introduction to motivation*. New Jersey: Van Nostrand.

Austin, J.T. & Bobko, P. (1985). Goal-setting theory. Unexplored areas and future research needs. *Journal of Occupational Psychology*, *58*, 289–308.

Benston, G.R. (1967). Published corporate accounting data and stock prices. *Empirical Research in Accounting: Selected Studies*, 1–54.

Beresford Dew, R. & Gee, K.P. (1973). *Management control and information*. London: Macmillan.

Berkowitz, L., Fraser, C., Treasure, F.P., & Cochran, S. (1987). Pay, equity, job gratifications and comparisons in pay satisfaction. *Journal of Applied Psychology*, November, 544–551.

Bjorn-Anderson, N. & Pedersen, P.H. (1977). Computer systems as a vehicle for changes in the management structure. *ISRG Working Paper No. 77-3*, Copenhagen.

Blackler, F. & Shimmin, S (1984). *Applying psychology in organisations*. London: Methuen.

Blauner, R. (1964). *Alienation and freedom*. Chicago: University of Chicago Press.

Bratkovich, J.R. (1989). Pay for performance boosts productivity. *Personnel Journal*, January, 78–86.

Brenner, V.C. (1970). Financial statement users' views on the desirability of reporting current cost information. *Journal of Accounting Research*, Autumn, 159–166.

Buchanan, D.A. & Huczynski, A.A. (1985). *Organisational behaviour: An introductory text*. London: Prentice-Hall International.

Carlson, R.E. (1969). Degree of job fit as a moderator of the relationship between job performance and job satisfaction. *Personnel Psychology*, *22*, 159–170.

Cassidy, T. & Lynn R. (1989). A multifactorial approach to achievement motivation: The development of a comprehensive measure. *Journal of Occupational Psychology*, *62*, 301–312.

Child, J. (1984). New technology and developments in management organisation. *Omega*, *12*, 211–223.

Child, I.L. & Whiting, J.W.M. (1954). Determinants of level of aspiration: Evidence from everyday life. In H. Brand (Ed.), *The study of personality*. New York: Wiley.

Conger, J.A. & Kanugo, R.N. (1988). The empowerment process: Integrating theory and practice. *Academy of Management Journal*, *13*, 471–482.

Cordery, J.L. & Wall, T.D. (1985). Work design and supervisory practice: A model. *Human Relations*, *38*, 425–441.

Crawford, J.W. (1960). *Advertising: Communications from management*. Boston: Allyn & Bacon.

Crawley, R. & Spurgeon, P. (1979). Computer assistance and the air traffic controller's job satisfaction. In R.G. Sell & P. Shipley (Eds.), *Satisfaction in work design: Ergonomics and other approaches*. London: Taylor & Francis.

Dupuy, J. (1990). Flexible jobs: Key to manufacturing productivity. *Journal of Business Strategy*, May-June, 28–32.

Earley, P.C., Connolly, T., & Ekegren G. (1989). Goals, strategy development and task performance. Some limits on the efficacy of goal-setting. *Journal of Applied Psychology*, *74*, 24–33.

Economist (1993). *Return of the stop-watch*. 23rd January, 77.

Estes, R.W. (1968). An assessment of the usefulness of current cost and price-level information by financial statement users. *Journal of Accounting Research*, Autumn, 200–207.

Goldthorpe, J.H., Lockwood, D., Bechhofer, F., & Platt, J. (1970). *The affluent worker: Industrial attitudes and behaviour*. Cambridge: Cambridge University Press.

Griffeth, R.W., Vecchio, R.P., & Logan, J.W. (1989). Equity theory and interpersonal attraction. *Journal of Applied Psychology*, June, 394–401.

Griffin, R.W. (1982). *Task design: An integrated approach*. Glenview, IL: Scott, Foresman.

Grube, C.S. (1947). How the public learned to pronounce "Suchard". *Advertising and Selling*, October, 68.

Guirdham, M. (1972). *Marketing: The management of distribution channels*. Oxford: Pergamon.

Hackman, J.R. (1977). Work design. In J.R. Hackman & J.L. Suttle (Eds.), *Improving life at work*. Santa Monica, CA: Scott, Foresman.

Hackman, J.R. & Oldham, G.R. (1975). Development of the job agnostic survey. *Journal of Applied Psychology*, *60*, 2, 159–170.

Hackman, J.R., Oldham, G.R., Janson, R., & Purdy, K. (1975). A new stage for job enrichment. *California Management Review*, *17*, 57–71.

Hall, D.T. & Nougaim, K.E. (1968). An examination of Maslow's need hierarchy in an organisational setting. *Organisational Behaviour and Human Performance, 3*, 12–35.

Harlow, H.F. (1953). Mice, monkeys, men and motives. *Psychological Review, 60,* 23–32.

Heneman, R.L., Greenberger, D.B., & Strasser, S. (1988). The relationship between pay-for-performance, perceptions and pay satisfaction. *Personnel Psychology*, Winter, 745–759.

Herzberg, F. (1966). *Work and the nature of man.* London: Staples Press.

Herzberg, F. (1968). How do you motivate employees? *Harvard Business Review*, January-February, 53–62.

Herzberg, F. (1974). The wise old Turk. *Harvard Business Review*, September-October, 70–80.

Hinrichs, J.R. & Mischkind, L.A. (1967). Empirical and theoretical limitations of the two-factor hypothesis of job satisfaction. *Journal of Applied Psychology, 51*, 191–200.

Hirst, M.K. (1981). Accounting information and the evaluation of subordinate performance: A situational approach. *The Accounting Review*, October, 771–784.

Hodgetts, R. M. (1991). *Organisational behaviour: Theory and practice.* New York: Macmillan.

Hodgetts, R.M. & Luthans, F. (1991). *International Management.* New York: McGraw-Hill.

Hofestede, G.H. (1968). *The game of budget control.* London: Tavistock.

Hollenbeck, J.R. & Klein, H.J. (1987). Goal commitment and the goal-setting process: Problems, prospects, and proposals for future research. *Journal of Applied Psychology, 72*, 212 220.

Hollenbeck, J.R., Williams, C.R., & Klein, H.J. (1989). An empirical examination of the antecedents of commitment to difficult goals. *Journal of Applied Psychology, 74*, 18–23.

Hopper, T. (1978). *Role conflicts of management accountants in the context of their structural relationship to production.* Unpublished M.Phil. thesis. Birmingham: University of Aston.

Hopwood, A. (1974). *Accounting and human behaviour.* London: Haymarket.

Horner, M.S. (1970). Femininity and successful achievement: A basic inconsistency. In Y. Bardwich et al. (Eds.), *Feminine, personality and conflict.* Belmont, CA: Brooks & Cole.

House, R.J. & Wigdor, L.A. (1967). Herzberg's dual-factor theory of job satisfaction and motivation: A review of the evidence and a criticism. *Personnel Psychology, 20, 4,* 369–389.

HSE (1992). Display screen equipment at work: Guidance on regulations. *Health and Safety Display Screen Equipment Regulations.* London: HMSO.

Hulin, C.L. & Blood, M.R. (1968). Job enlargement, individual differences, and workers responses. *Psychological Bulletin, 69,* 1, 41–55.

Hulin, C.L. & Smith, P. (1967). An empirical investigation of two implications of the two-factor theory of job satisfaction. *Journal of Applied Psychology*, October, 396–402.

Huseman, R.C., Hatfield, J.D., & Miles, E.W. (1987). A new perspective on equity theory: The equity sensitivity construct. *Academy of Management Review, 12*, 222–234.

Kanter, R. (1992). Address to the national conference of the Institute of Personnel Management. Harrogate, UK.

Kapstein, J. (1989). Volvo's radical new plant: The death of the assembly line. *Business Week*, 28th August, 92–93.

Katzell, R.A. & Thompson, D.E. (1990). Work motivation: Theory and practice. *American Psychologist*, February, 144–153.

Kenis, I. (1977). Effects of budgetary goal characteristics on managerial attitudes and performance. *The Accounting Review*, October, 707–721.

Klein, H.J. (1989). An integrated theory model of work motivation. *Academy of Management Review, 14*, 150–172.

Kling, R. & Scacchi, W. (1980). Computing as social action: The social dynamics of computing in complex organisations. *Advances in Computers, 19*, 249–347.

Laird, D.A. (1932). How the consumer estimates quality by subconscious sensory impression. *Journal of Applied Psychology, 16*, 241–246.

Landy, F.J. & Becker, W.S. (1987). Motivation theory reconsidered. *Research in Organisational Behaviour, 9*, 1–38.

Latham, G.P. & Locke, E. (1979). Goal-setting. A motivational technique that works. *Organisational Dynamics*, Autumn, 68–80.

Latham, G.P. & Steele, T.P. (1983). The motivational effects of participation versus goal-setting on performance. *Academy of Management Journal*, September, 406–417.

Lazarus, R.S. (1971). *Personality.* New York: Prentice-Hall.

Lewin, K. (1964). The psychology of a successful figure. In H.S. Leavitt & L.R. Pondy (Eds.), *Readings in Managerial Psychology*. Chicago: University of Chicago Press.

Likert, R. (1961). *New patterns of management.* New York: McGraw-Hill.

Locke, E.A. (1968). Toward a theory of task performance and incentives. *Organisational Behaviour and Human Performance, 3*, 157–189.

Long, R. J. (1987). *New office information technology: Human and managerial implications.* London: Croom Helm.

Lord, R.G. & Hanges, P.J. (1987). A control system model of organisational motivation: Theoretical development and applied implications. *Behavioural Science, 32,* 161–178.

Lord, R.G. & Hohenfeld, J.A. (1979). Longitudinal field assessment of equity effects on the performance of major league baseball players. *Journal of Applied Psychology,* February, 19–26.

Lowe, E.A. & Shaw, R.W. (1968). An analysis of managerial biasing: Evidence from a company's budgeting process. *Journal of Management Studies,* 5, October, 304–315.

Lowe, E.A. & Shaw, R.W. (1970). The accuracy of short-term business forecasting: An analysis of a firm's sales budgeting. *Journal of Industrial Economics, 18,* 275–289.

Maccoby, M. (1988). *Why work?: Motivating and leading the new generation.* New York: Simon & Schuster.

Manos, J. (1980). Stressless use of VDUs. *Health and Safety at Work,* August, 34–36.

March, J.G. & Simon, H.A. (1958). *Organisations.* New York: Wiley.

Maslow, A.H. (1954). *Motivation and personality.* New York: Harper & Row.

McClelland, D.C. (1967). *The achieving society.* New York: The Free Press.

McClelland, D.C. (1970). The two faces of power. *Journal of International Affairs, 24, 1,* 29–47.

McClelland, D.C. (1975). Good guys make bum bosses. *Psychology Today,* December, 69–70.

McClelland, D.C. & Boyatzis, R.E (1982). Leadership motive pattern and long-term success in management. *Journal of Applied Psychology, 67,* 737–743.

McDougall, C. (1973). How well do you reward your managers? *Personnel Management,* March, 38–43.

McGregor, D. (1960). *The human side of enterprise.* New York: McGraw-Hill.

Merchant, K.A. (1981). The design of the corporate budgeting system: Influences on managerial behaviour and performance. *The Accounting Review,* October, 813–829.

Meyer, J.P. & Gellatly, J.R. (1988). Perceived performance norm as a mediator in the effect of assigned goal on personal goal and task performance. *Journal of Applied Psychology, 73,* 410–420.

Miner, J.B. (1978). Twenty years of research on role motivation theory of managerial effectiveness. *Personnel Psychology, 31,* 739–760.

Mitchell, T.R. (1982). Motivation: New directions for theory, research, and practice. *Academy of Management Review,* January, 80–88.

Moorhead, G. & Griffin, R.W. (1992). *Organisational behaviour* (third edition). Boston: Houghton Mifflin.

Mumford, E. & Banks, 0. (1967). *The computer and the clerk.* London: Routledge & Kegan Paul.

Oborne, D.J. (1994). *Computers at work: A behavioural approach.* (3rd ed.). Chichester: Wiley.

Otley, D.T. (1977). Behavioural aspects of budgeting. *Accountants' Digest ICAEW (Institute of Chartered Accountants in England and Wales),* No. 49, Summer.

Otley, D.T. (1982). Budgets and managerial motivation. *Journal of General Management, 8, 1,* Autumn, 26–42.

Pankoff, L.D. & Virgil, R.L. (1970). Some preliminary findings from a laboratory experiment on the usefulness of financial accounting information to security analysts. *Empirical Research in Accounting: Selected Studies,* 1–61.

Pinder, C. (1984). *Work motivation.* Glenview, IL: Scott, Foresman.

Porter, L.W. & Lawler, E.E. (1968). *Managerial attitudes and performance.* Homewood, IL: R.D. Irwin.

Porter, L.W., Lawler, E.E., & Hackman, J.R. (1975). *Behaviour in organisations.* New York: McGraw-Hill.

Robbins, S.P. (1991). *Organisational behaviour: Concepts, controversies and applications* (fifth edition). New York: Prentice-Hall.

Ross, I.C. (1957). *Role specialisation in supervision.* Unpublished PhD thesis. Columbia University.

Salancik, G. & Pfeffer, J. (1978). A social information processing approach to job attitudes and task design. *Administrative Science Quarterly, 23,* 224–253.

Sayles, L.R. & Chandler, M.K. (1971). *Managing large systems: Organisations for the future.* New York: Harper & Row.

Smith, G.P. (1967). The motivation of sales executives. *Ashridge Papers in Management Studies,* No. 2, Autumn. Berkhamsted: Ashridge Management College.

Stahl, M.J. & Harrell, A.M. (1982). Evolution and validation of a behavioural decision theory measurement approach to achievement, power, and affiliation. *Journal of Applied Psychology,* December, 744–751.

Stedry, A.C. (1960). *Budget control and cost behaviour.* New York: Prentice-Hall.

Stedry, A.C. & Kay, E. (1964). *The effects of goal difficulty on performance: A field experiment.* MIT: Sloan School of Management.

Strassman, P.A. (1982). Overview of strategic aspects of information management. *Office: Technology and People, 1,* 71–89.

Strauss, G. & Sayles, L.R. (1960). Personnel: The human problems of management. New York: Prentice-Hall.

Strawser, R.H., Ivancevich, J.M., & Lyon H.L. (1969). A note on the job satisfaction of accountants in large and small CPA firms. *Journal of Accounting Research, 7, 2,* Autumn, 339–345.

Tannenbaum, A.S. (1962). Control in organisations: Individual adjustment and organisational performance. *Administrative Science Quarterly, 7,* 236–257.

Taylor, F.W. (1947). *Scientific management*. New York: Harper & Row.

Thomas, J. & Griffin, R.W. (1983). The social information processing model of task design: A review of the literature. *Academy of Management Review*, October, 672–682.

Turner, A.N. & Lawrence, P.R. (1965). *Industrial jobs and the worker*. Cambridge, MA: Harvard University Press.

Umstot, D.D., Bell, C.H., & Mitchell, T.R. (1976). Effects of job enrichment and task goals on satisfaction and productivity: Implications for job design. *Journal of Applied Psychology*, *61*, *4*, 379–394.

Veroff, J (1953). Development and validation of a projective measure of power motivation. *Journal of Abnormal and Social Psychology*, *55*, 1–8.

Vroom, V.H. (1964). *Work and motivation*. New York: Wiley.

Walker, C.R. & Guest, R. (1952). *The man on the assembly line*. Cambridge, MA: Harvard University Press.

Wall, T.D., Corbett, J.M., Jackson, C.W., & Martin, R. (1990). Advanced manufacturing technology and work design: Towards a theoretical framework. *Journal of Organisational Behaviour*, *11*, 201–219.

Wall, T.D., Kemp, N.J., Jackson, P.R., & Clegg, C.W. (1986). Outcomes of autonomous work groups: A long-term field experiment. *Academy of Management Journal*, June, 280–304.

Wernimont, P. (1966). Intrinsic and extrinsic factors in job satisfaction. *Journal of Applied Psychology*, *50*, *1*, 41–50.

White, R.W. (1960). Competence and psychosexual stages of development. In M.R. Jones (Ed.), *Nebraska Symposium on Motivation*, 97–141. Lincoln: University of Nebraska Press.

Wood, L. & Goodhart, D. (1993). *Workers give job security lower priority*. Financial Times, 20 September, p. 80

Yoell, W.W. (1952). Make your advertising themes match consumer behaviour. *Printers' Ink*, *238 (12)*, 82–87.

3

Perception and Communication

The process of perception is an important activity in the life of the individual. Our environment, including the business environment, is littered with numerous stimuli trying to attract our attention. The quality of our perception depends on the way we organise, process, and interpret the stimuli or information reaching our senses. When we interpret a situation or event, we are then in a position to respond. To sum up, the framework for perception can be described as follows: stimulus→attention→organisation→ interpretation→response. But the potential for misperception has to be recognised.

As an extension of interpretation, person perception is discussed, and, given the importance of perception in communication, the final section is devoted to an examination of communication processes from a number of different angles.

The issues discussed in this chapter have considerable relevance to matters examined elsewhere, for example ergonomic factors (Chapter 14), change and development (Chapter 12), and human resource practices (Chapter 13).

STIMULUS

Before any information can be registered it has to be sensed, and this is accomplished through the senses. The eventual response can be an intentional reaction to the stimulus received and processed, but equally it could be a reflex response that is generally outside the control of the person.

When focusing on a stimulus and how it is perceived, there are a number of philosophical views to consider. Although this subject is largely beyond the scope of this text, one such approach may be briefly acknowledged. The phenomenologists (see Introduction) are of the view that it is the way we cognitively construe or interpret the stimuli reaching our senses that determines our responses. So what we perceive as reality is a reconstruction of what is in our environment. This reconstruction involves adding information and ignoring parts of the information coming our way; the information added or ignored will depend not only on the experience, education, personality, and training of the perceiver, but also on the purpose for which the information is to be used. For example, the accounts of a company are to a greater or lesser extent a reconstruction of the economic reality of the business, though there are, of course, problems in finding a suitable unit of measurement and the most appropriate method of presenta...

The question is also perception is innate or learned.

that normal perception is to some extent learned. In one experimental study, kittens were brought up in the dark except during the period when the experiment was in progress (Held & Hein, 1963). One kitten was strapped into a basket and carried around by an active partner in a rotating arm during the experimental periods (see Fig. 3.1). The active kitten had the superior view and developed normal perception whereas the passive kitten remained effectively blind.

In another experiment (Gibson, 1969), young animals and human infants were exposed to a visual cliff (see Fig. 3.2). This is a patterned area with a steep drop in the middle, which is covered by glass to prevent a fall over the cliff. Both animals and human infants behaved in the same way by avoiding the deep side. The results of this experiment would suggest that perception is either innate or learned at a very early stage in the development of the animal or human.

THE SENSES

We rely on the senses in order to experience the world around us and to adapt to our environment. Normal stimuli impinging on our senses are taken for granted, and it is when we find ourselves in a situation of sensory isolation that we positively yearn for stimuli from the outside world. When deprived of sensory stimulation, people suffer from disorientation, confusion, and emotional disturbance and are vulnerable to persuasion and pressure. Also in these circumstances, people engage in warding-off depression by dwelling on past experiences.

Humans possess at least 10 sensory channels:

vision;	warmth;
hearing;	cold;
taste;	pain;
smell;	kinaesthesis;
touch;	vestibular

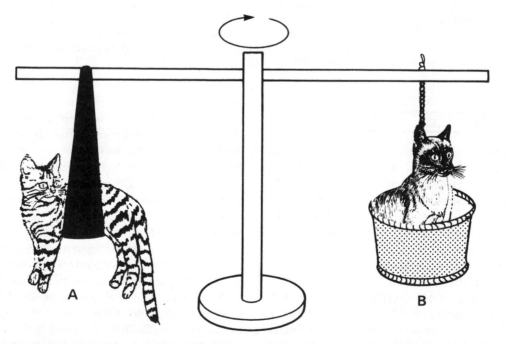

FIG. 3.1.   The active kitten (A) and the passive kitten (B). Source: Held, R. and Hein, A. (1963). Movement-produced stimulation in the development of visually guided behaviour. *Journal of Comparative and Physiological Psychology, 5, 56*, 872–876.

FIG. 3.2. The visual cliff. Source: Gibson, E.J. (1969). Principles of perceptual learning and development. New York: Appleton-Century-Crofts.

Each sense provides a channel through which information received from the world is transmitted to the brain. For each sense receptor at the surface of the body, there are nerves that connect it to the brain and certain areas of the central nervous system. These nerves are made up of a bundle of neurons that are responsible for transmitting information by electrical impulses. Because there are different channels through which qualitatively different information flows, each type of information has its own pathway to the brain, but perception, through the different senses, can be integrated. This is illustrated when we simultaneously hear the lecturer speak, feel the hardness of the chair we are seated on, and feel uncomfortably hot because of the high temperature of the room.

Vision

Vision is perhaps the most important and most often-used sense, and it has been suggested that we obtain three-quarters of our information about the world through sight.

The physical stimulation necessary for vision is electromagnetic energy, in the wavelength range between 380 and 780 nanometres (a nanometre is a millionth of a millimetre). All creatures see approximately the same wave band of electromagnetic energy as light, but there are some differences. For example, humans are blind to ultra-violet light, but honey-bees and ants can see it. Likewise, humans cannot perceive infra-red radiation either by vision or touch because it lies between light and heat, but rattlesnakes are sensitive to it.

The Eye

The eye encodes the information it receives as electromagnetic radiation (light) into a form that the human nervous system can use. The retina at the back of the eye transforms the light energy into electro-chemical energy; this manifests itself as an impulse in the group of nerves running from the eye to the brain (called the optic nerve). The nerve impulses are received by the brain, translated and identified, and the body's reaction to the information is then determined by nerve impulses from the brain to the muscles powering the actions of different parts of the body—legs, arms, hands, and so on.

As well as the wavelength of the light, the intensity of the light determines what we can or cannot see. The human eye is sensitive to light intensities ranging from a low of 5–10 lux to a high of 100,000 lux (a lux is 1 lumen per square metre of surface). Different tasks require different levels of illumination: imagine, for example, the amount of visual detail required to drive a car, with all the complex and changing visual information involved. A driver would, however, tolerate a much lower level of illumination when travelling at 20 mph than at 60 mph, as he or she would have more time in which to resolve dimly seen objects and distances.

When specifying an optimum light level in the workplace (i.e. finding a light level that provides sufficient illumination without causing glare), it is important to consider the nature of the tasks being performed, and also to take account of individual differences. For instance, the performance of people with abnormal vision—e.g. partial sight defect—can be greatly improved by brighter illumination.

Rods and Cones. The sensory receptors in the eye are divided into two types: rods and cones. The cones perceive different wavelengths of light—i.e. they are sensitive to different colours. The cones are clustered near the centre of the retina. The rods are distributed around the perimeter of the retina, and cannot distinguish between different colours, but are much more sensitive to very low levels of light.

Apparently the primates are the only mammals that can see in colour, but birds and a number of other animals have colour vision. One suggestion is that as most mammals are active at night, they are operating in low light levels; the colour receptors are either not functioning or not present. It has been proposed that mammals do in fact possess all the receptors needed to see colours, but that the process by which the brain recognises the nerve impulses triggered by different colours has not evolved. This type of example highlights the importance of the two sides of visual perception—the physical equipment of the eye and the nervous system, and the psychological processes occurring in the brain to analyse and identify nerve impulses.

The choice of green for use in the early VDUs was probably due to the availability of green phosphor. Red is a favoured choice for many displays where light-emitting diodes are used (e.g. in electronic calculators). Red appears to be identified as distinctive more frequently than any other colour of the same brightness, and red numerals are far more legible than green ones.

Colour Perception

A number of workplace problems connected with abnormal colour vision have been identified, such as inefficiency, financial loss, personal embarrassment, and danger (Voke, 1982). Mistakes in colour identification with unacceptable consequences that have occurred in the UK include: a day's production of colour-coded resistors had to be discarded; a crop of unripe tomatoes was picked too early; a buyer experienced difficulty in the selection of cured tobacco leaves; the wrong coloured thread was used in the weaving of a piece of carpet; a red entry was put in the place of a black one in an accountant's records; and a colour-blind electrician received an electric shock from faulty wiring on a piece of equipment.

It is therefore important to consider the implications of employing people with defective colour perception. In Britain alone, roughly 2,000,000 men and 150,000 women experience defective colour perception, though very few individuals are fully blind to colours (Voke, 1982). Red, orange, green, and brown pose the greatest difficulty for those with some degree of defective colour perception.

Glare

Light has to be evenly distributed, otherwise glare will result, causing discomfort, visual fatigue, and accidents. Glare is caused by a marked contrast in brightness between two surfaces, which has the effect of concentrating the light in one direction rather than diffusing it (e.g. the effect produced when light descends on shiny metal or glossy paper on a desk). It is advisable to darken the surroundings when vision is concentrated on a work surface in order to reduce visual strain. However, too great a contrast between the surroundings and the work area should be avoided.

Visual Displays

These are important in providing the individual with pertinent information. There are several displays in a car that provide the driver with information. The windscreen is a kind of display—sometimes called a real-time display—from which the driver obtains information through vision concerning the speed of the car on the road, and the position of other vehicles. Another display is the instrument panel, which provides information about the internal functioning of the car as well as its relation to other parts of the car–road system. The design of the displays and controls will influence performance. If the driver cannot see the instrument panel, or cannot see through the windscreen, his or her performance will suffer.

Visual displays to show readings can assume different forms. In Fig. 3.3 we have the following: (a) a vertical dial; (b) a horizontal dial; (c) a semicircular design; (d) a round design; and (e) an open window design. The smallest percentage of errors in reading the information on display was obtained with the open window design—the dial moves but the pointer remains fixed. The area to scan is the smallest and this could be an important consideration when it comes to accuracy of reading. However, when the direction and rate of movement of the pointer is required, as for example when assessing the speed of a car in motion, the moving pointer is more suitable (Feldman, 1971).

Auditory signals may complement visual ones when one is overwhelmed by visual displays. Even in circumstances where visual displays are not overwhelming—e.g. as when reading the speedometer of a car—it might be useful if an auditory signal was emitted whenever the speed exceeded the statutory limit.

Visual perception is an important consideration when a consumer is faced with making a decision, and product advertising and packaging are designed in order to provide visual cues. In packaging, for example, a particular detergent proudly displays colour stripes with the words "colour safe", obviously appealing to the customer's natural desire to preserve the colour of garments going into the wash. The appearance of the product is critical because it has to compete with other detergents in the same display position in the supermarket. Likewise, expensive cosmetics are found in attractive packaging in order to project a glamorous image.

Hearing

The physical stimulus for hearing is waves of pressure in the air. The sound waves vary in frequency (pitch, measured in Hz), intensity (loudness), and complexity (tonal quality).

Sounds that human beings can hear range from low tones of 20 Hz to high ones of 20,000 Hz. At the low end of the sound range we feel vibration more than we hear sound. We hear

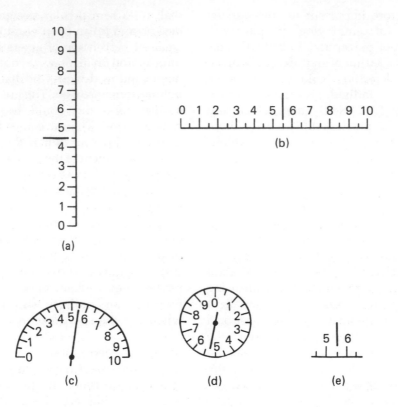

FIG. 3.3. Visual display types: (a) vertical dial; (b) horizontal dial; (c) semicircular dial; (d) round dial; (e) open window dial. Adapted from Feldman, M. (1971). *Psychology in the industrial environment.* Sevenoaks: Butterworth.

best in the range 1000–4000 Hz. Many animals, including cats and dogs, can hear high-pitched sounds that we cannot hear, and cats have an upper limit of approximately 150,000 Hz. Frequency and intensity are both important in determining perceived loudness. Tonal quality enables us to distinguish different musical instruments and different voices. But there are other sounds that have little or no tonal quality, and we call them noises—for example, the hissing noise made by blowing air across a microphone. A violin tone, by contrast, has many strong harmonics.

Loud noises are known to cause hearing loss; boiler-makers and footplate men, for example, have suffered impaired hearing because of loud noises (Feldman, 1971). Although people have the capacity to adapt to continuous loud noises, as happens in certain factories and at parties, the distracting noises are tolerated, but soon pose a psychological strain, leading to irritability and annoyance. Distraction, for whatever reason, causes errors. Of course, not all sounds are unpleasant or distracting, and people involved in marketing a product or service recognise the advantages of pleasant sounds. For example, advertisers use jingles—catchy tunes that people can hum or whistle—as a major awareness technique to associate a certain tune with a certain product through repetition. There has also been a trend in recent years to use popular music from many decades ago.

Other Senses

Smell and Taste

The senses of smell and taste are based on the recognition of chemicals by special receptor cells.

Smell receptors are located in the roof of the nasal passages and taste receptors are located in the taste buds on the tongue, cheeks, and throat. When chemicals that "smell" or "taste" come into contact with these cells, a nerve impulse is triggered and directed to the brain.

Whole industries have grown up around our perceptions of tastes and smells—many people regularly buy deodorant to suppress "unpleasant" smells, and perfume to make themselves smell attractive. In the late 1960s *Proctor and Gamble* added a fragrance with no functional benefit to a washing up liquid. Flavourings are added to many products to disguise unpleasant tastes. Our perception of what is a "good" taste or smell is influenced strongly by social and cultural considerations and, at the same time, we are more disposed to accept a product if it tastes or smells pleasant.

Skin-based Senses

Receptors for four different senses are found in the skin: touch; warmth; cold; and pain.

Touch. As for smell and taste, our sense of touch is conditioned by social and cultural factors. We think of smooth baby's skin as "pleasant" and work-roughened or chapped skin as "unpleasant" to touch. These conditioned responses are both used and reinforced by advertising: for example, an advertisement for hand cream which promises to "leave the skin silky soft" both appeals to our idea of soft skin as being pleasant, and reinforces the idea of soft skin being desirable.

Warmth and Cold. Warmth and cold are felt when the receptors in the skin pick up even and continuous temperature changes.

Pain. The pain receptors appear to be stimulated by tissue destruction—when cells are destroyed by touching a hot surface, for example, a nerve impulse is sent to the brain signalling "pain", which then initiates a series of quick responses, such as snatching the burnt limb away from the hot surface. Interestingly, it has been shown that loss of a limb can often result in the feeling of pain in the limb that is actually no longer there. It is as though we lack the right type of nerve receptors to tell us that a limb is missing, and so the pain signals are used instead.

Finally, the two remaining senses are kinaesthesis and the vestibular sense.

Kinaesthesis

This is the sense of where one's limbs and body are in space—the way in which you can know where your hand or foot is, even in pitch darkness. The kinaesthesis receptors are located throughout the muscles, tendons, and joints of the body.

Vestibular

This is the sense of balance and movement, the receptors for which are located in the inner ear.

The interlocking system of senses provides a network for registering stimuli both internal and external to an organism. Sense receptors can be overloaded and cease to register stimuli—after a while a person wearing perfume can no longer smell it, for example, whereas others are still immediately aware of it. Senses are also affected by changes in the individual's surroundings, habits, and circumstances. For example, it has been shown that confinement in an isolation chamber promotes an increased tolerance of pain (Feldman, 1971).

The importance of the senses to the world of work is seen when our attention focuses on people's relationship to machines and to the physical work environment. The way environmental hazards affect our senses is discussed in Chapter 14, and factors external to the person (physical stimuli) and the disposition of the person will be considered in the next section.

ATTENTION (SELECTIVE PERCEPTION)

In everyday life, many stimuli vie for the attention of the individual. On commercial television the consumer is bombarded with a large number of messages. Likewise when one enters a chemist shop to buy medicine, one is exposed to many products. The investor interested in the financial health of a company potentially has a welter of information from which to choose. However, we cannot attend to all stimuli, so selectivity must be exercised. Selective perception amounts to picking out those stimuli that are most likely to be important and ignoring the others.

Certain conventions govern selective perception, and are discussed with reference to external physical stimuli, absolute and differential thresholds, and the disposition of the perceiver.

External Physical Stimuli

Certain types of external physical stimuli attract our attention, such as size (e.g. large objects); repetition (e.g. events that occur repeatedly); position (e.g. of an advertisement on a newspaper page); colour; moving objects in a stationary setting; novelty; and contrast. All of these stimuli have particular properties that cause us to focus attention on them. These stimuli are discussed in the following sections and then general applications are explored.

Size
In studying the effects of advertising, physical stimuli such as size, repetition, position, and colour have been analysed (Anastasi, 1979). Increasing the size of an advertisement will generally increase its readership—it encounters less competition from other advertisements on a newspaper or magazine

page. But obviously there is limited scope for the enlargement of the advertisement. In a large advertisement there is an opportunity to include more illustrations and more text. Advertisements with a large proportion of unfilled background (or "white space") tend to attract attention because of their novelty, stark simplicity, and arresting appearance. With regard to print size, it is suggested that increasing the print size of an advertisement will increase the odds of gaining the consumer's attention (Finn, 1988).

Repetition
Repetition is an important factor aimed at increasing the readership of an advertisement. For those readers who notice the advertisement on more than one occasion, the repeated exposure strengthens the initial impact of the advertisement. This was borne out in an experimental study when pairs of advertisements were exposed in a stereoscope for a short time. The subjects were young women, divided into an experimental group and a control group. The experimental group had much more contact with the advertisements, which dealt with brassières and girdles and included a picture of a model, than did the control group. The result was that the experimental group recalled these advertisements significantly more often than did the control group (Berg, 1967).

Constant repetition is said to produce familiarity, and if a brand is relatively risk-free with some incentive given at the point of sale (e.g. a price discount), shoppers may purchase the product because of accumulated familiarity, even though they have not actively attended to the advertising message (Oliver, 1980).

Position
The position of an advertisement within a magazine or newspaper is crucial. Placing an advertisement near a popular editorial feature gives it an advantage, particularly where the content of the advertisement bears some relationship to the editorial: for example, it is

important to place advertisements for books on or near the book review pages. Such a location helps to select an interested audience and attract readers at a time when they are particularly receptive to the appeal of the product. It is claimed that placing advertisements on and inside the front cover, on page one, and both on and inside the back cover of a magazine creates a significant readership advantage of between 30% and 64% over positions on the inside pages (Starch, 1961).

With respect to position within a page, it seems that the upper half of a page gets more attention than the lower half, and the left-hand side of the page gets more attention than the right (Berkman & Gilson, 1978). A comparatively recent study reports greater attention for advertisements located in the front rather than the back part of the magazine, on the right-hand pages rather than the left-hand pages in the open magazine, and on the inside front, inside back, and outside back cover (Finn, 1988). Position is considered important when specific groceries are located in particular parts of a store, and certain items are displayed near cash tills.

Colour

Colour is often used as a device to attract attention and portray realism. In a mass of black and white, a modicum of colour catches the eye. Where colour is still a novelty, as with newspapers, the addition of even a single colour to an advertisement will enhance its attention-getting value.

Colour can be used to emphasise the attractive features of a product or to create a suitable atmosphere—high technology products such as cameras are usually produced in black or metallic finishes, although some have been marketed with a less serious, more sporty image, in bright primary colours. Some products, such as cars, come in a variety of colours, but others, such as toothpaste, are limited in colour range. It would somehow seem incongruous to use black toothpaste.

Standards (based on psychological research) for the optimum use of colour in coding systems have been adopted by the British Standards Institution after collaboration with industry. There are, for example, colour codes to denote different types of fire extinguisher, for industrial and medical gas cylinders, for the hatched yellow lines at busy crossroads, and for traffic signalling.

Colour can be used in the workplace for the enhancement of lighting effects, for creating pleasant surroundings, and for putting across and reinforcing safety messages. When planning the colour scheme or decor for a room it is important to consider the use to which the room will be put. For repetitive and monotonous activities the overall decor could be made more stimulating by providing small areas of bright colours. A large working area can be divided into smaller identifiable segments by using different colour schemes that complement each other. Where mental concentration is a necessary feature of office life, the colour scheme should be light and non-intensive.

The effects of colours on the psychological state of the individual should also be considered, because some colours act as a stimulant and others act as a depressant. A dark blue ceiling may appear to be refreshing to begin with, but in time the apparent coldness may become an irritant. Various effects are attributed to different colours and these are shown in Table 3.1 (Hayne, 1981).

Movement

Movement, or the illusion of movement, may also be used to capture attention. People are attracted by neon lighting and by billboards with rotating bars that carry a different message on each surface.

Novelty

People tend to notice distinctive or novel aspects of their environment. That which is novel—e.g. humour, animation, and unusual graphics in an advertisement—stands out and is noticed.

TABLE 3.1

The Effects of Different Colours

Colour	Psychological Effect	Temperature Effect	Distance Effect
Violet	Agressive and tiring	Cold	Very close
Blue	Restful	Cold	Further away
Brown	Exciting	Neutral	Claustrophobic
Green	Very restful	Cold/neutral	Further away
Yellow	Exciting	Very warm	Close
Orange	Exciting	Very warm	Very close
Red	Very stimulating	Warm	Close

Contrast

Another means of attracting attention is contrast. It is evident in the case of sound on television or in the cinema when there is a difference between the loudness of the programme soundtrack and that of the advertisement soundtrack. It is also manifest in the case of vision when, for example, there is a picture of a product on a completely white background.

The contrast between scenes in an advertisement and scenes in the television programme that carries the advertisement should not create undesirable impressions. In selecting programmes for its television advertisements, *Kraft Cheese* rejects programmes that are excessively violent. The contrast between a programme scene where excessive blood is spilled and a subsequent advertising scene showing a cheese spread in a tranquil setting could hardly be considered appropriate. The panel below carries an example of a case where the contrast between a TV commercial and a drama gave rise to criticisms (Engel et al., 1990).

Other Applications of Physical Stimuli

A number of the stimuli identified in the previous section could be incorporated in the following contexts.

Notices and Warnings

Employees must be alerted to dangerous equipment, areas, processes, etc. It is important to attract their attention to the

---

Undesirable Contrasts

In the screening of *The Holocaust* in the United States, the plight of the Jews under the Hitler regime was shown. Viewers complained about the bright and cheerful scenes that appeared in commercials just after the scenes of horror.

There was one particular contrast which was likely to have aroused passions. Lieutenant Dorf was sitting with Adolf Eichmann and other SS officers in their dining room at Auschwitz. Eichmann sniffed the air and remarked that the stench of the chimneys kept him from enjoying his meal. The scene was cut for an air freshener commercial, in which a woman called "Snoopy Sniffer" arrived at a houswife's kitchen and informed her that she had house odours (Engel, Blackwell, & Miniard, 1990).

hazards that are present, and to inform and remind them of the safety precautions they should take. This is usually done with notices. Notices and warnings should be varied from time to time in order to attract fresh attention. Warnings are necessary in the following conditions, especially on the factory floor:

- where a particular hazard cannot be "designed out" of a piece of equipment;
- where an operator cannot be removed physically from the potentially dangerous point of contact; and
- where effective guards cannot be installed.

In the UK an employer has a legal duty to inform employees about hazards at work. Employees are more likely to co-operate in keeping rules made for their benefit if they appreciate the risks and the reasons for the precautions.

Warnings may be either dynamic or static. Dynamic warnings consist of warning lights and audible sounds, and static warnings comprise pictures, symbols, and diagrams. Warnings should be universally understood, they should convey why something is a hazard, how it arises from the use or misuse of a piece of equipment or process, and what to do if an injury should occur. Such warnings should also be complete, allow for any literacy or language problems, be conspicuous and capable of attracting attention, and should be updated periodically. "Redundancy" should be built into the information provision process: redundancy in this context is the injection of essentially the same information through two or more sense channels—e.g. vision and hearing (Christensen, 1981).

In the UK there are statutory safety regulations requiring that dangerous sub-stances be supplied and conveyed in containers of sound construction carrying an appropriate warning label. Such labels would include information indicating the general hazards, such as "explosive", "highly inflammable", "toxic", or "corrosive", as well as important health and safety information.

The justification for this legislation is that inadequately labelled or badly packed dangerous substances cause accidents and injury.

Illustrations
Illustrations of a product are useful devices to attract attention, for instance, attractive photographs of the product—like pictures of various appetising foods that can be prepared using the product (e.g. a photograph of a cake along with the recipe for it, displayed on the packaging for flour). Illustrations serve to facilitate comprehension of ideas about the product, to arouse feelings about it, and to help identify the product when the consumer is out shopping. Pictures of people generally rate highly in attention value, but there is evidence suggesting that when human models are used in a printed advertisements the appropriateness of the model for the product may influence judgements about product quality (Anastasi, 1979; Kanugo & Pang, 1973). It is essential that the illustrated advertisement does not become an end in itself and detract attention from the product.

Cues
Cues are physical stimuli that act as symbols, giving us an indication of what to expect, and facilitating judgements. The names of supermarkets (e.g. *Sainsbury*), brand names (e.g. *St. Michael*), packaging, and price are cues that convey the quality of the store or product and help us make our decision to buy. Judgements are also made about a company from cues such as the helpfulness of the staff, and the image of the company (e.g. *Harrods*). Perhaps when we confront a situation where there is an absence of cues about a store, greater reliance is placed on the assessment of the quality of service and product at the time of purchase.

Sometimes reliance on a few cues could lead to stereotyping that might not be justified in particular circumstances. This might arise when someone calls at the door selling, for example, insurance. Because of a negative stereotype of a door-to-door salesman, which could be totally unjustified in given circumstances, the customer withdraws from what might otherwise be a fruitful commercial encounter.

A *trade-mark* is a *reduced cue*, serving as a conditioned stimulus for the recall of the product and company name. A trade-mark may symbolise some advantageous characteristic of the product—e.g. "Long Life" for milk—and often tends to evoke ideas and feelings associated with the product, either through previous advertising or through the customer's own contact with the product. When the trade-mark is a direct representation of the brand name of the product, as is the case with *Kellogg's Corn Flakes*, the association between the brand name and trade-mark is particularly easy to establish and the likelihood of confusion with other products or brands is minimised.

Sometimes a brand name is so strongly identified with a product that it is used as a generic term—e.g. *Kleenex* to denote any cleansing tissue. In circumstances such as these, there is a danger of associating dissatisfaction with the original brand if the customer is dissatisfied with the purchase of an inferior brand.

Financial Data

Published accounting information is a stimulus attended to by the investor. However, there are other sources of information at the disposal of the investor apart from these, such as commentaries and tips in the financial press, government reports on the state of the economy, employers' and trade association reports, stockbrokers' reports, merger reports, the latest inflation and balance of payments figures, and so on. The proposition that published accounts are only one of many sources of information is supported by at least one study (Brown, 1970). The results of this study indicate that most movement in share prices took place in the 12 months preceding the announcement of profits, and that on average there was only a

10% change in the value of shares at the time the profits were announced.

The accountant's image may also be important as a stimulus. Where the accountant is seen as conservative in outlook, the investor may adjust his or her judgement accordingly. There is a belief in some quarters that annual reports and accounts have become complex and cumbersome documents prepared by financial experts for financial experts, despite official exhortation to be realistic about the user's requirements (Lothian, 1978). Financial statements should be designed for users "who have limited authority, ability, or resources to obtain information and who rely on financial statements" (*Objectives of Financial Statements*, AICPA, 1973). The clarity or ambiguity of accounting stimuli is discussed again later in this chapter.

Clarity

In written official documents and forms, clarity is an important principle. It is very important, for example, for tax literature to be as clear as possible. In an annual report of the UK Inland Revenue it was stated that "good communications are crucial to our task of assessing and collecting the revenue due from the public efficiently with a minimum of friction.... Like any other organisation with millions of individual contacts with members of the public each year, we have to rely for the exchange of information largely on forms and standard printed materials" (Lewis & James, 1981). The accuracy of tax returns is obviously related to the degree of difficulty experienced in comprehending tax forms and guides.

In the 1980s, the Form P1 used by the Inland Revenue changed colour from blue to white, although the titles and subtitles remained blue. There were other improvements to Form P1 and the accompanying guide: the format improved, with much more space generally; the size of the print was enlarged; the number of introductory comments in the guide, in order to establish the right mental focus, was increased; and there were changes in wording—e.g. "correspondence" with the tax office has become "letters". Other revisions and changes affected the tax guide associated with Forms 11 and 11P, and a start had been made on revising all the main explanatory leaflets and booklets (Lewis & James, 1981).

These developments are indicative of a determination to strive for clarity in the presentation of a stimulus to the target audience.

Absolute and Differential Thresholds

Each sense receptor requires some minimum level of energy to excite it before perception is organised. The minimum level is called the *absolute threshold*—a point below which we do not perceive energy. The absolute threshold for light is a flame from a candle seen at a distance of 30 miles on a dark clear night; for sound it is the tick of a watch under quiet conditions at a distance of 20 feet; for taste it is one teaspoon of sugar in two gallons of water; and for smell, it is one drop of perfume diffused into the entire volume of a three-room apartment (Day, 1969).

The differential threshold is the smallest amount by which two similar stimuli must be different in order to be perceived as different. People differ in both absolute and differential thresholds. For example, the professional wine taster can frequently distinguish between two bottles of wine that the amateur finds identical. In the production of paper, the mixing foreman can ascertain exactly when the pulpy mixture is at the appropriate

consistency for the type of paper required— an example of an acute differential threshold (Bobbitt et al., 1978).

The concepts of absolute and differential thresholds are important in the field of safety. The safety engineer and the design engineer must acquaint themselves with people's absolute and differential thresholds and allow for these when designing signals.

Thresholds need not only concern the physical stimuli of the real world. For example in accounting, the absolute threshold could be considered as the minimum level of information required by the individual to perceive the overall profitability or financial position of a business. An example of a differential threshold might be a discrepancy in figures detected in the course of a financial audit. To the experienced and competent auditor this discrepancy is serious enough to warrant further investigation, but to the inexperienced auditor the detection of the discrepancy may not signal a need for further action.

It has already been acknowledged that stimuli below the absolute threshold level cannot be perceived. However, on the basis of an experiment conducted in the autumn of 1957 in the US, it was thought that subliminal perception—perception below the absolute threshold level—existed in and affected buying behaviour (see panel below).

However, it should be noted that in situations like this, factors other than subliminal advertising may influence the results: in the case in the panel below, for example, the presence of a high proportion of

---

Subliminal Advertising?

An experiment was conducted by a commercial firm in a New Jersey cinema. The words "Eat Popcorn" and "Drink Coca-Cola" were flashed alternately on the screen every 5 seconds for 1/3000th of a second during the showing of the regular film. These stimuli were described as subliminal, and the firm claimed that, over the 6-week period this procedure was followed, sales of popcorn in the foyer rose by 57.5% and

Coca-Cola by 18.1%.

The report of these results aroused widespread public alarm, and this type of advertising was described as the "super softsell" and the "invisible sell". The claims made for the experiments could not be evaluated because of the refusal by the commercial firm to reveal the details of the experimental procedure and results (Berkman & Gilson, 1978).

teenagers in the audience during the period, changes in the display of the two products and in the sales tactics, and the weather (McConnell, Cutier, & McNeil, 1958).

Subliminal perception is not a mysterious technique for projecting ideas directly into the mind by evading the individual's conscious defences. There is no evidence to suggest that weak stimuli—i.e. stimuli below the absolute threshold level—exert more influence on behaviour than strong stimuli; in fact the reverse is the case. Also, as the stimulus becomes weaker, the probability of mis-erception becomes higher. With regard to subliminal stimuli, individual threshold differences must be considered—a word flashed across a cinema screen for a short period may have significance for one person because it falls above his or her absolute threshold, but not for another because it falls below the minimum level.

Notwithstanding what has been said, the findings of a study by Zajonc and Markus (1982) would seem to indicate that subliminal stimuli have significance, and that there is a possibility that attitudes are influenced without the individual interpreting stimuli through a conscious cognitive process. Some argue that the subliminal messages of in-store music have a soothing and productive effect on shoppers. But, from another source (Moore, 1982), comes a challenge to the effectiveness of subliminal stimuli. It is claimed that subliminal stimuli are usually so weak that the recipient is not just unaware of the stimuli, but is also oblivious to the fact that he or she is being stimulated. Generally, people are preoccupied with normal stimuli.

Sensory Adaptation

Absolute and differential thresholds are known to fluctuate, and this fluctuation is referred to as sensory adaptation. One example is visual adaptation.

Visual Adaptation.   When dusk descends the rods take over from the cones in the retina of the eyes. The reverse is true when light reappears. We do not encounter too many difficulties when adapting to different levels of illumination, but the problem of temporary blindness appears with rapid changes in illumination. For example a change from darkness to light increases the level of illumination falling on the retina of the eyes. In such circumstances the rods are unable to function, and the cones have not had sufficient time to adapt to the new conditions. The natural reaction is to close the eyes, or wear dark or coloured glasses in order to allow the eyes to adapt. The cones react relatively fast—e.g. a couple of minutes—as we move from darkness to light.

As we move from light to darkness, the rods react much slower—typically half an hour or more. The period of adaptation depends on the previous intensity of illumination. It is for this reason that coloured goggles (e.g. red) are worn by people who work in a dark environment, such as is found in the photographic industry. They would normally wear the goggles for some time before entering the dark-room. Red is an appropriate colour for the goggles because it has little effect on the visual pigment in the rods (Cushman, 1980).

Colour Adaptation.   This is manifest in the following illustration. If a person views a bright red stimulus for a few minutes, and then focuses on a yellow stimulus, the yellow appears to be green. Gradually the eye will adapt and return to normality. Such processes have important implications for computer operators spending a long time viewing various colours on a screen.

Adaptation to Repeated Stimuli.   People have the capacity to adapt to stimuli that are repeated, by developing reduced awareness. For example, a worker becomes oblivious to the dangers of operating certain types of machines, and risks having an accident. To account for this phenomenon, one could argue that a stimulus that is repeated contains no new information.

This is akin to a situation whereby people living close to a nuclear power station adapt to the conditions in the absence of an accident. In the process, anxieties subside with the accompanying cognitive reassessment of the probability of an accident. Often, it is the people living furthest away from the nuclear plant who suffer the most anxiety, provoking rumours about the effects of radiation or melt-down. Rumour is the consequence of conditions in which good information is scarce; therefore, it can contain inaccuracies.

People living furthest away from the nuclear plant can be compared with those living close to it. The latter have the advantage of being able to see the plant on a daily basis and perhaps learn more about the nature of the hazard. As a consequence, they are better able to adapt to any unconscious fears about the dangers of nuclear power. Any resident living close to the nuclear plant who experiences severe anxiety has the option of moving away, although one recognises that in practice it may not be easy to exercise this option because of depressed labour and housing market conditions, as experienced in the early 1990s.

Familiarity with stimuli, where no adverse experience occurs, is a feature of repeated exposure to stimuli. Effectively the person adapts to the situation. However, there are situations when the person fails to adapt to stimuli (e.g. continuous noise) and the result is reduced powers of concentration, leading to poor quality work.

Disposition of the Perceiver

Unlike the physical stimuli discussed at length in previous sections, there are other less quantifiable variables that are unique to the individual. These can be classified as the internal state of the person—e.g. personality, motivation, and previous learning—and affect the way people perceive. The disposition of the individual will be discussed with reference to the preparatory set, orientation, intensity of motives and familiarity of stimuli.

Preparatory Set
The preparatory set basically refers to the range of things that, because of our internal state, we are almost programmed to see. Items outside the preparatory set are virtually ignored irrespective of what is contained in the stimuli to which we are exposed. The interest we have in certain things influences our attention. Perhaps more women are interested in advertisements for children's and babies' clothing than men, and the position could be reversed when attention focuses on cars and lawn mowers.

Users of accounting information may take insufficient interest in financial data for a number of reasons, such as failure to meet their requirements because of the accountants' preoccupation with the techniques of accounting rather than the use to which accounting information is put (Robson, 1965). In one study of the use of accounting control data by middle managers it was found that a significant amount of the information prepared for control purposes was not properly used because it was considered not totally relevant, too detailed, not detailed enough, or it arrived too late (Beresford Dew & Gee, 1973).

Orientation
The particular orientation—the attitude adopted by the perceiver towards a set of physical stimuli, based on interests, background, etc—is also critical. This is borne out in the results of two studies.

In the first (Cyert & March, 1963), a group of students was presented with a set of numbers in the form of cost and revenue statements. Both statements were analysed by all the students but there was a 10-week interval between the analysis of the two statements, with one half of the group working first on the revenue statements and the other half beginning with the cost statements. It was found that the context in which the students operated influenced their outlook; when analysing costs they tended to overestimate costs, but underestimated sales when analysing revenue. Perhaps people are somewhat conservative in outlook when engaged in information processing connected with money values. By overestimating costs there will be a tendency to minimise losses, whereas by underestimating sales the likelihood of overstating income is reduced.

In the second study a group of managers drawn from a large manufacturing company participated while attending a management course. The managers came from different functional backgrounds (e.g. accounting, marketing, and production) and they were asked to specify the major problem facing a company depicted in a case study that they had read. The majority of managers perceived the major problem as being related to their own area of specialisation (Dearborn & Simon, 1958).

Intensity of Motives
Perception is selectively affected by personal motives because we pay most attention to stimuli that appeal to fairly intense motives. Thus our perception may be distorted by our motivations. This point is emphasised in the following study. Ten-year-old children were asked to estimate the size of a coin in front of them by varying the size of a spot of light until they thought it was the same shape as a coin from a series, ranging from a penny to half-a-crown. It was found that the estimated size of every coin was larger than its true size. This type of overestimation did not occur with a control group, which tried to estimate the size of cardboard discs that were the same size as the coins. When the experiment was conducted among separate groups from both affluent and poor backgrounds, over-estimation was detected in both cases, but was more pronounced among children from the poorer background. Here we observe that perception is accentuated when valued objects are perceived (Bruner & Goodman, 1947).

Where a stimulus is related to a need deficiency, our perception of that stimulus could be acute. The hungry person will display selectivity by tuning into food-related stimuli in his or her environment because of their association with the reduction of a need deficiency (hunger).

Selective perception can also help us to cope with a threat. Here our value system assists us by ignoring messages, particularly mildly threatening ones, that tend to question our values, and this can be achieved without conscious awareness.

Studies have also demonstrated how perception acts as a defence in certain circumstances—e.g. McGinnies (1949, see panel below). On the basis of this study one

---

Perception as a Defence Mechanism

Words were shown to subjects only briefly so that they found it impossible to recognise them. The period of display was then lengthened until recognition occurred. An electronic measure of emotion—the galvanic skin response (GSR)—was used to gauge the electrical resistance of the skin when an emotional reaction was aroused.

The words comprised 11 that were neutral and 7 that were taboo (e.g. bitch, whore, rape). Each time a word was flashed the subject gave his or her opinion of what the word was. An emotional reaction (as gauged by the GSR) occurred even in circumstances when taboo words were shown so briefly that recognition was not reported by the subjects.

Taboo words had to be exposed for longer than neutral words before being read because they were apparently more difficult to recognise. When the words were flashed very briefly, and the subjects guessed what the words were, it was found that neutral words were construed in a structurally similar sense—e.g. instead of recognising the word "trade" as such, it was recognised as "trace"—but completely different words were substituted for taboo words.

One might conclude that subjects suppress the reporting of taboo words even when they clearly perceive them; or that they have a higher threshold with respect to these words and are therefore not alerted to them; or that because these words appear less often in print than other words, they are less familiar and are recognised more slowly (McGinnies, 1949).

might accept that stimuli of a mildly threatening nature (e.g. a distasteful advertisement) tend to be ignored. Conversely, one may hypothesise that strongly threatening stimuli can capture our attention. We are protected from the distraction of mildly threatening stimuli, but alerted to the danger of strongly threatening stimuli.

Familiarity of Stimuli

Experience of a particular stimulus, such as a particular piece of music, amidst a range of stimuli to which we may be indifferent, attracts our attention. Alternatively, a novel or unfamiliar object amidst a range of familiar ones—for instance, a strange face at a social event, or a novel piece of accounting data in a stereotypical accounting report—produces a similar effect. Experience may also predispose us to discount the claims of a product advertiser; we do so on the basis of dissatisfaction experienced as a result of previously using that product. Previous learning creates a tendency to pay attention to familiar patterns, though this might bring about problems when we accept a stimulus which bears a similarity to a familiar stimulus—we see what we expect to see rather than what is.

PERCEPTUAL ORGANISATION

Having focused our attention on relevant stimuli, the next step is to organise the information contained in the stimuli. This could be difficult in circumstances where the stimuli are ambiguous. Dots, lines, and other shapes can have meaning for us; likewise we attribute meaning to sounds—a sound that emanates from within the home invites questions about where it is coming from and what it is. The commentary in this section covers ambiguous figures, figure/background, the Gestalt laws of organisation, constancy, visual illusions, and applications.

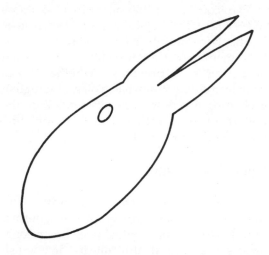

FIG. 3.4. An ambiguous figure—a duck or a rabbit.

Ambiguous Figures

When we first glance at the lines in Fig. 3.4 we may conclude that they epitomise disorganisation. Then we suddenly begin to realise that it is a drawing and could represent either a duck or a rabbit, and then it fluctuates between both images. Likewise, in Fig. 3.5 we see either a kneeling woman or a man's face, or perhaps both. With ambiguous figures there appears to be a need to create a whole image

FIG. 3.5. An ambiguous figure—a kneeling woman or a man's face. Source: Fisher, G.H. (1967). Preparation of ambiguous stimulus materials. *Perception and Psychophysics*, 2, 421–422. Reproduced by permission of the Psychonomic Society, Inc.

The concept of organisation also arises when a series of musical notes is perceived as a tune. For example *Yellow Submarine* would be immediately recognised by those who had heard this song previously, whether it was sung by a soprano or a bass voice, although in each case the notes are different. It is the pattern of notes rather than the individual notes that is important.

Figure/Background

We rarely encounter ambiguity with three-dimensional objects in our normal visual world. But with two-dimensional objects we find it difficult to distinguish between background and figure. Figure/background stimuli are presented in Figs. 3.6 and 3.7. Two different pictures could be derived from Fig. 3.6; at one moment we see a figure of a white vase against a black background, and the next moment we see two black profiles against a white background. In Fig. 3.7 we see either a black cross on a white background or a white cross on a black background.

The figure/background relationship is also found in senses other than vision. For

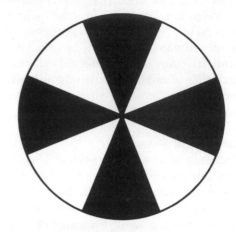

FIG. 3.7. A black or white cross.

example, when we listen to a symphony we perceive the melody or theme as a figure and the chords as background.

These reversible figure/background relationships illustrate the *multistability* of our perceptual organisation. This is depicted in Fig. 3.8 where each image can be "organised" in different ways, generating different three-dimensional or two-dimensional figures. For example, the right-hand image in Fig. 3.8 can be seen as a hexagon with lines from the points converging at the centre, or as a cube tipped forward.

Gestalt Laws of Organisation

A number of rules or laws governing the organisation of perception, sometimes

FIG. 3.6.An ambiguous figure—a vase or two profiles.

FIG. 3.8. Multistable figures.

referred to as the Gestalt laws of organisation, are examined in the following sections.

Area

Where one part of an area depicting an ambiguous figure is smaller in size than the remainder, it is more likely that the smaller area will be seen as a figure and the rest of the total area as background. Glancing at Fig. 3.9(A), it is usual to see the small areas of white as the figure of a white cross and the large area of black as the background. By contrast, in Fig. 3.9(B) a black cross set in a white background is more likely to be seen.

FIG. 3.10. Groupings of vertical lines.

Proximity

In Fig. 3.10 we see three pairs of vertical lines instead of six vertical lines. The law of proximity states that items which are close together in space or time tend to be perceived as forming an organised group, or belonging together. When one flicks through the pages of a book, small sections of text with headings stand out from the remainder of the text because of their distance from the previous section.

Similarity

In Fig. 3.11(a) most people would see one triangle formed by the dots with the apex at the top, and another triangle formed by rings (i.e. with the apex at the bottom). The triangles are perceived in this way because the dots and rings look different and therefore are organised separately. In a textbook, pictures and diagrams are instantly seen to be similar, and different from the body of the text. In Fig. 3.11(b) we do not see a triangle but a hexagon (a 6-pointed star) because all the dots are the same.

Grouping in accordance with similarity does not always occur. We see Fig. 3.11(c) more easily as a 6-pointed star than as one set of dots and another set of rings. In this illustration similarity is competing with the principle of symmetry or "good figure"; neither the circles

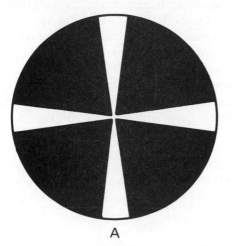

A

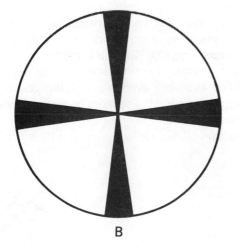

B

FIG. 3.9. Reversible figures.

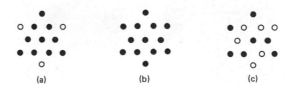

(a) (b) (c)

FIG. 3.11. Examples of perceptual grouping

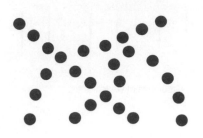

FIG. 3.12. An example of perceptual continuity.

nor the dots form a symmetrical pattern by themselves.

Continuation

There is a tendency to perceive a line that starts in a particular way as continuing in that way. For example, a line that starts off as a curve is seen continuing along a smooth curved course, and, if it changes direction, it is seen to form an angle rather than a curve. Equally a straight line is seen as continuing on a smooth straight course. Fig. 3.12 illustrates the principle of continuation. We see the curved and straight lines as crossing each other and having dots in common, but it requires some effort on our part to perceive a straight line becoming a curved line at one of these intersecting points or junctions.

A numerical illustration of continuation is shown when you are asked to specify a number to follow 4, 8, 12, 16. The most likely answer is 20 because of a tendency to follow a perceived pattern. But in fact any number would be good enough, because you were not asked to maintain the pattern.

Common Fate

This arises where elements that are seen as moving together take the shape of an organised group. The soldier in the jungle or wilderness who is perfectly camouflaged against his background is invisible until he moves; when he moves he becomes a figure and remains so while he is in motion. Two of the circles in Fig. 3.13 share a common fate because they move in the same direction.

Closure

We compensate for the missing portions of incomplete stimuli so that we perceive a whole rather than a disorganised group. In Fig. 3.14, the left-hand drawing is seen as a circle with gaps in it and the centre drawing as a square with gaps in it, rather than as disconnected lines. If these pictures were flashed very rapidly on to a screen, they might be perceived as complete pictures without gaps. The drawing on the extreme right will also be perceived as a form rather than disconnected lines (e.g. a man on horse-back).

All of the principles discussed here also apply to perception using senses other than vision.

Constancy

One way in which people organise their world and make it more understandable is by emphasising stability and constancy. Constancy refers to situations where we see objects as stable despite great changes in the stimuli reaching the sensory organs. An object remains constant despite variations in its size and this allows us to make an adjustment to

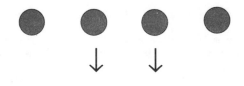

FIG. 3.13. A common fate.

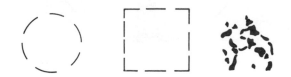

FIG. 3.14. Examples of closure.

the reality confronting us. The following are examples of perceptual constancies.

Size

The image on the retina of the eye produced by a nearer object is in fact bigger than that produced by a distant object, but we make allowances for that fact—e.g. we are not normally aware of a football player diminishing in size as he moves away from us across the field. We have a remarkable ability to keep the observed size of things constant in spite of large fluctuations in their retinal image.

Shape

The ability to maintain a constant shape in spite of different retinal images is called *shape constancy*. Like size constancy, it acts to our advantage by keeping our world of perception orderly. Imagine the confusion you would experience in a crowded car park if your car was seen as a different object according to the different retinal images produced from different viewing positions—front, side, back, etc.

Light

Different object surfaces absorb different amounts of light. If a surface absorbs all the light that falls on it, it is seen as black, but if it reflects most of the light it is usually seen as white. We make unconscious inferences about the colour and brightness of familiar materials because we have the advantage of experience of this type of phenomenon. Apparently, however, with unfamiliar materials, constancy still applies.

Person

Constancy can also apply to the perception of people. In one study it was demonstrated that there was considerable stability in people's judgements of politicians before and after reading newspaper reports about the politician in question. However, it appears that constancy is strongest when there is no great discrepancy between the position of the politician, in terms of his or her behaviour, before and after the newspaper reports. Even where a marked discrepancy exists, some degree of constancy still remains (Warr & Knapper, 1968). There is a detailed account of *person perception* later in this chapter.

Illusions

Under certain conditions constancy does not hold good, and what we see appears to be quite different from what we know to be true. These manifestations are called illusions. Visual illusions are illustrated in Figs. 3.15, 3.16, 3.17, and 3.18.

An illusion can be described as a reliable perceptual error; it is stable and not due to a hasty or careless exploration or processing of stimuli on our part. A widely discussed illusion is the Müeller-Lyer illusion shown in Fig. 3.15. Though the lines A and B in the figure are the same length, we see A as the shorter line. In Fig. 3.16 we see the two rectangles, A and B, as different even though they are the same size.

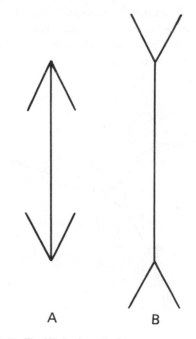

FIG. 3.15. The Müeller-Lyer illusion.

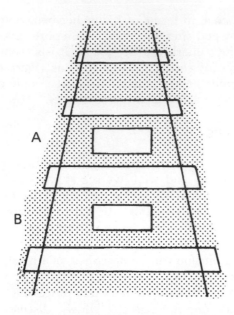

FIG. 3.16. The Ponzo illusion.

With regard to Figs 3.15 and 3.16, we can measure the lines A and B and likewise the rectangles A and B and establish that they *are* equal in length, yet we cannot, even consciously, make the necessary adjustments to *see* them as equal. It has been suggested that the difficulty encountered with many of the two-dimensional illusions is that we misinterpret them as three-dimensional

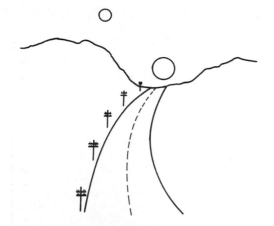

FIG. 3.17. The moon illusion.

figures which we expect to obey the laws of perspective (Gregory, 1966). For example, in Fig. 3.16 presumably we make some attempt at scaling sizes in accordance with their perceived distance.

The moon illusion is another illustration of this principle. In Fig. 3.17 the moon seems to be much larger when it appears on the horizon then when it is high in the sky. But it is the same distance away from us in both cases and the image projected on to the retina is also the same in both cases. Nevertheless, we still see the sizes as different.

The Ames room illusion (Fig. 3.18) shows the nearer woman in a room seeming taller than the woman further away, even though both women are about the same size.

How do these illusions occur, particularly as we have seen earlier how unconscious inference is introduced in order to maintain constancy? We may attempt to explain the moon illusion on the basis that the moon at the horizon looks further away because of all the information we are given on distance from the intervening terrain. Hence, when we see the moon in this position, we unconsciously "blow up" the image to compensate for this increased distance (Mackay, 1973). In much the same way, we are fooled into believing that the two women in the Ames room in Fig. 3.18, who are about the same size, are in a rectangular room and that they are at the same distance from us. But the room is not rectangular; the "short" woman is much further away than the "tall" woman. However, constancy is not maintained, and our judgement of the relative size of the two women is distorted because we have not allowed for distance.

Movement Illusions
Illusions of movement that arise from stationary stimuli are not uncommon. For example, an isolated stationary light in an otherwise dark visual field appears to wander after observing it for a while. This is called *autokinesis* and is typically encountered in flying (Hawkins, 1987). The autokinetic effect

FIG. 3.18. The Ames room. (Photograph copyright Eastern Counties Newspapers Ltd. and reproduced by permission.)

is a feature of the night flight environment (see panel below), when a stationary light in a dark visual field appears to move.

Another example of an illusion arising from a moving rather than a stationary stimulus occurs when a person on board a stationary train at a station looks out of the carriage window and sees a train at another platform. In reality the other train is moving, but the illusion is that the person's own train is moving, and this is called the illusion of induced movement. Illusions can also arise from the presentation of stimuli in rapid succession. An example of this phenomenon is the apparent slow backward movement of wagon wheels in an old western film.

Applications of Perceptual Organisation

The principle of the Gestalt psychologists that the "whole is more than the sum of its parts" is seen at work in the illustrations of

In-flight Movement Illusions

There are numerous reported cases of mistaken identity of light, such as the pilot "circling" round the wing-tip light of his or her own aircraft trying to identify it.

Another common illusory problem experienced in visual cruise flights relates to the evaluation of the relative altitude of approaching aircraft and the subsequent assessment of a potential collision risk. At a distance, an aircraft appears initially to be at a higher level, but eventually passes below the level of the observer. Mountain peaks, at a distance, seem to be above the height of the aircraft, but often are actually well below it. Two aircraft separated by only 1000 feet may appear to be approaching each other's altitude, and experience has shown that both pilots may resort unnecessarily to taking evasive action with the possibility of contributing to a mid-air collision (Hawkins, 1987).

perceptual organisation discussed here. The principle of organisation is frequently applied in our daily life. When an advertisement for a product is viewed on commercial television, the soundtrack and visual stimuli complement each other and help the consumer to organise the message. Repetition of a message in an advertisement also contributes to perceptual organisation.

For example, an advertisement for a lap-top personal computer at an attractive price is advertised in the colour supplement of a Sunday newspaper. This advertisement, which highlights the versatility and usefulness of the computer and associated software, as well as the price, is repeated over a period of time. Eventually, a consumer who has not responded to, or been aware of, initial exposures to the advertisement, sees the advantages of a computer of this size and decides to buy one. Repetition has been instrumental in bringing about the organisation of the consumer's perceptions.

In another case, perceptual organisation with respect to the features of a familiar product affects the consumer's decision when comparing it with competing products. For example, a consumer of *Maxwell House* instant coffee will pick out this brand from among other brands on a shelf in a supermarket, without comparing each brand of coffee feature by feature. He or she has an organised overall perception of the product— cost, taste, etc.

People's ability to organise their perception of individual stimuli into a coherent whole can be affected by particular situations, or blocked by the poor presentation or masking of the stimuli themselves. For example, at an annual general meeting of a public company, private shareholders may feel uncomfortable in a large conference room or hall, and be disconcerted by the need to use microphones to make themselves heard. It is easy for people to mishear or misunderstand the information being discussed or reported, and to form an incorrect impression of what is being discussed or reported. When they try to quiz

the senior management they may get to their feet, only to realise that they have not in fact been able to organise their thoughts and questions adequately, and are therefore easily fobbed off with evasions or bland assurances.

There is evidence to suggest that shareholders (particularly private shareholders) have difficulty in organising their perception of annual reports and prefer alternative sources of information because they are written for the user with limited financial ability (Lee & Tweedie, 1977). A further reference to this evidence is made in the next section concerning perceptual interpretation.

Where does the blame lie for the problems experienced by shareholders? According to an academic accountant interested in the problems of language in financial reporting (Lothian, 1978), the fault is in the accounting profession's unwillingness to use straightforward language to express essentially straightforward ideas and techniques. Though he acknowledges the need for technical language in every profession, it must not be a barrier to communicating with the public. Much of the accountancy profession's language is "bogus, existing only to impress the innocent and unwary; much of it is not essential, it cannot be justified on practical grounds and fulfils no purpose, except possibly to act as a kind of masonic glue between different members of the profession." All too frequently, accountants are complacent and pay insufficient attention to the user with limited financial expertise who finds the language at best confusing and at worst incomprehensible.

In a study of the information needs of middle managers in various companies, two researchers found what amounted to a language barrier between the producers and users of company information (Beresford Dew & Gee, 1973). The managers questioned did not like the form in which the information was presented and also noted that it was not in the language of their discipline; they would have preferred language that had meaning to them (i.e. in terms of weights or volume or hours), and not the language of costs and standards of output so dear to the accountants.

Where an apparently simple statement, such as "the accounts have been prepared on the historical cost basis of accounting", appears in published accounts, are users with limited financial expertise expected to know what comprises the historical cost basis and its limitations? Are they expected to know what the alternative bases are? The words "basis" and "convention" are used interchangeably in published accounts, but is the average private shareholder to know that the word "basis" means the same as "convention" when these terms are applied to historical cost accounting? Unlike the average private shareholder, the experienced financial analyst would not find it difficult to grapple with the contents of the annual accounts, though he or she might be critical of the low informational content (Lothian, 1978).

One recognises that there is a danger that financial reports would be of little value to the qualified accountant or experienced user of published accounts if they were over-simplified. One authority asks why accountants should accept the risks entailed in simplification when small shareholders have certain options open to them to deal with the status quo. For example, they can educate themselves in the interpretation of accounts, they can seek expert advice, or invest in mutual funds generally managed by experts. Oversimplification, apart from being prone to unreliability with the prospect of financial loss, would indeed be as great a mis-representation of reality as is the current, generally inadequate attempt by the account-ing profession to present complex concepts, such as inflation (Stamp, 1978).

On the question of complexity of financial reports, it is well to keep in mind a publication aimed at the accounting profession and called *SSAP2: Disclosure of Accounting Policies* (published by the Accounting Standards Committee). It says: "The accounting policies followed for dealing with items which are judged material or critical in determining profit and loss for the year and in stating the financial position should be disclosed by way of notes to the accounts. The explanations should be clear, fair, and as brief as possible." So as to introduce realism to the figures in the accounts "current cost" adjustments were advocated in the Accounting Standards Committee's *Hyde Report*, but companies are not asked to explain to readers of the accounts why these adjustments are required or what effects they are likely to have, although some companies do (Lothian, 1978).

The question of accounting standards is an ongoing debate. The successor to the Accounting Standards Committee is the Accounting Standards Board, headed by Professor Tweedie. In 1993, its main concern is the credibility of accountants and accounting as a specialism. It has therefore published principles offering guidance on all aspects of accounting practice, including disclosure of financial information and various technical accounting issues (see panel overleaf).

Shareholders are not alone in experiencing difficulties in organising perception when at the receiving end of the output of a professional group. A report from the Royal Society, the foremost learned scientific association in the UK, warned scientists to stop baffling the public with jargon and learn to communicate with ordinary people as a matter of urgency. The report goes on to say that the public should be helped to understand the scientific aspects of such issues as acid rain, nuclear power, and matters connected with in vitro fertilisation or animal experimentation, because of the importance of public opinion in influencing the country's decision-making process. Therefore, the language must be simple, free of jargon, and intelligible to the general lay public (Royal Society, 1985).

Recently a working party of the Institute of Chartered Accountants in England and Wales (Financial Reporting Committee), acting on behalf of the Accounting Standards Board, issued guidelines on disclosures in interim, rather than final, accounts. Half-year figures should contain such details as operating cash flow, and financial and investment payments required in FRS1, the cash flow statement which is mandatory in the year-end figures. Companies should provide a summarised balance sheet,. including details of fixed assets, creditors, provisions, capital and reserves. They should include basic profit and loss account information, such as turnover, interest payments and tax, and exceptional items as required by the FRS3, the profit and loss accounting standard (*Financial Times*, 1993).

PERCEPTUAL INTERPRETATION

Having organised our perception, the next step before an appropriate response can be made is interpretation. Perceptual interpretation occurs when we relate stimuli to a cognitive context. The cognitive context consists of various thought processes, ideas, and feelings about experiences and happenings in the world around us, which we have built up based on our own life experiences. It is a primary determinant of perception and response because it embraces such phenomena as our needs, goals, values, education, and training, and accounts for the selectivity in perception that was referred to earlier. As a result, the same objective stimulus or happening could be perceived differently by different people. For example, at the scene of an accident it is not unusual to come across conflicting eye-witness reports. Likewise, some people may think of soya in terms of animal feedstuff, whereas others see it as a cheap inferior meat substitute, and still others as an economical meat substitute for human consumption (Oliver, 1980).

It is now proposed to illustrate perceptual interpretation with reference to safety, financial reports, readability of documents, marketing information, and the role of the computer.

Interpretation of Safety Stimuli

There are times when stimuli are not accurately interpreted and this can have serious implications as far as safety is concerned. Misperception could arise when the individual's information processing capacity cannot cope with the stimuli registered, perhaps because of pressure of work, poor procedures, lack of appropriate experience, or lack of training or skill. An important source of error is the inability to analyse and reconcile conflicting evidence due to a less than satisfactory understanding of the work process in which the person is engaged, and failure to attach the proper meaning to information conveyed by instrumentation designed to facilitate effective performance on the job.

The official report on the accident at the Three Mile Island nuclear power station in the USA in 1979 cited poor control room design and poorly designed display systems as factors that resulted in the operators receiving misleading or incomplete information. The other factors mentioned were inadequate training and misleading and badly presented operating procedures (Health and Safety Executive, 1989).

At the British Association for the Advancement of Science Conference in 1982, a psychologist, having closely scrutinised the events leading up to the London (Moorgate) tube disaster of 1975, in which 42 people lost their lives and 74 were injured, challenged the suicide theory put forward at that time.

The driver of the train failed to slow down as he approached Moorgate Station, and it was suggested that he must have mistaken the stretch of track between Old Street and Moorgate for the distance between Essex Road (the station before Old Street) and Old

Street. The distance between Essex Road and Old Street Stations is longer than the distance between Old Street and Moorgate Stations. On the fateful trip, which was the third trip of that day, the driver may have been in a day-dream and picked up cues marking the approach to Moorgate Station incorrectly. The lights in the approaching tunnel were turned off, and the cue—i.e. the absence of lights—led him to believe that he was travelling between Essex Road and Old Street Stations instead of between Old Street and Moorgate Stations.

Therefore, the need to slow down was less critical, and the driver continued in a state of reduced vigilance for several seconds. Otherwise, he would have been confronted by a barrage of signals on his arrival at Moorgate Station. When the signals suddenly registered, and the driver realised he had made a mistake, this could have induced a state of "freezing". This amounts to an extreme state of involuntary immobility and is compatible with the fact that the driver had his hands on the controls at the moment of impact. Even a man intent on suicide would automatically have raised his hands to protect his face (Reason & Mycielska, 1982).

Reason (1987) throws further light on human error in his classification of errors and mistakes and, in Chapter 7, there is reference to group influences in the context of human error.

In the public inquiry into the circumstances surrounding the collision of two British Rail trains at Colwich Junction in 1986, there was evidence to indicate that the driver of the northbound train had difficulty in perceiving the significance of the red lights. The northbound train passed through the red lights before stopping, resulting in the death of the driver of the southbound train and injury to 52 passengers. The driver of the northbound train in his evidence to the inquiry stated:

As a railwayman with 42 years service I saw a double flashing yellow light which means caution, followed by a red signal. I

was surprised, as I expected the red signal to change to green, but it stayed at red. I am familiar with the use of flashing lights, but I never had formal training, nor have I seen training videos about the lights.

The signalman in his evidence said that he had given clear signals for the northbound train to stop, as the southbound train was coming from the tunnel. A point worth noting in connection with this accident is that the driver of the northbound train was accompanied in the cab by an off-duty trainee driver (*Guardian*, 1986; *Sunday Times*, 1986). Could an animated exchange between them at the critical moment have led to the delayed response to the stimuli in the form of the lights?

These reports highlight the problem of interpretation in perception and the devastating consequences that follow certain types of misperceptions or perceptual errors.

Interpretation of Financial Reports

In evaluating a business, the users of the annual report and accounts of a company emphasise one or more of the following perceptual categories:

- profit;
- growth in sales;
- capital employed;
- liquidity;
- responsibility to employees or customers;
- profile of the directors, and so on.

What sort of issues arise when examining the relevance of perceptual interpretation to accounting? There are a number of issues, but the ones examined here relate to the users of accounting data, the selection of such data, characteristics of accountants, and other issues.

Users of Data
Generally, the users of accounting information consist of the managers and employees of

the company, investors, bankers, other lenders, customers, and suppliers. They all have a common interest in the survival and profitability of the company and each group possesses its own particular needs with respect to the information required in order to monitor the health and prospects of the enterprise. Accounting information has an important contribution to make in filling the "knowledge gap" of the person receiving it (the perceiver). Users of accounting information are not really in a position to produce this information for their own use because, among other things, they do not normally have the knowledge, skill, experience, resources, and time to do so.

Selection of Data

Accountants produce information for the user, and so they are entrusted with the task of selecting data and putting it into a form suitable for communication. Accountants are thus well-placed to influence both what appears in accounting statements or reports and the quality of the information. Like everybody else, accountants can only focus attention on a limited number of factors simultaneously and naturally are subject to limitations when observing economic activity. It is unlikely that they perceive all that should be recorded and reported, and that begs an important question: How much vital information is missed? Also, if too much or too little is reported, how will this affect the user's perception of the business?

Characteristics of Accountants

Because accountants stand to influence the information user's behaviour, it is obviously highly desirable that they display honesty, credibility, and reliability in the pursuit of the compilation and dissemination of accounting data. Credibility is a crucial characteristic and on it rests the standing of the information system and the accountants that operate it. The audit, which reports on an annual or more frequent basis, is one means of establishing credibility for the benefit of the user. It is a formal procedure intended to remove the natural uncertainty and anxiety felt about the credibility of accounting information.

Other Factors

The issues discussed under this heading are the manipulation of accounting data by senior management, the credibility of accounting data, and difficulties encountered in understanding financial accounts.

There is scope for the directors of a company to manipulate reported profits by selecting accounting policies that give them the opportunity to provide results that are in their own interest and not necessarily to the advantage of the shareholder.

Private Shareholders and Accounting Information

In a survey of 301 private shareholders in *Scottish and Newcastle Breweries*, apparently 70% of those questioned doubted their ability to assess potential bankruptcy of the company on the basis of the way in which the information they receive was presented (Lee & Tweedie, 1977).

A mere 39% found accounting information relevant to their investment decisions, though the manner in which company reports were actually used in making investment decisions was not investigated. The term "current assets" had no meaning for 57% of respondents, and only 28% of respondents could give a reasonable definition of depreciation. The chairman's report was read by 52% of respondents, 39% read the profit and loss account thoroughly, but only 29% read the balance sheet thoroughly.

According to 53% of respondents, the reports should be less technical, written in lay person's language and summarised or, alternatively, they should be augmented by a simpler version. Most respondents merely glanced through the annual report, paying greatest attention to the chairman's summary of the main events of the year and his views on the prospects for the future.

Audited accounts may not be regarded as the only source of valid information about a company on which to base decisions about buying and selling shares, or whether or not to grant credit to a business. But the question of credibility for alternative sources of information remains. Perhaps a share tip in the *Sunday Times* or *Observer* may be perceived as having greater validity than one in the *News of The World*.

The interpretation of financial reports and statements appears to be problematic. In an analysis of footnotes that appear at the end of financial statements and reports, it was found that the messages in the footnotes were understood by only a limited number of people of high educational attainment (Smith & Smith, 1971).

The *Scottish and Newcastle Breweries* study reported in the panel identified not only the severe difficulties encountered by private shareholders in interpreting financial statements, but also the fact that available financial information about companies is generally not considered by an important group of financial report users. It also suggests that reporting accountants are failing to communicate with a large number of individuals and that existing financial reports have become documents that are prepared by accountants for accountants. The researchers at the time believed that the communication gap between companies and their private shareholders was so serious that the accountancy profession should give attention to a number of suggestions. The suggestions were that existing statements should be simplified, terms used in financial reports should be defined, reported financial results should be commented on and explained, and alternative systems of reporting which may mean more to the unsophisticated user of financial reports ought to be explored.

Readability

Making something readable and comprehensible is no easy matter. Layout, legibility of type, an interesting approach, absence of difficult words, and ease with which a passage can be read are obviously important factors.

Formulae, such as the Flesch readability formula, have met with a varied reception; they have been welcomed as guides to good writing and attacked vigorously as mechanistic devices used to stifle creativity and debase literature (Flesch, 1949). When the objective is to maximise the communication of simple messages—such as those found in advertisements, cookery books, instruction leaflets, and training manuals—they are said to be appropriate. However, literary or scientific writings may lose aesthetic value or intellectual precision when oversimplified.

The Flesch readability formula yields two measures—a *reading ease* score and a *human interest* score. The reading ease score is based on the average word length in syllables and the average sentence length in words. The human interest score is derived from the percentage of personal words, such as proper nouns and personal pronouns, and the percentage of personal sentences, such as spoken sentences, questions and other remarks directed to the reader, and exclamations. These measures are applied to a continuous 100-word passage.

When financial reports of companies were studied using the Flesch readability formula it was found that over a period of time these reports had become less and less readable and as a consequence less comprehensible (Soper & Dolphin, 1964). When measures of readability, such as the Flesch readability formula, were applied to the Form P1 tax guide, the overall results suggested that the guide is easier to read than *The Times*, but significantly harder than the *Sun* (Lewis & James, 1981).

Interpretation of Marketing Information

In this section brand image, price, and risk are discussed as important factors perceived by product consumers.

Brand Image

It is conceivable that perceived differences between products rest more with the efforts of marketing executives interested in building up a distinctive brand image than in differences in the physical make-up of products. Beer drinkers, who were credited with the ability to perceive differences between certain categories of beer on the basis of such characteristics as bitterness, strength, body, after-taste, foam, aroma, and carbonation, were asked to drink from unlabelled bottles of beer and distinguish differences in taste on a brand basis. None of the drinkers placed their preferred brand ahead of the others, and carbonation was the only characteristic where there was a significant difference noted between the beers tasted. When the same drinkers drank from labelled bottles, there was a marked tendency to express preferences for their favourite brand (Allison & Uhl, 1964).

There are a number of complex and interrelated factors that influence brand perception (Berkman & Gilson, 1978):

- the appeal of the label and packaging;
- the quality of advertising associated with the product;
- the consumer's experience of the product and disposition towards it;
- the product's reliability and the personal satisfaction derived from its use;
- the specification of attractive features of a product; and
- the desirable health or environmental factors associated with the product, such as health foods and lead-free petrol.

With regard to the perception of the quality of a brand, overstatements by a manufacturer of the product's quality tended to produce more favourable evaluations of the product and higher expectations of its performance in the mind of the consumer. When, for example, a tape-recorder did not perform well, the high expectations did not lead to disappointment and low evaluation of the product (Olshavsky & Miller, 1972).

Price

Information on price produces different responses among consumers and perception of price can easily be distorted. Sometimes people think that the higher the price the greater the risk if things do not work out, but at other times it is felt that the higher price produces less risk because of the association of an expensive product with greater reliability and quality. When different types of product were presented at three different price levels—low, medium, and high—it was found that 50% of the people tested chose the high-priced tennis rackets and portable stereo equipment, whereas 60% chose the low-priced toothpaste, coffee, and suntan lotion. The high-priced products were perceived as possessing quality and greater financial risk, as well as being socially conspicuous. The consumers who chose the low-priced products perceived an insignificant relationship between price and quality, felt that the choice of brand had little social meaning, and that the wrong purchase would not be disastrous (Lambert, 1972).

The more conscious consumers are of prices the more likely they are to have a developed price perception. A price that is compatible with quality is important for some consumers. Traditionally, *Marks & Spencer's* stores appeal to consumers who stress competitive prices in relation to quality, whereas *Tesco's* stores used to attract consumers who placed the primary emphasis on price. With the growth of competition among retailers, the situation depicted here is not as clear-cut today.

A strong emphasis on price generally comes from the full-time housewife who has the time to shop around, whereas the consumer who goes out to work full-time may be less discriminating in this respect. However, the situation is likely to be more complex than that. Perceptions of locational convenience, service, quality of the product, cleanliness of the shop, type of customer, and absence of queues at the check-out point are also important considerations. A number of studies point to the importance of price perception in relation to the quality of the product (Monroe, 1973). A high price is sometimes considered desirable for cosmetic products, such as perfumes, which puts them into the luxury class, though this is unlikely in the case of related products such as suntan lotion or hand cream.

Risk

The consumer tries to avoid psychological insecurity, does not like uncertainty, but has to live with the fact that all purchase decisions have unanticipated consequences. Certain purchases are high in psychological and social risks, such as purchases of clothing. Because clothing is so intricately associated with our self-image, and the image others have of us, it is to some extent a risk purchase.

Frequently there are risks attached to purchases, but in order to reduce risks we can engage in information seeking. A particular man may pay £20 for a London theatre seat to see a musical. He was initially attracted to the musical by one particular song from the show that he had already heard and liked. However, he was disappointed to find that a number of other songs from the show did not live up to his expectations. In future he is more likely to establish the quality of the repertoire of songs rather than just one song in order to reduce the risk.

To remove uncertainty about the outcome of a purchase, the following avenues are open to the consumer: speak to somebody with experience of the product; read an analysis of the product (for example, in the *Which* consumer magazine); read a detailed description of the product in an advertising leaflet, brochure, newspaper, or magazine; and finally, if possible, take advantage of a demonstration of the product. Another way to remove uncertainty is to develop loyalty to a brand known to be reliable. Sometimes the consumer is given an opportunity to try a new product without having to take risks. This could arise when the manufacturer distributes a free sample—e.g. a soap or detergent. Where a consumer has a strong brand loyalty, this might be the only way of getting him or her to sample an alternative brand.

Risk perception varies from one individual to another, and whereas some consumers actively engage in information seeking in order to reduce risks, others seem to enjoy the opportunity to sample new products and make purchase decisions with little or no attempt to reduce risk.

Interpretation by Computer

In the age of the computer, the interpretation of stimuli is not confined to human beings. A computerised surveillance system, consisting of a camera linked to a database, which contains the registration numbers of all recently stolen vehicles, has been developed by scientists at the British Home Office (Traini, 1983). The camera scans a stream of traffic and the computer checks the car numbers. When the computer comes across the number of a car reported as stolen, it automatically alerts the nearest police station or patrol. The whole process takes little more than a second. The computer supplies the police with a full description of the vehicle, and even the traffic lane in which it is travelling. The thief who tries to beat the system by using false number plates will not succeed because the computer has access to every valid registration number ever issued. If the camera picks up a number that is not on file, the alarm will be raised automatically. Stealing a car at night is not a way to get round the system because the camera uses infra-red light. However, dirty number plates or bad weather can create a problem. The expected recognition rate is 70%.

PERSON PERCEPTION

As an extension of the previous section on perceptual interpretation, we now turn to social interaction, in the context of the interpretations we place on other people's behaviour. Person perception is concerned with the manner in which we perceive the personal characteristics of others, in particular their current mood and their total personality. Various dynamic cues—such as posture, gesture, body movement, facial expression, direction of gaze, tone of voice, rate, amount and fluency of speech, orientation, and distance—are picked up in the course of social interaction and they influence the interpretations placed on other people's behaviour.

Misinterpretations

Where special factors apply, such as implicit personality, logical error, the "halo effect", stereotyping, and assumed similarity, misinterpretations are likely to arise. These should be borne in mind when we discuss the selection interview and staff appraisal in Chapter 13 and, later in the current chapter, in connection with communication processes generally.

Implicit Personality

Implicit personality theory is part of our "cognitive set"—in essence, a set of concepts and assumptions used to describe, compare, and understand people. We carry around in our heads the personality characteristics that go together. Therefore, we could arrive at a judgement of what constitutes, for example, the typical school bully. The resultant profile is implicit rather than explicit; therefore, we could experience difficulties if requested to articulate or make explicit the characteristics that constitute the profile.

Implicit personality theories vary with the individual, and the differences are greatest between people of different cultures. In one study, a number of children at a summer camp were asked to describe the others in their own words. There were wide variations in the descriptions used by different children to describe any specific child, but it was found that each child used the traits important to his or her central personality theory when describing all the other children (Dornbusch et al., 1965).

In attributing characteristics to people, we can arrive not only at static perceptual judgements (e.g. enduring characteristics such as age, beliefs, ability, manner, and personality traits) but also at dynamic perceptual judgements of characteristics that change, such as specific rather than general actions, moods, emotions, and intentions (Cook, 1971).

The use of implicit personality theories for making judgements of interviewees for jobs was found to be an acceptable mode of operation (Rothstein & Jackson, 1984). A number of issues connected with interviews are dealt with in Chapter 13.

Logical Error

Implicit personality theory could lead us to form hypotheses or assumptions about what traits go together in a person. Almost intuitively we use this interpretation to form an extensive and consistent view of other people when faced with incomplete information. This is often referred to as the logical error, the assumption being that certain traits are always found together.

An experiment was conducted to test this principle. Students on a psychology course were given descriptions of a guest speaker before he addressed the class. He was described to one half of the class as "warm" and to the other half as "cold". The lecturer then entered the class and led a discussion for about 20 minutes. When he left the classroom the students were asked to describe him. The students who were told that he was going to be "cold" were more likely to attribute to him traits such as self-centredness, unsociability, humourlessness, and ruthlessness than were the students who were told he was "warm". The students who thought of the lecturer as "warm" were also more likely to interact with him during the discussion (Kelley, 1950).

What appears to be happening is that changes in person perception arise from varying even minor cues or stimuli, leading to a totally altered view of the person perceived.

Halo Effect

Another tendency, similar to logical error, is called the "halo effect". This materialises when we perceive people in terms of the concepts of good and bad; all good qualities are possessed by the former and all bad qualities by the latter. Somebody given an adverse evaluation at a particular stage of his or her career may find that subsequently, when his or her profile has improved, an evaluation bears the scars of the earlier assessment. Likewise, in an interview situation, if an interviewer perceives in the interviewee a desirable attribute similar to one of his or her own, he or she may make a favourable overall assessment as a result.

The reverse would be true when a deficiency is identified at the outset. This is referred to as the "horns effect". There is evidence to suggest that our perceptions of people are influenced markedly by our initial good/bad evaluations of them. It has been suggested (Osgood, Suci, & Tanenbaum, 1955) that our overall attitudes towards others can to a large extent be determined by our evaluations of them along three dimensions: activity (active *vs* passive); strength (strong *vs* weak); and evaluative (good *vs* bad). The third dimension is considered the most influential.

Stereotyping

Another phenomenon similar to logical error is stereotyping. This is connected with our tendency to label people with traits or qualities that typically belong to a reference group. For example, we may consider a Scot to be mean or thrifty, or a Jew to be a shrewd business person. Therefore we attribute to a member of the race in question the characteristics of the stereotype. Biased perception arises when we rely on the stereotyped image and ignore critical information concerning the individual. Stereotyping does not necessarily result only in the creation of negative images; they can also be positive. Neither is it a wasteful activity, as one study has shown.

Subjects described a student in accordance with a stereotype, as they had no further information on which to work. At a later stage when the subjects became acquainted with the student, they described him for a second time and, on average, it was found that the initial descriptions were the more accurate. A further illustration is highlighted in the panel below.

What we should try to do is examine to what extent our impression of others is based on stereotype alone, so that we can make adjustments accordingly. How do we react when we are presented with information about an individual which contradicts our stereotyped image? The answer can best be presented by reference to a study (Haire & Grunes, 1950) in which two groups of college students were presented with different descriptions of a working man as follows.

- Group I: He works in a factory, reads a newspaper, goes to movies, is of average height, cracks jokes, is intelligent, strong and active.
- Group II: He works in a factory, reads a newspaper, goes to movies, is of average height, cracks jokes, is strong and active.

The only difference in the descriptions given to the groups was that for Group I the man was also described as intelligent. The actual description of the man given by the Group II students in response to the stimulus typified the description of the average American working man—i.e. likeable and well-liked, mildly sociable, healthy, happy, uncomplicated and well adjusted, down to earth, not very intelligent but tries to keep abreast of current trends, interested in sports and engages in simple pleasures. The introduction of the word "intelligent" in Group I had the effect of disturbing group members' set of beliefs about factory workers, but most of them tried to protect their original systems of cognition by the following means:

- Denial of the influential quality of intelligence: "He is intelligent but not so much, because he works in a factory."
- Modification of the influential quality of intelligence: "He is intelligent, but doesn't possess initiative to rise above his group."
- Denial of the fact that he is a shop-floor worker: some students maintained that the man was not a worker by promoting him to a foreman.
- Recognising the incongruity but adhering to the original cognition: "The traits seem to be conflicting but most factory workers I have heard about are not too intelligent."

The four responses serve as a defence of the stereotype. In fact this finding suggests that stereotypes can prevent accurate perception in a number of different ways.

Racial Stereotyping

In connection with stereotyping, a study was carried out in which students, whose attitudes towards black people were known to researchers, rated a number of pictures according to 25 traits. The pictures depicted ten Negroid faces and five Caucasian faces. The Negroid faces reflected a wide range of Negroid features. Ten of the traits described characteristics of the individual which could be determined from the features of the Negroid faces. The other 15 were personality traits widely accepted as part of the stereotype of the black person.

Once a student selected a picture as that of a Negroid face there was a tendency to assign to it the personality traits associated with black people as he or she construed them. The student paid no attention whatsoever to the individual differences depicted in the pictures. The results of the study were the same for students with either a less pronounced or more pronounced prejudice. Stereotyping occurred because of a strong tendency to assign traits to an individual on the basis of group membership, despite the fact that individuals vary in the extent to which they exhibit the characteristics of their group (Secord, Bevan, & Katz, 1956).

Do we recall information that is supportive of a stereotype better than information that challenges the stereotype? As a general principle, the answer would appear to be "yes". The main reason why this is so is that we are naturally reluctant to change a stereotype or belief when faced with evidence challenging it. But there must be times when the person is capable of recalling a lot of information which challenges the stereotype simply because he or she went through the motions initially of examining contradictory evidence in order to test that stereotype. However, there is a conclusion, based on empirical evidence, which suggests that we process information supportive of a stereotype more intensively than information inconsistent with it (Bodenhausen, 1988).

It seems that our desire to stereotype other people springs from our need to create a landscape of our social world in which our identity and the identity of others is expressed in the form of membership of groups. This line of thought is encapsulated in *social identity theory* (Tajfel & Turner, 1985), and has been applied by Ashforth and Mael (1989) to group interactions within organisations. A problem can arise when different groups, originating from various departments, functions, and hierarchical levels, perceive each other in terms of negative stereotypes. This could be done to bolster attempts to establish a group's own superiority, and justify a reduction in collaborative efforts with other groups. This behaviour could be more pronounced when groups have similar standing and where it is felt necessary to emphasise a groups's distinctiveness. Where status disparity between groups is clear-cut, groups of relatively low status may be overly concerned with trying to establish an identity, and they are likely to feel a certain sense of frustration if high-status groups show indifference to them.

Inter-group behaviour of the type just described could hamper understanding and tolerance with negative side effects. But does it have to be like that? The answer would appear to be "no". Where group members feel that differences in status or affluence between their group and other groups are legitimate, less negative stereotyped views could be found (Arnold, Robertson, & Cooper, 1991). Also, it is possible for a compromise to be reached where group members see themselves and members of other groups as having different but complementary abilities or characteristics (Van Knippenberg, 1984). Subscribing to the belief that organisational groups possess complementary strengths is a necessary first step for developing healthy collective effort. Inter-group conflict is discussed in Chapter 9.

As far as the individual prone to stereotyping is concerned, Devine (1989) has a simple recipe: inhibit the in-built prejudiced disposition and adopt an open-minded thinking process. In practice this is unlikely to be an easy transition.

Assumed Similarity

This is the tendency to see others as having characteristics more like our own than is really the case (Feshback & Singer, 1957). We are inclined to project our own emotional or motivational state on to others. In an experiment where subjects were anticipating the receipt of a painful electric shock, it was found that those subjects who reported feeling fear themselves were the subjects who predicted others would be afraid. In other experiments it was shown that those who were asked to predict the behaviour of others usually tended to make predictions more like their own behaviour than the behaviour of the person about whom the prediction was made.

This evidence may be explained as follows: we operate the ego defence mechanism of projection (see Chapter 1) by attributing to others the motives and emotions that we possess but feel uncomfortable about, and we act relying on our own experience with the disadvantage of not knowing the internal state of the other person.

Some of the pitfalls in person perception have been identified in this section, and it should be borne in mind that there are a number of situations in business where employees make unrealistic generalisations about the personal characteristics of those with whom they come into contact.

Impression Management

Impression management refers to the process by which individuals attempt to control the impression others form of them. It would therefore be a mistake to think that the person who is at the receiving end of the perceiver's attention—the target person—is merely passive, while the only person active in the process of person perception is the perceiver. For example, the target person in the employment interview is the job applicant and the perceiver is the interviewer. In reality the target person could be active in trying to create the right impression (impression management) by producing an image of himself or herself for consumption by the perceiver (Schlenker, 1980).

The target person could set out to generate a favourable impression through a variety of tactics, such as being highly selective in describing accomplishments, attempting to project strengths and conceal weaknesses, engaging in ingratiating behaviour, being apologetic, etc.

Of course the target person could study the way perceivers present themselves and use this information to inform their own mode of presentation of the self. Being sensitive to the way others present themselves, and using this insight to adjust one's own self-presentation strategies, can lead to improved performance in jobs where communication with many people is necessary (Gardner & Martinko, 1988). It would be foolish to overestimate the power of impression management. Eventually the charlatan or person lacking credibility may not be able to present the correct image all the time, and is exposed. But it is suggested that if the target person's presentation of the self is congruent with his or her self-concept, the perceivers could be convinced of the substance of the image projected (Swann & Ely, 1984).

Leary and Kowalski (1990) provide a useful review of the literature on impression management (a subject that is also relevant in the context of political behaviour discussed in Chapter 9).

Attribution Theory

A variation of the theories of person perception is attribution. Attribution theory has been proposed to develop explanations of how we judge people differently depending on the meaning we attribute to given behaviour (Kelley, 1971). The theory suggests that as we observe a person's behaviour, we try to establish whether it was caused by internal or external forces. When something is internally caused, it is under the personal control of the individual; if it is externally caused, it is the result of the power of the situation that confronts the individual. This can be illustrated by the use of a simple example. An employee is late for work. One might ask whether the cause is attributed to sleeping in because of being at a late-night party the previous night, or whether it is a matter of being caught up in a traffic queue due to a road accident. If the former were the case, that would be an internal interpretation. If the latter, it would amount to an external interpretation.

The concept of attribution is said to be subjected to the considerations listed in this section, which amount to judging actions in a situational context (Kelley, 1967).

Distinctiveness
This refers to how different the behaviour being observed is from other behaviour. Is it unusual or not? For example, if an employee's attendance record is exemplary, and this is reinforced by an overall satisfactory performance at work, a recent bout of absenteeism could be considered unusual. Therefore, in these circumstances the observer attaches an external attribution to this

behaviour (i.e. the absenteeism is outside the control of the employee). If, however, the absenteeism fits into a general pattern, and is not unusual, an internal attribution will be attached to the behaviour in question (i.e. the employee is personally responsible for his or her behaviour).

Consensus

If everyone who is faced with a similar situation reacts in the same way, we can conclude that the behaviour shows consensus. For example, a particular employee's late arrival at work is observed. When the observer establishes that all those who took the same route to work as the particular employee were also late, possibly because of delays due to bad weather, the conditions necessary for consensus arise. If consensus is high, one is likely to attach an external attribution to the particular employee's lateness. However, if the other employees who travelled the same route arrived at work on time, the consensus factor would be absent and an internal interpretation could be attributed to the particular employee's lateness (i.e. it was his or her fault).

Consistency

The observer of a person's behaviour takes consistency into account. For example, if an employee is responding in the same way over a period of time (e.g. he or she comes in late to work regularly over a six-month period), his or her behaviour is consistent. This could be contrasted with an example of an employee arriving late on the odd occasion. The more consistent the behaviour the more likely the observer is inclined to attribute the behaviour in question to internal causes.

Inference Model

Pennington (1986) suggests that, if we want to know more about considerations influencing an attribution based on internal factors, we should examine the following inference model. This model, put forward by Jones and Davis (1965), acknowledges that we draw inferences backwards from an observed event. This happens all the time with the most trivial of events. Public enquiries following major accidents are a ritualised form of drawing inferences. The model is shown in Fig. 3.19.

The following example illustrates the operation of the inference model. *A* (a manager) perceives the action of *B* (a subordinate) as tantamount to a grossly unsafe act in a factory resulting in an accident. *A*, starting at the left-hand side of the model, asks himself or herself whether *B* had the knowledge and ability to act in a safe manner? If *B* is perceived as having the appropriate knowledge and ability, *A* holds him or her responsible for the consequences of the unsafe act.

Another question could be whether *B's* action is intentional or accidental. If intentional, *B* is more likely to be held responsible for his or her actions, more so than if the action was accidental. A further question could be whether *B's* action is a response to external pressures? For example, the unsafe act occurred when *B* was under enormous pressure to meet a production deadline, at the instigation of a supervisor or chargehand, and involved short cuts at the expense of safety. In such circumstances, attribution of responsi-

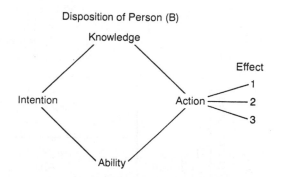

FIG. 3.19. Model for inferring a person's disposition from the action taken. Source: Jones, E.E. and Davis, K.E. (1965). From acts to dispositions: The attribution process in person perception. In L. Berkowitz (Ed.), *Advances in experimental social psychology, Vol. 12.* New York: Academic Press.

bility to *B* for the unsafe act is not as clear-cut as when action is seen as intentional.

Weiner et al.'s Scheme

A scheme to classify factors used to attribute causes to the outcome of a behavioural act (i.e. success or failure) was devised by Weiner et al. (1971). Success or failure are attributable to one of four causes: ability, effort, luck, and task difficulty. In Fig. 3.20 the four causal factors, together with the dimensions of stability and locus of control, are shown.

The dimension of locus of control, discussed in connection with personality in Chapter 1, can be either internal or external. When the outcome of a particular course of action is under the control of the person, it is referred to as internal. When the outcome is due to circumstances beyond the control of the person (e.g. fate), it is referred to as external. The dimension of "stability" refers to whether the four causal factors are fixed or variable over time.

Illustrations of the operation of this scheme, with numerical reference to the model, are as follows:

1. An individual performs a task, and the outcome is successful. The perceiver of the individual's performance attributes effort (something that is within the control of the individual—internal—and can vary over time) to successful performance. If the outcome was unsuccessful, lack of effort could be attributed to this eventuality.

2. An individual performs a task and the outcome is successful. The perceiver of the individual's performance attributes ability (something that is within the control of the individual—internal—and is relatively unchanged over time) to successful performance. However, if an error or mistake occurs, lack of ability is attributed as the cause of the error or mistake. Although ability is fixed in terms of stability, there may be some scope for

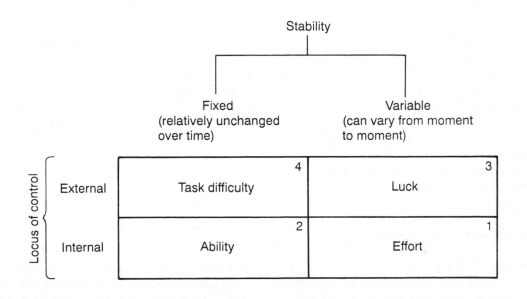

FIG. 3.20. A scheme for attributing causes to outcomes connected with achievement-type tasks. Source: Weiner et al., (1971). *Perceiving the causes of success and failure.* New York: General Learning Press.

improvement, and thereby for avoiding errors of this type in the future.

3. Where an individual exercising reasonable care is struck by falling masonry on a building site, bad luck is the attributed causal factor. Bad luck is perceived as outside the control of the individual and it can vary over time.

4. An individual may fail to perform well because of the difficulty of the task. This is a causal factor external to the individual, and for the time being it is fixed in terms of stability.

It is argued that the way people attribute causes to events can be learned, and distinctive ways of attributing causes emerge (Rotter, 1975). Where people develop in an enabling environment, exercising a fair amount of control over how to influence events in line with their needs, they are likely to attribute more outcomes or events to "internal" considerations. This group can be contrasted with externals—those who believe things happen without their intervention.

An attribution perspective is important because the way an observer perceives an action or behaviour will influence his or her response and provide a foundation for predicting future events. Therefore, it has significance in a motivational sense. (Sometimes, scholars approach attribution theory from the perspective of its important motivational properties, and the subject was therefore discussed alongside the theories of motivation examined in Chapter 2.) Of course there is a danger in attributing causation to particular actions or behaviour, because we may end up basing our attribution on an over-simplification of reality. As a result, there may be bias in the way we judge others.

As a broad generalisation we tend, as observers of social behaviour, to assume that other people's behaviour is internally controlled, but for ourselves we exaggerate the extent to which our own behaviour is externally determined (Nord, 1976). The tendency to take more account of the situation in explaining our own behaviour and less account of the situation in explaining other people's behaviour is sometimes called the "fundamental attribution error". In appraising the performance of an employee in an organisation (discussed in Chapter 13), effort or ability is often referred to when explaining performance with reference to internal factors. But when performance is explained with reference to external factors, often luck or the difficulty of the job is mentioned. Obviously the attitudes of the appraiser to the person being appraised will have an influence on the final outcome (Fletcher, 1984). Prejudice could be a factor in determining whether an event is seen as either internally or externally caused. For example, in one study (Garland & Price, 1977) the successful performance of female managers was attributed by prejudiced male managers to luck and being an easy task (an external interpretation), but in the eyes of unprejudiced male managers it was attributed to skill and hard work (an internal interpretation). Prejudice is discussed in the context of attitudes in Chapter 6.

COMMUNICATION PROCESSES

Perception is an important part of the communication process, and at work you will find different types of communication. That which is officially inspired is often referred to as formal communication, whereas communication that is unofficial, unplanned, and spontaneous is classified as informal. A communication system can transmit information up, down, and sideways within an organisation, and on a one-way or two-way basis. When communication is one-way there is no opportunity to receive a reaction from the receiver of the message. But in two-way communication the receiver of the message can provide a response and is encouraged to do so.

Ways of Communicating

There are many ways to communicate and these will now be examined.

Oral and Written Communication

When we use the spoken word, either face-to-face, in a small group, or over the telephone, the sender of a message has the opportunity to observe feedback, answer questions, and provide additional information by way of clarification. It is often faster than other forms of communication and has the advantage of being personal. For example, the safety practitioner may use the spoken word when he or she feels it necessary to impress upon a factory supervisor the absolute necessity of maintaining permanent machine guards around dangerous machinery where a certain laxity with regard to their use has developed. A disadvantage of the spoken word is the absence of a written record of the dialogue, though conversations can, of course, be taped.

A formal meeting usually consists of both the spoken and written word. The written component is the agenda, the minutes of the last meeting, and papers distributed previously or on the day. The meeting itself relies substantially on the spoken word. A meeting of a safety committee is an example of a forum to exchange information on health and safety matters, and decide on appropriate action. In certain meetings, visual aids could be used to emphasise technical issues. Apart from the use of the written word at meetings, a letter, memorandum, or report allows the communicator to organise his or her thoughts carefully, and provides a written record of happenings and transactions for future reference.

Although written communication is an impersonal process, it is generally possible to provide more information to the receiver by this means than through the spoken word. Written communication is somewhat more time-consuming than the spoken word, and it provides little opportunity for the sender to observe feedback and to provide clarification. Written communication amounts to a one-way communication system with a delayed response.

Non-verbal Communication

This covers all aspects of communication that are not expressed orally or in writing. It includes body movements, the emphasis and intonations we put on words, facial expressions, and the physical distance between the sender and receiver of a message. Non-verbal body language—e.g. raising an eyebrow for disbelief, shrugging our shoulders for indifference, winking an eye for intimacy, touching our forehead for forgetfulness—conveys meaning and constitutes an important facet of human communication.

Body language, coupled with verbal communication, can often give fuller meaning to the message of the sender, but equally the interaction between the two can be a source of confusion (Robbins, 1991). With the spoken word, a soft, smooth tone creates a different meaning from an *intonation* that is harsh with a strong emphasis placed on the last word.

Facial expression—e.g. an expressionless face, or a smiling face—also conveys meaning. On the basis of our perception we may conclude that a person is indifferent, sad, or happy. When coupled with intonations, facial expressions can exhibit fear, arrogance, aggressiveness, shyness, and so on.

Physical proximity or distance between people also conveys meaning. Our liking or disliking for a person may dictate physical proximity. Generally we prefer a shorter distance between ourselves and other people in intimate interpersonal relationships, than in other types of interpersonal relationships. However, this principle could vary depending on cultural influences. It is suggested that in casual interpersonal relationships, Greeks are likely to stand closest to the other person,

Scots furthest away, and Americans somewhere in between (Feldman, 1971). So if somebody stands too close or too far away from the other person, after taking into account cultural preferences, unease and difficulties in social encounters could arise.

Other examples of body language include:

- a handshake denoting a friendly greeting or farewell;
- eye contact indicating a willingness to continue a communication episode;
- sitting on the edge of a chair may convey a nervous disposition;
- sitting back with arms folded could indicate an unwillingness to continue with the dialogue; and
- the individual at a meeting constantly looking at his or her wristwatch might be expressing a preference to disengage mentally and to be "elsewhere".

Apart from body language, environmental factors such as a spacious office with quality carpeting and furniture conveys the impression to a visitor that the occupant of the office is likely to be a senior executive.

New Technology

The application of new technology to the communication of information includes computerised information processing systems, new forms of telecommunications systems, and a combination of the two. It is now possible for executives to send and receive letters using the computer. Also, the transmission of data between computers over long distances is a live issue. A growing trend is the office that contains a facsimile machine, a copier, and personal computers, all linked to create a single, integrated system, possibly attached as well to databases and electronic mail systems. These developments are often referred to as the "electronic office", whereby numerous categories of employees are plugged into a communication network that uses a combination of computerised data storage, retrieval, and transmission systems.

Moorhead and Griffin (1992) give examples of the computer-integrated organisation. For instance, in one company the sales, marketing, finance, distribution, and manufacturing functions exchange operating information continuously and rapidly through computers. A designer sends product specifications directly to those with responsibility for the machines on the factory floor, and accountants can receive on-line information about sales, purchases, and prices instantaneously. The challenge for the future is the integration of the various technologies, and ensuring that social structures and power relationships in organisations are congruent with the new electronic office systems. (New technology and organisation is discussed in Chapter 10, and new technology and job design in Chapter 2.)

Communication Networks

Within the organisation one finds networks of communication which are, in essence, systems of information exchange (small group communication networks are discussed in Chapter 7). The organisational communication networks that will be discussed here are not the same as the lines of communication found on an organisation chart. The reason for operating outside the formal hierarchical system of communication is that employees find it easier to perform their jobs, or to obtain necessary information, by going directly to employees in other departments. The roles and functions that are crucial for the proper functioning of the communication network and the organisation as a whole are as follows (Pace, 1983):

- *Gatekeeper:* This person occupies a strategic position in the network enabling him or her to control information moving in either direction through a particular communication line. The gatekeeper could be somebody who communicates most frequently with, say, the chief executive, even though he or she could be two levels removed from the latter.

- *Liaison*: This person acts as a bridge between groups by promoting closer relationships between them and ensuring that the necessary level of information to integrate group activities is available.
- *Cosmopolite*: This person acts as a link between the organisation and its external environment, and has a lot of contact with sources outside the organisation. He or she can be a valuable source of information on outside developments affecting the material well-being of the organisation. The cosmopolite could also be an opinion leader within the group.
- *Isolate*: This person tends to work alone, and communicates little with others.
- *Isolated Dyad*: Two people who interact with each other, but communicate little with others.

It is beneficial to develop an understanding of these roles in order to assist managers and subordinates to facilitate communication, to capitalise on the strengths and orientations of various individuals, and to foster much needed integration within the organisational system.

A well-known informal organisational communication network is called the "grapevine" (and can be an important aspect of informal organisation discussed in Chapter 10). It amounts to a network of relationships between people that arises in a spontaneous way, and can be used to supplement formal communication channels. The grapevine relies heavily on word of mouth, and opportunity to communicate (e.g. being in the same building) is a prime consideration.

A number of factors give rise to the formation of grapevines, such as the following (Davis, 1976):

- There is a lack of information through the formal communication channels.
- A state of insecurity activates people to communicate with each other and build a bulwark against likely threats.
- Conflicts and tensions, often between superiors and subordinates, can give rise to people talking about the issues informally.
- Where there is distrust and dislike between people, the protagonists will try to gain advantage by circulating informally negative information about their opponents.
- Where there is a need to spread new information quickly, informal communication channels will often be used.

The grapevine has the capacity to transmit rumour and gossip, as well as authentic information. Some argue that it is generally the carrier of incomplete and inaccurate information that creates negative side-effects (such as dissatisfaction and anxiety), whereas others say that one cannot discount its reliability on all occasions.

The proponents of the beneficial features of the grapevine are likely to put forward the following case (Zaremba, 1988):

- The grapevine is an emotional safety valve for the release of frustration in conditions where an individual's anger cannot be realistically directed at an authority figure.
- The grapevine provides groups with a feeling of security and belonging, which in turn fosters satisfaction and group stability.
- The grapevine can raise morale when it transmits positive information about the organisation.
- The grapevine's existence is a constant reminder to managers to be professional in their managerial role, because ineptitude and inefficiency can be highlighted by the informal network.
- The grapevine can act as a feedback mechanism, thereby providing managers with knowledge on how employees generally perceive problems.

Communication as Transactions

Transactional analysis, made popular by Berne (1964) and Harris (1969), is a theory or concept of personality (in the psychotherapy tradition) which can be used to analyse interpersonal communication. Personality can be viewed as having three major parts or ego states—the parent, the adult and the child. The ego states appear to resemble the id, ego, and super-ego referred to in Chapter 1. However, transactional analysis is concerned with the changing interactive aspects of the ego states in social intercourse.

An objective of transactional analysis training programmes is to help people relate better, ease tension, and accomplish things. A well-balanced person travels from one ego state to another in the light of the situational demands. The three ego states are defined as follows.

The Parent

A person is in the "parent" state when he or she is influenced heavily by childhood perceptions of the behaviour of parents or other important role models. This ego state is judgemental and moralistic in a pronounced way, and a person locked into this state displays characteristics such as being distant, dogmatic, self-righteous, and over-protective; but there are also times when it can be a nurturing mode. There may be certain cues to denote that the person is acting as a "parent"—e.g. shaking the finger to indicate displeasure, specific reference to rules and customs, and adherence to successful past strategies when offering guidance and help.

The Adult

A person is in the "adult" state when he or she is a seeker and processor of information. This ego state is characterised by rational analysis based on the accumulation of sound evidence, and the adult's behaviour reflects a high level of objectivity in discussions. A major objective of transactional analysis is to put the adult in the driving seat, in control of the parent and

child. Experiences in adolescence and adulthood are strong influences in the formation of the adult.

The Child

This ego state is characterised by needs, wants, and feelings associated with childhood, particularly from the earliest days of infancy to age five. The characteristics of the "child" ego state are creativity, conformity, immaturity, dependence, anxiety, fear, and hate. Evidence to indicate that the person is in the child state could consist of suggestions that the person is not logical in his or her position or approach, is intent on immediate gratification of impulses, and displays temper tantrums and attention-seeking behaviour.

Analysis of Transactions

If one wants to apply transactional analysis to interpersonal communication, a starting point is to identify the transactions going on between the different ego states. By recognising the ego states of two people engaged in a transaction, one is well placed to assist people to communicate and interact more effectively. Transactions can be categorised as complementary or non-complementary (crossed).

Complementary transactions can lead to effective interaction, positive strokes (e.g. praise and displays of affection), or ego enhancing compliments. By contrast, crossed transactions can lead to ineffective inter-action, negative strokes (e.g. criticism and harsh words), and ego belittling remarks.

The giving and receiving of strokes is associated with game playing in organisations. Complementary and crossed transactions are shown in Fig. 3.21. Complementary transactions are effective because both individuals in the exchange obtain the positive strokes they desire. Cross transactions lead to negative strokes and result in ineffective transactions between people, probably exemplified by interpersonal hostility and conflict.

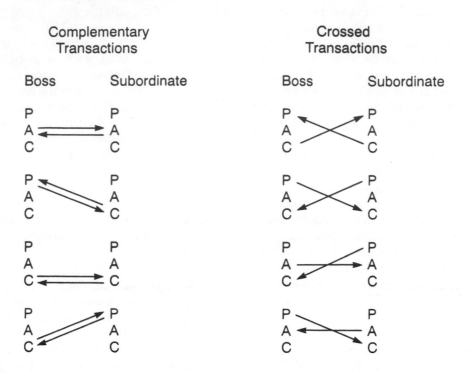

FIG. 3.21. Examples of complementary and crossed transactions. **Key:** P = parent; A = adult; and C = child. Source: Adapted from Dubrin, A.J. (1990). *Effective business psychology* (third edition). New York: Prentice-Hall.

It is often said that "parent–child" dialogue is functional in conditions where authority distinctions exist between two people in organisations. Some would argue that in problem-solving situations within organisations, a productive dialogue could take place between two people in the adult ego state.

An ulterior transaction happens when there is a failure of communication due to disguising the real meaning of the message—e.g. the sender of the message does not mean what he or she says. As a result, the receiver of the message is not sure whether the response should be to what is said or to its hidden meaning. Also, the body language of the speaker who initiates the communication seems to be at variance with the spoken word, leaving the receiver of the message unsure about its true meaning.

Another aspect of transactional analysis likely to affect interpersonal communication is the concept of "OK" or "Not OK". Unlike the concepts of the parent, adult, and child, the term OK means the same thing as it does in everyday language. Where a person is perceived as OK, the perceiver considers his or her views seriously. He or she is viewed as competent with an internal locus of control orientation (see Chapter 1). A person perceived as "Not OK" would possess the opposite characteristics, having an external locus of control with views not seriously entertained by the perceiver.

Transactional analysis has a lot of intuitive appeal, and is used by some organisations. However, there is a dearth of empirical evidence on its validity (Bowen & Rath, 1978).

Senz.

"WELL! IT'S EVANS IN ACCOUNTS,...AGAIN!.."

Communication Cycle

The communication cycle is depicted in Fig. 3.22. The message is transmitted to the receiver by word symbols, body postures, tone of voice, fluctuations in the voice, and various gestures. Other manifestations of non-verbal communication are: appearance; dress; facial expression; mannerisms; physical proximity; expression in the eyes; and attentiveness. Many of the senses are involved in sending and receiving messages

As can be seen in Fig. 3.22, a number of steps are involved in the communication process:

1. Have a clear idea of what you want to convey in your message.
2. Encode the communication by putting the ideas into a suitable form. Choose the proper words to convey the idea you have in mind, preferably using the language of the receiver.
3. Choose the most appropriate communication medium to transmit the message. For oral communication, you may ask yourself, "Shall I convey information by calling a meeting or, alternatively, by using the telephone?" When using the written word, the communication could take the form of a memorandum, a letter, a report, a telex, or some form of electronic transmission. Sometimes we build redundancy into the transmission process by providing the same information in more than one form. In a specific safety sense, the word "danger" can be flashed on a screen and at the same time an audible signal denoting danger can be used.
4. Make sure the message gets to the receiver, though the receiver should take it upon him or herself to listen to, or take note of, the message.
5. The communication should be decoded in such a way that the intended meaning is actually conveyed.
6. If the receiver is to take a specific course of action after receiving the message, check that this is done. Of course, the receiver may not be required to take positive action, other than to store the information for future use.
7. Elicit feedback from the receiver.

Understanding is a critical factor in the communication process, and it is often said that people are only 25% efficient when they are engaged in listening and remembering. Vital information with respect to important matters should be repeated at intervals.

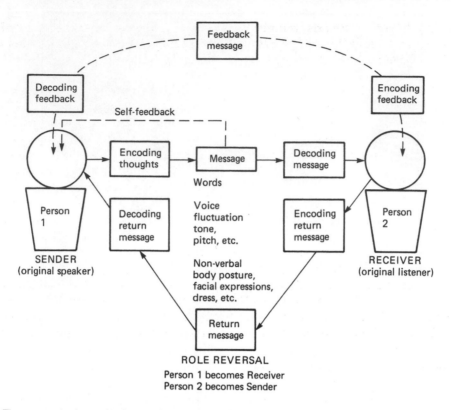

FIG. 3.22. The communication cycle. Source: Curtis, J.D. and Detert, R.A. (1981). *How to relax—a holistic approach to stress management.* Mountain View, CA.: Mayfield Publishing. Used by permission.

FIDO

The FIDO principle is worth noting; this states that learning through communication is enhanced by:

- *Frequency*: the more often a message is repeated, the more likely it is to be remembered.
- *Intensity*: the more vivid, enthusiastic, personalised and positive a communication is, the better it will be received and remembered.
- *Duration*: short, pointed messages are more likely to get the attention, understanding, and retention needed for good communication.
- *Over again*: learning is enhanced by spaced and frequent repetition; messages are imprinted in the mind bit by bit.

Communication Barriers

A number of pitfalls can hinder effective communication.

Inability to Think Clearly.   Communicators may be unable to think clearly about what they want to say.

Encoding Difficulties.   Though the communicator may have good ideas, he or she has difficulty in encoding the message properly—i.e. in putting ideas into a suitable form of words. Words mean different things to different people. Jargon can sometimes help communication, but there are occasions when it can hinder. "Politically correct" jargon, for example, is obviously understood by those who coined it, but for others its meaning may not be as clear as the words it replaces. Examples are: *Visually impaired* (blind);

Vertically   challenged   (dwarfs / midgets); *Physically challenged* (disabled / handicapped); *Senior* (old); *Differently-sized* (overweight). There has been some resistance to the acceptance and use of "politically correct" language.

Another encoding difficulty arises when communicators are unable to put themselves into the position of receivers, and, as a result, write or talk as if they are communicating only with themselves.

"Noise".   Transmission of the message can be interrupted by "noise". There are two categories of noise, one physical and the other psychological. Physical noise could be interference on a telephone line or in a television receiver. It is comparatively easy to recognise and eliminate. Psychological noise is different and is more difficult to cope with. It consists of biases, attitudes, and beliefs held by people in the communication process, and can block the transmission of ideas.

Information overload could also lead to noise. With regard to the design of displays, one should endeavour not to undermine the worker's reliability by providing too much information or providing information that cannot conveniently, easily, and accurately be used; in such circumstances the excessive information has become noise. Overload arises because of the temptation to include certain items on the basis of convenience, or when we act in the belief that there is a remote chance that the worker may find use for the information sometime.

Selectivity.   This refers to selectivity in the reception, interpretation, and retention of information. For instance, a manager receives a report on many facets of the company's operations, including advice on health and safety at work. This particular manager happens to be very interested in financial issues and ignores the safety considerations. Because of the manager's financial orientation, he or she may be adept at seeing the financial implications of various operational issues, but turns a blind eye to critical safety

matters. Likewise, he or she tends to be better at remembering the financial rather than the safety implications.

The "Bruised Ego".   The receiver of the message can be too quick to jump to conclusions or becomes defensive. As a result, the speaker may be offended by an unjustified interruption or a premature assessment of what he or she has reputedly said, and the quality of the delivery may be affected accordingly. If the ego of the receiver is bruised by what the speaker said, feelings of insecurity, inferiority, or hurt can develop. The receiver adopts a defensive stance, and may strike back, even though the speaker is offering a legitimate viewpoint or a constructive criticism. This can undermine the quality of the communication process. (In the earlier section on interpersonal processes, stereotyping and the halo effect were found to distort interpersonal perception.)

Environmental Factors.   An unsuitable environment acts as an impediment to good communication. A noisy factory setting is not the best place for the safety practitioner to give serious advice on health and safety matters to a chargehand or supervisor with only lukewarm interest in such advice.

Incomplete Feedback.   A misinterpretation by the speaker of feedback from the receiver, or no perceptible reaction from the receiver, represent communication barriers. In either case, the sender of the message is denied insight into the position of the receiver with regard to a particular communication.

Rumour.   Gaps in the formal communication system can be filled by rumour—and this is normally associated with the grapevine. The grapevine, however, which is part of the informal communication network discussed earlier, often feeds accurate information into the system. By definition, rumour is false information, and it frequently arises because people are kept in the dark about important matters.

Communication Problems

Perceptual problems are frequently encountered in organisations; these are often referred to as "communication problems":

- Communication within one function of a business—e.g. the finance department—is likely to be better than between groups drawn from, say, marketing and finance departments.
- Likewise, communication between people within a geographical location is usually better than between groups in different locations.
- As regards staff/line relationships (discussed in Chapter 10), sometimes we find that communication between the "staff specialist" on, say, product planning, and the line manager—e.g. the production manager—leaves much to be desired. This problem is often aggravated by a difference of outlook or orientation.
- The relationship between superiors and subordinates within the hierarchy of organisations can be (as highlighted in the studies that follow) another source of perceptual problems.

In a study of 58 pairs of managers, who were asked various questions about the duties of subordinates, only about half were able to agree on their duties (Maier et al., 1961). When it came to questions on the difficulties or obstacles that interfere with the performance of subordinates, only 8% of the pairs of managers were in agreement on more than half the topics discussed. In this study, therefore, it seems that either subordinates were not fully aware of what their superiors expected of them, or superiors did not know what work the subordinates were required to do. Whatever the cause, it would be useful to know more about the quality of communication that exists between the two with regard to specifying the requirements of the job of the subordinate. Obviously part of the problem arises from authority and status differences within organisations which inhibit individuals from communicating freely with their superiors about important job matters.

In a study of a large public utility, top management and foremen were asked to express their ideas on how free the foremen felt to discuss important aspects of their jobs with top management. About 90% of top management felt that foremen were very free to discuss such issues with them, but only 67% of the foremen felt this to be so.

The same question was asked of foremen and workers, and this time about 85% of foremen felt that the workers were very free to discuss important issues with them, but only 51% of the workers believed this to be so. (Perhaps superiors are more likely than subordinates to believe in high quality communication processes.)

It was also found that there were marked differences in perception between superiors and subordinates when it came to assessing the nature of consultation. For example, 70% of the top managers believed they almost always got their subordinates' ideas and opinions in problem-solving sessions on the job, but only 52% of foremen believed this to be so. Similarly, 73% of the foremen believed that they almost always got their subordinates' ideas and opinions in problem-solving sessions on the job, but only 16% of the workers believed this to be so (Likert, 1961).

In a survey of the opinions of full-time or part-time safety managers, together with a cross-section of shopfloor workers in 26 factories in the London area (Barrett & James, 1981), it was concluded that there were problems of communication with respect to safety. There was profound ignorance among employees about safety policy, but those who were aware of safety policy obtained details of it from a notice-board or from a personal copy of the document. Few employees knew about the Health and Safety at Work Act 1974, except that they were aware of the fact that an individual employee could incur criminal liability.

There was surprising ignorance of the operation of safety committees, and there were problems with the reporting of hazards. In fact, many employees were not very conversant with the business conducted in safety committees, though they were aware of the existence of them. Likewise, there were problems with reporting procedures for accidents, and there appeared to be little knowledge of first aid facilities. Apparently trade unions were a rather more important source of information on the Health and Safety at Work Act than management, though in one company management was a significantly more important source than trade unions.

Improving Communication

The response of the *General Motors Corporation* to criticism of the formality of its top-down communication system in the mid-1980s was to devise a large-scale communication improvement programme. This included public speaking workshops for employees, improving the numerous publications it circulated, providing videotapes of management meetings for employees, and using satellite links between the company's headquarters and the various operational sites to create two-way conversations around the world (Moorhead and Griffin, 1992).

Team Briefing
"Team briefing", a method used in the UK and pioneered by the Industrial Society, involves face-to-face communication in an organisational group setting. It is a two-way communication process whereby the manager or leader of the group provides up-to-date information to group members, and the latter are given the opportunity to ask questions.

The basic rationale for this process is to improve communication and to create a climate for more positive attitudes and employee involvement. This would be particularly appropriate at a time of organisa-

tional change when the reasons for the change can be stated and people can be given the opportunity to ask questions.

Team briefing can increase the standing of the supervisor or foreman as a provider of information, and creates a participative forum capable of confronting industrial strife, although (in the absence of good labour relations) it could be viewed by trade unions as a way of undermining their influence (Marchington, 1987).

The information transmitted should be relevant to the recipients and cover work-related issues such as corporate objectives, sales volume, and productivity, and how these impact on employees.

Team briefing starts at the apex of an organisation, and takes place at a maximum of four levels. The first could be a meeting of senior executives, and the notes from this meeting could be passed down to the next organisational level, with the addition of any information of particular significance at this level. This pattern is repeated until the stage is reached where the line manager or supervisor briefs the shopfloor workers.

Because the success of team briefing depends on the skill of the briefer, it is important that he or she is properly trained. Team briefing meetings are likely to be arranged well in advance, at intervals ranging from fortnightly to quarterly according to need. They should be seen as complementing communication systems generally within the organisation.

Expectations approach
A remedy for misperceptions encountered by managers and others in organisations, based on research carried out at Durham University, is a technique known as the "expectations approach" (Machin, 1980). It is claimed that it is operationally possible to audit the quality of communication among senior and middle management in any organisation and, where poor interpersonal communication is found, this is the starting point for improving it.

For a communication auditing system to be useful an effective audit is required of what Manager X says he or she wants from Manager Y, and of what Manager Y thinks Manager X wants from him or her. The expectations approach to auditing communication systems obtains information in the simplest way possible. Each manager in the group whose communication is to be audited goes through the following procedures:

- The manager writes down the expectations that he or she holds of each member of the group, identifying the various things others are expected to do (e.g. to provide essential information for inclusion in a management report).
- The manager then writes down the expectations that he or she perceives each member of the group has of the manager, identifying the various things others expect him or her to do (e.g. to keep them informed of critical happenings).

After writing down the various expectations, they can be processed and analysed on a computer. Participating managers receive a communication audit report that sets out the expectations held of them. This technique enables managers to identify rapidly where communication channels have broken down. The report gives no indication as to whether or not the expressed expectations are organisationally appropriate, but it does highlight the need to analyse whether or not communication should exist between the two managers concerned.

The expectations approach places the responsibility for auditing a manager's communication on the individual manager as opposed to the manager's superior or some other person. This is said to be advantageous for a number of reasons. After all, managers are immersed in the detailed content of the job, so their views about the job are crucial; they are well placed to judge how effective the other person's expectation of themselves are;

they are obviously concerned about how desirable and reasonable the expectations are; and they have a vested interest in the accuracy of the process.

Important Communication Skills

In any discussion of communications nowadays, the importance of active listening and the provision of feedback is underlined. In addition, the development of skills in listening and in the provision of feedback is advocated (Robbins, 1989). The skills listed in this section are important in the context of interpersonal perception. Also, they are critical for the efficient execution of certain human resource practices—e.g. selection and appraisal interviews examined in Chapter 13, and organisational development strategies discussed in Chapter 12.

Active Listening

Hearing is not the same thing as listening. While hearing amounts to registering stimuli based on sound, listening entails paying attention to what we hear, interpreting, and remembering the stimuli. Effective listening is an active rather than a passive process, whereby the listener is concentrating intensely on the communication and is keen to understand fully what the speaker is trying to get across. Of course it helps if the speaker is putting across his or her message in a clear and interesting way. Apart from intense concentration, other requirements for active listening are:

- Empathising with the speaker so that you try to see the subject or issue from his or her point of view, thus increasing the likelihood that the message put across by the speaker is interpreted in the way he or she intended.
- Accepting what is said, and reserving judgement on the content of the message until the speaker has finished. Otherwise the listener could be distracted from the content of the message if he or she were to

concentrate unduly on points of disagreement.

- Taking responsibility for getting the full picture, which means doing whatever is necessary to get the total intended meaning from the information that the speaker puts across. This entails not only absorbing content, but also listening for feelings, and asking questions to facilitate understanding.

It is claimed that effective listeners adopt the following patterns of behaviour (Robbins, 1989);

1. Establish eye contact. The absence of eye contact could signify lack of interest.
2. Show an interest in what has been said by a nod of the head and an appropriate facial expression. Together with eye contact, these responses convey to the speaker that the listener is interested in what has been said.
3. Avoid distracting actions or gestures. Distracting actions or gestures could include excessive glances at your watch and being fidgety. This could convey to the speaker that your thoughts are elsewhere and that disinterest or boredom has gripped the listener.
4. Ask questions. The perceptive listener seeks clarification of what has been said in order to aid understanding. Asking pertinent questions conveys to the speaker that the listener is tuned in to the communication.
5. Paraphrase. This amounts to a restatement by the listener of what the speaker has said, using his or her own words. Then the listener seeks verification of his or her interpretation of what has been said. Where paraphrasing bears a close relationship to what the speaker said, this could indicate careful listening.
6. Avoid interrupting the speaker. The speaker should be given the opportunity to develop his or her line of thought before an interruption takes place.

7. Do not overtalk. Some people may feel uncomfortable having to sit through a talk without having the opportunity to speak. However, where it is possible to ask questions and contribute to the debate, the good listener recognises that you cannot talk and listen at the same time, and refrains from overtalking.
8. Make smooth transitions between the roles of speaker and listener. In circumstances where there is one-way communication from speaker to listener (as with a formal lecture), generally conditions are conducive to stretches of uninterrupted listening. But in many situations at work, such as meetings, a person moves from the role of speaker to listener on a regular basis. The effective listener has to be adept at making a smooth transition between speaker and listener, and vice versa.

Feedback Skills

Managers are continually faced with providing both positive and negative feedback on various aspects of subordinates' performance. For obvious reasons, the provision of positive feedback is a function a manager could warmly embrace. The same cannot be said of the provision of negative feedback. The average manager could feel uncomfortable in the role of conveyor of bad news: he or she may fear offending the subordinate or does not relish the prospect of coping with a subordinate's defensiveness. It is, therefore, not surprising to find that the provision of negative feedback is frequently avoided or delayed, or when provided it is distorted (Fisher, 1979).

But managers have to face up to their responsibility for the provision of negative feedback, bearing in mind the potential resistance to it and the circumstances in which it is most likely to be accepted. It is suggested that negative feedback is most likely to be accepted if it is objective—i.e. supported by hard data—and originates from a person with high status and credibility in the organisation (Halperin et al., 1976). However, negative feedback that is given by experienced and respected managers of appropriate status can err on the side of subjectivity and still be accepted by subordinates.

The following suggestions have been made with a view to increasing the effectiveness of the feedback process (Robbins, 1991).

Focus on specific behaviours. Avoid making vague statements about performance; instead focus on a specific incident, informing the recipient of the reasons for the complimentary or critical remarks.

Keep feedback impersonal. This is particularly important in the case of negative feedback. Criticism should be directed at behaviour related to the aspect of the job the supervisor criticises (e.g. recent unsatisfactory delays in the processing of invoices). Refrain from criticism of a personal nature when commenting on less than satisfactory job performance or other job-related behaviour. The reason for this suggestion is that such action could provoke an emotional response from the recipient of the feedback and deflect attention from the issue of sub-standard performance or other inappropriate job-related behaviour.

Keep feedback goal-oriented. This is done by making sure that the feedback is directed at matters connected with the achievement of the recipients' goals. Using a feedback session, in the case of negative feedback to unleash a variety of criticisms, many of which are not directly related to the recipient's inappropriate behaviour currently under review, is a sure way of undermining the credibility and influence of feedback sessions.

Short time intervals. Ensure that the time interval between the relevant behaviour and the provision of feedback related to that behaviour is short. For example, a person is more likely to take suggested action to rectify a personal deficiency shortly after the mistake or malfunctioning occurred rather than after a formal performance appraisal session many months later. Feedback related to a fresh rather than a stale incident is likely to have greater effect. However, one should ensure that rapid feedback is complete and not half-baked because of an urgency to get it to the recipient quickly.

Ensure understanding. This can be fostered by a clear and concise exposition of the feedback and, if necessary, requiring the recipient to paraphrase its content.

Ensure control. Direct the negative feedback towards behaviour over which the recipient has control. Therefore, the recipient must be in a position to do something about the alleged deficiency. If output falls below target because of a failure of a supplier to supply raw materials, the poor output figures can hardly be the direct responsibility of the production manager. Where negative feedback relates to an event that is under the control of the recipient, an enlightened approach would be to offer guidance, where necessary, to improve the situation or solve the problem. This would also take some of the bite out of the criticism.

SUMMARY: PERCEPTION AND COMMUNICATION

- The basic processes in perception are reception of stimulus, attention, organisation, interpretation, and response. Stimuli are picked up by the senses, which consist of vision, hearing, smell, taste, touch, warmth, cold, pain, kinaesthesis, and vestibular.

- Safety practitioners, advertisers, producers of accounting information, and others recognise the importance of attracting the attention of the perceiver, although this is not always easy. In this context, absolute and differential thresholds are crucial. When they fluctuate this is known as sensory adaptation. The internal state of perceivers is something else to consider when trying to attract their attention.

- Before interpreting the information contained in a stimulus, it has to be organised. The Gestalt laws of organisation govern the organisation of perception. Marketing executives and accountants are naturally concerned with the question of grouping stimuli into an organised whole, but sometimes problems arise. The individual adheres to constancy when organising stimuli, though this can be undermined by illusions. Illusions were discussed with reference to stationary and moving stimuli.

- Perceptual interpretation follows organisation, and various cognitive aspects of our total personality are activated so that meaning can be ascribed to the information at our disposal. The interpretation of safety signals, published accounts, and tax forms can present some difficulties. The perception of a brand, the price of a product, and the risks attached to a purchase are important considerations for the consumer. The interpretation of stimuli by a computerised surveillance system is a feature of the era of new technology.

- In person perception the following factors feature in a prominent way: implicit personality; logical error; the halo effect; stereotyping; and assumed similarity. Additional factors are the concepts of impression management and attribution.

- Perceptual issues in organisations were explored through the medium of communication processes. These were discussed with reference to the following: formal and informal communication; oral and written communication; non-verbal communication; new technology; communication networks; transactional analysis; the communication cycle; barriers and problems with communication; and ways of improving communication. Finally, two important communication skills—active listening and the provision of feedback—were examined.

QUESTIONS

1. What steps can the marketing executive, accountant, and safety practitioner take to attract the attention of the target audience?
2. What significance is attached to the organisation of perception from a business perspective?
3. Distinguish between absolute and differential thresholds using examples from any business function.
4. What do we mean by sensory adaptation? Assess its significance in any business context.
5. Discuss the role of subliminal perception in a marketing context.
6. Why is it necessary to consider the disposition of the perceiver in the process of perception?
7. What do we mean by the concept of illusions in the field of perception? Illustrate your answer with suitable examples.
8. In what way does the private shareholder experience difficulties in interpreting financial reports?
9. What significance does the consumer attach to the brand image and price of a product, and the risk associated with it, before making a purchase?
10. Examine some adverse repercussions likely to arise from perceptual errors or misperceptions.
11. What insights derived from interpersonal perception should a sales representative, who is concerned with improving his or her social or communication skills, take into account?

12. What is the significance of stereotyping in person perception?
13. Define communication skills applicable to listening and feedback.
14. Explain what is meant by (a) attribution theory and (b) impression management.
15. Comment on (a) the grapevine, (b) non-verbal communication, and (c) the role of new technology in communication.
16. Examine typical communication problems that arise in organisations and suggest ways and means of solving them.

REFERENCES

Allison, R.I. & Uhl, K.P. (1964). Influence of beer brand identification on taste perception. *Journal of Marketing Research, 1,* August, 80–85.

Anastasi, A. (1979). *Fields of applied psychology* (second edition). New York: McGraw-Hill.

Arnold, J., Robertson, I.T., & Cooper, C.L. (1991). *Work psychology: Understanding human behaviour in the workplace.* London: Pitman Publishing.

Ashforth, B.E. & Mael, F. (1989). Social identity theory and the organisation. *Academy of Management Review, 14,* 20–39.

Barrett, B. & James, P. (1981). How real is employee participation in health and safety. *Employee Relations, 3,* 4–7.

Beresford Dew, R. & Gee, K.P. (1973). *Management control and information.* London: Macmillan.

Berg, D.H. (1967). An enquiry into the effect of exposure to advertisements on subsequent perception of similar advertisements. *Journal of Applied Psychology, 51,* 503–508.

Berkman, H.W. & Gilson, C.C. (1978). *Consumer behaviour: Concepts and strategies.* CA: Dickenson Publishing Co.

Berne, E. (1964). *Games people play.* New York: Grove Press.

Bobbitt, H.R., Breinholt, R.H., Doktor, R.H., & McNaul, J.P. (1978). *Organisational behaviour, understanding and prediction.* New York: Prentice-Hall.

Bodenhausen, G.V. (1988). Stereotypic biases in social decision making and memory. Testing process models of stereotype use. *Journal of Personality and Social Psychology, 55,* 726–737.

Bowen, D.D. & Rath, R. (1978). Transactional analysis is OK: Applications within the NTL model. *Academy of Management Review, 3,* 79–89.

Brown, P. (1970). The impact of the annual net profit report on the stock market. *Australian Accountant,* July, 277–283.

Bruner, J.S. & Goodman, C.C. (1947). Value and need as organising factors in perception. *Journal of Abnormal and Social Psychology, 42,* 33–44.

Christensen, J.M. (1981). The human element in safe man–machine systems. *Professional Safety,* March, 27–32.

Cook, M. (1971). *Interpersonal perception.* Harmondsworth: Penguin.

Curtis, J.D. & Detert, R.A. (1981). *How to relax—a holistic approach to stress management.* Mountain View, CA: Mayfield Publishing.

Cushman, W.H. (1980). Selection of filters for dark adaptation goggles in the photographic industry. *Applied Ergonomics, 11,* 93–99.

Cyert, R.M. & March, J.G. (1963). *A behavioural theory of the firm.* New York: Prentice-Hall.

Davis, K. (1976). Understanding the organisational grapevine and its benefits. *Business and Public Affairs,* Spring, 5.

Day, R.H. (1969). *Human perception.* Sydney: J. Wiley & Son.

Dearborn, D.C. & Simon, H.A. (1958). Selective perception: A note on the departmental identification of executives. *Sociometry, 21,* 140–144.

Devine, P.G. (1989). Stereotypes and prejudice: Their automatic and controlled components. *Personality and Social Psychology, 56,* 5–18.

Dornbusch, S.M., Hastorf, A.H., Richardson, S.A., Muzzy R.E., & Vreeland, R.S. (1965). The perceiver and the perceived: The irrelative influence on the categories of interpersonal cognition. *Journal of Personality and Social Psychology, 1,* 434–440.

Dubrin, A.J. (1990). *Effective business psychology* (third edition). New York: Prentice-Hall.

Engel, J.F., Blackwell, R.D., & Miniard, P.W. (1990). *Consumer behaviour* (sixth edition). Fort Worth, TX: The Dryden Press.

Feldman, M. (1971). *Psychology in the industrial environment.* Sevenoaks: Butterworth.

Feshback, S. & Singer, D. (1957). The effects of a vicarious aggressive activity. *Journal of Abnormal and Social Psychology, 63,* 381–385.

Financial Times, The. (1993, 25 September). *Accounts guidelines go beyond Cadbury.* (p. 8).

Finn, A. (1988). Print advertisement recognition readership scores: An information processing perspective. *Journal of Marketing Research, 25,* 168–177.

Fisher, C. (1979). Transmission of positive and negative feedback to subordinates: A laboratory investigation. *Journal of Applied Psychology,* October, 533–540.

Fisher, G.H. (1967). Preparation of ambiguous stimulus materials. *Perception and Psychophysics, 2*, 421–422.

Flesch, R. (1949). *The art of readable writing*. New York: Harper.

Fletcher, C. (1984). What's new in performance appraisal. *Personnel Management*, February, 20–22.

Gardner, W.L. & Martinko, M.J. (1988). Impression management: An observational study linking audience characteristics with verbal self-presentations. *Academy of Management Journal, 31*, 42–65.

Garland, H. & Price, K.N. (1977). Attitudes towards women in management and attributions of their success and failure in managerial positions. *Journal of Applied Psychology, 62*.

Gibson, E.J. (1969). *Principles of perceptual learning and development*. New York: Appleton-Century-Crofts.

Gregory, R.L. (1966). *Eye and brain*. London: Weidenfeld & Nicolson.

Guardian, The. (1986, 24 October). *An account of the Colwich Junction train accident*.

Haire, M. & Grunes, W.G. (1950). Perceptual defences: Processes protecting an original perception of another personality. *Human Relations, 3*, 403–412.

Halperin, K., Snyder, C.R., Shenkel, R.J., & Houston, B.K. (1976). Effect of source status and message favourability on acceptance of personality feedback. *Journal of Applied Psychology*, February, 85–88.

Harris, T.A. (1969). *I'm OK — You're OK*. New York: Harper & Row.

Hawkins, F.H. (1987). Human factors in flight. Aldershot, Hants.: Gower Press.

Hayne, C. (1981). Light and colour. *Occupational Health*, April, 198–204.

Health and Safety Executive Report (1989). *Human factors in industrial safety*. London: HMSO.

Held, R. & Hein, A. (1963). Movement-produced stimulation in the development of visually guided behaviour. *Journal of Comparative and Physiological Psychology, 5, 56*, 872–876.

Jones, E.E. & Davis, K.E. (1965). From acts to dispositions: The attribution process in person perception. In L. Berkowitz (Ed.), *Advances in experimental social psychology, Vol. 12*. New York: Academic Press.

Kanugo, R.N. & Pang, S. (1973). Effect of human models on perceived product quality. *Journal of Applied Psychology, 57*, 172–178.

Kelley, H.H. (1950). The warm–cold variable in the first impressions of person. *Journal of Personality, 18*, 431–439.

Kelley, H.H. (1967). *Attribution theory in social psychology*. Nebraska Symposium on Motivation. Lincoln: University of Nebraska Press.

Kelley, H.H. (1971). *Attribution in social interaction*. Morristown, NJ: General Learning Press.

Lambert, Z.V. (1972). Price and choice behaviour. *Journal of Marketing Research, 9*, 35–40.

Leary, M.R. & Kowalski, R.M. (1990). Impression management: A literature review and two-component model. *Psychological Bulletin, 107*, 34–37.

Lee, T.A. & Tweedie, D.P. (1977). *The private shareholder and the corporate report*. London: Institute of Chartered Accountants in England and Wales.

Lewis, A. & James, S. (1981). Understanding tax forms. *Certified Accountant*, February, 48–52.

Likert, R. (1961). *New patterns of management*. New York: McGraw-Hill.

Lothian, N. (1978). Bad language in financial reports. *Accountancy*, November, 42–46.

Machin, J.L.J. (1980). *The expectations approach: Improving managerial communication and performance*. New York: McGraw-Hill.

Mackay, K. (1973). *An introduction to psychology*. London: Macmillan.

Maier, N.R.F., Hoffman, L.R., Hooven, J.J., & Read, W.H. (1961). *Superior–subordinate communication in management*. New York: American Management Association.

Marchington, M. (1987). Employee participation. In B. Towers (Ed.), *A handbook of industrial relations practice*. London: Kogan Page.

McConnell, J.V., Cutier, R.L., & McNeil, E.B. (1958). Subliminal stimulation: An overview. *American Psychologist, 13*, 229–242.

McGinnies, E. (1949). Emotionality and perceptual defence. *Psychological Review, 56*, 244–251.

Monroe, K.B. (1973). Buyers' subjective perceptions of price. *Journal of Marketing Research, 10*, 70–80.

Moore, T.E. (1982). Subliminal advertising. What you see is what you get. *Journal of Marketing, 46*, 38–47.

Moorhead, G. & Griffin, R. W. (1992). *Organisational behaviour:. Managing people and organisations* (third edition). Boston, MA: Houghton, Mifflin.

Nord, W.R. (1976). *Concepts and controversy in organisational behaviour* (second edition). Pacific Pallisades, CA: Goodyear.

Oliver, G. (1980). *Marketing Today*. London: Prentice-Hall.

Olshavsky, R.W. & Miller, J.A. (1972). Consumer expectations, product performance and perceived product quality. *Journal of Marketing Research, 9*, 19–21.

Osgood, C.E., Suci, G.J., & Tannenbaum, P.H. (1955). *The measurement of meaning*. Urbana, IL: University of Illinois Press.

Pace, R.W. (1983). *Organisational communication: Foundations for human resource development*. New York: Prentice-Hall.

Pennington, D.C. (1986). *Essential social psychology*. London: Edward Arnold.

Reason, J. (1987). A framework for classifying errors (Chapter 1) and A preliminary classification of mistakes (Chapter 2). In J. Rasmussen, K. Duncan, & J. Leplat (Eds.), *New technology and human error*. Chichester: Wiley.

Reason, J. & Mycielska, K. (1982). *Absent-minded? The psychology of mental lapses and everyday errors*. New York: Prentice-Hall.

Robbins, S.P. (1989). *Training in interpersonal skills: Tips for managing people at work*. New York: Prentice-Hall.

Robbins, S.P. (1991). *Organisational behaviour: Concepts, controversies, and applications* (fifth edition). New York: Prentice-Hall.

Robson, A.P. (1965). Eliminating weaknesses in management accounting. *Management Accounting*, June, 200–205.

Rothstein, M. & Jackson, D.N. (1984). Implicit personality theory and the employment interview. In M. Cook (Ed.), *Issues in person perception*. London: Methuen.

Rotter, J.B. (1975). Some problems and misconceptions related to the construct of internal versus external locus of control of reinforcement. *Journal of Consulting and Clinical Psychology, 43*, 56–67.

Royal Society (1985). *The public understanding of science*. Report.

Schlenker, B. (1980). *Impression management*. Monterey, CA: Brookes Cole.

Secord, P.F., Bevan, N., & Katz, B. (1956). Perceptual accentuation and the Negro stereotype. *Journal of Abnormal and Social Psychology, 59*, 309–315.

Smith, J.E. & Smith, N.P. (1971). Readability: A measure of the performance of the communication function of financial reporting. *The Accounting Review*, July, 552–561.

Soper, F.J. & Dolphin, R. (1964). Readability and corporate annual reports. *The Accounting Review*, April, 358–362.

Stamp, E. (1978). The private shareholder and the corporate report, by T.A. Lee & D.P. Tweedie, ICAEW, 1977: book review. *Accounting and Business Research*, Autumn, 285–288.

Starch, D. (1961). Do inside positions differ in readership? Consultancy report cited in Anastasi, A. (1979), *Fields of applied psychology* (second edition). New York: McGraw-Hill.

Sunday Times, The. (1986, 21 September). *An account of the Colwich Junction train accident*.

Swann, W.B. & Ely, R.J. (1984). A battle of wills: Self-verification versus behavioural confirmation. *Journal of Personality and Social Psychology, 46*, 1287–1302.

Tajfel, H. & Turner, J.C. (1985). The social identity theory of inter-group behaviour. In S. Worchel & W.G. Austin (Eds.), *Psychology of inter-group relations* (second edition). Chicago: Nelson-Hall.

Thomas, A. (1978). Some perceptual illusions in accounting. *Accountancy*, June, 54–56.

Traini, R. (1983). Computer detection. *Sunday Times*, 16th January.

Van Knippenberg, A. (1984). Intergroup differences in group perceptions. In H. Tajfel (Ed.), *The social dimension: European developments in social psychology, Vol. 2*. Cambridge, UK: Cambridge University Press.

Voke, J. (1982). Colour vision problems at work. *Health and Safety at Work*, January, 27–28.

Warr, P.B. & Knapper, G. (1968). *The perception of people and events*. Chichester: J. Wiley & Son.

Weiner, B., Frieze, I., Kukla, A., Reid, L., Rest, S., & Rosenbaum, R.M. (1971). *Perceiving the causes of success and failure*. New York: General Learning Press.

Zajonc, R.B. & Markus, H. (1982). Affective and cognitive factors in preferences. *Journal of Consumer Research, 9*.

Zaremba, A. (1988). Working with the organisational grapevine. *Personnel Journal*, July, 38–42.

4

Learning, Memory, and Training

Learning and memory are related, even though they are concerned with different functions. Generally learning is concerned with the acquisition of knowledge and skills whereas memory is largely associated with retention and retrieval. The first part of this chapter is devoted to a study of learning, followed by a study of memory. The discussion of learning is sub-divided into classical conditioning, operant conditioning, and cognitive learning. Programmed learning and behaviour modification are discussed as techniques that derive their strength from operant conditioning.

Memory is sub-divided into short-term and long-term memory, and various processes concerning the functioning of memory are discussed.

The transfer of learning (training) is examined, and various aspects of training are discussed. The chapter covers material that provides a useful foundation for discussion in later chapters: e.g. information processing (Chapter 5); attitudes (Chapter 6); culture (Chapter 11); and management development (Chapter 12). Parts of this chapter also have relevance to material covered in earlier chapters: e.g. motivation (Chapter 2); and selective perception (Chapter 3).

LEARNING

Learning covers virtually all behaviour, and is concerned with the acquisition of knowledge, attitudes and values, emotional responses (such as happiness and fear), and motor skills (such as operating a computer keyboard or riding a bicycle). We can learn incorrect facts or pick up bad habits in the same way that we learn correct facts and acquire good habits. Learning can take place surreptitiously through the process of socialisation in a particular culture.

A generally accepted definition is that learning involves a relatively permanent change in behaviour that occurs as a result of previous practice or experience (Atkinson et al., 1987). This excludes the process of maturation, physical damage or disease and temporary changes in behaviour resulting from fatigue, drugs, or other causes. Learning cannot be observed directly; we can only observe a person's behaviour and draw the inference from it that learning has taken place. Sometimes a person may have the potential to perform and display what he or she has learned, but unfortunately anxiety intervenes to undermine actual performance. This could occur in an examination, when the anxious student does not perform in accordance with the tutor's expectations.

A distinction has to be made between learning and performance. Performance is evaluated by some quantitative and some qualitative measures of output—e.g. the number of calls a sales representative makes to customers or the quality of an executive's chairing of a committee meeting—but learning acts as a constraint on the outcome. Normally we cannot perform any better than we have learned, though there are occasions when the right motivational disposition and a supportive environment helps to raise the level of performance. Increased motivation may improve our performance up to a point but, beyond this, increased motivation may cause a lowering of the level of performance (Spence, Farber, & McFann, 1956).

The behaviourist approach to the investigation of learning has been very influential. This draws on the insights derived from classical conditioning and operant conditioning, discussed in this chapter.

CLASSICAL CONDITIONING

Classical conditioning is an association of one event with another that results in a pattern of behaviour. The name of Pavlov is associated with classical conditioning (Pavlov, 1927). He was a physiologist who originally experimented with digestive secretions in dogs, and noticed that the dogs not only produced secretions when they saw food, but also responded to any stimulus that had been regularly associated with the food—i.e. the sight of the food pan or the sound of the keeper's footsteps. These events prompted Pavlov to investigate the dogs' tendency to salivate in response to a stimulus; this was called a reflex action. Pavlov rang a bell each time he brought food to the dog, and gradually the dog began to associate the ringing of the bell with the presentation of food.

Unconditioned and Conditioned Stimuli

The unconditioned stimulus (US) is the presentation of the food; the conditioned stimulus (CS) is the ringing of a bell. The act of salivating by the dog is the response. This is often referred to as a conditioned response (CR) when associated with CS, and as an unconditioned response (UR) when associated with US. Before any learning can take place an association must exist between US and UR. Actual learning occurs from the pairing of the bell (CS) and the presentation of a pan of food (US).

Classical conditioning also functions in a human context. If a puff of air is blown into the human eye, a blink automatically occurs. There is an association between the puff of air (US) and the blink (UR). If, however, a new stimulus (e.g. a light) occurs close in time with the US, the new stimulus (CS) brings about the blinking of the eye (CR) (Hall, 1976).

Another example of human conditioning involves a physiological reaction. The small blood vessels close to the body surface constrict in order to try to keep the body warm when it is exposed to the cold; this is known as vasoconstriction. We are unaware of this response when our hands are placed in ice-cold water. After a number of joint presentations of a buzzer and putting a hand in ice-cold water it was established that vasoconstriction (CR) occurs in response to the buzzer (CS) alone (Menzies, 1937).

Extinction and Spontaneous Recovery

A conditioned stimulus will not last indefinitely unless it is accompanied by an unconditioned stimulus. If the conditioned stimulus is introduced repeatedly without being followed by the unconditioned stimulus, there will be a gradual weakening of the strength of the conditioned response. This is known as "extinction", and amounts to a reversal of learning. Pavlov's dog ceased to salivate at the sound of a bell because food did not appear after a number of occasions when the bell was rung.

A conditioned response that has been extinguished may spontaneously recover some of the strength lost in extinction after a period of rest. This is manifest when, after a night's rest, Pavlov's dog increases the number of drops of saliva to the first ringing of a bell the following morning. The degree of spontaneous recovery after extinction will depend on the strength of the association that exists between the conditioned and unconditioned stimuli, and the nature and frequency of the rest periods.

Illustrations of the Association Between US and CS

Classical conditioning has become a focus of growing interest as a basic framework for interpreting advertising effects (Allen & Madden, 1985). The marketing executive is interested in creating public awareness of the company's product, and through the medium of advertising attempts to establish a strong association between the conditioned stimulus—the image of the product portrayed in the advertisement—and the unconditioned stimulus (the product itself). With a limited advertising budget a decision will have to be made as to whether the expenditure should be allocated to one or two major campaigns in a year, or whether it should be spread through smaller but more frequent advertising campaigns throughout the year. For a new product it may be worthwhile to use the budget on an intensive campaign in order to create a strong association for the product, but for an established brand, the nature of the product and the likely activities of competitors would dictate the desired course of action (Williams, 1981).

The aim of a marketing strategy could be to associate some feeling of euphoria or satisfaction with the product, so that when consumers enter a store and see the product the associative feeling is aroused. This is reflected in a number of cinema and television advertisements. A scene showing a girl enjoying herself on a tropical beach is followed after a few seconds by a picture of a bottle of a particular brand of alcoholic drink. When the consumer is contemplating the purchase of an alcoholic drink at the off-licence or supermarket, the advertised brand on display can trigger off the image or emotional connotation of the beach and the girl. Similarly, a Hovis bread advertisement depicted the bygone rural conditions of life, followed by people eating brown bread. When this product is seen on the supermarket shelf it is hoped that the consumer will experience a pleasant association between it and the ancient country setting.

In order to entice a consumer to purchase a product, a price discount may be offered. The consumer purchases the product because of the price reduction and continues to do so after the discount has been withdrawn. In this example an association is established between the desirable reduction in price (unconditioned stimulus) and the product brand (conditioned stimulus). If the product in question compares well with the quality and performance of competing brands, the association initially established as a result of the price reduction strategy could continue. In the short term at least, the product may be chosen by the consumer despite the absence of a discount.

Once an action becomes repetitive, such as the continued purchase of the product with the initial price discount, a habit is formed. Many consumers rely on habit so as to alleviate the problem of choice. They tend to buy the same shampoo, coffee, and baked beans that they bought last time. A deliberate advertising strategy to foster brand loyalty is reflected in an overt association between the product and the brand. The slogan incorporating the misspelled name of the product and the name of the brand—"Beanz meanz Heinz"—is a good example of this strategy. A car manufacturer may adopt a different type of association in the form of a comparative claim, though the legal implications of such a strategy have to be considered. A comparative claim may take the following form: "The Ford Granada consistently rode as quietly as the Mercedes Benz" (Cohen, 1981).

Associations between social groups and life-style are exploited by advertisers, so as to promote products to particular social groups. It is highly unlikely that an advertisement would show a prestige car against the background of a dilapidated small house in a run-down area. A more likely image would be for the car to appear in a context of . affluence—near a large house, driven by an attractive, well-dressed woman, and so on. However, if an advertiser wishes to enlarge the market for a particular product, then the product will be shown in a number of different settings, each designed to appeal to a particular social group.

Generalisation

The phenomenon of generalisation, related to classical conditioning, occurs when we attribute to a similar stimulus the character-istics of the conditioned stimulus. For example, Pavlov's dog salivated, though to a lesser extent, to the sound of a buzzer. The greater the similarity between the conditioned stimulus (the bell) and the new stimulus (the buzzer) the more pronounced is generalisa-tion. The concept of generalisation can be viewed as the substitution of a new conditioned stimulus for the originally learned conditioned stimulus. It accounts for our ability to react to novel situations where we perceive similarities to familiar situations.

The accountant, when dealing with a new tax problem, may see certain similarities between it and a past problem, and as a consequence is able to draw inferences from the past situation to illuminate the present. This is an act of generalisation on the part of the accountant.

It is often assumed when a consumer has a satisfactory experience with a product—e.g. a *Phillips* or *Hitachi* radio cassette recorder—that this will be generalised to other products, such as a video recorder or camcorder, made by the companies concerned. But generalisa-tion may work to the firm's disadvantage, if an unfavourable experience with a product or service is transferred to a new product or service introduced by the firm. An example would be clients who are dissatisfied with the auditing service they receive from a firm of

chartered accountants. Subsequently, the firm creates a first-rate management consultancy service, but the clients concerned, although in need of consultancy advice, feel unable to use the services of this firm.

Generalisation is also evident in the following situation. A child, accompanied by a parent, pays a visit to the dentist. The child will probably respond with anxiety to the odd sensation as the tooth is drilled. But, while in the dentist's chair, the child registers a variety of stimuli: the dentist in a white coat, the "smells" of the surgery, the whine of the drill, and so on. The conditioned response of the child to pain is to be frightened, and this response becomes associated with the other stimuli registered by the child. On the way home the parent and child visit a chemist's shop to buy some medicine, and it would not be surprising if the child was frightened when the chemist appeared in a white coat. Many people experience strong emotional reactions to certain situations because in the past these reactions have been paired with some painful or unpleasant experience.

Anxiety could be produced following a car accident on a particular road. Subsequently when driving down a similar road (CS) the driver experiences anxiety (CR). In fact, an anxiety or fear could spread or be generalisable to other stimuli that bear some relationship to the original stimuli—e.g. riding a bicycle or motorcycle, or using a taxi.

Emotional Reactions

An experiment conducted by Watson many years ago shows how emotional reactions may be classically conditioned in humans (Watson & Rayner, 1920). At the beginning of the experiment, a child named Albert was presented with a small white rat and played quite happily with it. However, when the small white rat (CS) was paired with a loud noise (US), and this was done several times, Albert developed a very strong aversive reaction to the rat and would whimper and recoil when it came into sight.

Discrimination

The opposite of generalisation is called discrimination. This refers to the capacity to distinguish between two stimuli so that the appropriate response to the correct stimulus is made. If Pavlov's dog salivates to the ringing of a bell but does not salivate when the telephone rings, we can conclude that it has discriminated between the appropriate and inappropriate conditioned stimuli.

When product differences are easily recognisable—i.e. the distinctiveness of a *Mini Metro* or *Volkswagen*—it is relatively easy for consumers to discriminate. In other cases, terms such as "new" and "improved" are used in advertisements as discriminatory cues, though the continuing influx of new products to the market has deadened the impact of these frequently used words.

Stores, such as *Harrods* and *Marks & Spencer*, place overwhelming influence on the discriminatory cue of quality. Advertisers therefore have to give due care to the strategy of differentiating between the advertised product and competing products. Differentiation is evident when a car manufacturer highlights the positive design features of a particular car when compared with similarly priced competitive models.

However, generalisation that could result in a sales increase not only for the particular brand advertised but also for competing brands may be difficult to prevent in particular circumstances. Take for example an advertisement for *Pepsi Cola* which stresses that those who drink it are part of the in-crowd. There is a danger that this could be generalised to *Coca Cola* as well and result in increased sales of that product.

Thorndike (1911), a learning theorist, also gave much thought to the relationship between stimulus and response. He came to the conclusion that problem solving, at least in lower animals, involves a slow, gradual, and at times tortuous trial and error process. He considered learning as a gradual stamping in of correct responses and a gradual stamping out of incorrect responses.

Two basic principles govern trial and error processes: the law of repetition and the law of effect. The law of repetition is self-explanatory. The law of effect states that responses which satisfy the needs of the organism tend to be retained whereas those which fail to satisfy these needs tend to be eliminated. So if a person gets satisfaction from performing a particular act, that act will tend to be repeated. If you find that paracetamol is particularly effective in removing a headache over a period of time, this remedy is likely to be repeated.

Another theorist, Hull, recognised the importance of intervening variables in the stimulus response equation, though Pavlov and Thorndike played down their significance (Hull, 1943). Intervening variables consist of drive, habit strength, and incentive. A response to a need—e.g. consumption of a particular product—could reduce the search (drive) for this product, and satisfaction with its consumption could lead to the formation of a habit, though the habit could vary over time. Hull's theory is sometimes described as a theory of conditioned learning, and it incorporates aspects of the work of both Pavlov and Thorndike. However, Hull's real contribution is acknowledging that the internal state of the organism, and particularly motivation, must be considered in explaining learning.

OPERANT CONDITIONING

The basic difference between operant conditioning and classical conditioning is that, in operant conditioning, learners must make some response before their behaviour is reinforced or rewarded.

Reinforcement

The major proponent of the theory of operant conditioning is Skinner, and his work could be considered an elaboration of Thorndike's law of effect. In a basic experiment, Skinner (1951)

"HONESTLY GUYS... I KEPT PRESSING THIS LEVER....
AND THE FOOD JUST KEPT COMING..."

placed a hungry rat in a box in which there was a lever. When the lever was depressed it activated a mechanism to deliver a food pellet. The rat tended to explore the box and, by chance, pressed the lever and a food pellet dropped. It began to press the lever more and more frequently to obtain the food. The food is the reinforcement for the behaviour. This type of experiment was also conducted with pigeons: they pecked a disc in return for food pellets. The animals developed discriminatory behaviour in the sense that the lever was pressed, or the disc pecked, when a light was on but not when it was off. Food is a major form of reinforcement for animals, and this is evident in the training of circus animals to perform interesting manoeuvres in return for rewards.

With humans, factors such as attention, praise, approval, success, and money are major reinforcers. The teacher who pays attention to the troublesome behaviour of a pupil is reinforcing that behaviour. In certain circumstances, such behaviour might profitably be ignored, while acceptable behaviour ought to be reinforced by praise or reward. A child may find that asking a parent a question in a civil manner produces hardly any response; however, screaming and shouting in order to attract attention does produce a response, and subsequently the child may adopt this ploy again. Some examples of operant conditioning processes in an organisation are included in the panel overleaf.

For a reinforcer to work it must be perceived by the recipient as being useful and relevant. For example, receiving public praise in the classroom may not be regarded as a reinforcement by the young schoolchild who does not want to be seen as the teacher's favourite. The child might work less hard in the future to avoid this embarrassing situation.

Contiguity and Contingent
The principles of contiguity and contingent apply to reinforcement. The bigger the gap between behaviour and reinforcement, generally the less the likelihood that the behaviour will be strengthened or diminished. For conditioning to occur there

---

Operant Conditioning in Organisations

An executive is asked to speak at a board meeting. The stimulus is the request to speak, and the executive responds by giving certain views on matters within his or her area of responsibility. The executive's response may be reinforced by nods and smiles from a prominent director, and the effect of the reinforcement increases the likelihood that the executive will respond with the same or similar views at future meetings.

In another situation, a safety practitioner on an inspection in a factory is impressed by the system of control relating to potential hazards. He or she provides reinforcement by praising those responsible and writing in favourable terms about this experience in the company newsletter.

---

should be only a small delay between behaviour and reinforcement (contiguity). Therefore, when a consumer enters a store to buy a new product which has been intensively advertised, it is important that it appears on the shelf. Likewise, the commuter on the underground railway who is peckish would prefer to use a vending machine while waiting for the train, rather than satisfy his or her hunger at the end of the journey. Reinforcement should be contingent on the appropriate response; that is, it should be provided only when the desired behaviour occurs, and it should not come too late, otherwise it may be associated with more recent but inappropriate behaviour.

Extinction

If reinforcement is expected but is not forthcoming, the responses associated with it could become extinguished. For example, if the rat in Skinner's box no longer receives food after pressing the lever, it will gradually stop pressing and go back to the previous random exploratory behaviour.

Though reinforcement and reward are associated, reward is not synonymous with reinforcement. For example, a reward could be given without any effect on behaviour. A reinforcer is only a reinforcer if it maintains or increases the probability of responding at a high level (Burns & Dobson, 1984). The learning involved in operant conditioning is sometimes referred to as "instrumental conditioning", because the response of the organism is instrumental in obtaining the reinforcement.

Primary and Secondary Reinforcement

Reinforcers used in most animal-learning experiments are examples of primary reinforcers. Food, drink, and sex fit into this category. A secondary reinforcer is one that has derived and developed its reinforcement qualities from being associated with one or more primary reinforcers. Money would fall into this category. When monkeys performed certain actions to secure poker chips that could be exchanged for food (Wolfe, 1936), they responded to the secondary reinforcers (the poker chips). These became reinforcers because the monkeys learned that the chips could secure the food. To be effective, secondary reinforcers must be paired with primary reinforcers.

Positive and Negative Reinforcement

A number of examples of positive reinforcement have already been given. Skinner's rats and pigeons received positive reinforcement in the form of food. When a person picks up a magazine from a news-stand and derives satisfaction from reading it, then that person experiences positive reinforcement. The same would apply to other fast-moving consumer products; continuous satisfaction from the consumption of the product leads to a learned response and the development of brand loyalty.

Negative Reinforcement and Avoidance Conditioning

With negative reinforcement and punishment, the organism responds to avoid an unpleasant situation. The animal in a maze soon learns not to behave in a certain way in order to avoid receiving an electric shock (a negative reinforcement). An employee may work hard during a period in which the company is going through a difficult time to avoid being made redundant, rather than for the positive reinforcement of success. The motorist with little petrol left in the tank pulls in to a filling station with low standards of service, and unavoidably receives a negative reinforcer in the form of surly, discourteous service. Next time he or she will avoid, if possible, patronising this filling station. In this case, negative reinforcement can lead to avoidance conditioning because cues have been picked up indicating that the same standard of service is likely to prevail in the future.

Responses based on avoidance conditioning do not easily disappear, as most organisms are unlikely to try and establish whether or not the original negative reinforce- ment is still operating. Another illustration serves to highlight negative reinforcement and avoidance conditioning. A product is found to be faulty, or it does not live up to the customer's expectations in some way—i.e. it falls short of the manufacturer's claims. In this case, the purchase of the product will be negatively reinforced, and the customer may consciously avoid purchasing it again. This could create problems for the manufacturer because it could be difficult to extinguish a negatively reinforced response. A car manufacturer may experience problems if a product had developed a reputation for rust or faulty parts leading to an above average breakdown record. It could take a long time to overcome this reputation, even though corrective action was instituted soon after the difficulties were reported.

Punishment

Even though positive reinforcement is said to be more effective than punishment in regulating behaviour, punishment seems to be used in society as much as reward. The link between action or response and reward is visible in positive reinforcement, unlike punishment where it is evident that the action is wrong but the correct response is not specified. However, punishment can play a useful role in stamping out inappropriate behaviour and regulating behaviour, at least in the short term. If a lecturer shouts at a student guilty of disruptive tactics in the classroom, the misbehaviour is likely to cease immediately. The sudden cessation of the undesirable behaviour is very reinforcing for the lecturer. Though punishment has a role to play in changing behaviour, it should be used sparingly. If it is not severe, and there is a clear distinction between good and bad (for example, children playing on the road or with matches could be considered bad behaviour), then problems are unlikely to arise in terms of behavioural abnormalities.

But if punishment is very severe in conditions where it is not easy to distinguish between right and wrong, it may affect negatively both the bad behaviour and other similar good behaviour. For example, administering hard punishment to a child for answering back may not only extinguish this type of response but also it may eliminate intelligent discussions with parents and perhaps others as well, and so it produces unwanted side effects. Many chronically shy, unassertive individuals report that extremely punitive measures were used against them in childhood, not only when they challenged parental commands but also occasionally when they only tried to voice their opinions on some issue or other (Burns & Dobson, 1984). Often, people feel hostile towards punishment because it is viewed as a process that engendered anxiety in the first instance. Many children have failed to fulfil their scholastic potential because of negative feelings towards teachers and schools, which have arisen through earlier traumatic experiences in an educational setting.

To produce the maximum effect, the punishment should come immediately after the undesirable behaviour (Burns & Dobson, 1984). Note the paradox of the heavy drinker, for example, who, despite warnings about cirrhosis, has another drink. If death from cirrhosis was the immediate consequence of having another drink, he or she would decline it. But in reality the immediate pleasure of the alcoholic drink outweighs the distant worry of possible liver failure.

Generally, in order to stop the undesirable behaviour, enough punishment must be meted out early in the process and the recipient must know which aspects of his or her behaviour are looked upon with disapproval. It is always wise to have a positive reinforcement in mind.

Recognising that there are occasions when organisations have to rely on punishment or discipline, Moorhead and Griffin (1992) offer managers basic guidelines based on good practice on how to proceed. (These guidelines are relevant in the context of the use of management style, discussed in Chapter 8, and with respect to certain outcomes of performance evaluation in Chapter 13.)

1. Progressive discipline should be used. This means that each episode of undesirable behaviour (e.g. poor timekeeping, low work rate, curt treatment of clients) receives a stronger disciplinary measure than the one that preceded it. For example, the first infringement of the company's rules invites a verbal reprimand, the second is followed by a written reprimand, the third by a suspension, and the fourth by dismissal.

2. Given the benefits of autonomous groups (discussed in Chapter 7), why not give the team or group responsibility for using the disciplinary process? Provided this approach is used with caution, it could be successful.

3. Managers should realise that there is a need to tread a slender line between equity and specific situational circumstances.

Although the discipline received by two employees for breaking the same rule should normally be comparable, the interpretation of the event in the light of circumstance might dictate different treatment.

4. Punishment should be used before the undesirable behaviour has the opportunity to be strongly reinforced. This means that punishment meted out on the second infringement of a company rule, rather than the third, is better timed.

5. Punishment that immediately follows the undesirable behaviour has the effect of emphasising the connection between that behaviour and the sanctions imposed.

6. Punishment should be consistent over time and impartial, and should focus on the person's behaviour rather than the person.

7. The punishment should be accompanied by as much information as is practicable: for example, the offence to which the punishment relates should be clearly stated, as should the reasons for the punishment in the particular circumstances, and the likely consequences of repeating the undesirable behaviour.

Schedules of Reinforcement

Examples were given earlier of the nature of reinforcement with respect to animals and humans. Here we examine different ways in which reinforcement is administered. When behaviour is reinforced each time it occurs it is referred to as *continuous reinforcement*. However, reinforcement is not necessary every time a response is made; in fact intermittent or partial reinforcement may suffice.

Intermittent or Partial Reinforcement
Reinforcing responses only some of the time can be categorised as fixed ratio, variable ratio, fixed interval, and variable interval.

Fixed Ratio.   A fixed ratio could be the reinforcement of, say, every fifth response.

The fixed ratio schedule keeps the response fairly low after the moment of reinforcement, with a build up to a crescendo just before the next reinforcement when, for example, Skinner's pigeon would be extremely active pecking the disc in anticipation of obtaining more food pellets.

Variable Ratio.   A variable ratio could be the reinforcement of, for example, the third, tenth, and then the fifth response. Under the variable ratio schedule, the pigeon produces a very high and steady response rate as it has no idea when reinforcement will come. The variable ratio schedule is the one that is generally not resistant to extinction because the individual or animal never knows when reinforcement will appear again. Although continuous reinforcement is essential in establishing behaviour initially, once behaviour is learned it is best maintained on a partial reinforcement schedule such as the variable ratio basis (Burns & Dobson, 1984). An example of an application of this ratio is set out in the panel below.

It is the irregularity of the reward schedule that makes gambling so difficult to eradicate, because the gambler always feels he or she may be lucky next time. In an experiment (Lewis & Duncan, 1956) people were allowed to gamble using slot machines. The machines were tampered with so that some paid out on every operation of the lever (continuous reinforcement) while other machines func-tioned like normal slot machines and paid out on a periodic basis (partial reinforcement). Then a significant modification took place in the experiment whereby everybody played on a machine that was adjusted in such a way that it would never pay out; in other words there would be no reinforcement whatsoever. The subjects who had experienced partial reinforcement were much more resistant to extinction of their responses and they continued to play long after the subjects on continuous reinforcement had stopped.

Fixed Interval.   A fixed interval could be the reinforcement of response, say, every 10 minutes. With the fixed interval schedule there would be a reduction of activity just after the moment of reinforcement.

Variable Interval.   A variable interval could be the reinforcement of responses at varying time intervals. The variable interval schedule produces a steady and high response rate.

Applications of Partial Reinforcement

The most appropriate partial reinforcement schedule has to be considered in relation to work and business practice. It would be impossible to use the variable ratio schedule as the only method for providing rewards to employees. People expect to obtain their salary on a regular basis (fixed interval), whatever the evidence in support of the variable ratio schedule.

The Variable Ratio and Absenteeism

The variable ratio schedule in the form of a lottery has been used to reduce absenteeism. The *New York Life Insurance Company* devised a lottery that rewarded employees for attendance (Halcrow, 1986).

Every three months the names of central office employees—roughly 4000 of the total of 7500 employees—were placed in a drum. The first 10 names extracted were entitled to a bond worth $200, the next 20 names to a bond valued at $100, and a further 70 names received a day off with pay.

At the end of the year another lottery was held for employees with a year of perfect attendance, for which 12 prizes were given—2 employees each received a bond worth $1000, and a further 10 were entitled to five days off with pay.

Under this schedule of reinforcement, a good attendance record increased an employee's probability of winning, but a perfect attendance did not guarantee the award of a prize. The use of the lottery as a variable ratio schedule in this case resulted in lower absenteeism rates.

However, rewards such as bonuses and praise may materialise on a variable basis. A random partial reinforcement can be used as a basis for sales promotion schemes such as competitions. The consumer may be encouraged to purchase a certain product because it also provides an opportunity to enter a competition and a chance to win a holiday or car. But only a tiny minority of consumers are likely to receive the stated reinforcement (to win the competition). However, a large number of people may be persuaded to buy the product because of the competition, and then find that the product satisfies their needs. Its purchase has become a learned response.

Continuous Reinforcement
As stated earlier, continuous reinforcement amounts to the reinforcement of every response. Some research findings indicate that continuous reinforcement can be as effective as partial reinforcement. In a study of workers planting pine seedlings it was found that a variable ratio schedule based on incentives was no better than a continuous reinforcement schedule; if anything it was less effective (Yukl, Latham, & Elliot,, 1976). A further example is included in the panel below.

Such findings indicate that one should pay particular attention to differences between individuals when specifying the most appropriate reinforcement schedule. (An alternative theoretical framework for examining the relationship between rewards and performance is the expectancy theory of motivation, discussed in Chapter 2.)

Rules Governing Reinforcement

Hamner (1983) identified six rules that could be helpful when applying the concept of reinforcement in an organisational context:

1. Rewards should vary depending on performance. If everybody got the same reward, irrespective of performance, this would be tantamount to punishing the best performers and rewarding the poorer ones. It could lead to the best performers reducing their contributions or leaving the organisation.
2. Managers shape the behaviour of their subordinates by what they fail to do as well as by what they actually do. For instance, a failure to take action on a subordinate's lack of punctuality may be seen as a sign that it is acceptable to come to work late. It follows that managers have to consider the consequences in terms of performance of their lack of action as well as their actions. Therefore, a failure to respond has reinforcing consequences.
3. Managers should acquaint subordinates with what is expected of them to ensure

---

Rat Catching and Reinforcement

A study by Latham and Dossett (1978) focused on trappers who were paid to catch rats that were eating young trees planted for reforestation purposes. After an initial period on regular hourly pay, half the trappers operated on the basis of hourly pay plus a continuous reinforcement schedule (a specified bonus per rat trapped). The remaining trappers operated on the basis of hourly pay plus a variable ratio schedule (a bonus was paid for an average of every fourth rat trapped). Later these reinforcement schedules were reversed.

Both reinforcement schedules contributed to an improvement in the performance of the trappers, but the continuous reinforcement schedule was at least as effective as the variable ratio schedule. However, when the trappers were split into experienced and inexperienced groups, the variable ratio schedule was superior among the more experienced trappers. But the less experienced group, who were presumably still learning, operated better under a continuous reinforcement schedule.

they receive the appropriate rewards, without restricting their job freedom unduly.

4. So as to take the necessary corrective action, subordinates should be told when they are doing things wrong. Without feedback of this nature, subordinates do not understand why rewards are not given, or why punishment strategies are being used.

5. Subordinates should not be punished in front of colleagues. To do so would amount to a double punishment, and could incite an undesirable response. For example, a subordinate in such a situation may experience a badly dented self-image, and may decide to consider ways of settling scores with management.

6. In order to maintain the necessary level of commitment and motivation, managers should be fair with subordinates, and those doing a good job should receive the appropriate reward.

PROGRAMMED LEARNING

Programmed learning can be discussed with reference to linear programming and branching.

Linear Programming

Linear programming, which involves presenting very small pieces of information (a frame) at an acceptable level of difficulty to the learner (sometimes using machines), is linked to Skinner's concept of operant conditioning. It is a deliberate attempt to utilise in the classroom the experimental findings of the psychological laboratory, and is a major component of programmed learning.

The learner goes through a sequence of frames and makes a response. For learning to be effective under linear programming, reinforcement should follow immediately

after the response; only acceptable behaviour, such as the right answer, is reinforced, and there must be sufficient reinforcements otherwise lack of interest will lead to an extinct response. When the desired response is emitted, the learner is positively reinforced by being told that the correct answer has been given. An incorrect response is negatively reinforced by repeating the question. Linear programming can be reduced to the following basic principles:

- The subject matter, process or skill is defined, analysed, and broken down into its elements.
- Material is presented step-by-step in a pre-arranged sequence, with the steps being so small that the error rate should be close to nil.
- At each step, the learner is given just enough information to ensure he or she makes an active correct response before going on to the next item.
- Learners receive immediate confirmation of the results emanating from their responses, work at their own rate, and check their own progress.

While individuals work at their own pace, some take longer than others to get through the programme. The major disadvantages seem to be that, once written, programmes become inflexible and impersonal. They can also become boring after the initial novelty wears off. The personal intervention of the teacher (particularly the development of personal relationships, which is absent in programmed learning), is often considered to be critical in helping students to maintain their interest and motivation. (Perhaps this would not apply to the teacher with poor teaching skills.)

Skinner (1961) developed teaching machines because he believed that classroom learning was inefficient due to reinforcements being either delayed too long or being absent. This might be an over-simplification, because although animals like to receive reinforcements without much delay, the evidence for humans is that they generally favour delayed reinforcement. Humans have the capacity to retain information about reinforcements over a substantial period of time.

Branching

Another technique of programmed instruction is branching. Material presented in branching frames is usually more difficult and mistakes are more frequent. The questions at the end of the frame are designed to determine what, if anything, the learner has misunderstood. This can be achieved by directing the learner to remedial frames which deal with specific misunderstandings, and then directing the learner back into the mainstream of the programme.

Programmed learning is not in widespread use. An enormous number of prepared programmes would be required for large-scale use and presently the demand for, and supply of, programmes appears to be at a modest level. However, with a substantial growth in the use of computer hardware and software this situation could change in the future.

BEHAVIOUR MODIFICATION

This is a technique that draws its strength from operant conditioning. It is used to control and change behaviour by reinforcing in a systematic way those actions that are considered important or desirable. A related approach to the control and change of behaviour, which preceded the use of behaviour modification techniques, is that of shaping.

Shaping

With shaping, an appropriate reinforcer is selected to suit the occasion, and all positive reinforcements are contingent on the organism moving closer to adopting the desired behaviour. Gradually a chain of behaviour is built up and, once the desired behaviour is achieved, it will be reinforced continuously at first and subsequently on a variable basis.

For example, a pigeon can be taught to pick up a marble in its beak and deposit it in a box. The pigeon is accustomed to receiving food pellets in a small area, and when the pigeon happens to move near the marble the trainer uses the food reinforcement. As a result the pigeon will now be more likely to spend time near the marble. The trainer waits until the bird looks in the direction of the marble. The looking increases and the trainer then waits until the bird happens to bend towards the marble before it receives a reinforcement. So, in progressive steps, circumstances emerge whereby reinforcement is withheld until the bird performs the complicated movement that is required.

In another experiment, Skinner found that when a hungry pigeon engaged in a particular behaviour at the time it received a reinforcement (i.e. turning round in an anti-clockwise manner when the food came), this behavioural pattern developed into a conditioned response. Between the food-giving sessions the pigeon would perform anti-clockwise dances two or three times until the food was presented again. Skinner imputes to the pigeon a certain superstition, in the sense that the bird behaves as if its pattern of behaviour was the cause of the food. As mentioned earlier, shaping is used to control the behaviour of circus animals, and Skinner also trained pigeons to play tennis; they poked a table tennis ball across a table, trying to get it into a trough on their opponent's side (Skinner, 1951; 1961).

Shaping is also common in human learning. Tennis coaches, driving instructors, teachers, and parents all guide their subjects to the desired performance, be it manual, linguistic, social, or emotional behaviour (see panel overleaf).

Shaping and Sales Representatives

In an encounter between a customer and a sales representative, the customer emits an operant—e.g. a remark which need not be directly related to the topic that is of principal interest to the sales representative. The sales representative moves closer to the customer by a process of reinforcement. This could take the form of a nod, a smile, saying "that's a good point", "how interesting", and so on. Part of the behavioural strategy is to have a large repertoire of reinforcers and to select those most appropriate to a particular situation.

Reinforcement that the customer considers relevant can lead to the emission of another operant. Subsequently the sales representative should be selective in the use of reinforcers—that is, he or she should provide reinforcement when the conversation of the customer shifts a little nearer to the technical matter that interests the sales representative. The sales representative will tend to be effective if he or she is able to provide appropriate reinforcements to satisfy the psychological needs of the customer, on the assumption that the more the customer enjoys the encounter the more he or she will believe the technical case put forward by the sales representative.

Modelling

An applied learning procedure associated with shaping is modelling. The desired behaviour is firmly kept in mind before selecting the appropriate model capable of exemplifying the way to proceed: this could, for example, be an ideal style of supervision. Then a supportive learning situation is created, using role playing. The desirable consequences of adopting the model's behaviour are emphasised, and reinforcement is provided when the model behaviour is achieved. Initially reinforcement can be continuous, and subsequently provided on a variable basis. Modelling procedures can be illustrated with reference to a study (Goldstein & Sorcher, 1974) that was conducted at the *General Electric Company* in the US (see panel below).

A variant of the *GEC* study was the following exercise in behavioural analysis conducted in a small business (Komaki, Waddell,.& Pearce, 1977). Two employees in a grocery store were engaged in stock and sales activities. Their performance, covering a variety of duties, was initially monitored. Subsequently, the clerks were trained in desired work behaviour, through discussion, modelling and role playing. Reinforcement

---

Modelling at *GEC*

The aim of the study was to assist in facilitating the retention of disadvantaged employees. Films were developed to use with both employees and their supervisors. The supervisor films showed and modelled rewards for tact, coolness, patience, thoroughness, and control. The employee films emphasised the courage needed to succeed, the value of working at a job, and success in a job Other situations depicted were as follows: not quitting; how to teach a task; developing trust; pride in work; reactions to ostracism; the new environment; absenteeism; and lateness. Each film was introduced and summarised by a member of the management team, such as a plant manager in the case of the supervisors, and a famous black athlete in the case of the employees.

As part of the training session, role playing was introduced during breaks in the film show, and instructors and other members of the training group provided continuous social reinforcement when role playing behaviour was similar or identical to the behaviour of the models portrayed. In all, there were five two-hour sessions for both the supervisors and employees, and the outcome was very favourable from the point of view of the company (Goldstein Sorcher, 1974).

took the form of time off with pay, feedback in visual form, and self-recording undertaken by the employees. Following some behaviour modification interventions, performance increased significantly in terms of the employees' presence, assistance given to customers, and the completeness of the stock position.

Role modelling and shaping are relevant to training issues discussed later in this chapter, and to attitudes (Chapter 6), groups (Chapter 7), leadership (Chapter 8), culture (Chapter 11), and organisational change and development (Chapter 12).

Organisational Behaviour Modification

Two prominent contributors to behaviour modification in an organisational context are Hamner and Luthans. Both adopt a Skinnerian approach, though Luthans goes further than Hamner in his adherence to Skinner's ideas. There is clearly an overlap between the two, but it is useful to present their views separately.

Hamner's Approach
Hamner has proposed certain steps or stages that should be followed when introducing a positive reinforcement programme in a company (Hamner, 1977; Hamner & Hamner, 1976). The emphasis is on performance maximisation, maximum positive reinforcement, and minimum negative reinforcement. The attitudes of workers are generally ignored.

1. Performance should be defined in behavioural terms, and the company should be as objective as possible in devising measures of performance.
2. Specific and reasonable performance goals should be set for each worker in a form that can be measured; these goals are not meant to be personal goals—they are organisational goals.
3. The employee should maintain a continuous record of his or her work so

that the relationship between the performance goal and actual audited performance is clearly visible. The objective is to highlight behaviour that is associated with positive reinforcements; therefore, the measurement of performance should be frequent rather than infrequent.

4. The supervisor looks through the employee's own feedback report, as well as examining other indicators of performance such as sales or production records. With reference to the previously set goals and audited performance, the supervisor praises the positive aspects of the employee's performance. This amounts to positive reinforcement and it should strengthen the employee's resolve to achieve performance goals.

The withholding of praise for sub-standard performance in relation to the goals set should give the employee an incentive to improve performance. Working on the assumption that the employee is already aware of his deficiencies, there is no reason for the supervisor to be critical. In the final analysis the use of positive reinforcement leads to a greater feeling of self-control, whereas the avoidance of negative reinforcements keeps the individual from feeling controlled or coerced.

Luthans' Approach
The approach of Luthans is called *the behavioural contingency management model* for organisational behaviour modification. It seeks to identify and manage the critical performance-related behaviour of employees in organisations, and consists of a five-step procedure (Luthans & Kreitner, 1975).

First, the critical behaviour necessary for satisfactory performance should be identified. The causes of good performance or bad performance should be noted, and techniques such as discussion and observation may be used to carry out this procedure.

Second, a measure should be used to determine the strength or frequency of the relevant behaviour, using tally sheets, time sampling, and so on.

Third, a functional analysis of the behaviour is carried out, and this exercise poses a number of questions. What factors caused the behaviour in the first place, and what is sustaining it in terms of reward or avoidance of punishment? It is essential to have a view of the factors that may be maintaining the behaviour in question (see panel below).

Fourth, after conducting functional analysis, an intervention process gets under way to modify the appropriate behaviour. Care has to be exercised so that only desired behaviour is reinforced, and it is important to consider the context of the behaviour—e.g. tasks and organisation structure. A wide variety and range of rewards are available, and some do not involve costs, such as friendly greetings and compliments. In Table 4.1 there is a list of possible rewards for use in organisational behaviour modification. This approach represents a major alternative to the expectancy theory of motivation discussed in Chapter 2.

The fifth and final step in the procedure is evaluation. The primary aim of evaluation is to establish to what extent intervention has modified the behaviour. One way to achieve that aim is for the intervention process to be removed or reversed, and then the consequences are noted. Various combinations for manipulating the situation can be used in order to assess the impact of the behaviour modification programme.

Applications

Apparently, persuading workers to use personal protective equipment, such as ear-plugs or spectacles, is a significant problem in many manufacturing plants, and there is no doubt that a fair number of accidents at work could be avoided if personal protective equipment was used appropriately. The challenge then is to change the workers' behaviour as a means of avoiding work hazards.

This challenge was taken up in a study, using a behaviour modification programme to alter the habits of workers at two companies with regard to wearing ear protectors (Zohar, 1980). Some workers tend to be resistant to wearing ear protectors because they perceive certain costs associated with the practice, including a very unpleasant adaptation period, a continual concern for cleanliness when using ear-plugs, and increased sweating around the ear when using ear muffs. Because in a number of situations no

---

Sales Representatives and Behaviour Modification

The importance of understanding what is maintaining a behaviour pattern is exemplified by an example (Robertson & Cooper, 1983) of a sales manager who is concerned about the large number of visits by sales representatives to the home base; the visits are seen to be unproductive chats with colleagues.

The sales manager is acutely aware of the time wasting involved and is unhappy about the fact that the sales director keeps making comments that large numbers of the sales force are sitting at the home base doing nothing. It would be logical to establish the apparent rewards for returning to base. The chance to relax and avoid the pressures of being on the road may be one factor to consider. Another, and perhaps more important, may be that the sales representatives have the opportunity for social interaction with their colleagues. It is perhaps the reinforcing effect of the social interaction that is maintaining the undesirable behaviour from the company's point of view.

This analysis could lead to the adoption of a behaviour modification programme as a means of encouraging sales representatives to make fewer visits to the home base. However, the strategy of discouraging them from making frequent visits to the home base as a means to make better use of their time could be defeated if opportunities for relaxation existed elsewhere, or if it was possible to stagger the visits so that only small numbers were at the home base at any time.

TABLE 4.1

Organisational Behaviour Modification Rewards

Contrived On-The-Job Rewards				Natural Rewards	
Consumables	Manipulables	Visual and Auditory	Tokens	Social	Other
Coffee-break treats.	Desk accessories.	Office with a window.	Money.	Friendly greetings.	Job with more responsibility.
Free lunches.	Wall plaques.	Piped in music.	Stocks.	Informal recognition.	Job rotation.
Food baskets.	Company car.	Redecoration of work environment.	Stock options.	Formal acknowledgement of achievement.	Early time off with pay.
Easter hams.	Watches.		Passes for films.		Extended breaks.
Christmas turkeys.	Trophies.	Company literature.	Trading stamps.	Invitations to coffee/lunch.	Extended lunch period.
Dinners for the family on the company.	Commendations. Rings/tiepins. Appliances and furniture for the home.	Private office.	Paid-up insurance policies. Dinner and theatre tickets.	Solicitations of suggestions.	Personal time off with pay.
Company picnics.	Home shop tools.	Popular speakers or lecturers.	Holiday trips.	Solicitations of advice.	Work on personal project on company time.
After-work wine and cheese parties.	Garden tools. Clothing.	Book club discussions.	Coupons redeemable at local stores.	Compliments on work progress.	Use of company machinery or facilities for personal projects.
Beer parties.	Club privileges. Special assignments.	Feedback about performance.	Profit sharing.	Recognition in house organ.	Use of company recreation facilities.
				Pat on the back. Smile. Verbal or non-verbal recognition or praise.	

penalties accrue for not wearing the ear protectors, and the prospect of hearing loss is too distant to be considered significant, the incentive to wear personal protective equipment of this nature is weak.

Attempts were made to change the behavioural balance in favour of ear-plugs by introducing new reinforcers on a less-than-permanent basis. It was considered appropriate to enlist the support of supervisors in the design and execution of the programme. In this way it was felt that there could be mutual superior and subordinate reinforcement, and this could sustain the modified

behaviour after the programme had terminated.

In a metal fabrication plant of a company with 2000 employees, the management style was production-orientated and authoritarian, and industrial relations were poor as evidenced by the company's history of frequent strikes and high staff turnover. But the company was known for its outstanding safety record, due primarily to top management's involvement in all safety-related issues. Management had tried to increase the use of ear-plugs by workers before the study was conducted, using group lectures, poster campaigns, and disciplinary action. These efforts seemed to have had limited success.

Control and experimental groups were drawn from two departments involved mainly in lathe-type operations characterised by high-frequency noise levels averaging 90 decibels. Both groups received a standard lecture on hearing conservation, but only the experimental group received immediate feedback as a reinforcer. In order to gauge hearing loss, short audiometric tests were administered at the beginning and end of a work shift, and the audiograms from these tests were shown to the workers immediately after the test. The differences between the beginning of shift and end of shift tests were expressed in terms of temporary hearing loss.

One copy of the audiogram was given to each of the workers, and a second was placed on a special bulletin board in the production area. As well as the data on temporary hearing loss, other information such as a worker's name, age, and number of years in the department also appeared on the bulletin board. Workers were encouraged to try to use ear-plugs during one of their testing days so that they could observe the effect of noise on temporary hearing loss during that shift. On the other testing day there would be no such condition. The testing procedure was terminated after all the workers had been tested. For a period of five months thereafter (the follow-up period) the researchers sampled the behaviour of ear-plug use.

The resu'ts indicate that in the experimental ᴅepartment the use of ear-plugs had risen appreciably (from 35% to 85%) at the end of the five-month period. But the control group, who did not participate in the experiment except for listening to the standard lecture on hearing conservation, did not undergo any noticeable change. It took some time for the dramatic rise in ear-plug use in the experimental group to take place.

The effects of the experimental conditions were complemented by a management prescription requiring the compulsory use of ear-plugs in the production area. This was an important adjunct to the experiment because, in the changed environment, deviant behaviour (not wearing ear-plugs) could result in corrective or punitive responses by supervisors. Therefore, this altered the balance in favour of ear-plug use.

In the weaving department of a textile factory with 1200 employees, another company tried to encourage workers to use ear-plugs in a noise environment averaging 106 decibels. Previous promotion campaigns and disciplinary action aimed at increasing ear protector use proved to be ineffective. This company then decided to introduce a programme whereby tokens were dispensed at random times by managers to workers wearing ear-plugs. A token consisted of a slip of paper carrying the factory's official letterhead and a serial number used for monitoring purposes. The tokens could be used to acquire a variety of inexpensive consumer products, and each product had a price expressed in terms of the number of tokens required for its purchase. Wall charts were also used to show ear-plug usage rates. The results of the experiment indicated that a substantial improvement in ear-plug use occurred.

The experiments conducted at the two companies relied on individual feedback and the token economy system, and the expenditure involved was no higher than the costs of a conventional promotion campaign to encourage the use of personal protective equipment. The experimental evidence strongly supports the effectiveness of the behaviourist approach for promoting the use of personal protective equipment.

In a study conducted in a large hospital, a behaviour modification programme involving staff from many functions was used (Snyder & Luthans, 1982). Supervisors were given training in behaviour modification, and were encouraged to select problems and behaviours that could be measured, analysed, and adjusted by behaviour modification. Subsequently, intervention strategies were selected and applied. The results of the study indicated that behaviour modification as a process made a very favourable impact on performance in the hospital.

In another study, behaviour modification was used to improve teaching methods in schools for severely handicapped children (Parsons et al., 1987). The purpose of the programme was to encourage staff to use material and engage in classroom activities that had greater applicability in the real world. The programme was planned and executed by appealing to normal behaviour modification principles, with a successful outcome.

Criticisms of Organisational Behaviour Modification

Despite its apparent success, organisational behaviour modification has been the subject of a number of criticisms. The most favourable results emanating from the use of behaviour modification techniques are associated with highly controllable situations, such as a straightforward process in a small business, or variables that are independent and easily isolated (e.g. absenteeism). As research studies move into more complex situations involving subtle interactions between people, and where jobs are interdependent, the success of behaviour modification techniques is open to question.

Furthermore, almost all the research studies have focused on employees in the lower echelons of the organisation, paying less attention to the behaviour of managerial or professional staff. At these lower organisational levels, employees experience greater supervisory control and encounter less complex jobs, and it is said that these conditions facilitate the obtaining of positive results from the use of behaviour modification techniques (Miner, 1980).

The ethical problem of behaviour control and modification has to be considered, and some argue that the systematic manipulation and control of people undermines freedom and is an affront to the dignity of the individual (Robertson & Cooper, 1983). Others assert that operant conditioning principles lack the capacity to explain human action because they are not concerned with the internal functioning of the person (Locke, 1977). This criticism may have had greater validity in the past, because more recent work on behaviour modification acknowledges that behaviour is better understood as a function of both the situation and the person, and the interaction between the two (Davis & Luthans, 1980). There is a useful summary in Hodgetts (1991, p.118) presenting both the criticisms and the replies from proponents of behaviour modification.

Acknowledging the interaction between situational and personal factors, encapsulated in social learning theory, is said to be more productive than the purely situational view contained in operant conditioning. Reference has already been made to a social learning approach in the discussion of personality in Chapter 1.

The Relevance of Social Learning Theory

In social learning theory, internal cognitive processes are said to have some effect on behaviour. This could be reflected in a person's expectations about the outcome of a particular piece of behaviour. The individual realises from experience that certain actions will produce valuable benefits, and other actions will result in avoiding future trouble (Bandura, 1977). For example, business people do not have to wait until they experience the shock of a burning warehouse before they are prompted to take out fire insurance cover.

Another aspect of social learning theory is the notion that individuals adopt their own pattern of behaviour by observing and copying or modelling the behaviour of others. On the face of it, the act of modelling one's behaviour on other people's appears to provide no direct reinforcement. But what if the observer had expectations that certain desirable consequences could flow from adopting the behaviour of the model? The junior executive may copy the behaviour of the successful senior executive (e.g. mannerisms, work rate, management style) in the expectation that such behaviour leads to desired outcomes. Obviously cognitive activity comes to the fore in this example.

The socialisation processes involved in situations like the one described are informal, as opposed to formal processes like induction programmes for new recruits or the training programmes for established employees described later in the chapter. In some quarters there is a belief that the socialisation process should not be left to chance but should be formalised and used in a proactive sense by the organisation if the challenges of today's business world are to be successfully met (Nota, 1988). (Apart from the discussion of socialisation in connection with a behavioural perspective on personality in Chapter 1, there is reference in Chapter 11 to organisational socialisation in the context of the development of corporate culture.)

Social learning theorists maintain that although people respond to external reinforcement (e.g. money or praise), people often control and develop patterns of behaviour through the use of self-reinforcement. For example, a positive self-reinforcement could arise when an athlete, having appraised his or her performance in finishing in fifth place in an important race, nevertheless feels extremely satisfied because of the strong competition. Another athlete, having appraised his or her performance, feels intensely dissatisfied with the outcome and rebukes himself or herself.

It is now apparent that internal cognitive processes, such as self-reinforcement and expectations as to the outcome of behaviour, should be placed alongside external reinforcement when considering the application of behaviour modification techniques. According to Arnold, Robertson, & Cooper (1991), "more recent work has shown that the inclusion of ideas from social cognitive theory provides a theoretically more advanced, though still practical, basis for bringing about

behavioural change". For further comment on social cognitive theory (Bandura, 1986) see the section on behavioural role modelling later in the chapter.

COGNITIVE LEARNING

The main difference between a behaviourist approach to learning and a cognitive approach is that in cognitive learning there is a change in what the learner knows rather than what he or she does. The processing of knowledge is therefore important. Cognitive learning consists of two components—insight learning and latent learning.

Insight Learning

Much learning involves understanding what is being learned and thinking about it. Even animals behave sometimes as if they had insight into the situation to which they are responding. In a normal experiment in insight learning a problem is presented, followed by a period of time when no apparent progress is made, and finally a solution suddenly emerges. A feature of insight learning is that it can be generalisable to other similar situations (see panel overleaf).

Latent Learning

Latent learning is not manifest at the time learning takes place. The learning goes on in the absence of reward, but when a suitable reward is available the information previously learned can be used. We tend to store knowledge about positive and negative reinforcements acquired through past experience. For example, we may well have registered that a certain type of previous job was a source of satisfaction whereas another proved unsatisfactory. Likewise, the individual forms many kinds of cognitions about the way the career in which he or she is interested is structured, from the trainee stage right up to the highest position of responsibility.

Chimpanzees and Insight Learning

Kohler (1927) placed chimpanzees in an enclosed play area where food was kept out of their reach. Potential tools such as poles and boxes were placed in the enclosure, and the chimpanzees rapidly learned how to use a box to stand on or a pole to move the food in their direction. At times the poles were even used for pole-vaulting.

In this experiment, learning did not appear to develop as a result of trial and error and reinforcement, but came about in sudden flashes of insight. The chimpanzee would roam about the enclosure for some time, and then suddenly would stand on a box, grasp a pole and strike a banana suspended out of normal reach above the enclosure. When the chimpanzees were moved to new situations, the previous learning seemed to be transferred and the problems were solved quickly.

Cognitions from several different learning experiences may be integrated so that the individual can adapt to new situations and achieve personal goals. Tolman (1948) made an early contribution to the concept of latent learning. He placed a rat in a maze, and the rat developed a cognitive map or mental picture of the maze. The rat learned something about the spatial arrangement of the maze, but this learning was not evident until a reinforcement motivated the animal to behave—i.e. to use an alternative escape route when the original one was blocked.

Cognitive learning is closely related to other topics discussed elsewhere in this book. For example, selective perception (Chapter 3) and information processing (Chapter 5) are important ingredients in the cognitive process. But the heart of cognitive learning is memory.

MEMORY

Memory performs many functions and is involved in nearly every aspect of behaviour. In order to remember new information the individual needs to process or encode the information, store or retain it until it is called for, and be able to retrieve it when required to do so. If any of these processes breaks down for any reason, the result is a failure to remember; in other words, we forget.

Research on learning usually emphasises the acquisition of knowledge and skills, whereas research on memory is largely concerned with retention and retrieval—although, clearly, there is a relationship between these two concepts. The human memory can be supplemented by an external memory. There are many situations where information is available without the need for it to be stored in the individual's memory: brand packaging information, shopping lists, buyers' guides, or advertisements cut out by a consumer are all part of the consumer's external memory.

Research in cognitive psychology shows that the performance of memory is sensitive to the context surrounding the item committed to memory, and is dependent on factors related to the person, the information to be learned, the learning instructions given to the person, and the questions chosen to test memory (Jenkins, 1974). The importance of context is underlined by Horton and Mills (1984) who state that, "if there is a single principle that best describes the current status of the cognitive psychology of human memory, it is that the contextualist thesis is alive and well at both the empirical and theoretical levels".

It would appear that those interested in advertising should be aware of the importance of context—defined as consumer processing goals which determine the information committed to memory, and the interfering effects of competitive advertising—when it comes to information contained in advertisements that are committed to memory (Kellar, 1987). Memory is divided into two types: short term and long term.

Short-term Memory

Short-term memory (STM) is said to have limited storage capacity and is capable of holding a small amount of information for a short time. Normally we can remember around seven names, or seven letters in the alphabet, although each of the names may contain many more than seven letters. A feature of STM is the rapid loss of information; therefore, we tend to repeat the information over and over again in order to retain it.

An employee is verbally given a customer's telephone number and asked to ring the customer immediately. Without writing the number on a piece of paper, the employee retains the number in his or her STM while dialling it. After making the telephone call he or she is likely to forget the number. Likewise, an accounts' clerk holds a list of numbers in his or her STM for a brief period while engaged in mental arithmetic.

Long-term Memory

At some stage in the learning process, information is transferred from STM to long-term memory (LTM). When material can be recalled reliably after a day or a week, it is safe to conclude that the information is recalled from LTM. Before the transfer takes place, a fair amount of information can be lost but, unlike STM, the capacity of LTM is substantial and forgetting is slower. Other major functions of memory that will be discussed in this chapter are: encode or process; store or retain; retrieval; and recall.

Encode or Process

The storage capacity of STM is, as stated earlier, limited to around seven items or "chunks" of information (Miller, 1956). A chunk may be a single letter or digit or a combination of letters or digits, each combination being a chunk. We can remember a long telephone number (e.g. 35366673) because it can be chunked (35-36-66-73). In essence, a chunk is an organised cognitive structure that can grow in size as information is integrated into it. A brand name could be considered the summary of more detailed information about a product in the eyes of a consumer familiar with that product. When chunking words, the load on the memory is eased considerably. In order to facilitate memorising, the following words may be chunked to form a sentence:

company	a
The	acquisition
of	reorganisation
necessitates	another

The sentence reads: "The acquisition of another company necessitates a reorganisation".

Schemata

One important type of information in memory that is related to chunks is memory schemata. A schemata is an internal structure, developed through experience, that organises incoming information in relation to previous experience (Mander & Parker, 1976). The experienced stockbroker draws on a well-organised strategy (schemata) in buying or selling shares, and utilises a wide repertoire of dealing strategies, as well as interpreting the mood of the stock market, using his or her knowledge or experience. In addition, the broker may be able to rely on rapid recall from LTM about possible deals. The novice stockbroker would find each item of incoming information difficult to deal with. The information cannot be related quickly and easily to existing stored material because his or her schemata is underdeveloped. This could result in confusion and a lack of ability to process and respond to incoming information at the early stages of learning.

Scripts

A special subcase of a schemata is a script which describes a scenario of behaviour applicable to a particular setting, such as a restaurant script—the sequence includes being seated, looking at the menu, ordering food, paying the bill, and leaving (Gleitman, 1991). A script amounts to expectations about how various types of event will unfold, and its general function is to facilitate cognitive processing. When an incoming stimulus activates a person's script, a rich network of information is tapped that substantially reduces the burden of processing the stimulus. Scripts appear to exert significant influence on both the encoding and retrieval functions and as a result script-based information processing is highly automatic and efficient (Smith & Houston, 1985).

Scripts are said to provide an efficient framework for summarising what has been learned about a task, either derived from experience or observing others, and could be applied to the training of new employees. Because experts should have a greater repertoire of more thoroughly developed scripts for many activities within their task domain, teaching novices the scripts of experts may be an efficient way to train them (Lord & Kernan, 1987)

Rehearsal

As a means of keeping information activated in STM, rehearsal is used. Rehearsal is an activity that recycles the same items of information in STM. For example, a new word encountered in the study of a foreign language is repeated over and over again. Rehearsal is said to occur when items of information are repeated silently or overtly by the individual, and is limited by the capacity of STM to around seven items or chunks circulating in the system. It must not be confused with mere repetition, and it implies an active, conscious interaction with incoming information. Material that is rehearsed is then transferred to LTM.

Coding

It is suggested that there are two basic ways of representing information in memory—i.e. that there are two coding systems (Paivio, 1969). One is verbal, and the other is non-verbal and uses imagery. The latter could arise when you imagine a scene described by a sentence or caption, or a brand name may be associated with some mental image of that brand. On an aerosol can of freshener, a scene depicting a beautiful garden in springtime is obviously designed to create the appropriate imagery.

However, it is important from a manufacturer's point of view for the consumer to process the verbal or semantic information in the advertisement. Otherwise, a consumer who processes the imagery only (e.g. a waterfall or a beautiful scene) and fails to relate the claims made in the advertisement to his or her experience of the product, will be badly informed when confronted with product choice in a store. This is an example of the background of the advertisement diverting attention from the message. It is important to bear in mind that in processing material, individual differences with respect to priorities, preferences, and prejudices play a significant part.

Store or Retain

Various methods are employed to ensure the retention of incoming information. Obviously there is a limit to what can be stored in STM. An eight-digit number (e.g. 13456839) could be broken into manageable chunks (13-45-68-39), making four items, which will facilitate short-term retention.

Although LTM can be improved greatly by the individual becoming more proficient at encoding information, there is a distinct limit on the improvement of STM. A high priority is given to information that helps to achieve personal objectives, and information that can be easily stored (Shiffrin & Atkinson, 1969). For example, a consumer plans to compare specified foods in the supermarket on the basis of nutritional content, using only the information printed on the package. All that is required in this particular situation is to commit to memory the brands that the consumer plans to compare in the supermarket. However, if the information on nutritional content appeared in an advertisement or in an article in a health food newsletter, and not on the package, the consumer would have to put more information into his or her memory.

Events that are surprising, novel, inconsistent with our expectations, and so on, will often be given priority when it comes to processing and storage—e.g. a new price or an interesting new feature in a well-established home computer or word-processor.

Advertising can facilitate the retention of a message about a product. Frequently new products require the support of an intensive advertising campaign to capture the attention of the consumer. Special promotions such as free gifts or substantial discounts for a set

period produce a similar effect. A different strategy is likely to apply to advertising older, more familiar brands. The objective then is to foster long-term awareness and to mount a continuous but less saturated advertising campaign (Myers & Reynolds, 1967).

Hierarchical Models

A model for the structure of LTM to facilitate retention is the hierarchical model. This proposes that memory is structured with specific ideas categorised under more general ideas. Thus the concepts of a canary and an ostrich are categorised under birds, and birds are categorised under animals. At the highest level of the hierarchy (presented as a *conceptual hierarchy* in Fig. 4.1), there are a small number of general concepts, and at the bottom, many specific concepts (Collins & Quillian, 1969).

A similar model could be applied to the structure of information about accounting systems. Accounting could be sub-divided

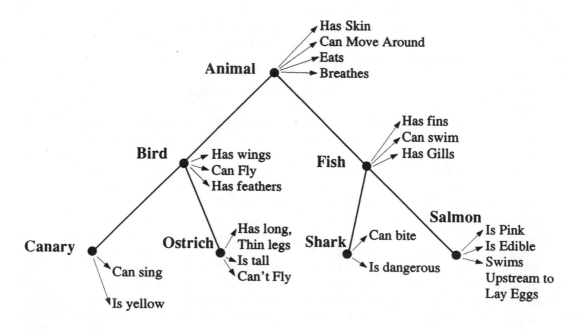

FIG. 4.1. A conceptual hierarchy. Source: Collins, A.M. and Quillian, M. (1969). Retrieval time from semantic memory. *Journal of Verbal Learning and Verbal Behavior, 8,* 240–247. Reproduced by permission.

into financial and management accounting. Financial accounting would include items such as trial balance, profit and loss account and balance sheet; and management accounting has sub-divisions such as direct and indirect costs and various methods of allocating them.

The conceptual hierarchy, depicted in Fig. 4.1, is a potent tool for facilitating learning. In one experiment, a group that had a brief exposure to 112 words presented in the form of a conceptual hierarchy were far more effective in reporting orally the words they could remember than a random group who did not receive the words in an organised form (Bower et al., 1969).

When a tree of items are associated, but not necessarily as a conceptual hierarchy, it is called an *associative hierarchy*. This is depicted in Fig. 4.2. The outcome of experiments on the associative hierarchy is similar to the results achieved with the conceptual hierarchy, but it would appear that the conceptual hierarchy is more organised and meaningful (Bower et al., 1969).

Conceptual Similarity
Another way of organising material is the use of a conceptual category. In examining the association between words, one may be able to conclude that certain things are similar conceptually, whereas others are not (Underwood, 1964). Words of both low and high similarity appear in Table 4.2. These were used in a memory experiment in which lists of words, high and low in conceptual similarity, were spoken by the experimenter. The subjects were told nothing about the differences between the lists shown in Table 4.2. After each list was read, subjects were asked to reproduce as many words as they could, in any order.

You will notice that the words listed under high similarity can be grouped under the names of people, animals, clergy, and dances. The scope to cluster words does not exist with

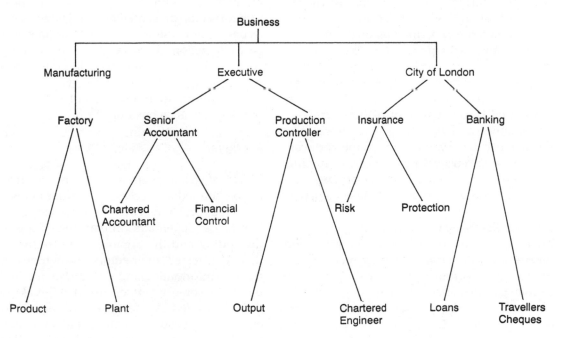

FIG. 4.2. An associative hierarchy.

TABLE 4.2

Words That are High and Low in Conceptual Similarity

Low Similarity		High Similarity	
Apple	Cruiser	Bob	Foxtrot
Football	Trumpet	Rabbi	Joe
Emerald	Doctor	Cow	Bishop
Trout	Head	Rumba	Dog
Copper	Wide	Bill	Tango
Theft	Blue	Priest	John
Hat	Gasoline	Horse	Minister
Table	Cotton	Waltz	Cat

Source: Adapted from Underwood, B.J. (1964). The representativeness of rote verbal learning. In A.W. Melton (Ed.), *Categories of human learning*. New York: Academic Press, (pp. 48–78).

the low similarity items. Those who participated in an experiment, but were unaware of the differences between the lists, experienced a high success rate when they unwittingly clustered the words in accordance with the type classification suggested earlier. Those who did not cluster the words on the basis of high similarity fared badly. When the experimental procedure was changed and participants were asked to be on the look out for word similarities, the best results in remembering were achieved. The message from these studies is that if the individual learns a way of relating items to one another and is able to place them in a particular category, then this framework can be used as a retrieval plan in reconstructing the items from memory. Performance in learning should improve as a consequence.

Personal System of Categorisation
There are many occasions when words or meaningful material are presented to us without the assistance of prior categorisation. In such circumstances, it can greatly assist the learner if he or she devises a personal system of categorisation. In Mandler and Pearlstone (1966), words arranged according to a classification system devised by the learner were more readily recalled than words

arranged in a predetermined sequence that the learner had to comprehend and follow. The very act of organising the material is in itself an aid to learning, particularly when the learner is involved in developing the system of organisation that is used. This appears to be at variance with the evidence on prior categorisation presented earlier. The principle of one's own system of categorisation can be seen in action in a management training course when, for example, a large group of participants is divided into syndicates to discuss information and present a summary of the syndicate's position.

Retrieval

Retrieval from memory can range from almost immediate access for familiar items to involved, problem-search processes for other items. It is dependent on both the quality of the coding and the organisation of information transferred to memory. Sometimes an item of information cannot be remembered, but then some event occurs that gives the "clue" needed to retrieve the item. For example, a consumer realises that some item which is not on the shopping list is needed, but is unable to recall the item unaided. However, while shopping in the supermarket the consumer sees a related item, or the item itself, which suddenly triggers recall.

People sometimes use real-life episodes to help them remember when certain events occurred. In a study of memory (Warrington & Sanders, 1972) the date of the assassination of President Kennedy was tied to the date of some event in the life of the person being questioned. A child of the respondent may have been born on that day, so the date of the assassination is then worked out by inference. A number of people of the older generation can vividly recall what they were doing when they heard the news of the assassination. When recalling what happened at a party, or who was there, a person may engage in imagery retrieval by visualising the room in which the event took place. This may facilitate the recall of the names of those present when the party-goers are known to the person engaged in recall. As regards marketing, an advertiser may use location and imagery to facilitate recall of the identity of the product; for example, the advertisement contains a picture depicting the user of a particular brand of air-freshener relaxing in the woods near a cool, idyllic stream.

Mnemonics

Mnemonics is a method of remembering items by imposing a structure of organisation on the material to be memorised. The example of the advertisement for the brand of air-freshener, referred to in the previous section, could be used as a mnemonic device. This device is known as the *method of loci*, in which people or objects to be remembered are associated with familiar locations. It is a peg system which provides an organisational framework for learning material as well as offering good retrieval cues. Many of the popular mnemonic devices rely on visual imagery. People tend to learn verbal materials better when they are connected with some visual image. For example, manufacturers incorporate imagery in the brand names of their products—"Thick and Zesty" tomato sauce, and "Easy-Off" oven cleaner.

If a learner wants to remember a particular item in a series (e.g. the third), then a peg system using numbering is useful. A popular system using numbers is as follows: one is a bun, two is a shoe, three is a tree, four is a door, five is a hive, six is sticks, seven is heaven, eight is a gate, nine is mine, and ten is a hen. This facilitates the development of a mental image of each item.

Another mnemonic device is the key word (e.g. cognition, bureaucracy) which publishers frequently use. In the March 1982 issue of *Protection* (a magazine about safety), a safety practitioner provided a mnemonic check list. Part of this list, which helped him to remember courses of action by heart, is reproduced in Table 4.3.

Mnemonic devices appear to be suitable when long lists of separate items need to be remembered. By relying on visual imagery, there could be problems when the learner tries to memorise abstract words. The mnemonic devices have been criticised because they do not foster the development of understanding and reasoning. But this criticism is unfair because really these devices are only appropriate to rote memory tasks (Eysenck & Keane, 1990).

Recall

The level of arousal (whether calm or active) can affect the ability of the person to recognise and recall. There is a difference between recognition and recall, and this is apparent when we recognise somebody but cannot recall their name. There is reason to believe that recognition and recall improve as a consequence of exposure to repeated messages, though eventually the effects are less pronounced (Bettman, 1984).

A number of difficulties arise with the recall of certain types of information. Material that is meaningful poses less of a problem. For example, the words "college" or "office" are associated with a number of events and experiences. But the same cannot be said of a nonsense syllable (e.g. "nac") (Ebbinghaus, 1885). Nonsense syllables, such as "dax" and

TABLE 4.3

Mnemonic Check-lists for Safety Practitioners

FIRST AID		ACCIDENTS AND INVESTIGATION	
P	— preservation of life	L	— looking after the injured
M	— minimising effects of illness and injury	I	— isolate the hazard
I	— immediate presence of trained personnel	F	— feeling for other employees
M	— minor injuries which do not need medical attention	E	— enquiry afterwards
		P	— persistence
HEALTH		R	— respect for witnesses' statements
I	— identification of hazard	O	— open mind
E	— eliminate	B	— background
S	— substitute	E	— explanation
I	— isolate		
P	— protection	I	— injury
		A	— accident
S	— first signs of over-exposure	U	— unsafe act or condition
I	— illness(es) due to over-exposure	H	— human failing
C	— conditions of over-exposure	B	— background
C	— consequences of over-exposure		
		LPG	
FIRE		C	— cutting off supply
R	— rapid spread in the early stages	E	— evacuation (erect barrier)
L	— late discovery	C	— containing spillage
L	— late call of the fire brigade	A	— avoid ignition sources
H	— harassment of fire fighting facilities	A	— approach downwind
		A	— avoid splashing on clothing
O	— occupancy		
C	— construction		
T	— time to evacuate building		
E	— number of exits		
T_	— travel distance to exit		

"ruf", are fairly unfamiliar to all learners, and we cannot rely on previous experiences to facilitate recall. However, there could be some familiarity with nonsense syllables—dax may be associated with a town in the south-west of France, and ruf sounds phonetically like rough. But not everybody would establish these associations (Burns & Dobson, 1984).

One can never know whether memory genuinely represents what was originally seen, or whether it represents a plausible reconstruction, with perhaps the addition of details that were never present in the first place. There is substantial evidence indicating that human beings have a tremendous capacity for describing what they believe to have happened, but these descriptions may have little relationship to what actually happened (Bartlett, 1932). Often people are unaware that their account of a happening is either invented or inaccurate. It is therefore not surprising to find conflicts of evidence in courts of law when two witnesses provide entirely different accounts of what happened and each swears that his or her account is the correct one.

When experimental subjects recalled stories, distortion occurred, changes were found in the meaning of passages, and reproductions got shorter with the omission of details (Bartlett, 1932). To achieve coherency, a story, though differing considerably from the original, would become a story in its own right, revamped with additional material in order to make sense out of it. People's names and other information appeared to get lost. Similarly, the example in the panel below shows how substantial inaccuracies in recall arise when we amend material to fit our preconceptions.

Though our preconceptions tend to promote inaccurate recall, there are occasions when this can be helpful as far as memory is concerned. In another experiment, two groups were presented with an account of a female patient, Nancy, who consults a medical practitioner (Owens, Bower, & Black, 1979). The experimental group was told that Nancy might be pregnant; the control group was not given this information. This was the only distinguishing feature in the reports given to the two groups, which were tested subsequently for the purposes of recall. The experimental group reported more items of information than the control group, and these items were not included in the original story; in fact, they were inferred or invented.

Forgetting

Forgetting arises when we cannot recall material at a particular time. It may not be due to a loss of information from our memory, but an inability to retrieve the information because the index system guiding the search is lost or inefficient, or because material has been classified in an inappropriate way so that the normal cues for retrieval are not effective (Tulving, 1968). A number of other explanations are put forward to account for why we forget. As time passes the "memory trace" of what was originally perceived decays. An alternative explanation is that certain processes interfere with the specific information committed to memory, and this undermines our ability to recall that information. There is experimental evidence to suggest that the interference explanation is more important than the decay explanation (Waugh & Norman, 1965).

Interference.   This can be expressed in a variety of forms. Some of the important ones are as follows:

- *Retroactive:* The placing of new information in the memory undermines the recall of previously recorded information. For example, a firm of accountants has changed its telephone number. After committing the new number to memory, the client may find it difficult to retrieve the old number.
- *Proactive:* Information that was previously committed to memory undermines the recording of new information. For example, a sales representative who has regularly dealt with the previous manager of a store finds it difficult to remember the name of the new manager.
- *Repression:* The individual subconsciously avoids retrieving information associated with unpleasant events. A patient might forget an appointment arranged with a

---

Inaccuracy in Recall

In this experiment, two groups were presented with a short passage of prose describing some aspects of the life of a girl. Group A was told that the girl's name was Carol Harris and group B was told that the girl's name was Helen Keller.

A week later the groups were asked whether the passage of prose included the statement that the girl was deaf, dumb, and blind. Only 5% of group A said "yes", but 50% of group B said "yes". The information on the girl's disability was not included in the original passage of prose, but apparently Helen Keller was known to a number of people in group B as actually being deaf, dumb, and blind, and they convinced themselves that they were given this information originally. (Sulin & Dooling, 1974)

doctor because of some traumatic experience associated with a previous visit to the doctor's surgery.

- *Emotion:* Anxiety can inhibit the retrieval of information. A student's anxiety about failing an examination may inhibit his or her attempts to retrieve information in the examination room.

The time that information enters memory, be it recent or at an earlier time, is something to consider. The advantage accruing to earlier information is that it is likely to receive more attention. However, it appears that the more recently acquired information can be retrieved more easily (the *recency effect*). But imposing a delay of 30 seconds before recall eliminates the recency effect completely, whereas it does not affect significantly the power of recall of information acquired earlier (the *primacy effect*) (Glanzer & Cunitz, 1966).

There are some ways of counteracting the effects of forgetting. It has been found that when a period of sleep intervenes between learning and recall, recall is greatly improved (Jenkins & Dallenbach, 1924). Perhaps the absence of the distractions of wakefulness, and the relative inactivity of sleep, may account for this finding. However, if one dreams during sleep (a period when the brain is relatively active), there is some evidence to suggest that more forgetting occurs (Ekstrand, 1972). More recent evidence indicates that

sleep has a beneficial effect on long-term memory (Idzikowski, 1984).

Rehearsal is said to prevent forgetting because it keeps replenishing the memory trace. An involved story about an event or happening must of necessity be repeated frequently to facilitate retention and avoid forgetting. A number of the measures discussed earlier in connection with the systematic organisation and arrangement of material prior to transfer to memory assist in combating forgetting.

Postscript. Finally, it should be noted that the study of human memory has been evolving and changing rapidly in recent times. There has been criticism of laboratory-based research on the grounds of artificiality, and an endorse- ment of human cognition that recognises the person's interaction with everyday environ- ments. The latter is called the *ecological approach to cognition*, and focuses on how people use knowledge from the past in present discourses. The ecological approach has, however, been vehemently attacked by the laboratory-based researchers. A feature of the ecological approach is discourse analysis, concerned with how people use knowledge of the past in current interactions with others in order to generate shared meanings and to communicate with each other (Conway, 1992).

TRAINING (TRANSFER OF LEARNING)

The basic psychological principle underlying the transfer of learning is that of generalisation of stimuli, referred to earlier in connection with operant conditioning. When a stimulus is similar to the original conditioned stimulus it tends to elicit the same response.

Transfer

The transfer of learning (or training) is the process by which the effects of training in one

form of an activity are transferred to another form. A claim often made is that the learning of mathematics, or at least the training involved, improves the learner's ability to solve problems requiring logic, whether these are of a mathematical nature or not. The classical curriculum of Latin, Greek, and Rhetoric was considered important in the development of logical reasoning. Many educational programmes are built on the assumption that people have the ability to transfer what they have learned in one situation to another. If transfer was not possible, there would be little justification for formal education; every element of knowledge, skill, and capacity would have to be taught separately.

Lateral Transfer. Lateral transfer involves performance at the same level of complexity as the initial learning, but in a different context. If a child has classroom experience of arithmetic calculations with the aid of blocks or beads, this understanding could be transferred laterally at home if the child, having removed two tennis balls from a box of six, realises that four are left.

Sequential Transfer. Sequential transfer occurs when we build on a learning foundation. A fact learned today in a subject may have some relationship to a fact or idea learned tomorrow. For example, multiplication draws on an understanding of addition.

Vertical Transfer. Vertical transfer occurs when learning at one level, such as comprehending facts about addition and subtraction, facilitates the solution of problems utilising these arithmetic operations. It amounts to a transfer from the simpler components of a task to the more complex ones.

Positive Transfer. When training or performance in one task can be transferred to another, positive transfer is said to occur. Positive transfer manifests itself in the following situations: learning Latin may aid the learning of Italian; having learned the skills of ice-skating could mean that learning to roller-skate is that much easier; and mastering the skill of driving a car results in positive transfer to lorry driving.

Negative Transfer. Negative transfer is said to occur when previous learning in a particular task hinders learning in another task. This is obvious when a motorist from the UK switches from driving on the left-hand side of the road to the right-hand side while holidaying in France.

Errors may arise in a factory when an employee with experience of driving one particular model of fork-lift truck drives another model. The pedals for braking, reversing and accelerating can differ in sequence from one model to the next. This can be contrasted with the standardisation universally applicable to cars, apart from the difference in the positioning of the steering wheel between cars made in different countries.

The typist of yesteryear may have experienced both positive and negative transfer when changing from a manual to an electric typewriter. Positive transfer occurs when the keys are tapped correctly, but negative transfer occurs when the typist takes action to return the carriage to the beginning of the line. On the manual machine this is done by hitting a lever on the carriage, and on the electric machine by depressing a key. When the typist changes from a manual to an electric machine, performance is initially slowed down by the persistent habit of raising the hand to hit the lever, which now does not exist, at the end of every line.

Skill Acquisition

Employee training can be defined as the systematic acquisition of skills, rules, concepts, or attitudes that result in improved performance on the job (Goldstein, 1986). Employee training may be very specific, as in the case of showing a telephone operator how to handle long-distance calls, or it may be less concrete as in training a manager to adopt a particular leadership style.

A number of factors are said to influence the acquisition of skilled performance. Most of these factors were proposed following simulated training sessions, rather than real-life training situations. However, they command a certain degree of acceptance.

Knowledge of Results or Feedback

Feedback comes from two sources—one from the external environment and one from the internal environment. The external environment could be the display section of a machine in front of an operator. The internal environment could be the operator's own muscles and nervous system. Both these sources provide continuous feedback so that, in effect, the operator is always receiving knowledge of results.

In driving a car the learner has a feel for the car while operating the clutch and accelerator pedals simultaneously (feedback from the internal environment), and receives feedback from the external environment when reading the dials on the dashboard. The driving instructor will provide augmented feedback in the form of verbal knowledge of results by telling the learner that he or she is engaged in movements that are either right or wrong. The instructor could also offer explanations to assist the learner.

Knowledge of results, preferably with appropriate comments, is important to the student on a course where continuous assessment is used, and to the business executive who wants to know how well operations are progressing, so that remedial action can be taken if necessary and objectives modified accordingly. Feedback should be precise and the trainee should be given adequate time to assimilate it (Rogers, 1974). Feedback should be appropriate to the stage of learning that the learner has reached, and it should concentrate on those aspects of the task that are critical for good performance. A trainee can become very dependent on feedback, and removing it could cause a deterioration in performance. This would be particularly so if its removal took place early on in learning.

Part or Whole Methods

Using the part method the task is broken down into sections, and this method is suitable where learning does not suffer from compartmentalising a body of knowledge. So if the task lends itself to chunking, and where some elements of the task are more difficult than others and require more time to be devoted to practising them, then this can be a useful method.

Typing is an example of an activity best learned by this method, where each letter is practised on the keyboard before attempting whole words. Likewise with swimming, where the components of breathing, arm stroke, and kicking are practised separately at first. Though the part method may appear appropriate for the actor learning the lines of a long play, and it may have beneficial motivational effects in the sense that the learner can reach the learning objective more quickly, it has disadvantages. For example, in linking the parts to form the whole the learner might get the sequence mixed up.

When the whole method is used, the total task is practised until mastered. Tasks that are best learned by this method include those where integration and rhythm are the critical features of the skill. For example, some tasks, like learning to drive a car, would lose their meaning if broken into chunks. In addition, the whole method is preferable when the total task is small enough to avoid resorting to numerous rests and when the learner is quick to learn and is intelligent.

A compromise between the part and whole methods is the *progressive (cumulative) part method*, which has been used for training older workers (Belbin, 1964). The task is broken into its constituent elements; the first element is practised until mastered, when the trainee proceeds to the second element and practises it in combination with the first. When this combination is mastered the third element is added, and so on until the whole task has been learned.

Older trainees often suffer from an impairment of short-term memory and, if the task is learned by the part method, the first element can be forgotten by the time the last element is learned. However, the whole method is also unsuitable because it tends to overload older trainees. The progressive (cumulative) part method attempts to prevent overload and minimises the likelihood of forgetting the earlier elements of a task by a constant process of rehearsal.

Massed or Distributed Practice

Should the elements of learning a task be massed together, or should they be spaced or distributed over a period of time? When the student is cramming in preparation for an examination, he or she is engaged in massed practice. In such circumstances some students could be highly motivated with less time to forget the study material. For some people, massed practice can result in boredom and fatigue and impair performance. However, this condition could be alleviated by the introduction of suitable rest pauses. (The role of rest pauses in motivated behaviour was discussed in Chapter 2.) Massed practice would appear to be particularly suited to a problem-solving exercise where it is important to persevere with the task until a solution is found.

Distributed or paced practice seems to be more beneficial for motor skill learning (e.g. typing) than for verbal or more complex

learning. But as the material to be learned increases in quantity and difficulty, then paced practice has a useful function (Bass & Vaughan, 1966).

In a verbal learning experiment, paced practice was found to be superior to massed practice (Hovland, 1938). Two groups of subjects learned a list of twelve nonsense syllables. One group, which adopted massed practice, had a six-second rest between each run through the list. The other group, which adopted paced practice, had a two-minute rest. The two groups were then given scores for the number of syllables that were reported correctly. The spaced practice group was superior to the massed practice group. It would be unwise, however, to generalise this result to all instances of verbal learning.

Learning Curves

The trainer must realise that learning takes place in a piecemeal fashion along increasingly difficult paths, and this can be depicted in the form of a learning curve (shown in Fig. 4.3). During the course of training, the learning curve sometimes shows

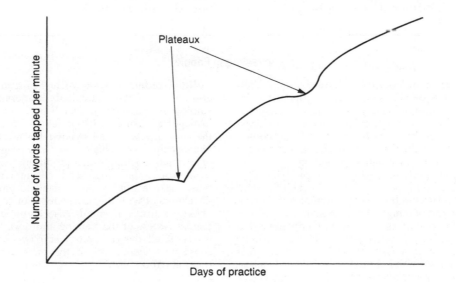

FIG. 4.3. A learning curve. Source: Adapted from Bryan, W.L. and Harter, N. (1899). Studies on the telegraphic language: The acquisition of a hierarchy of habits. *Psychological Review, 6*, 345–375.

a levelling off, after which it rises again. The point on the curve where little or no learning seems to be occurring was termed a plateau in a classic study of trainee telegraphists (Bryan & Harter, 1899).

One suggestion to account for the shape of the curve is that the first plateau denotes the point at which the trainees mastered the motion of tapping individual letters but had not yet progressed to tapping whole words. The second plateau denotes the point at which the trainees mastered whole words but not phrases. These plateaux were supposed to represent a period in the learning process when the skill concerned was in the process of reorganisation. This has been challenged in the light of subsequent studies in this field (e.g. Keller, 1959). It should be noted that the plateaux do not appear during the learning of all skills, but where they can be identified the trainer should take particular care in explaining to the trainees the reasons for their lack of progress, otherwise the trainees may become demotivated.

In a study of taxi drivers it was noted that driving performance improved by a factor of 50% in 7 weeks, but then it remained constant (a plateau) for 12 weeks. Over the following 10 weeks additional training brought about another 50% improvement in performance (Chisseli & Brown, 1955). When learning to drive, much effort goes into the development of hand–foot coordination. As driving proficiency increases the driver pays more attention to monitoring road conditions, predicting the reactions of other drivers, and so on.

TRAINING PROCESS

If an organisation is to function well, it is necessary for it to have an adequate system for employee training and development. The first step in the training process is to conduct a systematic assessment of training needs.

The importance of the training process in organisations is underlined by a number of initiatives taken at the national level (see panel below).

Needs Assessment

The assessment of needs can be considered at three levels of analysis—organisation, task, and person analysis (Wexley, 1984). A fourth level—demographic analysis—can also be added (Latham, 1988).

Investing in People

Training and Enterprise Councils and their Scottish equivalents have been responsible for persuading employers to strive to achieve national standards for effective training in order to address Britain's poor record in training. These bodies, backed by the British Government, are also involved in the validation of training.

A new body—Investors in People UK (IIP)—was created in early 1994 to ensure that the standards related to training assessment remain consistent and of a high quality. A main aim of IIP is to help companies to be more competitive and employees to be better skilled. This body will be predominantly a mechanism for assessing whether a company's training programme fits its business needs. The focus will be on the way training benefits a company in a measured financial sense.

IIP, according to the new Chief Executive, can also influence the individual development of employees. In one of Unilever's divisions, management using the IIP guidelines realised that the company was not making the most of its female employees. This resulted in a programme of affirmative action being introduced.

In order to be recognised by IIP, an employer must make a public commitment to employee development with the achievement of corporate objectives firmly in mind. Also required is the regular review of the training and development needs of all the company's employees, and a subsequent evaluation of the effectiveness of training (Wood, 1994).

Organisation Analysis

In examining the aims and objectives of the organisation it may be possible to identify barriers to their achievement. These could include poor production planning and control, unacceptable errors and waste, and poor management and work distribution. If we feel the barriers to the achievement of organisational aims and objectives can be removed by training rather than by some other activity, then we are, in effect, taking the first step in an assessment of training needs at the organisational level

Research in this area seems to be concerned with two strands of analysis. First, there is the recognition that training should be linked to corporate strategy, and, second, it is suggested that organisations have an ethical responsibility to minimise the technical obsolescence of their employees (Latham, 1988).

With regard to the first strand of analysis, Brown and Read (1984) make the point that the difference in productivity between UK and Japanese companies could be narrowed significantly by taking a strategic view of training policies. This would entail harmonising business and training plans. Hussey (1985) is in sympathy with this viewpoint when he argues that training objectives, particularly for management development, should be reviewed by top management when a major change in corporate direction is anticipated. Also, he believes that training should not be pursued for the improvement of the individual with the expectation that it will benefit the organisation. On the contrary, training should be undertaken for the benefit of the organisation in the realisation that this will eventually act to the advantage of the individual.

The second strand of analysis epitomises an approach to training whereby the organisation is committed to such activities as retraining workers to create a more flexible and adaptable work-force, with the added advantage of fostering corporate loyalty, training in job-search skills, and basic adult education.

Task Analysis

This approach focuses on (i) the objectives and (ii) the outcomes of tasks performed by employees. Tasks are broken down into their constituent elements or operations. For example, the assembly of an *MFI* kitchen or piece of furniture, consisting of certain main operations and a number of further operations which, in turn, are suitable for sub-division, is an example of the process involved in order to create a particular product. The latter is the outcome of the task.

The first step in task or job analysis is make sure that existing jobs produce outcomes that are consistent with the overall goals of the organisation. Where there is a significant discrepancy, it may be necessary to redesign existing jobs, or to design new jobs, to rectify the situation.

Given a suitable match between the goals of the organisation and the outcomes of tasks, the second step is concerned with identifying actual behaviours required of job holders if the requisite outcomes are to materialise. We have now arrived at a stage in the needs assessment process that has direct relevance to training. For example, if deficiencies in actual job behaviours are identified, this can signal the need for training. Techniques of job analysis are discussed in connection with personnel selection in Chapter 13.

Moving on from task analysis to the design of specific training programmes is one of the most challenging aspects of employee training (Goldstein, 1980). In this context it is wise to specify the knowledge, skills, and abilities (KSAs) that employees must possess in order to perform successfully the necessary job-related behaviours identified through task analysis:

- Knowledge refers to evidence of having absorbed and understood items of information.
- Skills are manifest when a person operates a machine, solves a difficult problem, and relates effectively in an interpersonal way to people.

- Attitudes in this context refers to the emotional or affective feelings and perspectives held by a person.

KSAs are normally identified with the help of job experts (e.g. industrial psychologists, management consultants in this field, and managers). Training programmes can then be designed to facilitate the learning of these KSAs.

The different types of learning (called capabilities) developed by Gagne (1977), and listed below, are considered more comprehensive than the list of items found in the KSAs:

1. basic learning, as found in the formation of simple associations between stimuli and responses in classical conditioning;
2. intellectual skills, at different levels;
3. cognitive strategy, as evidenced in such activities as learning to learn;
4. verbal information, as reflected in an ability to state specific information;
5. perceptual motor skills, as seen in driving a car; and
6. attitude.

Based on a study aimed at establishing the most relevant and difficult areas related to retraining, Downs (1985) maintains that the jobs of the future will require less memorising of facts and procedures, few physical skills, and far more conceptual ability. Such findings are relevant when considering training needs.

Person Analysis
This phase of the needs assessment process puts the spotlight on those who need training and on the type of training required. There are different ways of collecting data during this phase. Performance appraisal information could be available for those already holding down jobs. For those who are about to join the organisation, information derived from the use of selection methods could be used. Alternatively, the opinions of key individuals in the organisation could be sought, using questionnaires or interviews. Whatever method is used, it is no easy matter trying to establish who is in need of training (Latham, 1988).

Demographic Analysis
In recent years, a new phase in the needs assessment process, called demographic analysis, has been identified (Latham, 1988). This takes a macro view in the sense that it considers the needs of populations of individuals (e.g. women, people over 40, etc.) from a policy perspective rather from the standpoint of the individual employee within the organisation. Demographic studies have been conducted to identify the training needs of populations of workers by, for instance, age, sex, and position within the organisational hierarchy. For example, Berryman-Fink (1985), examined the views of male and female managers on the communication and training needs of women in management. Both male and female managers identified four communication skills for which female managers needed training—assertiveness, confidence building, public speaking, and dealing with men. By contrast, male managers needed training in listening, verbal skills, non-verbal communication, empathy, and sensitivity.

Training Objectives

Before formulating objectives for training, it is necessary to have conducted an assessment of training needs. This could have taken the form of, for example, task analysis, reported earlier, where a detailed view of the operation of a task is obtained. Such analysis is necessary in order to be in a position to state clearly the outcomes from the training programme. These outcomes will eventually manifest themselves in training objectives, which will state what the employee will be able to do at the end of the training session, and are often referred to as *behavioural objectives*. In addition, one would expect some reference to standards of performance and the conditions under which the behaviour takes place. For example, on completion of the training the trainee will be able to operate a word-processor to a specified degree of accuracy.

In some training sessions a list of behavioural objectives does not materialise in the manner just described. Instead, competence at the end of a training session is assessed by the use of various tests or job simulation exercises. Whatever system is used (setting behavioural objectives or some other method), it is important to specify the preferred outcomes from the training programme at the outset, so that trainees are offered programmes to help them achieve the desired standard.

There are particular training situations that do not lend themselves to the setting of specific and precise objectives. In this case—for example, experiential learning exercises discussed later in this chapter and also in Chapter 12—it is acceptable for objectives to be relatively general. The reason is that the learning taking place has unique significance for the individual, and each person derives different benefits from the experience.

Training Methods

From what has been said it is now apparent that the training methods used should have been chosen or developed following the statement of training objectives, and not the reverse. A variety of techniques, methods, and procedures are available. These include lectures, films, video tapes, computer-assisted instruction, case studies, conferences, simulation, behaviour modelling, coaching, and mentoring.

There are a number of questions one can ask about the various techniques. Does the technique emphasise content (information), process (behaviours), or both? Where does the training occur—on-site or off-site? Does the training emphasise psychomotor skills, cognitive skills, social skills, or a combination of all three? In the final analysis, what we must try to achieve is to ensure that the technique

or techniques chosen are appropriate in the light of the identified training needs.

One-way Communication
Lectures in their purest form, together with video tapes and films, are examples of a one-way flow of information from the trainer to the trainees. Unless the lecturer or trainer is prepared to respond to questions and provide feedback, the lecture method requires the recipients of information to be passive, with no opportunity to assess how well or how badly they are absorbing the message that is put across. Often the motivation of the audience is taken for granted, and their individual needs and abilities are ignored, with little or no rewards given. Sometimes lectures are considered quite boring and difficult to comprehend.

In defence of one-way communication through the methods described, it could be argued that these methods are efficient in the use of time and money, and are suitable for communicating substantial amounts of information to large numbers of trainees in the minimum amount of time.

Computer-assisted Instruction
This is similar to programmed learning discussed earlier in this chapter. Computer-assisted instruction adopts the principles of programmed instruction and adds the power and flexibility we associate with rapidly expanding computer technology. The phenomenal growth in the use of personal computers makes this method of training more accessible in the home and the office. Nowadays the trainee can interact with the computer in the form of a dialogue.

Computer-assisted instruction utilises two important learning principles—motivation and feedback. The motivation of trainees is normally high because of their interest in the process, and they are allowed to progress through the material at their own pace with the benefit of immediate feedback. However, transfer of learning is not always assured, except where, for example, the computer is used to enhance the realism of simulator training.

It is said that in order to impart a given amount of material, computer-assisted instruction places lower demands on the time of the trainer and trainee during the actual training session than do other methods, such as the lecture. However, there are no meaningful differences in the achievement scores between those trained under conventional training methods as opposed to computer-assisted instruction (Goldstein, 1986; Wexley, 1984). It should be noted that the preparation of packages used in computer-assisted instruction can be time consuming as well as expensive.

Conferences

A conference could be described as a carefully planned meeting with a specific purpose. The proceedings rely heavily on verbal communication between trainees, and this can help them understand concepts and influence attitudes.

Case Studies

This method relies on presenting a written report describing an organisational problem to trainees. On an individual basis, the trainee analyses the problem, makes certain assumptions about a number of events, and puts forward a set of solutions. Subsequently, trainees meet as a group and, with the assistance of the trainer, present and discuss their solutions and identify underlying principles.

A consistent criticism of lectures, conferences, and case studies, rests on the issue of transfer of learning. Information obtained from a conference, or lecture may have limited effect if the trainee returns to an organisational setting that does not support the application of such information. With regard to case studies, the outcome of these exercises may involve embracing principles that cannot easily be applied in the trainee's real-time organisational situation (Saal & Knight, 1988).

Simulations

When we provide approximations of real-life situations and events, we are essentially using simulations in training. The purpose of simulation is to reproduce an actual work situation under the control of a trainer, whereby the latter is able to provide trainees with useful and rapid feedback, and influence their motivational disposition. Training simulations can be used not only when trainees are working with materials and machines, but also when engaged in interpersonal processes. Simulations are generally far less expensive to run than training people in real-life situations, and the more realistic a simulation the greater the expected transfer of learning.

A good example of a machine simulator is the flight simulator used for training pilots. The trainee pilot can learn the appropriate response to all types of routine and hazardous conditions under controlled circumstances without the risk of injury or damage to the equipment. Advances in computer technology have created more complex and sophisticated flight simulators, but we are still rather ignorant about how seriously the trainee pilot reacts to these cleverly devised reproductions of reality with their impressive audio-visual effects. After all, the trainee pilot knows that when he or she "crashes" into a highly populated neighbourhood there is still a tomorrow!

In factories, trainees use simulators that are less complex than flight simulators. This is called *vestibule training*, and the trainees learn how to operate a piece of machinery away from the disrupting influences of the factory floor.

Role playing is a good illustration of an interpersonal simulation. Trainees go through the motions of playing a role related to work behaviour. If the trainees take the process seriously by eagerly embracing their assigned roles, role playing can be an effective method. It is suggested that if there is an acceptable level of motivation, and the role playing situation is a good representation of reality,

BEGINNING THE FINAL APPROACH, THE ULTIMATE TEST
OF CONTROL IS ADMINISTERED.

then there is some chance of the transfer of learning back to the role players' actual jobs (Saal & Knight, 1988).

There are variations in the way role playing is conducted. Reverse role playing is practised when a person takes on a role that is some other person's role. For example, *A* (a social security clerk) takes on the role of *B* (a claimant) in order to appreciate the client's perspective. There is also multiple role playing where a number of trainees are divided into teams. Each trainee acts out a situation, and subsequently compares and discusses the results with the other trainees.

Other types of interpersonal simulations include business games, as well as the case studies referred to earlier. With business games, trainees are required to make decisions in conditions that approximate circumstances found in the normal business environment. Nowadays, business games are operated using sophisticated computer packages like, for example, *Glass Inc.*, a six-hour, real-time organisational simulation in which participants manage a fictitious company (Stein, 1982). The design of this

business game has resulted in high content validity. It can be used as a diagnostic tool for identifying management training and development needs in an assessment centre, and for assessing team interaction as part of team-building programmes (Wexley, 1984). Team building is discussed in Chapter 7, and management development in Chapter 12.

Behavioural Role Modelling
This method, similar in some respects to the applied learning procedure referred to earlier, has captured the attention of practitioners and researchers in recent years and has grown in popularity. It is based on Bandura's social learning theory, more recently called *social cognitive theory* (Bandura, 1977; 1986). Apart from learning from one's direct experience, people may learn from observing the behaviour of others. This is referred to as vicarious (second-hand) learning. So trainees may learn new ways of behaving from observing the behaviour of role models. Vicarious learning is one of the major ways in which social cognitive theory differs from operant conditioning referred to earlier.

Originally, behaviour modelling was used in clinical psychology, treating people with phobias, but in the last couple of decades it has been applied to industry.

Mann and Decker (1984) summarise the components of behaviour modelling as follows:

- *Modelling*: the trainee observes another person engaging in desired behaviour for which he or she receives a reward. The trainee receives vicarious reinforcement by observing the role model receive the reward.
- *Retention processes*: the trainee encodes the observations for recall later.
- *Rehearsal*: the trainee goes through the motions where the actual observed behaviour is rehearsed or practised.
- *Social reinforcement*: the trainer and the other trainees reward the trainee for imitating the previously observed role model.
- *Transfer of training*: the trainee tries out the newly learned behaviours in his or her job and reports successes or failures back to the training group.

Behavioural role modelling is concerned with the trainee's motivation, provision of feedback, and the transfer of learning. By emphasising the importance of observation and vicarious reinforcement to learning, in addition to actual practice and direct reinforcement, it takes us a stage further than the traditional behaviour modification techniques discussed earlier. Closed-circuit television could be used to present role model behaviour that trainees should attempt to imitate. There is encouraging endorsement of this training method in the literature. For example, it was successfully used in a project designed to improve interpersonal relations among black employees and their predominantly white supervisors in a South African pharmaceutical company (Sorcher & Spence, 1982).

On-the-job Training

Among on-the-job training methods are induction courses, coaching, and mentoring. Induction courses are normally held during the first week of employment. New employees are usually informed about company policies, procedures, and where their job fits into the scheme of things. Coaching entails occasionally giving employees feedback and advice about aspects of their job performance, and is normally provided by the immediate supervisor or close colleagues. Mentoring is when senior organisational members take responsibility for the development and progression of newcomers.

Assessment of Training Methods

A problem encountered when making a global assessment of the effectiveness of the different training methods is that the literature to draw on has weaknesses. As Arnold et al. (1991) point out:

> One major problem in providing an overview of the effectiveness of different training methods is that much of the literature on training is theoretical rather than based on sound concepts, and descriptive rather than evaluative. Much of this literature is contained in various practitioner-orientated magazines and books. The scientific literature of work psychology does not contain such an extensive array of material, but in general the material is more rigorous and analytical.

Many of the approaches to training discussed here place a lot of control in the hands of trainers. They set training objectives, specify the contents of the training programme in terms of realistic tasks and skills, and, finally, ensure that the success rate in achieving objectives is sufficiently high. This overall approach has been referred to as the traditional approach to learning (Blackler & Shimmin, 1984). It is considered valid in the realms of operative, supervisory, and management training when knowledge and experience of a technical process are required. For example, the technical aspects of procedures governing machine operation and maintenance, budgetary control, and production planning and control would lend themselves to the traditional approach.

Alternative Approaches

One alternative approach incorporates the belief that learning is an active process best undertaken when individuals participate in and take responsibility for their own learning. This offers the trainee the opportunity to have a say in what the learning programme should accomplish, to exercise greater self-direction and control, and to remove the barriers to the attainment of learning objectives. The eventual outcome is said to increase sensitivity and lead to a continuing growth in self-awareness (Blackler & Shimmin, 1984).

Out of this training perspective has come management development with a firm humanistic flavour. The emphasis is on improving the sensitivity and self-awareness of the individual as a person and as somebody who interacts with others to bring about changes for the better in organisations. Stemming from this approach is sensitivity training (or T-groups), discussed as an organisational development intervention strategy in Chapter 12.

Approaches to management training and development at the present time are much broader than sensitivity training and related techniques. Two of these approaches—"action learning" and "competency based" management education—will now be examined. The concept of action learning is not new, but increasingly in recent years there has been noticeable interest in applying pure or adapted ideas of action learning to management training and development. Revans (1971) argues that traditional learning is concerned with providing knowledge to answer questions, the solutions to which are known in advance by the instructors. Action learning takes a different approach whereby students are asked to consider problems for which there are no obvious solutions, but which can be tackled by reinterpreting experience. Revans would view action learning as an activity whereby the student goes through a process of recognising that the relevant knowledge does not provide a solution to the problem under review; therefore, it is necessary to rely on experience to engage in "questioning insights".

The following is what one manager, who was a student on a formal action learning programme, had to say about his overall experience (Caie, 1988):

> There was a lot of learning from each other in sets (groups), either in a formal setting or at a distance. Often this learning involved insights into the person's character and how individuals performed in groups, rather than simply factual knowledge about members' businesses and experiences. Using real work situations as a learning environment for the project work proved invaluable and members learned a tremendous amount from the experiences of others.

There are two outcomes of action learning—one is the solving of problems right up to the implementation stage, and the other is learning while doing so. The latter involves developing a greater understanding of the learning process and of one's preferred approaches to learning. In addition, it could give rise to a reformulation of preferred approaches to learning with the potential to transfer them to the work situation. Concerning learning to learn, there is a recognition in Kolb's (1974) work that people learn in different ways. Practitioners in action learning have adapted these ideas (Caie, 1988). For example, a person may prefer to learn through new experiences (the pragmatist), by observation and reflection (the reflector), by conceptualisation (the theorist), and finally by experimentation (the activist). In practice it is unlikely that people adopt absolute positions on learning style, but they are more likely to have a leaning towards one style rather than another.

Once people have understood their own learning styles, derived from a question-naire, there is the opportunity in formal action learning programmes to become more balanced or broad-based learners by practising the learning styles that are less familiar to them. Alternatively, a conscious decision could be made to develop their strengths, and that could mean developing their particular orientation in learning style.

A systematic relationship has been established between learning style and personality. Individuals with different personalities were found to have different cognitive styles, and to resort to different decision-making strategies. Those with different cognitive styles approached learning in different ways (Furnham, 1992).

The current emphasis on management competencies (the technical term is competences) in management education and training stresses the nature of a manager's experience and the notion that experience is a great teacher. You will notice that learning from experience is enshrined in action learning. However, there are differences between the two approaches. One major difference is that the tutor or facilitator in action learning adopts a non-interventionist role to a far greater extent than does his or her counterpart in competency-based manage-ment education.

The following observation with regard to management competencies is from an executive director of the Council for Management Education and Development (Day, 1988):

> The emphasis on competence—the ability to put skills and knowledge into practice—stresses outputs from the management development process. This

approach stands in marked contrast to the traditional academic model of studying a body of knowledge and then being tested by a formal examination, primarily on retention of information rather than understanding and application.

Those of us who have respect for the traditional academic model would argue that it fosters understanding and perhaps limited application initially, but believe that managers need theories and concepts to assist them in interpreting their experience, otherwise they are unlikely to move outside the boundaries of their own experience with the real danger of becoming incompetent or even obsolete.

Berry (1991) refers to a recent study where managers were asked to express views on the value of their formal management education. Over 40% of the managers reported "that the greatest value of their education was the enormous range of ideas, theories and concepts to which they had been exposed and about which they had apparently learned. They reported that these were of significance to them in their managerial careers."

Finally, perhaps we can look forward to a future in which the academic model and the experiential model can coexist and complement each other for the betterment of the provision of management education and training

The Learning Organisation

It is interesting to reflect on the idea of a learning organisation, which has captured the imagination of trainers and others in recent times.

There is a view that for an organisation to grow and prosper, it has to develop a capacity to respond well to changes in its environment. A learning organisation can help with the development of that capacity by facilitating the learning of all its employees, and by being alert to the need for continuous transformation (Pedlar, Boydell, & Burgoyne, 1988).

In essence the aim is to create a culture of continuous learning for all employees. This goes beyond a narrow interpretation of training. Systematic self-analysis of a company's experience, especially its mistakes, is a necessary prerequisite for a company that wants to be a learning organisation. Garvin (1993) refers to the "3Ms" of learning organisations as follows:

- *Meaning:* A learning organisation is skilled at creating, acquiring, and transferring knowledge, and at modifying behaviour to reflect new knowledge and insights.
- *Management:* In a learning organisation, there is evidence of systematic problem solving, experimentation, learning from others, (see panel below) and transferring knowledge throughout the organisation by the rotation of personnel and by other means.
- *Measurement:* Ways are devised to assess the organisation's rate and level of learning to ensure that gains have been made. Rate and level of learning would be considered over a range of factors (e.g. cost, quality, delivery times, and innovations). The measures used would be concerned with the time taken to achieve improvement in relation to such factors.

The managerial qualities of the learning organisation have been described and operationalised (Senge, 1990; Beard, 1993). These embrace a serious approach to problem solving, objectivity, highly focused effort and patience, shared views of where the company is at, shared vision of the future, and team learning.

For a learning organisation to function well, it is said that one should pay attention to matters such as the following (Garvin, 1993):

- give employees time to reflect on innovative practices;
- equip them with the necessary skills;
- break down barriers (either internal or external to the organisation) that frustrate effort; and
- create learning forums.

Evaluation of Training

Essentially we are concerned with trying to establish the reliability (consistency) and validity (effectiveness in meeting objectives) of training programmes. This necessitates establishing a relationship between the training methods used and some measure (or criterion) of performance, and can only be done by examining the trainees' capabilities

---

Benchmarking and Conversations with Customers

Benchmarking, which amounts to learning from others, is an ongoing investigation and learning experience that ensures that the best industry practices are uncovered, analysed, adopted, and implemented. It is a disciplined process that begins with a thorough search to identify "best practice organisations", continues with a careful study of one's own practices and performance, progresses through systematic site visits and interviews, and concludes with an analysis of results, development of recommendations, and implementation.

Almost anything can be benchmarked. *Xerox*, the creator of the concept, has applied it to billing, warehousing, and automated manufacturing. AT&T's Benchmarking Group estimates that a moderate sized project takes 4 to 6 months and incurs out of pocket costs of $20,000. When personnel costs are included, the figure is three to four times higher.

Another way of gaining an outside perspective, which can provide an equally fertile source of ideas, is through customers. Conversations with customers invariably stimulate learning. Customers can provide up-to-date product information, competitive comparisons, insights into changing preferences, and immediate feedback about service and patterns of use. At *Motorola*, members of the Operating and Policy Committee, including the Chief Executive Officer, meet personally on a regular basis with customers (Garvin, 1993).

after training. If trainees meet the training objectives when they are assessed at the end of the programme, this shows internal or training validity. But if, after completing the training programme, it can be shown that the trainees' performance at work is up to the desired standard, then external or performance validity is achieved (Goldstein, 1978).

When evaluating a training programme it is desirable to go beyond a narrow concern with validation. One would obviously be interested in the trainees' general reactions to the programme—and make use of this information. The views of trainees should be carefully handled. It is known for trainees to be thoroughly satisfied with a programme merely because the instructor or trainer did a good job entertaining them. In other circumstances, the trainees come forward with a less than satisfactory evaluation because the instructor or trainer worked them very hard, or was unpopular for some reason. Feedback of this type may fail to inform us whether or not training was effective in achieving its objectives. Naturally, a major preoccupation is likely to be the extent to which there is a transfer of learning from the training programme to the place of work. For example, a trainee may pass the competency test at the end of the training programme but fail to transfer the learning to the job because of some inhibition, or continuing confidence in the old work methods.

When trying to relate training outcomes to organisational effectiveness, we run up against the problem of establishing whether the training variable, or a combination of other variables, was responsible for organisational success. For example, consider the case of where the training of sales representatives in an insurance company coincided with renewed public interest in life and endowment policies, and an upturn in the economy leading to increased earnings from the sale of policies. The extent to which training of sales representatives was responsible for increased sales revenue may be difficult to establish.

Such difficulties are often referred to as threats to validity. As a means to control the many threats to the validity of the evaluation of training, experimental designs can be used, although the typical conditions that prevail in real organisations may make this investigation impossible.

Probably it is true to say that there is a scarcity of good training evaluation studies, and that as a general principle one may state that it is easier to find reports of successful validation of training in perceptual motor skills, which are more amenable to straightforward testing of what has or has not been learnt, than in supervisory and management training. In the latter case, complex learning is at stake, involving the use of concepts and the transfer of learning to different situations. As a consequence, it is more difficult to demonstrate the effectiveness of supervisory and management training.

A final matter to consider is training people to improve their assessment skills, particularly in task analysis. This is referred to as "rater learning". According to Latham (1988), research in this area in recent years has focused almost exclusively on performance appraisal rather than training needs analysis.

Other observations related to training appear in Chapter 12 where there is a specific focus on the training and development of managers. From a current snapshot of training in the UK, many employers could be criticised (see panel overleaf).

Training within Organisations

Employers spend an average of £492 per head on training, with each employee spending a total of just over four days a year being trained, according to the Industrial Society's quarterly survey (*Training Trends*, 10, 1993).

A finding of particular note is that only 36% of personnel directors of organisations out of the Society's 12,000 member organisations defined objectives for each training and development programme. The majority of respondents did not know if training objectives were set.

With regard to the evaluation of training, most organisations did very little, apart from using questionnaires, to seek the employees' view on how effective their training had been. This made it very difficult to establish if training programmes had been successful.

The Industrial Society feels that organisations must take action to ensure that training has to be closely linked to business objectives, and not a sideshow with little connection to corporate strategy. The "Investment in People" initiative, administered by the British Training and Enterprise Councils, is intended to help companies link their training more effectively to their business plans. Finally, employers need systems to evaluate the aims of training before it happens, and the effectiveness of training after it has taken place (Wood, 1993).

SUMMARY: LEARNING, MEMORY, AND TRAINING

- Learning, which cannot be observed directly, embraces most of our behaviour and can be distinguished from performance. Three major approaches to the study of learning are: classical conditioning; operant conditioning; and cognitive learning.

- Classical conditioning was discussed, with the aid of a number of illustrations derived from business practice, under the following headings: unconditioned and conditioned stimulus; extinction and spontaneous recovery; generalisation; discrimination; and emotional response.

- Operant conditioning consists primarily of reinforcement. The principles of "contiguity" and "contingent" apply to reinforcement. This concept was discussed with reference to primary and secondary reinforcement, positive and negative reinforcement (including avoidance conditioning), punishment, and schedules of reinforcement. Schedules of reinforcement, appropriately illustrated, were sub-divided into intermittent or partial reinforcement and continuous reinforcement. The former were listed as fixed ratio, variable ratio, fixed interval, and variable interval.

- Programmed learning, which is linked to the concept of operant conditioning, consists of linear programming and branching. Linear programming and branching are techniques of programmed instruction. Behaviour modification, also related to operant conditioning, was discussed in terms of shaping and modelling, and specifically in an organisational context. Certain applications of behaviour modification were introduced. Criticisms of the concept of behaviour modification and the relevance of social learning theory were also discussed.

- Cognitive learning can be categorised as insight learning and latent learning. This concept is closely related to selective perception and information processing, and draws heavily on memory.

- Memory was classified as either short term or long term, and critical functions of memory were identified as encoding, storing, retrieving, and recalling information. The performance of memory is sensitive to context. Chunking, the use of schemata, scripts, and rehearsal, facilitate the encoding process prior to the transfer of information to long-term memory. Verbal and non-verbal coding systems are used to represent information in our memory. As a means to facilitate the storage of information in long-term memory, devices such as the conceptual hierarchy, the associative hierarchy, conceptual similarity, and a personal system of categorisation can be used.

- Retrieval depends on the quality of the coding system and the organisation of information transferred to memory. In this context, mnemonics and recall were explained. For a variety of reasons, distortions in the retrieval of information occur, and forgetting occurs when we fail to retrieve information. A number of possibilities were proposed to explain why we forget, and there was a brief reference to ways of counteracting the effects of forgetting.

- Transfer of learning (training) was referred to as a process by which the effects of

training in one activity are transferred to another. Different types of transfer were described—lateral, sequential, vertical, positive, and negative. Factors likely to influence skill development in a training context were identified as knowledge of results or feedback, part or whole, and massed or distributed practice. The relevance of learning curves was emphasised.

- Finally, the employee training process was discussed at length. The discussion focused on training needs assessment, training objectives, and training methods, with a distinction between trainer-centred and trainee-centred methods. A manifestation of the latter is action learning. The concluding section on training looked at the evaluation of training.

QUESTIONS

1. Distinguish between learning and performance.
2. Define the following processes in classical conditioning: (a) generalisation; (b) extinction; (c) conditioned stimulus; and (d) discrimination.
3. What is the significance of the association between an unconditioned stimulus and a conditioned stimulus in the field of marketing?
4. Explain the following terms: (a) primary and secondary reinforcement; (b) positive and negative reinforcement; (c) avoidance conditioning; and (d) contiguity and contingent.
5. Assess the relative strengths of different schedules of reinforcement in a business context.
6. Comment on the differences between programmed learning and behaviour modification.
7. Discuss behaviour modification as a technique used to promote good safety practice at work.
8. Compare and contrast operant condition-

ing and cognitive learning.
9. Identify the difference between short-term and long-term memory.
10. Using examples from business practice to illustrate your answer, what do you understand by: (a) an associative hierarchy; and (b) mnemonics?
11. Explain the following terms: (a) chunk; (b) schemata and scripts; (c) rehearsal; (d) interference and decay; and (e) primacy and recency effects.
12. Identify the activities involved in the assessment of training needs.
13. Review the training methods at the disposal of the trainer, and indicate the method(s) you consider appropriate in the training of: (a) airline pilots; and (b) sales representatives.
14. Explain the following terms: (a) action learning; and (b) competency-based management education.
15. Comment on why it is necessary to evaluate training, and mention the important issues involved in such an exercise.

REFERENCES

Allen, C.T. & Madden, T.H. (1985). A closer look at classical conditioning. *Journal of Consumer Research, 12*, 301–313.

Arnold, J., Robertson, I.T., & Cooper, C.L. (1991). *Work psychology: Understanding human behaviour in the workplace.* London: Pitman.

Atkinson, R.L., Atkinson, R.C., Smith E.E., & Hilgard, E.R. (1987). *Introduction to psychology* (ninth edition). New York: Harcourt Brace Jovanovich.

Bandura, A. (1977). *Social learning theory.* New York: Prentice-Hall.

Bandura, A. (1986). *Social foundations of thought and action: A social cognitive theory.* New York: Prentice-Hall.

Bartlett, F.C. (1932). *Remembering: An experimental and social study.* London: Cambridge University Press.

Bass, B.M. & Vaughan, J.A. (1966). *Training in industry: The management of learning.* Belmont, CA: Wadsworth.

Beard, D. (1993). Learning to change organisations. *Personnel Management*, January, 32-35.

Belbin, E. (1964). Training the adult worker. *Problems of Progress in Industry*, No. 15. London: HMSO.

Berry, A. (1991). Management development. *Manchester Business School Research Newsletter, 13*, 5.

Berryman-Fink, C. (1985). Male and female managers: Views of the communication skills and training needs of women in management. *Public Personnel Management, 14*, 307–313.

Bettman, J.R. (1984). Memory factors in consumer choice—a review. In I. Fenwick & J.A. Quelch (Eds.), *Consumer behaviour for marketing managers.* Newton, MA: Allyn & Bacon.

Blackler, F. & Shimmin, S. (1984). *Applying psychology in organisations.* London: Methuen.

Bower, G.H., Clark, M., Lesgold, A., & Winzenz, D. (1969). Hierarchical retrieval schemes in recall of categorised word lists. *Journal of Verbal Learning and Verbal Behavior, 8*, 323–343.

Brown, G.F. & Read, A.R. (1984). Personnel and training policies: Some lessons for Western companies. *Long Range Planning, 17*, 48–57.

Bryan, W.L. & Harter, N. (1899). Studies on the telegraphic language: The acquisition of a hierarchy of habits. *Psychological Review, 6*, 345–375.

Burns, R.B. & Dobson, C.B.L (1984). *Introductory psychology.* Lancaster: MTB Press.

Caie, B. (1988). Learning in style: Reflections on an action learning MBA programme. *Business Education, 9*, 109–117.

Chisseli, E.E. & Brown, C.W. (1955). *Personnel and industrial psychology* (second edition). New York: McGraw-Hill.

Cohen, D. (1981). *Consumer behaviour.* New York: Random House.

Collins, A.M. & Quillian, M. (1969). Retrieval time from semantic memory. *Journal of Verbal Learning and Verbal Behavior, 8*, 240–247.

Conway, M.A. (1992). Developments and debates in the study of human memory. *The Psychologist*, October, 439–440.

Davis, T.R.V. & Luthans, F. (1980). A social learning approach to organisational behaviour. *Academy of Management Review, 5*, 281–290.

Day, M. (1988). Managerial competence and the charter initiative. *Personnel Management*, August, 30-34.

Downs, S. (1985). Retraining for new skills. *Ergonomics, 28*, 1205–1211.

Ebbinghaus, H. (1885). *Memory: A contribution to experimental psychology.* New York: Columbia University Teachers' College.

Ekstrand, B.R. (1972). To sleep perchance to dream: About why we forget. In C.P. Duncan, L. Sechrest, & A.W. Melton (Eds.), *Human memory.* New York: Appleton-Century-Croft.

Eysenck, M.W. & Keane, M.T. (1990). *Cognitive psychology: A students' handbook* (second edition). Hove, UK: Lawrence Erlbaum Associates Ltd.

Furnham, A. (1992). Personality and learning style: A study of three instruments. *Individual Differences, 13*, 429–438.

Gagne, R.M. (1977). *The conditions of learning* (third edition). New York: Rinehart & Winston.

Garvin, D. (1993). Building a learning organisation. *Harvard Business Review*, July–August, 78-91.

Glanzer, M. & Cunitz, A.R. (1966). Two storage mechanisms in free recall. *Journal of Verbal Learning and Verbal Behavior, 5*, 351–360.

Gleitman, H. (1991). *Psychology.* 3rd Edition. New York: W.W. Norton & Co.

Goldstein, I.L. (1978). The pursuit of validity in the evaluation of training programmes. *Human Factors, 20*, 131–144.

Goldstein, I.L. (1980). Training in work organisations. *Annual Review of Psychology, 31*, 229–272.

Goldstein, I.L. (1986). *Training in organisations: Needs, assessment, development, and evaluation* (second edition). Monterey, CA: Brooks/Cole.

Goldstein, A.P. & Sorcher, M. (1974). *Changing supervisor behaviour.* New York: Pergamon.

Halcrow, A. (1986). Incentive! How three companies cut costs. *Personnel Journal*, February, 12.

Hall, J.F. (1976). *Classical conditioning and instrumental learning.* Philadelphia: Lippincott.

Hamner, W.C. (1977). Worker motivation programmes: The importance of climate, structure, and performance consequences. In W.C. Hamner & F.L. Schmidt (Eds.), *Contemporary problems in personnel.* Chicago: St. Clair.

Hamner, W.C. (1983). Reinforcement theory and contingency management in organisational settings. In R. Steers & L.W. Porter (Eds), *Motivation and work behaviour.* New York: McGraw-Hill.

Hamner, W.C. & Hamner, E.P. (1976). Behaviour modification on the bottom line. *Organisational Dynamics, 4,* 3–21.

Hodgetts, R.M. (1991). *Organisational behaviour: Theory and practice.* New York: Macmillan.

Horton, D.L. & Mills, C.B. (1984). Human learning and memory. *Annual Review of Psychology, 35,* 361–394.

Hovland, C.I. (1938). Experimental studies in rote learning theory—111: Distribution of practice with varying speeds of syllable presentation. *Journal of Experimental Psychology, 23,* 172–190.

Hull, C.L. (1943). *Principles of behaviour.* New York: Appleton-Century-Crofts.

Hussey, D.E. (1985). Implementing corporate strategy: Using management education and training. *Long Range Planning, 18,* 28–37.

Idzikowski, C. (1984). Sleep and memory. *British Journal of Psychology, 75,* 439–449.

Jenkins, J. (1974). Remember that old theory of memory? Well, forget it! *American Psychologist, 29,* 785–795.

Jenkins, J.G. & Dallenbach, K.M. (1924). Oblivescence during sleep and waking. *American Journal of Psychology, 35,* 605–612.

Kellar, K.L. (1987). Memory factors in advertising. *Journal of Consumer Research, 14,* 316–333.

Keller, F.S. (1959). The phantom plateaux. *Journal of the Experimental Analysis of Behaviour, 1,* 1–13.

Kohler, W. (1927). *The mentality of apes.* London: Routledge.

Kolb, D.A (1974). On management and the learning process. In D.A. Kolb, I.M. Rubin, & J.M. McIntyre (Eds.), *Organisational psychology,* (second edition). New York: Prentice-Hall.

Komaki, J., Waddell, W.M., & Pearce, M.G. (1977). The applied behavioural analysis approach and individual employees: Improving performance in two small businesses. *Organisational Behaviour and Human Performance, 19,* 337–352.

Latham, G. P. (1988). Human resource training and development. *Annual Review of Psychology, 39,* 545–582.

Latham, G.P. & Dossett, D.L. (1978). Designing incentive plans for unionised employees: A comparison of continuous and variable ratio reinforcement schedules. *Personnel Psychology, 31,* 47–61.

Lewis, D.J. & Duncan, C.P. (1956). Effect of different percentages of money reward on extinction of a lever pulling response. *Journal of Experimental Psychology, 52,* 23–27.

Locke, E.A. (1977). The myths of behaviour modelling in organisations. *Academy of Management Review, 4,* 543–553.

Lord, R.G. & Kernan, M.C. (1987). Scripts as determinants of purposeful behaviour in organisations. *Academy of Management Review, 12,* 265–277.

Luthans, F. & Kreitner, R. (1975). *Organisational behaviour modification.* Glenview, IL: Scott, Foresman.

Mander, J.M. & Parker, R.E. (1976). Memory for descriptive and spatial information in complex pictures. *Journal of Experimental Psychology: Human Learning and Memory, 2,* 38–48.

Mandler, G. & Pearlstone, Z. (1966). Free and constrained concept learning and subsequent recall. *Journal of Verbal Learning and Verbal Behaviour, 5,* 126–131.

Mann, R.B. & Decker, P.J. (1984). The effect of key behaviour distinctiveness on generalisation and recall in behaviour modelling training. *Academy of Management Journal, 27,* 900–910.

Menzies, R. (1937). Conditioned vasomotor response in human subjects. *Journal of Psychology, 4,* 75–120.

Miller, G.A. (1956). The magical number seven, plus or minus two: Some limits in our capacity for processing information. *Psychological Review, 63,* 81–97.

Miner, J.B. (1980). *Theories of organisational behaviour.* Fort Worth, TX: The Dryden Press.

Moorhead, G. & Griffin, R.W. (1992). *Organisational behaviour: Managing people and organisations* (third edition). Boston, MA: Houghton, Mifflin.

Myers, J.H. & Reynolds, W. (1967). *Consumer Behaviour and Marketing Management.* Boston, MA: Houghton, Mifflin.

Nota, B. (1988). The socialisation process of high commitment organisations. *Personnel, 65,* 20–23.

Owens, J., Bower, G.H., & Black, J.B. (1979). The soap opera effect in story recall. *Memory and Cognition, 7,* 185–191.

Paivio, A. (1969). Mental imagery in associative learning and memory. *Psychological Review, 76,* 241–263.

Parsons, M.B., Schepis, M.M., Reid, D.H., McCarn, J.E., & Green, C.W. (1987). Expanding the impact of behavioural staff management: A large-scale, long-term application in schools serving severely handicapped children. *Journal of Applied Behaviour Analysis, 20,* 139–150.

Pavlov, I.P. (1927). *Conditioned reflexes.* New York: Oxford University Press.

Pedlar, M., Boydell, R., & Burgoyne, J. (1988). *Learning company project.* Manpower Services Commission.

Revans, R.W. (1971). *Developing effective managers.* Praeger.

Robertson, I.T. & Cooper, C.L. (1983). *Human behaviour in organisations.* Plymouth: Macdonald & Evans.

Rogers, C.A. (1974). Feedback precision and post-feedback interval duration. *Journal of Experimental Psychology, 102.*

Saal, F.E. & Knight, P.A. (1988). *Industrial and organisational psychology: Science and practice.* Belmont, CA: Wadsworth.

Senge, P. (1990). *The fifth discipline: The art and practice of the learning organisation.* New York: Random House.

Shiffrin, R.M. & Atkinson, R.C. (1969). Storage and retrieval processes in long-term memory. *Psychological Review, 76,* 179–193.

Skinner, B.F. (1951). How to teach animals. *Scientific American, 185,* 26–29.

Skinner, B.F. (1961). *Analysis of behaviour.* New York: McGraw-Hill.

Smith, R.A. & Houston, M.J. (1985). A psychometric assessment of measures of scripts in consumer memory. *Journal of Consumer Research, 12,* 214–224.

Snyder, C. & Luthans, F. (1982). The application of OB modification to increase the productivity of hospital personnel. *HR Magazine* (formerly *Personnel Administrator*), August, 72.

Sorcher, M. & Spence, R. (1982). The interface project: Behaviour modelling as social technology in South Africa. *Personnel Psychology, 35,* 557–581.

Spence, K.W., Farber, I.E., & McFann, H.H. (1956). The relation of anxiety (drive) level to performance in competitionial and non-competitional paired-associated learning. *Journal of Experimental Psychology, 52,* 296–305.

Stein, R. T. (1982). Using real-time simulations to evaluate managerial skills. *Journal of Assessment Centre Technology, 5,* 9–15.

Sulin, R.A. & Dooling, D.J. (1974). Intrusion of a thematic idea in retention of prose. *Journal of Experimental Psychology, 103,* 244–262.

Thorndike, E.L. (1911). *Animal intelligence.* New York: Macmillan.

Tolman, E.C. (1948). Cognitive maps in rats and men. *Psychological Review, 55,* 189.

Tulving, E. (1968). Theoretical issues in free recall. In T. Dixon & D. Horton (Eds.), *Verbal behaviour and general behaviour theory.* New York: Prentice-Hall.

Underwood, B.J. (1964). The representativeness of rote verbal learning. In A.W. Melton (Ed.), *Categories of human learning.* New York: Academic Press.

Warrington, E.K. & Sanders, H. (1972). The fate of old memories. *Quarterly Journal of Experimental Psychology, 23,* 432–442.

Watson, J.B. & Rayner, R. (1920). Conditioned emotional reactions. *Journal of Experimental Psychology, 3,* 1–14.

Waugh, N.C. & Norman, D.A. (1965). Primary memory. *Psychological Review, 72,* 89–104.

Wexley, K. N. (1984). Personnel training. *Annual Review of Psychology, 35,* 519–551.

Williams, K.C. (1981). *Behavioural aspects of marketing.* London: Heinemann.

Wolfe, J.B. (1936). Effectiveness of token rewards for chimpanzees. *Comparative Psychology Monographs,* 12, Whole No. 60.

Wood, L. (1993). Employers criticised on training. *Financial Times,* 19 October.

Yukl, G.A., Latham, G.P., & Elliott, D.P. (1976). The effectiveness of performance incentives under continuous and variable ratio schedules of reinforcement. *Personnel Psychology, 29,* 221–231.

Zohar, D. (1980). Promoting the use of personal protective equipment by behaviour modification techniques. *Journal of Safety Research, 12,* 78–85.

5

Human Information Processing and Decision Making

Information processing and decision making are overlapping and related concepts, but there is a tendency among scholars to discuss them separately. In fact, the individual acts as a processor of information right through to the final decision stage. This chapter starts with a definition and illustrations of information processing, followed by an examination of three major approaches to the study of human information processing.

Next is a description of a decision cycle, followed by a discussion of three descriptive decision-making models. A distinction is made between structured and unstructured decision processes. This distinction is important when analysing decision making under conditions of uncertainty. A number of issues connected with decision making in conditions of uncertainty are raised. The development of decision support systems in the age of the computer is acknowledged, before closing the discussion with an examination of individual and organisational influences (e.g. decision styles, creativity, and bureaucratic factors) on human information processing and decision making.

This chapter draws on ideas developed in earlier chapters (e.g. personality, motivation, perception, and memory), and supports the discussion in later chapters (e.g. on attitudes, groups, leadership, and organisational culture).

HUMAN INFORMATION PROCESSING

A human information processing perspective is essentially a cognitive view of man. Human beings approach only a few situations in a unique way as information processors. Instead, information from a person's environment is processed through pre-existing systems of knowledge abstracted from various memory schemata (discussed in Chapter 4) and experiences. These would include beliefs, theories, propositions, and schemes. Effectively, they are structures of knowledge that provide people with an important interpretative function capable of attaching meaning to incoming information as well as augmenting it. These structures also help to resolve certain ambiguities and to draw inferences, sometimes unconsciously, from incoming information, and they create a much broader scene than could be justified by a literal interpretation of the material just received. The following illustrations refer to the handling of information.

Production managers, like most people, have personal goals and aspirations and are motivated to achieve goals. They are fortunate if their personal goals coincide with the goals of the organisation for which they work. In the pursuit of organisational goals, expressed as a specified quantity and quality of output, production managers have to place reliance on information, not always accurate, about such matters as the availability of raw material and manpower, stock levels, product quality, and the needs of customers. This and other information is used as a basis for making predictions about the business environment that influence the production function and to which it has to adapt.

The processor of information is essentially concerned with identifying and registering cues or stimuli that are perceived to be useful. The intelligent investor will not only pick up cues or information from the published accounts of a company, but will also rely on information from non-accounting sources, such as stockbrokers, financial analysts, and the financial press (although some of this information may have its origin in the accounting system of a company) (see panel below).

Information processing is considered by consumer researchers as an intermediate variable in the relationship between personality and behavioural outcomes. The focus of the research is the relationship between personality and information processing. The personality variable—need for cognition (or "N. Cog.")—has been investigated and found to be related to how advertisements may influence the formation of attitudes towards a consumer product. N. Cog. is a measure of the individual's tendency to enjoy thinking. Marketing experiments indicate that individuals high in N. Cog. are more influenced by the quality of arguments contained in an advertisement than are individuals low in N. Cog. who are apparently more influenced by peripheral advertising stimuli, such as the attractiveness of the person endorsing the product (Haugtvedt et al., 1988).

What are the implications of this personality orientation with respect to information processing? Those low in N. Cog. are said to need advertisements repeated more often, but those high in N. Cog. need less exposure to advertisements, though the advertisements should contain higher amounts of information. Further speculation indicates that those high in N. Cog. may rely more on newspapers and magazines for news, whereas those low in N. Cog. are likely to find television news coverage adequate. The

---

Auditors and Information Processing

The auditor establishes the appropriate starting point for an audit, and the extent of the assignment, after registering cues from early exploratory work. If the internal control system is perceived to be strong, less extensive tests of a substantive nature are likely to be performed. But if the internal control system is perceived at the outset to be on the weak side, more testing of entries in the accounting records is likely to be undertaken.

The next step is to translate and transform the cues or information into a meaningful pattern in order to facilitate the choice of an appropriate response. Before doing so, however, the information will be evaluated and that which is considered inappropriate will be rejected.

Having conducted the audit of the accounting information systems, and having evaluated the data at his or her disposal, an auditor is faced with the task of formulating opinions about the "true and fair" state of the client's financial statements. Before expressing an opinion, professional judgement will be exercised to determine the amount of information to collect, when to collect it, the manner in which it is to be collected, and the implications of the information collected.

The information is rarely, if ever, perfectly reliable or perfectly predictive of the "true and fair" state of the client's financial affairs. Nevertheless, the auditor may be held liable in law should the audited financial statements prove to be unrepresentative of the "true and fair" state when the latter is certified as being the case.

perspective described may be of assistance in the design of marketing communications, but one feels it would be difficult to arrive at market segmentation using the N. Cog. concept.

APPROACHES TO INFORMATION PROCESSING

There are at least three major approaches to the study of human information processing. These are the Lens model, the cognitive approach, and the process tracing approach.

Lens Model

The basic principles of this model are that the nature of the task environment exerts a powerful influence on behaviour; that the numerous cues from the environment within the grasp of the individual are usually imperfect; and that these cues are not very effective at predicting the environment with which the individual has to cope. As a result of the low level of predictability, the individual has to develop a range of processes that act as a response capability in order to achieve the objectives associated with the task (Brunswick, 1955).

The Lens model uses linear statistical procedures based on Bayesian decision theory. A primary objective of certain researchers using this approach in the accounting field is to build mathematical models designed to show the relative importance of different sets of information and to measure the accuracy and consistency of judgement. The measurement of consensus and predictability is also attempted.

The Lens model is a normative model. A normative model in this context is concerned with how people solve problems, how they predict events, how they make decisions, and so on. To test the model, actual behaviour can be compared with what the model predicts, and if there is a perfect match the model is said to be robust. If there is a mismatch, it is hoped that the discrepancies are reflected in a systematic way.

For a company making a major capital investment decision, techniques based on normative principles could be used. Subjective probabilities will also be considered, because certain benefits or costs are expected to accrue following the making of the decision. Subjective probabilities are really different degrees of belief in the truth of a particular proposition. People revise their subjective probabilities as new information is received, so in these circumstances we can expect the company to revise the predictions based on its investment decision.

Research on the Lens model identifies the prevalence of conservatism (Snowball, 1980). This means that when people receive new information, they revise their subjective probabilities in the direction indicated by the normative model, even though the revision may be very small. Misperception and bias in the handling of data emanating from a person's task environment explains to some extent the onset of conservatism. When significant revisions are built into a normative model, it would appear that one is gravitating towards a descriptive model; such a model would describe rather than prescribe the way the individual processes information.

A valid question to ask is whether individuals terminate the search for information at a point before the best or optimal stopping point as specified by the normative model? Sometimes it would appear that individuals have accumulated enough evidence to satisfy their own standards and stop short of the ideal position for the cessation of the search for information. Somebody wishing to buy a camcorder may be advised to consult the *Which* magazine report on camcorders. A thorough analysis of the strengths and weaknesses of the various brands covered in the report could be considered a prerequisite to a purchase decision. However, consumers may leaf quickly through the report without studying it closely or completely, and terminate the search for information before the optimal stopping point, feeling that they have enough information to make an acceptable decision.

In the last decade, the usefulness of Bayesian decision theory, which is used in the Lens model, has been questioned; criticism is levelled at the static nature of algebraic models for evaluating and combining information, and it is suggested that time would be better spent observing the decision-making process (descriptive theory) (Dillard, 1984).

Cognitive Approach

A cognitive approach has already been discussed in connection with the study of personality (Chapter 1) and motivation (Chapter 2). The focal point of attention with this approach in this section is information-seeking behaviour in a complex environment. The assumption is that it is both possible and useful to classify individuals according to how they use information—i.e. their customary style of processing information. (Related concepts—cognitive and decision styles—are discussed later in this chapter.)

Accounting studies based on the cognitive approach attempt to classify users of information by their personal characteristics, employing personality measures and decision style, the objective being to design information systems best suited to the individual style of the decision maker (Libby & Lewis, 1982). However, it is likely to be very difficult to accommodate a tailor-made information system compatible with the personality needs of various individuals in an organisation, though it is recognised that certain information processing tasks are performed more capably by people with particular cognitive approaches.

For example, in examining the problem-solving ability of schoolboys, it was found that those who were studying sciences and proposing to continue with their studies to degree level were showing tendencies to be

"convergers"—in other words, they tended to be analytical and symbolic in their thinking rather than being imaginative, fluent, and flexible. Those in the arts stream, however, showed a tendency to be "divergers"—i.e. imaginative, fluent, and flexible rather than analytical and symbolic (Hudson, 1966).

A rather crude extension of these different problem-solving orientations to work organisations might suggest that the converger may feel more at ease with tasks that are highly structured, whereas the diverger may find the less structured tasks more suited to his or her mode of operation. The highly structured tasks, exemplified by tight procedures and management techniques, are more prevalent further down the organisational hierarchy than at the top, where the number of relatively unstructured tasks is probably greater. Therefore a convergent outlook would seem to be particularly appropriate at the lower echelons of the organisation. But would a divergent outlook be suited to life at the top of the organisation? The likely answer is yes. Apparently, successful chief executives tend to rely more on "feel" and intuition (divergency type characteristics) than systematic reasoning—they synthesise rather than analyse, they intuitively know more than they can communicate, and they revel in ambiguity and dislike regularity (Bobbitt et al., 1978).

The cognitive approach is associated with the theories of Schroder, Driver, & Streufert, (1967). This work focuses on the reaction of a person's information processing system to changes in the complexity of the decision environment—particularly changes in the information load. Cognitive complexity has been referred to by Schroder et al. as having three main features: (i) differentiation (numbers of parts); (ii) integration (the degree to which the parts are related); and (iii) order (the clarity with which the layers are arranged in a hierarchy).

Cognitive complexity is a function of past experience, and this can be expressed as the amount of information received and the degree of success in negotiating problems in the past.

People facing increasing inputs of information to their processing systems are expected to develop relatively complex cognitive structures. These people tend to rely on more complex sources of information and spend more time searching for and processing information, as if to suggest that they can handle larger amounts of information and are motivated to seek an optimum level of information. A person with an ability to utilise complex conceptual processes (that are integrated in nature), is likely to understand and react favourably to complexity in his or her decision environment.

For example, a difficult tax problem is more likely to be resolved by a competent tax specialist than by an accountant with a peripheral interest in taxation. Speed and an ability to cope with a substantial amount of complex data would be a feature of the performance of the tax specialist. Apart from information load, the format for the display of information and the order in which the information is presented are also important considerations.

Process Tracing Approach

Unlike the other two approaches to human information processing, this approach goes beyond input–output analysis and attempts to obtain measures of events or processes between the input and output stages (Hayes, 1968). In both the Lens model and the cognitive approach, one draws inferences about how the information-processing system works by looking at the relationship between the information received from the task environment and the end result (i.e. the judgement or decision). With process tracing one seeks evidence relating to the actual information processing activities. The evidence is most commonly sought by asking individuals to describe their thought processes. Obviously, memory (discussed in

Chapter 4) plays an important part in the process tracing approach.

Protocol Analysis

In a study comparing the decision-making processes of experts and novices in the context of a financial analysis task, differences in the style and depth of analysis between the two groups were detected. The research method used in the study was process tracing or *protocol analysis* (Bouwman, 1984). Decision makers were asked to verbalise while engaged in financial analysis, and these verbalisations were recorded on tape. The resulting transcripts, called concurrent or thinking-aloud protocols, provide the data for the protocol analysis.

Each subject was given a number of financial cases to process during the financial analysis task. A case contained a general description of the firm and a three-year set of financial statements, consisting of a balance sheet, income statement, and pages with financial ratios, sales figures, and production data. Each subject was asked to evaluate quickly the financial position of the firm, and to identify the underlying problems, if any.

- Protocol analysis starts with splitting up the evidence provided by individuals into phrases, and coding or classifying these phrases with respect to the decision-making activity that they exhibit. (An example of a decision-making activity would be computing a financial trend or comparing costs and revenue.)
- Next the decision maker's goals are identified. (An example of a goal would be the objective of the individual to explore indicators of the economic health of the firm, or to discover unusual features of the financial statements.)
- The next step in protocol analysis is the identification of the decision-making processes in terms of the individual's analysis in relation to the goals he or she has set.

- The final step is to present a visual representation of the sequence of events leading from the initial examination of the information through to the making of the final decision.

A methodological weakness of protocol analysis stems from the difficulties in eliciting verbal descriptions from subjects. It is the degree of complexity of the task to be performed that exerts an influence on the way the information system functions in the process tracing approach. The task environment, or *problem space* as it is called, determines the extent of the problem. The problem space will then determine the processes used to come up with a solution. This is illustrated in the example in the panel below.

The accounting example provided is a simple problem, but the basic processes involved in solving it apply to more complex problems. For instance, if the land in question was leased rather than purchased, the problem would be more complicated. The student would have to establish whether it was a rental lease or a capital lease. He or she would go ahead with the construction of the problem space, combining his or her internal knowledge with the external information provided, using a process more difficult than that described in the example.

DECISION MAKING

Before examining decision-making models, a distinction should be made between different types of decisions made in organisations. Basically, there are two types—programmed or structured decisions, and non-programmed or unstructured decisions.

A programmed or structured decision is well defined; the decision maker is aware of the extent of the decision, and there exists a clear set of options from which a choice can be made. The method of evaluating the options has been established and is straightforward. Therefore the decision maker has a well specified and agreed decision procedure at his or her disposal (Simon, 1960). The following is an example of a programmed or structured decision (Cooke & Slack, 1984):

A manager has to choose a new packaging machine from a choice of two models, both of which are similar to an existing machine and are known to be reliable. The manager chooses the machine which offers the most attractive post-tax discounted return calculated over a five-year period. This involves collecting details (such as price and operating costs) of each machine, using a formula approved by the organisation for capital expenditure

---

Problem Space and an Accounting Problem

In an accounting exercise a student is confronted with a statement indicating that "land was purchased for £55,000 cash". The student is asked to make the required bookkeeping entry, and begins by constructing a problem space, which means identifying the type of problem to be solved (Dillard, 1984). In this case it is an accounting problem.

The student will then proceed to identify key words in the statement. The word "land" is compared with accounting words stored in long-term memory. When the word is identified, it is categorised by type. For example, a definition of an asset is recalled and is then checked to see if land possesses the characteristics of an asset. If it

does, it would be classified as an asset.

Next, the entry in the asset account will be determined by an evaluation of the word "purchased". The information with respect to acquiring an asset would be combined with the student's understanding of the principles of debit and credit. In this case, it would be a debit entry of £55,000 to the land account. The same process would apply to cash, but here it is a credit entry of £55,000 in the cash book. Obviously the manner in which the total process is activated will depend on the skill of the student. What is critical in this example is the interaction of the task environment and the expertise of the information processor in doing the exercise.

proposals. An order is then placed for the selected machine and the goods received section and accounts department are duly notified.

When decisions are unique and not routine, they can be classified as non-programmed or unstructured. This type of decision is illustrated later in the discussion of the implicit favourite model, and decision making under conditions of uncertainty.

Turning then to our main discussion of decision-making models, these are of two types: prescriptive and descriptive. Earlier in the analysis of the Lens model, a normative approach was considered prescriptive in the sense that the model tells us what ought to be done. The normative or prescriptive model attempts to impose on the decision maker the framework reflected in the assumptions of the model. A descriptive model, on the other hand, describes the steps involved in making a choice from among various courses of action open to the decision maker (as can be seen in the *Decision Cycle* section that follows). As we shall discover later, this is not always a rational process.

Decision Cycle

A study of over 2000 managers, supervisors, and executives was undertaken in order to determine what steps in the decision cycle they used and found helpful. Out of this study came a simple nine-step framework, though the outcome of other studies had a part to play as well (Archer, 1980). This is depicted in Fig. 5.1 as a decision process, and it is discussed with reference to a description of a relatively simple decision (Cooke & Slack, 1984).

1. Monitor. The environment should be monitored constantly to obtain feedback. The decision maker monitors the environment to detect deviations from plans or to pick up signals on the need to take a decision. For example, a company makes specialised quality testing equipment for the food

processing industry. The general manager of the company, having monitored the environment, has become aware of the fact that the number of late deliveries of testing equipment to customers is on the increase. Subsequently, this information is reinforced by a complaint from an important customer who has just received a second late delivery.

2. Define.   The problem or situation has to be defined precisely. The information picked up at the monitoring stage could relate to the symptoms of the problem, but not the causes. From initial inquiries it appears plausible that communication difficulties between the production and marketing functions are a contributory factor in the problem of late deliveries. The general manager writes a letter to both the marketing and production managers asking for information on the delivery service to customers and the present utilisation of manufacturing capacity.

3. Specify.   The decision objectives have to be specified, and the likely risks and the constraints should be considered. What the decision makers expected to be achieved is clarified.

4. Diagnose.   The problem or situation is analysed more thoroughly and the causes of the problem are scrutinised. The general manager discusses the problem with the production manager, who states that the reasons for the late deliveries are the unrealistic delivery promises made by sales staff, who are also said to be at fault in not giving manufacturing staff enough notice to plan production when large new orders are received.

Faced with this evidence the marketing manager in conversation with the general manager defends the sales staff. He or she maintains that prompt delivery is crucial in highly competitive market conditions, and that the company must react quickly to get new business. Inevitably the manufacturing

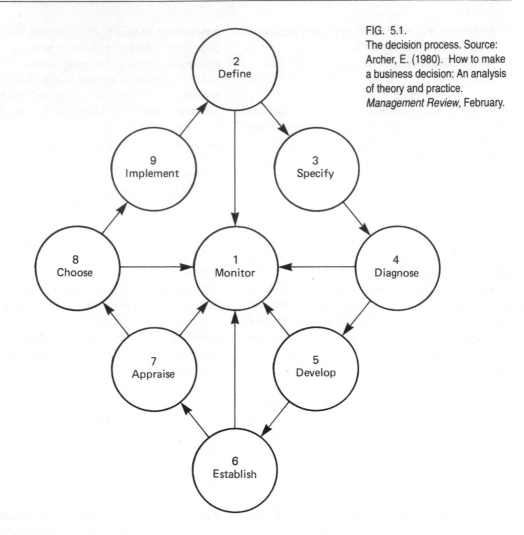

FIG. 5.1.
The decision process. Source:
Archer, E. (1980). How to make
a business decision: An analysis
of theory and practice.
Management Review, February.

staff cannot expect much notice of new orders. The marketing manager also maintains that the problem is inadequate capacity in the production area due to under-investment in plant over a period of time. Therefore the production function does not have sufficient flexibility to meet delivery times.

The general manager at this stage feels that, due to communication difficulties, neither the production manager nor the marketing manager has critical information at their disposal when making decisions.

5. Develop. Alternative courses of action or solutions are developed. The options open to the company are discussed at length and the critical options are listed as:

(a) introduce a computerised information system;
(b) all sales staff are required to check with production control before making promises related to delivery;
(c) put aside an afternoon each week for a meeting when operating managers can discuss matters of prime importance; and
(d) all sales staff are required to complete weekly reports on the likelihood of receiving orders from customers in the near future.

It is felt that any combination of these options is feasible.

6. Establish. At this stage the methods or criteria to be used in the appraisal of the options or alternatives are established. This could be any process that ensures the provision of an adequate amount of information to facilitate realistic promises with respect to deliveries of testing systems to customers, and to improve performance of the delivery service at acceptable cost levels.

7. Appraise. Alternative solutions or courses of action should be appraised. Each alternative or option is evaluated in terms of the quantity and quality of information it would provide for the production and marketing functions. The costs of implementation of the alternatives would also be appraised. Both costs and benefits would be expressed in quantitative and qualitative terms.

8. Choose. The best alternative solution or course of action is chosen. In this case a management committee made the decision, and chose two options (rather than one) for implementation. Options 5(a) and 5(d) were either too expensive or were unlikely to produce much useful information. The eventual decision was that 5(b) and 5(c) should be implemented.

9. Implement. The best alternative solution or course of action is implemented, and the detailed operational plan is discussed at the regular afternoon management meeting. In addition, the marketing manager issues instructions to sales staff to check with a certain person in production control before stating delivery times.

This decision process could revert back to stage 1, when monitoring activity resumes. In this case it was felt that the system had improved, but the general manager was not totally satisfied with the outcome. At a meeting of the management group, the problem was redefined to include some fundamental issues that affected the way the production function was organised, and the decision process started again.

In practice, the process of decision making is unlikely to be as smooth as the model depicted here would suggest. According to (Cooke & Slack, 1984):

> Real decision behaviours can exhibit frequent backtracks and jumps forward before an option is finally selected. Thus the decision process may not be smooth but a jerky and hesitant progression involving, at times, one step forwards and two steps backwards.

This descriptive decision process might be classified by Behling and Schriesheim (1976) as the "econological" model of decision making. Other descriptive models of decision making, which they acknowledge, and which will be analysed now, are the "bounded rationality" and "implicit favourite" models.

Econological Model

This model describes a logical and orderly way of processing information and arriving at a decision. The resultant decision is considered to be based on rationality. However, there is some evidence to suggest that consumers do not make decisions in the way outlined in the econological model. For example, in the literature on consumer behaviour a decision model similar to the econological model is adopted (Engel, Blackwell, & Kollat, 1978), but in a critical analysis of research studies on pre-purchase decision behaviour, it was concluded that for many purchases a decision process never occurs, or if purchase behaviour is preceded by a decision process, this process of choice is likely to be very limited. It typically involves the evaluation of only a few alternatives, it entails little external search for information, few evaluative criteria are used, and the evaluation process is a simple one. It may be more realistic to consider the potency of a personal recommendation from a friend or relative, coupled with limited search for and evaluation of information prior to a purchase decision. Other influences on purchase behaviour may be conformity to group norms, imitation, and so on (Olshavsky & Granbois, 1979).

Two main factors may account for the limitations of the econological model. One is concerned with the information available to decision makers, and the other with the processing capability of the individual.

With regard to examples of limitations on availability of information, only a small number of alternative courses of action in the decision situation come to mind, knowledge of a given alternative is incomplete, and when outcomes of the decision process are considered the values attached to these outcomes are imperfectly anticipated (Simon, 1957a). A real difficulty is the problem experienced by the decision maker in selecting even a limited number of alternative courses of action, because of knowledge deficiencies (Terry, 1968).

With regard to the information-processing capability of the individual, there are constraints in the way we seek solutions to problems. Even if the decision maker has full knowledge of all alternatives and outcomes, complete rationality could not be achieved because of the restrictions imposed on the decision process by the capabilities of the human mind as an information-processing system. The system accommodates only one process at a time, it cannot work in a parallel fashion and, as was stated in Chapter 4 with reference to memory, the inputs and outputs stemming from problem-solving activity are initially stored in a small short-term memory with very limited capacity. Of course the human information processing system has access to a substantial long-term memory with fast retrieval but slow storage. All these factors impose restrictions on the way in which the individual's information-processing system will seek solutions to problems (Simon & Newell, 1971).

Given the limiting factors identified earlier, it would appear that decision processes which are amenable to a consideration of a number of alternatives and outcomes cannot find expression in the form postulated by the econological model. Basically, we suffer deficiencies when comparing alternatives in a simultaneous fashion, rather than a sequential arrangement, and our memory storage system can be a handicap. Likewise, the exercise of placing values on various outcomes of the decision process, and ranking alternatives in order of preference, is constrained by the limitations of our memory. Again we find that being able to select the alternative that will generate the greatest benefit is extraordinarily difficult (Von Neumann & Morgenstern, 1953).

Bounded Rationality Model

This model is more reality-orientated, and it recognises the constraints acting on the ability of the individual to process information. Individuals and organisations seek the best solutions when faced with a choice among alternatives, but they usually settle for considerably less than they would like to have. The ideal decision would make too great a demand on their data processing capabilities. Bounded rationality explains decision making in terms of three main processes:

1. consideration of alternative solutions in a sequential fashion;
2. use of heuristics to identify the most promising alternatives; and
3. "satisficing".

1. Sequential Consideration of Alternatives
When things are going well there is a tendency not to scan the environment in a serious way. But if the external environment poses a threat to the organisation, then a search for solutions to the problems encountered takes place. This is akin to the notion of strategic planning. Fredrickson and Iaquinto (1989) underlined

the importance of search for information in particular circumstances. They found that a comprehensive information search and consideration of options contributed to effective strategic decision making in stable external environments (in their study, for example, the environment of the paints' industry), but this did not apply in unstable external environments (e.g. the forestry industry).

The search process is said to have three main characteristics (Cyert & March, 1963):

- The search is motivated in the sense that it is activated in response to a current problem.
- It is simple minded in that it begins with the obvious solutions, and only considers other solutions if the simple-minded solutions prove inadequate.
- It is biased because the search for solutions is influenced by the individual's ego, training, experience, hopes, aspirations, and other factors that serve to distort his or her view of the world.

Unlike the treatment of alternatives in the econological model, which requires that all alternatives under consideration be identified before any evaluation takes place, with the bounded rationality model the various alternatives are identified and considered one at a time. Those that prove inadequate in the light of the evaluative criteria are discarded before other alternatives are considered.

2. Use of Heuristics

Heuristics are rules which guide the search for alternatives into areas where there is a good chance of finding satisfactory solutions. They reduce to manageable proportions the number of possible solutions through which the decision maker must sift (Simon & Newell, 1971).

Heuristic models do not attempt to optimise, though they can do so by chance, but they aim to achieve satisfactory sub-optimal solutions. The heuristic approach adopts short cuts in the reasoning process, and it uses rules of thumb, such as the following, in the search for a satisfactory solution (Hinkle & Kuehn 1967):

- "Buy when prices on the stock exchange move rapidly in a particular direction with a heavy volume of trading".
- "When the stock of goods gets down to four, that is the time to buy more".
- "For accounting purposes, value assets at cost or market value, whichever is the lower".
- In production scheduling, the motto is "first come, first served" or "schedule urgent jobs first" (Weist, 1966).

Heuristic models are generally more complex than these rules of thumb, but equally they can be relatively simple.

Tversky and Kahneman (1974) recognise the influence of judgemental strategies in conditions of uncertainty, and analyse three heuristics—representative, availability, and anchoring.

Representative Heuristic. This is concerned with seeing a resemblance between objects or events. A person could be asked to state the extent to which an object or event has certain features to permit appropriate categorisation. In the application of this heuristic, consider the situation outlined in the top panel overleaf.

Availability Heuristic. This is concerned with our tendency to consider an event more probable if it can easily be imagined than if it cannot. The availability heuristic can be prone to error. For example, those who have been involved in crime may, when asked, overestimate the criminal statistics, unlike those who have not been involved. With the former group, bias creeps into the estimate, and this group is unlikely to consider the influence exerted by their own unique experience on their judgement, nor recall media comments on the statistics which could present a more authentic view.

Academic Specialism and the Representative Heuristic

A scholar, who is rather shy and small in stature, enjoys writing poetry. Which of the following areas is his specialism: (i) Psychology; or (ii) Chinese studies?

If the answer was Chinese studies, it is said you have been influenced overwhelmingly by the representative heuristic. You arrived at a judgement which conveys a view that the personality profile presented is a better description of a Chinese studies scholar than a psychologist. But the odds are that a given person is more likely to be aware of psychologists, and also psychologists are far more plentiful than Chinese studies scholars. Given this base-rate information, an appropriate answer from a statistical point of view would be psychology (Vecchio, 1991).

Anchoring Heuristic.

This is concerned with a tendency to pass judgement by starting from an initial position that is likely to influence the final outcome. But bias creeps in when we fail to adjust our position in the light of new information.

The heuristic techniques discussed here help us to draw inferences from events, but not all judgements are likely to be accurate. It has been argued (Vecchio, 1991) that "they are not, strictly speaking, heuristics in the sense of being explicit and not liable to change. Rather they represent automatic and unconscious processes that are frequently involved in judgement and decision-making processes".

3. Satisficing.

In the econological model, the best (or optimal) course of action is chosen after considering all possible alternatives. On the other hand, *satisficing* as a bounded rationality process, operates on the assumption that decision makers judge alternatives one at a time against certain standards of acceptability, and choose the first alternative which meets the minimal acceptable criteria or the minimum conditions for success. So the decision maker need not evaluate all possible alternatives, but only search until an adequate one is found. Therefore, satisficing means the acceptance of a satisfactory outcome. As a result, the decision maker engages in less information processing activity than would be the case if an optimal alternative was sought. An example of a decision situation relying on the satisficing process is included in the panel below.

An insight from an expectancy theory of motivation (discussed in Chapter 2), could be applied to the behaviour of the decision maker intent on satisficing. As decision makers explore the various alternative solutions, their aspiration level rises, and next time round they may be a little more adventurous in their search. But as they find it difficult to discover satisfactory solutions, their aspiration level falls and that makes it easier on the next occasion to obtain satisfactory solutions (Simon, 1957b). For a

---

Investment Decisions and Satisficing

An example of a computerised behavioural model to simulate an investment decision is provided by Clarkson (1963). The model relied heavily on satisficing criteria in the form of rules of thumb and standard operating procedures. An attempt was made to duplicate the investment decisions of a bank trust officer.

Before examining in detail the officer's decision behaviour, numerous bank officials were interviewed. Questions were asked of the officer about how decisions were made with respect to investment portfolios. Transcripts of the responses were studied, the officer was asked to read financial documents and comment upon them, and a model of the trust investment decision process used by the bank officer was constructed.

new perspective on satisficing, refer to Kaufman (1990).

Finally, the bounded rationality model appears to be a more accurate description of the individual's decision-making process than is found in the econological model, but the evidence to support this assertion is not totally conclusive (Behling & Schriesheim, 1976). Much of the supporting evidence comes from computer simulations of the decision-making process, and the decisions studied seem to have a number of characteristics found in programmed or structured decisions.

Implicit Favourite Model

In an analysis of the job-search behaviour of graduate business students it was concluded that decisions were made in a way that could not be explained adequately by either the econological model or the bounded rationality model (Soelberg, 1967). However, in accordance with the predictions of the econological model, the students searched for alternatives in a parallel fashion and evaluated several alternatives at a time. But a departure from the econological model was evident with respect to the lack of weighting attached to the evaluation criteria; nor were the evaluation criteria used in making the final choice. (The criteria used in evaluating alternative jobs may, for example, relate to a number of characteristics such as salary level, job interest and challenge, and location.) It was also established in this study that the alternatives were not ranked in some order of preference.

An important finding of the study was that the search for information continued after a satisfactory alternative (*the implicit favourite*) was identified—e.g. the choice of a particular type of job that offers interest and challenge with a modest initial salary. What happened next was a lengthy process of investigation soon after the search for alternatives ceased. This took the form of justifying the choice of the implicit favourite by offsetting against it

the most attractive of the rejected alternatives—e.g. a job with an attractive initial salary, but rather limited challenge and prospects. Then a rationale was created to show that the implicit favourite was superior to the best of the rejected alternatives.

Once the implicit favourite was chosen, information on the outcome of alternatives was biased in its favour. Also, evaluation elements (e.g. minimum salary and challenge) used in the choice of the most appropriate alternative were adjusted to fit the desired outcome. From an outside, objective assessment of the decision process, it was clear that the implicit favourite was based only on a limited number of dimensions of the decision criteria. A decision was not announced at the time of the choice of implicit favourite; it was not until the most attractive of the rejected alternatives was ruled out in a rather biased analytical exercise that a decision was declared. Further comment on the implicit favourite model is provided by Power and Aldag (1985).

In a criticism of the implicit favourite model, it is alleged that it is more a model of decision rationalisation than of decision making. It concentrates on the justification for the choice of the implicit favourite, but it says very little about how the implicit favourite is selected (Behling & Schriesheim, 1976). The model was created as a result of individual decision making in pursuit of a job, and may not be applicable to organisational decision making where bargaining and political processes could act as significant constraints.

Decision Making Under Uncertainty

The evidence discussed in the previous section relates to a non-programmed or unstructured decision, which is described further here.

Non-programmed or Unstructured Decisions
These decisions are not defined clearly either in terms of what the objectives are or who is involved in the decision. In fact the decision

situation is blurred, not well understood, and difficult to tackle. The alternative solutions to be considered are not immediately apparent, simply because the situation facing the decision maker has not been seen in its present form before, or under the prevailing circumstances. Because of the novelty of the decision, the decision maker has an unclear view of how to make it; in fact different executives are likely to have different views on both the decision itself and how to tackle it. The following is another example of a non-programmed or unstructured decision (Cooke & Slack, 1984).

A manager is keen to make a decision about the nature of the company's product portfolio in the medium term. Reports from sales representatives indicate that the existing product range appears somewhat obsolete in relation to that offered by competitors. The manager has to face a decision either to update the existing range of products or alternatively to offer a new range. This presents a dilemma, more so because the eventual decision will affect a number of areas within the company. The manager proceeds to consult and seek advice from colleagues in other functional areas of the business on the feasibility of his or her own initial ideas about the best way to go ahead. He or she recognises that a new product range will provide a firm foundation for the long-term security of the company, but also realises that any significant expenditure incurred at this stage could threaten the delicate cash flow position of the company in the short term. It is no easy task to take the right decision in these circumstances.

Apparently, the uncertainty associated with the making of a non-programmed or unstructured decision also makes its presence felt at the implementation stage. This was highlighted in Dufty and Taylor (1970), a study of the implementation stage of a non-programmed decision (see panel below).

As a final comment on unstructured decisions, it is worth noting that a certain type of unstructured decision—i.e. a strategic decision in an organisation—may be underpinned by a basic structure. From a field study of 25 strategic decision processes, together with a review of the related empirical literature, Mintzberg, Raisingham, and Theoret (1976) concluded that strategic decision processes, as opposed to tactical decision processes of a routine problem-solving nature, are immensely complex and dynamic, yet they are amenable to conceptual structuring.

To round off this section we shall examine an important decision process that exemplifies uncertainty—the process of negotiation.

Implementation of a Non-programmed Decision

A decision was made to transfer staff from one location within a company to another. The chief executive decided that a specified number of staff were involved in the move, and a senior personnel executive had responsibility to implement the decision. The personnel executive was given wide discretionary powers to use standard operating programmes and to develop new programmes or modify old ones through discussion and analysis. His first line of action was to initiate problem-solving activity by calling a meeting of individuals qualified to contribute to the process of implementing the decision. Out of this meeting came an action programme.

However, as the implementation process neared completion it was evident that matters were not progressing at the level originally anticipated. Because of a reluctance of some staff to move from the old to the new site, quality considerations had to be relaxed and, in certain circumstances, lower calibre staff were transferred. In addition, the reluctance of certain staff to move created organisational slack at the old site and this was condoned by the workers and union officials alike. The unanticipated consequences flowing from the implementation process, which acted to the disadvantage of the company, were the creation of organisational slack at the old site and the introduction of lower calibre staff at the new site (Dufty & Taylor, 1970).

Negotiation

Negotiation is an example of decision making under conditions of uncertainty. It pervades many aspects of organisational life—for example, negotiations are conducted between union representatives and management, between sales executives and clients, and between managers within an organisation on matters connected with the allocation of scarce resources. Before decisions are made, delicate behavioural processes can be detected during the course of negotiations. Morley (1984) has analysed these processes, and the more important ones will now be discussed.

Negotiators take certain courses of action on the basis of their perception of the likely response of the other party in the negotiation process. Negotiators will strive to attain the maximum benefits from the encounter, but equally they are aware of the need to reach an agreement acceptable to all parties. Obviously this will necessitate compromise and modification of positions when circumstances dictate such a course.

Negotiators have to come to terms with two major forces that impinge on the situation. First, there are the social processes and relationships built up with the opponents at the bargaining table. Secondly, negotiators are conscious of the fact that they are acting as representatives of a group that is outside the bargaining process. For example, union representatives are acting on behalf of their trade union, which may have specified the desired result. The relative strength of the two forces can change as negotiations proceed.

At the bargaining table it is possible for friendly relationships to develop between the protagonists. This in turn facilitates the free flow of information, and eventually contributes to a co-operative rather than a competitive spirit and the development of mutual trust and respect. Of course, there is also the potential for conflict, and this could be injected into the proceedings from the outside environment. Another source of conflict stems from inconsistencies in the judgements of negotiators. Deviousness may be attributed to a negotiator because his or her judgement is considered inaccurate or incomplete.

The bargaining process can be complex and clouded with uncertainty. Critical information may not be readily available or, if it is, it may be ambiguous. Alternatively, there may be a lot of information available in numerous documents and the negotiators may find it difficult to grasp their brief. As arguments are presented and manoeuvres worked out, the interests and power base of participants become critical. Uncertainty is often created when a negotiator tries to answer questions on the validity of information presented by the other party. Likewise, negotiators may doubt their ability to defend their position, and are concerned about giving too much away too quickly. ("Shall we continue in the hope of negotiating a better deal?") Negotiators are continuously trying to make sense out of the dialogue and to put it into an ordered perspective.

Eventually, the outcome of the negotiations will depend upon the accuracy of the negotiators' diagnosis of the delicate interpersonal processes, and the skill with which they make the appropriate moves. Those endowed with a perceptive outlook, who possess a good facility in presenting a case and are shrewd, operate at an advantage. In complex negotiations, particularly of a multilateral nature, a breakthrough in the negotiations may be difficult to achieve. The desired outcome of most negotiation processes is likely to embrace a favourable agreement, the avoidance of a disaster, and improved relationships between the parties concerned.

Other Issues

Apart from decision-making models, there are a number of other research issues that enter into the debate on decision making. Hodgetts (1991) recognises three such issues as simplification, subjective rationality, and rationalisation. To these could be added escalation of commitment.

Simplification

A simplified model of reality is adopted by the decision maker. Familiar situations invite similar responses and a different approach is adopted only if the previous approach did not work out well. Schwenk (1985) maintains that many people make decisions based on their recollections of the facts as opposed to diligently checking their records or other sources of information. However, circumstances could dictate a more refined strategy of data collection.

For example, this could arise where the information obtained is incomplete, or a major mistake occurred because of previous reliance on a recollection of facts. There is also a view that people who are attached to a particular belief underpinning behaviour show a resistance to new information that challenges that belief. For instance, the heavy drinker could turn a blind eye to new evidence on the dangers of excessive alcohol consumption.

Subjective Rationality

People frequently become more conservative as the complexity of the decision situation grows. At the same time, there is the tendency to cease seeking more information, even though such information could be useful and inexpensive to acquire, and start placing heavy reliance on personal judgement (Hodgetts, 1991). Research has shown that individuals often use subjective rationality even in circumstances where all the necessary information is available to permit judgements based on objective rationality (Fagley & Miller, 1987).

Fear of failure is evident when people place bets with their own money. People are likely to be risk takers with small bets, but with larger amounts they are likely to be more cautious, even with favourable odds. Fear of failure (subjective rationality) outweighs the favourable odds (objective rationality) (Schurr, 1987).

People show an aversion to losses greater than the attractiveness of possible gains where the same amount of money is involved. For example, most people would prefer the certainty of winning £750 over a 75% chance of winning £1000; but the same individuals would prefer a 75% chance of losing £1000 over a certain loss of £750. This points to risk-averse decisions when it comes to gains, and risk-seeking decisions when it comes to losses (Kahneman & Tversky, 1984). Therefore, companies facing financial difficulties may take more risks in an attempt to eliminate losses than companies who are doing well and experiencing gains (Fiegenbaum & Thomas, 1988).

People tend to create rules governing decision making, but in reality such rules are often fallacious. This can be seen when people predict the occurrence of a particular kind of event simply because that event has not occurred recently. For example, if a coin is tossed and comes up heads on three occasions, many people are likely to bet that tails will come up next time (Hodgetts, 1991).

The same information can be presented or "framed" in different ways, so that for one group it has particular appeal in one form, as opposed to another form which appeals to another group. This can have an effect on decisions made on the basis of that information, though not everybody would agree with this proposition (Arnold, Robertson, & Cooper, 1991).

Rationalisation

There is a view that decision makers not only invoke satisficing (discussed earlier in the chapter), but also that they frequently rationalise. Instead of being concerned with the identification of satisfactory alternatives, the decision maker, who may be in a hurry, rationalises choice by adopting the first feasible option even in circumstances where time was available for further exploration. As stated earlier, some argue that the implicit favourite model has rationalisation built into it, when decision makers rationalise their decision choice by finding some shortcomings with each of the other potential choices.

Escalation of Commitment

This arises when there is a tendency to persist in an ineffective course of action, even when evidence suggests that a problem exists and that a particular project is doomed to failure (see panel below).

Staw (1981) has offered explanations for the escalation of commitment. Some projects involve much up-front investment, with little return until the end. These projects require continuous commitment, and those who put up the capital, or provided the funds, must stay the course in order to receive any return on their investment. On other occasions, investors or project managers frequently become so egotistically involved with the project that their identities are immersed in it (Brockner et al., 1986). They support the project as potentially worthwhile despite evidence to the contrary, because failure signals a threat to their self-esteem. There are other occasions when organisational inertia or culture is responsible for allowing a less than satisfactory project to continue. But it is important for the organisation to recognise when it is necessary to stop a project before it results in throwing good money after bad.

Good information based on project reviews is a necessary course of action to prevent the problem of escalation of commitment. Staw and Ross (1988) put forward a solution to the problem by suggesting that one should create an "experimenting organisation" in which every project is reviewed regularly and managers are evaluated on the basis of their contribution to the total organisation rather than to specific projects.

Decision Support Systems

A decision support system is a system that provides information to supplement rather than replace managerial decision making (Cooke & Slack, 1984). It generally consists of a database that accommodates internally generated data (e.g. costs), but can also include external data (e.g. economic forecasts). The data can be analysed or rearranged using, for example, computer models of varying degrees of sophistication. There are those used in financial analysis where data on cash flow, financial forecasting, and balance sheet projections are available. By contrast, databases in a marketing information system might include sales figures, pricing data, and the costs of marketing a product. This data could be merged with an external marketing database to provide a forecast of sales, as well as effects of different marketing decisions.

Escalation of Commitment by an Investor

Imagine an investor who purchased shares in a company for £1.50 per share. Due to a deteriorating overall economic situation and adverse market conditions for the company, the share price falls to 50p.

At around this time, the company experiences problems with repayment of debt and decides to raise additional equity capital by way of a rights issue of shares (an offer of more shares to existing shareholders, pro rata to their holdings). The investor subscribes for the allocation of shares to which he or she is entitled at a price marginally below the prevailing market price. The share value falls still further, and the investor acquires additional shares in the expectation that one day the share price will recover when the company's fortunes change for the better. In this case, there was no such change because the company went into liquidation.

This is an example of a situation in which people remain committed to a particular course of action despite negative vibrations that all is not well.

The examples given here are related to systems providing decision-oriented data with the aid of a small computer model. A more sophisticated model would be a system that proposes a decision or a specific recommendation for action. In this situation, the decision support system has the capacity to provide solutions based on the appropriate software and data input. An example is a system for calculating the premium attached to an insurance policy. The premium is calculated by the system using standard statistical and actuarial data, and details of the proposed policy (Alter, 1977). At the other end of the scale is a simple decision support system that is effectively a file-drawer system. This is a computer-based version of a manual filing system. All it does is provide access to a particular item of data (e.g. the cost of a spare part in the offices of a dealer in the car trade).

How do policy makers respond to systems based on computer models? In one study (Greenberger, Crenson, & Crissey, 1976), the extent to which computer-based modelling systems were used by public agencies was investigated. It was found that the eventual choices of alternatives in decision processes were rarely influenced directly by the analyses from these systems. An interesting finding was that in relevant cases the computer analyses (results) were used to support policies already decided in advance. If the results were considered by the policy makers to be influential, they would call in the expert (computer modeller) who would play a prominent part in the making of a decision.

In another study, the constraints surrounding the operation of computer models in a changed context were emphasised (Bjorn-Anderson, 1979). The following computer systems, using small to medium-sized computers, carried out functions normally undertaken by middle managers:

- inventory and marketing analyses in a plant in the UK;
- patient scheduling in a hospital in the UK; and

- scheduling production in a radio factory.

The results emanating from these systems were unsatisfactory. All three systems were too inflexible to meet changing demands.

With regard to (1), bad weather accompanied by unexpectedly heavy snowfalls led to problems with transportation, and this disrupted inventory planning. With regard to (2), the system was disbanded because it failed to respond to the basic needs of doctors and patients. Finally, in the case of (3), changes in the taxation system resulting from new European Community regulations made the marketing of the radios extremely difficult.

Are certain types of decisions more amenable to decision support systems than others? It appears that decisions on the borderline between structured and unstructured decisions are compatible with the computer models of the decision support systems (McCosh & Scott-Morton, 1978). Well-structured decisions can be accommodated by the conventional management information systems. But when top management face novel and unpredictable conditions, which require the taking of unstructured decisions, programmed packages may be too restrictive to deal with these circumstances (Oborne, 1994). In decision situations that are highly unstructured, the decision maker will rely heavily on experience, judgement, and even intuition.

With regard to creativity (discussed in the next section), computer-aided creative problem solving could be of great assistance to both individuals and groups. Proctor (1991) provides a useful summary of the different kinds of computerised managerial creativity aids.

INDIVIDUAL AND ORGANISATIONAL INFLUENCES

Individual and organisational factors influence the way in which information is acquired, processed, and used in the making of decisions. The influence exerted by the group on decision making is reserved for discussion in Chapter 7, and some individual considerations in connection with cognitive complexity were discussed earlier, in the section of this chapter on the cognitive approach to information processing.

In this section the following influences will be discussed:

- Personality and Cognitive Style
- Creativity
- Trained Incapacity
- Division of Labour
- Organisational Hierarchy
- Grapevine

Personality and Cognitive Style

With respect to specific personality factors related to information processing, it has been suggested that dogmatic and authoritarian personality types display a marked lack of tolerance for ambiguity and uncertainty and consequently are less likely to search for information. They are less capable of dealing with inconsistent information and are unlikely to be flexible in the positions they adopt (Dermer, 1973). (A discussion of personality types appears in Chapter 1.)

Decision makers with machiavellian tendencies could view information as a tool for achieving their personal objectives, possibly resulting in the withholding of information so as to maintain control or to win favours from influential people. The withholding, ignoring, and distorting of information for whatever reason can be detrimental to decision making that rests on the combined or co-operative efforts of a number of employees. Social motives play an important part in interactive episodes or contacts between employees, and as a consequence can affect the quality of decisions where an exchange of information is critical in the decision process.

Decision Styles
Whatever decision model is applicable, managers are said to adopt a particular style of decision making as they collect and evaluate information. In Chapter 1, Jung's typology of personality was introduced (Jung, 1923), and this consists of four functions. The orientation associated with each function is as follows:

- *Sensation*: this type likes to solve problems in standard ways.
- *Intuitive*: this type likes to solve new problems, relying on hunches, spontaneity, and openness in redefining problems until they are solved.
- *Thinking*: this type tends to be unemotional, carefully considers all options, and uses intellectual processes in decision making.
- *Feeling*: this type tends to be sympathetic and relates well to others, and believes in harmonious and pleasant working relationships.

The first two functions—sensation and intuition—are compatible with the collection of information, whereas the last two—thinking and feeling—relate to the evaluation of information in a problem-solving context (Hodgetts, 1991).

The four functions can be expressed as four basic decision styles as follows:

1. Sensation–Thinking (ST);
2. Sensation–Feeling (SF);
3. Intuition–Thinking (IT); and
4. Intuition–Feeling (IF).

Taggart and Robey (1981) place these four decision styles in an organisational context (see panel overleaf).

Using the Myers–Briggs Type I indicator—a personality inventory drawing its substance from Jung's typology—Mitroff and Kilmann (1976) administered it to managers to determine their decision style. In addition, the researchers asked the managers

---

Decision Styles in Organisations

1. *Sensation–Thinking* (ST). People who are classified as ST attend to facts and handle them with impersonal analysis. They tend to be practical and matter of fact and develop their abilities in situations of technical clarity. Occupationally, ST is typified by a technician.
2. *Sensation–Feeling* (SF). People classified as SF attend to facts but they handle them with a warm personal touch. They tend to be sympathetic and friendly, and their abilities can be usefully applied helping people. Occupationally, SF is typified by a teacher.
3. *Intuition–Thinking*(IT). People who are classified as IT are logical and ingenious, like to explore a number of possibilities, and

approach the exercise with impersonal analysis. Their abilities find expression in developments from a theoretical and technical perspective. Occupationally, IT is typified by a planner.
4. *Intuition–Feeling* (IF). People classified as IF rely on intuitive and non-rational feelings in arriving at a judgement. They tend to explore possibilities with the human touch, are enthusiastic and insightful, and their abilities find easier expression in understanding and communicating. They tend to be sympathetic and friendly, and their abilities can be usefully applied helping people. Occupationally, IF is typified by an artist (Taggart & Robey, 1991).

---

to relate stories about their ideal organisation. They found a strong similarity between the stories of those managers who had the same decision style.

- STs depicted their organisation and its infrastructure in a factual way, emphasised the certainty and specific nature of things, and underlined impersonal organisational control.
- SFs also concentrated on facts and precision, but did so in a way that highlighted human relationships.
- ITs stressed broad global issues, and theorised about organisations in a rather idealistic but impersonal way.
- IFs underlined the global nature of things, laced with a concern for personal and humanistic values.

Henderson and Nutt (1980) used the Myers–Briggs Type I indicator to study management decisions. They studied risk taking and the acceptance of hypothetical capital expenditure proposals. STs were the most reluctant to accept the proposals, perceiving the most risk in making decisions. SFs had a tolerance for greater risk and shared the acceptance of the same proposals. ITs and IFs fell between ST and SF with regard to the acceptance of the proposals.

However, Nutt (1990) would elevate IFs to a position of greater risk taking when faced with hypothetical risky business ventures, and concludes that top managers' decisions were more influenced by their decision style than were middle managers' decisions. Obviously decision styles have real meaning to people: Hunt et al. (1989) found that people tend to select advisers with decision styles similar to their own when faced with evaluating hypothetical strategic business decisions.

There have been other attempts to classify decision styles. Arroba (1978) isolates six styles, among them the logical, emotional, and intuitive styles. Generally, the logical style was the style most often used. Janis and Mann (1982) also identify styles, but their emphasis is on decision quality, and they underline the way people cope with the conflict inherent in the decision-making process. Examples of coping strategies are "defensive avoidance" where the decision maker avoids the decision by delaying making it or denying responsibility for it; and "vigilance" where the decision maker conducts a careful search for relevant information and weighs it up in an impartial way. The latter is considered to be a good strategy.

Left-brain and Right-brain.   A preoccupation of some psychologists interested in decision styles is the issue of left-brain and right-brain hemispheres. Although the brain is usually viewed as a single structure, in actual fact it is divided into two halves, joined by the *corpus callosum*, which is a bundle of connecting fibres. For most people, the right side of the brain controls the left side of the body, and the left side of the brain controls the right side of the body. Although each hemisphere of the brain has the potential to undertake many functions, there tends to be specialisation.

Where the left brain is dominant, the person is predominantly involved with analytic, logical thinking, especially in verbal and mathematical functions. Where the right brain is dominant, the power to synthesise is evident, but language ability is limited. This hemisphere is primarily responsible for orientation in space, artistic endeavour, crafts, body image, and recognition of faces. It processes information more diffusely than does the left hemisphere, with a capacity to integrate many inputs at the same time (Ornstein, 1977).

There is speculation about the functions of both sides of the brain in the management literature. For example, left-brain dominant people tend to respond best to verbal instructions, whereas right-brain dominant people respond best to visual instructions. According to Lynch (1986), the different orientations in the decision-making process can be summarised in the proposition that when left-brain dominant people are compared with right-brain dominant people they:

- tend to be more conformist;
- prefer structured assignments to open-ended ones;
- discover things systematically as opposed to by exploration;
- recall verbal material better than spatial imagery;
- focus on specific facts, as opposed to main ideas;
- solve problems in a logical way as opposed to an intuitive way; and

- work best with ideas that flow in sequence, as opposed to those that show a relationship.

In connection with decision styles, Taggart and Robey (1981) claim a link between the left brain and the sensation–thinking (ST) type, and between the right brain and the intuition–feeling (IF) type. The other types were considered less important in this respect.

In today's world, with its numerous complex and difficult problems, it would seem appropriate to admonish managers on the need for flexibility in their information processing style. Ideally, it would appear to be beneficial for the organisation if the manager could move with ease from one decision style to another in the light of the demands of the situation. The same reasoning could apply to movement within the brain hemispheres where, for example, the logically minded manager could move in the direction of the more imaginative sphere. These are issues that can offer a challenge to management education and development.

According to Hodgetts (1990), this challenge has to some extent been taken up. He relates the experience of the Hawaiian Telephone Company, which introduced tests to identify left-brain dominant and right-brain dominant managers. They were then allocated to a group with thinking styles similar to their own. The left-brain dominant managers were asked to make decisions that required a creative approach, while the right-brain dominant managers were required to make decisions that required a logical and analytical approach. This form of training appeared to be successful.

Other examples of training in this field include encouraging left-brain dominant people to develop their right-brain by participating in unstructured activities such as creative day-dreaming, observing colours, listening to sounds in their immediate environment, and cracking jokes in other people's company. Right-brain dominant people are encouraged to developed their left brain by solving mathematical problems and engaging in analytical thinking (Hodgetts, 1990). Despite what has been said, one should be cautious in accepting the relationship between brain hemispheres and training, because there are some scholars who are extremely sceptical about its substance.

A further word of caution is called for when looking at the association between cognitive styles and neurological functioning. Robertson (1985) rightly points out that it is far from clear that cognitive strategy and style can be related to brain functioning in any straightforward way, although some researchers argue strongly that there are links. Levy (1985) maintains that any mental activity is carried out by both sides of the brain simultaneously, and that the two hemispheres work together in harmony.

Adaptors vs Innovators

Kirton (1984) identified differences in the way people prefer to process information. These differences can be expressed as cognitive or thinking styles, are referred to as adaptors and innovators, and occupy opposite ends of a continuum. Similarities can be found between Kirton's approach and the approaches discussed earlier. The main distinguishing characteristics of the adaptor and innovator are as follows:

- With regard to problem definition, adaptors are more inclined to wait to be handed a problem, whereas innovators seek problems.
- With regard to solving problems, adaptors can be effective in modifying existing systems in conditions of relative stability, whereas innovators derive a challenge from seeking new and possibly unexpected solutions.
- With regard to the implementation of decisions, the adaptors utilise precise, accurate, methodical, and disciplined approaches, unlike the innovators who appear undisciplined with a low tolerance for routine work.

- With regard to personal image within the organisation, adaptors are seen as safe, dependable, and conformist, whereas innovators are seen as mavericks, with lots of self-confidence, and are constantly generating ideas that are not always practical.

It is possible, of course, for the two styles to complement each other but, given the fundamental differences, the potential for a clash of personalities always exists. Kirton attributes the failure to implement innovative ideas in organisations to a clash of styles. Hopefully a way forward can be found to resolve these difficulties by understanding the other person's orientation and accepting it. It is said that adaptors may find some sectors of the economy—for example, public sector organisations—more amenable to their outlook, but it has to be said that these organisations are now becoming increasingly exposed to market forces and the consequent pressures to innovate.

The adaptor and innovator styles could find expression in the culture of departments within organisations, giving rise to inter-group conflict that is referred to in Chapter 9. If, within the organisation, such a state of affairs is frustrating efforts to innovate and change, Kanter (1984) is likely to suggest the need for "integrative thinking" to ensure a team-oriented, co-operative environment in which change is facilitated and innovation flourishes.

Creativity

A number of problems, especially in the area of non-programmed decision making, require creative solutions. It stands to reason that organisations which devise creative strategies for dealing with decision making are well placed to gain competitive advantage in a highly competitive business environment. In today's world, many companies are under pressure to improve old systems and products, and organisational growth and survival can be directly related to an ability to innovate (Proctor, 1991). Creativity has a part to play at each stage of the decision-making process. A critical perspective is beneficial in the way a problem is defined, in the generation of alternative solutions, and in the actual implementation of a solution.

Creativity has been defined by Richards (1990) as a universal human process resulting in an escape from assumptions and the discovery of new and meaningful perspectives, or as an escape from mental "stuckness". It seems that creative ideas arise purely by chance, but one has to recognise that generating ideas is not just a chance process: ideas appear to arise by chance only when people are actually looking for ideas. It is recognised that being immersed in one's own subject, and being detached in order to examine it critically, are important factors in gaining creative insights. It is probably safe to conclude that creative ideas do not float into the minds of people who are not curious, or inquiring, or who are not engaged in a hard search for opportunities, possibilities, answers, or inventions (Proctor, 1991).

Creative problem-solving stems from creativity. Creative problem-solvers allow the imagination to wander, tend to push back constraints that impose limitations on their thinking, make deliberate jumps in thinking, and welcome chance ideas whenever they come along. By contrast, the less creative person (or conformist) proceeds in an orderly way from point to point (Dubrin, 1990).

Nowadays, creativity is considered to be a valuable resource for somebody who aspires to a leadership role in an organisation. This view is examined in the discussion of transformational leadership in Chapter 8.

Creative Individuals
It is claimed that creative people possess different intellectual and personality characteristics from their less creative counterparts. However, there is one overall distinguishing characteristic, which is flexibility. Creative people are in general more flexible mentally than others, and this allows them to overcome the traditional ways of looking at problems (Dubrin, 1990). Drawing on his own work and the work of other writers in the field, Godfrey (1986) has produced a grouping of the characteristics of creative workers (see panel below).

Certain initiatives can be taken to measure individual creativity. A basic approach for measuring the creative potential of employees is for the manager to give them a challenging assignment and then assess both the way they

---

Characteristics of Creative Workers

Knowledge. It is necessary to have a broad background of information, including facts and observations.

Intellectual abilities. These would include intelligence and abstract reasoning. Creative people are expected to be adept at generating alternative solutions to problems in a short period of time, and display a youthful curiosity, not only in their own specialist field but beyond it as well.

Personality. Among the non-intellectual characteristics of creative people are reasonable self-confidence and the ability to handle criticism of their ideas. Although creativity can be fostered by interaction with others, creative people show a tolerance for working in isolation because it puts them into a receptive mood for ideas.

Creative people value their independence, tend to be non-conformist, and do not have strong needs for group approval. They tend to be thrill-seekers, because imaginative solutions to problems give them a thrill (a thrill-seeker has a higher than average need for stimulation, can become easily bored, and as a risk-taker is likely to pursue adventure). Creative people place value on persistence, because they recognise that finding creative solutions to problems involves a lot of concentration and hard work.

In summary, this profile of the creative person fits the popular stereotype of him or her as a maverick, both intellectually and socially (Godfrey, 1986).

went about completing it and the final outcome. Another approach is the use of standard creativity tests or, alternatively, tests of creativity devised by companies for their own use. A problem may be finding creativity tests that are occupationally specific. Tests of creativity bear a similarity to the cognitive tests discussed in Chapter 1.

Stages in the Creative Process

One can identify at least five stages in the creative process (Randall, 1955):

1. *Opportunity or problem recognition*: this is the stage when it crosses the mind of a person that either a problem or an opportunity is waiting to be tackled.
2. *Immersion*: this is the stage where a person either recalls or obtains information relevant to the problem or opportunity identified in stage one. The information is unlikely to be evaluated seriously at this stage. What is more likely is to hypothesise about the situation. For example, a manager might say, "I have a faint recollection that the problem or opportunity was tackled in a particular way by a professional acquaintance in another company a few years ago".
3. *Incubation*: this is the stage for reflection and consideration often at an unconscious level. The person is literally sleeping on the problem or opportunity that is beneath the surface. Even when the person is engaged in recreational activity, ideas are maturing and being rearranged.
4. *Insight*: this is the stage where, as a result of the previous stages, there is a desired outcome reflected as something new. This could be a novel but effective way of tackling the problem or taking advantage of the opportunity. Creative insight should be committed to writing immediately, as it could be easily forgotten.
5. *Verification*: this is the last stage of the creative process. A person subjects the solution to test by using logic or actual experimentation. It may then have to be verified by the person's superior, or an outside agency, such as a referee or assessor, as when, for example, the insight or solution to a scientific problem is scrutinised prior to publication in an academic journal.

Where the issue is connected with an innovative process within a company, resistance could mount at the point of implementation, when it may be branded as an impractical proposal. This could test the perseverance of the creative person.

This progression in the creative process commands a certain appeal. However, creative insight may not evolve in the manner described. The process may be repetitive because the initial outcome of the whole process is considered unsatisfactory, and therefore it requires reconsideration and revision. Also, incubation might very well occur during the verification stage.

Enhancing Creativity

Techniques are available to improve creative ability. One such technique is *brainstorming*. It is used to train individuals to be more creative and to tackle complex problems (Osborn, 1957). In a brainstorming session a group of people are encouraged to exchange ideas freely in an atmosphere characterised by little censorship or criticism. The important thing is to be tolerant of all suggested solutions to a problem, however unconventional or unworkable they appear to be. The latter are particularly encouraged because they may act as an impetus to subsequent ideas which, in turn, could form the basis of a useful solution.

With regard to brainstorming, one should point out there is evidence, at variance with Osborn's position, indicating that individuals acting on their own with instructions to produce as many ideas as possible, generated twice the number of ideas per person than did the groups (Lamm & Trommsdorff, 1973).

What explanation can be offered for this result? Perhaps individuals in groups are inclined to think that other group members will do their work for them. Also, individuals in groups may be too self-conscious about how others perceive them and their contributions, and show a reluctance to air their views, despite having registered the brainstorming instructions which should have reassured them on this point.

An alternative explanation, advanced by Diehl and Stroebe (1987) and known as *production blocking*, states that because only one individual at a time in a group can articulate his or her ideas, other individuals may forget or suppress their own ideas.

An alternative format of brainstorming is *brain writing* or private brainstorming. This entails individuals arriving at creative ideas by jotting them down. An important requirement of private brainstorming is that a regular time is set aside for generating ideas. Another technique is De Bono's imaginative system of lateral thinking, which is designed to help people escape from habitual mind patterns, called vertical thinking. Lateral thinking poses a deliberative and provocative challenge to ones preconceptions and the rejection of yes/no thinking (De Bono, 1970).

A number of organisations have experimented with a technique called SCIMITAR, which stands for systematic creativity and integration modelling in technical and research environments (Carson & Richards, 1979). It represents an attempt to combine rigorous and systematic searches for opportunities with imaginative thinking in three stages of new product development—idea search, development, and commercial exploitation. Training the team members in creative thinking is an important feature of this approach.

A creativity technique suitable for individual use is *mind mapping*, which is a form of visual thinking (Goman, 1989). Visual aids in various forms are used to enhance creativity. The technique starts with identifying and writing a central theme in the middle of a blank sheet of paper. This is then circled and lines like spokes are drawn whenever new ideas come to mind. The description of the idea will appear on the spoke. If a particular idea spawns another idea, a branch line is drawn with a description of the new idea.

Important principles that people intent on increasing their creativity should bear in mind are set out in the panel overleaf. The principles do not offer a prescription for tackling specific problems, but they can be a useful aid to personal development. To put these principles into action requires self-discipline and a fair amount of control over one's emotions and intellect in order to develop a new set of behaviour patterns and eliminate old ones.

From what has been said one may conclude that the path to creativity for the individual seems to be a rather arduous one.

Intrapreneur
During the last decade, the roles of the entrepreneur and the intrapreneur have been associated in the literature with creativity. The entrepreneur, who creates and manages a business in an innovative way, must have the creative talent to identify a new product or service.

By contrast, an intrapreneur is a company employee who works independently inside the company to develop a new product or service, and adopts an entrepreneurial perspective with the objectives of the organisation firmly in mind (Atkinson, 1986). The intrapreneur, who is a risk taker and operates within a small organisational unit, has the advantage of the company's backing, and the company benefits from his or her creativity. At the same time the company exempts the intrapreneur from many of the restrictions and controls associated with large organisations, and he or she is given special privileges. If the endeavours of the intrapreneur are successful, he or she commands more resources (De Chambeau & Mackenzie, 1986). There has been a trend in recent years to identify employees with intrapreneurial potential, particularly in high-tech companies.

Becoming More Creative

- Do not be intimidated by the fact that a large proportion of attempts at being creative are likely to fail.
- Work on your sense of humour; it can promote a lessening of tension and a relaxed disposition which, in turn, assists creativity. Also, insights can be cultivated by approaching a problem with a sense of humour.
- Build up a tolerance for the possibility of failure, and adopt a risk-taking attitude. It is the fear of failure that suppresses creativity.
- Develop self-confidence and courage and persist in your determination to solve your problems.
- Engage in creative hobbies which demand physical and mental effort, on the understanding that creative growth is possible only through constant and active use of mind and body.
- Build up your knowledge base in your specialist area, and maintain it in order to foster creative links between one piece of information and another.
- Read widely in fields not directly related to your specialist area, and be aware of links between what you already know and the new information.
- Be alert in your observations, looking out for similarities, differences, and unique features of ideas and things.
- Be open and alert to others ideas, realising that new ideas seldom arrive in finished form. Seize tentative, half-formed ideas and hunches.
- Keep track of your own ideas at all times, and record flashes of insight in a notebook for future reference.
- Identify a specific time of day when you are most likely to be creative, and schedule work sessions accordingly.
- Pose new questions every day, because a questioning and active mind is likely to be creatively active (Dubrin, 1985; Randsepp, 1978).

Trained Incapacity

A situation sometimes develops where the training provided by the organisation actually interferes with the individual's approach to decision making and problem solving. This arises, in particular, when the decision rules or procedures do not fit the problem or decision under review, but the individual has been trained to operate the rules and procedures, and is not prepared to modify or adjust them to suit the decision or problem in hand. This is referred to as *trained incapacity*, and it acts as a process to compartmentalise incoming information and problems into a limited number of categories in a procedure or decision process (Merton, 1957).

This may have an advantage from the employee's point of view because less time is spent on analysing the problem and searching for alternatives, and it provides consistency and predictability in the processing of information. However, it tends to produce rigidity and impairs the capacity of the organisation to react effectively to changed circumstances, when problems cannot be categorised neatly by a predetermined procedure. Trained incapacity is said to portray an approach to decision making whereby the decision makers become so accustomed to making programmed decisions that they even attempt to solve non-programmable problems in a programmed way (Kerr et al., 1975).

Division of Labour

Division of labour within organisations provides a number of operating advantages. It permits specialisation with the potential for greater efficiency, but the introduction of functional specialists breeds the growth of specialised language and terminology. Production managers have their own unique vocabulary, just as accountants have their technical language. These and other factors, such as conventions and outlook on commercial life, make the transmission of information for the purposes of decision making across functional or unit boundaries rather difficult, and may result in distortions and omissions (Litterer, 1973).

Organisational Hierarchy

Apart from the division of tasks into specialist functions, an organisation is invariably characterised by an arrangement of tasks in a hierarchical form (as described in Chapter 10). For example, senior managers perform different tasks from those performed by first-line supervisors. The organisational hierarchy may pose problems for the processing and transfer of information. Sometimes, information is modified by a subordinate so that it complies with the preferences and prejudices of the superior. This may be done in order to obtain the approval of the superior. There are many occasions when employees of the same status in the organisation provide information and feedback on performance to one another as a normal part of social interaction, but the incidence of feedback is much less between different layers of the organisation. There appears to be a tendency for subordinates to feel uncomfortable when they are engaged in exchanging information with superiors rather than with their peers (Blau & Scott, 1962). They tend to over-interpret and over-react to messages sent by superiors.

In addition to the problem of communication of information between layers of the organisation, there is the problem that results from the tendency of the organisational system itself "to filter information by providing less and less detailed information to the top of the organisation" (Richards & Greenlaw, 1972). As the information makes its way up the organisation, summaries with expressions of opinion, conclusions, and recommendations for action are very prevalent. So it is the inferences drawn from the primary data collected at the lower levels of the organisation, not the detailed data itself, that is transmitted upwards.

Therefore the people further down the organisation who prepare the summaries and draw inferences from the detailed information can exert considerable influence on the decision makers at the higher level. As the top decision maker is unlikely to inspect the raw primary data, he or she should be aware, to an acceptable extent, of the credibility of the major sources of information within the organisation (March & Simon, 1958). However, advances in information technology make it possible for senior managers in certain circumstances to gain direct access to information generated further down the hierarchy. A discussion of new technology and organisation appears in Chapter 10.

The Grapevine

Not all communication takes place within the formal hierarchy of organisation. Nearly all organisations make extensive use of informal communication processes, partly to compensate for the deficiencies generated by the formal processes. Informal communication can arise spontaneously within an organisation, and can be seen to make a contribution in terms of lightening the burden on the overloaded formal communication channels. The grapevine (discussed in Chapter 3) consists of a network of informal relationships and it transmits information unofficially. Sometimes this information is accurate, and sometimes it is inaccurate.

It is now clear that communication processes within organisations can have a material effect on the quality of information processing and decision making, particularly when the information flows through the layers of the hierarchy. A full discussion of communication can be found in Chapter 3.

SUMMARY: HUMAN INFORMATION PROCESSING AND DECISION MAKING

- Human information processing and decision making are related concepts.
- A human information processing perspective, which amounts to a cognitive view of humanity, was discussed with reference to the production manager, the investor, the auditor, and the marketing executive. Three approaches to the study of human information processing were identified. These are the Lens model, the cognitive approach, and the process tracing approach.
- Two types of decision models were referred to, but most of the discussion was devoted to an analysis of descriptive rather than prescriptive models. This reflects the interests of behavioural researchers who study applied decision making.
- The steps in a decision cycle were illustrated with respect to a description of a relatively simple decision. Three models of decision making were introduced—the econological model, the bounded rationality model, and the implicit favourite model. Heuristics and satisficing were examined as two important features of the bounded rationality model.
- Decision making was examined with respect to conditions of uncertainty. Two types of decision were defined as structured and unstructured. The unstructured decision lends itself to conditions of uncertainty, whereas stable or more predictable situations are compatible with a structured decision.

- Negotiation and bargaining were discussed as examples of decision making under conditions of uncertainty. Issues such as simplification, subjective rationality, rationalisation, and escalation of commitment were also discussed in the context of decision making in conditions of uncertainty.
- Decision support systems, using computer models, were acknowledged as a process that supplements managerial decision making, though one must recognise the constraints that affect the operation of computer decision models in changed circumstances.
- There was an examination of some individual and organisational influences on decision making. Apart from trained incapacity, division of labour, organisational hierarchy, and the grapevine, the role of personality and cognitive style, and creativity received due attention.
- Personality and cognitive style were examined from the perspective of the authoritarian personality, machiavellian tendencies, decision styles, left-brain and right-brain processing, and adaptors/innovators.
- Creativity was discussed with respect to characteristics of the creative individual, steps in the creative process, and ways of enhancing it. The significance of creativity for the intrapreneur was acknowledged.

QUESTIONS

1. Define human information processing with examples drawn from business life.
2. Describe three approaches to the study of human information processing. Select one approach and show how it can be applied to an accountancy problem.
3. Distinguish between a converger and a diverger in an organisational context.
4. Identify the steps in the decision cycle. To what extent do decisions in real life follow this process?
5. Comment on the conditions appropriate to (a) unstructured decisions, and (b) structured decisions.

6. List the models of decision making reported by Behling and Schriesheim.

7. Collective bargaining is a complex negotiation process. Discuss.

8. Examine the significance of subjective rationality and escalation of commitment in decision making under conditions of uncertainty.

9. Discuss the different types of heuristic techniques.

10. What do you understand by the notion of decision support systems?

11. Comment on the interaction between decision styles and neurological functioning in the way information is processed and decisions are made.

12. Distinguish an adaptor from an innovator.

13. Describe the characteristics of the creative person, and discuss ways in which organisations may cultivate creativity among employees.

REFERENCES

Alter, S. (1977). A taxonomy of decision support systems. *Sloan Management Review*, Fall.

Archer, E. (1980). How to make a business decision: An analysis of theory and practice. *Management Review*, February.

Arnold, J., Robertson, I.T., & Cooper, C.L. (1991). *Work psychology: Understanding human behaviour in the workplace*. London: Pitman.

Arroba, T.Y. (1978). Decision-making style as a function of occupational group, decision content, and perceived importance. *Journal of Occupational Psychology, 51*, 219–226.

Atkinson, K. (1986). Intrapreneurs: Fostering innovation inside the corporation. *Personnel Administrator*, January, 43.

Behling, O. & Schriesheim C. (1976). *Organisational behaviour: Theory, research, and application.* Glenview, Ill: Richard D. Irwin.

Bjorn-Anderson, N. (1979, June). Myths and realities of information systems contributing to organisational rationality. *Proceedings of the FIP second HCC conference*. Amsterdam: North-Holland.

Blau, P.M. & Scott, W.R. (1962). *Formal organisations*. San Francisco: Chandler Publishing.

Bobbitt, H.R., Breinholt, R.H., Doktor, R.H., & McNaul, J.P. (1978). *Organisational behaviour: Understanding and prediction*. New York: Prentice-Hall.

Bouwman, M.J. (1984). Expert vs. novice decision making in accounting: A summary. *Accounting, Organisations and Society, 9*, 325–327.

Brockner, J., Houser, R., Birnbaum, G., Lloyd, K., Deitcher, J., Nathanson, S., & Rubin, J.Z. (1986). Escalation of commitment to an ineffective course of action: The effect of feedback having negative implications for self-identity. *Administrative Science Quarterly*, March, 109–126.

Brunswick, E. (1955). Representative design and probabilistic theory in a functional psychology. *Psychological Review*, May, 193–217.

Carson, J. & Richards, T. (1979). *Industrial new product development*. Farnborough, UK: Gower.

Clarkson, G.P.E (1963). A model of trust investment behaviour. In R.M. Cyert & J.G. Marsh (Eds.), *A behavioural theory of the firm*. New York: Prentice-Hall.

Cooke, S. & Slack, N. (1984). *Making management decisions*. Hemel Hempstead, UK: Prentice-Hall.

Cyert, R.M. & March, J.G. (Eds.). (1963). *A behavioural theory of the firm*. New York: Prentice-Hall.

De Bono, E. (1970). *Lateral thinking for management*. New York: McGraw-Hill.

De Chambeau, F.A. & Mackenzie, F. (1986). Intrapreneurship. *Personnel Journal*, July, 40–45.

Dermer, J.D. (1973). Cognitive characteristics and the perceived importance of information. *Accounting Review*, July, 511–519.

Diehl, M. & Stroebe, W. (1987). Productivity loss in brainstorming groups: Towards the solution of a riddle. *Journal of Personality and Social Psychology, 53*, 497–509.

Dillard, J.F. (1984). Cognitive science and decision-making research in accounting. *Accounting, Organisations and Society, 9*, 343–354.

Dubrin, A.J. (1985). *Contemporary applied management*. Plano, TX: Business Publications.

Dubrin, A.J. (1990). *Effective business psychology* (third edition). New York: Prentice-Hall.

Dufty, N.F. & Taylor, P.M. (1970). The implementation of a decision. In L.A. Welsch & R.M. Cyert (Eds.), *Management decision making*. Harmondsworth: Penguin.

Engel, J.F., Blackwell, R.D., & Kollat, D.T. (1978). *Consumer behaviour*. Orlando, FL: The Dryden Press.

Fagley, N.S. & Miller, P.M. (1987). The effects of decision framing on choice of risky vs. certain options. *Organisational Behaviour and Human Decision Processes*, April, 264–277.

Fiegenbaum, A. & Thomas, H. (1988). Attitudes toward risk and the risk return paradox: Prospect theory explanations. *Academy of Management Journal, 31,* 86–106.

Fredrickson, J.W. & Iaquinto, A.L. (1989). Inertia and creeping rationality in strategic decision processes. *Academy of Management Journal, 32,* 516–542.

Godfrey, R.R. (1986). Tapping employees' creativity. *Supervisory Management,* February, 17–18.

Goman, C.G. (1989). *Creative thinking in business.* London: Kogan Page.

Greenberger, M., Crenson, M.A., & Crissey, B.L. (1976). *Models of the policy process: Public decision making in the computer era.* New York: Russell Sage Foundation.

Haugtvedt, C., Petty, R.E., Cacioppo, J.T., & Steidley, T. (1988). Personality and ad. effectiveness: Exploring the utility of need for cognition. *Advances in Consumer Research, 16.* Prova, UT: Association for Consumer Research.

Hayes, J.R. (1968). Strategies in judgemental research. In B. Kleinmuntz (Ed.), *Formal representation of human judgement.* New York: Wiley.

Henderson, J.C. & Nutt, P.C. (1980). The influence of decision style on decision-making behaviour. *Management Science,* April, 371–386.

Hinkle, C.L. & Kuehn, A.A. (1967). Heuristic models: Mapping to maze for management. *California Management Review, 10,* 59–68.

Hodgetts, R.M. (1990). *Modern human relations at work* (fourth edition). Orlando, FL: The Dryden Press.

Hodgetts, R.M. (1991). *Organisational behaviour: Theory and practice.* New York: Macmillan.

Hudson, L. (1966). *Contrary imaginations.* London: Methuen.

Hunt, R.G., Krystofiak, F.J., Meindl, J.R., & Yousry, A.M. (1989). Cognitive style and decision making. *Organisational Behaviour and Human Decision Processes, 44,* 436–453.

Janis, I.L. & Mann, L. (1982). A theoretical framework for decision counselling. In I.L. Janis (Ed.), *Counselling on personal decisions.* New Haven: Yale University Press.

Jung, C.G. (1923). *Psychological types.* London: Routledge & Kegan Paul.

Kahneman, D. & Tversky, A (1984). Choices, values and frames. *American Psychologist, 39,* 341–350.

Kanter, R.M. (1984). *The change masters.* London: Unwin.

Kaufman, B.E. (1990). A new theory of satisficing. *Journal of Behavioural Economics,* Spring, 35–51.

Kerr, S., Klimoski, R.J., Tolliver, J., & Van Glinow, M.A. (1975). Human information processing. In J. Leslie Livingstone (Ed.), *Managerial accounting: The behavioural foundations.* Columbus: Grid Publishing.

Kirton, M.J. (1984). Adaptors and innovators: Why new initiatives get blocked. *Long Range Planning, 17,* 137–143.

Lamm, H. & Trommsdorff, G. (1973). Group vs. individual performance on tasks requiring ideational proficiency (brainstorming). *European Journal of Social Psychology, 3,* 361–387.

Levy, J. (1985). Right brain, left brain: Facts and fiction. *Psychology Today,* May, 44.

Libby, R. & Lewis, B.L. (1982). Human information processing research in accounting: The state of the art in 1982. *Accounting, Organisations and Society, 7,* 231–285.

Litterer, J.A. (1973). *The analysis of organisations* (second edition). New York: Wiley.

Lynch, D. (1986). Is the brain stuff still the right (or left) stuff. *Training and Development Journal,* February, 23–26.

March, J.G. & Simon, H.A. (1958). *Organisations.* New York: Wiley.

McCosh A.M. & Scott-Morton, M. (1978). *Management decision support systems.* London: Macmillan.

Merton, R.K. (1957). *Social theory and social structure.* Glencoe, Ill: Free Press.

Mintzberg, H., Raisinghani, D., & Theoret, A. (1976). The structure of unstructured decision processes. *Administrative Science Quarterly, 21,* 246–275.

Mitroff, I.I. & Kilmann R.H. (1976). On organisation stories: An approach to the design and analysis of organisation through myths and stories. In R.H. Kilmann, L.R. Pondy, & D.P. Slevin(Eds.), *The management of organisation design, Vol. 1.* New York: Elsevier, North-Holland.

Morley, I. (1984). Bargaining and negotiation. In C.L. Cooper & P. Makin (Eds.), *Psychology for managers* (second edition). Basingstoke, UK: British Psychological Society / Macmillan.

Nutt, P.C. (1990). Strategic decisions made by top executives and middle managers with data and process-dominant styles. *Journal of Management Studies, 27,* 173–194.

Oborne D. J. (1994). *Computers at work: A behavioural approach* (3rd ed.). Chichester: Wiley.

Olshavsky, R.W. & Granbois, D.H. (1979). Consumer decision making—fact or fiction. *Journal of Consumer Research, 6,* 93–100.

Ornstein, R.E. (1977). *The psychology of consciousness.* New York: Harcourt Brace Jovanovich.

Osborn, A. (1957). *Applied imagination.* New York: Scribners.

Power, D.J. & Aldag, R.L. (1985). Soelberg's job search and choice model: A clarification, review, and critique. *Academy of Management Review,* January, 48–58.

Proctor, R.A. (1991). The importance of creativity in the management field. *British Journal of Management, 2,* 223–230.

Randall, F.D. (1955). Stimulate your executives to think creatively. *Harvard Business Review*, July/August, 121–128.

Randsepp, E. (1978). Are you a creative manager? *Management Review, 58*, 15–16.

Richards, M.D. & Greenlaw, P.S. (1972). *Management: Decisions and behaviour*. Glenview, Ill: Richard D. Irwin.

Richards, T. (1990). *Creativity and problem solving at work*. Farnborough, UK: Gower.

Robertson, I.T. (1985). Human information processing strategies and style. *Behaviour and Information Technology, 4*, 19–29.

Schroder, H.M., Driver, M.J., & Streufert, S. (1967). *Human information processing*. New York: Holt, Rinehart & Winston.

Schurr, P.H. (1987). The effects of gain and loss decision frames on risky purchase negotiations. *Journal of Applied Psychology*, August, 351–359.

Schwenk, C.R. (1985). The use of participant recollection in the modelling of organisational decision processes. *Academy of Management Review*, July, 496–503.

Simon, H.A. (1957a). *Administrative behaviour*. New York: Free Press.

Simon, H.A. (1957b). *Models of man*. New York: Wiley.

Simon, H.A. (1960). *The science of management decisions*. New York: Harper & Row.

Simon, H.A. & Newell, A. (1971). Human problem solving: The state of the theory in 1970. *American Psychologist, 26*, 145–159.

Snowball, D. (1980). On the integration of accounting research in human information processing. *Accounting and Business Research, 10*, 307–318.

Soelberg, P.O. (1967). Unprogrammed decision making. *Industrial Management Review, 8*, 19–29.

Staw, B.M. (1981). Escalation of commitment to a course of action. *Academy of Management Review*, October, 577–587.

Staw, B.M & Ross, J. (1988). Good money after bad. *Psychology Today*, February, 30–33.

Taggart, W. & Robey, D. (1981). Minds and managers: On the dual nature of human information processing and management. *Academy of Management Review*, April, 190.

Terry, G.R. (1968). *Principles of management*. Homewood, Ill: Richard D. Irwin.

Tversky, A. & Kahneman, D. (1974). Judgement under uncertainty: Heuristics and biases. *Science, 185*, 1124–1131.

Vecchio, R.P. (1991). *Organisational behaviour*, 2nd Edition. Orlando, FL: The Dryden Press.

Von Neumann, J. & Morgenstern, O. (1953). *Theory of games and economic behaviour*. Princeton, NJ: Princeton University Press.

Weist, J.D. (1966). Heuristic programs for decision making. *Harvard Business Review*, September/October, 129–143.

6

Attitudes and Job Satisfaction

After a definition of attitudes, this chapter continues with an explanation of the distinction between values and attitudes. A brief commentary on attitude formation is followed by a section on the functions of attitudes.

Next, the notion of prejudice is introduced, and this leads to an analysis of attitude change. The discussion then moves on to examine attitude measurement, followed by an analysis of the relationship between attitudes and behaviour.

The final part of the chapter is devoted to job satisfaction and organisational commitment. Job satisfaction straddles several related attitudes in the workplace, and is connected with organisational commitment (an individual's identification with and involvement in the organisation).

This chapter draws on a number of ideas raised in earlier chapters (e.g. socialisation and communication), and has particular relevance in the context of job design (Chapter 2), changes within organisations (Chapters 11 and 12), and human resource practices (Chapter 13).

DEFINITION

Attitudes are enduring systems of positive or negative evaluations, emotional feelings, and action tendencies with respect to an individual's social world (Krech, Crutchfield, & Ballachey, 1962). Attitudes can also be defined as mental states developed through experience, which are always ready to exert an active influence on an individual's response to any conditions and circumstances that the attitudes are directed towards (Allport, 1935). (For example, an attitude to safety could predispose the individual to react in a certain way to hazardous conditions at work.)

Three components of an attitude can be identified (see Table 6.1). They are classified as belief (cognitive), feeling (affective), and action (conative), and each component can be either positive or negative. The feeling or affective component of an attitude is of prime importance and it can have a significant impact on the other two components. There are occasions when the cognitive, affective, and conative components of an individual's attitudes will be consistent with one another; this is called *intra-attitude consistency*. The person who visits a pub or bar frequently (action tendency), probably believes that the bartender gives a good service (cognitive), and feels that the service and atmosphere is good (affective). However, intra-attitude consistency may not always be achieved, as will be seen later.

TABLE 6.1

Components of An Attitude

Component	Positive	Negative
Belief (cognitive)	JH is safety conscious	JH is careless in the way he operates machinery
Feeling (affective)	JH can be trusted	JH cannot be trusted
Action (conative)	It is easy to relate to JH	It is difficult to relate to JH

The distinctiveness of the attitude components and the interrelationships between them have been subjected to analysis (Kothandapani, 1971). An example of an empirical study in this area is provided by Breckler (1984). Subjects were presented with a live snake, and the next step was to record their reactions by the use of verbal measures of the three attitude components. In addition, the heart rate was measured for the affective components, and there was a measure of coping behaviour (e.g. avoidance of the snake) in the case of the behavioural component.

A subsequent variation of this experiment was not to present a live snake, but to ask subjects to imagine a live snake in their midst. This could invite a different reaction. For example, when you imagine a live snake in your midst which you believe to be harmless (cognitive component), it is likely that you would not be afraid of it (affective component), and that you would be prepared to handle it (behavioural component). However, a different reaction is likely to occur if you were actually confronted by a snake, however benign.

VALUES

There is a difference between attitudes and values. Having an attitude implies the existence of an object towards which an attitude is directed. A value is an ideal to which the individual subscribes, and it represents basic convictions that a specific mode of conduct is preferable (in a personal or social sense) to any other. Values contain a judgemental element of what is right or wrong, or desirable, and they offer a standard that will guide our conduct and act as a process to evaluate and judge our own behaviour and that of others. The motivational impact of a value is apparent when we strive to attain a particular ideal (Rokeach, 1973).

Certain values—e.g. co-operation and achievement—could be developed and reinforced over time and form societal values. Within a person's value system, there could be a hierarchy of values, with some more important than others. For example, we attach relative importance to concepts such as freedom, equality, honesty, and so on. Values can cloud objectivity and rationality, and when values clash with organisational reality, dissatisfaction can arise. Thus, a prospective employee may possess a value that reflects itself in pay being related to performance, but finds on entering the organisation that seniority is the crucial factor in the determination of pay. Understandably, the person concerned could experience dissatisfaction (discussed later in this chapter).

Values can be classified by type. A typology put forward by Allport, Vernon, and Lindzey (1960) was described in Chapter 1 as consisting of theoretical, aesthetic, social, political, religious, and economic values.

Later, a hierarchy of levels, descriptive of personal values, was advanced by Graves (1970). These levels (which could be used to examine the range of individual values within an organisation) are as follows:

1. *Reactive*. Individuals classified as reactive rarely inhabit formal organisations. Their basic orientation is to value fundamental physiological needs, and they are oblivious to their inner self and people around them.
2. *Tribalistic*. These individuals value dependence, and are strongly influenced by tradition and the power wielded by authority figures.
3. *Egocentric*. These individuals display determined individualism, and are easily seduced by power. They tend to be selfish and aggressive.
4. *Conforming*. These individuals would like other people to accept their values, have difficulty in accepting people with values that are opposed to their own, and have a low tolerance for ambiguity.
5. *Manipulative*. These individuals tend to be materialistic, with a strong penchant for significant status and recognition. In pursuit of their objectives they find it easy to manipulate people and events.
6. *Sociocentric*. These individuals value the gratification of social needs, and consequently place being liked and relating well to people higher than personal achievement. They are likely to react adversely to behaviour associated with levels 4 and 5.
7. *Existential*. These individuals do not take kindly to restrictive bureaucratic practices or symbols of status. They find it easy to relate to people with values different to their own and display a high tolerance for ambiguity.

The seven-level hierarchy of values might be used by recruiters to profile potential employees in order to determine if their values are in line with the dominant values of the organisation. An example of a mismatch is an egocentric individual operating in an organisation that seeks conformist behaviour from its employees. Where there is a fit between the person's values and those of the organisation, this could have a beneficial effect on performance and job satisfaction. In this respect, Robbins (1991) makes the following observation:

> Managers are more likely to appreciate, evaluate positively, and allocate rewards to employees who "fit in", and employees are more likely to be satisfied if they perceive that they do fit. This argues for management to pay close attention during the selection of new employees to not only finding job candidates with the ability, experience, and motivation to perform, but also with a value system that is compatible with the organisation's.

Attitudes and behaviour are the consequence of adhering to a particular value. For example, if an individual places a high value on equality for different races in society, one could expect him or her to have a positive attitude to ethnic minorities and behave accordingly. However, the relationship between attitudes and behaviour is not always predictable. An attitude can spring from a value; a person who places a high value on honesty may develop a negative attitude towards another person who consistently tells lies. In another context, a person who values justice may develop a positive attitude towards a public figure who is seen to be fostering this cause.

Business Ethics
Ethics—beliefs about what is right and wrong, and good and bad—has become a serious issue with some organisations. The principle of business ethics is that companies and their employees need a framework to deal with issues, internal and external to the organisation, that have a moral dimension. This framework can have a motivational

effect, influences corporate culture, and specifies desired behaviour. There is growing interest in business ethics in Europe as a consequence of financial scandals and environmental accidents. In recent years, some companies have adopted codes of ethics and corporate conduct, and these codes can refer to individual behaviour as well as corporate behaviour (see panel below).

However, there is a view in both Europe and the United States (where such codes have been in existence for a long time) that many of the codes of practice are either ineffective in themselves or they are enforced inadequately (Lorenz & Lorenz, 1989). According to Pocock (1989), there is a need for the personnel function within organisations to be proactive in raising awareness of business ethics, and to encourage consistency between values and behaviour in the age of the green consumer and ethical investor.

ATTITUDES AS FILTERS

A person tends to select information that is consistent with his or her attitudes and ignores information that is opposed to them. The expression of an opinion amounts to an interpretation of what has been observed after filtering it through the medium of attitudes.

In the processing and use of accounting information, for example, the attitudes of those involved assume a primary importance (Lee, 1972). The attitude of the accountant to the processing of accounting information will be influenced by the emphasis put on formal information processing systems by management in organisations, by the extent of the value placed by senior management on both accounting information and the contribution of accountants, and by the emphasis put on the notion of communicating data of a financial nature both inside and outside the organisation. The extent to which accounting information is used is likely to be influenced by the attitudes to accounting information held by the user (or decision maker).

Positive and Negative Attitudes

A positive attitude is likely to exist if decision makers consider the information to be useful,

---

Corporate Halo

About a third of large UK companies, and four-fifths of their US counterparts now have codes of ethics. Most set guiding principles for the organisation, as well as covering specific areas such as buying policies, safety, and environmental responsibilities. In April 1993 the *National Westminster Bank* produced a document setting out the proper behaviour for its 90,000 employees in cases where interests conflict, and on accepting entertainment from outsiders.

There are a number of reasons why organisations produce codes of ethics. Adopting ethics codes could be motivated by a need to avoid embarrassment in the future. *British Airways* produced a code of conduct after the bad publicity created by the dirty tricks campaign aimed at its competitor, *Virgin Atlantic*. In other cases, the rationale could be associated with altruistic or philosophical considerations in a world where the image projected by business is less than ideal.

And, of course, there are situations where self-interest has a powerful impact when it comes to embracing ethics. In such circumstances, ethics codes could be used in marketing the company. In 1992 the *Co-operative Bank* produced a 12-point code which included statements that the bank would no longer lend money to organisations involved in activities that include cruelty to animals or environmental destruction. This code could be viewed, although not necessarily so, as a marketing ploy to attract new business. At the end of the first year of the code's operation there was a 9% increase in deposits lodged with the bank.

The problems connected with the implementation of business ethics have been noted; in particular, the difficulty of sanctioning people who break the codes. Also, there are those who believe that the adoption of ethics codes could blunt the competitiveness of business (Jack & Dixon, 1993).

where they welcome it, have confidence in it, and place value on it when compared to other types of information about the business. The quality of accounting information and accounting systems is likely to be associated with the quality of the accountant as perceived by the users of accounting information. The decision maker or user of accounting information may have negative attitudes towards certain types of information because these are considered irrelevant, even though in practice the information may be of the utmost importance to the decision-making process. On other occasions, accounting information is wrongly or inefficiently used, or alternatively it is discounted, because, in specified circumstances, decision makers are attached to preconceived notions about the right decision.

An example of a negative attitude to safety at work could be the acceptance of a situation where machinery guards in a factory are frequently removed by workers, where workers are sometimes forced by supervisors to work in unsafe conditions, where supervisors do not listen when workers report unsafe conditions, where supervisors do not act to put right unsafe conditions when reported, and when they are not very receptive to requests for personal protective equipment (Re Velle & Boulton, 1981). The importance of adhering to positive attitudes when faced with machine hazards at work hardly needs stating.

A large number of accidents result from inadequately guarded machine tools and machinery in factories. Though certain machines are difficult to guard (for example, milling and grinding machines), the manager with a positive attitude towards safety will give serious consideration to the provision of sturdy and all-round guarding, and ensure that switches for emergency stops are placed in a prominent position. Automatic guards, using a trip device, are available to prevent access to dangerous parts of machines: when the trip device is activated, the dangerous parts stop. A similar principle is the photo-electric system, whereby the machine cuts itself off if a light curtain is interrupted.

Management can also adopt positive attitudes towards personal protective

NEVILLE'S FIRST, AND LAST, DAY ON THE JOB.

equipment. This type of equipment includes items such as safety glasses, ear-plugs, hard hats, face shields, gloves, knee pads, safety shoes, respirators, and the like. In a survey of worker attitudes to safety (Re Velle & Boulton, 1981), it was found that 75% of male respondents stated that they always or almost always wear the personal equipment available on the job. However, only 40% of female respondents used the equipment to the same extent. The female workers may be concerned with their appearance; if so, safety practitioners should work on the motto that the "safe look" is the "smart look".

ATTITUDE FORMATION

In the formation of attitudes, personality and socialisation are two important variables (Personality is discussed in Chapter 1 and socialisation in Chapters 1 and 4). Personality in terms of introversion or extraversion is said to create a disposition favourable or unfavourable to the acceptance of attitudes. Introverts are more susceptible to socialising influences and are more prone to accept the values of society than extraverts who tend to be under-socialised (Eysenck, 1970). It is said that the authoritarian personality is likely to display attitudes such as deference to superiors, hostility towards inferiors, disinclination to be introspective, with an inclination to project unacceptable impulses on to others. It is also suggested that highly authoritarian individuals are those who have been exposed to harsh and threatening discipline in the home early in life, and they retain an attitude of latent hostility towards their parents (Adorno et al., 1953). A more comprehensive discussion of personality types can be found in Chapter 1.

Membership of a group can be influential in determining the attitudes of individuals. This is illustrated in the Bennington College study on groups reported in Chapter 7. Socialising influences at work also play a part in the formation of attitudes. It is widely acknowledged that, during training, professional people develop attitudes towards the practice of their chosen vocation that colour their vision and affect their approach to the reality of the work situation.

This process of socialisation, by which members of a profession subscribe to the values and beliefs nurtured by the professional group, is termed *professionalisation*. It involves modification of attitudes during the training phase and conformity to group standards, and it embraces acceptance of specific obligations to colleagues, clients, and the public. Thus, entrants to the profession come into contact with various segments of it during training and, apart from acquiring necessary skills, they become acquainted with the typical responses, postures, thought processes and expectations of the qualified professional. For example, in a survey of chartered accountants (Hastings, 1968), the attitudes shown in Table 6.2 were said to be nurtured during their training.

Using the framework in Table 6.2, an exploratory study of the attitudes of chartered accountants working both in industry and the profession was conducted in the early 1970s (Buckley & McKenna, 1973; McKenna, 1972). The results are outlined in the panel overleaf. In the 1990s, such findings might have to be modified to reflect changes that have taken place within the accountancy profession over the past two decades, particularly with respect to the level of qualification for new entrants and subsequent professional education and training.

FUNCTIONS OF ATTITUDES

Attitudes help individuals to adopt a stable view of the world in which they live. We can only cope with our environment if that environment is reasonably orderly and predictable, so that the individual, the group, or society may know where they stand and what to do (Kelman, 1969). Attitudes facilitate the organisation of diverse thoughts into a

TABLE 6.2

Attitudes Developed by Chartered Accountants in Training

Caution	— a preference for certainty, predictability, and avoidance of risk
Exactitude	— a preference for the maximum attainable precision in output independent of the cost and value of achieving it
Anti-theoretical pragmatism	— a preference for convention-based rather than analytical approaches to problems, and for experience rather than theory
Professional exclusiveness	— a preference for the qualities of chartered accounants when compared with those of other accountants
Quantification	— a preference for numerical methods of working and items which can be quantitied
Rationality	— a preference for systematic logical approaches to problem solving as opposed to other methods such as intution

coherent pattern. This contributes to the reduction of uncertainty and allows individuals to operate without the discomfort of having to evaluate all stimuli impinging on their senses in order to make the correct response. The mere fact that we impose some order on our social universe makes it easier for others to communicate and relate to us, particularly when they have some insight into our attitudes.

Likewise, an insight into the attitudes of others helps us to understand and interact with them. However, as we saw in Chapter 3 on perception, we still experience difficulties in perceiving and evaluating people and events in everyday life. It is generally recognised that humans have a need to experience themselves as free agents, and are not just entities reacting to an ordered environment. In fact, there are a number of occasions when we exert influence on our environment.

A Study of Profession and Industry-based Chartered Accountants

The accountants showed a preference for caution in their approach to business problems, and this was more marked in the case of accountants employed in professional practice. Similarly with respect to exactitude, the accountants working in a professional practice displayed a firm attachment to this attitude, whereas their counterparts in industry were less concerned with exactitude.

With regard to anti-theoretical pragmatism, accountants in professional practice exhibited a strong tendency towards acceptance of this attitude. They tended to rely on experience rather than theory, and they showed a preference for the status quo as opposed to innovation in accounting and auditing. By contrast, the accountant in industry seemed distinctly less attached to anti-theoretical pragmatism.

Both the profession and industry-based chartered accountants seemed to regard their qualification as being better in most respects than that of other qualified accountants, although industry-based accountants considered themselves slightly less exclusive. Chartered accountants in professional practice frequently perceived their fellow members as possessing better education (both general and professional), higher professional integrity, more social presence, greater independence of mind, and a wider breadth of business vision than their certified and cost and management counterparts.

Finally, as one would expect, all the sampled accountants showed a very clear preference for quantification in dealing with problems; as one respondent observed, numerical ways of thinking and working are developed during training. (Buckley & McKenna, 1973; McKenna, 1972)

The major functions of attitudes, which have not been experimentally tested to any great extent, have been identified by Katz (1960) as: instrumental or adjustive; ego defensive; expressive; and acquisition of knowledge.

Instrumental or Adjustive Function

Individuals strive to maximise rewards and minimise sanctions or penalties in their external environment. They develop favourable attitudes towards objects that satisfy their needs, and unfavourable attitudes towards objects that thwart their needs. In the latter case, a consumer may develop a particular attitude towards a product category and avoid items in that category. For example, a consumer chooses not to use hotbrushes because of a previous bad experience with heated rollers. By contrast, a successful stay in a hotel may give rise to a favourable attitude that manifests itself in return visits to that or a similar hotel.

Ego Defensive Function

Individuals develop attitudes designed to protect themselves from exposure to undesirable basic truths or certain realities in their environment. Consumers may attempt to ward off threats to self-esteem by developing positive attitudes towards products, such as grooming aids or an impressive car, that may enhance their self-image. Others may develop favourable attitudes towards mechanisms of defence, such as mouthwashes or deodorants, in order to defend their ego.

There are other occasions when the individual projects his or her weaknesses on to others as a means of self-protection and, in the process, develops unfavourable attitudes towards the target group; this could arise in the case of prejudice directed at minority groups.

Ego defensive attitudes may be aroused by internal and external threats, by frustrating experiences, by the build-up of pressures previously repressed, and by suggestions or directives from an authoritarian source. Ego defensive attitudes are difficult to change because of the misdirected nature of the impulses associated with them. For example, an employee encounters a frustrating experience at work, and feels aggressive as a consequence because of the hurt to his or her ego. However, the employee displaces this aggression by directing it at a completely different target such as a member of the family or a pet. Though ego defensive attitudes are difficult to change, it is possible to remove the threats to the attitudes through therapeutic means in a supportive environment, by giving individuals insight into the dysfunctional parts of their defence mechanism.

Expressive Function

This attitudinal function contains three main aspects:

1. It helps to express the individual's central values and self-identity. Consumers express their values in the products they buy, the shops they patronise, and the life-style they exhibit.
2. The expressive function also helps individuals to define their self-concept, and facilitates the adoption of sub-culture values considered important. For example, teenagers may dress and behave in a certain way in order to foster their status in an in-group.
3. The expressive function helps individuals to adopt and internalise the values of a group they have recently joined and, as a consequence, they are better able to relate to the group. An individual who has joined an ecology group may now express values manifest in the purchase and use of a bicycle and the recycling of bottles.

Knowledge Function

Individuals need to maintain a stable, organised, and meaningful structure of their world in order to prevent chaos. Attitudes provide the standards or frames of reference by which the individual judges objects or events, and attitudes that provide consistency in our thinking are particularly relevant. The efficiency of the knowledge function of attitudes is readily observable in consumer behaviour.

Attitudes predispose purchasers to prefer a particular make of car, and they do not have to re-examine their values, habits, and life-style prior to the decision to buy. However, if existing attitudes are inadequate in resolving a particular issue, then the acquisition of new knowledge could bring about a changed attitude. Consumers are generally information-seekers; they have a need to know and this drives them to gain information that gives meaning to their social world. But sometimes individuals take the easy option and rely on stereotypes to simplify reality.

Of the four major functions of attitudes, the knowledge function is perhaps the weakest in theoretical significance (Reich & Adcock, 1976).

Demands of the Work Environment

The demands of the work environment are many and varied, but in this section they will be illustrated with reference to the earlier discussion of specific attitudes developed by chartered accountants during training. Whether these attitudes are functional depends on the type of job environment in which the chartered accountant works. With reference to the industrial (as opposed to the professional) accountancy environment, it has been suggested that adherence to quantification is generally functional, but adherence to caution, exactitude, and anti-theoretical pragmatism is, on balance, dysfunctional (Hastings, 1968).

Caution may manifest itself in the industrial or commercial world in an undue amount of checking of figures and records. Accountants who are very attached to caution may be ill-prepared to cope with decisions in

the work situation as they move up the organisational pyramid. An example of dysfunctional exactitude in business is the calculation of figures to many decimal places where approximations to the nearest thousand may suffice. Anti-theoretical pragmatism in the business situation can be seen, among many other instances, in the failure to approach decision problems on an incremental cash flow basis. An accountant's preference for caution, coupled with anti-theoretical pragmatism, may explain the emphasis on, and attachment to, conservatism in the preparation and presentation of accounting information.

At the level of professional practice, attachment to anti-theoretical pragmatism may help to explain much about stagnation in the development of a framework of financial accounting. Preference for experience rather than theory may lie at the heart of the profession's failure to get to grips with financial reporting relevant to the needs of existing and potential shareholders, rather than merely detailing stewardship in the traditional manner (Buckley & McKenna, 1973).

PREJUDICE

Although it is possible to encounter a continuum of prejudice, ranging from extremely favourable to extremely unfavourable in terms of attitudes, in practice the word "prejudice" is mainly used with a negative connotation. The prejudiced person tends to hold a negative view of, for example, racial groups or certain practices. In rural India it was not uncommon to find prejudice against the introduction of new farm machinery or the general acceptance of contraception. Also, prejudice may find expression in a negative view of certain safety procedures used by a company.

The prejudiced person with, for example, a stereotyped view of people of a particular race or creed, may have that view dispelled on meeting somebody who does not fit the stereotype. But equally, the prejudiced person is capable of rationalising the situation in such a way as to conclude that the person he or she met is unique in some respects, and is unlike the stereotype. Therefore the prejudiced view prevails. For example, an anti-Semite will not be swayed in his or her view of Jews by evidence of their charitable behaviour, nor will those who have a deep prejudice against black people be persuaded by coming in contact with intelligent and industrious people in this racial group. A successful encounter with an estate agent, whereby a person's house was sold in record time to a reliable purchaser, may not dispel that person's prejudice against estate agents—the experience may be viewed as atypical. The prejudiced person can easily slide into behaviour known as discrimination.

Despite legislation in the UK outlawing discrimination in employment, there is a general belief that prejudice based on sex and race leads to discrimination reflected in widespread inequalities at work. Cassell and Walsh (1993) considered the difficulties facing women at work and highlighted some of the barriers that prevent women achieving positions of power in organisations. They concluded that psychology as a discipline needs to understand ways in which gender determines work organisation—particularly the links between gender, power, and organisational culture. Another form of discrimination— age discrimination—has become a live issue in recent years (see panel below).

Influence of Personality and Culture

Factors such as personality, home background, culture, and conformity can influence prejudice. Earlier, the authoritarian personality was considered important in the context of attitude formation. In a study conducted by Adorno et al. (1953), it was concluded that the most seriously prejudiced people displayed an authoritarian personality. These people put a high premium on status both inside and outside the home, and had a clear view of dominance and submission. They were basically insecure and tended to repress or deny their own personal conflicts; they were conventional in their approach to life with explicit values and rules to guide behaviour; they adhered to socially acceptable behaviour that promoted their interests, and tended to be aggressive towards groups not sharing their views.

A study of anti-Semitism among female university students concluded that those girls

---

Ageism in the Workplace

Age discrimination is rife throughout the EC. This is evident from the practice of targeting employees over 50 for redundancy and retirement programmes, and advertising vacant positions specifying that applicants must be below a certain age (e.g. 35). Ageism unfairly curtails individual opportunity, and it is likely to become increasingly economically wasteful because older people who are still capable of making a contribution to society may instead become a burden.

A report produced by the pressure group *Eurolink Age* blames the restricted opportunities largely on *discriminatory* attitudes. It is said that too many employees believe that old people are not up to the job, and there is a widespread belief that older people's jobs are more expendable than young people's. Although some people lose their ability and enthusiasm to work in their fifties, it is unfair to lump all older people in that category. If people are fit, productive, and want to work, age should be no barrier.

However, where older people are forced out of work, it is often too simplistic to point at discriminatory attitudes. It could be that institutional arrangements give employees artificial incentives to do so. For example, due to the seniority system, the rewards (e.g. salaries) of older employees are greater than the younger people's, and barriers are created by pensions and retirement arrangements (*Financial Times*, 1993).

who harboured deep prejudice against Jews displayed repressed hatred, jealousy, and suspicion of parental figures (Frenkel-Brunswick & Sanford, 1945). In effect, they projected on to Jews feelings that would normally be directed towards parents and other authority figures in their life.

Culture can determine the nature and level of prejudice. In Japan the culture is supportive of flexible working practices whereas, until very recently, Britain had a reputation for rigid demarcation lines between jobs and skills.

From the results of a survey of South African whites, three main reasons were inferred to explain prejudice against black people (MacCrone, 1957). One reason was the manner in which the historical strife between black and white has been presented in schools, in textbooks, and at home. The whites were the "goodies" and the blacks were the "baddies", and invariably the blacks were presented as perpetrating atrocities on the whites. Another reason was associated with way of life. Blacks were poorer, had no political rights, and had the least attractive jobs. Finally, the way blacks were treated was considered important. Blacks had to carry identity cards and, if they were imprisoned, they were forced to work—a requirement not imposed on the whites.

Influence of Group Norms

Conformity to the dominant norm of a prejudiced group is a critical factor in prejudice. When the individual conforms to a prejudice held by the group, he or she can be seen as favouring the maintenance of this prejudice. Conformity can give legitimacy to extreme behaviour that is based on prejudice. At work this could lead to active discrimination and ill-treatment of minorities.

The victims of prejudice are generally held in low esteem by the prejudiced person, and this is considered an ample justification for prejudice and discrimination. Sometimes the social status of the prejudiced person is low or declining, and using a scapegoat to compensate for feelings of internal unease is one way of trying to cope with the frustration experienced.

Ways of Reducing Prejudice

A number of suggestions have been made about ways of reducing prejudice. As was mentioned earlier, contact with the victim of prejudice may help to change the attitude of the prejudiced person, but this does not always happen. There are circumstances where the prejudiced person, having worked with the victim of prejudice, concludes that, contrary to expectations, his or her colleague is not, for instance, lazy after all. However, the prejudice may remain firm when generalised to situations outside work (Secord & Beckman, 1974).

Discussion is said to reduce prejudice when the prejudice is of a lower order, but to intensify it when it is of a higher order (Mackay, 1973). When people with opposing prejudices work in an interdependent fashion to achieve a common objective, this can have the effect of reducing prejudices on both sides. As described in Chapter 7 on groups, hostility between two groups was reduced by creating situations that made it necessary for both groups to co-operate in removing obstacles.

ATTITUDE CHANGE

A variety of factors are responsible for bringing about a change in attitudes. For instance, marketing executives can attempt to modify those attitudes that strongly influence the purchase of a particular type of product by trying to bring them into line with what the company plans to offer. Take a past British Rail advertisement with the simple message, "Let the train take the strain". It draws attention to the convenience and relaxation of a train journey compared with a similar journey by car.

There are many instances of marketing strategies designed to change attitudes towards a product by attracting attention to the characteristics of the product that have an edge over the competition. For example, a manufacturer may add a supplement to the existing characteristics of a product—a mouthwash ingredient may be added to a toothpaste, and a fabric softener to a washing powder. In other situations, the emphasis could be placed on an important product attribute. For example, a car manufacturer may stress the special anti-rust proofing its cars receive, and a washing machine manufacturer may attract the consumer's attention to a "no-tangle" washing action.

Sources of Attitude Change

Kelman (1961) proposed three sources of attitude change—compliance, identification, and internalisation.

Compliance
Compliance arises when an attitude is adopted for ulterior motives, such as the desire to make a favourable impression on the individual's boss or client.

Identification
Identification arises when the individual adopts an attitude in order to establish or maintain a satisfying relationship with others. A student wishing to establish a good working relationship with a lecturer may adopt an attitude reflected in listening attentively at lectures and contributing intelligently at seminars.

Internalisation
Internalisation arises when the new attitude is embraced as part of a cluster of attitudes, because the individual feels comfortable subscribing to that attitude.

Factors Contributing to Attitude Change

A number of specific factors giving rise to a change in attitudes can be identified. These are:

1. Group Membership
2. Exposure to the Mass Media
3. Forced Contact
4. Rewards
5. Communication
6. Persuasion.

1. Group Membership
In a study conducted at Bennington College (Newcombe, 1943), there was evidence of a noticeable shift in attitudes as a result of group membership, though there were marked individual differences. It was concluded that the main factor influencing students' decisions to change or not to change their attitudes was their relationship to the family or college. Where students decided to be independent of their family, and affiliated with and derived prestige from the college group, they tended to adopt a radical position on the left of politics. But where they maintained strong family ties, coming from a home where conservative attitudes were more prevalent, there was a tendency to ignore the influence of the college. This was expressed as withdrawal or active resistance. Membership of a group at work, whereby the individual is influenced by some prevailing ideology or practice, can likewise contribute to a change in attitudes.

A "situational view" of attitudes, stressing the power of *social context*, could be considered under the heading of group membership. Social context can influence individuals' attitudes, and this is evident in Salancik and Pfeffer's (1978) social information-processing approach. Socially acceptable attitudes and behaviour could be prescribed through cues and guides in the social information-processing approach. The spotlight could focus on specific attributes of a particular setting (e.g. the office or factory) with an emphasis on the set of attitudes and behaviour of greatest importance (salience) to the individual. For example, a new recruit joins the accounting department in an organisation, which could be considered a well-established group. In a short space of time, members of the group will communicate with the new recruit on different matters, such as what is expected of a group member in terms of expenditure of effort, what members think of the competency of the boss, the acceptability or otherwise of the salary system, and so on. It would not be unusual to find the new recruit's attitudes and behaviour being at least partly influenced by this experience. In effect, social information emanating from the group influences the new recruit's perception of reality.

2. Exposure to the Mass Media

The mass media (press, radio, and television) are often held responsible for a change in attitudes. For instance, campaigns are mounted periodically in the mass media with a strong safety connotation—"clunk click, every trip" in connection with the wearing of car seat belts, or highlighting the risks of driving with excess alcohol in the bloodstream. The aim is to influence attitudes to safety.

On examining the influence of the mass media on attitudes to certain issues, an unexpected conclusion emerged in one study (Katz & Lazarsfield, 1955). Messages presented via newspaper, radio, and television produced insignificant attitude changes initially. However, having repeated the measurements of these attitudes some weeks later, the researchers found significant changes. They put forward the following explanation for the delayed shifts in opinion. Most people, to begin with, are affected in a very small way by what they see and hear in the media, but are then likely to discuss these issues with others whom they know and whose opinions they value and trust. It is only then that attitude change will occur to any marked degree.

3. Forced Contact

Closely related to the influence exerted by the group in changing attitudes is the notion of forced contact. For example, placing a worker with negative safety attitudes in a vibrant safety group, whose terms of reference are to promote good safety practice in a company, could result in a change in safety attitudes. But the success of such a venture is likely to depend on the degree of involvement of the recalcitrant worker in the work of the group.

When black and white people were forced to live in integrated housing schemes—i.e. where families were allocated flats and houses irrespective of their race—the three aspects of attitudes (beliefs, feelings, and actions) towards black people by white people improved. A control group observed in segregated housing schemes did not produce a similar effect (Deutsch & Collins, 1951).

A related finding was reported during the World War II, when black troops were integrated into previously all-white US combat divisions. Where black and white soldiers experienced field service together, only 7% of the white soldiers in the mixed units said they disliked this form of integration. But in units that were all-white, 62% of the troops opposed the integration (Stouffer et al., 1949).

It is clear that forced contact in these housing and military situations led to a decrease in racial prejudice.

4. Rewards

In certain cases, some form of reward may have to be forthcoming before a person changes an attitude. Take, for example, a prejudiced politician with strong views on immigration. Having had a number of refusals from selection committees in constituencies where he would have liked to have stood, paradoxically he is eventually adopted by a constituency with a strong immigrant community. In nursing the constituency, his behaviour is at variance with his private beliefs. But if he receives social approval for the way he conducts himself politically, it is conceivable that he will adopt the attitude implicit in his political role. In this case, social approval is the reward that leads to attitude change.

As a means to encourage workers to use personal protective equipment, changes could be made to both the design and the material to improve the comfort of the wearer (Zohar, 1980). In effect, this is offering the prospect of reward to those prepared to adopt a more positive attitude to safety practice. Also, campaigns could be initiated consisting of awards for success in safety competitions.

5. *Communication*

Various facets of the communication process were discussed in Chapter 3. Communication of a message designed to change attitudes may be "one-sided" or "two-sided". The following findings emerged when propaganda was used to change the attitudes of soldiers (Hovland, Lumsdaine, & Sheffield, 1949). A soldier who had received a high school education was more influenced by a two-sided communication, whereas the soldier with a poorer education was more influenced by a one-sided communication. Arguments contained in one-sided communication are effective if the receiver's attitude is in sympathy with the attitude embedded in the message. But an argument contained in a two-sided communication would be more effective if the initial attitude of the receiver was at variance with the attitude embedded in the message. These findings may not be valid in the long term and in conditions where counter-propaganda exists. This principle is illustrated by the following examples.

A productive social encounter in an organisation might arise when A, a credible communicator with a deep-seated positive attitude to safety, tries to influence B who has a lukewarm attitude to safety. If A and B held diametrically opposed views on safety, the encounter could be quite different.

A manufacturer of electrical appliances provides information in a one-sided communication when a user's manual is included with the product, although there is scope for two-sided communication when the consumer asks questions of a sales assistant in the store where the appliance was bought. This offers an opportunity to clear up any confusion or difficulties with respect to the operation or use of the product.

In the context of consumer decision making, Chattopadhyay and Alba (1988) maintained that the advantage of one-sided arguments was that the individual receiving the message has more time to think about the issues raised, and this would be of particular importance if the person concerned had limited cognitive ability and was not very familiar with the central issues of the argument.

Reflecting on the question of the relative merits of the two sides of an argument, Tesser and Shaffer (1990) proposed that two-sided communication encourages people to concentrate on receiving the message at the expense of thinking about its implications in detail, particularly when the issues under review are unfamiliar to the recipient of the message.

Primacy and Recency Effects. The order in which two opposing arguments are presented is likely to have a bearing on the effectiveness of the communication. Where the first argument put across has the greatest effect, this is referred to as the primacy effect. But where the second argument put across has the greatest effect, this is referred to as the recency effect. Attachment to the notion of the primacy effect may be implied from the behaviour of a lawyer acting for the prosecution in a court of law. He or she presents the prosecution's case before the lawyer acting for the defence has a say. On the other hand, a politician may feel that the best moment to make a final address before an election is the day after his or her major rival does so; this politician obviously believes in the recency effect.

There is support for the superiority of the primacy effect in certain circumstances (Hovland et al., 1957). A first communication is likely to be more effective if both sides of an argument are presented by the same person, and provided the listeners are unaware that conflicting views are to be presented. If at the end of the presentation the listeners make a public commitment, this is an important factor in endorsing the primacy effect.

Public Commitment. This is a powerful strengthener of attitudes (see panel below). The effect of making a public commitment is to make the person relatively resistant to change in the face of counter-propaganda. But situations like the one illustrated in the panel are rather complex because people differ in their interest in particular issues. Likewise, if the issues are difficult to grasp, the intelligence of the person is an important factor. Other factors to consider are the nature of the propaganda to which the individual is exposed, and the nature of the group making the public commitment.

Sequence of Presentation. Is the manner in which the message is put across critical in terms of changing attitudes? To answer this question, a group of researchers conducted two experiments based on the UK court system (Maslow, Yoselson, & London, 1971).

A written legal case was presented to subjects and they were asked to reach a decision on whether they considered the accused guilty or innocent. However, before they reached a decision they were asked to study the defence argument put forward by the accused. The defence argument was submitted to two groups, and though the content was identical the presentation was different in each case.

In the first group, the experimenters put forward the arguments in a confident tone of voice—a statement would be prefaced with, "Obviously ...", "I believe ...", "I am sure ...", etc.

In the second group, the experimenters presented the arguments with more tentative expressions in the text, for example, "I don't know ...", "I am not positive ...", "I am unsure ...", etc.

It was found that when the case for the defence was put forward in a confident verbal manner to the first group, the number of subjects agreeing with the submission for the defence was significantly higher than was the case in the second group.

In a second experiment, an actor used a tape to submit a plea of "not guilty" and this submission was presented in alternative forms—that is, in either a confident, a neutral, or a doubtful manner. So the subjects were exposed to three different modes of presentation. The number of subjects who were sure that the plea was correct was highest when the actor behaved confidently. This was followed by neutral and doubtful modes of presentation in that order.

It hardly needs stating that confidence is an important factor in influencing people in business, and one feels that the able

---

Public Commitment and the Voting Age

A group of students were asked to write essays on their attitudes to reducing the legal voting age to 18 years. This came after a session in which they were exposed to an argument favourable to the idea. Half the group members—the public commitment group—were asked to sign their essays and were told that their work would be published in full in the school newspaper the following week. The other group members—the private commitment group—were not asked to sign their essays, and in addition were assured that their views would remain anonymous.

Both groups were then presented with an argument that was strongly in favour of retaining the minimum voting age at 21 years, and they were invited to write a short paragraph stating their frank opinions on this matter.

The results of this experiment suggest that only 25% of the public commitment group shifted or changed their attitudes, whereas 50% of the private commitment group (whose views remained anonymous) decided to change their attitudes. (Hovland et al., 1957)

communicator is likely to rely on non-verbal expressions as a means of supplementing the verbal delivery when transmitting confidence to an audience. (Communication skills were examined in Chapter 3).

Threats and Fear.   When dealing with threats and fear, how gruesome should a message be? An advertisement on road safety showing a really horrific illustration of road accident victims may not produce the desired effect, whereas a more temperate reference to road accident victims might be more productive. On this theme, Janis and Feshbach (1963) conducted a study into the effects of different levels of threats to persuade high school students to adopt recommended practices of dental care (see panel). The conclusion from the study is that threats should be used with great care, and although a little fear may be a good thing, a lot of fear may be a bad thing.

The common sense view, unlike the view emanating from the Janis and Feshbach (1963) study, would suggest that a high-level threat is likely to produce a better response in terms of attitude change. Support for this view came from the findings of a study assessing the effect of a talk on the seriousness of tetanus and the need for anti-tetanus injections (Leventhal, Singer, & Jones, 1965). The talk created strong fear arousal leading to a behavioural change in the form of obtaining an inoculation if this was easily available (although such a course of action could be considered medically desirable behaviour requiring little prompting).

It is also suggested that a strong fear appeal in a message is superior to a mild fear appeal in changing attitudes when a threat is posed to an individual's loved ones, when the subject matter of the message is presented by a highly credible source, when the recipient, though vulnerable, has a high degree of self-esteem (Karlins & Abelson, 1970), and when the recipient has the ability to ward off the danger depicted in the message (Rogers & Mewborn, 1976). In a particular situation a speaker with high credibility can arouse high

fear in the recipients of the message, but the logical consequences of total acceptance of the message may not materialise. For example, when subjects were subjected to high fear arousal with respect to the hazards of smoking, they were willing to cut down on smoking but less willing to have a chest X-ray (Leventhal, Watts, & Pagano, 1967).

Sutton (1982), having reviewed a number of studies, concluded that fear arousal in messages produced a consistent improvement in intention to change behaviour, as well as actual changed behaviour, when compared with situations where no fear arousal was applied. Also, he maintained that higher levels of fear led consistently to more change than lower levels.

It is important to stress that the effects generated by fear arousal in a message must be placed in their proper context. For example, are the suggested remedies to counteract the threat likely to be perceived by the recipient of the message as effective measures, and also does the recipient have confidence in his or her ability to carry out the recommended action (Eiser & Van der Pligt, 1988)? Seasoned smokers, faced with persuasive messages to stop smoking or face dire consequences, must believe the advice that giving up smoking is an effective measure in reducing their chances of contracting lung cancer and other diseases, and must have confidence in their ability to successfully forego cigarettes if they try.

Another question to consider when people are exposed to horrific images, is how relevant the message is to the perceiver's personal predicament. For example, subjects exposed to a communication aimed at generating a high level of fear—where it is stated that improper dental care leads to teeth being extracted, inflamed gums, paralysis, and blindness (see panel facing)—may believe this message, but on reflection are convinced that their own oral hygiene practices are unlikely to result in these devastating consequences, and naturally infer that their teeth have been cared for properly. Therefore, they conclude

Dental Care Study

An illustrated lecture on dental care was given to three similar groups, but a different level of fear-arousing message was used in each group. In the mild-level threat group, the students were shown decayed teeth cavities, mouth infections, and visits to the dentist. In the moderate-level threat group, there were similar illustrations, but in addition warnings of pain from toothache and dental work were given. In the strong-level threat group, the threats already made clear to the other two groups were reiterated and these were reinforced by warnings of possible intense suffering from secondary diseases, such as blindness, cancer, and major dental surgery. In addition to the three experimental groups, a control group, which received a talk on a different topic, was used.

In order to measure the response to the message, the experimenters noted the students' reported changes in teeth-brushing practices and the extent to which they attended a dentist during the following week.

It was found that the mild-level threat produced the greatest change in responsive behaviour (37%), followed by the moderate-level threat (22%), with the strong-level threat producing a small change (8%). The mild-level threat group responded significantly more than the control group. But the strong-level threat group was no different from the control group that did not get a pep talk. These findings indicate that the greater the threat, or the higher the intensity of a fear-arousing message, the lower the intensity of dental protective action.

The three experimental groups were exposed to counter-propaganda (a different message) a week later. The mild-level threat group was more resistant to this message than the other two groups, and the least resistance was felt by the strong-level threat group. This is understandable because the mild-level threat group had already changed their attitudes significantly, whereas the strong-level threat group experienced an insignificant change of attitudes following the initial fear-arousing message.

An explanation put forward to account for the initial reaction of the strong-level threat group suggests that stimuli that appeal to intense fear arouse anxiety in listeners. To try and reduce this anxiety, people become hostile to the speaker and, as a result, are likely to reject the message (Janis & Feshbach, 1963).

---

that there is no need to change existing tooth-brushing behaviour (Fishbein & Ajzen, 1975).

A cardinal principle one must never lose sight of is that people with different attitudes are likely to perceive matters in different ways, and this can be seen clearly in some health campaigns carried out nationally. A fear-arousing message may be construed as a personal attack (and consequently avoided) by the target group whose behaviour the health authority is trying to change. For example, consider the possible reactions of gay men to certain AIDS campaigns.

Attitude Dissimilarity or Similarity.   The similarity or dissimilarity of the attitudes of both the communicator and listener also have to be considered. If the communicator advocates a position that is close to the one held by the listener, the listener will perceive a greater similarity between the two positions than exists in reality; this is referred to as *assimilation*. On the other hand, if the communicator advocates a position that is rather distant from the one held by the listener, the latter perceives it as more distant than it really is; this is referred to as *contrast* (Reich & Adcock, 1976).

Maximum attitude change can be expected when the listener does not hold an extreme attitude on the matter, the issue is not one that appeals to his or her ego, is likely to be considered neutral, and the communicator has high credibility. This might very well describe the conditions in a psychology laboratory, because the typical laboratory setting creates a high credibility source (academic or scientific staff), and the issues dealt with are unimportant when compared to real life events; therefore it is no wonder that experimenters usually obtain attitude change (Himmelfarb, 1974). However, this criticism may be unfair if levelled at all studies of attitude change, because attitude change as an outcome of field studies has been observed.

6. *Persuasion*

Persuasion is an important process in attitude change, and persuasive influences were conspicuous in the role of communication as a factor contributing to attitude change, discussed in the previous section. An extreme form of persuasion was employed by the Chinese with respect to the re-education (brainwashing) of prisoners of war. Soldiers were coerced into reading aloud pro-communist propaganda over the camp's loudspeaker system. The reason for this was that other prisoners were more likely to accept such ideas from their own colleagues than from the enemy. In one camp, a soldier reared in Brooklyn, New York, delivered the message with a deadpan expression in an exaggerated southern Dixieland drawl as an act of defiance (Mackay, 1973).

Persuasion exemplified in promotional efforts for marketing purposes would appear to be more subtle. A company may wish to change one or more of the attributes of its product or service in order to enhance its corporate image: for example, an airline, primarily a domestic carrier, now wishes to be considered an international carrier. In another situation the consumer is asked to reassess the value of a particular attribute of the product or service: thus, a building society, moving to a banking type of service, in addition to its normal service stresses the convenience of being open on Saturday mornings. (Partly in response to increased competition from the building societies, some commercial banks now offer a limited banking service on Saturday mornings.) A pharmaceutical company may stress the absence of an undesirable attribute in its product—e.g. paracetamol, unlike aspirin, is not very harmful to the stomach.

In order to increase the overall attractiveness of a brand, a new attribute of the product is given particular emphasis in advertisements. Here are a few examples: a birth control element in dog food; the addition of a deodorising feature in socks; the inclusion of a "light to show the way to escape" in smoke detectors; the incorporation of protein in a dishwashing product for "softer hands"; a revolutionary roll-on anti-perspirant that goes on dry; and the "wonder loaf" that is nutritionally superior. Also, a manufacturer of roll-on deodorants may wish to capitalise on a social trend and stress the advantages of roll-on over spray products.

Opinion Leaders. An advertiser may wish to influence opinion leaders either individually or in groups. Opinion leaders are people of roughly the same social standing as those who will be subjected to their influence. They tend to be better informed, often more intelligent, and pay more attention to the channels of communication than those subjected to their influence. There could be an opinion leader for different pursuits—e.g. fashion, sport, and politics.

Those who succumb too readily to persuasion are said to be anxious (Reich & Adcock, 1976). Their lack of self-confidence, as a result, may make them vulnerable, and their preoccupation with their own thoughts and fears may create a disposition whereby they do not pay enough attention to the persuasive message.

Credibility of Source. The credibility of the source of a message has been acknowledged earlier: it is equally applicable to persuasion. The perceived status (the position or role occupied by the persuader) is also important. Credibility depends on the general trustworthiness, qualifications, dynamism, or energy of the person (Mackay, 1973). What effect has the credibility of the persuader on whether or not one yields to his or her message? The impact of the credibility of the persuader in a classroom situation is demonstrated in a study (see panel overleaf) by Karlins and Abelson (1970).

In another experiment, the opinions of students on certain important issues were obtained (Hovland & Weiss, 1951). One week

The Power of Suggestion

A lecturer, introduced as Dr. Hang Schmidt, an internationally renowned research chemist, was presented to a group of students. Dr. Schmidt wore a white laboratory coat and spoke with a German accent. The students were asked to report, by putting up their hands, when they smelt a new chemical vapour he was about to release. The lecturer pulled the stopper of a small glass beaker giving the impression that he was releasing the vapour. Then the students sitting in the front of the lecture hall raised their hands, and their reaction spread throughout the hall. Later the students were told that the beaker had not contained any vapour, merely distilled water, and that Dr. Schmidt was a lecturer from the Department of German.

This experiment illustrates the power of suggestion emanating from an apparent expert or credible source. One wonders whether the same effect would be produced if a student dressed in jeans went through the same motions as Dr. Schmidt (Karlins & Abelson, 1970).

later the students were presented with four newspaper articles dealing with the issues on which they had earlier expressed an opinion. Each article dealt with one of the important issues, and the articles contained a mixture of arguments for and against the topics discussed. The students were unaware of the title of the publication from which the articles were extracted.

Subsequently, one group of students was told that an article came from a credible source—for example, from a medical journal in the case of the use of drugs. Another group was told that the article came from a low credibility source—for example, from a mass-circulation newspaper, again in the case of drugs. Once again the attitudes of the students to the issues raised earlier were assessed, and they were compared with the attitudes that prevailed prior to the experiment. A 22% change in attitudes was observed for the group exposed to the high credibility source, as opposed to 8% for the low credibility source.

What is the relevance of the notion of credibility to a commercial organisation? The credibility of a trading company can be enhanced by creating a corporate reputation. This could be achieved by reliable products, good after-sales service, sound warranties and guarantees, using friendly and helpful staff, and acting in a socially responsible manner. Likewise, a supplier could use well-respected stores or speciality shops for an unknown brand, and this could contribute to improved sales. The high credibility of the source is evident in a magazine such as *Which*, because of its established reputation for expertise in providing information on different products. A source with low credibility could be effective if it argues against its own interest (Koeske & Crano, 1968). For example, a tobacco company would have low credibility if it argued that there is no relationship between smoking and lung cancer, but the company could be very persuasive in changing people's attitudes if it argued publicly that smoking definitely leads to lung cancer.

When considering source credibility, what is called the *sleeper effect* should be acknowledged. This develops when, after a lapse of time, a person will be more persuaded by the content of a message and less influenced by the credibility or non-credibility of the source.

It is said that credibility is of importance only in relation to attitudes on issues in which subjects have a mild interest. But if the latter's ego involvement in an issue is high, the importance of credibility is minimal (Johnson & Scileppi, 1969). Perhaps where there is greater involvement of the self in an issue, this leads subjects to a position whereby they pay more attention to the content of the message and less to the source. The subject's firm attitudinal attachment to a particular issue is the crucial factor in this situation, and the credibility of a source that may challenge this state of affairs is likely to be considered unacceptable.

It has sometimes been suggested that "overhearing" and taking notice of a message on an issue in which one has a high personal involvement—instead of being the direct recipient of the message—can produce the intended effect. At least the communicator cannot be accused of attempting to influence directly the eventual recipient who overheard the message. But where the communication is presented directly, the communicator may be suspected of giving desirable information to further his or here own ends (Brock & Becker, 1965; Waister & Festinger, 1962).

It is probably better to think of credibility as applicable to a particular situation, rather than having general applicability, because the credible source may have only a specific expertise to offer. Is it important for the persuader to draw an explicit conclusion at the end of the message? The persuader, on the grounds of effectiveness, does not have to be explicit if the listener is motivated or intelligent enough to draw his or her own conclusion. However, the explicit conclusion is more likely to be effective with the less intelligent listener (McGuire, 1968).

Persuasion Routes. Petty and Cacioppo (1985) have postulated the so-called "elaboration likelihood model" of persuasion. According to this model there are two routes to persuasion—the central route and the peripheral route. The central route to persuasion entails handling the message received with careful thought, and considering the various arguments along with our own ideas in deciding what position to take. We take this route if the issue interests us, where we take notice of the content of the message and the information contained in it, and where the arguments are significant and can withstand serious scrutiny. People who are likely to process persuasive messages through the central route are likely to enjoy thinking, are able to concentrate, feel involved in the issues under review, and consider that they have a personal responsibility for evaluating the message. A critical aspect of the persuasive message for these people is the arrangement of the arguments, and they play down simply remembering the arguments (Cacioppo & Petty, 1989).

The situation is quite different if the message comes by way of the peripheral route to persuasion. Along this route we resort to a more simplistic processing of information, possibly because we do not care much about the issue in question, or because the message is not clearly heard because of background noise or we are otherwise distracted. In such circumstances the content and arguments matter little. What matters more are peripheral cues. Such cues may embrace the speaker's apparent expertise ("experts know their subject"), or likeability ("nice people can be trusted"), or the sheer number or length of the arguments presented, irrespective of how meaty they are ("the more arguments put forward, the greater the likelihood that they are correct"). Also, the reaction of other recipients to the message ("it appears to be well received") is a cue that might be considered (Wood & Kallgren, 1988).

Balance and Consistency

A key concept in attitude change is balance and consistency. It is suggested by Festinger (1957) that people try to establish internal harmony, consistency, or congruity among their opinions, attitudes, knowledge, and values. Consistency theory was developed in a climate of conformity in the USA when it was believed that people do not like to behave in a manner inconsistent with their attitudes.

Consistency could equally be applied to the structure of a given attitude, whereby the cognitive, affective, and conative components of an attitude are consistent with one another. In a sense, consistency could be internally rewarding and this is tantamount to experiencing internal reinforcement. The concept of consistency can be applied to a cluster of attitudes within the attitudinal frame of the individual, though it is possible to condone minor inconsistencies (Sherif & Sherif, 1967).

Consistency Theories

Consistency theories have been divided into three categories—balance theory, congruity theory, and cognitive dissonance theory.

Balance Theory

Balance theory is concerned with both balance and imbalance in attitudes (Heider, 1946). There are times when our intuition tells us that a particular situation is unbalanced or uncomfortable in a cognitive sense.

For example, the finance director of a company welcomes the appointment of a new marketing director because he or she believes they share an outlook in common about efficiency and the future direction of the company. However, the finance director suddenly senses that the marketing director has serious reservations about proposed cost-cutting plans. As a result the finance director expects friction to arise at the next board meeting. This creates imbalance and produces tension, which the finance director attempts to alleviate. In these circumstances the finance director, in order to restore balance, could change his or her attitude to the marketing director from positive to negative, or revise his or her opinion about the matter on which there is likely to be fundamental disagreement, or alter his or her perception of the marketing director's attitude towards the proposed cost-cutting plans.

It should be recognised that people have different thresholds or levels of tolerance for imbalance, and some people may function well in certain states of imbalance and not feel it necessary to reduce the accompanying tension.

Congruity Theory

Congruity theory is also concerned with positive and negative attitudes but, in addition, attempts to measure the strength of these attitudes (Osgood & Tannenbaum, 1955). For example, if someone such as a first class actor for whom we have great respect and who we evaluate as +3 (highly favourable) on an Osgood semantic differential scale (see Table 6.5, p. 278), praises a product in a television advertisement (again which we evaluate at +3), then there is no discrepancy. However, if somebody whom we admire greatly (say, +3) makes many complimentary remarks about a product or service for which we have a low regard (say, –2), then there is a discrepancy of 5. To reduce the discrepancy, the individual could think less well of the admired figure and view the product or service in a less negative way; this might help to bring the attitudes in question more into line.

Factors to consider when adjustments to attitudes are contemplated are the strength of the attitudes (because generally speaking the stronger the attitude the more difficult it is to change), and the extent to which the person believes in the information disseminated by the admired figure. A consumer could arrive at a conclusion that the admired figure is putting forward favourable views about the product, not because he or she thinks highly of it, but merely because there is a handsome fee for promulgating the message.

There are occasions when people actively seek information consistent or consonant with their attitudes. In one study, recent purchasers of new cars were asked to read advertisements for various makes of car including their own (Ehrlich et al., 1957). The results showed that they were much more likely to read advertisements for their own car, which they presumably had favourable attitudes towards, than advertisements for cars which they had either seriously considered buying at one stage or cars that had been given little or no consideration. There are other occasions when people strive for consistency by bringing their attitudes into line with newly adopted behaviour. When workers were promoted to the job of foreman they tended to acquire managerial attitudes consistent with their new organisational role. However, when some of them returned to their previous positions as workers they experienced a significant dilution of their recently acquired managerial attitudes (Liberman, 1956).

The consistency between attitudes and behaviour may not prevail in every situation. In a study of hotel owners' attitudes towards certain racial groups it was concluded that there were discrepancies between attitudes and behaviour. In their response to items on a questionnaire, some hotel owners resident in the southern part of the USA expressed an intention to discriminate against a Chinese couple, accompanied by a white American, in the provision of accommodation (La Piere, 1934). But when they came face-to-face with a well-dressed Chinese couple, travelling with a white American, the travellers were not refused accommodation. Perhaps it is more difficult to discriminate in a face-to-face situation than in private on paper. But equally, it is often easier to be liberal on paper than in face-to-face encounters. In this situation the hotel owner may have had to come to terms with conflicting attitudes, and perhaps the business attitude to making a profit took precedence over the racial attitude or prejudice.

Cognitive Dissonance Theory

Cognitive dissonance theory is probably the most important cognitive consistency theory. Cognitive dissonance arises when individuals act in a manner inconsistent with what they feel. If an attitude is not terribly important to the individual, then the behaviour that is inconsistent with it creates relatively little dissonance. Different situations create different levels of dissonance.

For example, a child may experience greater dissonance when having to choose between buying a book and going fishing, than between going to the cinema and going to the theatre. Choice in the face of alternatives then becomes a critical issue. The positive aspects of a rejected alternative and the

negative aspects of the chosen alternative are inconsistent or dissonant with the action taken (Festinger, 1957). The easiest way to get rid of this psychological discomfort—i.e. to reduce the dissonance—is to change the attitude to the decision so that it corresponds more closely with the outward behaviour.

One may hypothesise that this may be achieved by deliberately playing down the attractiveness of the rejected alternative and reinforcing the chosen alternative by providing supportive information after the decision was made (Brehm, 1966). This hypothesis has been subjected to favourable empirical testing (see panel overleaf), although some doubt has been cast on the findings.

Punishment or Reward. The threat of punishment or the promise of reward is relevant in the context of cognitive dissonance (Festinger & Carlsmith, 1959). If individuals are forced to comply, following the use of sanctions or rewards, there will be a tendency for them to change their attitude so that it is brought into line with their behaviour. However, this statement needs qualification in the light of whether or not the force to bring about compliance is strong or weak. If the pressure used to force compliance is strong, the individual is much less likely to change his or her attitude so as to bring it into line with enforced behaviour. Why should this be so? Because it could be argued that if you were made to change your actions or behaviour by a strong force, you can always say that if you had the freedom to express yourself you would do so and would not take the enforced action. In this case, dissonance would be minimal because the individual has little choice in the matter.

On the other hand, if the pressure to force compliance is weak—i.e. the force exerted to make you act or behave in opposition to your inner attitude is weak—then dissonance is strong. This might arise, for example, when under the threat of a minor social sanction you behave in a manner contrary to your privately

Post-decision Information and Dissonance

A group of women was asked to rate the desirability of a number of household products. They were told that the manufacturer wanted consumer reactions for which they would receive a reward of one product from a set of two that was available for this purpose. The researcher then manipulated the magnitude of dissonance likely to be experienced. Half the group could choose from two products where there was only a slight difference in the attractiveness of the products (high dissonance group)—this makes the act of choice more difficult. The other half could choose from two products where the difference in the attractiveness of the products was great (low dissonance group)—this makes the act of choice easier.

When both groups made their choice of product they were asked to read four research reports which contained commentaries on the products used in the study. The high dissonance and low dissonance groups were divided into sub-groups, whereby half the members in each sub-group were given a report on the products that constituted the first choice, and the other half were given reports dealing with products not the subject of choice. Therefore, those provided with reports on products chosen had the opportunity to peruse relevant technical data after they had made their decisions.

The experimental test was repeated when the subjects were asked to rate the desirability of the household products once again. The results showed that the attractiveness of the previously chosen product increased and the attractiveness of the previously rejected product decreased in the high dissonance group, irrespective of whether or not relevant information about the product was received. In other words, the provision of relevant or irrelevant post-decision information did not have a material effect on individual efforts to reduce the state of dissonance. In the low dissonance group it was the irrelevant information that increased the attractiveness of the previously chosen product and decreased the attractiveness of the previously rejected product.

Because the results show that dissonance was reduced by the provision of information unrelated to the product choice after a decision was made, the hypothesis cited in the main text (i.e. that the use of supportive information reinforces the chosen alternative and plays down the attractiveness of the rejected alternative) must be rejected. However, the manner in which the research was conducted in this study has been subjected to criticism (Brehm, 1966).

held attitude. To reduce the dissonance would necessitate bringing the attitude into line with the behaviour.

These hypotheses were subjected to experimental laboratory tests by Festinger and Carlsmith (1959). Students were asked to carry out boring, repetitive tasks. One group was paid $1 to participate in the test and the other group was paid $20. The first batch of students who performed this task was told to tell the next batch that the tasks were interesting and enjoyable; in fact the students were asked to tell a lie. The students complied with the experimenter's request, and later the two groups were tested privately on their attitudes towards the original laboratory tasks. The first group, who received the smaller payment, said that the tasks were enjoyable, but the second group, who received $20, said the tasks were boring and uninteresting.

Therefore, in accordance with the prediction specified in the previous paragraph, the first group of students had little pressure applied to them and they changed their attitude by acknowledging that the tasks were interesting and enjoyable. This group could hardly justify telling a lie for the money, so dissonance was high. To reduce the dissonance the students had to change an inner attitude by an unconscious means to arrive at the view that the tasks were quite interesting and enjoyable. But the second group of students were subjected to greater pressure to tell a lie, in the form of an incentive of $20, and felt it unnecessary to change their inner attitude to the task; the students were prepared to tolerate dissonance because the rewards for doing so were worthwhile.

In experimental studies like the one described, we cannot always be sure of the exact nature and seriousness of the subject's response and when it is the best time to introduce the rewards.

Consumer Dissonance. The following are examples of observations on cognitive dissonance in the literature on consumer behaviour. In advertisements one should be careful not to exaggerate the positive features of a product, because if the product does not live up to the expectations of consumers, dissonance is likely to occur. Disappointed consumers may feel more at ease later when, having received some unfavourable word-of-mouth communication about the product from members of their consumer peer group, they evaluate the product negatively. This could reduce dissonance.

Incentives, such as free samples or coupon offers, can be used to entice consumers to experiment with a product they might not normally buy. Dissonance could occur if the act of acquiring and using the product is inconsistent with the specific attitude towards the product. Of course, the consumer could avoid dissonance by not responding to the incentives because of a firm view of the unacceptable nature of the product (Engel, Blackwell, & Miniard, 1990). In practice, one might encounter a number of situations in which free samples may result in the product not being given a fair trial, in the sense that consumption ceases when the supply of free samples is depleted. In such circumstances, dissonance may be of a small magnitude. This could account for the mixed success of incentive offers in contributing to a larger market share for products.

A consumer chooses a product that has created dissonance and, subsequently, reads an advertisement that emphasises the desirable features of this product. The effect of this could be that dissonance is reduced to such an extent that, at a future date, the consumer develops a favourable attitude towards the brand in question. For example, a car manufacturer, by emphasising the desirable features of the vehicle—e.g. its high

trade-in value and the length of time the car will remain fashionable—is trying to reassure the consumer that the right purchase decision was made and, in the process, is contributing to the reduction of post-purchase dissonance. In a study of consumer behaviour with respect to cars, it was found that, although the consumer considered a large number of alternative models, more advertisements connected with the make of car finally chosen were read (Ehrlich et al., 1957). The notion of post-decision dissonance is likely to be more important for consumer durables than for convenience goods.

Do individuals appraise critically the information they seek in order to reduce dissonance? It is suggested that people tend to prefer information supporting consonance or cognitive consistency rather than avoiding information likely to promote dissonance (Ehrlich et al., 1957). Festinger (1957) identifies some of the possible reactions to a state of dissonance as follows:

- Individuals seek new information that is supportive of their outlook, and will avoid sources of new information that are likely to increase the existing state of dissonance.
- New information likely to increase the existing state of dissonance could be misperceived or misinterpreted.
- The company of others who agree with a particular attitude that one wants to establish or maintain is sought, and efforts are made to solicit greater social support for one's desired position.
- The individual plays down the importance of the factors contributing to the state of dissonance, and loss of memory intervenes and helps remove key dissonant elements.

Criticism. Cognitive dissonance theory has been subjected to much criticism on the grounds that attitudes have often been found not to predict behaviour, and that results supporting the theory often turn out to be based on vulnerable experimental evidence. In addition, most people seem able to tolerate great logical inconsistencies, and do not necessarily avoid information favourable to alternatives not chosen. Neither do most people over-expose themselves to favourable information and, finally, dissonance seems to explain the past rather than predict the future (Tedesch, Schlenker, & Bonoma, 1973). A particular criticism of the measures used to gauge cognitive dissonance is the rarity of circumstances in which subjects engage in self-reporting. With regard to our tolerance of inconsistencies, it is argued that people grow used to and expect a certain amount of imbalance in their cognitive make-up and over time have managed to adapt to a certain level of incongruity (Driver & Streufert, 1966). Therefore, up to a point, they are not too concerned with means of coping with dissonance reduction.

Cognitive dissonance theory focuses attention on what happens when we act in ways that are inconsistent with our attitudes. An alternative view, put forward by Bem (1967), is that we frequently determine what our attitudes are from observing our own behaviour (self-perception). For example, if a person repeatedly takes various safety precautions at work (safe behaviour), that person might conclude that he or she possesses positive safety attitudes through observing his or her own behaviour. It is said that self-perception theory is less applicable when somebody holds a strong attitude related to the observed behaviour, and is more applicable when an attitude or set of beliefs towards the behaviour in question does not exist (Pennington, 1986).

ATTITUDE MEASUREMENT

How do we measure attitudes? Attitude measurement usually implies measurement of the cognitive component (i.e. the thinking aspect) of an attitude. The most basic way of doing this is to ask a single question, but this is rarely a satisfactory method because it does not take into account the many components of attitudes. Many general attitudes possess a number of facets, and therefore it is preferable to use an attitude scale composed of many questions.

Attitudes cannot be directly observed as such, but can be measured indirectly. We need measures to help us compare the attitudes of individuals or groups, and to be able to register changes in an individual's attitudes over time. The aim is to record numerically what a person thinks about a particular issue (e.g. the new world order, or the political party most suited to governing the country) and it is important that the questions asked have the same meaning for all those who participate in the attitude survey. Among the widely used techniques are the following methods.

Thurstone Scale

This was one of the first systematic approaches to attitude measurement and was developed by Thurstone and Chave (1929). The first step is to write out a large number of statements (perhaps 100 or more), each of which expresses a particular view. These statements should express all possible viewpoints from extremely favourable to extremely unfavourable. An example of statements used for the measurement of employees' attitudes using this method is illustrated in Table 6.3.

Each statement is typed on a separate piece of paper, and a judge is asked to place each statement in anything up to 11 piles. There are 9 statements in the example in Table 6.3, so the piles range from statements judged to express the least favourable viewpoint (pile 9) to statements judged to express the most favourable viewpoint (pile 1). Statements judged to express varying degrees of favourableness in between these extremes on a continuum are put into the appropriate pile. In the construction of the attitude scale the services of as many as 100 judges or assessors are used. The judges are asked not to express their own attitudes, but to be as objective as possible in indicating the extent to which the

TABLE 6.3

An Example of a Thurstone Scale Measuring Employee Attitudes

Statements	Scale Value*
The company values my contribution	9.50
My job is safe as long as I turn out good work	8.25
My boss lets me know what he or she thinks of me	7.20
The company offers rewards commensurate with efforts	6.50
The company needs to improve its training programme	4.80
The company's policy of dealing with people is rather vague	3.00
My job offers little opportunity for the exercise of discretion	2.65
My boss never lets me know what he or she thinks of me	1.50
Many employees stay with the company because they cannot find another job	0.70

* These values would not appear on the scale

statement is favourable or unfavourable towards the topic in question. The purpose of allocating statements to piles is to determine the scale value of the various statements. For example, if all judges place a statement in piles towards the favourable end of the continuum of attitudes, we could conclude that the statement expresses a favourable attitude towards the company.

The number of times each statement is placed in each pile is calculated, and a further calculation is made to determine the average location of the statement in order to arrive at a scale value. An imaginary scale value is shown in Table 6.3. The consistency of the judges' assessments for each statement is analysed, and statements placed by all judges in one or a limited number of categories have the greatest degree of reliability. Statements that are placed by the judges over several categories are eliminated. It is sensible to begin with many more statements than are required for the final scale, and to settle for 10 or more statements that are spread over the entire range of the continuum; these statements would have been consistently evaluated by the judges.

The final material for the attitude scale comprises the selected statements and their scale values. In the administration of an attitude scale, statements appear on printed paper in random order without the scale values that appear in Table 6.3. All employees participating in the attitude survey are requested to tick all statements they agree with: participants remain anonymous. The attitude of each employee is usually calculated as the average or median scale value of the statements ticked. An average of 6.52 would be the outcome of an attitude survey where the second, fourth, and fifth statements shown in Table 6.3 were ticked by an employee. The calculation is as follows:

$$\frac{8.25 + 6.50 + 4.80}{3} = 6.52$$

This employee's average score is at the favourable end of the scale, and therefore it indicates a favourable attitude towards the company (the higher the scale, the more favourable is the attitude in this illustration). On the other hand, an average of 1.73 would emerge if the sixth, eighth, and ninth statements reflected the preferences of the employee. This score would be arrived at as follows:

$$\frac{3.00 + 1.50 + 0.70}{1.73} = 1.73$$

The average of 1.73 would indicate an unfavourable attitude towards the company.

Likert Scale

This method of measuring attitudes is somewhat simpler than the Thurstone method, and is probably the most commonly used attitude scale (Likert, 1932). The individual is asked not only to indicate agreement or disagreement, but also to signify how strongly he or she agrees or disagrees with a number of statements relevant to the attitude being measured. This is normally done on a five-point scale, though it is possible to use a seven-point scale. The normal practice is to incorporate the various statements in a questionnaire. The following selection of items is extracted from a questionnaire used in a study of union and management attitudes to safety (Price & Lueder, 1980).

1. Many accidents happen because a worker tries to make things easier or faster at the expense of safety.
2. Industrial accidents are part of life and must be accepted as such by management and workers.
3. Many of the present-day occupational illnesses from which people suffer cannot be anticipated or avoided.
4. The benefits of safety outweigh its costs.
5. Safety is the most important element of the working environment.

The subject is asked to respond to these statements, indicating the extent of his or her agreement or disagreement and using the scoring method illustrated in Table 6.4.

In the example, a value is given to each response category in order to produce a numerical score, and the different scores in each category are added together to arrive at a total score. A high overall score can be viewed as a positive attitude to the issues

TABLE 6.4

An Example of a Likert Scale

Scoring Attitude Intensity	
1.	Strongly Disagree
2.	Disagree
3.	Tend to Disagree
4.	Neither Agree nor Disagree
5.	Tend to Agree
6.	Agree
7.	Strongly Agree

raised in the questionnaire, whereas a low overall score denotes a negative attitude.

The statements chosen for inclusion in the Likert scale are usually found from experience to be connected with the attitude concerned and would be provided by knowledgeable people. In order to analyse statistically the data on the scale, it is important that a zero point is absent. However, this entails forcing a subject to express an attitude when in fact he or she does not hold one, and this reduces to some extent the validity of the exercise. Because of the way the Likert scale is constructed, most of the scores will fall at the two ends of the scale, and there is less power of discrimination as we move nearer the neutral point.

Osgood's Semantic Differential

This technique was devised by Osgood and his colleagues as part of a study of the meaning of words; it consists of pairs of adjectives opposite in meaning (Osgood, Suci, & Tannenbaum, 1957). An abbreviated example of pairs of words used by Fiedler (1967) to create a profile of the least preferred co-worker in the contingency model of leadership (referred to in Chapter 8), is shown in Table 6.5.

In the Table, a seven-point rating scale is used with zero standing for neutral or "don't

TABLE 6.5

An Example of a Semantic Differential Rating Scale

	+3	+2	+1	0	−1	−2	−3	
Pleasant	–	–	–	–	–	–	–	Unpleasant
Friendly	–	–	–	–	–	–	–	Unfriendly
Accepting	–	–	–	–	–	–	–	Rejecting
Helpful	–	–	–	–	–	–	–	Frustrating
Enthusiastic	–	–	–	–	–	–	–	Unenthusiastic
Relaxed	–	–	–	–	–	–	–	Tense
Close	–	–	–	–	–	–	–	Distant
Warm	–	–	–	–	–	–	–	Cold
Co-operative	–	–	–	–	–	–	–	Unco-operative
Supportive	–	–	–	–	–	–	–	Hostile
Interesting	–	–	–	–	–	–	–	Boring
Self-assured	–	–	–	–	–	–	–	Hesitant
Cheerful	–	–	–	–	–	–	–	Gloomy

know". Numerical values cover a scale from +3 to –3. Alternatively, a scale ranging from 7 to 1 can be used, with 4 as a mid-point. The respondent is asked to give an immediate reaction to each pair of words listed in the Table and describe the person he or she prefers the least by placing a cross in one of the seven spaces between each pair of words. The individual's score is his or her total score on all scales of the measure used; the higher the score the more favourable is the respondent's impression of the person assessed.

The semantic differential deals with factors concerned with evaluation (good–bad), with potency (strong–weak), and with activity (active–passive). It could be used in the study of interpersonal perception, and also in measuring attitudes to work where the emphasis is on the emotional reaction of the subject. The semantic differential technique measures attitudes in a rather global way and can be used to advantage among less literate subjects.

Social Distance Scale

This scale was designed by Bogardus (1925) and comes closest to measuring the conative or the "tendency to act" component of an attitude. The concern of Bogardus was to design, for example, a measure that would give an indication of the extent to which a native would accept or reject foreigners. A native would be asked, with respect to a foreigner, which of the following statements were acceptable:

1. I have no objection to intermarriage.
2. I would invite this person to my club as a personal friend.
3. I feel this person should have only visitor status in my country.
4. I would exclude this person from my country.

It is a very useful and relatively simple method, though its main limitation is its preoccupation with issues that are often perceived in a negative way (e.g. foreigners).

Sociometry

Using a natural group, every member of the group is asked to name their preferred partner for a specified activity (Moreno, 1953). They then rank the remainder of the group in order of preference, with reference to questions such as, "Who would you most like to sit next to?".

Some knowledge of the "thinking" and "emotional" aspects of an individual's attitude can be obtained by asking, "Why do you want to sit next to JH, the most popular person?". The least popular person can also be identified by this method. This technique, though useful in establishing the popularity of group members, has not been used extensively in the measurement of attitudes.

Reliability and Validity

Qualities that are essential to any kind of measure are reliability and validity. A reliable measure is one that will provide the same reading if that which is measured remains constant. If the same jar of marbles is weighed twice within a day, one expects it to weigh the same on both occasions. This procedure can then be used to test the scales, because the jar's weight can be relied on to remain the same. However, with attitudes one cannot get away with the assumption that they remain the same over time; in fact attitudes may change as a result of being measured. Therefore, the reliability of an attitude measure is more difficult to establish.

A valid measure is one that measures what it claims to measure, though this is sometimes difficult in psychology because we normally try to measure something that cannot be observed from the outside (i.e. how somebody thinks and feels about an issue). So the appropriate criterion for establishing validity is often difficult to determine. For a measure to be valid it must first be reliable, though a measure may be reliable but lack validity. A fuller exposition of reliability and validity can be found in the section on selection methods in Chapter 13.

Finally, one of the reasons why work attitudes are measured is to try to establish how satisfied or dissatisfied employees are with their jobs. The concept of job satisfaction is discussed later in the chapter.

ATTITUDES AND BEHAVIOUR

The relationship between attitudes and behaviour is more complicated than one might expect. A positive attitude towards road safety is just one factor among many that influence safe driving (behaviour on the road). Other factors have to be considered, such as driving habits, social conventions, temperament when provoked by another driver, and the attitude of the police to speeding or reckless driving.

The relationship between an intention to behave and actual behaviour has been the subject of rigorous investigation (Fishbein & Ajzen, 1975). Intentions with regard to behaviour, such as intentions to devise safety procedures for a paint shop in a factory, are influenced by the safety practitioner's attitude towards implementing safety policy and by various organisational and social influences about the acceptability of this activity. Safety practitioners may ask themselves the following questions. What will the group of workers in the paint shop think of my ideas for their safety, and what is likely to be the most acceptable formula for devising a workable procedure? If the workers object to some or all of my ideas, how should I proceed?

Planned Behaviour

In Ajzen and Fishbein's (1980) *theory of reasoned action* there is a recognition that people's actions are best predicted by their intentions. In turn, intentions are determined by people's attitudes as well as by what they see as expectations of them held by others. The theory of reasoned action, now slightly amended by Ajzen and Madden (1986) and called the *theory of planned behaviour*, is shown in Fig. 6.1.

The theory defines an attitude in a particular way. An attitude is expressed as a belief about the consequences of behaviour; it is not concerned about general beliefs or feelings related to the object or subject matter of the attitude. As such it has something in common with expectancy theories of motivation. As a result, it is said that this is a good predictor of behaviour.

Along with "attitude" we have to consider "subjective norm" before arriving at "intention". Subjective norm embraces the beliefs of other people whose opinions we value with regard to performing or not performing the behaviour. It would also

accommodate a person's desire or lack of desire to comply with the opinions of others. Before arriving at a final position on intentions, one should realise that people differ in the relative weighting they attach to "attitude" and "subjective norm".

The theory of reasoned action has been successful in predicting behaviour in a range of areas such as smoking, alcohol abuse, contraception, and consumer behaviour (Sheppard, Hartwick, & Warshaw, 1988), but as Eiser and Van der Pligt (1988) rightly point out, the theory has not escaped criticism at both theoretical and empirical levels. In the revised version of the theory by Ajzen and Madden (1986), the idea of perceived behavioural control is introduced. This is concerned with the extent to which people believe they can perform the required

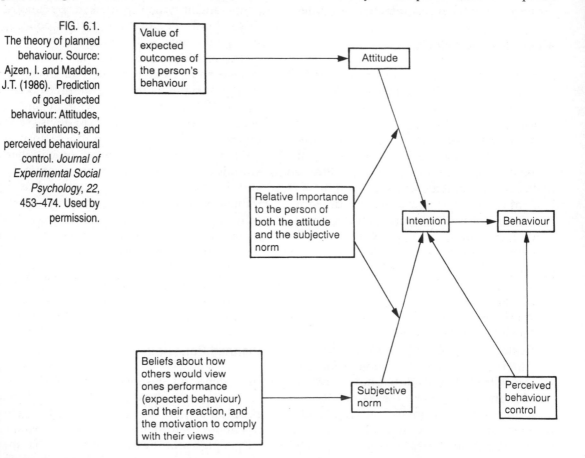

FIG. 6.1. The theory of planned behaviour. Source: Ajzen, I. and Madden, J.T. (1986). Prediction of goal-directed behaviour: Attitudes, intentions, and perceived behavioural control. *Journal of Experimental Social Psychology, 22,* 453–474. Used by permission.

behaviour in particular situations. As a new variable, perceived behavioural control in Fig. 6.1 has the potential to influence behaviour in a direct fashion or indirectly through intentions.

Influenced by the ideas of Fishbein and colleagues, Allegrante, Mortimer, and O'Rourke (1980) conducted a study attempting to identify attitudes and social influences that would predict a motorcyclist's behavioural intention to wear a helmet in a US state without a helmet-use law (see panel below).

Consumers tend to give different weightings to different attributes of a particular product. With regard to paper towels, one consumer wants extra absorbency, another wants colourful paper, and somebody else stresses price and the cheapest brand available. The evaluation placed on a product amounts to an aggregation of individual attitudes attached to each attribute (e.g. price, design, packaging, durability, etc.) that the consumer perceives as important.

A distinction has to be made between an attitude towards an object (e.g. a product) and an attitude towards behaviour (e.g. buying the product). For instance, a consumer may have a positive attitude towards a particular brand, but may not have a positive attitude towards buying that brand for perfectly understandable reasons. This is exemplified in the following example (Cohen, 1981). A consumer believes that high-pile carpeting is warm, comfortable, luxurious, and prestigious. Having positively evaluated these attributes, the consumer is likely to have a positive attitude towards high-pile carpeting. But is it practicable to buy this type of carpeting if there are pets and young children in the consumer's house? Therefore, a consumer's intention to purchase a product is dependent upon an assessment of how favourable the outcome is likely to be in terms of utility or satisfaction.

Motorcyclist's Behavioural Intentions

Attitudes in the form of beliefs about the advantages and disadvantages of helmet use were far more important than social influences in determining the intention to wear a helmet. This was particularly so for users of helmets rather than non-users.

It is interesting to note the beliefs held by the motorcyclists with respect to the use of helmets. On short trips and riding in city and suburban streets there appeared to be a low frequency of helmet use, even though the risk of accidents is high. The miles recorded for these journeys were relatively high over a set period of time. Apparently 65% of motorcyclists, who reported that they used helmets on and off depending on conditions, indicated that they always used a helmet when riding on long highway trips.

Is the risk of an accident or threat of hazardous conditions on the road perceived to be greater in the eyes of the long-distance traveller? If it is, this explains the need for precautionary measures, although the helmet's effect in providing protection from injury at high speed appears to diminish! This is reminiscent of the attitude to wearing seat belts in motor vehicles in the UK on long journeys prior to the statutory requirement to wear seat belts by the driver and front-seat passenger.

The frequency of helmet use was also influenced by weather conditions. It is a comfortable prospect to wear a helmet in cold or wet conditions, and the perceived possibility of having an accident in wet road conditions could prompt the motorcyclist to take protective action.

Helmet users appeared to be generally better informed about the benefits, in terms of safety and prevention of injury when wearing a helmet, than were the non-users.

Those who did not use a helmet appeared to be misinformed about the effects of wearing helmets, and were possibly unaware of the likely serious consequences that could befall non-users. The type of belief held by the motorcyclist who did not wear a helmet was as follows: "Using a helmet would adversely affect the motorcyclist's ability either to hear or see, or both, when riding, and therefore would interfere with the safe operation of the motorcycle; and there is a likelihood that a helmet might actually result in the wearer receiving a neck injury if he or she was involved in an accident when riding the motor-cycle."(Allegrante et al., 1980).

Sometimes the attributes of a product gain in importance as a result of external factors, quite independent of any marketing strategy used by a company. For example, dietitians promulgate the view that products high in fibre content are good for people's health. This in turn is likely to influence substantially the sale of selected high-fibre foodstuffs. An interest in jogging has led some bra manufacturers to develop "sweat" and "support" bras for female joggers. The widespread use of tea bags in the UK has fundamentally changed some people's attitudes to the purchase of tea bags, although initial promotion campaigns may have been influential in changing consumer attitudes.

Alternative Viewpoint

An alternative view of the relationship between attitudes and behaviour is put forward by Fazio (1986). He maintains that an attitude influences behaviour by selectively activating various thought processes stored in the person's memory. The consequence of this development is that selective perception of the object to which the attitude relates is created. For example, a lecturer holds a positive attitude towards an object— attending academic conferences. If so, it is likely that he or she will recall positive rather than negative thoughts or associations (evaluative beliefs) with respect to academic conferences. These associations or thoughts will shape the person's selective perception of what academic conferences are like, which in turn will influence a decision to attend one.

From Fazio's perspective, an attitude is dependent upon previous positive or negative experiences, but it influences (rather than being merely influenced by) the evaluative beliefs (e.g. recall of positive thoughts and associations from memory) at the time the person decides on a course of action. This perspective underlines the view that people with different attitudes may see different aspects of an issue as important or salient.

Eiser and Van der Pligt (1988) feel that the theory of reasoned action is better suited to a situation where a person is deciding on a course of action for the first time. But many times in life the action we consider will be similar if not identical to actions performed many times before. Therefore, a model of the relationship between attitude and behaviour should have the capacity to explain "habit" resting on previous behaviour, which unlike normal attitudes and beliefs can be very resistant to change. Note the predicament of the "habitual" smoker who continues to smoke cigarettes despite recognising that this behaviour is damaging to his or her health. However, one has to recognise that some smokers' behaviour is physically determined—that is their behaviour is activated by an addiction to nicotine, as well as being a functional means of counteracting stressful conditions in daily life.

JOB SATISFACTION

When attitudes are examined in a work context, we often make reference to job satisfaction and organisational commitment. Locke (1976) captured the *affective* aspect of job satisfaction when he defined job satisfaction as "a pleasurable positive emotional state resulting from the appraisal of one's job or job experiences". Organisational commitment will be looked at later. Job satisfaction is associated with how well our personal expectations at work are in line with outcomes. For example, if our expectations indicated that hard work generated equitable rewards, and that was the case, job satisfaction could ensue. The opposite situation of shattered personal expectations could lead to job dissatisfaction.

Job satisfaction straddles several related attitudes. For example, people experience fairly strong affective or emotional responses to such things as remuneration, promotion opportunities, relations with superiors and colleagues, and the work itself. In turn, these and related factors could be classified as important causal agents in determining job satisfaction.

Causes of Job Satisfaction

The following are some of the factors one might consider in attempts to establish the causes of job satisfaction (Hodgetts, 1991):

- *Pay and benefits*. The importance of equitable reward is a factor to consider here.
- *Promotion*. The level of satisfaction will depend on the acceptability of the system in operation, be it a system based on merit, or seniority, or whatever combination of the two.
- *Job*. This would embrace skills variety (the extent to which the job allows a worker to use a number of different skills and abilities in executing his or her duties); interest and challenge derived from the job; and lack of role ambiguity (how clearly the individual understands the job). Glisson and Durick (1988) found that job satisfaction is most influenced by skill variety and clarity of role.
- *Leadership*. There has been endorsement of people-centred or participative leadership as a determinant of job satisfaction (Miller & Monge, 1986).
- *Work group*. It would appear that good intra-group working and supportive colleagues have value in not permitting job dissatisfaction to surface, rather than in promoting job satisfaction.
- *Working conditions*. Where working conditions are good, comfortable, and safe, the setting appears to be appropriate for reasonable job satisfaction, though not necessarily high job satisfaction. The situation with respect to job satisfaction would be bleaker if working conditions were poor.

To these factors can be added personality—job fit as a factor influencing job satisfaction. This arises when there is congruence between personality type and the

FIVE MINUTES INTO THE OPERATION, HARVEY'S UNSUITABILITY FOR SURGERY BECAME RATHER APPARENT.

demands of the job. Initially this could be expressed as successful job performance, eventually leading to high job satisfaction (Feldman & Arnold, 1985).

Measuring Job Satisfaction

The most frequently adopted approach to measuring job satisfaction involves the use of rating scales. These are standard instruments that are designed to provide feedback on specific examples of employee satisfaction and dissatisfaction. When attitude measurement was discussed earlier in this chapter, reference was made to various rating techniques. A brief restatement or reinforcement of some of the earlier observations is appropriate here.

Rating scales in their simplest form consist of a single "global" rating, whereby an individual is asked to respond to one question—for example: "By and large, how satisfied are you with your job?". The respondent is asked to circle a number between one and five that corresponds with answers ranging from highly satisfied to highly dissatisfied. An alternative rating scale is called the "aggregate score", made up of a number of job facets. This is considered a more refined technique. It identifies key elements in the job and invites employees to express their feelings in numerical form about each element using the method identified earlier in connection with single global rating. The individual scores are added up to create an overall job satisfaction score. The elements could refer to the nature of the job, promotion opportunities, remuneration, supervision, relations with peers, and so on. An example of the type of items appearing in a measure of job satisfaction is contained in Table 6.6.

One might well ask which one of the two approaches discussed has the edge as a measure of job satisfaction? A subjective evaluation might lead to a conclusion that the aggregate score approach is superior. However, there is evidence to indicate that single global rating has the edge (Scarpello &

TABLE 6.6

Items extracted from a Measure of Job Satisfaction from the Occupational Stress Indicator

How do you feel about your job?	6	5	4	3	2	1
The relationship you have with other people at work						
The job itself						
Current career opportunities						
Your level of salary relative to your experience						
The degree to which you feel motivated by your job						
The degree to which you feel extended in your job						
The style of supervision that your supervisors use						
The amount of participation which you are given in important decision making						

Note: 6 = very much satisfied: 1 = very much dissatisfied
Source: Cooper, C.L., Sloan, S., & Williams, S. (1987) *Occupational Stress Indicator*. Windsor: : NFER/Nelson. Used by permission.

Campbell, 1983). The main advantages and disadvantages of measures of job satisfaction based on rating scales are listed in the panel below.

Other techniques for measuring job satisfaction are *critical incidents* and interviews.

Critical Incidents

Employees are requested to focus their attention on some situation or incident that is related to job satisfaction. For example, employees are asked to relate what they particularly like or dislike about their jobs. The next step is to have the content of this specific job-related information analysed in order to identify factors that can either cause job satisfaction, or prevent it. With the critical incidents technique, respondents experience greater freedom to express themselves, unlike the situation with rating scales. However, using the critical incidents approach is time consuming, with the likelihood of respondent

bias. The latter could arise when respondents equate intrinsic job factors (e.g. challenging and stimulating assignments) with liking the job, whereas extrinsic job factors (e.g. style of supervision) are equated with disliking the job. Another way of putting this statement would be to suggest that people tend to like events over which they exercise control, but tend to dislike events or situations that are determined environmentally, and over which they have little, if any, control.

Interviews

As a more open-ended approach than critical incidents, interviews offer the interviewee wider scope in terms of response. Also, the interviewer can probe because he or she has the opportunity to ask questions and seek clarification on responses or observations that are unclear. A shortcoming of this technique is that it is time-consuming; also there is the possibility of interview bias, which can arise when the interviewer's preconceptions

---

Measuring Job Satisfaction With Rating Scales—Advantages and Disadvantages

Advantages

- They are normally short in length and can be completed rapidly.
- The language used is general, as opposed to being occupationally specific, and therefore it caters for a broad spectrum of employees.
- The responses can be quantified and this facilitates comparisons between groups (e.g. the attitudes of employees in a particular organisation are compared with those in similar organisations) and between periods of time. Normative data is available for certain job satisfaction questionnaires, including the distribution of responses in a representative population.
- The outcome of surveys of job satisfaction could lead to the diagnosis of problems amenable to solutions. At the very least, the survey could provide a forum for eliciting constructive feedback from employees.

Disadvantages

- Not everybody may be honest and straightforward when completing the questionnaire.
- The results may be distorted by the wording of questions and the choice of topics contained in the questionnaire.
- The results may be contaminated by attitudes or dispositions that bear an indirect relationship to job satisfaction. For example, a person may respond negatively to job-related items because of transport problems affecting getting to work on time. Likewise, short-term considerations, such as perceived lack of progress in writing a report with the deadline date looming, may provoke a certain anxiety. Matters such as these may create an inaccurate picture of the real state of job satisfaction.
- There may be problems with the validity of the measuring instrument—do the questions really measure job satisfaction?
- There may be problems with the reliability of the measuring instrument—do the questions measure job satisfaction consistently?

concerning the issues raised, and misunderstanding of the responses, contaminate the outcome. A fuller discussion of interviews and critical incidents can be found in the section on employee selection in Chapter 13.

Consequences of Job Satisfaction

A commonplace view is that if an organisation does not create conditions for the provision of a minimum level of job satisfaction, one can expect certain outcomes or consequences to follow—e.g. a deterioration in productivity, employee turnover, absenteeism, and morale. In the light of evidence, however, the relationship between job satisfaction and the outcomes just mentioned may not be as clear-cut as many people think (Hodgetts, 1991). The outcomes, which will now be examined, are performance, employee turnover, and absenteeism.

Performance
Apparently there is empirical evidence to show that the link between job satisfaction and performance is weak (Iaffaldano & Muchinsky, 1985). Reflecting on the relationship between job satisfaction and performance, at least two moderating variables—i.e. job level and machine-paced work—come to mind. Forces such as these could improve the relationship between job satisfaction and performance (Petty, McGee, & Cavender, 1984).

With regard to job level or position in the hierarchy, the correlations between job satisfaction and performance are stronger for groups of employees in the supervisory and managerial class. Also, the relationship between job satisfaction and performance is likely to be weaker in the presence of factors outside the control of the worker. For example, an operative on the factory floor may have his or her productivity much more influenced by the speed of the machine or assembly line (something outside the person's control) than by the level of job satisfaction.

Another way of looking at job satisfaction and performance is to reverse the relationship and examine how productivity could influence job satisfaction (Petty et al., 1984). This could be achieved in an indirect way. For example, good job performance could not only lead to feeling good about oneself, but could lead to organisational recognition in the form of improved rewards and opportunities which, in turn, could raise the level of job satisfaction.

Employee Turnover
With regard to the relationship between job satisfaction and employee turnover, Lee and Mowday (1987) conclude that individuals who are satisfied with their jobs are less likely to leave the organisation than those who are dissatisfied. However, it would be wise to acknowledge the potency of moderating or intervening variables in the relationship between job satisfaction and employee turnover. There is a recognition that labour market conditions, expectations about alternative job opportunities, and job tenure within the organisation, all act as intervening variables (Carsten & Spector, 1987; Hulin, Reznowski, & Hachiya, 1985).

In a specific sense, as job tenure increases it is suggested that the employee turnover rate tends to decline, irrespective of the level of job satisfaction (Hodgetts, 1991). This might be explained as follows. There is still commitment to the organisation from long-standing employees who may not be as satisfied with their jobs as previously because they are close to retirement. Also, they are of an age where it may be difficult to get another job of similar status and remuneration package; they cannot see themselves doing any other kind of work; and they are on top of the job to such an extent that its demands put little pressure on them.

Another example of a moderating or intervening variable is the competence of the employee (Spencer & Steers, 1981). For example, competent performers may stay with the organisation irrespective of the level of job satisfaction because the organisation is intent on retaining their services and bestows certain benefits (e.g. increased pay and promotion opportunities, praise, and other forms of recognition). But the organisation is unlikely to go out of its way to retain the services of poor performers or incompetent employees. In fact, the latter may be encouraged to seek opportunities elsewhere.

Absenteeism

There is said to be an inverse relationship between job satisfaction and level of absenteeism—that is, when job satisfaction is low, absenteeism tends to be high (Scott & Taylor, 1985). Apparently, high levels of job satisfaction will not guarantee low levels of absenteeism (Clegg, 1983).

But yet again one has to accept the influence exerted by intervening variables. The relationships between job satisfaction and absenteeism could be moderated by the importance of the job to employees, the opportunity to use a variety of skills in the job where clear objectives exist, and the existence of good relationships with superiors and peers. These variables could enhance the level of job satisfaction. Even when satisfaction is high, absenteeism could occur when people, feigning illness, take time off work to go to some important sporting fixture or attend to some domestic problem, in the realisation that they are not going to lose pay.

Finally, one has to acknowledge the importance of the interaction between job satisfaction and job design (discussed in Chapter 2), and the relationship between job satisfaction and occupational health (examined in Chapter 14).

ORGANISATIONAL COMMITMENT

Whereas job satisfaction focuses narrowly on the job, commitment to the organisation could be affected by a range of considerations. For example, people may be dissatisfied when they did not receive an expected promotion, or when a salary increase is less than expected. In such circumstances, organisational commitment could be adversely affected.

Commitment, a key ingredient in human resource management, could be defined as the relative strength of an individual's identification with and involvement in an organisation (Mowday, Porter, & Steers, 1982). Involvement could be reflected in the person's willingness to undertake duties beyond the standard requirements of the job. Organisational commitment arises when the employee strongly identifies with the organisation, agrees with its objectives and value systems, and is willing to expend effort on its behalf. But commitment is not just a global organisational phenomenon; it can be directed to specific aspects of the employee's experience at work—for example, the individual's geographic location, his or her section or department, or a trade union (Barling, Wade, & Fullagar, 1990; Reichers, 1985).

An attempt has been made (see Table 6.7) to identify the component parts of commitment along similar lines to the descriptions of the three components of attitudes (Allen & Meyer, 1990). Using the framework in Table 6.7, one could offer explanations for the causes of organisational commitment (Arnold, Robertson, & Cooper, 1991). A view, applicable to affective commitment, might convey the following sentiment: "If the organisation is good to me, I will be loyal and hard working." It appears that intrinsic job factors (e.g. taxing assignments and personal autonomy) rather than extrinsic factors (e.g. working conditions, remuneration, and supervision) are most salient in fostering commitment (Mottaz, 1988).

A view applicable to continuance commitment unfolds itself as follows. People take stock of their track record, as well as their current worth in the open market. The outcome of this analysis could determine organisational commitment (Myer et al., 1989). A view that might apply to normative commitment suggests that commitment is in

TABLE 6.7

The Component Parts of Commitment

Attitude	Commitment
Affective	**Affective** A person's emotional attachment to the organisation
Behavioural	**Continuance** A person's perception of the costs/risks of leaving the organisation
Cognitive	**Normative** The obligation and responsibility felt by the individual in the organisation

Source: Allen, N.J. and Meyer, M.P. (1990). The measurement of antecedents of affective, continuance, and normative commitment to the organisation. *Journal of Occupational Psychology, 63*, 1–8.

some way influenced by the person's nature rather than what happens at work, and that some people are naturally committed, whereas others are not (Bateman & Strasser, 1984).

There are other causal factors to note, such as age and time spent in the organisation, the extent of participation in decision making, and perceived security of employment (Romzek, 1989; Steers, 1977). The participative leadership factor is endorsed by Glisson and Durick (1988), who also stress the importance of the age of the organisation and the educational attainment of employees. An explanation derived from Bem's (1967) self-perception theory, discussed earlier, might suggest that if employees do something which is of obvious benefit to the organisation (e.g. expend exceptional effort), they may reflect on this and then conclude that they must be committed to the organisation.

Instruments are available to measure the various dimensions of organisational commitment examined earlier. One such instrument, developed by Warr, Cook, and Wall (1979), tends to measure affective commitment.

With regard to consequences of organisational commitment, one should note the following. Organisational commitment is said to influence outcomes such as employee turnover and absenteeism (Mowday et al., 1982). As far as work performance is concerned, a distinction could be made between the different components of commitment examined earlier. For example, employees rated "high" on affective commitment tended to be better performers than those rated "low" (Myer et al., 1989). However, this relationship does not stand firm for those rated high on continuance commitment. High, as opposed to low, continuance commitment is partly based on one's poor external job marketability, and a contributory factor for the lack of employment opportunities could be that the person concerned is not very efficient or competent.

SUMMARY: ATTITUDES AND JOB SATISFACTION

- In defining attitudes, the three components of an attitude (cognitive, affective, and conative) were identified.

- A distinction was made between attitudes and values. With regard to values, a hierarchy of levels was examined. It was stated that attitudes, which can be either positive or negative, act as filters in the selection of information.

- Personality and socialisation are important influences in the formation of attitudes. The influence of socialisation at work, in the context of attitude formation, was mentioned with reference to the training of chartered accountants.

- Attitudes perform an important function in helping individuals adopt a stable view of the world in which they live. The functions of attitudes were discussed with reference to Katz's system of classification—i.e. instrumental or adjustive, ego defensive, expressive, and knowledge functions. In this context, a brief reference was made to the demands of the work environment.

- With respect to prejudice, which mainly has a negative connotation when discussing attitudes, the influence exerted by personality, group, and culture was noted. Suggestions were made about ways of reducing prejudice.

- Attitude change was examined from three angles: sources of attitude change, factors contributing to attitude change, and balance and consistency. Using Kelman's classification system, the sources of attitude change are compliance, identification, and internalisation.

- Factors contributing to attitude change were identified as group membership (where the power of social context reflected in the social information-processing approach was acknowledged), exposure to the mass media, forced contact, rewards, communication, and persuasion. With respect to persuasion, the elaboration likelihood model was examined. The factors contributing to attitude change were illustrated with reference to appropriate examples.

- A key concept in attitude change is balance and consistency. Basically this means that people strive for consistency between the components of an attitude as well as between attitudes and behaviour. Consistency theories were discussed with reference to balance theory, congruity theory, and cognitive dissonance theory. The relevance of the latter to consumer behaviour was noted. An alternative view to cognitive dissonance, in the form of self-perception theory, was introduced.

- The notion of attitude measurement was acknowledged, and the following techniques were described: the Thurstone scale; the Likert scale; Osgood's semantic differential; the social distance scale; and sociometry. The qualities essential to any kind of measure—reliability and validity—were briefly explained.

- The relationship between attitudes and behaviour (drawing on the work of Fishbein and Ajzen) was introduced and illustrated, with examples drawn from safety and marketing. The updated version of the theory of reasoned action in the form of the theory of planned behaviour was examined. An alternative view of the relationship between attitudes and behaviour with the emphasis on the role of selective perception was put forward.

- Job satisfaction and organisational commitment straddle several related attitudes in a narrow and broad sense within organisations, and their nature, cause, measurement, and consequences were analysed.

QUESTIONS

1. Explain what is meant by the components of an attitude.
2. Distinguish between attitudes and values.
3. Examine the significance of a hierarchy of levels with respect to values.
4. Give examples of attitudes developed during the course of professional or occupational training.

5. Reflect on the significance of business ethics.

6. How do attitudes act as filters?

7. What functions do attitudes perform?

8. Explain what is meant by prejudice and discuss the factors that give rise to it.

9. In what way does compliance differ from internalisation when the focus is on sources of attitude change?

10. Why is the social information-processing approach referred to as a situational view of attitudes?

11. Examine the merits and demerits of one-sided and two-sided arguments in the communication of messages designed to change attitudes.

12. What is "the elaboration likelihood model" of persuasion?

13. In connection with communication and persuasion, explain the following terms: (a) primacy effect; (b) public commitment; (c) threats and fear; (d) opinion leaders; (e) credibility; and (f) the sleeper effect.

14. Discuss any one of the consistency theories and explore its application to business practice.

15. What is the alternative view to cognitive dissonance?

16. Examine the methods for measuring attitudes.

17. Explain the theory of planned behaviour.

18. "The relationship between job satisfaction and outcomes (e.g. performance and absenteeism) may not be as clear-cut as many people think". Discuss.

19. What is the difference between job satisfaction and organisational commitment?

20. Identify the component parts of commitment.

REFERENCES

Adorno, J.W., Frenkel-Brunswick, E., Levinson, D.J., & Sandford, R.N. (1953). *The authoritarian personality*. New York: Harper & Row.

Ajzen, I. & Fishbein, M. (1980). *Understanding attitudes and predicting social behaviour*. New York: Prentice-Hall.

Ajzen, I. & Madden, J.T. (1986). Prediction of goal-directed behaviour: Attitudes, intentions, and perceived behavioural control. *Journal of Experimental Social Psychology, 22*, 453–474.

Allegrante, J.P., Mortimer, R.C., & O'Rourke, T.W. (1980). Social-psychological factors in motorcycle helmet use: Implications for public policy. *Journal of Safety Research, 12*, 1115–1126.

Allen, N.J. & Meyer, M.P. (1990). The measurement and antecedents of affective continuance and normative commitment to the organisation. *Journal of Occupational Psychology, 63*, 1–8.

Allport, G.W. (1935). Attitudes. In C. Murchison (Ed.), *Handbook of social psychology*. Worcester, MA.: Clark University Press.

Allport, G.W., Vernon, P.E., & Lindzey, G. (1960). *A study of values: A scale for measuring the dominant interests in personality*. Boston: Houghton Mifflin.

Arnold, J., Robertson, I.T., & Cooper, C.L. (1991). *Work psychology: Understanding human behaviour at work*. London: Pitman Publishing.

Barling, J., Wade, B., & Fullagar, C. (1990). Predicting employee commitment to company and union: Divergent models. *Journal of Occupational Psychology, 63*, 49–61.

Bateman, T. & Strasser, S. (1984). A longitudinal analysis of the antecedents of organisational commitment. *Academy of Management Journal, 27*, 95–112.

Bem, D.J. (1967). Self-perception: An alternative interpretation of cognitive dissonance phenomena. *Psychological Review, 74*, 3, 183–200.

Bogardus, E.S. (1925). Measuring social distance. *Journal of Applied Sociology, 9*, 216–226.

Breckler, S.J. (1984). Empirical validation of affect, behaviour, and cognition as distinct components of attitude. *Journal of Personality and Social Psychology, 47*, 1191–1205.

Brehm, W.J. (1966). *A theory of psychological reactance*. New York: Academic Press.

Brock, T.C. & Becker, L.A. (1965). Ineffectiveness of overheard counter-propaganda. *Journal of Personality and Social Psychology, 2*, 654–660.

Buckley, A. & McKenna, E.F. (1973). The practising chartered accountant: Job attitudes and professional values. *Accounting and Business Research*, Summer, 197–204.

Cacioppo, J.T. & Petty, R.E. (1989). Effects of message repetition on argument processing, recall, and persuasion. *Basic Applied Social Psychology, 10*, 3–12.

Carsten, J.M. & Spector, P.E. (1987). Unemployment, job satisfaction, and employee turnover: A meta-analytical test of the "Muchinsky Model". *Journal of Applied Psychology*, August, 374–381.

Cassell, C. & Walsh, S. (1993). Being seen but not heard: Barriers to women's equality in the workplace. *The Psychologist*, March, 110–113.

Chattopadhyay, A. & Alba, J.W. (1988). The situational importance of recall and inference in consumer decision making. *Journal of Consumer Research*, 15, 1–12.

Clegg, C.W. (1983). Psychology of employee lateness, absence and turnover: A methodological critique and an empirical study. *Journal of Applied Psychology*, February, 88–101.

Cohen, D. (1981). *Consumer behaviour*. New York: Random House.

Cooper, C.L., Sloan, S., & Williams, S. (1987). *Occupational stress indicator*. Walton-On-Thames, UK: NFER/Nelson.

Deutsch, M. & Collins, M.E. (1951). *Inter-racial housing*. Minnesota: University of Minnesota Press.

Driver, M.J. & Streufert, S. (1966). *The general incongruity adaptation level (GIAL) hypothesis: An analysis and integration of cognitive approaches to motivation*. Paper No. 114, Krannert School of Industrial Administration: Purdue University.

Ehrlich, D., Guttman, I., Schonbach, P., & Mills, J. (1957). Post-decision exposure to relevant information. *Journal of Abnormal and Social Psychology*, 54, 98–102.

Eiser, J.R. & Van der Pligt, J. (1988). *Attitudes and decisions*. London: Routledge.

Engel, J.F., Blackwell, R.D., & Miniard, P.W. (1990). *Consumer behaviour* (sixth edition). Orlando, FL: The Dryden Press.

Eysenck, H.J. (1970). *Psychology is about people*. London: Allen Lane Press.

Fazio, R.H. (1986). How do attitudes guide behaviour? In R.M. Sorrentino & E.T. Higgins (Eds.), *Handbook of motivation and cognition: Foundations of social behaviour*. New York: Guildford Press.

Feldman, D.C. & Arnold, H.J. (1985). Personality types and career patterns: Some empirical evidence on Holland's model. *Canadian Journal of Administrative Science*, June, 192–210.

Festinger, L.A. (1957). *Theory of cognitive dissonance*. Evanston, IL: Row, Peterson.

Festinger, L. & Carlsmith, J. (1959). Cognitive consequences of forced compliancies. *Journal of Abnormal and Social Psychology*, 58, 203–210.

Fiedler, F.A. (1967). *Theory of leadership effectiveness*. New York: McGraw-Hill.

Financial Times, The. (1993). *Ageism in the Workplace* (Editorial Comment). 7 October (p. 23).

Fishbein, M. & Ajzen, I. (1975). *Beliefs, attitudes, intention and behaviour: An introduction to theory and research*. Reading, MA: Addison-Wesley.

Frenkel-Brunswick, E. & Sanford, R.N. (1945). Some personality factors in anti-Semitism. *Journal of Psychology*, 20, 271–291.

Glisson, C. & Durick, M. (1988). Predictors of job satisfaction and organisational commitment in human service organisations. *Administrative Science Quarterly*, March, 61–81.

Graves, C.W. (1970). An open systems' theory of values. *Journal of Humanistic Psychology*, Fall, 131–155.

Hastings, A. (1968). *The chartered accountant in industry: A study of values*. Unpublished PhD thesis: University of Birmingham.

Heider, F. (1946). Attitudes and cognitive organisations. *Journal of Psychology*, 21, 107–112.

Himmelfarb, S. (1974). Resistance to persuasion induced by information integration. In S. Himmelfarb & A. Eagley (Eds.), *Readings in attitude change*. New York: John Wiley and Sons.

Hodgetts, R.M. (1991). Organisational behaviour: Theory and practice. New York: Macmillan Publishing.

Hovland, C.I., Harvey, O.J., & Sherif, M. (1957). Assimilation and contrast effects in reactions to communication and attitude change. *Journal of Abnormal and Social Psychology*, 55, 244–252.

Hovland, C.I., Lumsdaine, A.A., & Sheffield, F.D. (1949). *Experiments in mass communication*. Princeton, NJ: Princeton University Press.

Hovland, C.I. & Weiss, W. (1951). The influence of source credibility on communication effectiveness. *Public Opinion Quarterly*, 15, 635–650.

Hulin, C.L., Reznowski, M., & Hachiya, D. (1985). Alternative opportunities and withdrawal decisions: Empirical and theoretical discrepancies and an integration. *Psychological Bulletin*, July, 233–250.

Iaffaldano, M.T. & Muchinsky, P.M. (1985). Job satisfaction and job performance: A meta-analysis. *Psychological Bulletin*, 97, 251–273.

Jack, A. & Dixon, H. (1993). What price a corporate halo? *Financial Times*, 17 September (p. 16).

Janis, I.L. & Feshbach, S. (1963). Effects of fear-arousing communication. *Journal of Abnormal and Social Psychology*, 48, 78–92.

Johnson, H.H. & Scileppi, I.D. (1969). Effects of ego involvement conditions on attitude change to high and low credibility communications. *Journal of Personality and Social Psychology*, 13, 31–36.

Karlins, M. & Abelson, H. (1970). *Persuasion*. London: Crosby Lockwood.

Katz, D. (1960). The functional approach to the study of attitudes. *Public Opinion Quarterly*, 24, 163–204.

Katz, E. & Lazarsfield, P.F. (1955). *Personal influence*. New York: Free Press.

Kelman, H.C. (1961). Processes of opinion change. *Public Opinion Quarterly*, 25, 57–78.

Kelman, H.C. (1969). Patterns of personal involvement in the national system: A social psychological analysis of political legitimacy. In J.N. Rosenau (Ed.), *International politics and foreign policy*. New York: Free Press.

Koeske, G. & Crano, W. (1968). The effect of congruous and incongruous source statement combinations upon the judged credibility of a communication. *Journal of Experimental Social Psychology*, 4, 384–399.

Kothandapani, V. (1971). Validation of feeling, belief, and intention to act as three components of attitude and their contribution to prediction of contraceptive behaviour. *Journal of Personality and Social Psychology*, 19, 321–333.

Krech, D., Crutchfield, R.S., & Ballachey, E. (1962). *Individual in society*. New York: McGraw-Hill.

La Piere, R.T. (1934). Attitudes vs. actions. *Social Forces*, 13, 230–237.

Lee, T.A. (1972). Psychological aspects of accounting. *Accounting and Business Research*, Summer, 223–233.

Lee, T.W. & Mowday, R.T. (1987). Voluntarily leaving an organisation: An empirical investigation of Steers and Mowday's model of turnover. *Academy of Management Journal*, December, 721–743.

Leventhal, H.R., Singer, P., & Jones, S. (1965). Effects of fear and specificity of recommendation upon attitudes and behaviour. *Journal of Personality and Social Psychology*, 2, 20–29.

Leventhal, H., Watts, J.C., & Pagano, F. (1967). Effects of fear and instructions on how to cope with danger. *Journal of Personality and Social Psychology*, 6, 313–321.

Liberman, S. (1956). The effects of changes in roles on the attitudes of role occupants. *Human Relations*, 9, 385–402.

Likert, R. (1932). A technique for the measurement of attitudes. *Archives of Psychology*, 22, 1–55.

Locke, E.A. (1976). The nature and causes of job satisfaction. In M.D. Dunnette (Ed.), *Handbook of industrial and organisational psychology*. Chicago: Rand McNally.

Lorenz, C. & Lorenz, C. (1989). Business ethics: Will the practice ever emulate the theory? *Financial Times*, 13 November.

MacCrone, I.D. (1957). *Race attitudes in South Africa*. London: Oxford University Press.

Mackay, K. (1973). *An introduction to psychology*. London: Macmillan.

Maslow, C., Yoselson, K., & London, M. (1971). Persuasiveness of confidence expressed via language and body language. *British Journal of Social and Clinical Psychology*, 10, 234–240.

McGuire, W.J. (1968). Personality and susceptibility to social influence. In E. Borgatta & W.W. Lambert (Eds.), *Handbook of personality theory and research*, Vol. 3. Chicago: Rand McNally.

McKenna, E.F. (1972). *Leadership styles in industry*. Unpublished MSc thesis: University of Lancaster.

Miller, K.I. & Monge, P. (1986). Participation, satisfaction, and productivity: A meta-analytic review. *Academy of Management Journal*, March, 748.

Moreno, J.L. (1953). *Who shall survive?* New York: Beacon.

Mottaz, C.J. (1988). Determinants of organisational commitment. *Human Relations*, 41, 467–482.

Mowday, R.T., Porter, L.W., & Steers, R.M. (1982). *Employee–organisation linkages: The psychology of commitment, absenteeism, and turnover*. New York: Academic Press.

Myer, J.P., Paunonen, S.V., Gellatly, I.R., Goffin, R.D., & Jackson, D.N. (1989). Organisational commitment and job performance: Its the nature of the commitment that counts. *Journal of Applied Psychology*, 74, 152–156.

Newcombe, T. (1943). *Personality and social change: Attitude formation in a student community*. New York: Holt, Reinhart, & Winston.

Osgood, C.E., Suci, G.J., & Tannenbaum, P.H. (1957). *The measurement of meaning*. Urbane, IL: University of Illinois Press.

Osgood, C.E. & Tannenbaum, P.H. (1955). The principle of congruity in the prediction of attitude change. *Psychological Review*, 62, 42–55.

Pennington, D.C. (1986). *Essential social psychology*. London: Edward Arnold.

Petty, R.E. & Cacioppo, J.T. (1985). The elaboration likelihood model of persuasion. In Berkowitz, L. (Ed.), *Advances in experimental social psychology*, Vol. 19. New York: Academic Press.

Petty, M.M., McGee, G.W., & Cavender, J.W. (1984). A meta-analysis of the relationship between individual job satisfaction and individual performance. *Academy of Management Review*, October, 712–721.

Pocock, P. (1989). Is business ethics a contradiction in terms. *Personnel Management*, November, 60–63.

Price, D.L. & Lueder, R.K. (1980). Virginia union and industry management attitudes toward safety and the Occupational Safety and Health Act. *Journal of Safety Research*, 12, Fall, 99–106.

Reich, B. & Adcock, C. (1976). *Values, attitudes and behaviour change*. London: Methuen.

Reichers, A.E. (1985). A review and re-conceptualisation of organisational commitments. *Academy of Management Review*, 10, 465–476.

Re Velle, J.B. & Boulton, L. (1981). Worker attitudes and perceptions of safety: part 1. *Professional Safety*, December, 28–34.

Robbins, S.P. (1991). *Organisational behaviour: Concepts, controversies, and applications* (fifth edition). New York: Prentice-Hall.

Rogers, R.W. & Mewborn, C.R. (1976). Fear appeals and attitude change: Effects of a threat's noxiousness, probability of occurrence, and the efficacy of coping responses. *Journal of Personality and Social Psychology, 34,* 54–61.

Rokeach, M. (1973). *The nature of human values.* New York: Free Press.

Romzek, B.S. (1989). Personal consequences of employee commitment. *Academy of Management Journal,* September, 649–661.

Salancik, G. & Pfeffer, J. (1978). A social information-processing approach to job attitudes and task design. *Administrative Science Quarterly, 23,* 224–253.

Scarpello, V. & Campbell, J.P. (1983). Job satisfaction: Are all the parts there? *Personnel Psychology,* Autumn, 577–600.

Scott, E.D. & Taylor, G.S. (1985). An examination of conflicting findings on the relationship between job satisfaction and absenteeism: A meta-analysis. *Academy of Management Journal,* September, 599–612.

Secord, P.F. & Beckman, C.W. (1974). *Social psychology.* New York: McGraw-Hill.

Sheppard, B.H., Hartwick, T., & Warshaw, P.R. (198). The theory of reasoned action. A meta-analysis of past research with recommendations for modifications and future research. *Journal of Consumer Research, 15,* 325–343.

Sherif, M. & Sherif, C.W. (1967). Attitude as the individual's own categories: The social judgement-involvement approach to attitudes and attitude change. In C.W. Sherif & M. Sherif (Eds.), *Attitude, ego-involvement, and change.* New York: John Wiley & Sons.

Spencer, D.G. & Steers, R.M. (1981). Performance as a moderator of the job satisfaction–turnover relationship. *Journal of Applied Psychology,* August, 511–514.

Steers, R.M. (1977). Antecedents and outcomes of organisational commitment. *Administrative Science Quarterly, 22,* 46–56.

Stouffer, S.A., Suchman, E.A., Devinney, L.C., Star, S.A., & Williams, R.N. (1949). *The American soldier,* Vol. 1 (adjustment during army life). Princeton, NJ: Princeton University Press.

Sutton, S.R. (1982). Fear-arousing communications: A critical examination of theory and research. In J.R. Eiser (Ed.), *Social psychology and behavioural medicine.* Chichester: Wiley.

Tedeschi, J., Schlenker, B., & Bonoma, T. (1973). Cognitive dissonance: Private rationalisation or public spectacle. In W. Scott & L. Cummings (Eds.), *Readings in organisational behaviour and human performance.* Homewood, IL: Richard Irwin.

Tesser, A. & Shaffer, D. (1990). Attitudes and attitude change. In M.R. Rosenzweig & L.W. Porter (Eds.), *Annual review of psychology,* Vol. 41. Palo Alto, CA: Annual Reviews Inc.

Thurstone, L.L. & Chave, E.J. (1929). *The measurement of attitudes.* Chicago: University of Chicago Press.

Waister, E. & Festinger, L. (1962). The effectiveness of overheard persuasive communications. *Journal of Abnormal and Social Psychology, 65,* 395–402.

Warr, P., Cook, J., & Wall, T. (1979). Scales for the measurement of some work attitudes and aspects of psychological well-being. *Journal of Occupational Psychology, 52,* 129–148.

Wood, W. & Kallgren, C.A. (1988). Communicator attributes and persuasion: Recipients' access to attitude-relevant information in memory. *Personality and Social Psychology Bulletin, 14,* 172–182.

Zohar, D. (1980). Prompting the use of personal protective equipment by behaviour modification techniques. *Journal of Safety Research,* Summer, 12, 78–85.

PART II

The Group

7

Groups and Team-building

The opening sections of this chapter cover a definition of a group and different types of groups. There follows an analysis of important characteristics of groups, and some reasons are given as to why people join groups. Next, the main focus is on key processes within groups, and this is followed by an examination of inter-group behaviour. Finally, various approaches to team-building or group development are discussed.

This chapter examines topics connected with issues raised in earlier chapters (e.g. autonomous groups in Chapter 2 and decision making in Chapter 5). It also provides a foundation for issues considered in later chapters (e.g. leadership in Chapter 8, conflict in Chapter 9, and organisational change and development in Chapter 12).

DEFINITION

How do we go about defining what we mean by a group? In the first instance, we can observe interpersonal relationships in a group and note that people communicate verbally and non-verbally. The behaviour of members of the group is influenced by shared norms (e.g. standards of behaviour or expectations). Members strive to achieve a common objective, normally under the influence of a leader or chairman.

Interdependency is apparent when members of the group are dependent on each other for support and help. The more the members of the group interact to finish a job, the greater is the level of interdependency. When members of a group subscribe to common values, beliefs, and objectives, and there is a high level of agreement between them on these matters and how best to achieve the objectives of the group, a state of

cohesiveness is said to exist. Cohesive groups emphasise the need for close co-operation in order to complete their various tasks in an effective way, and to create conditions in which the personal needs of members are satisfied.

This definition of a group might not include a silent order of nuns who do not interrelate in a dynamic way; also, there are occasions when members of a committee (a group) may not share group norms and, although they work together, one member could achieve his or her goals at the expense of the others. So it is difficult to arrive at an all-embracing definition of a group.

TYPES OF GROUP

Groups can be referred to as belonging to certain types, and a classification of groups by type follows.

Formal or Informal

Groups can be classified as either formal or informal. In a formal group, important objectives and roles performed by members are predetermined. For example, the quantity and quality of output, the requirement to adhere to safety standards, and desired behaviour in dealing with charge-hands and colleagues are either implicit or made explicit. In formally constituted groups it is also possible to find informal norms and behaviour.

By contrast, the informal group develops in a spontaneous fashion, and the objectives and roles found in this type of group arise from the current interactions of members. Once these objectives and roles are established, members normally subscribe to them because they consider themselves a group member or wish to be considered as such.

Primary or Secondary

Groups can also be classified as either primary or secondary. A primary group is small in size, face-to-face contact is generally frequent, and relationships tend to be close and often intimate. A family, a play-group, a sports team, or a tightly knit group of accountants in an organisation could constitute a primary group. A secondary group assumes more of an impersonal nature and may be geographically distant. A company, a hospital, or a school could fall into this category. This type of group is not necessarily a psychological group, but membership of it could influence a member's outlook.

Co-acting

A feature of a co-acting group is the level of independence experienced by group members. They may undertake either similar or dissimilar tasks within the group, but they do so independently of each other. The interdependency and cohesiveness referred to earlier would not apply to the co-acting group. However, members are likely to relate more to each other at the advanced stages of work processes or assignments where there may be a need for co-operation and co-ordination.

Counteracting

Counteracting groups have opposing aims and compete for scarce resources. In the process they may engage in a struggle for power and advantage. With regard to what goes on within each individual group, unity of purpose and mode of operation may feature prominently.

Reference

Reference groups may possess a certain attraction and, as a result, individuals may wish to join them, or merely to identify with them in some way. Therefore, a reference group can influence a person's outlook without that person being a member of it.

Classification by Skill and Level of Interaction

Sayles (1958) maintains that the technology of a plant has the effect of creating different types of work groups, which he distinguishes primarily on the basis of skill and level of interaction.

1. *Apathetic*: a relatively unskilled group, the members of which tend to work as individuals. There is little sense of group solidarity, morale is low, and the group is regarded as unsatisfactory by management.
2. *Erratic*: the group is unskilled with a relatively large amount of interaction among members. On occasions, the group develops solidarity. It is not usually shrewd about choosing the right situation in which to express grievances. The group consists of unpredictable members led by authoritarian leaders.

3. *Strategic*: the group consists of skilled members who interact to a great extent. The group is highly calculating in its strategy and is accepted by management.
4. *Conservative*: this is the most highly skilled group. It maintains a strong sense of group identity, even when its members are dispersed. It is primarily concerned with the stability of traditional wage differentials.

Because the workers categorised here were drawn from mass production industries only, one could question the validity of this exercise if generalised to other groups. However, it shows that groups in industry display different orientations. For example, as a result of introducing new technology in the coal-mining industry, Trist et al. (1963) showed how group loyalty and cohesion were adversely affected by the change, and the miners reacted strongly against having to forego their traditional independence.

CHARACTERISTICS OF GROUPS

The following key characteristics of groups will be discussed in this section:

- norms;
- cohesiveness;
- communication and interaction;
- structural factors; and
- group dynamics.

Related topics, such as reference groups and decision making, will be discussed later in this chapter in the section on "Group Processes".

Norms

Social norms regulate the relationships between individuals in groups; in fact they are guides to behaviour. Norms are collective because they are shared by many members of a group. They are only guides or expectations about what behaviour should be and, as such,

allow us to anticipate other people's behaviour in specified circumstances. They are not necessarily followed in all circumstances. However, they can be enforced, and people are either positively rewarded for complying with them or punished for not complying. Norms usually reflect the values of the group (Zaltman & Wallandorf, 1979).

Though norms regulate behaviour in groups, some norms can be viewed more seriously than others simply because of the sanctions associated with contravening them. To depart from a group norm in a street gang could produce significant sanctions, and so members of the gang may break society's laws in order to escape the sanctions. Yablonsky (1967) has shown how an ordinary youth, a member of a violent gang, gets involved in brutal behaviour as a response to group pressure. This illustrates a powerful compulsion to adhere to group norms considered by many people, in this case, to be crude and unacceptable. But for the individual member of the gang, the fear of sanctions far surpasses general moral inhibitions. There are other circumstances depicted in experiments where deviation from a group norm would not activate any significant sanctions apart from the anxiety that would arise as a result of departing from the consensus established by a group. These are examples of internally imposed norms.

Externally imposed norms in, for example, an active military group, are various forms of discipline to which military personnel are required to adhere. Sanctions for the infringement of these norms can be heavy. By contrast, a sports team may typify a situation where norms are externally imposed, but sanctions applicable to deviations from the norms are modest; for instance, a footballer may receive only a caution for indulging in illegal play.

Somebody who chooses to ignore a group norm by, for example, persistently ignoring safety regulations at work, can be referred to as a deviant. Pressure can be put on deviants to conform to group norms and this can take the form of verbal abuse, physical assault, silence, blacklisting, and physical exclusion from the group. Sometimes, one or more of these sanctions are levelled at a worker who fails to respond to officially approved strike action—he or she is considered to be a deviant by contravening the norm to withdraw labour in specified circumstances.

Norms are associated with the internal working of the group, but to the outsider it is generally the group's external image that is visible. The outsider recognises private language, technical slang, and in-jokes as alien, but may attribute them to a particular group. Likewise, the distinctive way in which members of the group dress conveys the group's identity (e.g. a nun or priest).

Norms can cover a variety of work situations. For instance, they could apply to the quantity and quality of output; production practices; the manner in which individuals relate to each other; the appropriate dress to wear; demonstrations of loyalty to the organisation; times when it is important to look busy even if the workload is light; who to socialise with at work and outside work; conventions with regard to the allocation of resources; and other issues considered relevant by the group (Goodman, Ravlin, & Schminke, 1987). Some norms are beneficial from the organisation's point of view when they help to maintain the quality of output—i.e. the desire to do a job well. Other norms are considered by the organisation to be counter-productive; for example, norms supportive of restrictive practices.

Characteristics of Norms

Norms possess the following characteristics (Chell, 1987):

- the majority of group members generally find them acceptable;
- only the significant aspects of group life are covered by them;
- group behaviour, rather than the thoughts and feelings of members, is the focal point of attention;

- members of the group accept them in varying degrees;
- there is variation with regard to the degree of toleration members will accept when it comes to deviations from the norm;
- the process of managing the group is facilitated by them;
- they develop slowly and change slowly;
- conformity to norms can be a function of a person's status within the group—e.g. this is conspicuous when some members, normally of high status, are given latitude to deviate from the norm; and
- there is usually an accepted set of rewards and punishment associated with compliance or non-compliance with certain norms.

Purpose of Norms

Four main purposes can be served by norms (Feldman, 1984):

1. Norms express the central values of the group and, in doing so, can inspire members and project to others the nature of the group.
2. Norms simplify and make more predictable the behaviour expected of group members, so that members' behaviour can be anticipated. This can smooth the functioning of the group.
3. Norms assist the group in avoiding embarrassing situations when, for example, members may avoid discussing certain issues likely to hurt the feelings of a particular member.
4. Norms help the group to survive. This could arise when the group rejects deviant behaviour that poses a threat to its existence. However, a successful group that does not feel threatened may be more tolerant of deviant behaviour.

Difficulties with Conformity

The normal expectation (mentioned earlier) is that conformity to norms or standards will be encouraged by offering rewards or imposing punishment. In some situations the group

'CRUSHER' (A.K.A. NIGEL) IS RUMBLED.

may go overboard in using such a strategy to promote the group's interest, almost at the cost of stifling individuality.

A number of problems can arise if pressure to conform is applied in the following circumstances (Chell, 1987):

- The personal goals of the individual and those of the organisation are in conflict.
- The individual does not feel a sense of pride from belonging to the group.
- The individual seems to be more preoccupied with achieving his or her own ends, rather than those of the group.
- The individual is not recognised as a fully fledged group member because of occupying a peripheral position within the group.
- The individual considers the price of conformity to be too high; for example, the person could harm his or her career as a result of compliance.
- The individual refuses to conform, because the effort by the group to force compliance appears to be unconvincing, or on this occasion the group's judgement is perceived as unsound.

Opposition to Norms

There are occasions when it may be possible for group members to oppose norms without the fear of punishment, personal strain, feelings of guilt, or loss of self-esteem. Zander (1982) has suggested the following action strategies as a means to promote opposition to norms:

1. Establish where you stand on relevant issues, and where you think the group should be going. Then join forces with like-minded members of the group. This action has the advantage of deriving comfort from others who share your view, and it sows the seed for joint action as an opposition force.
2. Resist pressure from the group by concealing from others what you think and feel.
3. Have the courage of your convictions and do not jettison that which you consider precious for the sake of harmony within the group.
4. If it is necessary to make some concessions, explore ways in which you can enter some

form of compromise without appearing to have capitulated, but at the same time retaining your major principles.

5. Consider the effects, rewards, and punishments for you personally of conformity and non-conformity respectively. Then make a decision whether or not to conform.

Avoiding Punishment

Earlier it was stated that a member of a group who does not conform to a significant norm could be considered a deviant, and therefore liable to be punished for non-conformity. However, a deviant could, in circumstances such as those listed here, avoid punishment (Zander, 1982):

- the deviant is an influential member of the group;
- the deviant is a member of a very large group in which it is easy for deviancy to go unnoticed;
- the deviant deviates on matters or issues of no great importance;
- the deviant absents himself or herself temporarily from the group and fails to take his or her share of the work load;
- the deviant is a member of a group that somehow has a soft spot for the antics of deviants.

Cohesiveness

Cohesiveness is likely to exist when there is a high level of agreement among group members with respect to values, beliefs, and objectives. This promotes the sharing of similar ideas and the mutual acceptance of such ideas. One would expect members of a cohesive group to agree among themselves on how best to achieve the objectives of the group, with an emphasis on the need for close co-operation in order to complete the various tasks and create conditions in which the personal needs of individuals are satisfied. In connection with the last point, it should be noted that the greater the benefit derived from group membership, the greater the likelihood of cohesiveness.

Those who have studied cohesiveness emphasise the attractiveness of the group to members, the motivation of members to remain in the group, and their resistance to leaving it (Piper et al., 1983; Shaw, 1981).

What factors induce and sustain group cohesiveness? The following seven determining factors, together with the effects created by cohesiveness, ought to be considered:

1. *Similarity of attitudes and goals*. The assumption here is that people with similar attitudes and objectives will find each other's company a source of satisfaction.

2. *Time spent together*. As people spend more time together they are given the opportunity to explore common interests and experience greater interpersonal attraction (Insko & Wilson, 1977). Physical proximity is a factor that could determine the frequency of contact. A closer relationship is likely to exist between group members who are located near to each other rather than far apart.

3. *Isolation*. Groups that are isolated from other groups may perceive themselves as special. The need to close ranks and be in a state of readiness to counteract threats may also be prevalent.

4. *Threats*. One would expect the cohesiveness of the group to solidify in the face of external competition or threats. In such conditions, the importance of interdependency is underlined. For example, a co-operative mode of thinking and functioning could be fostered within a work group faced with unreasonable demands by management for changes in working practices. However, cohesiveness could be dented where the group feels it is unable to withstand the external threat or attack. Here the members feel that the group is now less important as a source of security.

5. *Size*. With an increase in size comes less opportunities for interaction, and the growth of bureaucratic rules and procedures that could dilute the informal nature of relations and communication among group members. By contrast, smaller groups tend to create conditions for the advancement of cohesiveness because of the greater opportunities for interaction among members.

6. *Stringent entry requirements*. The more difficult it is to get into a group, the greater the likelihood that the group is cohesive. This is likely to apply to a club with exacting entry requirements. Once admitted, the member feels that it is important to uphold the standards that contribute to the exclusive nature of the group. Groups with a record of success (e.g. football teams or academic departments) can specify exacting entry requirements in their endeavour to attract the most talented people.

7. *Rewards*. It is sometimes said that incentives based on group performance cultivates a group-centred perspective where co-operation rather than internal competition prevails. As a consequence, cohesiveness is enhanced.

With regard to the effects of cohesiveness, communication between members is significantly greater in highly cohesive groups than in less cohesive groups, as one would expect, and likewise satisfaction is much greater because of the strong attraction among members. But it is likely that highly cohesive groups are more resistant to change than are less cohesive groups—in particular changes to the status quo that threaten the group's networks and social supports (Vecchio, 1991).

Cohesiveness and Productivity

In the relationship between cohesiveness and group productivity, highly cohesive groups seem to be more effective at meeting their objectives than groups low in cohesiveness—especially in research and development groups in US companies (Keller, 1986). It appears that it is important for the group's goals to be compatible with the organisation's goals if the relationship between cohesiveness and productivity is to stand (Moorhead & Griffin, 1992).

Another intervening variable one might consider in the relationship between cohesiveness and productivity is performance-related norms within the group (Robbins, 1991). If performance-related norms with respect to output, quality, co-operation, etc., are well established (i.e. high), a cohesive group will be more productive than a less cohesive group. On the other hand, if performance-related norms are low in a cohesive group, productivity will suffer.

It thus appears that goal congruency and performance-related norms are key variables in the relationship between cohesiveness and productivity. It stands to reason that low productivity aspirations in highly cohesive groups will lead to relatively low output, as Schachter et al. (1951) found in an empirical study many years ago.

When focusing on group cohesiveness it is worth reflecting on the success of Japanese car manufacturers. They believe strongly in nurturing group cohesiveness. Apart from the emphasis on careful selection of employees and training, a lot of attention is given to building and maintaining group morale. There is also an emphasis on participative management and encouraging employees to promptly correct any mistakes without stopping the production line. There is an expectation that employees will commit themselves fully, and gladly take up the slack for colleagues absent due to illness.

Some people believe that the over-whelming emphasis on high productivity generates stress, whereas others applaud the job security that success brings in its wake. It is claimed that Japanese management practices in car plants result in greater effort by employees, lower absenteeism, and lower staff turnover (Hodgetts, 1991). The danger of too much cohesion is that it could lead to an insufficient exploration of issues considered by the group. This is a topic that will be elaborated on later when discussing "groupthink".

Other Issues
In a marketing study the cohesiveness of the group as a determinant of the degree of brand loyalty of members was subject to analysis (Witt & Bruce, 1970). Apparently the power of group cohesiveness is greater in predicting choice of products high in social involvement (e.g. cigarettes and beer) than of products low in social involvement (e.g. deodorants).

Members can improve their self-concept with the help of the reflected impression they make on others in certain groups. The "therapeutic" nature of face-to-face contact is generally recognised. In a group such as Alcoholics Anonymous, members who are dependent on drink can unburden themselves and expect to receive sympathy and support from the group. Likewise, a member may derive moral strength to control his or her weight from membership of a group such as Weight Watchers. But groups can also produce negative effects. According to Laing (1970), mental illness has its origins in faulty interactions in the patient's primary group (i.e. the family). Deviance can spring from group membership when young people are integrated in groups with norms at variance with those of wider society, as was described earlier with reference to a street gang.

Communication and Interaction

In studies of communication networks, groups of four or five people were engaged in problem-solving tasks in different forms of groupings (Leavitt, 1951). Each person in a group receives a list of symbols (e.g. star, circle, wavy line). Although each list is different, all lists contain one symbol in common. The task is to find out as quickly as possible which is the common symbol. Subjects are only permitted to communicate with one another by written notes. The situations depicted in these studies are not like the small group in which communication is face-to-face and everyone can hear everyone else. They are rather more like situations found in large organisations where a number of people in different parts of the organisation are in touch with one another only indirectly or, if directly, then frequently through relatively impersonal media such as a telephone or memorandum.

The communication networks studied by Leavitt are shown in Fig. 7.1. Problems were solved more quickly, there were fewer mistakes, and fewer messages were required in the more centralised network—i.e. the wheel. The person at the centre enjoyed himself much more than the other members

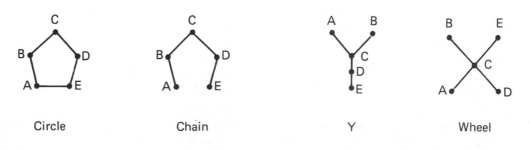

FIG. 7.1. Communication networks. Source: Leavitt, H.J. (1951). Some effects of certain communication patterns on group performance. *Journal of Abnormal and Social Psychology, 46,* 38–50.

of the group, and he was perceived as leader. In the decentralised network—the circle—performance was slower, more erratic, but enjoyable.

It is suggested that centralised networks, such as the wheel, lend themselves to the efficient execution of simple tasks, but more complex tasks were found to be more effectively performed by less highly centralised networks, such as the circle or a network in which everybody communicates with everybody else (Shaw, 1964). The complex tasks required more than the mere collation of information in exercises connected with the construction of sentences and solving arithmetic problems. The central person in the wheel could be overwhelmed and overloaded when dealing with incoming messages and manipulating data in the complex tasks; so a centralised network would be inappropriate in these circumstances.

Reflecting on the managerial implications of communication networks, a number of observations can be made. For a work group confronting a variety of tasks and objectives, no single network is likely to be effective. For example, the wheel, with its simplicity and efficiency, can be less than functional in the event of low job satisfaction having an adverse effect on the motivational disposition of group members. If a situation exists where the work group is not adept at sharing information and considering alternatives in decision making, then there is the danger of not being able to handle complex problems requiring high interdependency among group members. Preference for a particular network and the nature of the task have to be considered. For example, a work group that prefers a network in which everybody communicates with everybody else (high interdependency), could experience difficulties in handling simple problems that require little interdependency between members (Hodgetts, 1991).

When people are interacting at work they are essentially engaged in two sets of activities—the accomplishment of tasks and the maintenance of the social fabric of the group. But a balance has to be struck between behaviour related to a task, and behaviour of a socio-emotional nature (i.e. social maintenance of the group).

A well-known system embracing the two streams has been developed (Bales, 1950). It is called "interaction process analysis", and the 12 categories used are as follows.

Socio-emotional: positive behaviours are:
1. Shows solidarity, raises others' status, gives help, rewards.
2. Shows tension release, jokes, laughs, shows satisfaction.
3. Agrees, shows passive acceptance, understands, concurs, complies.

Task: attempted answers are:

4. Gives suggestion, direction, implying autonomy for others.
5. Gives opinion, evaluation, analysis, expresses feelings, wish.
6. Gives orientation, information, repeats, clarifies, confirms.

Tasks: questions are:

7. Asks for orientation, information, repetition, confirmation.
8. Asks for opinion, evaluation, analysis, expression of feeling.
9. Asks for suggestions, direction, possible ways of action.

Socio-emotional: negative behaviours are:

10. Disagrees, shows passive rejection, formality, withholds help.
11. Shows tension, asks for help, withdraws out of field.
12. Shows antagonism, deflates others' status, defends or asserts self.

The 12 categories comprising the interaction process analysis system are claimed to be mutually exclusive. Verbal or non-verbal contributions by members of the group can be classified by a trained observer using this system as an aid in interactive skills training.

Bearing some similarity to the interaction process analysis system, is a list of functional and non-functional behaviour devised by Benne and Sheats (1948) (see panel facing). They recognise, as Bales does, a balance between task and social factors in the life of a group; they refer to the social dimension as group-building and maintenance. A, B, and C in the lists in the panel facing are considered functional because they serve the interests of the group. By contrast, D is non-functional because this behaviour tends to make the group weak or inefficient.

In using a classification, such as D in Benne and Sheats' (1948) analysis, people need to guard against the tendency to blame any person (whether themselves or another) who falls into "non-functional behaviour". It is more useful to regard such behaviour as a symptom that all is not well with the group's ability to satisfy individual needs through group-centred activity. People need to be alert to the fact that each person is likely to interpret such behaviours differently. What appears to be non-functional behaviour may not necessarily be so, for the nature and content of that behaviour as well as group conditions must also be taken into account. For example, there are times when some forms of being aggressive contribute positively to the scene by clearing the air and instilling energy into the group.

Spatial Factors

Spatial factors such as geographic proximity can also affect group communication and relationships, and the greater the opportunity to interact with other people the greater the likelihood that such meetings will give rise to the development of group norms and consensus (Festinger, Schacter, & Back, 1950). It would appear that homogeneity among subjects (in terms of age, intelligence, and social class) is important in this context. Different seating arrangements in groups were associated with different types of group task. Where children were given a competitive task, they chose to sit at right angles at a table, but when they were given a co-operative task they sat side-by-side.

Students participated more in discussions when the seating arrangement was a circular layout of chairs (Sommer, 1967). It is clear that decisions customarily taken by architects and interior designers have a marked effect on group structures and relationships. It is sometimes suggested that the ideal arrangement is the loose oval seating plan adopted by five or so people meeting for informal discussion. A rule of thumb is to increase the distance of people from the hub or centre until they are almost out of the bounds of communication. Then the desks and apparatus required for work can be positioned. Ancillary facilities, such as communal files, rest areas, and soft drink dispensers should be spread widely so that people are encouraged to stand up and walk around for at least 2 in every 20 minutes. It should be borne in mind that our bodies do not like immobility and our span of attention is limited (Lately, 1982).

Personal Space. In interactions with others, we allow people we know well to enter our personal space. A stranger entering into this territory could be perceived as a threat. Effectively, he or she violates our personal space by entering a zone not reserved for the invader. The invasion of personal space may cause discomfort, tension, and flight, and could lead to an over-aroused state. A state of over-arousal can be associated with reduced performance. Also, people whose space is invaded could turn away or withdraw, or alternatively ignore the fact that their space has been invaded by creating greater distance between them and the intruder. In public transport, as a train becomes overcrowded, the contraction of space is evident and this could lead to discomfort. To cope with such a

Benne and Sheats' (1948) Classification of Functional and Non-functional Behaviour

A: Task Roles (functions required in selecting and carrying out a group task)

- *Initiating activity*: proposing solutions, suggesting new ideas, new definitions of problems, new attack on problems, or new organisation of material.
- *Seeking information*: asking for clarification of suggestions, requesting additional information or facts.
- *Seeking opinion*: looking for an expression of feeling about something from the members, seeking clarification of values, suggestions, or ideas.
- *Giving information*: offering facts or generalisations, relating one's own experience to the group problem to illustrate points.
- *Giving opinion*: stating an opinion or belief concerning a suggestion or one of several suggestions, particularly concerning its value rather than its factual basis.
- *Elaborating*: clarifying, giving examples or developing meanings, trying to envisage how a proposal might work if adopted.
- *Co-ordinating*: showing relationships among various ideas or suggestions, trying to pull ideas and suggestions together, trying to draw together activities of various sub-groups or members.
- *Summarising*: pulling together related ideas or suggestions, restating suggestions after the group has discussed them.

B: Group-building and Maintenance Roles (functions required in strengthening and maintaining group life and activities)

- *Encouraging*: being friendly, warm, responsive to others, praising others and their ideas, agreeing with and accepting contributions of others.
- *Gatekeeping*: trying to make it possible for another member to make a contribution to the group by saying, "We haven't heard anything from Jim or Jane yet", or suggesting limited talking time for everyone so that all will have a chance to be heard.
- *Standard setting*: expressing standards for the group to use in choosing its content or procedures, or in evaluating its decisions, reminding the group to avoid decisions that conflict with group standards.
- *Following*: going along with decisions of the group, thoughtfully accepting ideas of others, serving as an audience during group discussion.
- *Expressing group feeling*: summarising what group feeling is sensed to be, describing reactions of the group to ideas or solutions.

C: Both Group Task and Maintenance Roles

- *Evaluating*: submitting group decisions or accomplishments to comparison with group standards, measuring accomplishments against goals.
- *Diagnosing*: determining sources of difficulties, appropriate steps to take next, analysing the main blocks to progress.
- *Testing for consensus*: tentatively asking for group opinions in order to find out whether the group is nearing consensus on a decision, sending up trial balloons to test group opinions.
- *Mediating*: harmonising, conciliating differences in points of view, making compromise solutions.
- *Relieving tension*: draining off negative feeling by jesting or pouring oil on troubled waters, putting a tense situation in wider context.

D: Types of Non-functional Behaviour

From time to time, more often perhaps than anyone likes to admit, people behave in non-functional ways that do not help, and sometimes actually harm, the group and the work it is trying to do. Some of the more common types of such non-functional behaviours are as follows:

- Being aggressive: working for status by criticising or blaming others, showing hostility against the group or some individual, deflating the ego or status of others.
- *Blocking*: interfering with the progress of the group by going off at a tangent, citing personal experiences unrelated to the problem, arguing too much on a point, rejecting ideas without consideration.
- *Self-confessing*: using the group as a sounding board, expressing personal, non group-oriented feelings or points of view.
- *Competing*: vying with others to produce the best idea, talk the most, play the most roles, gain favour with the leader.
- *Seeking sympathy*: trying to induce other group members to be sympathetic to one's problems or misfortunes, deploring one's own situation, or disparaging one's own ideas to gain support.
- *Special pleading*: introducing or supporting suggestions related to one's own pet concerns or philosophies, lobbying.
- *Horsing around*: joking, mimicking, disrupting the work of the group.
- *Seeking recognition*: attempting to call attention to one's self by loud or excessive talking, extreme ideas, unusual behaviour.
- *Withdrawal*: being indifferent or passive, resorting to excessive formality, daydreaming, doodling, whispering to others, wandering from the subject.

situation, people often stare at the floor or into space.

Personal space considerations can be influenced by cultural factors. It is said that the Germans have larger personal space areas, and are less flexible than the Americans. The Latin Americans, the French, and particularly the Arabs require smaller space zones than the Americans (Oborne, 1994).

Landscaped Office.   One solution to people's need for space is to allow them freedom to arrange the workplace as they wish. The landscaped office does not have boundaries, and offers flexibility in the use of space. In the absence of walls and partitions, the need for personal space and privacy is met by having low moveable screens, and by allowing employees to arrange desks—within limits—as they see fit. The way work groups are scattered would normally reflect the pattern of the process of work.

It has been suggested that all staff—managerial, supervisory, and clerical—should participate in the open-plan office in order to foster overall group cohesiveness and increased productivity. Also, the flow of information between the different groups of employees could be facilitated (Brookes & Kaplan, 1972), and there would be an incentive to create a colourful design for the office.

But the concept of the landscaped office has been criticised. It has been said that there would be a pronounced loss of privacy, increased noise, distractions, and inter-ruptions (Nemecek & Grandjean, 1973). In addition, people's absences can be readily seen; the nature of what people are doing is also visible, as are the various interactions in which they are engaged. As a consequence, the question of monitoring and surveillance arises, which can make people feel uneasy. Because of the lack of privacy, people may feel a certain lack of control even though they may have physical control over the arrangement of the immediate space. There appears to be no strong research evidence to support the claims of the proponents of the landscaped office (Oborne, 1994).

Structural Factors

Work groups have a structure that influences the behaviour of members. In this section certain characteristics of groups, often called structural factors, will be examined. These include the nature of the structure or atmosphere, roles, status, composition, size, and management of the group (leadership).

Structure and Atmosphere

The structure and atmosphere of a group has a part to play in facilitating the performance of tasks and the satisfaction of individual needs. The connection between innovation and group structure has been emphasised (Meadows, 1980a; 1980b). Innovation in this sense means the ability to generate and implement new ideas and to cope with change in the application of new technology or work practices, and developing new products. The characteristic of group structure that was related to innovation was the "organic" type.

In the organic structure there tends to be less of a bureaucratic outlook on the part of group members, with built-in flexibility manifested in greater awareness of organisa-tional objectives, less reliance on formality with respect to jobs and organisational relationships, and far more consultation and discussion. The research described earlier conveys the message that the management process should be flexible, and that work groups should be handled with a certain sensitivity, particularly when they are involved in problem-solving activities.

Other features of the organic work group are:

- the group has a high level of autonomy on matters connected with the use of technology and appropriate organisational arrangements;
- there tends to be flexibility in taking decisions as to when it is appropriate to deploy groups;

- there exists an appropriate mix of relevant knowledge, abilities, and skills in the group with members having similar values and beliefs, and agreeing on goals to be achieved;
- people work well together as a team supported by effective communication.

The opposite of the organic group is the mechanistic group, which tends to be bound by rules with established norms for making decisions, and in which it is difficult to move outside the organisational guidelines. Features of overall organisational structure, including mechanistic and organic systems, are discussed in Chapter 10.

Roles

Members play a particular role in a group, and the way an employee perceives and performs his or her role in a group has a material influence on how the group functions. A role could be defined as a set of expected patterns of behaviour attributable to a person occupying a particular position.

Frequently, a role is prescribed by the role occupant's job description. In life we all play a number of roles inside and outside work, and our behaviour can vary with the role we are playing. There are three aspects to roles that should be noted.

The first, which has been referred to earlier, is the "expected role". For example, financial accountants are expected to participate in the process of preparing the statutory accounts of the company. The concept of role expectations can be considered in the context of the "psychological contract". This is an unwritten agreement that exists between employers and their employees, and it sets out what management expects from its staff and vice versa. In essence this contract defines the behavioural expectations that accompany each role (Baker, 1985). If management fails to honour its side of the bargain, the commitment and motivation of staff could suffer, whereas dereliction on the part of staff could give rise to disciplinary action or severance.

The second aspect of roles is the "perceived role", which embraces those activities or behaviours the individual or role occupant believes are necessary to fulfil the expected role. Financial accountants, having realised what is expected of them in the preparation of accounts, engage in various interactions with colleagues that they consider are part of the overall duties. So, from the expected role, a person develops the perceived role.

The third aspect of roles is the "enacted role" which springs from the perceived role. This is the way a person actually behaves. As financial accountants interact with colleagues, they adopt a pattern of behaviour, such as asking questions, discussing issues, uttering words of encouragement, providing information, and so on. Many of the things financial accountants say and do during the exchanges will be determined by their understanding of the best way of executing the perceived role.

Role Ambiguity. As a person moves from the expected to the perceived role, a big problem is role ambiguity. This arises when people are uncertain about their duties, responsibilities, or authority, or all three. Role ambiguity can arise because of lack of sufficient guidance in job descriptions or explanations by superiors, and results in confusion, conflict, and lower levels of performance (Hodgetts, 1991).

Role Conflict. This arises when a person performs more than one role, and performance in one role makes performance in the other more difficult. For example, successful senior executives may experience role conflict, and attempt to reconcile the expectations placed on them as a spouse, parent, and corporate official. An extreme form of role conflict arises when two or more role expectations contradict each other. There are five types of role conflict:

1. Intra-role conflict occurs when a person experiences conflicting requirements in the job. For example, in a study of

supermarket cashiers it was found that the greatest demands originated from the customers as opposed to managers and co-workers, and that the demands of customers often conflicted with managerial or organisational rules and instructions (Rafaeli, 1989).

2. Inter-role conflict occurs when a person experiences conflict between a number of roles to which he or she has been allocated. For example, in the performance appraisal process a manager may experience conflict between the role of the evaluator about to make a negative assessment and the day-to-day role of the supportive manager when faced with a subordinate whose performance is unsatisfactory.

3. Intra-sender conflict is seen, for example, when a manager conveys the impression to a subordinate of being very satisfied with his or her performance, and that an upgrading is a mere formality. However, to the great surprise of that subordinate the upgrading goes to another subordinate. In this case, contradictory messages originating from a single source reach the recipient.

4. Person–role conflict emerges when a person's values are incompatible with the behaviour appropriate to the performance of the role. For example, on the issue of ethics in business one study found that 57% of *Harvard Business Review* readers had to confront the dilemma of having to choose between what was profitable for the organisation and what was ethical (Brenner & Molander, 1977).

5. Role overload conflict arises when a person is inundated with work, and considers it almost impossible to perform the expected role. In such circumstances it is obviously necessary to prioritise the various activities in order to handle them to an acceptable level (Jackson & Schuler, 1985).

A number of avenues are open to those afflicted by problems connected with role ambiguity and role conflict. One approach could be to live with them, but this does not seem to be an acceptable way to proceed. Role problems, as reported in Chapter 15, can be a significant source of stress, and eventually the person could become a victim of stress leading to resigning from the organisation or withdrawing from certain activities to the detriment of the organisation.

Alternatively, a proactive stance can be taken and, in the event of role ambiguity, the person approaches the superior seeking clarification. In the case of role conflict, a number of approaches may be worth pursuing (Hodgetts, 1991). For example, where conflict due to role overload occurs, prioritise the tasks to be done, and if possible delegate the activities you cannot complete, or arrange for them to be reallocated. Where person–role conflict is experienced, cite the organisation's code of ethics if there is one and it is supportive of your position, or simply refuse to engage in behaviour that contravenes your system of values. Where inter-role conflict is experienced, recognise that it is necessary to function in a number of areas, and seek the advice and support of others in approaching the unpalatable tasks.

Status

Status is the social ranking given to an individual because of the position he or she occupies in a group. Various factors may contribute to status, such as seniority, title, salary, and power, and any one of these factors could be critical in bestowing status. Naturally, status must exist in the eyes of those who confer it. Because status plays an important role in how people are treated, it assumes importance for many people.

Sometimes status is acquired as a birthright, but generally nowadays people acquire status in an organisational system on the basis of merit. Position in the organisational hierarchy conveys status—for example, the position of the chief executive. In other situations, groups of employees could be at the same hierarchical level, but the jobs they do are critical determinants of status. For example, a senior accountant and a senior production executive, although attached to different functions, occupy positions at the same level within the organisation. But there may be a general perception within the organisation that accountants enjoy higher status relative to production executives.

There are people in groups whose status is influenced primarily by their personal attributes, but the most powerful combination arises when status rests on both personality and position. Symbols of status, such as titles, are badges of identification that communicate differences in organisational rank, and are said to provide stability and predictability concerning role expectations and the appropriateness of conduct and behaviour. In addition, they provide incentives for people to strive for improved performance and advancement.

Two common problems with status are "status incongruency" and "status discrepancy" (Hodgetts, 1991). Status incongruency arises when there is disagreement among members of the group about an individual's status. For example, a particular executive is perceived to be on the same level in a number of respects with colleagues. However, the particular executive is in receipt of an inferior remuneration package. So there is incongruency between the executive's position and an important status symbol, and this could create some confusion in interpersonal relations.

Status discrepancy happens when people engage in activities considered to be out of keeping with their status. For example, if the chief executive of an industrial company was to lunch with the operatives in the factory canteen, this could be viewed as discrepant behaviour in a status sense. It is as if there is an expectation that people should stay within their reference groups—i.e. groups with which they can identify and the values and behaviour of which they have adopted.

Composition

When the composition of a group is considered, there tends to be an emphasis on *homogeneity* and *heterogeneity*. A homogeneous group is said to exist when the profile of members (e.g. age, experience, education, specialism, and cultural origins) is similar in one or more ways that are relevant to the functioning of the group.

In the heterogeneous group, the profile of members is dissimilar. However, one could encounter in a particular work group aspects of both homogeneity and heterogeneity. This could arise where there is dissimilarity with regard to some factors—e.g. age or experience—but similarity in respect of a major factor such as a technical specialism (e.g. a research chemist in a drug company). In this example, the tendency would be to describe the group as homogeneous because the major factor is critical in terms of group functioning.

In recent years "group demography" has captured the interest of researchers. This amounts to the degree to which members of a group share a common demographic attribute such as age, sex, race, educational level, or time spent in the organisation. Heterogeneity within a group with respect to age and time spent within the group has been associated with staff turnover (O'Reilly, Caldwell, & Barnett, 1989). That means that groups with members who are of different ages or who possess different levels of experience are likely to show frequent changes in membership due to turnover.

Why should this be so? One explanation is that staff turnover is likely to be greater among those with profoundly dissimilar experience because communication is more difficult, and conflict and power struggles are more likely and more potent when they occur. The increase in conflict makes membership of the group less attractive, leading to the likely departure of members. Also, the losers in a struggle for power are likely to leave or be forced to go (Robbins, 1991). By contrast, a homogeneous group is likely to have less conflict, fewer differences of opinion, freer communication, and more interaction.

Certain variables are said to intervene in the relationship between type of group and effectiveness (Moorhead & Griffin, 1992). A homogeneous group is likely to be more productive in situations where the tasks facing the group are simple and in sequence, co-operation is necessary, and prompt action is required. An example of such a situation would be a minor disaster facing a group of fire fighters from the local fire brigade.

A heterogeneous group is more likely to be productive when the task is complex and requires creative effort, and the group draws on a diverse range of skills in its collective effort. A group of advertising executives with mixed backgrounds asked to prepare interesting and novel advertisements projecting the attractiveness of, say, the Channel Tunnel, would fall into this category. A wide range of perspectives could be explored in such a group, with the potential for much discussion and differences of opinion.

Finally, the composition of a group becomes a critical issue when companies enter into joint ventures with other companies overseas—for example, British Aerospace's proposed alliance in recent years with a Taiwanese company.

Size

The size of the group has some bearing on its performance. Smaller groups give people the opportunity to interact frequently, facilitate the free flow of information, and provide a setting in which it is easier to reach agreement. The larger group has at its disposal more resources, and is more likely to have formalised communication processes and bureaucratic practices. In the larger group the potential influence of any individual is limited, but it is said that groups with more members tend to produce more ideas and seem to be better at problem solving than smaller groups.

Beyond a certain point, the rate of increase in the number of ideas diminishes swiftly as the group grows (Shaw, 1981). Also, a stage is reached in the growth of the size of the group when the corresponding increase in the complexity of interactions and communications makes it more difficult for the larger group to co-ordinate activities, retain cohesiveness, and arrive at a consensus. The larger group may also inhibit participation by some members who despair at the lack of an opportunity to make a meaningful contribution to the deliberations.

Other observations about the consequences of increasing size in groups are:

- Directive leadership becomes more acceptable.
- Job satisfaction is lower than in smaller groups.
- Sub-groups may spring into existence, and problems could arise when the sub-groups do not share the main group's objectives and prefer to pursue rather parochial interests.
- An odd number of members in a group is preferred over groups with an even number because this eliminates the possibility of a tie after votes are cast.
- Members may engage in "social loafing", whereby the average productivity of each member decreases. In other words, the productivity of the group as a whole is not at least equal to the sum of the productivity of each group member.

Explanations for social loafing embrace views such as, that if one perceives others in a group not pulling their weight then the perceiver adjusts his or her contribution downwards. In addition, diffusion of responsibility may take root. For example, because a group member realises that his or her contribution to the group effort is incapable of measurement, there is the temptation to ride on the back of the group and coast along at idling speed (Latane, Williams, & Harkins, 1979).

In recent years it has been suggested that social loafing is likely to occur in an individualistic culture dominated by self-interest, because it will maximise an individual's personal gain. An example of a society fitting this description is the United States. Social loafing is not expected to appear in collective societies (e.g. China) as it is believed that individuals in such cultures are motivated by group goals rather than self-interest. It was found in one study that the social loafing effect existed among American management trainees but not among their Chinese counterparts. The Chinese seemed to perform better in a group situation than working alone (Earley, 1989).

Therefore, it would appear that the social loafing effect is culture specific, being most prevalent in individualistic cultures. The most obvious way to counteract the effects of social loafing in work situations where co-operation is necessary is to make serious attempts to identify individual contributions.

Finally, many organisations might consider a group of five to seven to be ideal. However, hard evidence about an ideal size for groups is thin on the ground.

Leadership
Leadership is an important structural characteristic of a group. It can be both formal and informal.

Formal leadership is bestowed on the leader or manager of the group by the organisation with the authority to use rewards and sanctions. By contrast, an informal leader derives a mandate from the group members and usually reflects the group's values. In addition, the informal leader can be of practical assistance to members in a number of ways, including acting as spokesperson for the group. Rarely does one find formal and informal leadership residing in one person, though it is possible. The informal leadership role could be short-lived if the person lacks the ability and skills to exert influence in coping with the changing scene.

The current vogue is for "self-directed" groups, whereby leadership rotates naturally to the person best qualified to run specific parts of a task. However, this could present some real problems in terms of managing and appraising employees (Golzen, 1993). A discussion of leadership appears in Chapter 8.

Group Dynamics

A psychoanalytical view of the dynamics of a group recognises the group's emotional impact on the individual's behaviour because of considerations of conformity, loyalty, and identification with and reaction to the group. According to Freud, libidinal or sexual impulses are inhibited, and identification with the leader takes place, though this could lead to envy and competition between members for the chance to replace the leader (Freud, 1955). A discussion of the psychoanalytical view appears in Chapter 1 on personality.

It is conceivable that when the individual is acting alone, he or she is more reality-orientated and more efficient intellectually than when exposed to the stultifying effect of interaction in a group. From his observational experiments with groups of soldiers undergoing therapy, Bion (1961) refers to the unconscious contributions by members to the group mentality. For example, an atmosphere of hostility in a group does not come out of nowhere; members unconsciously contribute to it even though individually they may deny it. Bion recognises the existence of a mechanism existing below the surface of the group and made up of three functions, which has the express purpose of resolving group tensions. The three functions are flight or fight, dependency, and pairing:

1. *Flight or fight.* Although designed to protect the group and ensure its survival, this could be destructive. The group appears to want to fight somebody in the group, including the leader, or ignore issues by replacing them with anything other than the appropriate issues.

2. *Dependency*. The group is concerned with procedural matters (e.g. good committee practice) so that it can feel secure. The concern is to ensure that the group continues to exist and function in a predictable way.

3. *Pairing*. Two members of the group, one of whom could be the leader, enter into discussion, while the remaining members listen and are attentive. The matters under discussion could hinge on a change of leadership or a change in the direction of the group in order to improve its effectiveness.

Anxiety and discomfort can arise as a result of the flight or fight function, complacency and security can stem from dependency, and guilt can follow on from pairing because the group is not making headway in the task of changing the situation. Pressures are generated internally, arising from the dynamics of the group, as well as imposed externally—for example, nursing mentally handicapped patients in understaffed conditions. The psychoanalytical view emphasises the dysfunctional aspects of group dynamics, but it should be noted that the working life of the group is not always dominated by these pressures.

REASONS FOR JOINING GROUPS

People have a need to develop relationships with others, and therefore companionship is one reason why people join groups. Sometimes a job may not be very interesting, but belonging to a work group could provide the interest and diversity that is lacking in the job. When a person enters a new situation or encounters unfamiliar surroundings he or she may feel lost or lonely; it is in circumstances like these that a friendly group can be of immense benefit.

Another reason for joining a group is the need to identify with the group. Belonging to a group where one can share the experiences of one's immediate colleagues can be an important source of job satisfaction and, as a result, loyalty to the group can override loyalty to the organisation. The group may also provide a sympathetic ear when we experience tension or frustration. Likewise, we rely on the group to provide guidance on the correct behaviour to adopt in particular circumstances, or to provide answers to difficult questions. This could apply to an inexperienced recruit in an organisation.

People sometimes join groups in order to obtain power because they wish to control others or want the status that accompanies a leadership role. Some, however, have a desire to be dependent or submissive. Associating with others may not be prompted by a need for dependence; instead it may be a self-protection strategy employed by an individual when, for example, he or she joins a trade union. Finally, groups provide a refuge for those who seek a certain degree of anonymity in a social setting.

GROUP PROCESSES

Group processes are discussed by focusing on the following:

- reference groups;
- social comparison;
- co-action and affiliation;
- social control;
- decision making; and
- inter-group behaviour.

Groups can exert a powerful influence on the attitudes and behaviour of members. People are not only influenced by groups to which they currently belong, but also by reference groups, which they consult in arriving at an opinion or judgement.

Reference Groups

Reference groups may provide a normative or comparative reference point or both. They may not always be real groups; it may be a single individual who symbolises a group perspective on life, or it may be a group that never meets—e.g. "well-rounded people". A *normative* reference group is one from which the individual obtains certain standards. The individual is influenced by the norms, values, and attitudes of the group as well as its total outlook on life. The aspiring entrant to a profession, such as chartered accountancy, may be influenced profoundly by the persona of chartered accountants before being admitted to professional membership. This is referred to as *anticipatory socialisation*.

A *comparative* reference group is used as a focus when the individual compares the predicament and characteristics of members of the reference group with his or her own situation or that of his or her group. Reference groups chosen may be those seen as very similar to the individual's own group or those with which he or she can identify. These groups are important in determining whether the individual feels relatively satisfied or dissatisfied after engaging in the comparative exercise. Both normative and comparative reference groups may be used as positive frames of reference when the groups are admired or envied or, alternatively, as negative frames of reference from which individuals disassociate themselves, or which they reject.

In the study reported in the panel below, Newcombe (1943) concluded that a change in attitude is affected by the way in which an individual relates himself or herself to the total membership group and one or more reference groups within it.

A change in attitude could also depend on the strength of the initial attitude prior to exposure to group influences, the perceived discrepancy between the person's attitudes and the attitudes of members of the membership group, and the personality of the individual in the light of perceived pressures from the group. Therefore, a factory operative with regressive safety attitudes who works in a progressive safety environment may not necessarily be influenced by the enlightened

---

Reference Groups and Bennington College

Newcombe (1943) uses the "reference" concept in his study of women students at an expensive American residential college (Bennington College). In the 1930s most of the girls came from wealthy conservative families and, on arrival at college, held conservative political views. During their four-year stay at the college they were exposed to the more liberal or radical attitudes of the teaching staff and senior students. A feature of the educational approach at the college at that time was discussion of a wide range of social problems; in part this was prompted by the experience of the Great Depression and President Roosevelt's New Deal. There was also a belief that the girls should be exposed to issues affecting the contemporary world. Over the four years a number of the girls experienced a marked shift in their attitudes, from relatively conservative to relatively liberal.

How can this phenomenon be explained? Bennington College was the girls' membership group, but this in itself would not explain the shift towards attitudes held in high regard by the college. The crucial factor appears to be that the college community was taken as either a positive or negative reference group for the political attitudes of the students. The college community was taken as a negative reference group for the girls who remained conservative in outlook; they used the home or family group as a positive reference group. For some girls the college remained a negative reference group for political attitudes, but a positive reference group for social attitudes. But the vast majority of the students did alter their political outlook, taking the college as a positive reference group and possibly the parents and family as a negative reference group.

The girls who remained unaffected by the college's political attitudes may have had well thought out conservative opinions, rather than mere compliance with parental views, prior to joining the college. Alternatively, in the estimation of Newcomb, they were overdependent on their home and parents, or they had other interests and did not take either the college or home as a reference point for their political attitudes.

attitudes of his or her membership or reference group. Likewise, a stubborn and obstinate character may resist group pressures even though acceptance of such pressures could be beneficial to all concerned.

Reverting to the Bennington College study, Newcombe (1967) and his colleagues carried out a follow-up study 25 years later. They found that very few of the women had reverted to the conservative attitudes that they had on entering the college. The women and their husbands, where appropriate, expressed more liberal attitudes than a comparable sample of American women of the same socio-economic grouping. One interpretation of this finding might indicate that the college remained a vital reference group and focus in the lives of the women, and the persistence of their liberal views was assisted by their choice of spouse and friends.

Reference Groups and Marketing
Reference groups influence consumer behaviour in at least two ways. They set levels of aspiration for individuals by offering cues as to what life-style and related purchasing patterns they should strive to achieve. They also define the actual items considered acceptable for displaying this level of aspiration—i.e. the kind of housing, clothing, car, etc. appropriate for a member to retain his or her status in a group. Manufacturers place importance on getting their brand identified with a particular reference group, and advertisers have made effective use of reference groups in marketing a wide range of products.

The conspicuousness of a product is said to be the attribute that has the greatest general bearing on consumers as far as their susceptibility to reference group influence is concerned (Bourne, 1957). To be conspicuous the product must be seen and identified by others, and it must stand out and be noticed. To satisfy the second condition, wide ownership of the product must not prevail. A high-performance car is open to more reference group influence than fresh vegetables!

Advertisers have to be careful in the identification of the reference group. More than 20 years ago, a toothpaste company launched a new product in the UK aimed specifically at girls in their teens. The television advertisement alluded to a likely friendship between a member of a band and a girl at a dance hall. Unfortunately the band chosen had an image and musical style 10 years out of date. The next advertising campaign dropped this particular approach and reverted to a yachting scene featuring a much older girl (Oliver, 1980).

In addition to the conspicuous nature of the product, three other factors affect reference group influence:

1. The amount of information and experience that the individual can draw upon is important. Where the consumer has limited information and personal experience of the product, he or she may seek the advice of informed people or observe the behaviour of influential consumers or role models.
2. The perceived risk in purchasing the product may be significant. A group discussion can influence the amount of risk to accept in a purchase decision, and the amount of risk individuals are prepared to accept can be increased or reduced as a result of any discussions they may have with others whom they respect.
3. The greater the credibility of the reference group, as perceived by the individual, the greater the likelihood that its standards will be accepted (Schiffman & Kanuk, 1978).

Social Comparison

A reasonable degree of conformity, and hence predictability, is necessary for successful living in a social environment. When we find ourselves in a particular group situation, it is of immense value to have previously given some thought to what others consider the correct response to make in a particular situation—e.g. the best way to behave at an interview. Also, we may consider other people's views before deciding on the most suitable views to express on religious, social, and political issues, as well as the use of a particular vocabulary in conversation, or the most suitable clothes to wear at a party.

An able safety practitioner is continually comparing his or her views on safety with those of other experts in the field, as well as line managers who have something useful to say about the implementation of safety policy. It is natural for people to compare their own judgements on a particular issue with the judgement of others who are in close proximity to them so that they can check out the validity of these judgements.

Kelman (1961) identifies three processes of social influence that have an impact on the individual—compliance, identification, and internalisation (referred to in the previous chapter as the sources of attitude change):

- Compliance arises when individuals conform to the expectations of the group because the group has the power to reward them if they conform to the group's norms or values, and to punish them if they fail to do so.
- Identification refers to the process of adopting the characteristics of the group in order to sustain a valued relationship.
- Internalisation develops when individuals accept the group's influence because it appeals to their own values and can be instrumental in attaining personal goals.

These processes of social influence have been examined in relation to their influence on the evaluation of a brand of instant coffee (Burnkrant & Cousineau, 1975). People perceived the product more favourably after seeing others evaluate it favourably. The researchers, however, concluded that although people frequently buy products that others in their group buy, this purchase behaviour may not establish a role relationship with others (identification), or

lead to a reward or punishment mediated by others (compliance). But the evaluation of products by other people provides information about the products, and the idea of a "good product" may be derived from the group. This influence could be invaluable in comparing and contrasting different brands or products (internalisation).

Group Norms in Social Comparison

As a social comparative influence, norms in work groups can assume a position of significant importance. A deviation from significant norms may initially invite disapproval that amounts to no more than reminding the culprit that a deviation has taken place. Subsequently, disapproval may assume a stricter and harsher form. Norms, which were discussed earlier in connection with characteristics of groups, can relate to work targets, sharing of resources, and mutual help, and can be affected by events such as changes in work practices, rewards, and employment and economic circumstances.

The Bank Wiring Group, consisting of men engaged in wiring up telephone banks in the celebrated "Hawthorne studies", developed clear norms about what represented a fair day's work for a fair day's pay. The group set an output level below that which was possible, but that was, none the less, acceptable to management. Sanctions were used to denote disapproval when deviation from norms occurred. If a worker produced at a level far above the output norm, he was described as a "rate buster". Where the level of production was far below the output norm, the worker was described as a "chiseller". A norm unrelated to output was called "squealer", which meant that divulging information on colleagues to superiors was frowned upon. The pressure brought to bear on deviants to conform ranged from the use of derogatory names, to being ostracised, to "binging"—i.e. a hard blow on the upper arm. In addition, the Bank Wiring Group had a standard with respect to what was acceptable behaviour for those in positions of authority. As a consequence, the group applied social pressure on the inspectors and group supervisor to get them to conform to this standard (Roethlisberger & Dickson, 1939).

One of the findings in a study conducted by Lupton (1963) confirmed the Bank Wiring Group finding, but another finding did not. There was a restrictive productivity standard in one factory, *Jays*, engaged in light engineering, and all employees referred to it as the "fiddle". In the other factory, *Wye*, which was engaged in the manufacture of waterproof garments, each employee sought to maximise his or her earnings. Various explanations were put forward to account for the differences in group standards or norms. *Jays* operated in a stable market, had a history of union organisation, a predominantly male labour force with interdependent work, and relatively low labour costs. *Wye* operated in a small unstable market, had a weak union, a predominantly female labour force with independent tasks, and high labour costs. What appears to be fairly clear is that attempting to maximise earnings in one organisation was tantamount to deviant behaviour, but such behaviour in the other organisation amounted to conformist behaviour.

Group norms can also be related to accounting control systems. Standard costs, as part of the accounting system in an organisation, are typically used to evaluate individual performance. However, individuals may be faced with a conflict between the standards imposed by the formal organisation and the informal peer group. It is suggested that formal control systems, of which standard costing is part, should be consistent with group norms. Otherwise individuals will face conflicting requirements and some will certainly bow to small group pressure rather than conform to the organisation's formal requirements (Flamholtz, 1975). Therefore, the task for the accountant is to design systems that do not pit the individual against the group, and this necessitates basing the

system on group performance standards rather than individual standards. In examining congruency or fit between the requirements of the standard costing system and the small group, the accountant should be aware of variables such as group norms, cohesiveness, and control by members.

The Hawthorne and Lupton studies reported earlier deal with the technical or task-related aspects of group norms. But norms can also be social in nature ("social norms"). This was highlighted in the study of a small group in which the researcher was a participant (Roy, 1960). The group under observation was involved in simple and repetitive work (operating a punch during a long work day). Ritualistic behaviour emerged within the group, which was not apparent to the observer at first, and this became an important part of the group culture. For example, on a frequent basis the long day of boring work was interrupted by events that gave employees the opportunity to interact. The first interruption was "peach time" when one worker provided a pair of peaches for his colleague to eat. Invariably, there were then complaints about the quality of the fruit. "Banana time" followed peach time when the worker who brought in the peaches produced a banana intended to be consumed by himself. Every morning another worker would steal the banana, calling out "banana time", and would eat it while its owner made futile protests. Nevertheless, the latter continued to bring the bananas to work with the intention of consuming them, but never managed to do so. There were other forms of ritualistic behaviour of an inter-personal nature—e.g. "fish time", "cake time", and "window time". Ritualistic behaviour of the type described here can be used to counteract boredom at work, and make the passage through the day a little bit easier.

A classic study dealing with the emergence of group norms in ambiguous or uncertain conditions was conducted by Sherif (1936) (see panel facing). The study illustrates dramatically the powerful effects of group

Emergence of Group Norms in Uncertain Situations

Individuals who participated in the experiment were given the job of judging the apparent movements of a stationary pinpoint of light. When the light is viewed in a completely dark room, without any reference points, it appears to move. This is a phenomenon known as the "autokinetic effect". Perception of the magnitude of this movement varies from individual to individual and is influenced by psychological factors residing in the person.

When individuals work alone on different occasions, each develops a stable perception of the light. One individual may perceive relatively little movement (e.g. a few centimetres) in a particular direction, whereas another individual may perceive a large movement in a different direction. An individual norm or standard develops and this is repeated consistently from one episode of the experiment to another.

When individuals work in groups of two or three, announcing their judgements aloud without any collusion between them, each individual is affecting the other's judgement. Gradually, group norms (shared expectations) rather than individual norms or standards are established. The group norm tends to reflect a compromise between the individual norms, whereby extreme estimates of the movement of the light are moderated. Individuals who had previous experience of the autokinetic phenomenon, and had established their own individual norms, gradually gave them up in response to the behaviour of the group. In fact, the group norms persisted even after the individuals were allowed subsequently to work on their own. A more rapid acceptance of group norms occurred among individuals who had no experience of the experiment before becoming a member of the group. As before, these group norms persisted in the period when individuals later worked alone (Sherif, 1936).

membership on the individual and has some fascinating features. The individual has negligible past experience that can be applied in judging the position of the pinpoint of light. There is the absence of a yardstick, ambiguity is present and, as a consequence, the individual is highly dependent upon others in arriving at judgements. In everyday life this happens with different degrees of ambiguity, but in many situations each of us usually has some past experience (knowledge, facts, beliefs, values, attitudes) that forms a basis for our judgement.

In a laboratory study (Venkatesan, 1966), where subjects were asked to evaluate and choose the best suit from three identical men's suits, it was concluded that individuals who are exposed to a group norm will tend to conform to that norm in a decision-making situation that confronts them when no objective standards are available. However, if the individual's freedom is threatened by being induced to comply with a group norm, then there will be a lesser tendency to conform. The marketing implications of this study would indicate that when objective evaluation is difficult consumers accept information on product quality or style provided by their peer, or reference, groups.

Thus peer groups, friends, and acquaintances may be a major source of influence and information that deserves our attention at the stage of buying major products or services. But any attempt to restrict the independent choice of the consumer may be resisted under certain conditions. For example, a neighbour or relative may sell you an idea about a product, but not necessarily the brand to buy or the store to patronise because this advice could very well be ignored (Cohen, 1981).

Even when a situation is clear-cut, where conditions of uncertainty are absent, a group can exert a significant influence on the judgements of the individual. This would be particularly noticeable in situations where one individual is in the minority, and the majority holds a view that is contrary to the view of reality held by the individual.

In a well-known study conducted by Asch (1952), groups of eight individuals each had the job of comparing a series of standard lines with several alternatives. They were then required to announce, in the presence of the investigator, which of the alternative lines was the same length as the standard line in each case. Unknown to the one genuine subject in each group, seven individuals colluded with the investigator; each of them was secretly instructed on exactly how to respond. They offered the same incorrect answer before it was the turn of the genuine subject to pass comment. From this experiment emerged the sobering thought that, for one-third of the time, the genuine subjects were prepared to deny the information being conveyed by their senses and shifted their judgements, thereby making an error, so as to conform with the group norm or standard.

It is interesting to note that before the group task, each individual performed on a solo basis with virtually no errors. This suggests that perceiving the similarity or otherwise of the paired lines was not a particularly difficult task and errors can hardly be attributed to an ambiguous stimulus.

After the experiments, the researcher confronted each individual who had succumbed to group pressure or influence with the fact that they had yielded to the group in the specified instances. When faced with their mistaken judgements, some individuals admitted that they had realised the seven other members of the group were wrong, but the unanimity in outlook of these members led them to experience severe distress about being deviant, which culminated in yielding to the perceived pressure. Others reported experiencing equal distress but, sensing the considerable weight of evidence against them, concluded they must have misunderstood the instructions and were wrong. A small proportion of those who succumbed to group influence were amazed at discovering their errors, and reported not being aware of any conflict and could not recall being influenced by other group members.

Here we observe three quite different processes of social influence:

1. There is the threat of disapproval or rejection because one is a deviant, and it is up to the person to cope with the stress brought about by ignoring the group pressure, or to succumb to group pressure and avoid the stress.
2. There is the threat arising from doubts about whether the requirements of the task have been correctly interpreted. This could give rise to a search for confirmation or disconfirmation of the accuracy of one's judgement, and, dependent on the outcome of this search, yielding or not yielding to the group.
3. There is an attempt to neutralise the threat by denial or repression without being aware of this and, as a consequence, accommodating oneself to the wishes of the group.

Apparently the subjects who did not yield to group pressure, and who remained independent, were those who experienced the greatest stress and discomfort. However, this condition was substantially alleviated when the genuine subject was supported by an ally (another genuine subject). Also, a growth in the minority representation—i.e. another genuine subject joining the group—gave rise to a lesser degree of compliance with the group judgement.

Whether the individual yields to the group or resists it is likely to depend on the clarity of the stimulus (i.e. the degree of similarity of the paired lines), whether or not the genuine subject is the only deviant from the group norm, and the personality disposition of the genuine subject. A genuine subject, acting on his or her own, who perceives only a small difference between the standard and alternative lines, and acts invariably in a conformist way, may side with the group judgement.

Group influence may be particularly important in budgeting discretionary costs. These costs would be associated with non-programmable and non-routine tasks and would cover areas such as advertising, research and development, training, and so on. There is no optimal solution as to the amount to spend and there is considerable latitude for the use of judgement in the determination of discretionary costs. The group may exert pressure to achieve uniformity of opinion or consensus, even though this may not be the most appropriate way to act in given circumstances.

In accordance with Asch's conclusions, a solitary voice of dissent within the budgeting group may yield to the majority view in circumstances when such a course of action is unwise. But a growth in the minority view may add strength to a position of justifiable resistance. Therefore this may suggest a vote in favour of heterogeneity in group composition so as to increase the likelihood that minority viewpoints will have at least some peer group support, and not face unanimous opposition in the budgeting process. It may also suggest the need for group leaders to develop a group norm embracing the encouragement of responsible disagreement. The importance of minority influence as an enriching experience has been recognised in the literature in recent years (Nemeth, 1986).

The conformity hypothesis has been discussed in the context of the psychology of the stock market (Eachus, 1988). Because investors are presented with a mass of competing investment opportunities, and are uncertain on how to act, they look around to see what others are doing. For example, when a share price is rising, or the stock market is bullish, it is very difficult for individual investors to resist the pressure to behave as they believe others are behaving.

Co-action and Affiliation

Being in the company of others has a material bearing on the behaviour of the individual. In emergency situations it is said that we are more likely to respond quickly if we are on our own than if we are in a co-active situation in the presence of another person (Latane &

Darley, 1968). When we are in the presence of others in a group situation, we are inclined to leave it to other members and, if they do not react, perhaps the situation is perceived as not being serious enough. Until we see others acting in a decisive way, there may be a reluctance to act because of the lack of clarity surrounding what is happening. This may occur in an emergency situation when life or property is at risk. If an individual experiences smoke in a room, he or she is likely to respond fairly quickly. However, if a group is confronted with the same stimulus, rapid response may be less likely because of the inclination to discuss the nature of the threat and how to tackle it (Zajonc & Sales, 1966).

In the company of others, be they colleagues or observers, we tend to get aroused and this creates a state of drive that manifests itself in a behavioural response (Latane & Darley, 1968). If the observer of the behaviour is an expert who evaluates the subject's performance, the behavioural response of the subject is likely to be greater; in these circumstances the subject is likely to be apprehensive. A lesser behavioural response is likely when the audience consists of peers who are watching out of interest, and the least behavioural response was noted when subjects acted on their own (Henchy & Glass, 1968). Imagine a situation when your own performance as a student or worker is being evaluated by an expert in your field!

Do people prefer the company of others to remaining in isolation? A classic experiment conducted by Schachter (1959), who was concerned with the concept of affiliation, may throw some light on this question (see panel overleaf). The results suggest that people affiliate with others when suffering from fear. Why should this be? Perhaps they want to compare their situation with others to see if their fears are justified. Apparently people are likely to reduce their anxieties while waiting for a painful experience, but more so when waiting in the company of others, irrespective of whether the people in the group communicate (Wrightsman, 1960).

Affiliation and Fear

Groups of college girls in an American university were selected to participate in an experiment in a mythical Department of Neurology. They were greeted on arrival by Dr. Gregor Zilstein, the psychologist performing the experiment, who wore a white coat and used a stethoscope. This image was intentional in order to influence the students' behaviour.

The psychologist told the girls that they were about to receive electric shocks that would be either painful (but would do no permanent harm) or not painful, and in either case the electric shock would resemble more of a tickle or a tingle than anything unpleasant. The key question was what the girls would do in this frightening situation. They were told to choose whether to wait with other girls or alone, and to state their preference on a questionnaire. It should be noted that the instructions the girls received, and the presence of the doctor with his apparatus was merely a deception, in order to make the subjects feel afraid.

When the girls experienced strong fear, they generally preferred to wait with others, and they preferred to wait alone in conditions of low fear (Schachter, 1959).

Sometimes it is argued that knowledge about what might happen in a future fearful event could have a beneficial effect. For example, uncertainty as to the outcome of a visit to a hospital for a medical check-up is obviously a factor that contributes to anxiety. From this one might conclude that increasing a patient's knowledge and understanding of what is going to happen reduces uncertainty, and in turn reduces the level of distress and anxiety.

The latter statement was subjected to testing in a research study consisting of a sample of 40 women undergoing colposcopy (a diagnostic investigation for the detection of cervical cancer). Half the group received a 20-minute verbal and visual presentation of what they were to expect in terms of the medical procedures they would go through and the likely range and intensity of sensations they would experience. The other half received much less information, although the same amount of time was devoted to the talk. Various techniques were used to obtain the views of the women at different stages—i.e. after the information-giving stage (the briefing session), after the medical examination, and after the women returned home (Miller & Magnan, 1983). Surprisingly, the group that received the most information showed increases in anxiety and tension after the briefing session. This level of anxiety and tension decreased somewhat after the medical examination, but still was only marginally below the level that prevailed prior to the briefing session.

How can we explain this result? First, the research took place within a short space of time, with the information-giving (briefing) and the medical examination carried out at one session. This may not have allowed the women sufficient time to integrate and synthesise the information. Second, it seems that the information was presented to the women in a one-way communication mode in a formal setting without the women having a chance to ask questions or to check out their understanding (Harvey, 1988), as they would be able to do if a discussion group was used. In exercises of this type, it is suggested that comprehensive information, previously distributed in booklet form well in advance of hospitalisation, together with checking whether the patient has received, understood, and acted on the information presented, is a wise course of action. In such circumstances, one can expect to find a real reduction in anxiety after a briefing session based on the giving of comprehensive information (Wallace, 1986).

Social Control

In social control the influence is exercised from above on a vertical basis, rather than on a horizontal basis as in social comparison. Experiments on obedience to authority, such as the famous study by Milgram (1965), have shown that a significant number of people are prepared to inflict pain on others because an authority figure instructs them to do so. Subjects representing a cross-section of the population in an American university town were induced to inflict pain and danger on other people by increasingly large doses of electric shock as a punishment for making mistakes in a learning experiment. Those at the receiving end of the electric shocks—the victims—protested in a dramatic fashion and pleaded for the experiments to cease.

This put the subjects into an awkward and difficult position. They had to cope with the demands of the experimenter to continue with the experiment, the pleas of the victims for the experiment to cease, and the demands of their own conscience. A number of people refused to take part in the experiments, and some withdrew after administering a small dose of electric shock. However, others continued to participate and, though troubled by their participation, they accepted the experimenter's logic that it is legitimate to administer electric shock to a learner who makes mistakes.

When colleagues of the experimenter were present, and they refused to continue with the experiments, this gave subjects encouragement to do likewise in most situations. The effects of group pressure are evident in this situation. The behaviour of the colleagues of the experimenter conveyed to the subjects that first of all disobedience is possible, that no adverse consequences stem from disobedience, and anyway the act of giving a victim an electric shock is improper. The good news is that the electric shocks were not real, though the subjects were not aware of this during the experiment. The cries of the victim's distress came from a tape recorder which was activated by pressing the "shock" lever. When victims were visible to the subject, through a glass partition, the role of the victim was played by an actor.

What was surprising in this series of experiments was the number of people who were prepared to administer electric shocks to somebody who made a mistake in a learning experiment. Another striking aspect of the experiment was that the subjects were in a situation where demands were made on them while they could not compare themselves with somebody in a similar situation. As such, the conditions of the experiment do not correspond with those found in formal organisations.

It is worth noting the operation of social comparison in one phase of the experiments. This occurred when colleagues of the experimenter decided to challenge his authority. From this incident we may conclude that social comparison may play an exceedingly important part in limiting the potency of demands from authority figures.

Milgram's aim was to establish conditions under which a person would blindly carry out the orders of another, even when the task was objectionable and the orders could not be supported by any kind of reasoning. He saw his research as contributing to a reduction of the threat of totalitarian authority systems. His critics felt that he should not have exposed his subjects to the stress they experienced from participating in the experiments, and that studies of such destructive forms of obedience are open to misuse by totalitarian authority figures. Nowadays the ethics of research of this nature is a live issue, and many scholars would subscribe to the view that it is important to protect participants in research studies from threatening or traumatic experiences. The question of deception is also important in this context.

Other forms of social control are institutional control and brainwashing. In institutional control the inmate in a prison is frequently stripped of personal props to his or her identity. For example, personal clothing and furniture are not permitted, the mail can be controlled, and frequent association with relatives and friends is not allowed (Goffman, 1961). In brainwashing there is an attempt to undermine people's stability of mind and self-image by not permitting them to relate to friends or identify with their normal group. This is achieved by measures such as segregating members of the group, prohibiting group formation, fomenting mutual distrust, manipulating the news so that only the bad news gets through, and finally exposing the individual to the desired message in a state of social isolation (Schein, 1956).

Individual differences have to be taken into account when considering the degree of difficulty in altering a person's values. It would be more difficult to induce sincere Catholic missionaries to renounce their faith than to persuade army conscripts who are peace-loving civilians at heart to renounce their country's involvement in an unpopular war. Some manipulative measures manage to secure compliance only, but not identification and internalisation. The value of this type of social control is lost when the individual returns to his or her old environment, but in severe situations the effect of coercive persuasion cannot be reversed.

Decision Making

Models of decision making and constraining influences (individual and organisational) were discussed in Chapter 5. Using groups to make decisions has been both strongly endorsed and seriously questioned by behavioural scientists and managers. From early studies of group dynamics the implication appears to be that people are more likely to accept new ideas from their colleagues and leader in the course of discussion than from a leader telling them what to do. It is believed that the individual sees a clearer picture of the situation and, as a consequence, feels involved in the decisions, and finds it easy to bow to the will of the group.

This involvement is considered effective when the focus is on overcoming resistance to change. It is claimed that group discussion makes better use of the available talent or abilities of members. It promotes acceptability

of decisions because people have had the opportunity to raise their anxieties or concerns in connection with the problems under discussion. Also, it is considered a democratic way of going about things, although this could be somewhat invalidated if the information put before the group is chosen selectively.

The early studies referred to at the start of this section were conducted by Lewin (1958). Groups of housewives were persuaded to buy cheaper, unattractive cuts of meat, which were nutritional, to help economise as part of the war effort.

Interesting and attractive lectures were given with supporting leaflets, emphasising the vitamin and mineral value of offal as well as stressing the health and economic aspects of this type of food, with hints about the preparation of dishes.

In the method devoted to group discussion a different approach was adopted. The group leader explained the link between diet and the war effort and the discussion focused on the reasons why housewives were not keen to experiment with cheap foods (hearts, kidneys, etc).

It was found that 32% of those who discussed the issues in a group said a week later that they had served at least one of the dishes recommended by their group, but only 3% of the housewives who attended the lectures took the minimum advice of the lecturer. Is the lecture an unsuitable medium in these circumstances? The listener is generally in a passive role, using personal experience to accept or reject the proposals advocated by the lecturer; the listener is generally ignorant of what others are going to decide and there is no "new social norm" to offer guidance.

By contrast, in the discussion group, people are encouraged to exchange views and consider the merits and demerits of buying different cuts of meat. There is an acknowledgement that other people have a valid point of view, and this could lessen a resistance to change. The advisability of buying offal is discussed openly, and recipes are introduced when the housewives are mentally prepared for a change. The decision that emerges from the discussion becomes a norm, and when members publicly support the group's decision this can consolidate the individual's intention to buy and, in effect, change her purchasing behaviour.

Lewin accepts the power of group decisions in influencing individual behaviour. To him, the exercise of freedom of choice rather than high pressure salesmanship is critical. In the discussion group a minority position (to buy the cheap meat) developed into a majority position. In fact the previous majority position (not to buy the cheap meat) could now be considered deviant.

One particular facet of this experiment should be noted, which is that the advocated new behaviour (save money and assist the war effort) was obviously an attractive proposition.

In some organisational settings, efforts are made to change the individual's outlook, and group decision making may be used as a vehicle to achieve this objective. In a study adopting similar methods to those used by Lewin, housewives were encouraged to consume greater quantities of fresh and evaporated milk (Radke & Klisurich, 1958). It was found that the group discussion was more effective in changing behaviour than the lecture. The influence of the personality of the leader of the discussion group was considered not to be an influential factor. The group was drawn from the same neighbourhood, and unlike the Red Cross Group in Lewin's experiment, members of the neighbourhood group were not members of a club meeting regularly. This might suggest that group decision making can be effective in ad hoc groups.

Lewin is of the view that group discussion could be used as an important method of bringing about social change which is potentially adaptive. However, group discussion as a method could be undermined (as is shown later in the analysis of "groupthink") if the discussion is limited and the group leader manipulates proceedings in a manner that is contrary to the interests of the group.

Group decision making is not without its limitations. Assembling a group can consume much time, and reaching a decision may be a more prolonged exercise than if individuals did so on their own.

There may be a tendency to conform too readily to social pressures, and domination by a few individuals in a group situation is not uncommon. The latter could be particularly disadvantageous if the members concerned are of below average ability. Responsibility for the final outcome of group deliberations is ambiguous, unlike a situation when a single individual is responsible for a decision and it is clear who is accountable.

In comparing groups with individuals to establish who is best at decision making, it appears that the effectiveness of either will depend on the criteria (e.g. accuracy, speed, creativity, acceptance) used. With regard to accuracy, there is evidence to indicate that groups outperform the average individual in the group (Michaelsen, Watson, & Black, 1989), but the most accomplished individual in the group is likely to outperform the group (Miner, 1984). With regard to speed, the individual is likely to be superior to the group, but the group appears to be superior to the individual on creativity and acceptance of the final decision. However, as stated earlier, groups can fall short of standards of efficiency (e.g. time spent arriving at a decision) normally associated with individual decision making.

Types of Decision-making Group
Management has to give thought to devising the best format for a group faced with problems solving and decision making. Three formats for decision making are suggested— interacting, nominal, and delphi groups (Van de Ven & Delbecq, 1974).

Interacting Groups.   These groups are widely used and involve members interacting in the process of generating ideas about ways of tackling a problem, leading eventually to a group decision using majority voting if necessary. These groups suffer from the deficiencies associated with group functioning discussed elsewhere in this chapter.

Nominal Groups. Discussion is restricted during the decision-making process. Members physically present at the meeting state their opinions independently with respect to the problem before the discussion takes place, and remain silent in relation to such opinions during the discussion. Hence the term nominal to describe groups of this type. The procedure adopted after presenting the problem to the group is as follows:

- Before discussion takes place, each member writes on paper his or her ideas about the problem under review.
- Then each member in turn presents one idea to the group, using a flipchart or blackboard. There is no discussion at this stage.
- Next, the group discusses the ideas presented, with the emphasis on clarity and evaluation.
- Finally, each member reverts to silence and ranks independently the ideas already presented to the group. The idea with the highest aggregate ranking constitutes the final decision.

A particular advantage of nominal groups is that independent thinking in a group situation is cultivated, unlike the circumstances in interacting groups.

Delphi Groups. These groups bear a similarity to nominal groups, except for the fact that members do not meet face-to-face. The following procedure is used:

- Members are told what the problem is and asked to provide a solution. This is done through a structured questionnaire approach.

- The questionnaire is completed independently by each member whose anonymity is maintained.
- The responses of all members are tabulated and each member receives a copy of the set of results covering all responses.
- After having an opportunity to see the range and types of answers, each member is asked again to provide an answer to the original problem. At this stage an individual could change his or her solution.
- The last two steps could be repeated until a consensus position is arrived at.

Delphi groups, like nominal groups, require limited exposure to group influence, but in the case of nominal groups there is a forum for discussion. Delphi groups have a certain appeal when group members are scattered geographically and it would be expensive for them to meet at a central location. However, they consume a lot of time and certainly are not appropriate when a quick decision is necessary. Because of the absence of interaction, obviously there is a total lack of useful insights which could emanate only from discussion and from people bouncing ideas off each other.

As an overview of the three group formats, reference will now be made to the conclusions of a study conducted by Van de Ven and Delbecq (1974). They maintain that the nominal and delphi groups are more effective than the normal discussion group in problem situations where the pooled judgement of a group of people is necessary. In particular, nominal groups are suitable for situations where people can come together without much difficulty, and for problems needing data that can be produced quickly. By contrast, delphi groups are suitable for situations where the cost and inconvenience of people congregating in one place is high, and for problems that do not require immediate solutions.

Risky Shift

Is there a danger that a group is more conservative and cautious than an individual in arriving at decisions and, as a result, may produce poorer decisions? Or, alternatively, are groups prepared to take greater risks? Apparently, some groups are prepared to take greater risks than are individuals, and this is known as the "risky shift" phenomenon (Stoner, 1961). The following is an item from a questionnaire on choice dilemma used for measuring risk taking (Kogan & Wallach, 1967).

A corporation, dealing in light metals, is prosperous and has considered seriously the possibility of expanding its business by building an additional plant in a new location. It is faced with a dilemma of choice. It can build a new plant in the home country which is politically stable, and where a moderate return on the initial investment could be achieved; or, it could build a plant in a foreign country where there are lower labour costs and easy access to raw materials. The latter action would mean a much higher return on the initial investment, but there is a history of political instability and revolution in the foreign country. In addition, the leader of a small minority party in the foreign country is committed to nationalising all foreign investments.

As finance director, imagine you are advising the chief executive of the corporation. Several probabilities or odds of continued political stability in the foreign country under consideration are listed in Table 7.1, and you are asked to tick the lowest probability that you would consider acceptable in order for the chief executive to go ahead and build the new plant in that country.

The dilemma is a two-choice situation where the finance director is faced with a choice between a risky but highly desirable course of action, and a cautious but less desirable one. Failure in terms of the risky alternative can be assumed to lead to very unfavourable consequences. For the risky choice there are two possible consequences: (1) the probability of political stability and no nationalisation; or (2) the probability of political instability and nationalisation. In Table 7.1, a 1 in 10 chance represents a risky choice whereas a 9 in 10 chance represents a cautious one.

When business executives decided on the ranking of investment projects, in a study outside the normal risky shift research studies, they agreed as a group to take more risky decisions than they had chosen as individuals. An appropriate question to ask at

TABLE 7.1

Choice Dilemma Questionnaire: Probabilities of Political Stability

Tick the lowest probability that, as finance director, you would consider acceptable for the chief executive to decide to build a new plant in the foreign country.

The chances that the foreign country will remain politically stable are:

1 in 10	_____
3 in 10	_____
5 in 10	_____
7 in 10	_____
9 in 10	_____

Or tick here if you feel that the chief executive should not build, no matter what the probabilities _____

this stage is whether people would generally be more willing to take risks in their behaviour when decisions are for real in the world of work?

What aspects of the group's experience account for the risky shift phenomenon? Before a consensus is reached certain aspects of the group discussion are important:

- An upward influence on the level of risk an individual proposes to take emanates from information about the risks other members in the group are prepared to take.
- The emotional interaction arising from the discussion may create a disposition for a shift towards risk to take place.
- The act of committing oneself to a group decision is tantamount to lifting the burden off one's shoulders and transferring it to the group and, in the process, the commitment becomes more risky. Because each member feels less personal responsibility for a potential loss, consensus is likely to move towards acceptance of more risk (Wallach & Kogan, 1965).

Cautious Shift.   It is also suggested that there may be a possibility of a "cautious shift" in group decision making, and this would coexist with a risky shift. For example, certain items under review might be interpreted in a cautious direction after the discussion, whereas other items are biased towards risk. In other circumstances, risk taking may be ingrained in the culture of the members of the group. In such a case, cultural values could act as a filtering process whereby information generated by the group discussion is interpreted in a particular way. For example, risk-taking business executives from the US engaged in committee deliberations to justify a decision, may select observations arising from the discussion that support their cultural disposition. On the other hand, cautious business executives from the UK may place a different interpretation on the group discussion. In the former case it is likely that

persuasive arguments favoured risk, and in the latter case they favoured a conservative view.

Risky or cautious shifts are referred to as "group polarisation". Isenberg (1986) stresses the importance of the influence of the group (in terms of social comparison and persuasion) in promoting group polarisation.

Cohesion and Loyalty
Sometimes the advantages of group decision making are undermined by powerful psychological pressures resulting from members working closely together and sharing the same set of values. At a time of crisis this puts people under considerable stress. Where a group is cohesive—that is, the group is very important to its members or they have a strong need to stay in it—a high level of conformity can be demanded of members. The conformity is likely to express itself in loyalty to the group, even in circumstances when the policies of the group are malfunctioning. A detailed discussion of cohesiveness appeared earlier in the chapter.

There are occasions, for example, when group loyalty makes a mockery of accident prevention (see panel facing).

Groupthink
It has been suggested by a perceptive observer of the functioning of in-groups that as a group becomes excessively close-knit and develops a strong feeling of "we-ness", it becomes vulnerable to a pattern of behaviour known as groupthink (Janis, 1972). When consensus seeking becomes a dominant force, groupthink develops; this is a thinking process that tends to push aside a realistic appraisal of alternative courses of action. It is the outcome of group pressure, impeding the efficient execution of members' mental faculties and interfering with members' ability to test reality and preserve their judgement. Groupthink amounts to an unintentional erosion of one's critical faculties as a result of adopting group norms. This is to be distinguished from a similar occurrence as a

---

Group Loyalty and Accident Prevention

In one particular case, the function of factory units was to modify rod-shaped machine tools by cutting or banding them (Chapman, 1982). Before modifying them, one end of each pen-sized tool was dipped in a protective molten plastic substance. After modification some of the tools were sandblasted to make them look better. Almost every one of these actions was undertaken in a grossly unsafe manner.

One Monday the manager told six of his subordinates to make the place presentable because the Factory Inspector was coming round. Three of them were asked to tidy up around the machine and the other three to pick up the boxes of machine tools from the gangway and place them on a long bench.

The manager told the group that they could replace the boxes as soon as the visit was over, and gave them a wink, because the bench was required for other things. The Inspector seemed to be viewed as an enemy. The men grumbled about the visit, but the manager said, "Surely we don't want people like Inspectors finding fault with our unit, lads!" This prompted jokes about setting booby traps for the Inspector.

When the Inspector left, there was evidence of a lot of anti-safety behaviour. This behaviour would suggest that there appeared to be mindless devotion to the group, particularly in the face of an outside authority figure with powers of sanction.

---

result of external threats of social punishment. Although groupthink is more likely to affect cohesive in-groups, this is not always the case, and is particularly unlikely to be so where an atmosphere of critical inquiry is a normal feature of the decision-making approach.

The outward signs of groupthink are likely to manifest themselves in a number of ways. Members of groups formed to make decisions show a tendency to be lenient in their judgement of the ideas of their leader or fellow members for fear of being ostracised or disciplined. They go so far as being unnecessarily strict with themselves, placing controls on their own freedom of thought. There is an amiable atmosphere with an absence of aggravation so as to retain the comfortable "we-feeling". As cohesiveness in the group continues to develop, there is a strong urge on the part of each member to avoid "rocking the boat" and this can be instrumental in persuading the individual to accept whatever proposals are promoted by the leader or a majority of the group's members.

On the face of it, the scope for deviant thought is considerable in a highly cohesive group; nevertheless, the desire for consensus on all important issues is so prevalent as to discourage the individual from utilising this advantage. When groupthink is forcefully present, deviant thoughts are relegated to insignificance by individuals establishing that their own reservations are not so overwhelming after all and should be set aside, and that the benefit of the doubt with regard to the remaining uncertainties should be given to the group so as to promote consensus.

Also, perhaps agreeing is considered more beneficial than the insecurity that is likely to be created should the individual suffer rejection because of persistent deviant thoughts. Groupthink places greatest emphasis on team-work with an inherent striving for unanimity within the collective membership. This presents a number of difficulties ranging from over-optimism and lack of vigilance to ineffectiveness and lack of realism in the formulation and implementation of policy. Janis (1972) proposes the following key characteristics of groupthink:

- illusion of invulnerability;
- belief in the rectitude of the group;
- negative views of competitors;
- sanctity of group consensus;
- illusion of unanimity; and
- erecting a protective shield.

Illusion of Invulnerability. Many, if not all, members of the in-group share an illusion of invulnerability. This has some reassuring effect as regards obvious dangers, and is responsible for members becoming over-optimistic and keen to take unjustifiable risks. It also causes them to fail to respond to clear warning signals. Here the group displays an unshaken belief in its endorsed course of action, and in the face of information or views to the contrary its belief remains intact. The group goes as far as discounting warnings or negative feedback by indulging in rationalisations of its action on a collective basis.

Inevitably this leads to a reconsideration and renewed commitment to both the underlying assumptions of policy pursued and the policy itself. A further line of action might be reflected in an approach whereby evidence to support the status quo is chosen selectively from any available source or, if necessary, by inventing specious forecasts. Some members of the group or committee may be aware of the misgivings of an outsider about the wisdom of pursuing the policy in question, but display a reluctance to voice concern. Where the group believes it is invulnerable, this can reduce anxiety about taking risks.

The following is an example of a situation where an employee performing a staff role encounters the illusion of invulnerability. An accountant acting in an advisory capacity may find that members of a management committee fail to respond to clear warning signals with regard to the financial advisability of pursuing a particular course of action. Because of the illusion of invulnerability, the group discounts the warnings and engages in collective rationalisation in order to maintain its view or belief.

Belief in the Rectitude of the Group. There will develop an unquestionable belief in the morality or self-righteousness of the in-group. In this way members can choose to ignore the ethical or moral consequences of the decisions taken. A war cabinet, having placed the minimisation of civilian casualties high on its priority list, may find it easier to prosecute or escalate the war without feelings of guilt. In much the same way a working party or committee within an organisation, having reached a decision to introduce a scheme related to quality circles or industrial democracy, may appeal to the justness and ethical nature of the scheme when fully operational—i.e. it provides employees with potential benefits.

A member whose doubts, following consideration of the scheme, are committed to writing, is likely to suppress them when attending meetings. When an outsider is invited to express his or her observations on the feasibility or otherwise of the scheme, the chairperson is likely to be quick off the mark when the speaker finishes, and to move on to the next item on the agenda if the speaker's observations express misgivings or doubts. At crucial meetings the obvious tactic would be for the chairperson or leader not to call on the doubters to speak. Instead, an attempt would be made to tame the doubters, and in any case not to permit them to go so far as questioning the fundamental assumptions of strategy. This would be particularly so if the doubters are members of the in-group.

Negative Views of Competitors. There is a tendency to subscribe to negative stereotyped views of the leaders of enemy or competitor groups. Here we find the prevailing attitude of mind supporting the view that these leaders are either too weak or too stupid to meet the challenge of the in-group. In a military campaign this disposition could create an underestimation of the numerical strength of the enemy, or a totally inaccurate assessment of their true intentions. For example, it is reported that because of the rigid attachment of President Johnson's advisers to the domino theory, they ignored the nationalistic yearnings of the North Vietnamese and their wish to ward off the Chinese. Similarly, it was suggested by a social scientist in Britain, who has made a special study of decision making, that the UK government did not pick up certain critical signals prior to the Falklands War (Heller, 1983). Similarities to the military analogy can be found within organisations among groups competing for scarce resources, and in an external context when policy-making groups make certain assumptions about the quality of the company's competitors.

Sanctity of Group Consensus.   There appears to be a natural tendency to steer clear of a deviation from what is perceived as group consensus. Members sharing this disposition remain reticent about personal misgivings or doubts and, in addition, are quite capable of convincing themselves of the lack of substance in these doubts. Outside the group situation, in the corridor or dining room, such people may, however, feel strongly about the issues in question and convey the antithesis of their true feelings on the matter at the meeting. These individuals may subsequently feel guilty for having kept silent, but it is probable that the circumstances surrounding the group discussion were such as to permit only the raising of matters of minor importance.

Illusion of Unanimity.   The illusion of unanimity creates the belief that all members' judgements are unanimous when they subscribe to the majority view. No doubt unanimity is fostered when members are insulated from outside views between meetings, and where the emerging majority view reflects the declared choice of an influential figure (e.g. the chief executive) in the organisation. The presumption of unanimity is upheld when members remain silent. There is an almost unstated assumption that members who respect each other will arrive at a unanimous view. The result of this proneness to validate group consensus is, in the absence of disagreements among members, the sweeping away of critical thinking and testing of reality. This can lead to serious errors of judgement, though it could

be argued that the mutual bolstering of self-esteem and morale, which emanates from the process of seeking agreement, enhances the group's capacity to take action.

A range of divergent views about the riskiness of the preferred course of action could be mildly traumatic. The existence of disagreement could give rise to anxieties about the likelihood of making a serious error, and once unanimity is severely dented it is difficult to remain confident about the correctness of the group decision. The onus then falls on members to confront the uncertainties and assess the seriousness of the risks. Therefore, to eradicate this painful state, members are inclined, without realising it, to prevent latent disagreements from coming to the surface, particularly when they are proposing to initiate a risky adventure.

However, a nagging doubt may persist if information about difficulties surfaces and is provided by a previous supporter of the group who is of high calibre. There now develops a movement towards emphasising areas of convergence in thinking at the cost of fully exploring divergencies that might expose unresolved issues. The illusion of unanimity is maintained simply because, generally speaking, the major participants in the group discussion fail to reveal their own reasoning or discuss their assumptions or reservations.

An overview of the processes involved in the making of an investment decision by a policy group in a public corporation, screened on British television some years ago, provided ample evidence of unnatural striving for unanimity engineered by the chairman of the corporation. The rationale for his preference was not always clearly stated, but alternative solutions that challenged the preferred solution seemed to be all too easily discredited and discarded in circumstances that justified more serious consideration of them.

Erecting a Protective Shield.   Groupthink has the effect of erecting a shield to protect the leader and fellow members from adverse information that might shatter their shared complacency about the morality and effectiveness of past decisions. This situation arises when an influential group member calls a doubter or dissenter to one side and advises him or her on the desirability of backing the leader and the group.

Where outside expert opinion is sought, invariably the chairperson will retort by questioning the legitimacy of the assumption underlying it, or ensuring that insufficient time is devoted to discussing it, finally stating why the original decision seems to be a wise one. This type of behaviour manifested itself in the investment decision process referred to earlier, and can also be seen in the following example.

An accountant may be asked to submit a financial appraisal of a project to which the chief executive has a total commitment. Having presented the report, the accountant is horrified to find that the chief executive, instead of assessing the report on its merits, questions the legitimacy of the assumptions underpinning it, and puts aside insufficient time to discuss it. In effect, a shield is erected to protect the group members from what they consider to be adverse information likely to dislodge commitment to the chosen course of action. The accountant then faces a dilemma: having presented an opinion, should he or she accept a committee decision which is quite contrary to it?; would it be better to insist that the report goes on record?; by being too persistent or regularly opposing the group, is there a possibility of increasing isolation and eventual rejection by the group or its leader?

Consequences of Groupthink. The consequences that flow from these groupthink symptoms, are synonymous with the consequences of poor decision-making practices, and it follows that inadequate solutions to the problems under review are found. Discussion tends to be limited to but a few alternatives, and there is a conspicuous absence of evaluation of many alternatives that should be considered in the decision process. No systematic consideration is given to the question of whether gains, which do not appear obvious in the normal course of events, have been overlooked; neither is any cost assessment placed on the alternatives that have been rejected by the group. Similarly, no serious attempt is made to obtain the views of experts on potential losses or gains.

A noticeable trend is for group members to display a positive interest in facts and options that support their preferred policy, while ignoring facts and opinions that test it. The decision to launch the ill-fated *Challenger* space shuttle in 1986 may very well be an example of this frame of mind. Negative information was ignored by the group that made the decision (Moorhead et al., 1991).

Finally, there tends to be a failure to establish contingency plans to deal with foreseeable setbacks such as bureaucratic inertia, mishaps, or subtle political manoeuvring by opponents, which could pose a threat to the successful outcome of the course of action chosen.

In the discussion so far the importance of groupthink to processes within organisations was emphasised. In the panel facing, the concept is applied to a particular incident within an organisation concerned with generating commercial nuclear power.

Given the dysfunctional effects created by groupthink, what steps can we take to try to prevent it? There are a number of steps suitable to counteract groupthink:

Steps to Counteract Groupthink

1. Encourage individual members to evaluate what has been said in a critical fashion and place a high priority on an open discussion of doubts and objections where it is perfectly legitimate to disagree or be sceptical. The leader must be prepared to accept criticisms of his or her own judgement, which could have a healthy effect in arresting the rapid slide towards consensus with its adverse effect on critical thinking.

The Chernobyl Disaster

In a psychological analysis of the events leading up to the Chernobyl disaster in 1986—the worst accident in the history of commercial nuclear power generation—Reason (1987) focuses on two perspectives. The first deals with the cognitive difficulties people have in coping with complex systems. The second, which is examined here, is concerned with the "pathologies" of small cohesive groups (groupthink). Reason identified a number of groupthink symptoms as being attributable to the Chernobyl operators, as follows:

- "The actions of the operators were certainly consistent with an illusion of invulnerability. It is likely that they rationalised away any worries (or warnings) they might have had

about the hazards of their endeavour."
- Their single-minded pursuit of repeated testing implied "an unswerving belief in the rightness of their actions".
- They clearly underestimated the opposition: in this case, the system's intolerance to being operated within the forbidden reduced-power zone.
- Any adverse outcomes were either seen as unlikely, or possibly not even considered at all.
- Finally, if any one operator experienced doubts, they were probably "self-censored" before they were voiced.

These speculations suggest that the group aspects of the situation were prominent (Reason, 1987).

---

2. At the beginning of the discussion, as a means of encouraging open inquiry and an objective investigation of a wide range of policy alternatives, the leader should exercise impartiality and avoid stating preferences and expectations with regard to outcomes. Avoid arriving at conclusions on the basis of a consideration of an inadequate number of alternative courses of action. Encourage members to offer suggestions, and be aware at all times that early evaluation of a limited choice of alternatives could have a detrimental effect on ideas that are different, novel, or lacking support.

3. At the stage of the meeting when an evaluation of policy alternatives is required, one member of the group should play the role of devil's advocate, challenging the evidence put forward by those promulgating the majority point of view.

4. Do not rush into a quick solution of the problem. When you arrive at a first solution or preliminary choice, let it rest for a while, come back to it later and analyse the problem afresh. Where security considerations permit, allow each group member to report back to his or her section

or department to establish what people feel about the proposals before a final decision is reached. Expose the problem to outsiders with different special interests from those of group members and ask them to challenge its assumptions and content. The outcome of this exercise would be reported back to the group.

5. Where appropriate, break up the group into sub-groups (each having a chairperson) to examine the feasibility and effectiveness of the proposed policy alternatives. Then the main group should reconvene to settle any differences. Ideally, create more than one group to examine the same question, each group working under a different leader.

6. Where the group is in competition with another group, it may be advisable to put aside a session to monitor information reaching the group from this source and write alternative models of the rival group's intentions.

The strategy outlined here, though desirable, could be costly in execution and might be considered inappropriate at a time of crisis.

Research on Groupthink. Reflecting on the research basis of groupthink, there is a view that although the arguments for its existence are well stated, the concept has not been subjected to rigorous empirical investigation. Apart from interviews with participants in some cases, there is a heavy reliance on news reports and memoirs. Nevertheless, part of the groupthink phenomenon is supported by research, although a number of questions remain unanswered (Montanari & Moorhead, 1989). Another challenge to groupthink is made by Whyte (1989), who conceives it as the outcome of risk seeking in a group faced with impending losses.

Inter-group Behaviour

As well as intra-group behaviour, organisations are also concerned with the way groups interact with other groups. This is called inter-group behaviour, and is seen when, for example, organisations use cross-functional teams to tackle difficult technical problems. At a more basic level, it is manifest in normal liaison between different groups in an organisation in order to settle routine matters (e.g. between marketing and production departments).

Tajfel (1970) states that membership of a group is in itself a sufficient condition for the creation of "inter-group discrimination". Turner (1981) explains discrimination resulting from group membership as being due to individuals perceiving greater similarities within their own group, and greater differences between their own group and other groups than actually exist in reality. Also, individuals assess and compare themselves using their own group as a yardstick in a quest for "positive social identity" (the source of self-confidence and a sense of belonging).

Sometimes inter-group interactions breed hostile behaviour and may result in open conflict. Inter-group conflict is discussed in Chapter 9.

Reason (1987) recognises inter-group behaviour in his analysis of the Chernobyl disaster. He makes reference to two groups at the plant—the operators and the experimenters—and the relationship between them in trying to explain the catastrophe. Key observations from his analysis are as follows:

The operators, probably all Ukrainians, were members of a high-prestige occupational group, and had recently won an award. They probably approached the task with a "can do" attitude with some confidence in their ability to "fly" the reactor. Like other nuclear power plant operators, they would operate the plant using "process feel", rather than a knowledge of reactor physics. Their immediate aim was to complete the test as quickly as possible, get rid of the experimenters and shut down the plant in time for the start of the Tuesday maintenance programme. But they had forgotten to be afraid of the dangerous beast they were driving. As the Russian report put it: "They had lost any feeling for the hazards involved."

The experimenters, akin to a development group, were electrical engineers from Moscow. Their aim was quite clear: to crack a stubborn technical problem once and for all. Although they would have set the goals for the operators before and during the experiment, they would not, themselves, have known much about the actual operation of a nuclear power station. The Russian report makes it evident that the engineer in charge of this group knew little or nothing about nuclear reactors.

Together the two groups made a dangerous mixture. The experimenters were a group of single-minded but non-nuclear engineers directing a group of dedicated but over-confident operators. Each group probably assumed that the other knew what it was doing. And both parties had little or no understanding of the dangers they were courting, or of the system they were abusing.

As individuals identify strongly with a group, their views of other groups become biased, and harmonious relations may be difficult to achieve (Ashforth & Mael, 1989). The two groups at the Chernobyl plant had some difficulties in relating to each other. In general it is important for groups to relate well when interactions are required for the achievement of the organisational objectives.

Inter-group performance can be affected by the following variables (Moorhead and Griffin, 1992):

- task uncertainty;
- task interdependence;
- time and goal interdependence; and
- resources and location.

Task Uncertainty

This arises when groups lack information about courses of action to take or what to do about future events that may affect them, the task, or the organisation. Uncertainties arise from a diverse range of factors relating to technology, markets, the economy, regulatory agencies, etc. Groups may confront these uncertainties on their own, or seek help from another group in an attempt to reduce uncertainties. For example, the personnel department may be able to assist the production department on legal practices with respect to handling staff redundancies.

Task Interdependence

This is concerned with the extent to which groups have to depend on each other, necessitating co-ordination to achieve common objectives. For example, when the output of one group becomes the input for another ("sequential interdependence") interactions occur and co-ordinative effort is necessary. The research and development department in a pharmaceutical company provides an output that is used as an input to the production department which, in turn, provides an output that the sales and marketing department handles.

Time and Goal Interdependence

Goals set at the top of the organisation are expressed further down the hierarchy as sub-goals to which various groups subscribe. It is common for deadlines to be attached to the achievement of particular sub-goals—e.g. complete a project or task by a certain date—because of the need to harmonise the operations of various groups. Problems arise when groups do not share the same time frames. For example, the research engineer feels that more time is needed before a new product is ready for production—a view not shared by the production department. Those responsible for co-ordinating the work of diverse groups should be sensitive to the need to resolve such differences so that group interactions flow smoothly.

Resources and Location

Groups interact over the availability of organisational resources. There is a greater likelihood of interaction if groups share the same or similar resources, or if one group can affect the availability of resources to another group. Budgetary processes are used to allocate resources between groups. Often one finds heated discussions among groups about rights to floor space and facilities. It is necessary to resolve these matters on an equitable basis.

In connection with location, the closer work groups are to each other the more likely that they will interact. Often the relocation of groups on a single floor or in one building is prompted by a deliberate strategy to promote greater interaction. In other situations it may be appropriate to separate groups who are having difficulty relating to each other, in which case the objective is to decrease the frequency of interactions. However, this could create problems if there is a high degree of interdependency between these groups.

"RELEASE THE PROTOTYPE NOW, BOB, THAT'LL GIVE US
TIME TO IRON OUT ANY WRINKLES... BOB?..."

TEAM-BUILDING.

Teams and groups are words that are used interchangeably, but when group concepts are applied to certain features of organisational functioning, it is customary to refer to *teams* and *team-building*. A journalist in the management field had this to say recently: "New ideas about management generally originate in America or Japan, but there is one debate where Britain is at the forefront—the contribution that teamwork can make to business success" (Golzen, 1993)

The concept of group or team-building originated from developments in organisational development. The latter in its broadest sense (i.e. trying to fulfil the twin objectives of meeting organisational goals and satisfying individual needs) is discussed in Chapter 12. It is natural for an organisation to be concerned about the effective operation of the various work groups (e.g. autonomous groups—see Chapter 2) on both the technical and interpersonal fronts. Team-building is the process of enhancing the effectiveness of teams, and the term is often used interchangeably with team development (Hogg & McInerney, 1990). This section will examine:

- a model of group development;
- effective groups;
- project teams; and
- management team development.

Tuckman's Model of Group Development

In its development a group is said to pass through four main phases in a set sequence (Tuckman, 1965), with each stage having both dominant task-related and social considerations. The four stages are:

1. *Forming*. At the level of the task, the primary consideration is to focus on the nature of the job to be done and how best to do it with the available resources. At the social level, members try to establish the most appropriate behaviour to adopt (perhaps cautiously to begin with), and

look to the leader or a powerful figure for guidance.

2. *Storming*. At the level of the task, there appears to be emotional resistance to the demands of the job, particularly when the individual experiences a mismatch between the demands of the job and his or her own interpretation of what the job entails. At the social level, opinions of members seem to be polarised, particularly on key interpersonal issues. There is resistance to the control exercised by the group leader, and members are inclined to stress their own needs and concerns, and attempt to resist group influence.

3. *Norming*. At the level of the task, there is an open exchange of views and feelings. Co-operation is conspicuous, with a willingness to listen to and accept the views of other members. At the social level, group cohesion develops. New standards (norms) and roles emerge and are accepted by group members. There is an emphasis on harmony, and mutual support is noticeable as members perceive themselves to be part of a sound group that they wish to preserve. There is a conscious effort to avoid situations typified by conflict.

4. *Performing*. At the level of the task, solutions to problems are emerging, and constructive attempts are made to complete jobs. The task and social aspects of work are coming together. At the social level, the group has developed a purposeful way of members relating to each other in the performance of tasks and functions with flexibility being apparent. Interpersonal problems have been resolved, and the energy of the group is channelled into the tasks in hand.

These four stages are referred to as the Tuckman model. The model implies that the group must go through the four stages before it can be effective in terms of performance. Time could be an important factor as far as successful progression within the model is concerned; too little time and issues may not be adequately resolved at a particular stage. Also, issues that are not resolved may go underground only to find expression at a later stage, but the Tuckman model would not accommodate such an eventuality because of its linear nature.

More recently in connection with team development, a slightly different four-stage model has been advanced by Woodcock (1979). The stages of development (in a concise form) are as follows:

1. This phase suggests that many aspects of life in a team leave much to be desired. There appears to be an unnecessary level of authoritarian management and bureaucratic control. Group objectives are not very clear to members, and predictably there is a low level of involvement in the planning process. The stage is also characterised by poor listening, feelings are not seriously considered, and weaknesses are covered up.

2. At this stage, suddenly there are indications that the group is prepared to experiment, risky ventures are debated, and wider options are considered. There is now concern for others, more listening, and personal feelings are aired.

3. In addition to what is happening in stage 2, now there is evidence that the group is more methodical with respect to working practices. Procedures are agreed and ground rules are established.

4. This stage builds on the foundation laid in stages 2 and 3, by developing new activities from a healthy base. The situation now is characterised by in-built flexibility and appropriate leadership, with the creative use of members' abilities and energy. The group is sensitive to members' needs and cherished principles, and development is a priority.

The development of groups and teams on the lines indicated, cannot be isolated from the prevailing ethos or culture in the organisation.

An organisational culture having an impact on team development could be either achievement-orientated or help-orientated. According to Zander (1982), in the achievement-orientated organisation people place value on achieving their own personal ends, with a desire to get ahead and compete with colleagues. They tend to be individualistic and are not too concerned about the needs of the group.

The help-orientated organisation has quite a different culture in which people make an effort to help their colleagues grow as people. They ask questions, listen attentively to the answers or observations made, and at all times they are seeking to understand people and situations. There tends to be a determined effort to explain issues in order to assist comprehension of what is entailed.

The culture or atmosphere of the organisation, referred to in the previous paragraph (and discussed in more detail in Chapter 11), cannot be ignored when the operation of teams or groups is considered. In today's organisation, certain groups (for example, the innovative project group, the multi-disciplinary research team, the project planning group) are growing in importance, and as a consequence it is necessary for the organisational culture or climate to be supportive of them. An organisation with a supportive culture is likely to have the following features (Thomsett, 1980):

- There is a view that people are an asset to be developed.
- The organisation has a flat rather than a tall shape, and the management style is participative rather than autocratic.
- Innovation is prevalent, with a tendency to take significant risks.
- The control system within the organisation places more stress on internal controls (where the individual or group exercise self-regulation) rather than having an undue reliance on external controls (i.e. controls stemming from close supervision, specialist staff, as well as procedural control).

- The grouping of staff is enlightened, in the sense that people with skills and expertise tend to be brought together in appropriate groups, rather than having people with skills dispersed and located in isolated units.
- The level of commitment is impressive, with a noticeable lack of alienation, and people tend to collaborate rather than compete in a congenial environment.
- People's skills should match the roles they are expected to play, and natural groups should be allowed to form.

The central idea behind the notion of a supportive organisational climate is that one is creating an infrastructure in which effective groups can flourish.

Effective Groups

The features of both the effective and ineffective group are highlighted in Table 7.2 (McGregor, 1960). The profile and performance characteristics of the highly effective group are specified by Likert (1961), and are set out in Table 7.3. They may be viewed as a supplement to the features of effective groups listed in Table 7.2.

Many of the characteristics of effective groups listed in Tables 7.2 and 7.3 are ideal types, and although people may strive to operationalise them there are formidable behavioural and organisational constraints likely to undermine the process. Nevertheless, they are indicative of good practice with respect to the functioning of groups.

On reviewing the research evidence on making groups effective, Zander (1982) proposes key steps to promote problem solving within the group and to avoid ineffective decision making (see Table 7.4).

A recent concern has been to identify person-centred factors related to effective performance (Larson & La Fasto, 1989). These include being knowledgeable about the problems faced, having well specified and inspiring goals with members committed to a problem-solving approach, and having the

TABLE 7.2

McGregor's (1960) Characteristics of Effective and Ineffective Groups

	Effective	*Ineffective*
a)	Informality; relaxed atmosphere; involvement; interest	Formality; tense atmosphere; indifference; boredom
b)	Much discourse,; high contributions	Domination by few; contributions often lack relevance
c)	Understanding/acceptance of common aims	Aims ill-defined and misunderstood; conflict between private aims and common aims exists
d)	Listen; consider; forward ideas	Unfair hearing; irrelevant speeches; members fear ridicule/condemnation
e)	Examine disagreements; dissenters are not over-powered	Disagreements are suppressed or conflict develops; large minority is dissatisfied; disruptive minority imposes its views
f)	Consensus decision making; member feels free to disagree	Lack of consensus; premature decision making; formal voting (simple majority)
g)	Constructive criticism	Personalised destructive criticism
h)	Feelings and attitudes are aired	Feelings remain under the surface
i)	Awareness of decisions/actions; clear assignments	Lack of awareness of decisions; unclear assignments
j)	Leadership role undertaken by most suitable member	Leadership role is jealously guarded
k)	Frequent review of group operations	Not too concerned with deficiencies of the group

From D. McGregor *The Human Side of Enterprise*. Copyright © 1960 by McGraw-Hill, Inc. Reproduced by permission.

capacity to tap external sources of repute. Generally, the impact of personality and abilities on group performance (a feature of Belbin's approach considered later) is receiving increasing attention.

Project Teams

As is now apparent, a team is a particular type of group. We speak of teams in sport, and in business we have groups or teams that come together at various stages to work on a project. Different specialists could make a contribution to a project at different times. In the early stages of a construction project, the architects, planners, and clients will be actively involved. Later, the surveyors, construction engineers, and builders will have a part to play. The project team changes in composition over time, though some members continue to serve throughout the life of the project and, of course, the contracting agent plays an integrating role, co-ordinating the various elements. Teams of this nature can be difficult to manage, and to complicate matters they cut across organisational boundaries, as well as permeating inter-departmental barriers.

Project teams, drawing their membership from within the organisation, are essentially multi-functional groups that may only have a temporary existence. They could be formed to solve particular problems and are likely to draw on representatives from different departments, with different backgrounds, values, skills, and affiliations. The problem of

TABLE 7.3

Likert's (1961) Characteristics of the Effective Group

1.   Social interaction skills (e.g. ability to relate to others) required by both the leader and members are well developed

2.   Relaxed working relationship among members of the group

3.   Identification with the group and loyalty to all members, including the leader

4.   High degree of confidence and trust among members, including the leader

5.   Individual values and needs find expression in the group's values and goals. Because the individual members have helped to shape the group outlook, they feel satisfied with the way in which the group is going

6.   Acceptance of important group values (e.g. loyalty or safety) by members

7.   Because individuals wish to achieve something and enhance their personal worth, they channel this motivation to achieve the important goals of the group and at the same time they abide by the major values of the group (e.g. achieve a high level of production without compromising safety standards)

8.   Commitment to the group springs from sharing the group's values and deriving satisfaction from membership. The individual is keen to do his or her best and not let his or her colleagues down

9.   Supportive atmosphere governs all interactions, problem-solving and decision-making activities of the group. Suggestions, comments, ideas, information, criticisms, are forthcoming

10.   Linking functions with other groups: the group endeavours to adopt the values and goals of the groups with which it has a link

11.   The leader of the group who is carefully chosen adopts a participative management style

12.   The group is capable of setting attainable goals for members

13.   Mutual help is forthcoming in order to accomplish the group's goals

14.   The supportive atmosphere of the group stimulates creativity

15.   The group has a healthy respect for necessary bureaucratic practices

16.   A premium is placed on efficient communication processes, and there is little reason to doubt the credibility of the information communicated

17.   Members tend to exert influence on each other for the common good; this would apply to exerting influence on the leader. The ability of members of the group to influence each other contributes to the flexibility and adaptability of the group

18.   The attachment to common goals and shared values contributes to the stability of group activities. Members feel secure in using their initiative to make decisions in these circumstances

From R. Likert *New Patterns of Management*. Copyright © 1961 by McGraw-Hill, Inc. Used by permission.

integrating members' contributions from diverse specialist areas can be difficult. The appointment of an "integrator" could be crucial in this respect. He or she could oversee the situation, deal with unusual problems that cut right across the group, resolve inter-sectional conflict, and facilitate decision making. In the final analysis, the organisational climate and structure needs to be supportive of this approach. In identifying the problems of introducing change and innovation, Kanter (1984) maintains that there should be "integrative thinking" within organisations in order to cultivate team-

TABLE 7.4

Promoting Effective Group Problem Solving and Decision Making (Zander, 1982)

- State the problem clearly, indicating its significance and what is expected of the group when faced with solving it
- Break a complex problem into separate parts, and make decisions affecting each part
- Focus discussion on the key issues and, when all avenues are explored, put a stop to analysis, and call for a vote, if necessary, when the time is right
- Assist members on how to cope with other people's ideas, and then ask them to substantiate the correctness of their own ideas
- Choose the least objectionable alternative, if no clearly appropriate or appealing solution emerges
- Before making a final decision, encourage members to consider any adverse repercussions likely to flow from a given solution
- Be suspicious of unanimous decisions, particularly those arrived at quickly, and avoid them
- Make sure that those who are charged with the implementation of a group's decision understand exactly what they are expected to do
- Be on one's guard in order to prevent "groupthink"
- Avoid wide differences in status among members, or alternatively help members recognise these differences and explore ways of reducing their inhibitions with respect to "status" in the group
- Use brainstorming to generate improved participation within the group, as well as a device for the enhancement of the quality of ideas
- Prepare procedures in advance to deal with urgent or crisis decisions
- Protect the group from the damaging effects of external criticism, but at the same time let the group benefit from critical ideas or observations of a constructive nature that are likely to improve the quality of its deliberations
- Encourage members to evalue the skills residing in the group and find ways of improving them

---

orientated, co-operative environments in which change is facilitated and innovation flourishes.

What has been discussed so far with respect to project teams is the notion of the project team as a group concerned with developments where innovation features prominently. However, in recent years, due to cut backs and rationalisation, groups or teams have been created to plan and execute changes in organisations against a background of anxiety and fear of job losses due to redundancy. What often happens in these circumstances is that these emotional and psychic issues begin to find expression at the level of the group and the organisation, with a regression to primitive thought processes and behaviour and the use of defence mechanisms (Kanter, 1984). The end result can be irrational behaviour and illogical group decision making.

Management Team Development

A conscious attempt can be made to develop managerial teams already in existence. Before any decision is made to implement a team development programme, several matters have to be considered (Dyer, 1977). For example, one could ask the following questions:

- Why is it necessary?
- Can an appropriate programme be devised?
- Who will be included as part of the team?
- What is the duration of the programme?
- Where should the programme be located?
- Should an external consultant be appointed?

Dyer's Approach
A straightforward team development programme has been put forward by Dyer (1984), and it consists of the following steps:

1. A day should be set aside, away from the place of work and free from interruptions, for team-building.

2. Each individual should provide answers to the following questions before going to a meeting with other members. (i) What prevents you from being as effective as you would like to be in your position? (ii) What prevents staff in your unit from functioning as an effective team? (iii) What do you like about the unit that is worth maintaining? (iv) What suggestions do you have for improving the quality of the working relationships and the functioning of the unit?

3. At the meeting each person makes a presentation of responses to the questions in step 2, and these are written on a blackboard or a flipchart, under four headings: barriers to individual effectiveness; barriers to team effectiveness; matters people enjoy; and suggestions for improvement.

4. The group is asked to list, in order of priority, the problems it wants to raise. The list forms the agenda for the meeting.

5. The group begins addressing the major objective of the session. This would be to remove as many barriers as possible to the smooth functioning of the group. The barrier-removing activity may consist of clarifying the role each member plays, putting right misunderstandings, going in for more sharing of information, changing assignments, or instituting other innovative measures.

These processes are characterised by collecting data to determine the causes of the problem. As a catalyst, a consultant must be sensitive to the group's desire to handle issues through open discussion. There will be a recognition that certain issues can be confronted here and now, other issues perhaps could be dealt with by a task force later, while the remaining issues are not open to change and will have to be left as a constraint that one has to accept. In the quest for solutions to a problem a manager acts as the group leader, while the consultant acts as an observer/facilitator, concentrating his or her attention on the process by which the group arrives at its conclusions along the lines of Schein's "process consultation" (discussed in Chapter 12). The final stage of the process is where action strategies, planned and approved during the team-building session, are put into practice. This requires commitment on the part of the manager, with support from the consultant.

Belbin's Approach

While Dyer's approach to team development is used largely with existing teams of managers, an approach that will now be examined starts with the proposition that the best way to proceed is to bring together people with a range of skills and expertise to form a balanced and effective team. This concept was advanced by Belbin (1981) and his colleagues, who were concerned with analysing what team member roles were necessary to constitute an effective team.

Before members were allocated to a team, they underwent a series of psychometric tests designed to measure the individual's personality and mental ability. With regard to personality types, the measures used would shed light on dimensions of personality listed here, which are similar to those used by Eysenck (see Chapter 1):

- stable extravert (e.g. social, responsive, talkative, enthusiastic, leader);
- unstable extravert (e.g. restless, aggressive, impulsive, optimistic);
- stable introvert (e.g. passive, thoughtful, reliable, calm);
- unstable introvert (e.g. moody, anxious, pessimistic, quiet).

Measures of mental ability were also used, and these were designed to detect cleverness, and also creativity, using Cattell's formula for creative disposition.

You will notice that the first step is to classify team members by personality type and mental ability. The next step is for members to be formed into teams and then to engage in an activity testing their skills. Trained observers would frequently record the way members interacted and the nature of their contributions. Categories of behaviour that were observed are as follows:

- asking;
- informing;
- proposing;
- opposing;
- delegating;
- building; and
- commenting.

Numerical scores would be given to each participating member on each category of behaviour. The scores would reveal who, for example, was doing the most talking, or what type of intervention strategy was used by a particular team member. Performance in the activity testing team members' skills could be related to a certain aspect of personality or ability. For example, was the person who was active in "proposing" one of the cleverest team members, or alternatively was he or she a stable extravert?

Examples of the work-related tests were the executive management exercise (*EME*) and *Teamopoly* (based on *Monopoly*). The EME is a computer-based game that requires users to be involved in producing calculations and analysis in the context of models of business. With Teamopoly the success of teams was measured in financial terms; so a financial yardstick was used to indicate the effectiveness of the teams in attaining their objectives. Also, in this exercise it was possible to detect the reasons for team failures—e.g. a poor team or inefficient use of the team's resources.

Many experiments were conducted by Belbin and his colleagues over a period of nine years. The following are examples of the tests whereby attempts were made to come up with the right mix of talent in a team on the basis of (1) mental ability and (2) personality:

1. A high-powered management team was formed consisting of those who scored high on the mental ability tests (i.e. clever people). This group was called the Apollo group, but unexpectedly was placed last among the teams. Apparently, the observers noted that the team did not function very well. In fact, there was fruitless debate, there was a lack of logical consistency in decision making, a number of priority tasks were neglected, members were prone to act independently, and there was an absence of co-ordinated effort.

2. A team was formed of particular personality types, using the personality measure referred to earlier. Generally, the extraverts performed better than introverts. In particular, a team of stable extraverts had members who functioned in pairs; they were flexible in the way they operated and communicated well. They used the record sheets of the observers in order to modify or adjust their team's style. But note that when the teams of stable extraverts were engaged in planning activities, they had difficulty in concentrating; as a result, social activities, such as playing snooker, assumed a certain attraction. This led to a situation where they were likely to commit minor errors, and these errors were left uncorrected because of the easygoing manner of members. Apparently, the approach to team-building using similar personality types had clear weaknesses.

We can now conclude that management teams categorised solely by either mental ability or personality were less than satisfactory.

Team Roles.   The next series of experiments focused on teams composed of one particular type of worker. Eight key team roles were identified as follows: company worker; plant; resource investigator; chairperson; shaper; monitor-evaluator; team worker; and completer-finisher. A profile of each team role follows.

1. *Company Workers (CW)*.   A CW possessed the following characteristics:

- disciplined;
- tough-minded;
- practical;
- trusting;
- tolerant;
- conservative;
- conscientious;
- exercised self-control;
- firm self-image;
- outward looking.

The experimental CW groups were composed of one team high in mental ability and the other low in mental ability. By and large, the results were negative; these groups failed to get good results and they tended to be inflexible and were lacking in substantive ideas. However, they were strongly committed to achieving the objectives of the team, and generally worked well together towards that end. If the situation in which they operated matched their style, the teams could be reasonably successful, but they did not have the versatility to respond well to new and different situations.

2. *Plants (PLs)*.   For this role, creative individuals who scored high on the mental ability and creative disposition tests were chosen. PLs had the following characteristics:

- individualistic;
- intellectual;
- serious minded;
- knowledgeable;
- unorthodox;
- aloof;
- genius;
- impractical;
- lacking managerial skills;
- loner.

PLs were planted in different teams, and were known as "ideas people". They were skilful at getting their ideas across and having them accepted. But, paradoxically, teams with more than one PL fared no better than those with none.

3. *Resource Investigator (RI)*.   An RI tended to be creative, and possessed the following characteristics:

- versatile;
- curious;
- sociable;
- low on anxiety;
- extravert;
- innovative;
- communicative;
- social skills.

Both the RI and PL share creativity in common and could be considered innovative. By contrast the PL was more extravert and more capable in a managerial sense. The RIs looked beyond the boundaries of their group and, as a consequence, injected new ideas from outside into the team's deliberations. Being outgoing, they liked to work closely with people, and were particularly good at utilising resources. I suppose the real strength of the PL was that of collecting incompletely developed ideas from others and making something of them, rather than originating ideas.

4. *Chairperson (CH)*.   Given the importance of the leadership role in a team, the characteristics of the effective CH should be noted:

- calm;
- average intellect;
- self-confident;
- average ability;
- trusting;
- impartial;
- dominant;
- self-disciplined;
- enthusiastic;
- positive thinker;
- reasonably extravert.

Successful team performance was associated with the effective CH profile. Their behaviour at meetings of the group indicated that they were capable of making the best use of resources at their disposal. They showed tolerance when listening to others, but were quite capable of rejecting people's advice when feeling justified in doing so. They had a canny way of intervening at critical points in the discussion, were adept at handling people, and never lost their grip on a situation. They injected a sense of purpose and direction into a meeting and, as a consequence, the discussion was highly focused. They were proficient at making assessments of situations in terms of practical implications.

Reflecting on this personal profile, and noticing that the effective CH is of average ability, a conclusion could be that the ability level is not compatible with his or her impressive track record. It is suggested by Belbin that average mental ability is an advantage, because it facilitates communication with colleagues or team members. Apparently CHs with below average mental ability had difficulty in following the threads of an argument, were unsure of the number of alternatives open to them in a discussion, and showed signs of indecision. By contrast, CHs well above average mental ability tended to be too erudite in their reasoning at the cost of losing the attention of team members. The intellectual power, underpinned by the status factor (e.g. chairperson's role), had an adverse effect on the quality of communication and had an inhibiting effect on likely opponents within the group; as a result they advocated a cautious stance.

5. *Shaper (SH).*   Another role, similar to that of the CH, was the shaper. SHs had the following characteristics:

- high achievers;
- highly strung;
- argumentative;
- outgoing;
- impatient;
- dynamic;
- provocative.

SHs were full of nervous energy, and winning was an important goal. They tended to be both a disruptive influence and an arousing force in a group.

6. *Monitor-evaluator (ME).*   With regard to ME, it was said that in a team with PL and RI one could find a situation whereby there were a number of conflicting ideas floating about. Therefore, there was a need for a team member who had the ability to evaluate conflicting proposals put forward by the group. Hence the need for ME, whose characteristics are as follows:

- sober;
- clever;
- unemotional;
- uninspiring;
- discreet;
- detached;
- hard-headed;
- low arousal.

MEs are pretty shrewd in their judgements, and have a tendency to think that they are invariably right in their decisions, and anyway their disposition is conducive to taking an impartial view.

7. *Team Worker (TW).*   When one or more team members with real ability and skill cannot work well together or with colleagues, this can undermine the effectiveness of the team. TW is the sort of person who is needed to make the necessary interventions in order to minimise friction and encourage members to divert their energies to constructive ends. TWs characteristics are:

- responsive;
- gregarious;
- sensitive;
- team player;
- somewhat indecisive.

8. *Completer-finisher (CF)*. Because many teams are reasonably good at instituting initiatives, but poor at sustaining the effort necessary for successful completion, there is a need for somebody like a CF. The characteristics of CF are as follows:

- perseverance;
- perfectionist;
- conscientious;
- attention to detail;
- anxious.

CFs' role is a real asset to a team. They put enormous effort into the job, with an eye for detail, and show consistent performance. Though CFs appear to be calm and seemingly never frightened or upset, they absorb a fair amount of stress, and though highly controlled they are prone to anxiety.

When one is reflecting on these eight roles, it is well to remember that there are certain individuals, perhaps a very small minority, who can perform more than one role in a group or team. There are other individuals who lack the necessary competence to perform any of the team roles in a satisfactory way; as a result, they contribute to a team's lack of success. Other factors contributing to a team's lack of success are:

- Where the culture of the situation interferes with the team's ability to confront particular problems and it is not supportive of members acting as specialists.
- Where individuals are not fully aware of what their roles entail, or they are performing a role that accords with their previous experience rather than the role allotted, or the role is changed in an unpredictable way.
- Where there is an unsuitable mix of characters in the team.
- Where the team has no strategy.

In the light of the analysis of Belbin's research work at the theoretical level, it is possible, through careful selection and matching of team members, to arrive at an optimal solution in terms of group effectiveness. That would entail the right mixture of team roles. However, in practice it must be extremely difficult to balance the team role with that of the role in which the manager feels comfortable as a technical expert. Also, for each member to use his or her skill and expertise in a way complementary to existing resources of the group in relation to the job in hand is no mean task. The team can only operate to its best advantage when it has the required set of roles to function as an efficient team. Belbin's approach to the design of successful management teams would hardly be appropriate in a very small company not possessing a management team of eight members.

One thing that is certain about the discussion of Belbin's work is that it is a rigorous piece of research, but to design a successful team with reference to the prescription for the eight roles would be a challenge requiring considerable knowledge and expertise, and it would in itself rank as one of the most creative of tasks!

Recently, Belbin (1993) referred to six factors connected with team roles behaviour. These are depicted in Fig. 7.2. Also the titles used to describe two team roles have been changed. Co-worker is now referred to as *Implementer*, and Chairperson has become *Coordinator*.

There has been a recent challenge to the psychometric properties of the measure used by Belbin in his research. Belbin's measure is known as the *Team Role Self-Perception Inventory*. Furnham et al. (1993) subjected it to empirical test and concluded that there is little psychometric support for the structure of Belbin's inventories which, as already stated, have been used in many applied settings. Furnham et al. point out that if Belbin's inventory is to be used for employee selection, it is important that the psychometric properties of the scale are investigated.

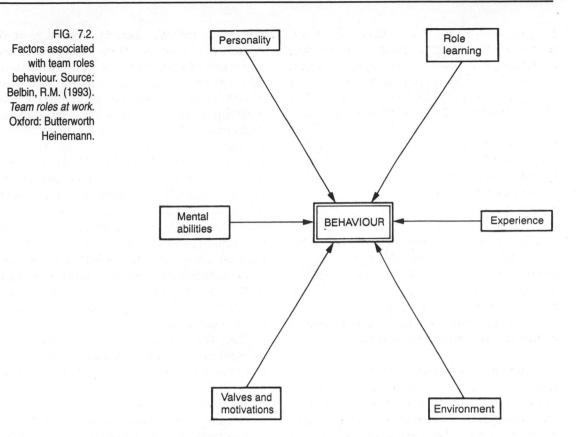

FIG. 7.2.
Factors associated
with team roles
behaviour. Source:
Belbin, R.M. (1993).
Team roles at work.
Oxford: Butterworth
Heinemann.

Team Management Wheel

Margerison and McCann (1991) go a stage further than Belbin by developing a basic model that links job functions with the roles team members are expected to perform. This model is depicted in Fig. 7.3 as the team management wheel, and is based on necessary behaviour (i.e. exploring and controlling) and preferred roles (i.e. advisory and organising).

Exploring behaviour includes contacting people, searching for opportunities, and creative pursuits. Controlling behaviour is reflected in adhering to rules and regulations, and operating systems with an eye for detail and precision in the performance of tasks.

Advisory roles are associated with the provision of support services—e.g. planning, research, and training for main-line activities such as the production and distribution of products and services. Organising roles focus on the main-line activities.

The team roles identified in Fig. 7.3 are as follows:

1. Reporter-Advisers, who collect and use information in performing a support role.
2. Creator-Innovators, who concentrate on generating new ideas, and are likely to emphasise experimentation and new designs.
3. Explorer-Promoters, who represent the group or the organisation in establishing outside contacts so as to publicise new ideas, and attract funds and resources.
4. Assessor-Developers, who identify the best way to develop ideas in practice, assessing the viability of proposals with reference to market research and other intelligence data. They may make a prototype, where appropriate, as a means to test their ideas.
5. Thruster-Organisers, who show an eagerness to establish exacting objectives,

FIG. 7.3. Team management wheel. Source: Margerison, C.J. & McCann, D. (1991). *Team management: Practical approaches*. London: Mercury Books.

and ensure that the appropriate procedures and systems are in place to facilitate the attainment of those objectives. They show a keenness to remove any obstacles that stand in their way.

6. Concluder-Producers, who show consistency and determination in seeing a process or project through to completion, adhering to quality considerations and deadline dates.

7. Controller-Inspectors, who emphasise the inspection function to ensure that jobs are done in the correct way, with an emphasis on control.

8. Upholders-Maintainers, who place weight on the maintenance of valuable social and organisational systems and relationships. They try to preserve the best of the old traditions and cultural heritage in an organisational sense, but at the same time they are receptive to the notion of grafting new ideas into the ongoing system without too much disruption.

9. Linkers are those who link people within the team, but they also act as representatives for the team in its contacts with other units and organisations. The emphasis is on co-ordinating and integration, a common managerial function.

Overview

In recent years, Sundstrom, De Meuse, and Futrell (1990) called for a broader perspective when focusing on team effectiveness. Apart from team development, with its emphasis on the internal processes of the group, they draw our attention to the need to consider contextual factors and team boundaries. Key contextual factors include:

• organisational culture;
• clarity of mission;
• technology and task design;
• group autonomy;
• rewards;
• performance feedback;
• training/consultation; and
• the physical environment.

Boundaries differentiate one group from another, creating real or symbolic barriers to access or flow of information, and serve as points of external contact. If the boundary is too open or indistinct, the team risks becoming overwhelmed and in danger of losing its identity. If it is too closed, the team might become too isolated and lose touch with peers, management, customers, and suppliers. Team boundaries are likely to mediate the impact of organisational context on team development. In the final analysis, it would appear that team effectiveness is a function of the interaction of team development, organisational context, and group boundaries.

SUMMARY: GROUPS AND TEAM-BUILDING

- Having briefly introduced the notion of what is meant by a group, it was suggested that groups can be classified by type—i.e. formal or informal, primary or secondary, co-acting, counteracting, and reference groups—as well as by skill and level of interaction.

- The characteristics of groups were identified as norms, cohesiveness, communication networks and interaction episodes, spatial and structural factors, and group dynamics. Before examining group processes, some reasons for joining groups were briefly stated.

- Group processes were identified as: reference groups; social comparison; co-action and affiliation; social control; decision making; and inter-group behaviour. Reference groups were classified as normative or comparative, and as positive or negative. The relevance of the concept of the reference group to marketing was noted.

- The significance of social comparison was explained. Group norms as a social comparative influence were illustrated with reference to production targets and standard costs. The influence exerted by the group in different experimental conditions (e.g. the studies conducted by Sherif and Asch) was acknowledged. Group influence was briefly discussed with respect to budgeting discretionary costs and investor behaviour.

- With regard to co-action and affiliation, relating to others in different conditions (e.g. being evaluated by an expert or being in a state of fear) can have a material bearing on the behaviour of an individual in a group setting.

- Social control is the influence exercised by an authority figure on a vertical basis, rather than on a horizontal basis as in social comparison. Social control was illustrated with particular reference to Milgram's experiments (i.e. obedience to authority). Other forms of social control are institutional control and brainwashing.

- The nature and likely benefits of group decision making were discussed, initially with reference to the experiments conducted by Lewin. The limitations of group decision making were noted. The different types of decision making groups were examined. The risky shift phenomenon was explained and illustrated using an investment decision as an example. The focus on decision making was concluded with a discussion of groupthink. The key characteristics of groupthink were explained along with possible steps to counteract it. Reflections on groupthink research were introduced.

- The importance of inter-group behaviour was noted, and the variables likely to affect inter-group performance, such as task uncertainty, task interdependence, time and goal interdependence, and resources and location, were identified.

- Team-building as a process to enhance the effectiveness of teams or groups was discussed at length, with reference to a model of group development, effective groups, project teams, and management team development.

QUESTIONS

1. Define what is meant by a group, and give examples of different types of group.
2. What is the difference between an internally imposed norm and an externally imposed norm? Into which category would you place a production target?
3. Explain the following terms which are used to describe the characteristics of a

group: (a) communication networks; (b) group dynamics; and (c) geographic proximity.

4. Examine the relationship between cohesiveness and productivity.

5. Identify the structural factors discussed in the context of the characteristics of the group, and single out the factors(s) that you consider are critical for our understanding of groups.

6. Give the reasons why you joined your favourite group other than your family.

7. What is the difference between: (a) a membership group and a reference group; and (b) a normative reference group and a comparative reference group?

8. Discuss the suggestion that reference groups influence consumer behaviour.

9. What is the significance of the Hawthorne studies in the context of group norms as a social comparative influence?

10. "Formal control systems, of which standard costing is part, should be consistent with group norms." Discuss.

11. Comment on the relevance of the findings of Asch's experiment to a group involved in the budgeting process.

12. Describe Milgram's work on obedience to authority, and suggest the most appropriate type of organisation where social control is legitimate.

13. With reference to decision-making groups, explain the following with examples from business practice: (a) group discussion; (b) risky shift and cautious shift; and (c) groupthink.

14. Discuss the factors likely to influence inter-group performance.

15. Select the approach to team-building that has the greatest appeal to you, and give reasons for your choice.

16. Explain the "broader perspective" on team effectiveness, as outlined by Sundstrom and colleagues.

REFERENCES

Asch, S.E. (1952). Effects of group pressure upon the modification and distortion of judgements. In C.E. Swanson, T.M. Newcombe, & E.L. Hartley (Eds.), *Readings in social psychology*. New York: Holt, Rinehart, & Winston.

Ashforth, B.E. & Mael, F. (1989). Social identity theory and the organisation. *Academy of Management Review*, January, 20–39.

Baker, H.G. (1985). The unwritten contract: Job perceptions. *Personnel Journal*, July, 37–41.

Bales, R.F. (1950). A set of categories for the analysis of small group interaction. *American Sociological Review, 15*, 257–263.

Belbin, R.M. (1981). *Management teams*. London: Heinemann Educational Books.

Belbin, R.M. (1993). *Team roles at work*. Oxford: Butterworth Heinemann.

Benne, K.D. & Sheats, P. (1948). Functional role of group members. *Journal of Social Issues, 4*, 41–49

Bion, W.R. (1961). *Experience in groups*. London: Tavistock.

Bourne, F.S. (1957). Group influences in marketing and public relations. In R. Likert & S.P. Hayes (Eds.), *Some applications of behavioural research*. Paris: UNESCO.

Brenner, S.N. & Molander, E.A. (1977). Are the ethics of business changing. *Harvard Business Review*, January–February, 57–71.

Brookes, M.J. & Kaplan, A. (1972). The office environment: Space planning and effective behaviour. *Human Factors, 14*, 373–391.

Burnkrant, R.E. & Cousineau, A. (1975). Informational and normative social influences in buyer behaviour. *Journal of Consumer Research, 2*, December, 206–215.

Chapman, J. (1982). After the inspector's visit: When group loyalty made a mockery of accident prevention. *The Safety Representative*, March, 5.

Chell, E. (1987). *The psychology of behaviour in organisations*. London: Macmillan.

Cohen, D. (1981). *Consumer behaviour*. New York: Random House.

Dyer, W.G. (1977). *Team-building: Issues and alternatives*. Reading, MA: Addison-Wesley.

Dyer, W.G. (1984). *Strategies for managing change*. Reading, MA: Addison-Wesley.

Eachus, P. (1988). The psychology of the stock market. *The Psychologist*, March, 100–103.

Earley, P.C. (1989). Social loafing and collectivism: A comparison of the United States and the People's Republic of China. *Administrative Science Quarterly, 34*, 565–581.

Feldman, D.C. (1984). The development and enforcement of group norms. *Academy of Management Review*, January, 47–53.

Festinger, L., Schachter, S., & Back, K. (1950). *Social pressure in informal groups: A study of human factors in housing.* New York: Harper & Row.

Flamholtz, E. (1975). Small group interaction and task performance: Its implications for managerial accounting. In J. Leslie Livingstone (Ed.), *Managerial accounting.* Columbus, Ohio: Grid Inc.

Freud, S. (1955). Group psychology and the analysis of the ego. In J. Strachey (Ed.), *The complete psychological works of Sigmund Freud*, Vol. XVIII. London: Hogarth Press.

Furnham, A., Steele, H., & Pendleton, D. (1993). A psycho-metric assessment of the Belbin Team-Role Self-Perception Inventory. *Journal of Occupational and Organizational Psychology, 66*, 245–257.

Goffman, E. (1961). *Asylums: Essays on the social situation of mental patients and other inmates.* New York: Doubleday.

Golzen, G. (1993). Team up for business success. *The Sunday Times*, 21st February, 4.2.

Goodman, P.S., Ravlin, E., & Schminke, M. (1987). Understanding groups in organisations. In L.L. Cummings & B.M. Staw (Eds.), *Research in organisational behaviour*, Vol. 9. Greenwich, CT: JAI Press.

Harvey, P. (1988). *Health psychology.* Harlow, Essex: Longman.

Heller, F. (1983). The danger of groupthink. *The Guardian*, 31st January, 9.

Henchy, T. & Glass, D.C. (1968). Evaluation of apprehension and the social facilitation of dominant and subordinate responses. *Journal of Personality and Social Psychology, 10*, 445–454.

Hodgetts, R.M. (1991). *Organisational behaviour: Theory and practice.* New York: Macmillan.

Hogg, C. & McInerney, D. (1990). Team-building. *Personnel Management*, October, Factsheet 34.

Insko, C. & Wilson, M. (1977). Interpersonal attraction as a function of social interaction. *Journal of Personality and Social Psychology*, December, 903–911.

Isenberg, D.J. (1986). Group polarisation: A Critical review and meta-analysis. *Journal of Personality and Social Psychology, 50*, 1141–1151.

Jackson, E. & Schuler, R.S. (1985). A meta-analysis and conceptual critique of research on role ambiguity and role conflict in work settings. *Organisational Behaviour and Human Decision Processes*, August, 16–78.

Janis, I.L. (1972). *Victims of groupthink: A psychological study of foreign policy decisions and fiascos.* Boston: Houghton Mifflin.

Kanter, R.M. (1984). *The change masters.* London: Unwin.

Keller, R.T. (1986). Predictors of the performance of project groups in research and development organisations. *Academy of Management Review*, December, 715–726.

Kelman, H.C. (1961). Three processes of social influence. *Public Opinion Quarterly, 25*, 57–78.

Kogan, N. & Wallach, M.A. (1967). Risk taking as a function of the situation, person, and the group. In T.M. Newcombe (Ed.), *New directions in psychology*, Vol III. New York: Holt, Rinehart, & Winston.

Laing, R.D. (1970). *The divided self.* Harmondsworth: Penguin.

Larson, C.E. & La Fasto, F.M.J. (1989). *Team-work.* London: Sage.

Latane, B. & Darley, J. (1968). Group inhibition of bystander intervention in emergencies. *Journal of Personality and Social Psychology, 10*, 215–221.

Latane, B., Williams, K., & Harkins, S. (1979). Many hands make light the work: The causes and consequences of "social loafing". *Journal of Personality and Social Psychology, 37*, 822–832.

Lately, P. (1982). Computing can damage your health. *Practical Computing*, July, 126–127.

Leavitt, H.J. (1951). Some effects of certain communication patterns on group performance. *Journal of Abnormal and Social Psychology, 46*, 38–50.

Lewin, K. (1958). Group decision and social change. In E.E. Maccoby, T.M. Newcombe, & R.L. Hartley (Eds.), *Readings in social psychology* (third edition). New York: Holt.

Likert, R. (1961). *New patterns of management.* New York: McGraw-Hill.

Lupton, T. (1963). *On the shop floor.* Oxford: Pergamon.

Margerison, C.J. & McCann, D. (1991). *Team management: Practical approaches.* London: Mercury Books.

McGregor, D. (1960). *The human side of enterprise.* New York: McGraw-Hill.

Meadows, I.S.G. (1980a). Organic structure and innovation in small work groups. *Human Relations, 33*, 369–382.

Meadows, I.S.G. (1980b). Organic structure, satisfaction and personality. *Human Relations, 33*, 383–392.

Michaelsen, L.K., Watson, W.E., & Black, R.H. (1989). A realistic test of individual versus group consensus decision making. *Journal of Applied Psychology*, October, 834–839.

Milgram, S. (1965). Some conditions of obedience and disobedience to authority. *Human Relations, 18*, 57–76.

Miller, S.M. & Magnan, C.E. (1983). Interacting effects of information and coping style in adapting to gynaecologic stress: Should the doctor tell all? *Journal of Personality and Social Psychology, 45*, 223–236.

Miner, F.C. (1984). Group versus individual decision making: An investigation of performance measures, decision strategies and process losses/gains. *Organisational Behaviour and Human Performance*, February, 112–124.

Montanari, J.R. & Moorhead, G. (1989). Development of the groupthink assessment inventory. *Educational and Psychological Measurement*, *49*, 209–219.

Moorhead, G., Ferrence, R.K. & Neck, C.P. (1991). Group decision fiascos continue: Space shuttle "Challenger" and a revised groupthink framework. *Human Relations*, *44*, 539–550.

Moorhead, G. & Griffin, R.W. (1992). *Organisational behaviour: Managing people and organisations* (third edition). Boston: Houghton Mifflin.

Nemecek, J. & Grandjean, E. (1973). Noise in landscaped offices. *Applied Ergonomics*, *4*, 19–22.

Nemeth, C.J. (1986). Differential contributions of majority and minority influence. *Psychological Review*, *93*, 23–32.

Newcombe, T.M. (1943). *Personality and social change: attitude formation in a student community*. New York: Holt, Rinehart and Winston.

Newcombe, T.M. (1970). Attitude development as a function of reference groups: The Bennington study. In *Understanding society*. London: Macmillan (for the Open University).

Oborne, D.J. (1994). *Ergonomics at work* (third edition). Chichester: John Wiley & Sons.

Oliver, G. (1980). *Marketing today*. London: Prentice-Hall.

O'Reilly, C.A., Caldwell, D.F., & Barnett, W.P. (1989). Work group demography, social integration and turnover. *Administrative Science Quarterly*, *34*, 21–37.

Piper, W.E., Marrache, M., Lacroix, R., Richardson, A.M., & Jones, B.D. (1983). Cohesion as a basic bond in groups. *Human Relations*, February, 93–108.

Radke, M. & Klisurich, D. (1958). Experiments in changing food habits. In E.E. Maccoby, T.M. Newcombe, & R.L. Hartley (Eds.), *Readings in social psychology* (third edition). New York: Holt.

Rafaeli, A. (1989). When cashiers meet customers: An analysis of the role of supermarket cashiers. *Academy of Management Review*, *32*, 245–273.

Reason, J. (1987). The Chernobyl errors. *Bulletin of The British Psychological Society*, *40*, 201–206.

Robbins, S.P. (1991). *Organisational behaviour: Concepts, controversies, and applications* (fifth edition). New York: Prentice-Hall.

Roethlisberger, F.J. & Dickson, W.J. (1939). *Management and the worker*. Cambridge, MA: Harvard University Press.

Roy, D.F. (1960). Banana time: Job satisfaction and informal interaction. *Human Organisation*, *18*, 156–168.

Sayles, L.R. (1958). *The behaviour of industrial work groups*. New York: John Wiley & Sons.

Schachter, S., Ellertson, N., McBride, D., & Gregory, D. (1951). An experimental study of cohesiveness and productivity. *Human Relations*, August, 229–239.

Schachter, S. (1959). *The psychology of affiliation*. Palo Alto, CA: Stanford University Press.

Schein, E.H. (1956). The Chinese indoctrination programme for prisoners of war. *Psychiatry*, *19*, 149–172.

Schiffman, L.G. & Kanuk, L.L. (1978). *Consumer behaviour*. New York: Prentice-Hall.

Shaw, M.E. (1964). Communication networks. In L. Berkowitz (Ed.), *Advances in experimental social psychology*, Vol. 1. New York: Academic Press.

Shaw, M.E. (1981). *Group dynamics: The psychology of small group behaviour* (third edition). New York: McGraw-Hill.

Sherif, M. (1936). *The psychology of social norms*. New York: Harper & Row.

Sommer, R. (1967). Small group ecology. *Psychological Bulletin*, *67*, 145–152.

Stoner, J.A.F. (1961). A comparison of individual and group decisions involving risk. Unpublished School of Industrial Management, M.I.T. thesis, quoted in R. Brown, (1965) *Social Psychology*. New York: Free Press.

Sundstrom, E., De Meuse, K.P., & Futrell, D. (1990). Work teams: Applications and effectiveness. *American Psychologist*, February, 120–133.

Tajfel, H. (1970). Experiments in inter-group discrimination. *Scientific American*, *223*, 96–102.

Thomsett, R. (1980). *People and project management*. New York: Yourdon Press.

Trist, E.L., Higgin G., Pollock, H.E., & Murray, H.A. (1963). *Organisational choice*. London: Tavistock.

Tuckman, B.W. (1965). Development sequence in small groups. *Psychological Bulletin*, *63*, 384–399.

Turner, J.C. (1981). The experimental social psychology of inter-group behaviour. In J.C. Turner & H. Giles (Eds.), *Inter-group behaviour*. Oxford: Blackwell.

Van de Ven, A.H. & Delbecq, A.L. (1974). The effectiveness of nominal, delphi, and interacting group decision-making processes. *Academy of Management Review*, December, 606–615.

Vecchio, R.P. (1991). *Organisational behaviour* (second edition). Orlando, FL: The Dryden Press.

Venkatesan, M. (1966). Experimental study of consumer behaviour: Conformity and independence. *Journal of Marketing Research*, *3*, November, 384–387.

Wallace, L.M. (1986). Communication variables in the design of pre-surgical preparatory information. *British Journal of Clinical Psychology*, *25*, 111–118.

Wallach, M.A. & Kogan, N. (1965). The roles of information, discussion, and consensus in group risk taking. *Journal of Experimental Social Psychology, 1,* 1–19.

Whyte, G. (1989). Groupthink reconsidered. *Academy of Management Review, 14,* 40–56.

Witt, R.E. & Bruce, G. (1970). Purchase decisions and group influence. *Journal of Marketing Research, 7,* November, 533–535.

Woodcock, M. (1979). *Team development manual.* Farnborough, UK: Gower Publishing.

Wrightsman, L. (1960). Effects of waiting for others on changes in level of felt anxiety. *Journal of Abnormal and Social Psychology, 61,* 216–222.

Yablonsky, L. (1967). *The violent gang.* Harmondsworth: Penguin.

Zajonc, R.B. & Sales, S.M. (1966). Social facilitation of dominant and subordinate responses. *Journal of Experimental Social Psychology, 2,* 160–168.

Zaltman, G. & Wallandorf, M. (1979). *Consumer behaviour: Basic findings and managerial implications.* New York: John Wiley & Sons.

Zander, A. (1982). *Making groups effective.* San Francisco: Josey-Bass.

8

Leadership and Management Style

This chapter examines the leadership process from a number of angles. It begins with a distinction between leadership and management, followed by a commentary on traits, personal qualities, and skills. Next there is an examination of studies in leadership where behavioural styles feature prominently. A number of contingency theories of leadership are then introduced, and it is acknowledged that this is a fertile area of research. Contemporary trends in the study of leadership are discussed, and the influence of transformational leadership is noted.

This chapter leads on naturally from the previous chapter on groups, and is complementary to the next chapter on power, politics, and conflict. It also has relevance to other chapters—e.g. on personality (Chapter 1), motivation (Chapter 2), organisational culture (Chapter 11), and organisational change and development (Chapter 12).

LEADERSHIP VERSUS MANAGEMENT

In this section, the similarities and differences between leadership and management will be explored. Some researchers who have studied leadership in organised settings tend to state that people endowed with authority are leaders. Therefore, supervisors and managers within organisations can be called leaders. Many theories of leadership are concerned with managerial influence, and the terms "leadership" and "management" are sometimes used interchangeably. However, some scholars can see differences between management and leadership. Kotter (1990) felt that leadership and management are two distinctive and complementary systems, each having its own function and its own characteristic activities, but both are necessary for the management of complex organisations. A definition of leadership and management that has a particular appeal to the author is as follows (McKenna, 1991):

Leadership is a force that creates a capacity among a group of people to do something that is different or better. This could be reflected in a more creative outcome, or a higher level of performance. In essence, leadership is an agency of change, and could entail inspiring others to do more than they would otherwise have done, or

"...I DUNNO,..WOULD A MANAGER DO... INSTEAD OF A LEADER...?"

were doing. By contrast, management is a force more preoccupied with planning, co-ordinating, supervising, and controlling routine activity, which of course can be done in an inspired way. Managerial leadership could be viewed as an integral part of the managerial role, and its significance grows in importance as we move up the organisational hierarchy.

Researchers have focused on the nature of managerial jobs. For example, Stewart (1982) has been very active in the UK over the years trying to understand what managers do. At the outset of this research she simply focused on identifying how managers spent their time. Subsequently, she moved towards developing a scheme for classifying managerial behaviour in terms of the amount of choice managers have in coping with their specific circumstances.

The overlap between leadership and management can be seen clearly in the contrast between the two in the work of Mintzberg (1980) and Yukl (Van Fleet & Yukl, 1989) shown in Table 8.1. Mintzberg identifies

a diversified range of managerial roles of senior managers, of which the leadership role is an important ingredient. The list of leadership behaviour categories provided by Yukl covers general management activities, but is derived from an exhaustive review of the research literature on leadership. (Aligned entries in Table 8.1 indicate similarities.)

TRAITS, PERSONAL CHARACTERISTICS, AND SKILLS

The traits, motives, and abilities associated with leadership in general, and managerial leadership in particular, will now be examined. (See Chapter 1 for a discussion of the trait approach to personality.) In the early part of this century, the development of psychometric assessment procedures was felt to be very appropriate to the study of leadership. This was a time when there was a belief that abilities and leadership characteristics were inherited, and perhaps finally we could shed some light on the quality of charisma.

TABLE 8.1

Contrasting Leadership and Management

Leadership Behaviour Categories (Van Fleet & Yukl, 1989)	*Managerial Roles (Mintzberg, 1980)*
	1. Interpersonal roles — Symbolic duties as a figurehead
Recognising and rewarding Developing Motivating task commitment	— Exercising leadership (i.e. creating the necessaary culture, and providing the motivational stimulus to achieve organisational tasks)
Interfacing	— External contacts (i.e. obtaining the necessary information and resources through contacts outside the department/organisation)
	2. Handling information
Monitoring operations	— Monitoring (i.e. examining actual performance in relation to targets using appropriate information)
Informing Clarifying roles and objectives	— Disseminating — internal (i.e. information that originated from outside the department/organisation is disseminated internally)
	— Transmitting — external (i.e. internally generated information is transmitted externally)
	3. Decision making
	— Strategic change focus (i.e. shaping or reshaping the organisation to adapt to external events)
Problem solving and crisis management	— Fire fighting (i.e. handling disturbances or unforeseen events)
Representing, planning and organising	— Resource allocating (i.e. making policy decisions about the use of resources; negotiating or bargaining with other individuals/organisations; budgeting)

Source: McKenna, E.F. (1991, May). *Managerial leadership —emergent trends*. Unpublished professorial inaugural lecture, University of East London.

Traits

In a typical early study, Terman (1904) asked teachers to describe playgroup leaders. They were reported to be active, quick, and skilful in devising and playing games. Over 50 years later, Bavelas (1960) saw leadership traits as quickness of decision, the courage to take risks, coolness under stress, intuition, and even luck. Other traits often mentioned in popular journalism are vision, willpower, cultivating team spirit and loyalty, inspiring followers, integrity, honesty, and sheer physical stamina.

Recently an international magazine did a special feature on leadership entitled "Where have all the leaders gone?" (*Time*, 1993). This survey of leadership appeared on the eve of the Tokyo Economic Summit. It was stated that a terrible form of gridlock and an absence of vision seemed to have gripped the globe's most prominent nations. There was the inevitable contrast of the characteristics of great past political leaders wtih those currently in office, with conclusions not very complimentary to the latter.

Stogdill (1948) and Mann (1959) conducted independent reviews of the vast literature on personality as a factor in leadership, and concluded that personality had a minor effect in shaping leadership behaviour. Stogdill (1948) proposed that a person does not become a leader by virtue of the possession of some combination of personality traits—what is important is that the leader's personality must be compatible with the personal characteristics, activities, and goals of the followers.

By and large, the studies that Stogdill and Mann reviewed were predominantly concerned with the behaviour of children and students in unstructured settings, such as those found outside bureaucratic organisations. But the findings have often been raised with reference to the behaviour of leaders in formal organisational settings where a different set of conditions are likely to be important. A point worthy of note is that very few of the studies looked at the effectiveness of the leaders studied. Instead, the focus was on people who emerged as leaders—an emphasis to be expected given the nature of the research site (i.e. unstructured settings outside formal organisations).

In a subsequent review, Stogdill (1974) seems to mix personality traits with abilities or skills, though not intentionally, and concludes that the following factors are frequently linked with leadership:

- activity;
- dominance;
- self-confidence;
- achievement drive; and
- interpersonal skills.

Taking four of the traits and abilities identified by Stogdill as a framework, the author used observations on Margaret Thatcher, the former British prime minister, based on *The*

Whitelaw Memoirs (Whitelaw, 1989), and similarly the views of MacArthur (1988) on Eddy Shah, the founder of *Today* newspaper and the first newspaper proprietor to introduce sweeping changes in the production methods and staffing levels in the UK newspaper industry. The analysis appears in Table 8.2.

Both leaders could be considered successful in their respective fields, and from this comparative analysis certain common elements emerge. These are drive and a determination to succeed, perhaps touching on ruthlessness—but equally there are significant differences as well. This non-empirical comparative analysis shows the difficulties encountered with the trait approach to leadership. The Stogdill reviews, referred to earlier, essentially halted leadership research involving traditional personality traits.

Managerial Talent

Now the emphasis switched to the identification of managerial talent. In some studies this is undertaken through assessment centres (discussed in Chapter 13), which create simulations of the settings managers are likely to encounter in their work. In other studies managerial performance is measured and related to self-reports by managers of personality and motivation. In the latter studies, unlike the early leadership studies, leadership was viewed as being synonymous with the occupancy of a managerial role. Different criteria of managerial effectiveness arose, ranging from the promotion potential of managers, as perceived by top management, to ratings of competence by the manager's superior.

The requisite managerial qualities reflected a mixture of personality traits, motives, and skills. Bray and Campbell (1974) found that managers most frequently promoted with the *American Telephone and Telegraph Company* were those who had been assessed early in their careers as scoring high on:

TABLE 8.2

Managerial Leadership—Personality Traits

Stogdill (1974)	M. Thatcher	E. Shah
1. Activity	Very energetic Very vivacious	Energetic
2. Dominance	Dominant	
3. Achievement drive	Determined to succeed	Achievement-orientated
4. Interpersonal skills	Argumentative but listens carefully Not a conciliator	Relaxed, informal, pleasant and unassuming style
5. Other traits	Assertive Obstinate Reserved (with strangers) Not a clubable person	Courageous Impulsive Emotional Temperamental Inspired workaholic

Source: McKenna, E.F. (1991, May). *Managerial leadership—emergent trends*. Unpublished professorial inaugural lecture, University of East London.

- oral communication;
- human relations skills;
- need for advancement;
- resistance to stress; and
- tolerance for uncertainty.

Ghiselli (1971) compared effective and ineffective managers and reported that effective managers scored higher on:

- intelligence;
- self-assurance;
- supervisory ability;
- need for occupational achievement;
- decisiveness;
- need for self-fulfilment.

But they scored low on need for security.

McClelland (1975) sees a need for power as a prerequisite to assuming a managerial role. This finding was endorsed by Miner (1978), who, when specifying the motives most strongly linked to those who were most frequently promoted, added the desire to compete with colleagues for limited resources, to be active and assertive, to be visible and influential in handling subordinates, and having a positive attitude towards authority. A summary of this evidence appears in Table 8.3. From this analysis it seems that achievement-orientation, effective communication and interpersonal skills, and the need for power are the characteristics most commonly shared by effective managers.

Skills

The weakness of the traditional trait approach has led to a consideration of managerial talents, abilities, and skills, as well as aspects of personality. Today, the operationalisation of the leadership role would not be complete without an acknowledgement of the deployment of cognitive, affective, and administrative skills. This entails the use of skills in diagnosing problems and suggesting sound solutions, as well as having sufficient insight or personal awareness and the necessary interpersonal skills to relate effect-

TABLE 8.3

Personal Characteristics of Effective Managers

Ghiselli (1971)	McClelland (1967; 1975)	Miner (1978)	Bray & Campbell (1974)
Intelligence Self-assurance Supervisory ability		Effective interaction with subordinates	Communication and interpersonal skills
Need for occupational achievement	Need for achievement		Need for achievement
Need for self-fulfilment			
	Need for power	Need for power Competitive Asertive	
			Resistance to stress Tolerance for uncertainty

Source: McKenna, E.F. (1991, May). *Managerial leadership—emergent trends*. Unpublished professorial inaugural lecture, University of East London.

ively to colleagues in the implementation of decisions (Chell, 1987; Wright & Taylor, 1984).

Hosking & Morley (1988) offer an approach to leadership that is concerned with how leaders process information, understand the leadership environment, and use the knowledge they acquire as an input to a bargaining and negotiating process with others. Construing leadership in this way would inevitably lead to regarding it as a skill.

According to Hosking and Morley, a skilful leader is one who can construct and maintain social order, underpinned by systems of power and values. Within this framework, the skilful leader is likely to be very knowledgeable about the environment that governs his or her work, and is adept at interpreting information and making decisions on the basis of an analysis of that information. To develop information about his or her work environment, the leader is expected to build extensive networks of collaborative relationships, which will provide benefits in terms of awareness of matters of perhaps no immediate

relevance, but certainly with long-term significance as an information source. Hosking and Morley feel that the excessive emphasis in leadership studies given to superior–subordinate relationships has resulted in a neglect of lateral relationships.

BEHAVIOURAL STYLE

This major section is devoted to a discussion of topics and issues that can be broadly classified as the behavioural style approach to leadership. Topics covered are:

- styles of leadership;
- the impact of personality on leadership style;
- Likert's four styles;
- consideration and initiating structure;
- the managerial grid;
- participative leadership as a prominent style, and its application in production, budgeting, systems design, and safety;

- criticisms of participative leadership;
- macro participation; and
- offshoots of the participative process (e.g. quality circles).

Styles of Leadership

The lack of success of the early personality trait approach to leadership, which viewed leadership as a quality anchored in particular individuals to enable them to play roles in society where the exercise of influence is required, gave rise to a new approach. This was known as the behavioural style approach to leadership and was based on the view that leadership processes did not reside solely in the person, but could be cultivated as distinctive patterns of behaviour. The behavioural style approach became popular from the late-1930s onwards, and was promoted by the work of Kurt Lewin (see panel below).

The studies featured in the panel below showed that the effectiveness of a leadership style depended on what criterion of effectiveness was used—a criterion of effectiveness could be the morale of the group or productivity. For instance, the morale of the group in the example was better under democratic leadership, but under autocratic leadership a greater number of aeroplane models were constructed by the children (at least while the leader remained present).

The choice of subject matter or topic in these studies was probably influenced by Lewin's experience of totalitarian systems in Nazi Germany. The outcome of the studies had a significant effect on the development of leadership research in the US after World War II.

In other cultural settings, different results were achieved when the earlier studies were replicated (Smith & Peterson, 1988). For example, in Japan the democratic style was more effective when the task was easy, and the autocratic style was more effective when the task was difficult. In India the autocratic style was superior on all criteria. (The impact of culture on organisations is considered in Chapter 11).

A criticism levelled at these studies is that the findings suffer severe limitations if they are applied to the field of industrial leadership.

Both the ideal autocratic and democratic leadership style have been considered in an organisational setting (Lowin, 1968). In the autocratic model there is a noticeable absence

---

Early Studies of Behavioural Styles

In order to investigate some aspects of how a group functions under different types of group atmosphere and different types of leadership, experiments were conducted by Lewin and his colleagues with groups of children (Lippit & White, 1968). The groups were engaged in mask-making, model-making, and similar activities. Different styles of leadership—autocratic, democratic, and *laissez-faire*—were introduced by the (adult) experimenters. For example, the formulation of policy, the techniques and methods to be used, the division of work activities, and the allocation of individuals to work were determined by the autocratic leader without reference to the group, whereas the democratic leader actively involved the children in policy making and generally in the job of dividing and allocating the work. The autocratic leader was very subjective in his criticism and praise and remained aloof from the group except when demonstrating how to do the work.

On the other hand, the democratic leader was objective in his criticism and praise and tried to be a regular group member in spirit without doing much of the actual work. The groups appeared to react very favourably to the imposition of democratic leadership practice. There appeared to be greater group purpose, the individual group members related well to each other, and they displayed less aggression and hostility and more group unity than in the autocratic groups. The reaction of group members to the *laissez-faire* style was marked with a lower degree of efficiency, organisation and satisfaction.

of credit for suggestions emanating from subordinates and a lack of formal recognition of the efforts of subordinates. The subordinate does not have the opportunity to participate in the decision-making process, and is therefore deprived of feedback that could contribute to a useful learning experience. He or she is prevented from developing an insight into the factors that must be considered in choosing among alternatives in a decision situation. Should the subordinate make a contribution, he or she probably gets no credit for it and, as a result, has little motivation to contribute beyond what is minimally expected.

Under an ideal democratic system, participation by subordinates is more frequent and more constructive. Managers are more prepared to discuss relevant issues with subordinates and to respect their suggestions. When suggestions are received and evaluated, the reaction is transmitted to the subordinate in the form of feedback. This is believed to contribute to a desirable level of motivation and to promote the quality of future suggestions. It

is also said to lead to greater involvement and to contribute to high performance standards. A summary of the characteristics of the two styles appears in Table 8.4.

Impact of Personality

A number of writers and researchers subscribe to the view that personality interacts with behavioural style. This would apply to the personality of both the superior and the subordinate. The subordinate is said to react adversely to the imposition of autocracy. When the subordinate is denied pertinent information because the superior monopolises official communication, this creates certain problems. The subordinate is unable to perceive the significance of a number of dimensions in the work situation, and this results in emotionalism, lack of direction, and alienation. Because the superior can interfere with the subordinate's freedom of action and the realisation of personal objectives, the subordinate may feel frustrated (Thompson, 1961).

TABLE 8.4

Managerial Leadership—Ideal Behavioural Styles

Autocratic Style	*Democratic Style*
Direction/obedience	Open communication/Positive attitudes
Close supervision	Frequent and constructive dialogue
Control and accountability	Evaluation of suggestions/availability of feedback
Absence of participation and feedback	Consensus, rather than coercion/compromise
Subordinates are poorly informed	Self-direction/self-control
Absence of credit for suggestions	Atmosphere that permits emotional expression
Minimum level of motivation	Conflict is confronted Group-based problem solving Influence (based on technical expertise) Personal/organisational goal congruence

Source: Adapted from Lowin, A. (1968). Participative decision making. A model, literature critique and prescription for research. *Organisational Behaviour and Human Performance, 3*, 69–106.

An autocratic style of leadership is also said to interfere adversely with spontaneity and creativity on the part of subordinates, and is likely to undermine processes of co-operation (Coch & French, 1948). It can also promote significant hostility and aggression, leading to the harbouring of latent discontent (Lippit & White, 1968).

However, there may be conditions where the subordinate's personality is compatible with an autocratic style of leadership. According to Argyris (1973), autocracy appeals to the "infant" in the subordinate's personality, and promotes a state of dependency and submissiveness. So if the subordinate has not sufficiently matured and has not moved to the "adult" end of the personality continuum, then perhaps autocracy can be agreeable.

It is suggested that those with poor productivity records are prone to suffer some anxiety and, as a consequence, they prefer a more autocratic style (Wispe & Lloyd, 1955). By not disclosing at the outset the sequence of steps in the work cycle (having decided instead to reveal them in a piecemeal fashion), an autocratic leader may unintentionally reduce anxiety and promote dependence (Lippit & White, 1968). This is understandable because it is easier to cope with a partial rather than a global view of the work cycle.

What conditions are required to ensure that the subordinate's personality is compatible with a democratic style of leadership? The subordinate with a high need for independence is likely to prefer a democratic style (Tannenbaum & Schmidt, 1958). In a study of insurance salesmen it was concluded that the more successful salesmen, who felt the least threatened, preferred a democratic leadership style (Wispe & Lloyd, 1955).

Sometimes a person who acts as a subordinate in one capacity acts the role of superior in another. The exercise of authority by a superior has a number of psychological meanings. It relates to superiority, dominance, submission, guidance, help, criticism, and reprimand (Tannenbaum, 1962). Superiors whose feelings of insecurity in an uncertain situation do not allow them to release control over the decision-making process, may be unable to involve subordinates to the extent required by democratic leadership (Tannenbaum & Schmidt, 1958). If such superiors have a strong need for predictability and stability, they may consider the act of releasing control as something that reduces the predictability of the outcome.

In other situations, an executive in a new job may feel uncertain about the circumstances he or she is to confront, and is likely to seek elaborate counsel, whereas the self-contained manager prefers to deliberate alone, and acts in an autocratic manner with hardly any subordinate involvement in the decision-making process (Litchfield, 1956). Though this evidence may have credibility in some circumstances, there must be other occasions when the self-contained manager, who may well display self-confidence, invites a high level of subordinate involvement in the decision-making process.

There are complicated reasons why superiors adopt autocratic leadership. Some superiors may identify with their own superiors who also use autocratic leadership (Thompson, 1961). A superior may use an autocratic style as an outlet for repressed aggression brought about because of being subjected to autocracy as a subordinate (Fromm, 1942). Others may resort to harsh discipline bearing the hallmark of autocracy in order to express a deep-seated hostility need (Tannenbaum & Massarik, 1963). All these interpretations border on the realm of unconscious motivations in leadership behaviour and, though important, it is difficult to identify and measure these processes.

Likert's Four Styles

An expansion of the notion that leadership style consists of two extreme positions—autocratic and democratic—is provided by Likert (1967). He puts forward four styles of leadership to capture the management culture of an organisation:

1. *Exploitive authoritative*. The leader uses fear and threats, communication is downwards, superior and subordinates are psychologically distant, and almost all decisions are taken at the apex of the organisation.
2. *Benevolent authoritative*. The leader uses rewards to encourage performance, the upward flow of communication is limited to what the boss wants to hear, subservience to superiors is widespread, and although most decisions are taken at the top of the organisation there is some delegation of decision making.
3. *Consultative*. The leader uses appropriate rewards, communication may be two-way although upward communication is cautious and limited, by and large, to what the boss wants to hear; some involvement is sought from employees, and subordinates have a moderate amount of influence in some decisions, but again broad policy decisions are the preserve of top management only.
4. *Participative*. The leader discusses economic rewards and makes full use of group participation and involvement in fixing high performance goals and improving work methods and procedures. The emphasis is on a network of accurate information; subordinates and superiors are psychologically close, and group decision making is widely spread throughout the organisation. There is a tendency for a number of individuals to belong to more than one work group in order to promote inter-group links and understanding.

Consideration and Initiating Structure

Consideration and initiating structure, as dimensions of leadership behaviour, were isolated and identified by researchers at the Ohio State University (Fleishman & Harris, 1962). Both factors can be evaluated after an individual completes a questionnaire.

Consideration indicates friendship, mutual trust, respect, and warmth. A high score on this dimension reflects a climate of good rapport and two-way communication, and seems to resemble a participative (employee-orientated) approach to leadership.

Initiating structure indicates a concern with defining and organising roles or relationships in an organisation, and establishing well-defined forms of organisation, channels of communication, and ways of getting jobs done. A high score on this dimension characterises individuals who play an active role in directing group activities through planning, communicating information, scheduling, trying out new ideas and practices, and so on.

The job-centred manager (task-orientated) would appear to rank high on initiating structure and low on consideration. The Ohio studies found that the two factors were independent of each other—that is, how a leader scores on one factor has no influence on what he or she scores on the other, although other studies show that the two dimensions are related. This means that a leader can be directive in managing subordinates and at the same time can establish highly supportive relations with them (Weissenberg & Kavanagh, 1972). The outcome of early studies indicated that a leader rated high on both initiating structure and consideration was most likely to be a successful manager. However, some subsequent studies did not endorse this position.

It is maintained that behavioural styles that bear a close relationship to consideration and initiating structure are likely to be influenced by cultural norms. For example, in Japan and Hong Kong, the operationalisation of the consideration dimension in specific behavioural terms varied from that in the UK and the US (Smith et al., 1989).

Features of both consideration and initiating structure are acknowledged by implication in a report on *Managing Safety* prepared by the Accident Prevention Advisory Unit of the Health and Safety Executive (Health & Safety Executive, 1981). The report states that high standards of safety should be a management objective pursued in the same way as other management objectives. It goes on to suggest the need to stimulate managers to recognise the contribution that they can make to the assessment of safety and health problems for which they are responsible in the workplace.

The development and application of effective solutions to these problems would require effective information systems to assist in the identification and assessment of hazards so that resources can be earmarked and priorities allocated to control or eliminate the hazards. A successful manager is described in the report as somebody who:

- sets understandable and practical goals for safety;
- motivates and obtains commitment from the work-force;
- provides realistic resources for the implementation of safety policy;
- instils a need in the work-force to accept personal responsibility for safety; and
- evaluates standards of safety achievement in ways that clearly mark approval or disapproval of individual and group performances.

The Managerial Grid

Another approach to depicting different leadership styles is the managerial grid developed by Blake and Mouton (1985). In this concept of leadership style, concern for people and production are treated as separate dimensions. Leadership style is not shown as a point on a leadership continuum but rather as a point on a two-dimensional grid. In Fig. 8.1, the horizontal dimension of the grid represents the individual's concern for production, and the vertical dimension represents his or her concern for people.

This concept is similar to the concept of employee-centred and job-centred leadership discussed earlier. In the managerial grid the individual can score anything between the maximum number (9,9) or the minimum

number (1,1) on either dimension. The ideal of the managerial grid is to move towards the 9,9 style (team management) where there is an integrative maximum concern for both production and people; this appears to be in the same mould as participative leadership.

Blake and Mouton advocate a phased organisational development programme with the adoption of the 9,9 style in mind. The 9,1 style (task management) focuses wholly on production, and the manager in this category can generally be said to have acute problems in dealing with people, but is exceptionally competent in a technical sense. This style is entirely geared to a high level of productivity, at least in the short term. The superior makes the decision and the subordinate carries it out without question. Traditionally, shopfloor conditions in the motor industry were considered to be a good example of the 9,1 leadership style, and the fact that its past record of industrial relations was punctuated with disputes might be indicative of the shortcomings of task management. It is conceivable that this style of leadership is a major contributor to the polarisation of the superior and subordinate, resulting in the "them" and "us" thinking that is at the root of many industrial disputes.

By contrast, the 1,9 style (country club management) emphasises people to the exclusion of their performance. People are encouraged and supported, but their mistakes are actually overlooked because they are doing their best—the maxim of "togetherness" applies. Direct disagreement or criticism of one another must be avoided and, as a consequence, production problems are not followed up. This style of leadership can evolve easily when competition is limited.

Participative Leadership

The participative style of leadership has been endorsed in a number of studies. In an early Michigan study of the role of first-line supervisors, it was concluded that the supervisor who often checked up on

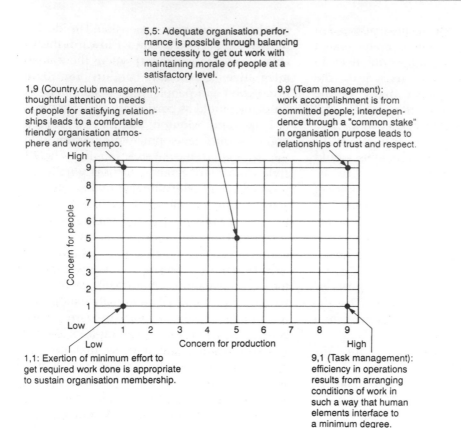

5,5: Adequate organisation performance is possible through balancing
the necessity to get out work with
maintaining morale of people at a
satisfactory level.

1,9 (Country.club management):
thoughtful attention to needs
of people for satisfying relationships leads to a comfortable
friendly organisation atmosphere and work tempo.

9,9 (Team management):
work accomplishment is from
committed people; interdependence through a "common stake"
in organisation purpose leads to
relationships of trust and respect.

1,1: Exertion of minimum effort to
get required work done is appropriate
to sustain organisation membership.

9,1 (Task management):
efficiency in operations
results from arranging
conditions of work in
such a way that human
elements interface to
a minimum degree.

FIG. 8.1.
The managerial
grid®. Source: Blake,
R.R. & Mouton, J.S.
(1985). *The
managerial grid III*
(revised edition).
Houston, TX: Gulf
Publishing Co.
Reprinted by
permission.

subordinates, gave them detailed and frequent instructions, and generally limited the employees' freedom to do their work in their own way (i.e. a directive or autocratic style), had a low productivity record. This result was contrasted with the record of high productivity units where there was a high frequency of contact between superior and subordinates, where decision making tended to be pushed down the hierarchy, where superiors were helpful in a constructive way, and generally where good relationships between superiors and subordinates were evident. This profile is congruent with a participative style. In low productivity units, on the other hand, contact between superior and subordinates was low and there existed a high degree of pressure to finish jobs and meet production targets (Likert, 1961). The

following statements seem to encapsulate the essence of participative leadership:

- The participative style is often conceived largely in terms of a "system of values" governing behaviour with a commitment to full and free communication, a reliance on consensus rather than on the more customary forms of coercion or compromise to tackle and manage conflict, and an atmosphere that permits and encourages emotional expression as well as a healthy attitude to work (Bennis, 1966).
- It is argued that as the individual moves from the infant end of a personality continuum (basically dependent and submissive, with few and shallow abilities and a short time perspective) to the adult

end (endowed with relative independence, autonomy, self-control, many abilities and a few in depth, and a long time perspective) then we have to create conditions to permit self-regulation, self-evaluation, self-adjustment, and participation in the setting of goals. By doing so, it is alleged, we bring about an improvement in productivity and attitudes (Argyris, 1973).

• Contrary to general misconceptions, humans have within themselves the capacity to exercise self-direction and self-control in the achievement of objectives to which they are committed. Individuals are likely to assume responsibility rather than to shed it, and if they are lazy, indolent, or passive, it is not due to inherent human weaknesses but attributable to previous organisational experience (McGregor, 1960). There is a recognition that the full potential of human resources is not realised in organisations.

This last point is a theme very much in evidence in a "human resources model" of organisation, not to be confused with human resource management as conceived in the 1980s, and referred to in Chapter 13. The human resources model maintains that there exists in organisations reservoirs of untapped resources and that these resources include not only physical skills and energy but also creative ability and the capacity for responsible, self-directed, self-controlled behaviour. The model also has something to say about the improvement of the quality of decisions and company performance through effective delegation, and that involvement in decisions applies to non-routine as well as to routine matters. Also, it is felt that providing the opportunity for the exercise of self-direction and self-control should come about in progressive steps in line with the growth in the ability and experience of the individual (Miles, 1965).

Participation in Production

In the following studies, the positive consequences flowing from the application of participative leadership are very much in evidence. In one factory a group of female employees were given the opportunity to determine their work rate by controlling their own conveyor belt. As a result, quality was maintained and production rose appreciably. It was not until the earnings of the female workers outstripped the earnings of many of the male workers in the plant, chiefly due to the size of productivity bonuses, that various pressures were brought to bear on management to remove the alleged inequality. In these circumstances the plant superintendent arbitrarily revoked, without consultation, the productivity bonuses the women had come to expect and he returned the plant's operations to the previous state. The end result was that things moved again at their "time study" speed, production dropped and, within a month, all but two of the eight women had left the company (Bavelas & Strauss, 1970).

In another factory, an investigation was undertaken because the company experienced acute resistance by employees to changes in both jobs and methods of work. The consequences of this resistance to change were high rates of staff turnover, many complaints, low efficiency, and restriction of output. It was decided to create both an experimental and a control group, the experimental group participating in the evaluation and redesign of their jobs. The experimental group, unlike the control group, surpassed their previous performance, but only after experiencing an unsatisfactory contribution for a transitional period (during which 62% of employees whose jobs were modified suffered a chronic substandard performance or left the job during the retraining stage). An encouraging note to these experiments was the impressive performance of control groups when they worked in the same conditions experienced by the experimental groups—i.e. exposed to the participative process (Coch & French, 1948).

Management at *ICI* saw three main benefits accruing to participation at the shopfloor level (Daniel & McIntosh, 1972):

1. The employees' unique knowledge of their job enabled them to identify waste that only they could know about.
2. Proposed changes were discussed in a positive co-operative spirit with both management and employees making suggestions and evaluating them together, as opposed to management making proposals that would subsequently be rejected by the workers' representatives.
3. After formal acceptance of changes, the changes took place with speed and without disruption to the life of the enterprise.

However, though management was encouraged to discuss matters with shopfloor workers, a disadvantage appeared to be the apparent erosion of the middle manager's role.

Participation in Budgeting

The concept of participation has been applied to planning and control processes (e.g. budgetary control) within organisations. At one time this was a fashionable line of enquiry. There is a long stream of studies indicating the desirability of participation in the budgetary process (see panel below for examples), though one should take note of the qualifying statements.

Sometimes participation in budgeting falls short of ideal practice. In budgetary control the illustration of "pseudo-participation" is embodied in a classic study which commented on the tactics of the controller who encourages an exchange of opinions but, believing that the line supervisors have little to contribute anyway, is very keen to get their signatures on the new budget signifying their approval (Argyris, 1953). The signatures are then evidence of their approval.

One should note however that if supervisors accept half-heartedly a budget target or budget changes, and are bound by their signatures, it will almost inevitably follow that the initiators of the targets or changes will have to be constantly vigilant, and will have to pressurise the acceptors of the suggested course of action in order to ensure compliance. This is not a favourable situation to be in for somebody who subscribes to the notion of participation as a motivational tool.

Participation in the Budgetary Process

It is maintained that higher levels of participation in the budgetary process lead to a higher level of motivation to meet budget standards, though this does not extend to the setting of financial standards (Hofestede, 1968).

In one particular study it was found that those who participated in the setting of standards performed better than those who did not, but the outcome from another study suggests that the favourable consequences of participation are limited to the creation of favourable attitudes rather than improving performance (Bass & Leavitt, 1963; Milani, 1975). In a participative process there is an opportunity to obtain feedback on the acceptability of the individual's proposals, and this is said to be a necessary prerequisite for the individual's commitment to the budget (Foran & De Coster, 1974). Likewise, the budget process is likely to be improved by the contribution of the individual's unique and localised knowledge of his or her area of work (Parker, 1979).

In more recent studies the clarity of the budget goal or standard goes hand in hand with participation as factors giving rise to higher levels of motivation to meet budget standards, the actual attainment of budget targets and an improvement in job satisfaction (Kenis, 1979; Merchant, 1981).

It appears that the personality of the manager involved in the budgetary process is an important variable in the relationship between participation and positive outcomes in terms of satisfaction and performance. According to Bromnell (1981), the relationship is said to be good for those individuals who feel they have a large degree of control over their destiny (internal locus of control), but bad for those who feel their destinies are controlled by luck, chance or fate (external locus of control). (The concept of locus of control was discussed earlier in Chapter 1).

There is also the danger of "budget biasing" taking root in a participatory budget system. This amounts to managers inflating costs or reducing revenue at the budget stage (Schiff & Lewin, 1970).

In the context of meeting the requirements of the corporate master budget, there is a view that the ability of large groups of lower level personnel to participate in budget planning must be the subject of some doubt for the following reasons (Parker, 1979):

- They may lack the interest and expertise required for comprehending the range of factors to be balanced in the planning of sales, production, materials, and administration.
- They may find it difficult to understand the need for identifying limiting factors, and may be unable to co-ordinate their estimates with those of other draft sub-budgets.
- There may be difficulties in comprehending the more sophisticated forecasting and simulation techniques, as well as a lack of full understanding of the broader economic and other environmental factors affecting operations.
- To finalise a budget with so many people contributing would present many problems for the accountant, and if planning were to start much earlier in order to accommodate this constraint, estimates may be out of date.

Participation in Systems Design
With the growth in the computerisation of administrative systems, the question arises as to the extent to which employees will be involved in the rearrangement of work and the redesign of jobs. Dickson and Simmons (1970) suggest that the atmosphere implicit in the human resources model of organisation referred to earlier, together with a supportive top management, is a necessary requirement. On occasions the specialists (systems analysts) have too much responsibility for design and modification of information systems, and operating managers and their staff have too little. Therefore it is a prime requirement for systems analysts to communicate with the users of information. This view would find favour with Mumford (1980), who puts forward participation as an effective process to bring about desired change in administrative systems.

"Consensus participation" is the preferred strategy of Mumford, which she construes as an advanced democratic approach. It aims to involve representatives of all staff in the user department continuously throughout the systems design process. Representatives would be elected, and the services of analysts would be at the disposal of the group. The object is for colleagues to exchange ideas about new forms of work organisation, and to allow the final decision to be taken by the department as a whole.

The first task of the design group is to gather information about the impediments to efficiency and job satisfaction. This would be followed by proposals for alternative systems of work designed to overcome the problems identified, leading to the adoption of the most preferred alternative. The likely outcome is the advocacy of autonomous or self-managing groups for the most skilled employees, and job rotation for those who do not mind doing routine jobs.

Participation in Safety
The pursuit of high standards of health and safety practice at work is a desirable objective, and the use of participative processes to attain that objective has been recommended. The Robens Committee in the UK, which, in the early 1970s, deliberated on safety and health at work, recognised the prime importance of worker co-operation with management if places of work were to be made safer. The committee believed that worker involvement would assist in overcoming the apathy that it felt was the primary cause of accidents at work (Robens' Report, 1972). The report went on to say that health and safety problems, unlike most other matters, have a greater

effect in promoting common ground between management and workers: "There is no legitimate scope for bargaining on safety and health issues but much scope for constructive discussion, joint inspection, and participation in working out solutions." The report sought to encourage employees to accept health and safety both as a personal responsibility and an important organisational objective, and to work co-operatively towards improving health and safety practices and standards.

The views of the Robens Committee were subsequently incorporated in the Health and Safety at Work Act 1974, and this created a legal framework for individual and collective involvement in health and safety issues at the workplace. The Act provides recognised trade unions with the right to appoint safety representatives from among their members. These representatives have the right to investigate potential hazards and dangerous occurrences, examine employee complaints concerning health and safety, and carry out routine inspections of the workplace. They are entitled to make representations to their employers on health and safety matters. The code of practice accompanying the statutory regulations stresses the need for open dialogue between management and representatives in order for participation to be effective.

Evidence on health and safety practice at work indicates that the consultative process was in some respects deficient. One of the most common problems was simply the lack of responsiveness by line managers to the requests of safety representatives for information or action, though sometimes the managers did not have the information to give (Gibson & Kidd, 1982).

Criticism of Participative Leadership

A challenge to the alleged benefits accruing to a participative style comes from a study conducted in four divisions within a company (Morse & Reimer, 1956). In two divisions a participative style was used, decision making was deliberately pushed down the hierarchy,

supervisors were trained to use democratic supervisory methods, and there was an appreciable increase in their freedom of action. In the other two divisions greater hierarchical control was introduced by an increase in the closeness of supervision, and there was a noticeable shift upwards in the level at which decisions were made. These conditions prevailed for a year and approximately 500 employees were involved. It was found that both programmes contributed to a significant increase in productivity, surprisingly with a slight advantage accruing to the autocratic system.

Critics of the participative leadership school (Crozier, 1964; Strauss, 1968) harbour a number of reservations:

- There is a tendency to place overwhelming emphasis on personal co-ordination and control to the detriment of bureaucratic or impersonal control techniques.
- The important role played by bargaining and the use of power in interpersonal relationships is overlooked.
- The democratic or participative style is conceived largely in terms of group harmony and compatibility between personal goals and organisational goals, but the importance of organisation structure is neglected.
- Although generally people would like to exercise some degree of control over their own environment, they may fear the participation process because it threatens their integrity and independence, or they believe they will be controlled to some extent by other participants.
- Should the rewards or benefits that result from co-operating with others prove inadequate, then withdrawal from the participative process is a likely outcome.
- Participation might lack appeal for those who do not trust each other, who feel intellectually superior to their peers, and who do not have the patience to bother with it and feel it consumes too much valuable time.

Macro Participation

The foregoing discussion dealt with participation at the micro level (primarily at the operational level). Participation at the policy or macro level is discussed briefly here. In Britain, participation at the macro level has never been a significant practical proposition, though the worker director scheme at the *British Steel Corporation* in the past was a notable exception. The Bullock Committee report in 1976 was followed by a White Paper on industrial democracy in 1978. The White Paper proposed a structure of joint representation committees composed of all unions at each place of work with a statutory right to discuss company strategy and have access to information. These measures were never enacted.

The European Commission's revised 1983 Draft Directive on *Procedures for Informing and Consulting Employees* (the "Vredeling Directive") recommended giving employee representatives, in organisations employing 1000 or more workers within the EC, substantial general information on the group as a whole and specific information on their own company within the group. Certain business secrets would be withheld.

The British Employment Secretary in Margaret Thatcher's government said in a press release in November 1983:

> The government welcomes moves to promote involvement of employees in the enterprises for which they work, but it believes that the main initiative is best left to employers and employees, who are in the best position to judge what best suits their particular circumstances. I am very dubious of the value in the European Community issuing directives which conflict with well-established and perfectly legitimate differences in industrial relations policy and practice between member states. There is evidence of significant growth in recent years of employee involvement under the voluntary approach preferred in the UK, and the Commission has not even attempted to show why this approach should now be discarded.

Interestingly, in 1993 the British government led by John Major is still not too keen on the European Commission's (now European Union) prescription to protect workers' rights. Alone among EC states, the UK opted out of the Social Chapter of the Maastricht Treaty. The Social Chapter is concerned with individual and collective rights, and provides standards and conditions governing employment, among them the right to information, consultation, and worker participation. By contrast, the main opposition party in Britain—the Labour Party—recently restated its commitment to worker participation or industrial democracy.

In Sweden, employee directors on the boards of companies have proved a successful venture, and in Germany, the *Mitbestimmung* provides an opportunity for employee representatives to influence policy formulation on supervisory boards.

A significant extension to industrial democracy practices in Sweden came about with the 1976 Act on Employee Participation in Decision Making. In this legislation there is provision for collective agreements between employers and unions to embrace questions relating to the conclusion and cancellation of employment contracts, supervision and distribution of work, and other aspects of management. The 1976 Act, though welcomed by trade unionists and certain politicians, has been received with hesitancy and anxiety by many employers and managers. They are afraid of increased union influence, and "cannot believe that it will be possible to run their companies in an efficient and profitable way under the new conditions" (Lind, 1979).

The reality surrounding the operation of Works Councils in the former Yugoslavia highlights some of the difficulties with participation at the macro level. For example,

90% of those contributing in the council were experts who had received higher education, the workers were inadequately motivated, and the influence of a power elite and a small circle of competent and responsible people was conspicuous (Mulder, 1971). However, the rank and file workers participated more actively when the discussion moved from technical problems to human relations problems such as standards of living, social welfare, and the hiring and placement of workers (Obradovic, 1975).

A British social scientist, on reviewing some critical evidence of self-management in the former Yugoslavia, feels the problems of alienation in the workplace cannot be magically solved by simply installing workers' councils, but is himself inclined to the view that much less might be achieved in terms of industrial democracy if an even weaker system of worker participation had been arrived at, or is set up in future (Warner, 1975).

On the basis of a personal impression of the drawbacks of participation in a sympathetic culture, the following observation was made by Child (1977) in studying Israeli industrial practices:

> The role of socialist principles in the establishment of Israeli institutions, and indeed in the political life of the country even today, cannot be overlooked. Bearing these factors in mind, one might conclude that if in that type of society schemes of participation and industrial democracy have on the whole become transmuted into techniques of management and have not substantially modified the industrial management hierarchy, then in societies where social stratification is more strongly entrenched there is even less prospect that the establishment of formal systems of industrial democracy will lead to any fundamental change of social relationships within industry.

Offshoots of the Participative Process

Quality Circles

The quality circle could be considered an extension to the basic philosophy of the participative process. As a group phenomenon, it has relevance to the discussion in Chapter 7. The quality circle advocates participation in the setting of objectives, together with participation in processes leading to a removal of obstacles frustrating the achievement of agreed objectives. The consequences of the implementation of quality circles are said to be enhanced commitment to necessary changes in work practices. The quality circle became an integral part of the management system in Japan, and the key factor appears to be the involvement of employees at all levels. It is used to improve productivity, product quality and safety at work, and the benefits claimed following its use are reduced waste, improved communication between management and workers, the creation of a problem-solving environment, increased job involvement, and improved morale.

A quality circle is a small group of employees (4 to 15) who do similar work and report to the same supervisor. The group meets regularly on a voluntary basis to identify and analyse work problems and provide solutions. A large plant could have many quality circles. Employees are encouraged to join a circle, not told to, and they can expect to experience a greater sense of control over their job environment. Members of a circle receive training in the basics of the technical aspects of the job, and in the skills of problem solving and making presentations to management. Interpersonal skills training is an important means of removing the barriers to interactions between people.

The usefulness of the concept of the quality circle must be properly understood, and to this end a publicity campaign could be launched within the company to explain the concept to employees and to request volunteers. The objectives of the circle must be endorsed by management. Some of the main functional considerations concerning quality circles are set out in the panel below.

The following conditions should also be given serious consideration (Collard, 1981). The management should be modest in its expectations initially, and perhaps start with a low-profile pilot scheme. The support and commitment of management, and particularly senior management, is crucial. They should demonstrate their support for the programme, in both words and actions, by explaining what is involved, by providing training resources and other assistance, by attending regular presentations made by the circle, and by using the circle for its own purposes. The terms of reference of the quality circle should be clearly stated and communicated.

The safeguards and assurances with respect to the impact the quality circle may have on bonuses, overtime earnings, and job security have to be considered. The union is likely to be sensitive to the question of productivity gains and the way they are to be distributed. The importance of anticipating problems, rather than merely reacting to them, has to be stressed, as well as the need to engage in innovative activities, such as new systems and products. Naturally, circle members would like to see their successes recognised at all levels of the organisation.

In an empirical study of how quality circles work in practice in four US companies, it was concluded that quality circles lend themselves to the solution of basic localised problems of an immediate and solvable nature. They also provide employees with an opportunity to

---

The Workings of Quality Circles

A quality circle consists of circle members, a circle leader, a facilitator, a steering committee, and circle management. Circle volunteers are those who do the work and are interested in improving the quality of the work environment. The circle leader is a specially trained supervisor or somebody chosen from among the voluntary group. A facilitator, who has to be carefully selected and trained, provides training to circle members, provides a communication channel between different circles, and acts as liaison between the steering committee and management. He or she provides feedback on various activities, exerts influence where appropriate, and deals with conflicting groups.

A steering committee normally comprises first-line supervisors, who have a brief to provide quick responses to requests for funds, and to make sure that the circles get support from technical specialists in the organisation. Circle management provides support, funds, and facilities, and it reviews the solutions recommended by the circle in its management presentations. The presentations are the vehicle through which the group obtains recognition for the work done.

A quality circle meeting, in a quiet room, could last for no more than one hour per week. Members of the circle would identify problems that could affect the overall company plan; for example, how to improve productivity by 10% over the next year. The circle would prioritise the order in which problems are to be tackled and, having selected a problem (e.g. how to reduce product defects from 5% to 2%), circle members set realistic goals. Using appropriate analytic methods, a general plan and schedule for the solution of the identified problem is established. Drawing on internal expertise and invited external specialists who act in an advisory capacity, and using external sources of data, the circle discusses several solutions to a problem.

The preferred solution would be tested and implemented after presenting management with a full analysis using appropriate statistical techniques. Where management decide to implement the solution, this should be publicised widely so as to provide circle members with the necessary recognition. Any rejection of a circle recommendation should have the reasons for non-acceptance well stated. The results emanating from circle initiatives should be monitored, and presentations of successful outcomes could go beyond the organisational level in which the circle functions. As an incentive for circle members, in Japan it is not uncommon for directors of a company to be present and participate directly by asking questions at the presentation.

learn how to influence their work situation (Burpeau-Di Gregorio & Dickson, 1983).

The Work Research Unit of the Department of Employment in Britain did much in the past to publicise the concept of the quality circle, and has been concerned with the practical application of the concept. In a publication of the unit it was stated that it is too soon to draw conclusions about the applicability of the concept in the UK, and acknowledged that the response to it has not been dramatic (Russell, 1983). In the mid-1980s the Work Research Unit organised a national conference on quality circles, sponsored by the National Economic Development Office. This was considered to be useful in creating and stimulating a renewed interest in quality circles, and had as its objectives the dissemination of knowledge based on practical experience, the sharing of useful ideas and suggestions, and the consideration of options and strategies for the future (Work Research Unit, 1983).

In Japan the enthusiasm for the quality circle is evident, and the concept is adapted to meet particular organisational circumstances. As a result, there are variations in the manner in which the quality circle is implemented (Collard, 1981). One practice common to all quality circles is that discussions go beyond quality; they include cost, use of equipment, efficiency, errors, and safety. In some cases there is a formal training programme for members; in other cases only leaders receive formal training, and there are also instances where no formal training is provided. In the latter case the skills of supervisors and experts in the group would be used. The circle leader can be the immediate supervisor of the group; in other cases the leadership role rotates, though it is likely that the majority of leaders come from the ranks of supervisors. Sometimes the norm is to hold meetings in the employees' time without payment, but there are also precedents for meetings to take place in the company's time, with overtime payments for meetings held in the employees' time.

In the late-1980s there was evidence to indicate that although quality circles had a short-term favourable effect, their effectiveness over time began to diminish (Griffin, 1988). Also there have been examples of lukewarm commitments to quality circles by management, as well as trade union opposition. In the latter case it is possible that quality circles were seen as a vehicle to create a more expansive participative culture throughout an organisation that could be construed as a threat. It could become a live issue if there is no agreement between management and the trade union about setting up quality circles. Van Fleet and Griffin (1989) provide a recent review of quality circles.

Total Quality Management. Speaking of quality, a recent development, not directly related to quality circles but no doubt complementary to them, is called "total quality management". It starts with the vision that concentrated management action can improve the quality of an organisation's services and products at very competitive cost levels, while still satisfying customer needs and increasing market share. Various action strategies are suggested, including securing a high level of involvement and commitment from organisational members (Kanji, 1990).

There is a belief that if total quality management (TQM) is handled properly it can deliver gradual but continuous improvements in many aspects of business performance. This is a view likely to be bolstered by the findings of recent research conducted by the Delta Consulting Group in the United States.

Although the study of around 200 large corporations was generally supportive of TQM, problems were identified. Chief executives reported two particular problems with TQM: it took longer than expected to produce results, and some senior managers were not sufficiently skilled in handling it. By contrast, quality officials in the organisations studied emphasised negative views with respect to senior management's knowledge and skill, and identified conflicting values among senior managers, a lack of perceived need for change, and strong resistance to change (Lorenz, 1993b).

A complementary development to TQM is "process re-engineering" (see panel below) which is related to job design (Chapter 2) and organisational design (Chapter 10).

CONTINGENCY THEORIES

By the early-1960s there was a recognition that leadership could not be explained satisfactorily in terms of behavioural styles,

and there was a general belief that the particular circumstances in which leaders find themselves (situational circumstances) are influential in determining the most appropriate leadership style. In this section the following important contingency or situational perspectives on leadership are considered:

- leadership continuum;
- influence–power continuum;
- Fiedler's model;
- a normative model (revised);
- vertical dyad linkage theory;
- path-goal model;
- Hersey-Blanchard situational theory; and

Process Re-engineering

This employs some of the same tools and techniques as TQM, and attempts to create a more dramatic impact on business processes over shorter periods of time.

The twin cores of process re-engineering are the radical redesign of business processes and their operation by cross-functional teams. Process re-engineering poses a direct challenge to the division of labour and the need for hierarchical control. In many organisations, orders and projects pass up, down, and across a succession of separate vertically structured "functional" departments, often waiting hours or days for the next task to be carried out. In a process re-engineered organisation, tasks which were previously separate are replaced by a seamless process, and functional boundaries are either bridged or removed entirely, with a "process owner" often overseeing everyone involved. Narrow job descriptions are abandoned, and multi-skilling is warmly embraced, supplemented by a small pool of specialist staff to be called on as necessary (Hammer & Champy, 1993).

The concept of process re-engineering has been applied at *Bell Atlantic* and *AT&T*. There has been an abandonment of the numerous, traditionally fragmented, start-stop work tasks, routines, and procedures, which have been replaced by a handful of unitary processes designed from scratch to operate smoothly, from first contact with the customer through to order completion (Lorenz, 1993a).

In 1989 the condition of the manufacturing facility at *HarperCollins Publishers* in Glasgow was

described as "enormously serious", if not terminal. The cosy days of long print runs were gone. In the new cut-throat market place, customers demanded smaller orders more frequently, and the inflexible plant could not respond. According to the business development director, the option of doing nothing expired.

A strategy was formulated on the following lines—develop people, simplify processes, and then automate. The implementation of the strategy resulted in a reduction in paperback book production lead times from 5 weeks to 10 days, and hardback lead times from 8 weeks to 4 weeks. Also, 33% was taken off the cost base. According to the chief executive, "top-level commitment was important, but equally people and their commitment was crucial. If companies embark on this journey without their employees understanding what is happening, or why, they are lost. With re-engineering, everything people have banked on is no longer there. If they do not know *why*, they get insecure—you have to communicate. Once they are committed, they generate ideas, and drive change forward"(Rees, 1993).

One has to bear in mind that changes in processes have implications for cultural change, examined in Chapter 11, particularly when the old command and control mentality of managers and employees is replaced with new sets of behaviour, such as empowerment, team-work, feedback, and customer responsiveness. Also, there is the danger that radical culture change could undermine the effectiveness of process re-engineering.

- other approaches (the attribution perspective and substitutes for leadership).

Leadership Continuum

The first theory to be examined is the revised continuum of leadership behaviour proposed by Tannenbaum and Schmidt (1973). They conceive a continuum (depicted in Fig. 8.2) with an autocratic style on the left-hand side, a democratic style on the right-hand side, and varying degrees of influence in between.

The term "non-manager" is used as a substitute for "subordinate" and this is said to reflect the organisational processes such as industrial democracy and participative management, where subordinates have a greater say in matters that affect them as well as frequently sharing managerial functions. The arrows indicate the continual flow of interdependent influence. The authors of the leadership continuum are inclined to associate a subordinate-centred style with the achievement of the following common objectives shared by managers: to raise the level of employee motivation; to increase the capacity of subordinates to accept change; to improve the quality of decisions; to develop teamwork and morale; and to foster the development of employees.

The theory also considers the situation in which leadership style operates. Situational factors that determine the manager's choice of leadership style are forces in the manager, forces in the subordinate, and forces in the situation.

Forces in the Manager

A useful starting point is an understanding of the manager's attitudes and predispositions towards an appropriate leadership style. A manager may not subscribe to a participative style because he or she prefers to act alone. Likewise, managers may not wish to involve their subordinates because they lack confidence in them; or if the situation is

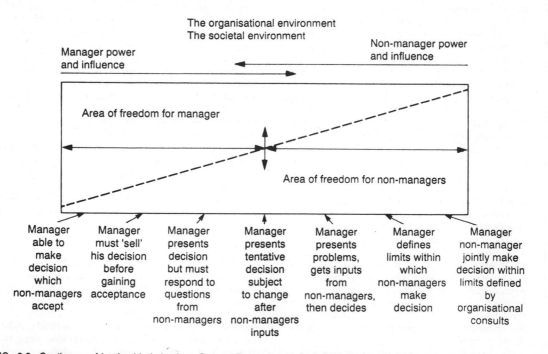

FIG. 8.2. Continuum of leadership behaviour. Source: Tannenbaum, R. & Schmidt, W.H. (1973). How to choose a leadership pattern. *Harvard Business Review*, May–June, 167. Reprinted by permission of the *Harvard Business Review*. Copyright © 1973 by the President and Fellows of Harvard College; all rights reserved.

uncertain, they may feel insecure and prefer to act independently.

Forces in the Subordinate
Ideally a manager would expect the following conditions to exist before being prepared to allow the subordinate to participate in decision making. The subordinate:

- has a relatively high need for independence;
- shows a readiness to assume responsibility for decision making;
- possesses a relatively high tolerance for ambiguity;
- is interested in the problem that is considered important;
- has the necessary knowledge and experience to deal with the problem;
- understands the goals of the organisation with which he or she can identify; and
- has developed expectations to share in decision making.

Forces in the Situation
The prevailing organisational culture may determine to some extent the type of leadership style that is best suited to a given organisation. For example, behavioural characteristics of an autocratic nature may be considered functional in some organisations and are therefore reinforced.

Other Factors
Other forces in the situation which may somehow restrain the manager's manoeuvrability with respect to leadership style are:

- the size of the working group;
- the geographical dispersion of subordinates;
- the secrecy of the issues in question;
- the level of relevant expertise of the subordinate; and
- the pressure of time.

For example, where the size of the group is large, subordinates are scattered over many company sites, the issues are highly confidential and secret, the subordinate does not have the kind of knowledge that is needed, and the organisation is in a state of crisis, then an autocratic style may be appropriate. The opposite may be true when these situations are reversed.

In the Tannenbaum and Schmidt model there is an interdependent relationship among and between the situational factors and leadership style, because what happens to one variable may have a bearing on another. The model is of some value as a conceptual scheme for identifying different leadership styles and the circumstances that influence them, but it lacks precision in suggesting the appropriate point on the continuum to choose in a given set of circumstances.

The Influence–Power Continuum

Another leadership continuum has been formulated by Heller (1971). He calls it the influence–power continuum (IPC) and it is used to evaluate the various degrees of sharing influence and power between superiors and subordinates. The main feature of the IPC—depicted in Fig. 8.3—is that it extends the normal concept of participation to incorporate the sharing of power through delegation.

A detailed description of the five styles in the IPC is as follows:

1. Own decision without detailed explanation. These are decisions made by the manager, without previous discussion or consultation with subordinates, and no special meeting or memorandum is used to explain the decisions.
2. Own decision with detailed explanation. The same as in style 1, but afterwards the manager explains the problem and the reasons for the decision in a memorandum or special meeting.
3. Prior consultation with subordinates. Before the decision is taken the manager explains the problem to his or her subordinates and asks for their advice and help. The manager then makes the decision.

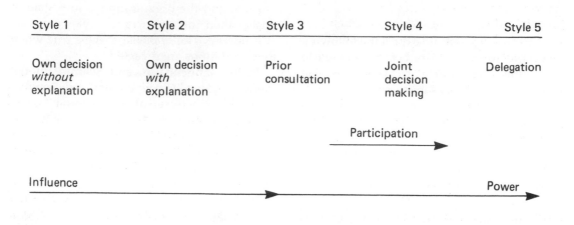

FIG. 8.3. The influence–power continuum. Source: Adapted from Heller, F.A. (1971). *Managerial decision making: A study of leadership styles and power-sharing among senior managers*. London: Tavistock.

The manager's final choice may, or may not, reflect the subordinates' influence.

4. Joint decision making with subordinates. The manager and his or her subordinates together analyse the problem and come to a decision. The subordinates usually have as much influence over the final choice as the manager. Where there are more than two individuals in the discussion, more often than not the decision of the majority is accepted.

5. Delegation of decision to subordinates. The manager asks the subordinates to make decisions regarding a particular subject. The manager may or may not request the subordinates to report back, and seldom vetoes such decisions.

Heller related the various leadership styles to specific situational circumstances and established certain relationships. The following sample of the findings of a study conducted in the US is illustrative of a situational perspective:

• A large span of control on the part of a senior manager, indicating a large number of immediate subordinates, is associated with time-saving decision styles at the extremes of the continuum—either highly centralised (style 1) or decentralised (style 5).

• When senior managers see big differences in skill between themselves and their subordinates, they use centralised or autocratic styles (styles 1 and 2). When they see little difference in skill, they are more willing to share power with their subordinates and use democratic styles (styles 3 and 4). The latter appeals to common sense, in that there is little point in sharing influence with a subordinate who is perceived as not possessing the necessary skill.

• Closely related to the last conclusion is the finding that where senior managers have experienced subordinates (measured by age and length of time in the company), they are noticeably more inclined to use delegation (style 5) and to avoid centralised or autocratic styles (styles 1 and 2).

General managers and personnel managers used the greatest amount of power sharing, whereas production and finance managers used the least.

Later, Heller's research programme was extended to a number of European countries, providing tests of the original US research. It also introduced some new variables—for example, skills and educational levels, and environmental turbulence and complexity. Taking the US and European studies together, it appears that managers in the UK, Germany, and the US are inclined to be more autocratic, whereas Swedish and French managers are more democratic (Heller & Wilpert, 1981). The influence of national cultures on management style is reported in Chapter 11.

The author adopted Heller's leadership continuum to measure the leadership style of chief accountants in the UK Among the situational factors that influenced their style were:

- the nature of the decisions they faced;
- the extent of job specialisation in the finance function;
- the calibre of section heads;
- the qualities or skills of their subordinates;
- the number of subordinates reporting to them; and
- the psychological distance or closeness between chief accountants and their subordinates.

Contrary to a general impression at that time which suggested that accountants are autocratic in orientation, chief accountants placed almost equal emphasis on both autocratic and democratic leadership styles. What was particularly interesting was that they modified their style to suit prevailing situational circumstances (McKenna, 1978).

Fiedler's Model

One of the most widely discussed theories of situational leadership in the last couple of decades is the contingency model of leadership effectiveness, postulated by Fiedler (1967). This theory attempts to predict how style of leadership, leader–member relations, the power vested in the position of leader, and the structure of the job or task

harmonise to determine the leader's ability to achieve productive output.

Style (LPC)

The measure of the style of leadership is the esteem of the leader for his or her least preferred co-worker (LPC). The LPC is the person with whom the leader has found it most difficult to co-operate. To arrive at an LPC score, leaders were asked to rate both their most preferred co-worker (MPC) and their least preferred co-worker (LPC). Leaders who describe their MPCs and LPCs similarly are classified as "high LPC" leaders, whereas those who describe their LPCs much more negatively than their MPCs are classified as "low LPC" leaders. The co-worker evaluated in this way need not be someone the leader is actually working with at the time. According to Fiedler, the LPC score is best interpreted as a dynamic trait that results in different behaviour as the situation changes.

Leaders with high LPC ratings would be psychologically close to their group members; with low LPC ratings they would be psychologically distant. Leaders who describe their least preferred co-workers in a relatively favourable manner (high LPC) tend to be employee-centred in their relationships with group members. They gain satisfaction and self-esteem from successful interpersonal relations. Leaders who describe their least preferred co-workers in a relatively unfavourable manner (low LPC) tend to be autocratic, task-centred, and less concerned with the human relations aspects of the job. They gain satisfaction and self-esteem from successful task performance. Therefore, the high and low LPC leaders seek to satisfy different needs in the group situation.

The three major variables in the work situation which can impede or facilitate a leader's attempt to influence group members are, as stated earlier:

- the structure of jobs or tasks;
- the power in the position of the leader; and
- leader–member relations.

Task Structure

The organisation generally provides support for the leader by structuring jobs with the help of procedures, rules, and regulations. The degree of structure in the job or task can be measured by establishing the extent to which work decisions can be verified, the degree of clarity surrounding the stating of the work goal, the number of methods available for achieving the goal, and the extent to which one can be specific about the solution to the work problem. The leader finds it easier to force compliance in a structured job situation than in an unstructured job situation. In the latter, leaders may find it difficult to exercise influence because neither they nor the group members can be dogmatic about what should be done; in fact, the leaders will have to pay attention to inspiring and motivating their followers.

Position Power

Power in the position is the authority vested in the leader's position as distinct from any power arising from his or her skill and ability in handling matters arising within the group. It would include the rewards and punishment at the leader's disposal, the leader's authority to define the group's rules, and his or her appointment being immune from termination by the group.

Leader–Member Relations

The most important of the three dimensions is leader–member relations. A liked and respected leader, or one working in a smoothly functioning group, can do things that would be difficult for a leader in different circumstances. Power in the position is the least important of the three dimensions because a well-liked leader can get results without institutional power, and likewise, will not need the power if the task is clearly structured.

Fiedler arrives at a continuum depicting the favourableness of the situation for the leader. This is shown in Fig. 8.4. For example, when executive functions in complex organisations were examined, the leader with a low LPC who is autocratic and task-centred (controlling, etc), was found to be effective in both favourable and unfavourable situations for the exercise of influence. A favourable situation has high task structure, good leader–member relations and strong power in the position. An unfavourable situation has low task structure, moderately poor leader–member relations, and weak power in the position.

But in between these two extreme positions, where the situation is intermediate in favourableness, the employee-centred leader (permissive, etc) who has a high LPC, was found to be effective. This type of leadership orientation was associated with policy decision making.

The implications of Fiedler's model for improving organisational effectiveness are either to change the manager's leadership orientation (as reflected in the LPC score) so it is compatible with the situational conditions or, alternatively, to modify the situational conditions in order to bring them into line with the leadership orientation. Fiedler's contingency theory of leadership has been the subject of a considerable amount of criticism (Graen, Orris, & Alvares, 1971).

Fiedler has consistently defended his approach, theory, research, and interpretations of the research evidence. There are numerous rejoinders in the literature on the contingency theory of leadership. Criticisms hinge on the difficulty of measuring task structure, the problem of using the LPC score to differentiate task and human relations-oriented leadership, and in particular the absence in many studies of a leader with an LPC score somewhere between high and low. Fiedler's view, with regard to the latter point, is that middle LPC leaders are not concerned with either task or human relations issues and perform poorly in most leadership situations. But others would dispute this view. Fiedler's model focuses heavily on performance to the neglect of employee satisfaction and, as a consequence,

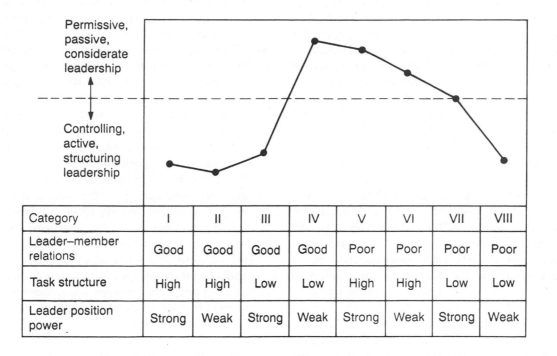

FIG. 8.4.Contingency model of leadership effectiveness. Adapted from: Fiedler, F.E. (1972). The effects of leadership training and experience: A contingency model interpretation. *Administrative Science Quarterly*, December, 455.

provides an incomplete picture of leadership effectiveness (Gray & Starke, 1984).

Fiedler has added refinements to his earlier work and has come forward with a cognitive resource theory that takes into account the intelligence and experience of the leader (Fiedler & Garcia, 1987). Leaders are said to use their intelligence more than their experience in conditions of low interpersonal stress (a favourable situation). However, they use their experience more than their intelligence in conditions of high stress (an unfavourable situation). It is suggested that in the latter situation the use of intelligence would be dysfunctional because of the negative impact of stress on cognitive functioning. As a final comment on Fiedler's work, one might suggest that the intelligence and experience variables should now join LPC

and the old situational variables before any pronouncement is made on the contingency model of leadership effectiveness.

A Normative Model

A "normative" or "prescriptive" model of leadership style has been put forward by Vroom and Yetton (1973). Certain assumptions are made about the consequences of exercising different leadership styles. A significant feature of this model is that it provides a list of considerations a manager may dwell on before selecting a leadership style in different circumstances. Vroom and Yetton believe descriptions of leadership behaviour, such as employee-orientation and task-orientation, are not strictly operational because they are too imprecise. They maintain that a normative theory of leadership must be sufficiently precise in specifying the behaviour of a leader so that a person may be confident that he or she is acting in accordance with the prescription offered by the theory. To achieve this, they put forward different forms of leadership or decision-making behaviour to cope with both individual and group problems. These are depicted in Table 8.5, and they bear a similarity to the autocratic–democratic continuum shown in Fig. 8.2.

In Table 8.5 the approaches or styles classified as "A" are autocratic; "C" are consultative; "G" are group-dominated; and "D" are delegative. There are variations within each letter classification. The right-hand column of the Table refers to problems where only one subordinate is involved, and the left-hand column refers to situations in which a group of subordinates is involved. The leader should only use an approach after considering seriously the type of problem faced and the context in which it is placed. Before selecting the most appropriate approach or style in a given situation, leaders must pay particular attention to what they would like the outcome of their deliberations and actions to be. Vroom and Yetton maintain that the leaders' approach to making a decision, or their leadership style, will be determined by the attributes of the various problems and situations they face (see panel on page 384).

Following on from this, it is important to consider the rules for choosing a particular approach to decision making or leadership style. These are derived by an elimination of the approaches or styles (listed in Table 8.5) that seem to be inappropriate, leaving us with a feasible set of decision-making approaches:

- Where the quality of the decision is important, and the leader does not possess enough information or expertise to solve the problem alone, eliminate the A1 decision-making approach in order to avoid the risk of a low-quality decision.

- Where the quality of the decision is important and the subordinates cannot be trusted to contribute to the solution of the problem with the goals of the organisation firmly in mind, eliminate the G2 approach.
- Where the quality of the decision is important, the leader lacks the necessary information or expertise to solve the problem alone, and the problem is unstructured—i.e. the leader does not know what information is needed or where it is located because access to it is difficult—then eliminate the approaches A1, A2, and C1. The approach A1 militates against collecting the necessary information, and the approaches A2 and C1 are cumbersome and less effective when a problem-solving orientation is required. In this situation approaches C2 and G1, which require interaction among subordinates who are knowledgeable with respect to a particular problem, are likely to generate high-quality solutions.

In the three cases above, the major preoccupation is to make sure that a high-quality decision is made in circumstances where quality is relevant. In the following four cases, the major preoccupation is to ensure that the decision is acceptable to subordinates when their acceptance of it is important.

- Where the acceptance of a decision by the subordinate is crucial for its effective implementation, and one is not sure that an autocratic decision-making approach would be acceptable, eliminate the A1 and A2 approaches because neither provide an opportunity for the subordinate to participate in the decision process. By taking this course of action the risk of the subordinate rejecting the decision is minimised.
- Where the acceptance of the decision by the subordinate is critical, and it is uncertain that a decision imposed autocratically will be accepted and

TABLE 8.5

Decision Methods for Group and Individual Problems

Group Problems	*Individual Problems*
A1. You solve the problems or make the decision yourself, using information available to you at the time.	A1. You solve the problem or make the decision by yourself, using information available to you at the time.
A2. You obtain the necessary information from your subordinates, then decide the solution to the problem yourself. You may or may not tell your subordinates what the problem is in getting the information from them. The role played by your subordinates in making the decision is clearly one of providing the necessary information to you, rather than generating or evaluating alternative solutions.	A2. You obtain the necessary information from your subordinates, then decide on the solution to the problem yourself. You may or may not tell the subordinate what the problem is in getting the information from him/her. His/her role in making the decision is clearly one of providing the necessary information to you, rather than generating or evaluating alternative solutions.
C1. You share the problem with the relevant subordinates individually, getting their ideas and suggestions without bringing them together as a group. Then you make the decision which may or may not reflect your subordinates' influence.	C1. You share the problem with your subordinate, getting ideas and suggestions. Then you make a decision, which may or may not reflect his/her influence.
C2. You share the problem with your subordinates as a group, obtaining their collective ideas and suggestions. Then you make the decision, which may or may not reflect your subordinates' influence.	G1. You share the problem with your subordinate, and together you analyse the problem and arrive at a mutually agreeable solution.
G2. You share the problem with your subordinates as a group. Together you generate and evaluate alternatives and attempt to reach agreement (consensus) on a solution. Your role is much like that of chairman. You do not try to influence the group to adopt "your" solution, and you are willing to accept and implement any solution that has the support of the entire group.	D1. You delegate the problem to your subordinate, providing any relevant information that you possess, but giving him/her responsibility for solving the problem. You may or may not request the subordinate to tell you what solution he/she has reached

Source: Vroom, V.H. & Yetton, P.W. (1973). *Leadership and decision making*. Pittsburgh: University of Pittsburgh Press, p.13. © 1973 University of Pittsburgh Press, reprinted by permission of the publisher.

subordinates are likely to be in conflict over the most appropriate solution, then eliminate the approaches A1, A2, and C1. The reason for this is that A1, A2, and C1 are approaches that generally require a one-to-one relationship and involve no significant interaction. These approaches do not provide enough opportunity for those in conflict to resolve their difficulties; as a consequence, some subordinates may lack the necessary commitment to the final decision. The most appropriate approach to adopt in these circumstances is either C2 or G1, which allow those in disagreement to resolve their differences, provided they possess full knowledge of the problem.

Problem Attributes and Situations Faced by Leaders (Vroom & Yetton, 1973)

I. *Decision Quality*

The importance of the quality of the decision.

II. *Leadership Information/Expertise*

The extent to which the leader possesses sufficient information or expertise to make a high-quality decision alone. It is obvious that a leader who makes a decision alone utilises the knowledge and skills he or she possesses. But there are a number of occasions when the leader draws on the resources of the group. Subordinates, as a group, may have the necessary information to generate a high-quality decision.

For example, a decision to rationalise the administrative structure of an organisation may require more knowledge and expertise than the leader possesses. In such circumstances one may ask if subordinates can make a valid contribution to the decision process. If not, it may be necessary for the leader to go outside the group for information.

III. *Structured or Unstructured Problems*

The extent to which the problem is structured or unstructured is significant. Structured problems are those for which the alternative solutions or methods for generating and evaluating solutions are known. An example of a structured problem is deciding when to take legal action for arrears on a customer's account where the amount involved is significant and long overdue. Unstructured problems cannot be dealt with in a clear-cut manner and they appear to be elusive or complex. An example of an unstructured problem is defining the expected life of a new fixed asset for depreciation purposes.

IV. *Subordinate Acceptance or Commitment*

This is the extent to which acceptance or commitment on the part of subordinates is critical to the effective implementation of the decision. Acceptance of the decision by subordinates is critical when the effective implementation of the decision requires the display of initiative, judgement, or creativity by all concerned. It is recognised that participation by subordinates in the making of a decision is likely to increase the probability of their accepting it.

V. *Acceptance of Autocratic Decision*

The likelihood that the leader's autocratic decision will be accepted by subordinates is a further factor. There might be circumstances when subordinates accept an decision imposed autocratically. This may occur when the proposed course of action enshrined in the decision appeals to reason and is intrinsically attractive (e.g. the leader awards his or her subordinates extra holiday entitlement because of their exceptional performance at work).

VI. *Subordinate Motivation*

This factor comprises the extent to which subordinates are motivated to achieve the organisational goals as reflected in the problem under review. It is possible to find situations where the personal goals of an employee are in line with those of the organisation. But in other cases the employee's self-interest, as reflected in his or her personal goals, is out of line with organisational goals, expressed as targets and objectives that he or she is expected to achieve. In such circumstances a leadership style, such as G2 in Table 8.5, could pose a potential risk to the quality of the decision because significant control resides in the group.

VII. *Subordinate Disagreement*

The final factor is the extent to which subordinates are likely to be in disagreement or conflict over preferred solutions. If there is disagreement, it may be possible to bring about agreement by allowing the group to interact. This could be achieved by using a group-dominated approach to decision making (e.g. C2 or G2 in Table 8.5) where subordinates interact in the process of solving the problem.

- Where the quality of the decision is unimportant, and there is doubt about the acceptability of an decision imposed autocratically, then the approaches that are likely to produce a lesser degree of acceptance by subordinates—A1, A2, C1, and C2—should be eliminated. A participative approach (e.g. G2) would appear to be more suitable in these circumstances.
- Where acceptance of the decision by subordinates is critical, where subordinates can be trusted, and where acceptance is unlikely to be forthcoming if an autocratic

approach is imposed, then eliminate the approaches A1, A2, C1, and C2. If these approaches to decision making were used, it would create the risk of a lower level of acceptance of the decision by sub-ordinates. The approach to decision making that would appear functional in these circumstances is G2, which suggests that a high level of influence is exerted by subordinates.

Having now eliminated the inappropriate approaches to decision making, the leader is still left with more than one approach. Vroom and Yetton suggest that decision rules can be used to help with the selection of the most appropriate approach to decision making. To apply this procedure a decision tree can be used. Decision rules are presented pictorially as a decision tree in Fig. 8.5.

Before examining Fig. 8.5, a brief case is introduced, which is subsequently used to follow the flow of the decision process in the figure.

An office manager, who has not yet embraced new technology, is dissatisfied with having to place such heavy reliance on electric typewriters in the office and wishes to explore alternatives. He or she is not very knowledgeable about the purchase and operation of substitute equipment in the form of word-processors. However, it is appreciated that word-processors perform all of the normal functions of the conventional typewriter, as well as providing the user with many other facilities to alter text and to produce higher-quality copy at a faster speed.

The office manager recognises that the secretarial staff must feel comfortable and confident using word-processors, otherwise the level of productivity will fall. The office manager's relationship with the secretarial staff is good and they can identify easily with the company's goals or objectives. However, because of the calibre of the secretarial staff, and the nature of their work, they would like to have a say in any decision to replace the electric typewriters. The problem facing the

office manager and his or her staff is not clear-cut. For example, why is a word-processor necessary? Is the expense justified if the word-processor is to carry out a specific but perhaps infrequent task that is not possible on a typewriter? What about the additional costs, such as maintenance of equipment, insurance, and staff training or recruitment?

Which decision-making approach or leadership style for group problems (see Table 8.5) should the office manager use in this situation? (The letters at the end of the decision tree in Fig. 8.5 denote leadership style and they correspond to those listed in Table 8.5.) On the horizontal line of Fig. 8.5 is a list of questions, posed by the office manager, relevant to the problem. We can go through questions I to VI, using the information provided in the case just described, and arrive at the following answers. (Note that arrows show the flow of the decision process in the decision tree.)

I. Yes, there is a quality requirement (the office system based on word-processors must function).
II. No, the leader (office manager) is not very knowledgeable about word-processors.
III. No, the problem is not structured because it is not obvious how to go about the purchase, installation, and operation of an office system based on word-processors.
IV. Yes, the subordinates' (secretarial staff) involvement in the making of the decision to replace the electric typewriters is crucial for the acceptance of the decision by the subordinates.
V. No, because the acceptance of the decision by the subordinates is critical, and a decision imposed autocratically is unlikely to be accepted.
VI. Yes, the subordinates have the interests of the organisation firmly in mind with regard to the efficiency of the office, and therefore they identify with the goals of the organisation.

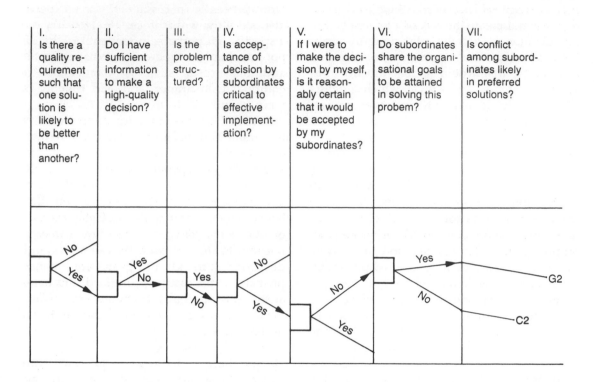

I.	II.	III.	IV.	V.	VI.	VII.
Is there a quality requirement such that one solution is likely to be better than another?	Do I have sufficient information to make a high-quality decision?	Is the problem structured?	Is acceptance of decision by subordinates critical to effective implementation?	If I were to make the decision by myself, is it reasonably certain that it would be accepted by my subordinates?	Do subordinates share the organisational goals to be attained in solving this probem?	Is conflict among subordinates likely in preferred solutions?

FIG. 8.5. Decision tree for group problems. Adapted from: Vroom, V.H. & Yetton, P.W. (1973). *Leadership and decision making.* Pittsburgh: University of Pittsburgh Press, p.194.

In this example, conflict among the subordinates (VII) did not arise. Following the arrows in Fig. 8.5 you will notice that the decision-making approach or leadership style associated with this case is G2 (a highly participative style). Given the circumstances reported in the case, it seems to be a sensible outcome. What would be the outcome if the circumstances were slightly different? Suppose the answer to question VI was "No", then the recommended style is C2, in which the leader permits limited participation but takes the final decision alone. The rationale for this may be that, as the subordinates do not share the organisational goals, it is wise for the leader to imprint his of her authority on the decision.

In the Vroom and Yetton prescriptive model, more than one of the five decision-making approaches or leadership styles shown in Table 8.5 may be effective depending on the answers given to the questions in Fig. 8.5. If time is of critical importance, the leader may use an autocratic style, but a participative style could be used when the leader feels it is preferable to spend time developing subordinates. A particular strength of the model is the identification of the factors that influence the effectiveness of the leader. These were referred to earlier as the quality requirement in decisions, the availability of relevant information or expertise, the nature of the problem, the acceptance of the decision by the subordinates, and the commitment and motivation of subordinates.

The theory has a number of attractive features, among them the issue of the involvement of subordinates in decision making. But the research methodology of the model has been criticised. It is suggested that the technique of self-reporting used by managers in devising a decision tree may be open to socially desirable responses (Field, 1979). This could arise when they report that their leadership style is more participative than it really is because they feel it is fashionable to say so.

The Vroom and Yetton model was revised by Vroom and Jago (1988). The attributes of the various problems and situations faced by the leader (listed as questions in Fig. 8.5) have now been extended to incorporate the following attributes and questions:

- Subordinate information: Do subordinates have sufficient information to make a high quality decision?
- Time constraint: Does a critically severe time constraint limit your ability to involve subordinates?
- Geographical dispersion (group problems only): Are the costs involved in bringing together geographically dispersed subordinates prohibitive?
- Motivation (time): How important is it to minimise the time it takes to make the decision?
- Motivation (development): How important is it to maximise the opportunities for subordinate development?

Another modification to the original model involved the replacement of a yes/no answer to most of the questions (now numbering 12) by a 5-point scale. Vroom and Jago (1988) point out that the original model assumed that all situations are black and white, "while managers tell us that the most difficult situations they encounter are those that are found in varying shades of grey. Yes and no answers simply do not capture all the meaningful differences that exist among situations".

The revised model is more complex but is said to be more sensitive to differences in the various situations. Computer software has been developed that makes it possible for managers to input their answers to the 12 questions. This helps them assess a particular situation quickly so as to arrive at the appropriate leadership style. However, this could be a difficult exercise for the average manager. The revised model is too recent to have been subjected to empirical examination.

Vertical Dyad Linkage Theory

Like the other leadership perspectives, this theory—sometimes also called the leader/member exchange model—places emphasis on subordinate participation and influence in the decision-making process, but it has distinctive features as well (Dansereau, Grean, & Haga, 1975). It attempts to explain how the nature of the relationship (or linkage) between leader and follower can affect the leadership process.

A distinction is drawn between subordinates who are members of particular sub-groups, called in-groups and out-groups. An in-group consists of workers who the superior believes are competent, trustworthy, and motivated to work hard and accept responsibility. These traits are said not to be possessed by the out-group. As a consequence, the leader feels confident to allocate responsibility for important tasks to members of the in-group, thereby making his or her job that much easier. The leader is grateful to in-group members for making his or her life easier, and reciprocates by offering support, understanding, and a more personal relationship.

What is the nature of the relationship between the leader and subordinates in the out-group? The leader does not bestow favours on members of the out-group. They are given tasks requiring less ability and responsibility. Also, out-group members do not benefit from a personal relationship with the leader. In fact the leader's interactions with out-group members is based on his or her formal authority, rather than respect or friendship.

An important implication of the vertical dyad linkage theory is that leadership can be understood better by examining dyads (pairs of relations) made up of leader and member (a vertical relationship) rather than concentrating on what one might call the average leadership style, which, in effect, assumes that all subordinates are treated in the same way. It is unclear how the leader classifies subordinates as belonging to either the in-group or the out-group. However, there is evidence to suggest that leaders consider subordinates to be in-group members where the latter have personal characteristics compatible with those of the leader and are likely to have a higher level of competence than out-group members (Duchon, Green, & Taber, 1986).

The theory predicts that subordinates privileged to be classified as in-group members will enjoy better performance, experience lower staff turnover rates, and enjoy greater satisfaction with their superiors. There have been criticisms of the predictive power of the theory (e.g. in the area of staff turnover), and reservations about the performance measures used. Nevertheless, there is strong support for this theory of leadership (Vecchio & Gobdel, 1984).

Path-goal Model

A path-goal theory of leadership, which is somewhat similar to the expectancy theory of motivation discussed in Chapter 2, was developed by House (1971). The main functions of the leader are, according to this theory, to assist the subordinate to attain his or her goals and to ensure that the subordinate finds the experience satisfying. The theory is concerned with explaining the relationship between the behaviour of the leader and the attitudes and expectations of the subordinate.

The description of leadership behaviour is similar in a number of respects to leadership behaviour discussed in previous sections—particularly initiating structure and consideration—and consists of four dimensions:

1. Directive leadership: the leader lets subordinates know what is expected of them and provides specific guidelines, rules, regulations, standards, and schedules of the work to be done.
2. Supportive leadership: the leader is concerned about the status, needs, and well-being of subordinates, is friendly, and endeavours to make work more pleasant.
3. Participative leadership: the leader goes through consultation processes with subordinates, seeking their suggestions and being considerate towards them in the decision-making process.
4. Achievement-oriented leadership: the leader sets challenging goals for subordinates and shows confidence and trust in the way concern is expressed about their ability to meet exacting performance standards. The leader is also concerned with trying to improve performance.

The four dimensions of leadership behaviour are related to three dispositions of the subordinate:

- Satisfaction of the subordinate. Subordinates will feel satisfied if they perceive the leader's behaviour as being responsible for their present level of satisfaction, or as being instrumental in bringing about future satisfaction.
- Acceptance of the leader by the subordinate.
- Expectations of the subordinate. Subordinates expect appropriate effort will lead to effective performance, and that effective performance leads to the acquisition of acceptable rewards. The leader's behaviour produces a motivational effect, and this increases the effort put into the job by subordinates, particularly where subordinates perceive the leader as being supportive and

responsible for creating a situation in which they can satisfy their personal needs as a result of effective performance.

The three dispositions of the subordinate can be influenced favourably by the leader, who uses initiating structure to clarify the path to goal achievement, and consideration to make the path easier to travel, in the following ways:

- The leader should arouse, where appropriate, the needs of subordinates for achieving results or outcomes over which subordinates have some control.
- The leader can ensure that subordinates are personally rewarded for attaining their goals.
- The leader can offer coaching and direction to subordinates and therefore make it easier for them to derive a rewarding experience from attaining their goals.
- The leader can help subordinates clarify their expectations about their work experiences.
- The leader can minimise or remove frustrating obstacles in the subordinates' path to the attainment of their goals.
- The leader can increase the opportunities for personal satisfaction that arise from effective performance.

There are two types of situational variables that have to be accommodated in path-goal theory (House & Mitchell, 1974). First, the personal characteristics of subordinates have to be considered. If subordinates feel that their behaviour influences events at work (internal locus of control) then they are more likely to be satisfied with a participative leadership style. However, if subordinates believe that their accomplishments are due to luck (external locus of control) they are more likely to be satisfied with a directive leadership style. (The internal and external loci of control were discussed in Chapter 1.) Where subordinates have a high need for affiliation they are likely to be more satisfied with a supportive leadership style, whereas a directive leadership style is more acceptable when a high need for security exists.

Second, there are a number of demands or pressures in the job environment that relate directly to both leadership style and the motivational disposition of the subordinate, and they influence the ultimate performance of the subordinate.

Where jobs are highly structured and the objectives or goals set for the subordinate are clear (e.g. the processing of an application for a television licence or a road fund licence for a motor vehicle), a supportive and participative style is likely to lead to increased satisfaction. The reason for this is that jobs are already routine and therefore little direction is necessary. By contrast, a more satisfactory arrangement for unstructured jobs would be the use of a directive style, because a directive style helps to clarify an ambiguous task for subordinates (for example, a clerk in an insurance office finds it hard to handle a difficult claim and the manager explains the best way to proceed).

Apart from job structuring, the complexity of the task is an important situational variable. This is said to interact with the individual's desire to develop his or her knowledge and ability within the job (i.e. a need for personal growth). Not all subordinates share this desire with the same degree of intensity, so it is possible to find two categories of subordinate—one with a strong need and the other with a weak need for personal growth. The subordinate with a strong need for personal growth who performs a complex task (e.g. negotiating the terms of a deal to merge two companies in conditions of uncertainty) is more likely to perform better under a superior exercising a participative and achievement-oriented style. The subordinate with a strong need for personal growth faced with a simple task (e.g. extracting the names of companies on a random basis from a directory of companies) is more likely to perform better when subjected to a supportive style.

Where the subordinate has a weak need for personal growth, and faces a complex task, then a directive style is more likely to be effective. But the same subordinate who performs a simple task is more likely to be effective with a supportive and directive leader (Griffin, 1979). These relationships are depicted in Table 8.6.

Path-goal theory deals with specific leadership behaviour and shows how it might influence employee satisfaction and performance. It recognises the importance of situational variables and accepts individual differences. However, studies evaluating the model have generated conflicting results. Overall, empirical evidence indicates that the theory (like many others) offers useful insights into employee satisfaction, but has problems predicting employee performance (Gray & Starke, 1984). More recent evidence suggests that the "path-goal" leader, who is able to compensate for weaknesses residing in the subordinate or work situation, is likely to have a beneficial effect on employee

satisfaction and performance, provided competent subordinates are not over-supervised (Keller, 1989).

Hersey-Blanchard Situational Theory

This model adopts consideration (relationship behaviour) and initiating structure (task behaviour) and extends these two dimensions of leadership to form four styles (tell, sell, participation, and delegation). The model places particular emphasis on matching a style of leadership to the maturity of subordinates, and this relationship is said to be crucial in the determination of leadership effectiveness (Hersey & Blanchard, 1982).

Maturity is considered in the context of a particular task, and consists of two parts—job maturity and psychological maturity. Job maturity relates to technical knowledge and task-relevant skills. Psychological maturity relates to feelings of self-confidence and ability, and people's willingness to take responsibility for directing their own

TABLE 8.6

Interaction of Leadership Style and Situational Variables in Path-goal Theory

Situational Variables		*Effective Leadership Style*
Characterists of Subordinate	*Features of the Job Environment*	
Internal locus of control	—	Participative
External locus of control	—	Directive
High need for affiliation	—	Supportive
High need for security	—	Directive
—	Structured Jobs	Supportive and participative
—	Unstructured jobs	Directive
Strong need for personal growth	Complex task	Participative and achievement-orientated
Low need for personal growth	Complex task	Directive
Strong need for personal growth	Simple task	Supportive
Low need for personal growth	Simple task	Supportive and directive

behaviour. A highly mature subordinate would be rated high on both job maturity and psychological maturity, and would be in possession of both technical competence and self-confidence for a particular task. A low-rated subordinate on the two maturity factors for a given task would be considered to lack both ability and confidence. Examples of the relationship between leadership style and maturity are as follows:

- Subordinates who are highly immature would be told what to do (tell). This is a task-orientated and directive style.
- Subordinates who are hovering on the low side of maturity, would be persuaded that a particular course of action is the most appropriate (sell). Here there is a tendency to move towards a relationship-orientated style.
- Subordinates who are hovering on the high side of maturity will be treated with a certain amount of consideration and support (relationship orientation) and are allowed to "participate" in decision making.
- Subordinates who are highly mature will be considered capable of exercising self-direction and self-control, and will enjoy a high degree of autonomy. Delegation is the style applicable in this situation.

These relationships are depicted in Fig. 8.6.

The Hersey and Blanchard model has intuitive appeal and is used widely in training programmes, but the theory has not undergone significant evaluation to test its validity. Vecchio (1987) carried out an empirical test of the model and concluded that its predictions were most accurate for subordinates with low maturity, but not very accurate for subordinates with high maturity.

Recently, a researcher at the University of East London used the Hersey and Blanchard model in an investigation of leadership in British secondary schools (Gersch, 1992). The qualities of effective school leadership with respect to pupil behaviour were studied. Effective school leadership was characterised by promoting teamwork and varying leadership behaviour, taking into account the nature of the task and member of staff. School leadership was a critical factor in the determination of pupil behaviour in class and school.

Other Approaches

The last two contingency approaches to be discussed are the attribution perspective and substitutes for leadership.

Attribution Perspective

Unlike a number of leadership theories, this approach focuses on antecedents or causes of the behaviour of leaders (Green & Mitchell, 1979). (Attribution theory is discussed in Chapter 3). In a nutshell, it suggests that we observe the behaviour of others, and then attribute causes to that behaviour. A leader may react to a subordinate's poor performance in a number of ways. For example, if the leader attributes poor performance to internal factors (e.g. lack of ability or inadequate effort) he or she may issue a reprimand or consider the subordinate as a candidate for training. The leader may adopt a different pattern of behaviour when he or she attributes the subordinate's poor performance to external factors (e.g. poor operating procedures or inadequate allocation of duties), in which case corrective action focuses on the organisation rather than the subordinate. Apparently, there is evidence to suggest that men and women differ in their response to poor performers in an attributional context (Dobbins, 1985). Finally, it appears that there has been little research undertaken with respect to the attribution perspective (Martinko & Gardner, 1987).

Substitutes for Leadership

Are there situations when leadership is irrelevant? Kerr and Jermier (1978) have provocatively suggested that there are

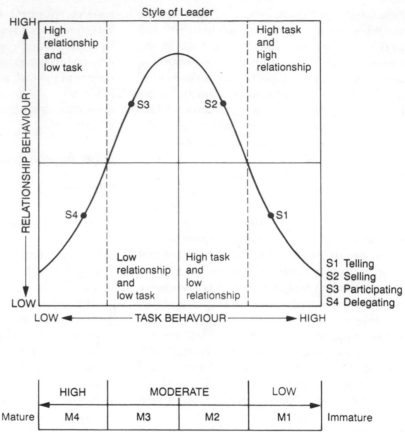

FIG. 8.6. The Hersey-Blanchard Situational Model. Source: Hersey, P. & Blanchard, K. (1982). *Management of organisational behaviour.* New York: Prentice-Hall. Used by permission.

occasions when forces in a situation, independent of leadership, offer subordinates sufficient assistance, and they do not have to rely on leaders.

For example, forces independent of leadership could be the ability, training, and experience of the subordinate, and these could account for effective performance even though the leader of the group is unsatisfactory. To explain situations in which leadership is considered irrelevant, reference is made to "leadership substitutes" and the "leadership neutraliser". Leadership substitutes could be the forces referred to earlier (e.g. subordinates' abilities and skills), intrinsically satisfying tasks, and knowledgeable officials other than the leader whom the subordinate can consult. By contrast, a leadership neutraliser stops a leader from

taking action in some way. For example, the leader's position may not be endowed with sufficient power, or the leader does not have adequate organisational rewards to dispense, and there may be physical distance between the leader and subordinates.

The work of Kerr and Jermier seems to be suggesting that effective group performance is dependent on factors other than leadership.

CONTEMPORARY TRENDS

A redefinition of leadership seems to be taking place and inspirational leadership qualities are back in fashion. It could be implied that the emphasis given to leadership earlier in this chapter is in the tradition of a transactional model of leadership.

Transactional Leadership

This type of leadership arises where the leader enters into various transactions with subordinates, explaining what is required of them in terms of contributions, and specifies the compensation or rewards they will receive if they fulfil these requirements. It is said that transactional leadership is appropriate to stable conditions in the marketplace and the environment generally, and in the application of technology in the workplace. Management by exception and a reliance on bureaucratic processes can be functional under these circumstances (Bass, 1990). This is exemplified by inward-looking and self-satisfied feelings, and a managerial culture more appropriate to keeping the organisation running smoothly in conditions of equilibrium. But its legacy can be over-control and risk aversion (Adair, 1990).

Transformational Leadership

This type of leadership needs to be fostered at all levels in the organisation when the organisation faces the following conditions:

- a turbulent environment where products have a short shelf life;
- greater international competition and deregulation of markets;
- where technology becomes obsolete before it is fully depreciated; and
- demographic changes are anticipated.

Here the emphasis is on people of vision, who are creative, innovative, and capable of getting others to share their dreams while playing down self-interest; and who are able to co-operate with others in reshaping the strategies and tactics of the organisation in response to a fast changing world (Tichy & Devanna, 1986). To these qualities could be added the pursuit of high standards, taking calculated risks, challenging and changing the existing company structure, with even the potential for the display (when considered

appropriate) of directive tendencies (Bass, 1990).

Bass (1990) lists the major characteristics of transformational leadership as:

- charisma;
- intellectual stimulation; and
- consideration of the emotional needs of each employee.

He claims such characteristics are based on the findings of a series of surveys, and on clinical and case evidence. Each of the characteristics will be discussed in turn.

Charisma

House (1977) identified charismatic leadership qualities in an ideal form. Charismatic leaders, through the force of their personalities and interpersonal skills, are said to have an extraordinary effect on followers or subordinates, without resorting to any formal authority. They have great power and influence and subordinates want to identify with them, as well as having a high degree of trust and confidence in them. Charismatic leaders— endowed with determination, energy, self-confidence, and ability—inspire and excite their subordinates with the idea that together, with extra effort, great things can be accomplished.

More recently, Conger and Kanugo (1987) attempted to create key components of behaviour that could be used as a framework to account for differences between charismatic and non-charismatic leaders. Examples of these components are expertise, articulation, trustworthiness, conception of status quo and future states, environmental sensitivity, and power base.

Intellectual Stimulation

The leader is willing and able to show subordinates new ways of looking at old problems, and emphasises that the difficulties they encounter in their work are problems to be solved in a rational way. A climate of intellectual stimulation should be nurtured and cultivated within the organisation.

Consideration

The leader pays close attention to differences in abilities and skills among subordinates, and acts as mentor to those who need to grow and develop. The leader places emphasis on coaching skills, is willing to delegate, and shows a preference for two-way, face-to-face communication. Kotter (1990) places much emphasis on the leader creating conditions in which people satisfy intrinsic needs, such as the needs for achievement, recognition, self-esteem, control over one's destiny, and the ability to live up to one's ideals.

In addition to these three major characteristics of transformational leadership identified by Bass (1990), we can add:

- vision;
- creativity; and
- the selection and training of talented people.

Vision

It is certainly fashionable nowadays to enunciate the important role of vision in transformational leadership. Vision in this context has been defined as the ability to be sensitive to changes in the organisation's environment, and to be able to perceive a future advantageous position to which the organisation must move if it is to survive (Selznick, 1984). Handy (1989) feels a vision must be reasonably concise, understandable, the leader must be seen to believe it, and that it will remain a dream without the commitment and work of others. It is reasonable to ask how well a vision serves the interest of important constituencies—e.g. customers, shareholders, employees—and how easily it can be translated into a realistic competitive strategy.

Bad visions tend to ignore the legitimate needs and rights of a particular constituency (e.g. favouring employees over customers). Or, alternatively, visions are strategically unsound as, for example, when a company that has never been superior to a weak competitor in an industry starts talking about

being number one in the not too distant future. That is a pipe-dream, not a vision (Kotter, 1990). The able leader is intent on articulating the organisation's vision in a manner that has meaning to followers, and is keen to involve them in deciding how to achieve it, or the part of it that is relevant to them. The leader also is aware of the significance of providing followers with the necessary technical and psychological support, and believes in recognising and rewarding success. Attending to the courses of action suggested earlier is said to produce real, intrinsic, motivational effects (Kotter, 1990).

In recent years the concepts of corporate strategy and leadership have been brought together to form strategic vision. The role of visionary leadership is an important ingredient in this combination. Westley and Mintzberg (1989) describe various types of visionary leadership.

Examples of visionary leaders from the USA are Lee Iacocca, who revitalised the *Chrysler Corporation*, and Land, the founder of the *Polaroid Corporation* and the inventor of the polaroid camera. A British example might be Clive Sinclair who pioneered the development of the personal computer in the early 1980s. As Westley and Mintzberg rightly point out:

Visionary leadership is not always synonymous with good leadership, and despite their great skills it is a mistake to treat visionary leaders as possessing superhuman qualities. In effect they are products of their times, of their followers, and of their opportunities. As times and contexts change the visionaries of yesterday fade into obscurity, or worse, become the villains of today.

Allied to the notion of intellectual stimulation, a dimension of transformational leadership identified by Bass (1990) is the concept of creativity (also discussed in Chapter 5). Adair (1990) sees the creation of new ideas as enriching the organisation's lifeblood in times of fundamental change, and sees an important role for leadership in tapping the fertile minds of young people in the organisation and providing opportunities for their personal development. He extols the virtue of involving layers of management, not traditionally consulted, in the process of strategic decision making. It is only then, he says, that we can expect to secure the necessary commitment for the implementation of strategic decisions. The maxim must be teamwork, with a shared sense of purpose, common objectives, and excellent communication.

In Sadler's (1988) view of creative leadership, there is a recognition that leaders do not have to be innovators themselves, but should be able to recognise the potential for creativity in others and make every effort to develop it. Facilitating the expression of creativity in the organisation is crucial, and a variety of ways of cultivating it are suggested. For example, the company could sponsor artists, invite creative people to exhibit their work in the organisation, encourage individuality, create conditions for people to be exposed to good external sources of ideas, create organic organisational structures, and encourage the formation of networks.

Selection and Training

Given the qualities residing in transformational leaders, it is understandable that attention turns to their selection, training, and development. The new emerging leadership culture is likely to emphasise the value of service and high quality products or services, an entrepreneurial spirit, the removal of unnecessary layers of management, flexible work groupings, and decentralised decision making with people as the key resource (Adair, 1990). Therefore, human resource strategies should focus on selection and training of transformational leaders. Recruiting people with leadership potential is obviously a first step. Thereafter, managing the career patterns of potential leaders is

crucial. They must be provided with opportunities to take risks, and to learn from successes and failures. By doing so, they develop a wide range of leadership skills and perspectives, and appreciate early on in their careers both their potential and limitations for producing change.

The value of lateral career moves, unusually broad job assignments, experience in special task force assignments, lengthy general management courses, and the creation of internal and external networks, are considered to be of tremendous importance later in broadening the leader's base as he or she develops (Kotter, 1990). The value of learning by doing is heavily underlined in the development of the experience suggested.

This is also endorsed by Sadler (1988) who favours a developmental experience for chief executives that uses the leader's own work situation, and the problems encountered therein, as the main vehicle for learning. However, he points out that if people are to learn from experience they will need skilled coaching and counselling, as well as the opportunity to receive feedback. This could best be achieved on a formal action learning programme in management studies, or a similar programme. There is a discussion of action learning in Chapter 4, and its role in management development in Chapter 12.

The issues raised in this discussion of transactional and transformational leadership are summarised in Table 8.7. At the bottom of the table there is reference to personality, motivation, leadership, and organisational intervening variables that are related to the two perspectives of leadership. For instance, similar motivational patterns and leadership style are applicable to both perspectives. Thereafter, there are differences. Leadership of management (as espoused by Sir John Harvey-Jones when at ICI) is more applicable in transformational leadership, whereas leadership in management applies to transactional leadership. Personal qualities feature prominently in transformational leadership, but situational leadership is

TABLE 8.7

Contrasting Leadership Perspectives

Transactional (Leader as Facilitator)	*Transformational (Leader as Shaper)*
Stable conditions	Turbulent environment
Managerial culture that maintains status quo	Adaptive organisational systems
Bureaucratic processes	Entrepreneurial spirit
Management by exception	Emphasis on quality
Over-control	Realistic visions
Risk aversive	Creativity
	Intellectual stimulation
	Innovation
	Charisma
	Reshaping

Intervening Variables Related to the Above Profiles

1. Intrinsic/extrinsic motivation	Intrinsic/extrinsic motivation
2. —	Personal qualities
3. Participative style	Participative style
4. Directive style	Directive style
5. Situational leadership	—
6. Leadership in management	—
7. —	Leadership of management
8. Lower levels of the organisation	Higher levels of the organisation

Source: McKenna, E.F. (1991, May) *Managerial Leadership—Emergent Trends*. Unpublished professorial inaugural lecture, University of East London.

pronounced in transactional leadership. Transactional leadership is better established at lower organisational levels, whereas the reverse is the case with transformational leadership. These associations are speculative, but interesting.

SUMMARY: LEADERSHIP AND MANAGEMENT STYLE

- A number of perspectives can be found in the study of leadership. This chapter opened with a discussion of the difference between leadership and management.
- There followed an examination of the trait approach and the personal characteristics of the leader, recognising the relevance of a mixture of leadership traits, motives, and skills.
- Leadership or management style can find expression in various forms—behavioural styles—ranging from autocratic to democratic styles. The democratic style is akin to participative leadership which was

examined in a number of contexts. A distinction was made between micro and macro participation.

- Under the umbrella title "Offshoots of the participative process", there was a discussion of quality circles, which led to an examination of total quality management and process re-engineering.
- A study of leadership would not be complete without an analysis of contingency theories or situational leadership. These theories point to the potency of the leadership environment in determining styles of leadership.
- The major contingency theories examined were the leadership continuum, the influence-power continuum, Fiedler's contingency model of l effectiveness, the revised normat of leadership style, the verti linkage theory, the path-goal n Hersey-Blanchard situational theory, the attributional perspective, and leadership substitutes.
- In looking at contemporary trends in leadership, a transactional model was contrasted with a transformational model. Transformational leadership, unlike transactional leadership, seems better suited to conditions of change requiring inspirational or visionary leadership qualities. Finally, variables related to the last two leadership perspectives were acknowledged.

QUESTIONS

1. Leadership and management complement each other. Discuss.
2. Distinguish between the early trait approach to leadership and the later emphasis on personal characteristics.
3. In what way does personality interact with leadership?
4. Identify the strengths and weaknesses of participative leadership, with particular reference to the budgeting process.
5. Compare micro participation with macro participation and emphasise the distinctive points of difference.
6. In what way can quality circles be used to enhance standards at work?
7. Identify one contingency theory of leadership which you feel has greatest practical significance, and comment on its features.
8. Analyse the conditions necessary for transformational leadership to take root.
9. Briefly explain the following: (a) transactional leadership; (b) attributional perspective in leadership; (c) leadership substitutes; (d) TQM; (e) process re-engineering.

REFERENCES

Adair, J. (1990). *Great leaders*. Talbot Adair Press.

Argyris, C. (1953). Human problems with budgets. *Harvard Business Review*, *31*, January–February, 97–110.

Argyris, C. (1973). Personality and organisation theory revisited. *Administrative Science Quarterly*, *18*, 141–167.

Bass, B.M. (1990). From transactional to transformational leadership. *Organisational Dynamics*, *18*, 19–31.

Bass, B.M. & Leavitt, H. (1963). Some experiments in planning and operating. *Management Science*, *4*, 574–585.

Bavelas, A. (1960). Leadership: Man and function. *Administrative Science Quarterly*, *4*, 344–360.

Bavelas, A. & Strauss, G. (1970). Group dynamics and inter-group relations. In W.G. Bennis, D. Benne, & R. Chin (Eds.), *The planning of change* (second edition). New York: Holt.

Bennis, W. (1966). *Changing organisations*. New York: McGraw-Hill.

Blake, R.R. & Mouton, J.S. (1985). *The managerial grid III* (revised edition). Houston, TX: Gulf Publishing Co.

Bray, D.W. & Campbell, R.J. (1974). *Formative years in business: A long-term AT&T study of managerial lives.* New York: Wiley.

Bromnell, P. (1981). Participation in budgeting, locus of control, and organisational effectiveness. *The Accounting Review,* October, 844–860.

Burpeau-Di Gregorio, M.Y. & Dickson, J.W. (1983). Experiences with quality circles in the south-west United States. *Employee Relations,* 5, 12–16.

Chell, E. (1987). *The psychology of behaviour in organisations.* Basingstoke, UK.: Macmillan Press.

Child, J. (1977). *Industrial participation in Israel.* Working Paper series No. 42, University of Aston in Birmingham.

Coch, L. & French, J.R.P. (1948). Overcoming resistance to change. *Human Relations,* 1, 512–532.

Collard, R. (1981). The quality circle in context. *Personnel Management,* September, 26–30 & 51.

Conger, J.A. & Kanugo, R.N. (1987). Toward a behavioural theory of charismatic leadership in organisational settings. *Academy of Management Review,* October, 637–674.

Crozier, M. (1964). *The bureaucratic phenomenon.* London: Tavistock.

Daniel, W.W. & McIntosh, N. (1972). *The right to manage.* London: Macdonald.

Dansereau, F., Grean, G., & Haga, W.J. (1975). A vertical dyad linkage approach to leadership within formal organisations. A longitudinal investigation of the role-making process. *Organisational Behaviour and Human Performance,* 13, 46–78.

Dickson, C.W. & Simmons, J.K. (1970). The behavioural side of management information systems. *Business Horizon,* August, 59–71.

Dobbins, G.H. (1985). Effects of gender on leaders' responses to poor performers: An attributional interpretation. *Academy of Management Journal,* 28, 587–598.

Duchon, D., Green, S.G., & Taber, T.D. (1986). Vertical dyad linkage: A longitudinal assessment of antecedents, measures, and consequences. *Journal of Applied Psychology,* February, 56–60.

Fiedler, F.E. (1967). *Theory of leadership effectiveness.* New York: McGraw-Hill.

Fiedler, F.E. (1972). The effects of leadership training and experience: A contingency model interpretation. *Administrative Science Quarterly,* December, 453–470.

Fiedler, F.E. & Garcia, J.E. (1987). *New approaches to effective leadership: Cognitive resources and organisational performance.* New York: John Wiley.

Field, R. (1979). A critique of the Vroom-Yetton model of leadership behaviour. *Academy of Management Review,* 4, 249–257.

Fleishman, E.A. & Harris, E.F. (1962). Patterns of leadership behaviour related to employee grievance and turnover. *Personnel Psychology,* 15, 43–56.

Foran, M.F. & De Coster, D.R. (1974). An experimental study of the effects of participation, authoritarianism, and feedback on cognitive dissonance in a standard setting situation. *The Accounting Review,* October, 751–763.

Fromm, E. (1942). *Fear of freedom.* London: Routledge & Kegan Paul.

Gersch, I.S. (1992). *School leadership and pupil behaviour in the secondary school: An investigation into the perception of the disciplinary role of school leaders.* Unpublished PhD thesis. London: The University of East London.

Ghiselli, E.E. (1971). *Exploration in managerial talent.* Santa Monica, CA: Goodyear.

Gibson, M. & Kidd, J. (1982). Some managerial implications of the Health and Safety at Work Act. *Employee Relations,* 4, 21–26.

Graen, G., Orris, J.B., & Alvares, K.M. (1971). Contingency model of leadership effectiveness: Some experimental results. *Journal of Applied Psychology,* 55, 196–201.

Gray, J.L. & Starke, F.A. (1984). *Organisational behaviour: Concepts and applications* (third edition). Columbus, OH: Charles E. Merill.

Green, S.G. & Mitchell, T.R. (1979). Attributional processes of leaders in leader–member interactions. *Organisational Behaviour and Human Performance,* 23, 429–458.

Griffin, R.W. (1979). Task design determinants of effective leader behaviour. *Academy of Management Review,* 4, 215–224.

Griffin, R.W. (1988). A longitudinal assessment of the consequences of quality circles in an industrial setting. *Academy of Management Journal,* June, 338–358.

Hammer, M. & Champy, J. (1993). *Re-engineering the corporation.* Nicholas Brealey.

Handy, C. (1989). *The age of unreason.* London: Hutchinson.

Health and Safety Executive (1981). *Managing safety,* Accident Prevention Unit (OP3). London: HMSO.

Heller, F.A. (1971). *Managerial decision making: A study of leadership styles and power-sharing among senior managers.* London: Tavistock.

Heller, F.A. & Wilpert, B. (1981). *Competence and power in managerial decision making.* Chichester: John Wiley.

Hersey, P. & Blanchard, K. (1982). *Management of organisational behaviour.* New York: Prentice-Hall.

Hofestede, G.H. (1968). *The game of budget control.* London: Tavistock.

Hosking, D.M. & Morley, I. (1988). The skills of leadership. In J.G. Hunt, B.R. Baliga, H.P. Dachler, & C.A. Schriesheim (Eds.), *Emerging leadership vistas.* Boston: Lexington.

House, R.J. (1971). A path-goal theory of leader effectiveness. *Administrative Science Quarterly, 16,* 321–338.

House, R.J. (1977). A 1976 theory of charismatic leadership. In J.G. Hunt & L.L. Larson (Eds.), *Leadership: The cutting edge.* Carbondale, IL: Southern Illinois University Press.

House, R.J. & Mitchell, T.R. (1974). Path-goal theory of leadership. *Journal of Contemporary Business, 3,* 81–97.

Kanji, G.K. (1990). Total quality management: The second industrial revolution. *Total Quality Management, 1,* 3–12.

Keller, R.T. (1989). A test of the path-goal theory of leadership, with the need for clarity as a moderator in research and development organisations. *Journal of Applied Psychology,* April, 208–212.

Kenis, I. (1979). Effects of budgetary goal characteristics on managerial attitudes and performance. *The Accounting Review,* October, 707–721.

Kerr, S. & Jermier, J.M. (1978). Substitutes for leadership: Their meaning and measurement. *Organisational Behaviour and Human Performance, 22,* 375–403.

Kotter, J.P. (1990). What do leaders really do? *Harvard Business Review, 68,* 103–111.

Likert, R. (1961). *New patterns of management.* New York: McGraw-Hill.

Likert, R. (1967). *The human organisation.* New York: McGraw-Hill.

Lind, O. (1979). Employee participation in Sweden. *Employee Relations, 1,* 11–16.

Lippit, R. & White, R. (1968). Leader behaviour and member reaction in three social climates. In D. Cartwright & A. Zander (Eds.), *Group dynamics—research and theory.* London: Tavistock.

Litchfield, E.H. (1956). Notes on a general theory of administration. *Administrative Science Quarterly, 1,* 3–29.

Lorenz, C. (1993a). Process re-engineering is sweeping across the Atlantic. *Financial Times,* 24th May, 11.

Lorenz, C. (1993b). TQM: Alive and kicking in the US. *Financial Times,* 23rd July, 15.

Lowin, A. (1968). Participative decision making: A model, literature critique, and prescription for research. *Organisational Behaviour and Human Performance, 3,* 69–106.

MacArthur, B. (1988). *Eddy Shah, Today and the newspaper revolution.* London: David & Charles.

Mann, R.D. (1959). A review of the relationship between personality and performance in small groups. *Psychological Bulletin, 56,* 241–270.

Martinko, M.J. & Gardner, W.L. (1987). The leader/member attribution process. *Academy of Management Review,* April, 235–249.

McClelland, D. (1975). *Power: The inner experience.* New York: Irvington.

McGregor, D. (1960). *The human side of enterprise.* New York: McGraw-Hill.

McKenna, E.F. (1978). *The management style of the chief accountant.* Farnborough, UK: Saxon House.

McKenna, E.F. (1991, May). *Managerial leadership— emergent trends.* Unpublished Professorial Inaugural Lecture, University of East London.

Merchant, K.A. (1981). The design of the corporate budgeting system: Influences on managerial behaviour and performance. *The Accounting Review,* October, 813–829.

Milani, K. (1975). The relationship of participation in budget setting to industrial supervisor performance and attitudes: A field study. *The Accounting Review,* April, 274–284.

Miles, R.E. (1965). Human relations or human resources. *Harvard Business Review, 43,* 148–163.

Miner, J.B. (1978). Twenty years of research on role motivation theory of managerial effectiveness. *Personnel Psychology, 31,* 739–760.

Mintzberg, H. (1980). *The nature of managerial work.* New York: Prentice-Hall.

Morse, N.C. & Reimer, E. (1956). The experimental change of a major organisational variable. *Journal of Abnormal and Social Psychology, 52,* 120–129.

Mulder, M. (1971). Power equalisations through participation. *Administrative Science Quarterly, 16,* 31–38.

Mumford, E. (1980). Social aspects of systems analysis. *The Computer Journal, 23,* 5–7.

Obradovic, J. (1975). Worker participation: Who participates? *Industrial Relations, 14,* 32–44.

Parker, L.D. (1979). Participation in budget planning—the prospects surveyed. *Accounting and Business Research,* Spring, 123–137.

Rees, R. (1993). *Transformation Scenes— Re-engineering. Back to the Black.* The Sunday Times, 17 October, p. 90.

Robens' Report (1972). *Safety and health at work.* London: HMSO Cmnd. 5034.

Russell, S. (1983). *Quality circles in perspective.* Occasional Paper 24, Work Research Unit, Department of Employment, February.

Sadler, P. (1988). *Managerial leadership in the post-industrial society.* Farnborough, UK: Gower Publishing.

Schiff, M. & Lewin, A.J. (1970). The impact of people on budgets. *The Accounting Review,* April, 259–268.

Selznick, P. (1984). *Leadership in administration.* Berkeley: University of California Press.

Smith, P.B., Misumi, J., Tayeb, M., Peterson, M., & Bond, M. (1989). On the generality of leadership style measures across cultures. *Journal of Occupational Psychology, 62,* 97–109.

Smith, P.B. & Peterson, M.F. (1988). *Leadership, organisations and culture.* London: Sage.

Stewart, R. (1982). A model for understanding managerial jobs and behaviour. *Academy of Management Review, 7,* 7–13.

Stogdill, R.M. (1948). Personal factors associated with leadership: A review of the literature. *Journal of Psychology, 25,* 35–71.

Stogdill, R.M. (1974). *Handbook of leadership.* New York: Free Press.

Strauss, G. (1968). Human relations—1968 style. *Industrial Relations, 7,* 262–276.

Tannenbaum, A.S. (1962). Control in organisations: Individual adjustment and organisational performance. *Administrative Science Quarterly, 7,* 236–257.

Tannenbaum, R. & Massarik, F. (1963). Participation by subordinates in the managerial decision-making process. In R.A Sutermeister (Ed.), *People and productivity.* New York: McGraw-Hill.

Tannenbaum, R. & Schmidt, W.H. (1958). How to choose a leadership pattern. *Harvard Business Review, 36,* 95–101.

Tannenbaum, R. & Schmidt, W.H. (1973). How to choose a leadership pattern. *Harvard Business Review,* May/June, 162–180.

Terman, L.W. (1904). A preliminary study of the psychology and pedagogy of leadership. *Journal of Genetic Psychology, 11,* 413–451.

Thompson, V.A. (1961). Hierarchy, specialisation and organisational conflict. *Administrative Science Quarterly, 5,* 485–521.

Tichy, N.M. & Devanna, M.A. (1986). *The transformational leader.* New York: John Wiley.

Time. (1993). *Where are the leaders?* 12 July, pp. 12–17.

Van Fleet, D.D. & Griffin, R.W. (1989). Quality circles: A review and suggested future directions. In C.L. Cooper & I.T. Robertson (Eds.), *International review of industrial and organisational psychology.* Chichester: John Wiley.

Van Fleet, D.D. & Yukl, G.A. (1989). A century of leadership research. In W.E. Robsenbach & R.L. Taylor (Eds.), *Contemporary issues in leadership* (second edition). London: Westview Press.

Vecchio, R.P. (1987). Situational leadership theory: An examination of a prescriptive theory. *Journal of Applied Psychology, 72,* 444–451.

Vecchio, R.P. & Gobdel, B.C. (1984). The vertical dyad linkage model of leadership: Problems and prospects. *Organisational Behaviour and Human Performance, 34,* 5–20.

Vroom, V.H. & Jago, A.G. (1988). *The new leadership: Managing participation in organisations.* New York: Prentice-Hall.

Vroom, V.H. & Yetton, P.W. (1973). *Leadership and decision making.* Pittsburgh: University of Pittsburgh Press.

Warner, M. (1975). Whither Yugoslav self-management. *Industrial Relations Journal, 6,* 65–72.

Weissenberg, P. & Kavanagh, M.J. (1972). The independence of initiating structure and consideration: A review of the evidence. *Personnel Psychology, 25,* 119–130.

Westley, F. & Mintzberg, H. (1989). Visionary leadership and strategic management. *Strategic Management Journal, 10,* 17–32.

Whitelaw, W. (1989). *The Whitelaw memoirs.* London: Aurum Press.

Wispe, L.G. & Lloyd, K.E. (1955). Some situational and psychological determinants of the desire for structured interpersonal relations. *Journal of Abnormal and Social Psychology, 51,* 57–60.

Work Research Unit, Department of Employment (1983). *Small group activities: Quality circles.* Review of a conference organised by the Work Research Unit and sponsored by the National Economic Development Office: London, March.

Wright, P.L. & Taylor, D.S. (1984). *Improving leadership performance.* New York: Prentice-Hall.

9

Power, Politics, and Conflict

This chapter, with its group-based perspective, covers three related concepts—power, politics, and conflict. First, definitions of organisational power, politics and conflict are given, followed by an examination of the bases of power, and types of power. Then the tactics used to gain power and manipulate the bases of power are examined. Following a definition of organisational politics, the causes of political behaviour as well as political tactics (both legitimate and devious) are discussed. The pros and cons of political behaviour are given. Conflict is defined and different types of conflict are stated. The sources of conflict are identified, and ways of using and managing conflict are discussed.

This chapter has particular relevance to the previous chapter on managerial leadership. It also has a bearing on the chapters covering groups (Chapter 7), organisational culture (Chapter 11), and organisational change and development (Chapter 12).

DEFINITION

Power refers to a force at the disposal of one person that can influence the behaviour of another. Therefore, X has the capacity to influence the behaviour of Y in such a way that Y performs tasks he or she would not otherwise do. Politics or political behaviour in an organisational context has been defined as activities undertaken by individuals or groups to obtain, enlarge, and use power and other resources to obtain outcomes they desire in situations where there is uncertainty or disagreement (Pfeffer, 1981). A state of conflict is said to exist when one party frustrates the attempts of another to achieve his or her goals.

POWER

After reflecting on this definition of power, one could conclude that the concepts of power and of leadership, which was discussed in Chapter 8, are closely related. For example, leaders use power to facilitate the achievement of their goals. Both concepts are preoccupied with the ability of an individual to control or influence others and to get someone else to engage in some activity. But there are some differences. For instance, power, unlike leadership, is not the preserve of supervisors and managers because individuals and groups with different status in the organisation can be involved in the exercise of power (Blackler & Shimmin, 1984).

One important feature of power is that its strength is heavily influenced by dependence.

For example, the more Y is dependent on X, the greater is X's power in this particular relationship. In turn, Y's dependence on X is determined by the fact that X controls something that Y values or wants, such as the power to bestow a reward (e.g. a salary increase or promotion).

Dependency is enlarged when the resource under the control of a person or group is important, scarce, and cannot be substituted (Mintzberg, 1983). To create dependency the forces or resources controlled must be seen as important. In a technologically based company the contribution of engineers or scientists may be crucial to the organisation, and consequently others are highly dependent on them.

If a resource is seen as scarce, this contributes to dependency. The possession of specialised knowledge about critical operations of the company by somebody in a modest position in the organisational hierarchy could create the situation where the highest ranked employee is dependent on a person who is lowly ranked. The scarcity factor also raises its head in normal economic conditions when certain occupational groups in short supply are able to exercise power to obtain increased salaries and benefits.

On the question of substitutability, the ability of one person to exercise power over another is dependent on how the latter perceives alternatives to the present job. For example, the greater the number of employment opportunities outside the organisation open to an individual, the less he or she is dependent on the organisation and the less influence is likely to be exerted by his or her boss. By contrast, a higher level of dependence would be expected where the person's external marketability is restricted.

Bases of Power

In a classic study, French and Raven (1958) distinguished between five different types of power:

- reward power;
- coercive power;
- referent power;
- legitimate power; and
- expert power.

"AS YOU RIGHTLY POINTED OUT, EVERYTHING'S NEGOTIABLE..."

Reward Power

The leader is able to control rewards—e.g. pay and promotion—which subordinates consider to be worth striving for. This type of power can extend beyond material rewards, because many people are motivated by a desire for intrinsic rewards, such as recognition and acceptance. Therefore, reward power also exists when a manager acknowledges and praises good performance by a subordinate. However, if a leader has rewards at his or her disposal to which subordinates attach no value, that leader has no reward power. But if the leader is astute enough to disguise the valueless rewards, he or she may still have reward power.

Coercive Power

If subordinates are of the view that the leader is able and willing to use penalties that they dislike—e.g. withdrawal of privileges, allocation of unattractive assignments, denial of promotion opportunities and pay increases, verbal abuse, withdrawal of friendship and emotional support—then the leader has coercive power. In this situation the penalties must be perceived by the subordinates as significant, and there must be a strong probability that they will be used if necessary. This type of power can still be found in organisations, though it should be noted that certain legislation (e.g. employment protection laws in the UK) offers protection against summary dismissal of disliked employees. The more extreme form of this type of power is physical coercion, but this is less common than it once was. Finally, the use of coercive power breeds the likelihood of employee hostility and resentment, but there are some who argue that coercive power employed prudently can be useful in ensuring the necessary compliance (Hodgetts, 1991).

Referent Power

This type of power, similar in concept to charisma, is visible when subordinates think the leader has desirable characteristics that they should imitate. Imitation could mean working the same hours, dressing like the boss, adopting his or her other mannerisms, and so on. It could result in an indiscriminate identification with the leader.

Legitimate Power

This type of power arises if subordinates believe that the leader is endowed with the right to issue orders that they are obliged to accept. In this case, subordinates tend to look at a title—e.g. director—as conferring on the leader the right to give orders. However, the lines of legitimate power are often blurred in the more organic type of organisations.

Expert Power

This type of power emerges when the leader is seen by subordinates as having superior knowledge and expertise which is relevant to the tasks or activities under consideration. The more important the information base underpinning expert power, and the fewer the alternative sources of such information, the greater the power. In practice, this type of power may be confined only to narrow specialist activities and functions, though leadership based on expert power could also be reflected in the other categories of power.

It should be noted that expert power can be found in many parts of an organisation; it transcends positions and jobs, and tends to be less attached to roles with formal authority. For example, a research scientist in an organisation who is privy to information on scientific breakthroughs of immense value to the enterprise, could be endowed with expert power. The person with expert power has to be able to demonstrate the right type of ability, and he or she must be perceived as somebody with credibility, trustworthiness, and honesty, as well as having access to the required information (French & Raven, 1958).

Other Power Categories

There are other categories of power, and these are referred to as position power, personal power, and opportunity power.

Position Power

This category of power is attached to a post, irrespective of who is performing the job, and is limited to the activities within the boundaries of that power. For example, a directive to a subordinate to commit a crime would fall outside the boundary. Subsumed under position power are legitimate, reward, expert, and some coercive categories of power.

Personal Power

Personal power is attached to the person and it subsumes referent and some traces of expert, coercive and reward power (Moorhead & Griffin, 1992). Those who use personal power can rely on rational persuasion, or appeal to the subordinate's identification with the leader in order to influence events. This type of power inspires much loyalty and commitment, with subordinates acting out of choice rather than necessity. Consequently, they are more likely to accede to requests to adopt a particular line of action. In the final analysis, of course, the subordinate is free to ignore the superior's suggestions.

Opportunity Power

This category of power is said to exist when someone can exert power by reason of being in the right place at the right time (Brass, 1984), and by taking advantage of a subordinate position close to a cell of power in the organisation.

Applications of French and Raven's Power Bases

Using the French and Raven bases of power, Yukl (1981) provides a framework for understanding how power can be employed under different conditions. The bases of power are related to forces residing in the subordinate—namely, those of commitment, compliance, and resistance.

- A committed subordinate will have little difficulty in accepting and identifying with

the leader, and may put in the extra effort necessary to complete a project of importance to the leader.
- A compliant subordinate is likely to carry out the leader's wishes provided they do not involve extra effort, but will nevertheless work at a reasonable pace.
- A resistant subordinate is likely to be in conflict with the leader, and may neglect the project as a means of contravening the leader's instructions or guidelines.

When the disposition of the subordinate interacts with the five bases of power, the outcomes listed in Table 9.1 are said to materialise. The following are matters to consider with respect to the use of the bases of power.

Reward Power

The use of reward power has a certain appeal for the leader because it amounts to giving positive reinforcement to subordinates. Rewards should be administered in a fair and equitable way and be related to performance, otherwise the power base of the leader could be eroded. The leader must have the capability to provide the expected rewards, and the rewards must be perceived by subordinates to have value. For example, a promotion without an adequate compensation package may not motivate a subordinate. Rewards should not be proffered as bribes or as a means to promote unethical behaviour.

Coercive Power

The use of this type of power could cause resentment and also erode referent power because of the adverse effect it may have on the subordinate's identification with the leader. Therefore, it should be used sparingly. If used in a hostile or manipulative way, resistance is a likely outcome. Where coercive power is used in a helpful, non-punitive way, whereby the sanctions employed are mild (such as a minor reprimand) and fit the person's failure to respond appropriately, compliant behaviour is all that can be expected from the

TABLE 9.1

Yukl's Adaptation of the French and Raven Model

Type of Power Used	Outcome as a Result of Subordinate		
	Commitment	Compliance	Resistance
Reward	If the follower believes that the request is important to the leader, the person will respond appropriately.	If a reward is given in an impersonal way, it is likely that the followers will comply.	If the reward is applied in a manipulative or arrogant way, the followers are likely to resist it.
Coercive	The individual is unlikely to commit himself or herself under the threat of coercion.	If applied in a helpful and non-punitive way, it is possible that the followers will go along with the directive.	If used in a hostile or manipulative way, the followers are likely to resist.
Legitimate	The follower is likely to go along with the request if it is viewed as appropriate and is politely presented.	If the order is viewed as legitimate, the followers are likely to comply with it.	If the request does not appear to be proper, it is possible that the leader will encounter resistance to it.
Referent	If presented in a subtle and personal way, the follower is likely to go along with the request.	If the request is viewed as important to the leader, it is possible that the followers will comply with it.	If the followers believe that the request will bring harm to the leader, they are likely to resist it.
Expert	If the request is persuasive and the followers share the leader's desire for goal attainment, they are likely to be commited to it.	If the request is persuasive and the followers are apathetic about the goals, it is possible that they will comply with it.	If the leader is arrogant or insulting, the followers are likely to oppose the directive.

Source: Hodgetts, R.M. (1991). *Organisational behaviour: Theory and practice*. New York: Macmillan Publishing Company. Used by permission.

subordinate. However, a serious misdeed, such as a significant theft or physical violence, would justify an immediate and severe punishment, but the disciplinary procedure should be appropriate and impartial.

With regard to sanctions for misdeeds, it is important that rules governing unacceptable behaviour are well communicated. Also, when the rules are broken, a clear picture of what happened and why it happened needs to be created so that the penalty fits the "crime" and to make sure that the wrong person is not penalised.

Legitimate Power

Instructions given by a manager in his or her formal capacity carry a certain amount of influence—and more so in a crisis situation where effective leaders are viewed as having more legitimate power than they actually possess (Mulder et al., 1986).

Certain behavioural traits are considered desirable in the exercise of legitimate power. For example, politeness in the issue of orders; being courteous when dealing with people, in particular those who are older than the manager; and confidence and calmness when dealing with subordinates who are nervous or anxious about the situation. In some situations subordinates may be unsure of the rationale for courses of action for which they are held responsible, or why in particular it is they that are expected to undertake the task. Therefore, it is important for the leader to explain the order or request given to the subordinate.

Referent Power

An important condition with respect to referent power is that subordinates identify with the leader. A common way of achieving this is by selecting subordinates who have similar backgrounds, education, or training. The reasoning is that people will identify with those who remind them of themselves. However, it would appear that a more delicate means of using referent power is through role modelling, whereby the leader behaves in way that he or she would like subordinates to act. The expectation is that the subordinates will emulate the leader's behaviour.

Expert Power

The central thrust of expert power is a leader's projection of an image that he or she possesses the appropriate expertise. This is achieved through subtle remarks about their education, experience, and achievements. For example, a manager well conversant with the application of information technology in the office situation, states that when he or she "used to work with *IBM* on computer applications in business, we did it in a particularly innovative way": such a statement is transmitting a clear message with respect to relevant expertise.

The maintenance of expert power depends on the continuation of the leader's credibility, and the latter cannot be achieved by pretending to know about things of which one has little or no knowledge. Managers using expert power update their knowledge of issues in their area of responsibility, and are sensitive to the concerns of subordinates. Also, they are keen not to intimidate subordinates by displaying their expertise in an ostentatious manner.

Knowledge Power. A base of power which, on the face of it, seems similar to expert power, is knowledge power. However, it is different because it relates to the control of unique information. When that information is required for decision making, it is easy to recognise power based on this source. This type of power is claimed to be effective in terms of satisfaction and performance, and places its holder in a strategic position to exact compliance (Bachman, Bowers, & Marcus, 1968; Robbins, 1991).

Finally, a comprehensive review of studies using the French and Raven typology suggests that a majority of them suffer from severe methodological shortcomings, and that much more research is badly needed in this area (Podsakoff & Schriesheim, 1985).

When our interest shifts to an analysis of organisational power, what immediately comes to mind is Etzioni's (1975) three types of organisational power, which are matched with three types of involvement on the part of organisational members (see Table 9.2). The crosses in the Table denote the best fit between power and involvement. Any other matching could generate dysfunctional effects.

A description of the three types of power and involvement is as follows:

- An organisation using coercive power attempts to obtain compliance by threats and punishment. This type of organisation may be associated with prisons and similar institutions. The involvement of members that is compatible with this type of power is alienative, exemplified by hostile, rejecting, and negative attitudes. These conditions provide a justification for the use of coercive power.

- An organisation using utilitarian power offers rewards to those who comply with directives, in the belief that it is in their best interests to do so. The involvement of members compatible with this type of power is calculative, exemplified by a rational approach aimed at optimising personal gain.

TABLE 9.2

Types of Organisational Power

Types of Involvement	Type of Power		
	Coercive	Utilitarian	Normative
Alienative	X		
Calculative		X	
Moral			X

- An organisation using normative power operates in the belief that members accept directives because of their commitment to the values embedded in the organisation. The use of normative power to influence members is prevalent in professional and religious organisations. The involvement of members compatible with this type of power is moral. They are committed to the ethos of the organisation.

Power Tactics

People use certain tactics to gain power, as well as tactics to manipulate the bases of power. A rich source of power tactics can be found in Pfeffer's (1992) book on managing with power. He argues that all managers must learn the subtle and demanding craft of "politicking" if they want to succeed, and often even survive. Power tactics are used by individuals on their own, within groups (intra-group) and between groups (inter-group).

Individual and Intra-group Tactics

In an empirical study of how managerial employees influence others (including superiors, subordinates, and co-workers) and the conditions under which one tactic is more suitable than another, it was concluded that seven tactics could be identified (Kipnis, et al., 1984):

- *Assertiveness*: this would entail setting a deadline date for others to comply with a request, ordering others to do what they were asked to do, emphasising the importance of complying with the request, and repeatedly reminding others of their obligations to perform.
- *Friendliness or ingratiation*: this is designed to make the person favourably disposed to comply with a request. It could amount to flattery by lavishing praise on the person prior to the request, exaggerating the importance of complying with the request, acting in a humble and friendly way when seeking the person's co-operation, and waiting until the person is in a receptive mood before striking.
- *Rationality*: this amounts to using facts and information in a logical way so that the request for action is seen to be detailed and well prepared. The rationale for the request is given together with a statement of what is required of the person. The originator of the request is portrayed as a competent individual.
- *Sanctions*: this amounts to the use of coercive power, whereby organisational rewards and punishments are activated— e.g. a promise of an increase in salary or a promotion, or, alternatively, ruling out a salary increase or withholding a promotion and threatening to give the person an unsatisfactory performance appraisal.
- *Higher authority*: this consists of efforts to secure support from people further up the

organisational hierarchy, and could be exemplified by securing the informal support of superiors and others in higher positions.

- *Bargaining*: this could amount to exchanging favours and benefits through a process of negotiation. Also, the person seeking a favour may remind the other person of benefits the former has bestowed on him or her in the past.

- *Coalition*: this consists of getting help from other parties in the organisation, by building up alliances with subordinates and co-workers. In numbers there is strength, which is evident when employees join trade unions. Coalitions are more likely to be formed where interdependency exists between organisational units, and where broad-based support is necessary for the implementation of decisions.

Kipnis et al. (1984) found that these tactics differed in importance. For example, the most popular tactic was the use of reason, irrespective of whether the influence was going up or down the hierarchy. Table 9.3 shows the tactics, ranging from the most popular to the least popular; but note that (for

obvious reasons) the sanctions tactic is excluded from the scale that measures upward influence.

Yukl and Falbe (1990) conducted two studies that extended and, to an extent, replicated the research of Kipnis et al. Certain measures of influence tactics were used that did not appear in the earlier research. Also, the research methodology was employed in a slightly different way. This research only partly replicated the Kipnis et al. findings for differences in upward, downward, and lateral use of influence tactics. The overall pattern of results suggests that the Kipnis et al. conclusions for influence tactics are considerably overstated, and that—aside from rational persuasion—consultation and inspirational appeals are important additional tactics, irrespective of the direction of influence.

For a collection of practical suggestions based on research into managerial influence behaviours, refer to Keys and Case (1990). They discuss the tactics most frequently used and those most effective in their impact on superiors, subordinates, and peers. Then five steps necessary to develop and maintain managerial influence are outlined. These are as follows:

TABLE 9.3

Use of Power Tactics

	When Managers Influenced Superiors	When Managers Influenced Subordinates
Most popular	Reason	Reason
	Coalition	Assertiveness
	Friendliness	Friendliness
	Bargaining	Coalition
	Assertiveness	Bargaining
	Higher authority	Higher authority
Least Popular		Sanctions

Source: Kipnis, D., Schmidt, S.M., Swaffin-Smith, C., & Wilkinson, I. (1984). Patterns of managerial influence: Shotgun managers, tacticians, and bystanders. *Organisational Dynamics*, Winter, 58–67.

- Develop a reputation as a knowledgeable person or as an expert.
- Balance the time spent in each critical relationship according to work needs rather than on the basis of habit or social preference.
- Develop a network of resource persons who can be called on for assistance.
- Choose the correct combination of influence tactics for the objective to be achieved and for the target to be influenced.
- Implement influence tactics with sensitivity, flexibility, and adequate levels of communication.

Situational Influences
It is suggested that four situational variables determine the choice of a power tactic:

1. *Relative power*. The manager who controls valuable resources, or who occupies a position of dominance uses a greater variety of tactics than the manager with less power. However, the former shows a penchant to use assertiveness more often than the latter. Assertiveness and directive strategies generally come into play where there is a refusal or a reluctance to comply with a request. By contrast, the manager with less power is more likely not to persevere with trying to influence others when resistance is experienced.
2. *Manager's objectives*. Managers attempt to match tactics to objectives in their dealings with both superiors and subordinates. When the objective is to derive benefits from superiors there tends to be a reliance on friendliness or ingratiation. By contrast, when the objective is to get superiors to accept new ideas, the most likely tactic is to use reason.
3. *Manager's expectations of success*. The degree of success in influencing either superiors or subordinates in the past is a strong determinant of the tactic to be used currently. Where managers have been successful in exerting influence, they are likely to use simple requests to obtain compliance. By contrast, where the success rate is low, they are tempted to use the tactics of assertiveness and sanctions.
4. *Organisational culture*. This is likely to be an important situational variable. For example, some cultures are supportive of a friendly approach, whereas others may favour reason. A detailed discussion of the impact of organisational culture appears in Chapter 11.

Inter-group Power Tactics

Inter-group power is related to influence and dependence. When one group can exert influence over another, the former has power over the latter. Inter-group power is determined by at least three factors (Hickson et al., 1971):

- *Uncertainty absorption*: there exist within organisations specialised groups performing a variety of functions—e.g. industrial relations, pay bargaining, etc. When complex issues arise, the expertise of the appropriate specialist group can be brought to bear on the problems and, in the process, these groups absorb the uncertainty normally associated with such matters. Consequently, the specialist group gains some power over the users of its service.
- *Substitutability*: in the example just given, if the user of the service can obtain a substitute provider (e.g. an external consultant), then the power of the specialist can be reduced or eliminated. However, in practice it might not be possible to substitute external for internal providers in circumstances where an available competent internal facility exists.
- *Integrative importance*: when a group's services—e.g. central computing services—are needed to a significant extent by other groups within the organisation in order that the latter can function effectively, the provider has a lot of inter-group power.

The level of power would be less if the group providing the services was needed only to a rather limited extent.

Having endorsed the power tactics already mentioned, a group of researchers underline the importance of third party intervention when the services of another organisation are used to negotiate on behalf of the organisation trying to influence events. Advertising is also a tool to consider in the context of the use of power tactics (Butler & Wilson, 1989; Hickson et al., 1986).

As we saw earlier, individuals and groups form alliances or coalitions to acquire or enhance a power base. Thompson (1967) identifies some of the co-operative tactics used on occasion by groups in order to expand their power. These are referred to as contracting, co-opting, and coalescing.

- Contracting, which does not necessarily culminate in a formal legal agreement, is a tactic arrived at between two or more groups to regulate future action. For example, a management group not wishing to maintain a confrontational stance with a trade union, which is likely to undermine its position, signs an agreement of co-operation with the union.
- Co-opting is a process whereby others are admitted to membership of a group, in this case in order to avoid threats to the group's stability or survival. For example, nominees of a bank take their seats on the board of a commercial company after an injection of substantial funds by the bank.
- Coalescing comes about when there is a joint venture between one group and another. There is strength in pooling resources for the benefit of the organisation. This would be particularly beneficial when two groups combine their efforts, rather than engaging in wasteful competition.

Reflections on Power

Thompson and McHugh (1990) provide a very useful critical evaluation of the literature on power from the perspective of organisational studies. They distinguish between micro and macro perspectives on power. For example, a micro perspective such as that taken by French and Raven earlier, would not explain the prior distribution of power, or how some people manage to get access to resources that bestow power, whereas others do not. A macro perspective would recognise that power within organisations has its origins in deeper structures of economic domination in society that give it legitimacy (Clegg, 1977). According to Thompson and McHugh (1990):

A prime example is the concentration of ownership and control in the transnational company. The power to switch resources and relocate operations simply cannot be explained at the level of the single enterprise and its sub-units. Without such a structural framework, we are left with a micro-level analysis capable only of explaining the skills of "politicking" rather than political power. We are also left with a view of managers solely as self-interested manipulators and power-seekers with little understanding of the broader dynamics and constraints that dispose management to use power in the first place.

An alternative route to the origin of power takes us to a position where we need to consider the behaviour of people whose actions are not very conspicuous because of their lack of presence in the scene of action. Power in this sense is attributable to powerful groups outside the immediate scene who prevent various options from being considered (Bachrach & Baritz, 1962). This is referred to as the "power of non-decision making", and is exemplified by a suppression of choices but is not necessarily ridden with resistance or overt conflict. The latter might be encountered if unattractive options were imposed on people in a decision-making forum by an authority figure vested with power.

Lukes (1974) calls for a radical view of power. His explanation of power is similar to radical perspectives on power in organisations, which rely on Weber's and Marx's analysis of class domination based on solid economic foundations.

POLITICS

Although the terms politics and power are used interchangeably, they have distinct meanings. However, they are related (Eisenhardt & Bourgeois III, 1988). Politics in organisations has been defined as those activities carried out by people to acquire, enhance, and use power and other resources to obtain preferred outcomes in situations where there are uncertainties or disagreements (Pfeffer, 1981). Another definition of organisational politics emphasises the fact that it operates outside the narrow confines of formal role behaviour. Political behaviour in organisations is comprised of those activities that are not required as part of one's formal role in the organisation, but nevertheless influence or attempt to influence the distribution of advantages and disadvantages within the organisation (Farrell & Petersen, 1982).

A valid question to ask is how prevalent is politics at work? According to Gandz and Murray (1980) it is a common phenomenon in organisations but it is more prevalent at the higher level. They also found that half the managers in their study felt that politics were unfair , bad, unhealthy, and irrational, but recognised that it is necessary to behave politically to progress within the organisation, and that successful executives have to be good politicians. A smaller but still significant proportion of the managers believed that political behaviour influenced decisions in

connection with employee selection and the determination of salaries. The results of the study indicate that political behaviour is an undesirable but unavoidable aspect of organisational life.

The connection between politics and motivation is emphasised by Lee and Lawrence (1985), particularly in the context of decision making in organisations. (Bargaining and negotiating in the decision-making process were discussed in Chapter 5).

Causes of Political Behaviour

A number of elements contribute to political behaviour, ranging from organisational to individual factors.

Organisational Factors
Apart from organisational change (discussed in Chapter 12), Miles (1980) identifies four contributory factors as ambiguous goals, scarce resources, technology and environment, and non-programmed decisions.

Ambiguous Goals. A certain ambiguity surrounds the meaning of organisational goals; and goals which espouse that the organisation will grow organically (e.g. through acquisitions) in some quantifiable form offer much scope for the adoption of political behaviour to achieve those goals. Behaviour that is politically inspired could rest on strong personal motivation. For example, a top manager in a conglomerate could be arguing strongly for a particular acquisition strategy where it is proposed the company should make a takeover bid for a target company at a very attractive price. Coincidentally, the top manager's family has a substantial stake in the target company!

Scarce Resources. A shortage of resources could come about as a result of cutbacks to improve efficiency, or when there is a significant reallocation of resources that creates difficulties in some areas. When resources are scarce, inevitably some people will lose out in the allocation process. Therefore, it is understandable that certain people engage in political behaviour in an attempt to maintain or increase their share of resources. Managers may present misleading information and lobby key people to obtain a larger budget to expand their departments. In a sense the existence of scarce resources, which is a common occurrence, offers lots of potential for the use of political behaviour.

Technology and Environment.   The ways in which technology and the environment affect organisational design are discussed in Chapter 10. The existence of advanced technology and complex environments invariably heralds a need for organisational change. Among the activities incorporated in various responses to change are political manoeuvring to restructure aspects of the organisation in order to preserve or enhance the power base of the politically inspired manager.

Non-programmed Decisions.   The nature of non-programmed decisions was discussed in Chapter 5. Situations related to non-programmed decision making can be clouded with a poor definition of events and much ambiguity. As a consequence, the scene is set for political manoeuvring.

Commenting on political activity associated with organisational factors, Robbins (1991) isolates the following variables:

- *Reductions in resources*. This was examined earlier.
- *Low trust*. The lower the level of trust, the greater the likelihood of political behaviour of a negative kind.
- *Role ambiguity*. In conditions of ambiguity surrounding organisational roles the behaviour prescribed for the role occupant is not clear. Therefore, it is more difficult to establish to what extent the employee is engaged in behaviour demanded by the formal role, as opposed to political behaviour.

- *Unclear performance evaluation*. The art of performance appraisal (discussed in Chapter 13) is far from perfect. The greater the use of subjective criteria in the appraisal process, the more emphasis that is placed on a single measure of performance, and the greater the lapse of time between the actions measured and the appraisal process, then the greater the likelihood of individuals adopting a political stance to further their aims.
- *Organisational culture*. The nature of organisational culture is discussed in Chapter 11. It is suggested that the more the culture of the organisation emphasises a win-lose outlook to the allocation of rewards, the greater the likelihood that employees will be motivated to engage in political behaviour. The win-lose approach takes total rewards as fixed, so that the gains of any individuals or groups are at the expense of others.

Also, the emergence of a culture supportive of participative management or industrial democracy may not be to the liking of managers who were previously attracted by the legitimate power of their positions, which gave them ample opportunity to engage in unilateral decision making. In the new situation it could go against the natural grain to share power with others, but reluctantly these managers use the prescribed committee system and group meetings. However, they do it in a half-hearted way, and seem to be committed to manipulating tactics.

Individual Factors

Apart from the organisational factors discussed earlier, there are individual factors contributing to political behaviour. Normally these relate to the personality or motivational disposition of people.

At one time there was a tendency to translate basic propositions in Machiavelli's writings into attitude scales to be used to measure the extent to which somebody agrees with his views. In one study it was found that employees having views highly compatible with Machiavelli were generally able to control social interactions and were adept at manipulating others (Gemmil & Heisler, 1972). Therefore, one could argue that Machiavellian individuals are better disposed than others to engage in political behaviour. Authoritarian personalities, with a propensity to take high risks, have been shown to engage in fairly reckless political behaviour (Mayes & Allen, 1977).

With respect to motivation, a high degree of power, autonomy, security, or status can predispose an individual to behave politically (Madison et al., 1980). The adoption of devious political behaviour is said to be influenced by one's investment (in terms of time and effort) in the organisation, by the alternative job opportunities available, and by expectations of using such behaviour successfully (Farrell & Petersen, 1982).

So the more a person works conscientiously in the expectation of securing increasing future benefits in the corporation, the more he or she stands to lose if eased out of the job or organisation. Such a person is less likely to use devious political action. By contrast, the individual with greater alternative job opportunities available because of a favourable job market or standing in his or her occupation or profession, is more likely to risk the use of devious political action. Finally, where there is a low expectation of using devious political action successfully, there is less likelihood it will be used, but those with refined political skills may not fall into this category.

Political Techniques or Tactics

The use of techniques or tactics to promote the political interests of certain organisational members is acknowledged by a number of writers, but there appears to be a dearth of strong empirical evidence on this topic. There has been the suggestion in recent years that political skills applicable to managers should become an increasingly important element of management education. To this end a two-dimensional model showing both politically competent and incompetent skills, particularly in a local government context, has been proposed (Baddeley & James, 1987). In the use of political behaviour, the following techniques are acknowledged (Mintzberg, 1983; Pfeffer, 1981):

- controlling information;
- controlling lines of communication;
- using outside experts;
- controlling the agenda;
- game playing;
- image building;
- building coalitions; and
- controlling decision parameters.

Controlling Information

The objective is to control as much information as possible. The more crucial the information, and the fewer the number of people having access to it or part of it, the stronger the influence of the person who is privy to the total picture. For example, a senior manager has at his or her disposal an important report about the company's future. Though it is necessary to confide in some colleagues about certain features of the contents of the report, the senior manager is strategically placed to exert political influence in decision making and related issues.

Controlling Lines of Communication

Certain people can, as gatekeepers, control the lines of communication as far as access to others is concerned—in particular, access to an important executive. For example, secretaries and personal assistants wield political influence when they regulate access to their boss.

Using Outside Experts

A manager may achieve his or her objective by using an outside consultant who happens to share his or her views about the matter under review. Although the consultant may approach the assignment in a professional manner, the recommendations made may be unconsciously biased towards a course of action favoured by the manager. Because the consultant is perceived as somebody occupying a position of neutrality, the recommendations are accepted by others in the organisation and the manager has the satisfaction of having successfully exerted influence to achieve the desired result.

Controlling the Agenda

The manager may not feel comfortable with the prospect of having a particular controversial issue thoroughly discussed and acted on at a meeting. The issue could be placed on the agenda as the last item, or alternatively it could be excluded from the agenda, with the manager claiming that it is rather premature to discuss such an important issue that requires further thought.

Where the item is placed on the agenda, a tactic open to the manager would be to develop allies by siding with colleagues' views on earlier items in the expectation that they will give him or her their support when the controversial item is discussed. Alternatively, the manager may rely on a combination of factors. For example, when the controversial item is to be discussed, he or she could rely on what one might refer to as committee fatigue if it was a long meeting, the desire of members to close the meeting, and on support from allies. Other tactics could include exhaustive discussion of prior agenda items, so that the meeting never discusses the controversial item, or only gives it cursory attention. Of course, the issue could be discussed, but the manager may display adeptness in raising new angles to the problem, and concludes that the matter needs further attention before the proposal can be considered firm.

Game Playing

Managers operate within the rules of the organisation when playing games. For example, a manager could arrange to visit an important customer outside the company at a time that coincides with a crucial internal meeting on which the manager would have to declare his or her hand on some policy issue, in circumstances where the manager's preferred action is to sit on the fence.

People can also play games with the management of information. This could amount to disseminating good or bad news at a time when it is likely to have the greatest impact. By doing so, the self-interest of the manipulator of the news is served but the hopes of others could be dashed. The disseminators of information in this context are unlikely to tell lies or circulate misinformation, because their future credibility would be undermined. But they rely on a carefully considered release of genuine information to serve their needs.

Image Building

People may cultivate an outward appearance and style in order to impress influential individuals within the organisation. This is a subtle technique to enhance one's power base in readiness for the exploitation of future opportunities, and could also be used as a supplement to the development of expert power referred to earlier in the chapter.

A more manipulative manifestation of this technique is making over-zealous efforts to be seen to be associated with successful projects, taking credit for the work of others, and overstating one's personal achievements.

Building Coalitions

An obvious tactic is to befriend people, often in the higher echelons of the organisation, who can help the user of this technique gain access to useful information. Also, being on good terms with the boss's secretary could be considered beneficial by some in developing greater awareness of what is going on.

The person using the technique of building coalitions often conveys the impression that by subscribing to his or her aims one would be contributing to the attainment of organisational objectives. Another tactic could be lobbying by a manager prior to a committee meeting to gain support for certain items on the agenda to which the manager has a deep commitment. Some would consider such an approach acceptable if support for the items concerned would lead to the achievement of organisational goals. Of course, the acceptability of the approach would be questioned if the prime beneficiary of the concerted action was the manager. The technique of building coalitions is used in the form of reciprocal action. This could arise when X votes for a particular measure sacred to Y, the adoption of which does not materially affect X. In return, Y reciprocates to the mutual advantage of the parties concerned. There are occasions when this behaviour is dysfunctional, but on other occasions it could be functional.

Controlling Decision Parameters

With this technique managers take a step backward in the organisational process by trying to control the parameters set for making decisions, rather than controlling the decision itself. For example, managers could adopt a stance whereby influence is exerted towards defining or redefining the criteria on which the decision will be based.

With respect to a selection decision, the manager could display considerable skill in shaping the criteria—e.g. depicting the ideal candidate for a particular job in terms of age, education, training, experience, etc—and in doing so creates a profile that happens to resemble that of the favoured internal candidate. In this way the manager has created a situation where the preferred candidate has an excellent chance of getting the job. Therefore, the manager can afford to be less active in the actual selection decision confident in the belief that the preferred outcome will materialise. Anyway, if he or she were to influence the selection decision directly, there may be accusations of bias because of the way questions were asked or the nature of the discussion.

In addition to these eight techniques, two more deserve mention (Vecchio, 1991). One is to eliminate a political rival by helping that person become more successful and marketable so that he or she is promoted to an attractive post elsewhere in the organisation.

The other is to seek earnestly an opening for the rival in the line organisation, and this tactic would be particularly appropriate for a staff specialist wishing to progress within the hierarchy. Securing a line manager's job is often considered a prerequisite to eventually wielding real power, and the base from which top-level executive appointments are made. However, one must not devalue the role of staff specialists who, of course, can wield power within their own function.

A Study of Tactics

Finally, of the tactics or techniques discussed in this section, control of information and image building were two of the three most important tactics perceived by a diverse group of managers. The other tactic was attacking or blaming others (Madison et al., 1980). Attacking tactics involved portraying rivals in a poor light in front of the influential members of the organisation. This was often done to create less competition for scarce resources. On the other hand, blaming tactics involved putting the spotlight on somebody else for an unfavourable result or situation in order to deflect attention from oneself. The fourth tactic in order of importance identified in the above study was building support for ideas. This was common among upper-level managers, and it involved getting others to understand one's views prior to a meeting at which a decision is going to be made, setting out the ideal scenario, and inviting others to contribute. Eventually, it is hoped that the others may embrace the views as their own, thereby fostering their commitment to the decision at the meeting.

Political tactics have been described as legitimate—e.g. forming coalitions or bypassing the chain of command—or alternatively as illegitimate or devious, such as sabotage (Farrell & Petersen, 1982). Extreme illegitimate tactics are not widespread because of the likely consequences (e.g. harsh sanctions or dismissals) that may result when the culprits are exposed and successfully charged for wrongdoing.

Devious Tactics

The following are devious political tactics that are morally difficult to defend (Dubrin, 1978):

- It is quite possible for managers or executives to create enemies because of unpopular or distasteful actions they have taken in denying promotion opportunities, freezing or reducing salaries, displacing people and terminating contracts of employment following, for example, major reorganisations or mergers. One tactic in dealing with this type of problem is to get rid of the individuals who survived but who still bear resentment against the manager's or executive's past unpopular actions.

- A tactic referred to as "divide and rule" amounts to a definite ploy to encourage a feud or conflict between subordinates or colleagues by spreading rumours or by promoting competition. The competing individuals may be rivals in the promotion stakes or may be competitors for favours bestowed by the boss. The logic of this approach is that the warring factions will be continually feuding, and therefore unable to mount an attack against the instigator of this tactic. However, the ploy could backfire if the tactics used become too visible.

- Where opposing factions are rivals, another tactic is preventing them from attending key meetings or gatherings. The ploy adopted here would be to schedule important meetings or events when the opposition is absent—for example, at another meeting, or on holiday. The instigator of this ploy could then be free to exert much influence in decision making, and perhaps unjustifiably claim credit for the ideas of rivals in their absence.

Serious Blunders

Among tactics considered to be costly political mistakes are the following (Vecchio, 1991).

Violating the Chain of Command.   Where a subordinate approaches the superior of his or her boss, without seeking the latter's permission, in order to act as an informant or complain about his or her predicament, this can be fraught with difficulties.

Losing Control.   Although behaving aggressively and displaying temper tantrums to achieve one's objectives may be tolerated to a certain extent in competitive sport, such behaviour in the office or factory is unlikely to be condoned. It could earn the person a reputation as being difficult to relate to, and could easily lead to them being typecast as a troublemaker. A sinister twist to events could arise when the person who loses control easily is deliberately provoked in, for example, a public forum, and reacts aggressively. A number of incidents of this nature could adversely affect that person's image and reputation.

Saying No to Top Management.   It may be considered unwise to reject a request from somebody high up in the organisation to undertake a specific assignment. Individuals receiving such a request may feel overburdened with work already and, because they feel that their reputation as an employee is very satisfactory, may conclude that it is acceptable behaviour to decline participation in the assignment. Such a course of action could well be an unwise move. A more acceptable reaction would be to explain the situation with respect to the work-load, stating that, if one were to undertake the special assignment, assistance with one's normal duties would be necessary.

Challenging Cherished Beliefs.   Where there are cherished beliefs about the nature of the organisation, it could be unwise (in the presence of influential loyalists) to criticise the

VINNIE EARNS HIMSELF A PAIR OF CONCRETE SHOES....

myths, folklore, and special feats of the organisation's revered founder. One recognises that people should be free to express their opinions; nevertheless, it may be politically insensitive and unwise to challenge in open debate the truth of widely held beliefs within the organisation.

Pros and Cons of Political Behaviour

What are the advantages and disadvantages of the use of political tactics? The advantages, according to the findings of a study examining the perceptions of managers on this topic, are career advancement, recognition, status, achievement of goals, effective co-ordination, and organisational survival. By contrast, the disadvantages were perceived as loss of credibility, demotion, feelings of guilt, divisiveness, and a negative climate (Madison et al., 1980).

Ethics in Organisational Politics
In the last decade there has been a focus on ethics in organisational politics, and naturally questions are asked as to whether people who engage in political activity end up subscribing

to unethical practices, such as lying and cheating, to achieve their objectives.

There has been much adverse publicity in recent years about practices such as insider trading in company shares, bribes to acquire large contracts, and raiding pension funds. However, it would be a mistake to view all political activity as unethical. Cavanagh, Moberg, and Velasquez (1981) consider political behaviour to be ethical and appropriate under two conditions— if it respects the rights of all interested parties, and if it is fair and equitable.

Coping With Political Behaviour

One recognises that it is impossible to eliminate all political behaviour. However, it is possible to take certain action to counteract its worst effects. In an optimistic tone, Moorhead and Griffin (1992), recognising the virtual impossibility of eliminating political activity in organisations, suggest that the manager can limit its dysfunctional effects by resorting to open communication, reduction of uncertainty, and awareness.

Open Communication.   This would amount to making known to everybody the basis for the allocation of scarce resources, and curtailing the ability of any individual to control information or lines of communication.

Uncertainty.   This is a phenomenon that inhabits our daily work life and, as was discussed earlier, a number of internal and external factors generate it. Strategies of organisational change and development can create much uncertainty, so it is important for change agents and others to state clearly the way likely future events will unfold, rather than remaining silent on key issues and fuelling speculation and rumour as a consequence.

Awareness.   Being aware of what has been discussed in this chapter about political techniques and tactics, and what gives rise to political behaviour, is a very useful first step to controlling the negative effects of organisational politics.

Vecchio's (1991) recipe, offered to managers to help them combat the dysfunctional aspects of political action, includes setting an example, giving clear job assignments, eliminating coalitions and cliques, and confronting those who play political games.

- Setting an example is evident when the manager acts as a role model by encouraging truthfulness and fair and equitable treatment of others.
- Giving clear job assignments entails the allocation of well-defined and discrete assignments that remove the potential for ambiguity.
- Eliminating coalitions and cliques which are detrimental to work performance could be achieved by transfers or dismissals, but it may be preferable for individuals to be rotated through different job assignments that could have the effect of enriching their total experience.

- Confronting people who play political games could mean suggesting to the game player that he or she should raise questionable information about an individual in a more appropriate setting, or, if feasible, have it discussed at the next meeting of the group as a matter that requires serious consideration. Adopting this approach conveys to the game player that political games are not condoned.

CONFLICT

Conflict is a phenomenon related to power and politics. In fact, it can be triggered off by political behaviour and can occur between individuals or groups. Conflict is defined as a process that materialises when an individual or group perceives that another individual or group is frustrating, or about to frustrate, the attempts of the former to attain a goal (Thomas, 1976). It can involve incompatible differences between parties that result in interference or opposition, often finding expression in antagonism and the violation of rules and procedures. In its more subtle form it can be reflected in highly controlled forms of interference. Conflict can be distinguished from competition: when groups strive for the same goal, harbour little or no antagonism towards each other, and operate according to the rules and procedures, we can expect to find competition (Robbins, 1974).

As Robbins (1974) explains, conflict has been interpreted differently at different times—i.e. the unitary, pluralist, and interactionist perspectives (see panel facing). The type of conflict supported by current thinking—the interactionist perspective—is described as "functional" or "constructive" conflict, and is said to facilitate the attainment of the group's goals and to improve performance.

Functional conflict is probably best described as low to moderate levels of subtle and controlled opposition which is likely to lend itself to activities such as creative or

---

Differing Perspectives on Conflict

Unitary Perspective

The early interpretations of conflict—the unitary perspective—amounted to a definition of a process that was harmful and should be avoided. In early research into groups (i.e. the Hawthorne experiments), conflict was seen as a negative outcome of poor communication, lack of openness and trust between people, and the inability of superiors to respond to the needs and aspirations of subordinates.

Pluralist Perspective

A later school of thought, spanning the period from the early-1950s to the mid-1970s, acknowledged the existence of conflict as a natural phenomenon, and went as far as suggesting that there may be times when it could have beneficial effects on the performance of the group. This outlook is called the pluralist perspective and claims that conflict stems from individuals and groups pursuing their own interests. It is the task of management to mediate conflicting claims and bring about an acceptable form of compromise to ensure the functioning of the organisation.

Interactionist Perspective

The current school of thought is called the "interactionist" perspective. This perspective encourages the adoption of a minimum level of conflict—that is, enough conflict to make sure the group is viable, self-critical, and creative. Implicit in this perspective is the belief that harmony, peace, tranquillity, and co-operation might create apathy and produce too great a tolerance of the status quo, with a lack of responsiveness to the need for change and innovation.

---

non-programmed decision making. Therefore, conflict may be more functional in groups that adopt new and novel approaches to tackle problems—e.g. research, advertising, or organisational change—than in groups performing highly programmed activities found in mass production systems.

Functional conflict can be contrasted with "dysfunctional" or "destructive" forms of conflict. Dysfunctional conflict produces uncontrolled opposition and discontent, hampers communication, undermines cohesiveness, elevates in-fighting between members to a position higher than the achievement of group goals, and eventually has an adverse effect on group effectiveness. In its extreme form this type of conflict can gravely disrupt the functioning of the group, and has the potential to threaten the group's survival.

In the final analysis one must recognise that the demarcation line between functional and dysfunctional conflict is not clear. The issues raised in this section would normally be of concern to commentators who examine the implementation of human resource management policies from an industrial relations perspective.

Types of Conflict

Conflict in organisations is manifest at both the level of the individual and the group.

Individual Conflict

Individuals experience frustration when their pathway to achieving personal goals is blocked. Candidates for an internal promotion may feel aggrieved at the way a job description for the vacant post is framed if it appears to hamper their chances of securing the job.

Sometimes employees feel so alienated by organisational conditions that the ensuing conflict expresses itself as sabotage. In the past this could have taken the form of damage to tools or equipment at work, and emanated from general feelings of powerlessness in circumstances where, perhaps, avenues for the expression of dissatisfaction did not exist. Though the underlying causes may remain the same, sabotage takes new forms with changes in technology. For example, computing facilities have to be guarded against errors invented by operators, including computer viruses (Huczynski & Buchanan, 1991).

Individuals perform a number of roles both at work and at home. There are occasions when the expected behaviour in one work role affects that in another work role, resulting in role conflict. A classic example of this conflict applies to the "person in the middle"—the first-line supervisor—who is expected by management to be part of its team, while the workers feel he or she should represent them and act as their link with management. Another example is that of the individual who is torn between the demands of management for higher productivity and the norms of the group that reflect more modest productivity aspirations.

Role conflicts can also exist where there is a clash between the demands of roles and an individual's values and beliefs—i.e. when the individual is expected to do something that goes against the grain. Another form of role conflict that is experienced by professionals is expressed as the conflict between the need for professional autonomy and the demands of bureaucratic organisation (Child, 1982). (Further discussion of role conflict can be found in Chapter 7.)

Group Conflict

At the level of the group, particularly in the context of industrial action, reference can be made to collective or organised conflict (Reed, 1989). A group of workers, assisted by a trade union, could engage in certain behaviour (e.g. a go-slow, withdrawal of labour, work-to-rule, or overtime ban) in order to accomplish an objective, such as increased earnings. In industrial action of this nature there could be a high degree of cohesion among those involved with respect to the aims of the action and the best way to fulfil those aims, but the workers group could be in conflict with the management group.

While focusing on conflict between groups within the organisation, Hodgetts (1991) classified this type of conflict as institutionalised and emergent conflict.

Institutionalised Conflict.   This is evident when, for example, the marketing and production groups vie for advantage during the budgetary process when resources are allocated. In such circumstances, particular groups are preoccupied with their own vested interests, and given that resources are normally scarce, a gain for one group could be a loss for another.

The hierarchical arrangement of occupational groups could inspire institutionalised conflict, because each level of the hierarchy experiences some degree of conflict with the level above it. This is often due to a concern with different sets of priorities. For example, top managers are naturally concerned with the future direction of the organisation, and may place undue demands on lower-level managers who are already burdened with short-term problems connected with the scheduling of work and the meeting of production quotas or other targets.

Emergent Conflict.   This is seen when two social forces collide. For example, the formal organisation calls for greater productive effort which the informal organisation resists. The seeds of emergent conflict are sown when the subordinates are convinced that their level of expertise surpasses that of their superiors. It is also evident where staff specialists rely on the influence of senior managers (with whom they may have a special relationship) to impose recommendations for action on subordinate line managers, rather than convincing the latter on the strength of their case.

Sources of Conflict

Conflict emanates from a number of sources. Robbins (1974) identifies three specific sources: communication, structure, and personal factors.

1. Communication

As can be seen from the discussion of the problems of communication in Chapter 3, the potential for misunderstanding is significant. The communication barrier variables said to be associated with conflict are semantic difficulties, insufficient exchange of information, and noise in channels of communication.

With respect to semantic difficulties, these are said to arise as a result of people's selective perception, inadequate information about others, and differences in training. As regards volume of information, too much as well as too little information is said to provide the foundation for conflict. As numerous people in the communication process filter the information, there is plenty of room to create incorrect, distorted, or ambiguous messages, all of which can lead to hostility. The channels used to convey information (such as circulars, meetings, or the grapevine) have also been considered in the context of the generation of conflict.

2. Structure
The interpretation of structure in this context includes size, specialisation, ambiguity, leadership, rewards, and interdependency.

Size and Specialisation.   These are said to interact; the larger the group and the more specialised its activities, the greater the likelihood of conflict. With specialisation and differentiation within organisations (e.g. marketing, finance, etc.) comes the development of distinctive expertise, and the adoption of a diverse range of goals, with sometimes a parochial outlook. The diversity of goals among groups is a major source of conflict.

Members of other functional groupings are likely to be seen as competitors for scarce resources. This can be aggravated by power imbalances between the functional groups, thereby stoking the flames of conflict.

Ambiguity.   The greater the ambiguity in defining where responsibility for action lies, the greater the likelihood of inter-group feuding to control resources and organisational domains.

Leadership.   Unexpectedly, one may find that too heavy a reliance on participative leadership may stimulate conflict, on the understanding that participation encourages the expression of different points of view.

Rewards.   Operating reward systems is fraught with difficulties. If one party secures rewards at the expense of another party, conflict can spring into existence.

Interdependency.   An interdependent type of relationship is not uncommon between various groups within organisations. In particular the relationship between line managers and staff specialists is worthy of note. The role of the line manager has been viewed traditionally as that of a generalist concerned with the primary activities (e.g. production) of the organisation. By contrast, the efforts of the staff specialist are directed at supplementing the contribution of the line manager by providing specialised assistance in areas such as accounting, purchasing, marketing, personnel, and research and development.

Over 40 years ago, Dalton (1950) recognised that the staff–line relationship had tremendous potential for conflict. He considered it a delicate relationship whereby the staff specialist must reach a tacit agreement with the line manager in order to foster a workable relationship. But the potential for disagreement and conflict is omnipresent. For example, line managers could resist the innovative proposals of the staff specialists because the former may feel a lowering of status owing to their inability to formulate such proposals, as well as the fear that the implementation of the proposals would cause disruption, and the exposure of shady practices and inefficiency in their departments.

Woodward (1965) made specific reference to the ill-feeling that existed between management accountants and line managers residing outside of the finance function. Hopper (1978) reported conflict between management accountants and production managers in the budgetary process, due to the failure of the accountants to present information in an easily understandable form relevant to the needs of managers. It is well to note that there is a significant amount of dissatisfaction with the concept of staff–line, and its applicability has been questioned in conditions of product diversity and increasing complexity in a company's operations (Fisch, 1961). The case in the panel below highlights the difficulties certain specialist groups may encounter in organisations.

3. *Personal Factors*

This heading covers personality characteristics and value systems to which people adhere. It is understandable that individuals who are highly authoritarian and dogmatic, with a leaning towards low esteem, have within themselves the capacity to generate conflict. "Value systems" are a significant variable in the study of social conflict. They determine one's outlook and behaviour, and can be seen as a significant force in prejudice, expressions of views about good and bad practices, and notions of equitable rewards.

Use of Conflict

When examining the interactionist perspective of conflict earlier, it was maintained that a certain level of conflict is necessary if a group is to be viable, self-critical, and creative. Certain cues signal the need for managers to stimulate conflict—e.g. when there is an unusually low rate of staff turnover, a shortage of new ideas, strong resistance to change, and the belief that co-operation is more important than personal competence. Conflict stimulation is the formation and constructive use of conflict by management, and its purpose is to create situations where differences of opinion are brought to the surface. Conflict is constructive when it improves the quality of decisions, stimulates creativity and innovation, encourages interest and curiosity among group members, provides the medium through which problems can be aired and tensions released, and fosters an environment of self-evaluation and change (Robbins, 1974). It is also an antidote for groupthink (discussed earlier in Chapter 7).

Management might profitably stimulate conflict where, for example, it is recognised that competing organisations are improving their product design and production systems and this is likely to lead to the competitor increasing market share. It is therefore concluded that the time is ripe for managers to stimulate innovation and creativity by challenging the status quo. This could entail taking a fresh view of prevailing attitudes, behavioural patterns, and the existing

---

Hostility Towards Computer Specialists

A computer was installed in an expanding retail establishment in the 1950s, when mechanised data processing was comparatively new. The organisation became heavily dependent on a group of computer programmers in charge of the installation. This specialist group—graduates who behaved informally and worked outside normal hours—had total control of computer applications (i.e. the group was endowed with expert power).

However, the group members did not fit well into the organisation, and they considered the other employees as staid and bureaucratically minded. The other employees viewed the programmers as immature and full of themselves.

Hostile feelings developed between the two groups, resulting in a failure of the programmers to become integrated into the organisation.

Senior managers were unhappy about having to rely on the programmers' skills, and an attempt was made to undermine the programmers' control of technical information. This took the form of a proposal to dismantle the programming function and allocate parts of it to other staff. The programmers responded by projecting their skills as exclusive and withholding information in order to retain the organisation's dependence on them (Pettigrew, 1973).

distribution of power (Van de Vliert, 1985). Creating a conflict situation may provide the impetus for employees to disclose differences of opinion previously kept secret.

In an experimental study, where students played the roles of supervisors and assembly workers, it was concluded that conflict can improve rather than impede decision making. When those with opposing views go through the motions of trying to reach agreement they develop an improved understanding of each other's points of view, focusing on their differences, and arriving at mutually acceptable decisions. The conditions considered best for decision making were called co-operative rather than competitive controversy conditions. Under these conditions feelings of curiosity, trust, and openness were cultivated, and decisions were arrived at that brought together the views of both workers and supervisors (Tjosvold & Deemer, 1980).

Among the measures proposed by Robbins (1974) to produce conflict are the following:

- Appoint managers who are receptive to change.
- Encourage competition by providing incentives (e.g. salary increases, bonuses, recognition) that are related to performance. However, the competitive situation needs to be properly managed so as to produce creative conflict.
- Restructure the work unit. This would entail rotating staff among jobs and altering lines of communication. Although this is one way to restructure, there is another, and this involves creating new jobs to be occupied by external candidates with values and styles that are the antithesis of the prevailing placid norms.
- Adopt the role of "devil's advocate" in group discussions so that a number of alternatives can be critically appraised and analysed.
- Train people to be more adept at identifying potential problems.

Management of Conflict

Because conflict has potentially damaging consequences, it is important that managers are aware of how to manage it. Conflict situations that are disruptive or counter-productive will have to be resolved.

Styles of Conflict Management
Thomas (1976) identified five major styles of conflict management at the disposal of the manager:

- competition;
- collaboration;
- avoidance;
- accommodation; and
- compromise.

As can be seen in Fig. 9.1, Thomas places the five styles in a two-dimensional framework comprising assertiveness (the desire to satisfy one's own concerns) and co-operativeness (the desire to satisfy another's concerns).

1. Competition. The use of this style in conflict resolution amounts to an attempt to overwhelm an opponent by utilising formal authority, threats, or the use of power. It is a win-lose struggle and is reflected in assertive and uncooperative behaviour.

2. Collaboration This style involves mutual problem solving, whereby all the parties to the conflict come face-to-face with each other and discuss the issues. For example, the office manager is convinced that the selective application of new technology to work will improve efficiency, but subordinates feel threatened by the changes that are contemplated. This creates a certain amount of conflict among the parties concerned. However, co-operation and the search for a mutually beneficial outcome can emerge when the parties to the conflict are determined to satisfy the genuine reservations of all concerned.

FIG. 9.1.
A two-dimensional model of
conflict management. Source:
Thomas, K.W. (1976). Conflict
and conflict management. In M.
Dunnette (Ed.), *Handbook of
industrial and organisational
psychology*. Skokie, IL: Rand
McNally.

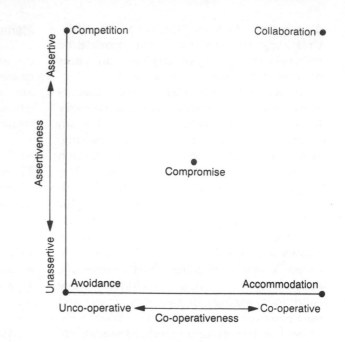

When the collaborative style is used, participants attempt to clarify their differences and consider the full range of alternatives with a view to solving the problem. Collaboration is frequently viewed as a win-win approach because the solution sought by the group is advantageous to all the participants. This style is used by marriage counsellors and by social scientists who place emphasis and value on openness, trust, genuineness, and spontaneous behaviour in relationships. The collaborative style is reflected in assertive but co-operative behaviour.

3. *Avoidance.*   One way in which parties to a conflict can deal with the situation is by avoiding the other person in order to prevent an overt demonstration of disagreement. Avoidance takes two forms—withdrawal and suppression. With respect to withdrawal, we may encounter a situation where, for example, the health and safety official finds it difficult to relate to key production executives. The former withdraws from interaction with the latter by sending safety reports up the hierarchical line for downward

action. In other cases within a particular department, parties to the conflict could stake out a territory in which each party decides what should be done and does not interfere with the other party. This could be workable if co-ordination of effort between the parties is not a live issue.

Where withdrawal is not possible or acceptable, because of, for example, the necessity for co-ordinative effort, the parties may suppress their differences by withholding information or not airing their feelings so as not to upset the other party. The adoption of this style has no effect on the cause of the conflict, but by removing the conditions for overt disagreement a win-lose struggle is avoided. Probably suppression is more widely practised than appears to be the case from casual observation. This style is reflected in unassertive and uncooperative behaviour.

4. *Accommodation.*   This style is similar to appeasement, where one party in a conflict situation places his or her interest below the opponent's interest. It amounts to self-sacrificing behaviour, and can be found in personal relationships where one party, for

altruistic or other reasons, puts the other party's interest first. This style is reflected in unassertive but co-operative behaviour.

5. *Compromise.* A compromise situation is created when each party to the conflict gives up something, and there is no winner or loser. If one party concedes ground on a particular issue, one would expect the other to yield something of equivalent value. In the field of industrial relations compromise is evident in discussions between management and trade unions. In order to arrive at a settlement to, for example, an industrial dispute, compromise is required. This style is reflected in intermediate amounts of assertiveness and co-operativeness.

Influence of Culture Attempts have been made to assess the influence of culture on conflict handling styles. For example, managers from Jordan and Turkey shared with their US counterparts a first preference for a collaborative style, but the managers from the three countries studied differed in their preferences for the remaining four styles depicted in the Thomas model, a version of which was used by the researcher (Kozan, 1989).

In another study where a similar model of conflict handling was used, culture also had an effect on styles. For example, Chinese managers in Hong Kong tended to favour harmony and adopt the less assertive styles—e.g. compromise and avoidance— whereas British managers favoured the more assertive styles—e.g. collaboration and competition (Tang & Kirkbridge, 1986).

Situational Factors No particular style of conflict resolution discussed above is applicable in all situations. Following a survey of chief executives, Thomas (1977) specifies the most appropriate situations in which to use the styles of conflict manage- ment. These are shown in Table 9.4.

The message from Table 9.4 is that individuals can adapt their conflict management behaviour to particular situations. However, this could be challenged, and one could argue that people are predisposed to deal with conflict situations in particular ways (Sternberg & Soriano, 1984), and in fact they may have preferred styles on which they place heavy reliance irrespective of prevailing circumstances. If so, it may be better to consider the five conflict handling styles as relatively fixed rather than as a set of alternative styles from which people can select the most appropriate style for a given situation (Robbins, 1991).

Surprisingly, the managerial grid (Blake & Mouton, 1964), discussed in Chapter 8, appears to be coming into its own as a means of assessing the conflict management styles referred to earlier (Van de Vliert & Kabanoff, 1990). People are classified into the five conflict management styles on the basis of which of the locations on the two-dimensional grid (i.e. concern for people, concern for production) they occupy.

Superordinate Goals
As well as the five styles of conflict management proposed by Thomas (1976), one could consider another strategy. This is known as the setting of common or superordinate goals by feuding groups. It is well established that membership of a particular group could predispose members to view other groups with suspicion and sometimes hostility.

A classic study of inter-group conflict is provided by Sherif (1967). Boys attending summer camps in the USA were allocated to two different groups, and initially were unaware of the other group's existence. The boys participated in the normal activities of a summer camp, and developed norms of behaviour within their groups. An example of the type of conflict situation created by Sherif was informing both groups that the other camp would be using certain equipment, such as canoes, and as a result they would not be able to pursue that activity. This created a win-lose situation,

TABLE 9.4

Uses of Five Styles of Conflict Handling

Conflict Handling Styles

1. Competition

   When quick decisive action is vital
   On important issues where unpopular actions need implementing
   On issues vital to the organisation's welfare and when you know you're right
   Against people who take advantage of non-competitive behaviour

2. Collaboration

   To find an integrative solution when both sets of concerns are too important to be compromised
   When your objective is to learn
   To merge insights from people with different perspectives
   To gain commitment by incorporating concerns into a consensus
   To work through feelings that have interfered with a relationship

3. Avoidance

   When an issue is trivial, or more important issues are pressing
   When you perceive no chance of satisfying your concerns
   When potential disruption outweighs the benefits of resolution
   To let people cool down and regain perspective
   When gathering information supersedes immediate decision
   When others can resolve the conflict more effectively
   When issues seem tangential or symptomatic of other issues

4. Accommodation

   When you find you are wrong—to allow a better position to be heard, to learn, and to show your reasonableness
   When issues are more important to others than to yourself—to satisfy others and maintain co-operation
   To build social credits for later issues
   To minimise loss when you are outmatched and losing
   When harmony and stability are especially important
   To allow subordinates to develop by learning from mistakes

5. Compromise

   When goals are important, but not worth the effort or potential disruption of more assertive modes
   When opponents with equal power are committed to mutually exclusive goals
   To achieve temporary settlements to complex issues
   To arrive at expedient solutions under time pressure
   As a backup when collaboration or competition is unsuccessful

Source: Thomas, K.W. (1977). Toward multi-dimensional values in teaching: The example of conflict behaviours. *Academy of Management Review*, 2, July, 484–490.

and the two groups harboured strong resentment towards each other. Also, competitive games were used to develop a competitive relationship between the two groups and, when a hostile inter-group relationship emerged, various procedures to resolve the conflict were used.

Bringing members of the hostile groups together socially as a means of reducing conflict did not seem to work. Neither did it help when accurate and favourable information about one group was communicated to the other group. Even bringing the leaders of the two groups together to enlist their influence was not productive. In fact social contact of the type described earlier can act as a means of intensifying conflict because favourable information about a disliked group may be ignored or reinterpreted to fit negative stereo-typed notions about opponents. (Inter-group discrimination was referred to in Chapter 7.)

Apparently the best strategy for achieving harmony between the groups in conflict is to bring the groups together to work towards the achievement of a common or superordinate goal, and in these circumstances favourable information about a disliked group is seen in a new light. In addition, leaders are in a better position to take bolder steps towards co-operation. Examples of superordinate goals set by Sherif included the breakdown of the camp water supply, which required inter-group co-operation to find the fault, and the breakdown of a lorry used for excursions, which required all members of the groups to pull together on the same rope to get it started. After a series of activities based on different superordinate goals, inter-group conflict was progressively reduced and the two groups began to integrate.

These principles can also manifest themselves in an organisational setting. An organisation consists of different groups (e.g. the production and marketing functions) and one effect of group membership, in whatever function, is the development of group loyalties. This can result in a parochial view of overall organisational events, and there is a likelihood that each group actively pursues its own ends to the disadvantage of the organisation as a whole. Conflict can arise when there is competition for scarce resources among the different groups. Budgeting can be used as a process for resolving inter-group conflict, but it may not always be successful in doing so. A significant threat to the survival of the organisation may be instrumental in bringing about more constructive inter-group co-operation and the resolution of conflict.

Although the principle of setting superordinate or common goals as a means to reduce inter-group conflict is appealing, Sherif felt it may not be applicable in all industrial settings because some groups in industry possess much more power than others. There is now greater interest in the significance of power (discussed earlier in this chapter) as a dimension of inter-group relations (Hartley, 1984). Finally, a special issue of the *Journal of Organizational Behaviour* (Vol. 13, No. 3, 1992) is devoted to conflict and negotiation in organisations.

SUMMARY: POWER, POLITICS, AND CONFLICT

- Power, politics, and conflict are interrelated. With regard to power, dependency is an important consideration.
- The bases of organisational power identified by French and Raven were discussed, with particular reference to the circumstances in which they can be used. Etzioni's types of organisational power were acknowledged.
- Power tactics used by individuals and groups were discussed, and situational variables that determine the choice of power tactic were examined. There was a brief section reflecting on power at the macro level.

- Politics in organisations was described, and the causes of political behaviour were noted. The techniques or tactics to promote the political interests of organisational members were described in some detail, as were examples of devious political tactics and political mistakes.
- The advantages and disadvantages of the use of political tactics were stated. Hints on how to combat the dysfunctional aspects of political action were offered.
- Conflict was examined as a phenomenon related to power and politics; it can occur between individuals or groups. Over time

conflict has been interpreted differently—e.g. the unitary, the pluralist, and interactionist perspectives.

- The types of conflict manifest at both individual and group levels in the organisation were discussed, and there was a recognition that conflict emanates from a number of sources.

- There was the suggestion that management might profitably stimulate conflict in specified circumstances, but as conflict has potentially damaging consequences, it is imperative for managers to be able to manage it. Styles of conflict management were outlined.

QUESTIONS

1. Distinguish between power, politics, and conflict in organisations.
2. What is meant by the bases of power?
3. Describe the power tactics at the disposal of individuals within groups, and isolate the ones considered the most important.
4. Define organisational politics.
5. What are the organisational factors that contribute to political behaviour?
6. Distinguish between devious and legitimate political tactics in organisations.
7. List the advantages and disadvantages of political behaviour in organisations.

8. How does the interactionist perspective on conflict differ from other recognised perspectives?
9. Define the following terms: (a) institutionalised conflict; (b) dysfunctional conflict; (c) opportunity power; (d) alienative involvement; and (e) building coalitions.
10. Identify the measures proposed to produce conflict in organisations.
11. Comment on styles of conflict management.

REFERENCES

Bachman, J.G., Bowers, D., & Marcus, P.M. (1968). Bases of supervisory power: A comparative study in five organisational settings. In A.S. Tennenbaum (Ed.), *Control in organisations*. New York: McGraw-Hill.

Bachrach, P. & Baritz, M.S. (1962). Two faces of power. *American Political Science Review, 56*, 947–952.

Baddeley, S. & James, K. (1987). Owl, fox, donkey or sheep: Political skills for managers. *Management Education and Development, 18*, 3–19.

Blackler, F. & Shimmin, S. (1984). *Applying Psychology in Organisations*. London: Methuen.

Blake, R.R. & Mouton, J.S. (1964). *The managerial grid*. Houston, TX: Gulf Publishing.

Brass, D.J. (1984). Being in the right place: A structural analysis of individual influence in an organisation. *Administrative Science Quarterly*, December, 518–539.

Butler, R.J. & Wilson, D.C. (1989). *Managing voluntary and non-profit organisations: Strategy and structure*. London: Routledge & Kegan Paul.

Cavanagh, G.F., Moberg, D.J., & Velasquez, M. (1981). The ethics of organisational politics. *Academy of Management Review*, July, 363–374.

Child, J. (1982). Professionals in a corporate world. In D. Dunkerley & G. Salaman (Eds.), *The international yearbook of organisation studies*. London: Routledge & Kegan Paul.

Clegg, S. (1977). Power, organisation theory, Marx, and critique. In S. Clegg & D. Dunkerley (Eds.), *Critical issues in organisations*. London: Routledge & Kegan Paul.

Dalton, M. (1950). Conflict between staff and line managerial officers. *American Sociological Review, 15*, 107–120.

Dubrin, A.J. (1978). *Winning at office politics*. New York: Ballantine.

Eisenhardt, K.M. & Bourgeois III, L.J. (1988). Politics of strategic decision making in high velocity environments: Towards a mid-range theory. *Academy of Management Journal*, December, 737–770.

Etzioni, A.(1975). *A comparative analysis of complex organisations*. New York: Free Press.

Farrell, D. & Petersen, J.C. (1982). Patterns of political behaviour in organisations. *Academy of Management Review*, July, 403–412.

Fisch, G.G. (l961). Line–staff is obsolete. *Harvard Business Review, 39*, 67–79.

French, J. & Raven, B. (1958). The bases of social power. In D. Cartwright (Ed.), *Studies in social power*. Ann Arbor, Michigan: Institute for Social Research.

Gandz, J. & Murray, V.V. (1980). The experience of workplace politics. *Academy of Management Journal*, June, 237–251.

Gemmil, G.R. & Heisler, W.J. (1972). Machiavellianism as a factor in managerial job strain, job satisfaction, and upward mobility. *Academy of Management Journal, 15*, 53–67.

Hartley, J. (1984). Industrial relations psychology. In M. Gruneberg & T. Wall (Eds.), *Social psychology and organisational behaviour*. Chichester: J. Wiley & Sons.

Hickson, D.J., Butler, R.J., Gray, D., Mallory, G.R., & Wilson, D.C. (1986). *Top decisions: Strategic decision makers in organisations*. Oxford: Blackwell.

Hickson, D.J., Hinings, C.R., Lee, C.A., Schneck, R.E., & Pennings, J.M. (1971). A strategic contingencies theory of inter-organisational power. *Administrative Science Quarterly*, June, 216–229.

Hodgetts, R.M. (1991). *Organisational behaviour: Theory and practice*. New York: Macmillan Publishing Co.

Hopper, T. (1978). *Role conflicts of management accountants in the context of their structural relationship to production*. Unpublished M.Phil. thesis: University of Aston in Birmingham.

Huczynski, A.A. & Buchanan, D.A. (1991). *Organisational behaviour: An introductory text* (second edition). Hemel Hempstead, UK: Prentice-Hall.

Kipnis, D., Schmidt, S.M., Swaffin-Smith, C., & Wilkinson, I. (1984). Patterns of managerial influence: Shotgun managers, tacticians, and bystanders. *Organisational Dynamics*, Winter, 58–67.

Keys, B. & Case, T. (1990). How to become an influential manager. *Academy of Management Executive, 4*, 38–51.

Kozan, M.K. (1989). Cultural influences on styles of handling interpersonal conflicts: Comparisons among Jordanian, Turkish, and US managers. *Human Relations, 42*, 789–799.

Lee, R. & Lawrence, P. (1985). *Organisational behaviour: Psychology and work*. London: Hutchinson.

Lukes, S. (1974). *A radical review*. London: Macmillan.

Madison, D.L., Allen, R.W., Porter, L.W., Renwick, P.A., & Mayes, B.T. (1980). Organisational politics: An exploration of managers' perceptions. *Human Relations*, February, 79–100.

Mayes, B.T. & Allen, R.W. (1977). Toward a definition of organisational politics. *Academy of Management Review*, October, 672–678.

Miles, R.H. (1980). *Macro organisational behaviour*. Glenview, IL: Scott, Foresman.

Mintzberg, H. (1983). *Power in organisations*. New York: Prentice-[

Moorhead, G. & Griffin, R.W. (1992). *behaviour* (third edition). Boston: H[

Mulder, M., de Jong, R.D., Kippelaar, [(1986). Power, situation, a effectiveness: An organisational field study. *Journal of Applied Psychology*, November, 566–570.

Pettigrew, A. (1973). *The politics of organisational decision making*. London: Tavistock.

Pfeffer, J. (1981). *Power in organisations*. Marshfield, MA: Pitman Publishing.

Pfeffer, J. (1992). *Managing with power*. Boston: Harvard Business School Press.

Podsakoff, P.M. & Schriesheim, C.A. (1985). Field studies of French and Ravens' bases of power: Critique, re-analysis, and suggestions for future research. *Psychological Bulletin, 97*, 3, 387–411.

Reed, M. (1989). *The sociology of management*. Hemel Hempstead, UK: Harvester Wheatsheaf.

Robbins, S.P. (1974). *Managing organisational conflict*. New York: Prentice-Hall.

Robbins, S.P. (1991). *Organisational behaviour: Concepts, controversies, applications* (fifth edition). New York: Prentice-Hall.

Sherif, M. (1967). *Group conflict and co-operation: Their social psychology*. London: Routledge & Kegan Paul.

Sternberg, R.J. & Soriano, E.J. (1984). Styles of conflict resolution. *Journal of Personality and Social Psychology*, July, 115–126.

Tang, S.F.Y. & Kirkbride, P.S. (1986). Developing conflict management in Hong Kong: An analysis of some cross-cultural implications. *Management Education and Development, 17*, 287–301.

Thomas, K.W. (1976). Conflict and conflict management. In M. Dunnette (Ed.), *Handbook of industrial and organisational psychology*. Skokie, IL: Rand McNally.

Thomas, K.W. (1977). Toward multi-dimensional values in teaching: The example of conflict behaviours. *Academy of Management Review, 2*, July, 484–490.

Thompson, J.D. (1967). *Organisations in action*. New York: McGraw-Hill.

Thompson, P. & McHugh, D. (1990). *Work organisations: A critical introduction*. Basingstoke, UK: Macmillan.

Tjosovold, D. & Deemer, D.K. (1980). Effects of controversy within a co-operative or competitive context on organisational decision making. *Journal of Applied Psychology, 65*, 590–595.

Van de Vliert, E. (1985). Escalative intervention in small groups. *Journal of Applied Behavourial Science, 21*, 19–36.

Van de Vliert, E. & Kabanoff, B. (1990). Toward theory-based measures of conflict management. *Academy of Management Journal, 33*, 199–209.

Vecchio, R.P. (1991). *Organisational behaviour* (second edition). Orlando, FL: The Dryden Press.

Woodward, J. (1965). *Industrial organisation: Theory and practice.* London: Oxford University Press.

Yukl, G.A. (1981). *Leadership in organisations.* New York: Prentice-Hall.

Yukl, G.A. & Falbe, C.M. (1990). Influence tactics in upward, downward, and lateral influence attempts. *Journal of Applied Psychology, 75,* 132–140.

PART III

The Organisation

10

Organisational Structure and Design

The opening sections of the chapter are devoted to a definition of organisation, a statement of the principles of organisation, and a criticism of classical theory. An analysis of Weber's ideal bureaucracy and its dysfunctional effects is followed by an examination of the various arrangements for organisational structuring, and descriptions of Mintzberg's co-ordinating mechanisms and forms of organisation.

The next section takes a broad view of the impact of contingency factors (i.e. internal and external environment, and technology) on organisation structure, and there is a recognition of the mediating effect of strategic choice. Technology is viewed from both a narrow perspective (e.g. production technology) and a broad perspective. Finally, there is reference to socio-technical systems as open systems, and an overview combined with a discussion of future trends.

This chapter provides the structural framework for the discussion of issues raised in subsequent chapters (e.g. organisational culture, change, and development), and is also relevant to topics discussed earlier (e.g. job design in Chapter 2).

DEFINITION

An organisation could be described as a collection of individuals who "interact" with each other in an "interdependent" relationship. The individuals work towards "common goals" and the way they relate is determined by the structure of the organisation (Duncan, 1981). Because organisations are complex, this simple definition fails to capture the true reality of this social phenomenon. However, as the chapter unfolds, the nature of organisational complexity will become clearer.

To elaborate on the definition, people employed by the organisation are expected to work, to some extent, towards the achievement of common goals, and structures and processes are designed to "co-ordinate" a wide range of activities. In practice there is a certain tension between personal goals and organisational goals, because not everybody has the same set of goals or priorities, and these do not always coincide with organisational goals. Sometimes one finds that the goals of the organisation are not sufficiently clear to members.

Organisations exist in all sectors of society, and although relationships and contacts operate within the formally established structure, the prevalence of an informal organisation (numerous informal contacts) has to be accepted as a necessary complement to the formal structure. (A related matter was discussed in Chapter 7 when a distinction was drawn between formal and informal groups.) Finally, an organisation is barren without a culture. The issue of culture will be examined in Chapter 11.

THE NATURE OF BUREAUCRATIC ORGANISATION

Over the years there have been a number of attempts to identify the key features of organisation. In this major section, the following contributions will be examined:

- principles of organisation;
- Weber's ideal bureaucracy;
- Mintzberg's structural arrangements and forms of organisation.

Principles of Organisation

The formal structure of an organisation can be depicted with the help of an organisation chart (see Fig. 10.1).

Hierarchy
Fig. 10.1 illustrates the shape of the organisation, and the different layers of decision making, in the form of a hierarchy. One would expect to find that positions higher up the hierarchy have more power associated with them than positions further down.

Communication Channels
The lines connecting the positions depict the communication channels through which authority is exercised. An organisation chart also shows the relationship between particular jobs or "roles", and the name of the person occupying the role can be inserted.

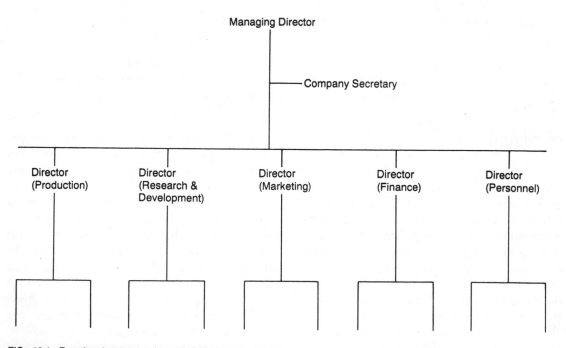

FIG. 10.1. Functional structure of a manufacturing organisation.

Specialisation

As organisations grow in size, it is inevitable that specialisation or division of labour becomes more pronounced. When activities within the organisation are sub-divided and tasks are distributed among people, division of labour takes place.

Horizontal division of labour occurs, as can be seen in Fig. 10.1, when the organisation is divided into separate departments or units on a functional basis (e.g. production, marketing, finance). With horizontal division of labour comes the opportunity for people to specialise in particular tasks (e.g. cost accounting, production engineering, etc). But specialisation has some negative side effects. For example, employees engaged in specialised activities can lose sight of the overall objectives of the organisation. Therefore, their work must be co-ordinated to ensure that it contributes to the welfare of the organisation.

Chain of Command

Organisations can be sub-divided on a vertical basis. Fig. 10.1 shows the chain of command going downwards from senior management positions to junior positions.

Centralisation

If the exercise of significant authority and decision-making resides in the hands of a relatively small number of people at the top of the organisation, reference is made to centralisation. The opposite phenomenon would be decentralisation, when there is greater autonomy further down the organisation. For example, a significant marketing decision affecting a particular product division could be taken in that division rather than being referred to corporate headquarters. (This could happen within a "product grouping" structure discussed later.)

Span of Control

Another characteristic of organisation structure is span of control, or span of management. Basically, this means the number of people reporting directly to, for example, a manager or supervisor. The classical management theorists were of the view that narrow spans of control were better than wide ones because they allowed close supervision. Also, it was suggested that spans should vary from three at the upper end of the hierarchy to six at the lower end. However, later empirical work took an opposing view and concluded that wide spans of control tend to create conditions for improved attitudes, better supervision, and more individual responsibility and initiative among employees (Worthy, 1950). This matter has not been resolved, although research is continuing (Van Fleet, 1983).

Mintzberg (1979) adopts a sensible position which finds expression in the proposition that the optimum size of the span of control depends on:

- The extent of co-ordinating activities within the unit or department, including the level of job specialisation.
- The extent to which tasks are similar.
- The type of information required by members of the department.
- The differences between people's needs for autonomy.
- The frequency with which subordinates need to have direct access to the superior.

The size of the span of control has a material influence on the closeness of supervision and the flatness of the structure. For example, when the span of control is narrower it is possible to exercise closer supervision with fewer subordinates reporting to a manager or supervisor. In such circumstances the structure is taller because of the inverse relationship between the size of the span of control and the number of layers in the hierarchy. Generally, an organisation structure is flatter, with fewer layers, when the span of control is wider.

These principles owe their origin to the classical principles of organisation propounded by Fayol (1949). Six of these principles, which are related to structure and are listed below, have been criticised as being too general. Nevertheless, they have some value as basic concepts:

- *Division of labour*: employees specialise in a particular task, and this can bring about increases in efficiency.
- *Authority and responsibility*: authority—the right to give orders and the power to exact compliance—is related to bearing responsibility for one's actions. Authority can be delegated, but not responsibility.
- *Unity of command*: subordinates receive orders from one supervisor.
- *Unity of direction*: there should be one manager and one plan for all operations with the same objective.
- Centralisation: the proportion of total discretion in decision making vested in the manager, as opposed to that given to subordinates.
- Hierarchy: a scalar chain of authority runs from the top to the bottom of the organisation.

Ideal Bureaucracy

Serious interest in studying the features of formal organisations started with the work of Max Weber many years ago (Gerth & Mills, 1948). Weber identified the typical or ideal features of bureaucratic organisation (see panel below) that were considered to be the most efficient form of organisation. The reason for believing that this model of organisation has much to commend itself is because the structure (the means) is designed to accomplish organisational objectives (the ends). Also, it is immune from the disruptive tactics of charismatic leaders, or inefficient traditional practices.

Dysfunctional Aspects of Bureaucracy

In criticisms of Weber's model of organisation, the central issue is that it neglects the human characteristics (Joseph, 1989; Vecchio, 1991). In particular, the disadvantages, or dysfunctions, of bureaucracy are neglected. These could be expressed as follows:

Weber's Ideal Features of Bureaucratic Organisation

- A hierarchy of offices or positions is clearly stated, with a clear chain of command.
- The functions attached to the positions are known. Tasks should be sub-divided and assigned to people with the appropriate level of expertise. Then each person should have the necessary authority and resources to execute his or her duties.
- Officials or employees are appointed on the basis of a contract.
- Selection is based on the possession of an appropriate qualification gained through an examination. Technical competence (rather than personal connections) is the important consideration.
- A salary, and usually pension rights, should be attached to each position, and should vary depending on the position in the hierarchy.
- Officials are only required to honour the impersonal duties of their positions, and are free to tender their resignation. The impersonal bias helps to maintain objectivity in decision making, rather than favouritism or personal prejudice. In order to ensure

objectivity in decision making, ownership is divorced from control in that employees, and particularly managers, should not share in the ownership of the organisation.
- It is possible to progress within the bureaucracy through a career structure, and promotion is based on seniority or merit, as judged by superiors.
- Officials must treat their positions as their sole or major occupation, and must not abuse their position by profiting in an illegal sense from the post held.
- Each official is subjected to an organisational system of control and discipline. Standard operating procedures provide greater certainty and help in the co-ordination of activities.
- Written records are effectively the organisation's memory, and contain not only rules and procedures but also details of past performance that are open to inspection. Written records also provide an information base to facilitate the training of officials.

- *Goal displacement*: gradually over time the "means" may displace the "ends", when the job itself may become more important than what is supposed to be achieved.
- *Conflict*: there appears to be an underestimation of conflict based on ambition because of the assumption that employees would be content with the organisational roles allocated to them. In fact, feelings of alienation or estrangement among employees could arise because of having to execute highly specialised tasks. Related to this is the lack of challenge and novelty that could result in job dissatisfaction and turnover.
- *Informal organisation*: the importance of informal work groups as a key source of influence is neglected.
- *Division of labour*: in today's world, extreme division of labour may be out of step with integrated computerised technologies that require teams of highly skilled workers.
- *Relevance*: the model may be more applicable to public sector organisations than to commercial organisations in the private sector.
- *Impersonality*: taking an impersonal stance, and adhering rigidly to rules, could lead to an inability to cope with special cases for which the "rule book" does not provide a solution. Also, excessive red tape can result from the emphasis on rules and procedures. Overall, people could feel frustrated with the bureaucratic system's lack of a human face.
- *Adaptation*: organisations are subjected to pressure from outside to adapt to their environment. In times of rapid change—for example, in markets and in the application of technology—the structure of the organisation could be subjected to profound changes. Managers may resist proposed changes in rules and procedures where they see the price of adaptation as the surrender of authority. Conservatism and inflexibility may prevail to the detriment of innovation.

In defence of Weber's model it should be stated that he put forward a system that focused on the ideal characteristics of a pure bureaucracy, rather than an organisation that already existed.

Structural Arrangements

There are a variety of ways to structure organisations. The ones examined here are the functional, process, product, customer, and territorial groupings, together with the matrix system of organisation.

Functional Grouping

In the functional grouping (see Fig. 10.1) employees have most contact with those working in the same function, and this helps to foster good communication and co-operation, as well as the sharing of ideas. But a disadvantage is that there is insufficient contact with those in other functions in the organisation. The preoccupation with one's own patch contributes to a narrowing of focus and can hinder the co-ordination of work activities across functional groups. For example, the finance function fails to provide the marketing function with product costings because it is over-stretched preparing end-of-year accounts.

Process Grouping

The grouping by process is similar to a functional grouping, but there is one material difference—that the grouping of specific jobs is influenced by a particular work activity. For example, an organisation's manufacturing jobs are divided into well-defined manufacturing processes as follows: drilling, milling, heat treatment, painting, and assembly. Each process would represent a department, reporting directly to the top manager with responsibility for manufacturing (Moorhead & Griffin, 1992). This type of structure promotes specialisation and expertise among employees, with enormous potential for the sharing of information. But then, as in the case of functional groups, it can engender a parochial perspective.

Product Grouping

As organisations grow in size the adequacy of a functional structure to serve the needs of the organisation may be called into question. This is said to be particularly the case for multi-product organisations such as *Ford*, *DuPont*, and *Coca-Cola*, in which a product grouping works well (Hodgetts, 1991). Grouping by product or service materialises when employees who work on a particular product or service belong to the same unit or department, irrespective of their specialism.

In the late 1980s, *IBM* reorganised its business operations into five autonomous units—personal computers, mainframes, medium-sized office systems, communications equipment, and components (*Fortune Magazine*, 1988). It was hoped that this type of structuring would develop greater communication and technical awareness among employees producing the same product or providing the same service. (However, one should recognise that *IBM* experienced a downturn in its market in 1993.)

A major advantage of product groupings is that specialisation and co-ordination is facilitated by bringing together all activities connected with a particular product or service. Also, each product line can become a semi-autonomous profit centre, making the detection of profitability, or the lack of it, that much easier.

A disadvantage is that as employees align themselves enthusiastically to their own product or service, they lose sight of significant developments and breakthroughs in other product groupings. Also, top management may experience problems connected with overall control if product groupings try to become too autonomous. Another drawback is the demands such a structure makes on managers with general management ability, because they are required to oversee a number of semi-autonomous units. This is obviously a

management development issue to be faced by an organisation adopting this type of structure.

A recent example of the creation of product groupings in a UK company appears in the panel facing

Customer Grouping

Structures are created to satisfy the needs of particular types of customers under a customer grouping arrangement. A department store may have major departments serving different customers (e.g. men's clothing and women's clothing), and a bank has separate departments for commercial and retail banking. The major advantage of this type of structure is that highly focused attention is paid to the needs of the customer. For example, a buyer in the men's department of a store can concentrate his or her attention on the needs of a particular client group and, overall, possesses a high degree of flexibility when it comes to finding ways and means to improve the relationship with the customer. A disadvantage of this type of structure is that the employee is isolated from his or her counterpart in another customer grouping.

Territorial Grouping

When an organisation is geographically dispersed, groupings are created by region within a country or, where appropriate, by world regions. Frequently sales or marketing groups are divided by geographic region. A significant benefit accruing to this type of structure is that the organisation can cater for the specific needs of a given location. Other benefits are cost reductions, better market coverage (Moorhead & Griffin, 1992), and the provision of a training ground for managers to familiarise themselves with operations in the field (Hodgetts, 1991).

A drawback could be the isolation the work groups in the regions feel when distanced from the nerve centre of the organisation. This could cultivate loyalty to the regional work group of greater magnitude than commitment

---

Product Grouping at JCB

JCB, the UK's largest construction equipment company, recently created product divisions which will have exclusive responsibility for the future of the main product lines—everything from design and product development to marketing. However, basic manufacturing such as welding will still be done centrally, but the new product divisions will each be responsible for painting and final assembly. The stated aim was to create multidisciplinary teams that will sit together and concentrate solely on one product line. The hope is that by identifying more closely with a particular product, the employees at all levels will understand the need for increased profitability, and be encouraged to participate in achieving it.

Certain mechanisms are being put into place to cope with various risks attached to the new structure. For example, one section of the organisation would act as central buyer for parts and components used by the product divisions, in order to take advantage of the company's considerable purchasing power, although decentralised buying could be justified in some circumstances. Other matters needing attention will be how to avoid duplicating contacts with dealers who sell the entire *JCB* product range.

Early benefits of the new structure are said to be that things are moving faster, the incentive to look at new ideas is much greater, and there is much more of a team spirit, with implications for quality improvement. Some grey areas, such as training, remain. According to the chairman of the company, it is believed that the new organisation structure will bring a marked improvement in profitability by next year (Baxter, 1993)

---

to the larger organisation. A difficulty for top management is the exercise of overall control in the face of significant devolution of authority to territorial groupings.

Matrix Organisation

The matrix structure integrates two different groupings—for example, a project department is superimposed on a functional grouping. This arrangement is shown in Table 10.1.

Each function and project has a manager, and each subordinate is a member of each grouping, effectively having two supervisors. This type of structure used to be popular among US firms in the aerospace and high-technology fields. It is a complex system of organisation that requires careful handling for it to be effective. A matrix structure is said to be appropriate when three conditions exist (Davis & Lawrence, 1977):

1. Factors in the organisation's environment require the organisation to give equal weight to responding to both external forces and internal operations. This could mean satisfying the customers' requirements, as well as embracing technological developments in turbulent and highly competitive conditions.

TABLE 10.1

Matrix Organisation

	Marketing	*Finance*	*Production*	*Personal*
Project A	X	X	X	X
Project B	X	X	X	X
Project C	X	X	X	X

2. There are pressures for a high capacity in information processing. Because of the environmental uncertainty (referred to in the previous condition) there is an added need for information processing.

3. There are pressures for shared resources because companies are expected to achieve good results despite limited resources.

In the matrix system described, the project leader draws on resources from the different functional areas, and members can work on one project for a set period of time, then they return to the "functional" home base, and afterwards are reassigned to another project. The matrix system is said to improve project co-ordination by assigning project responsibility to a single co-ordinator rather than having it dispersed among a number of heads of functional departments. Also, communication is said to improve because employees have the opportunity to talk about the project with both colleagues in the project team and in the functional department. This increases the possibility that solutions to problems arising from the project can come from either group.

However, problems do arise with the implementation of matrix organisation (Davis & Lawrence, 1977; Larson & Gobeli, 1987):

• The dual system of reporting may give rise to role conflict among subordinates.

• Power struggles may come about with regard to who has authority in given circumstances.

• In a matrix system there may be the mistaken view that all decision making is vested in the group. As a result, decision-making techniques may be used in inappropriate circumstances.

• It could be difficult to achieve full co-operation from the members involved in particular transactions.

• Where the design entails many matrices, one on top of the other, establishing who is accountable and who has real authority could be difficult.

A matrix organisation in a business school, at a college or university might assume a form similar to that set out in Table 10.2. In this structure, a lecturer or professor has a dual commitment, one to the subject group and the other to the programme(s) he or she teaches on. The problems mentioned earlier in connection with the operation of a matrix system of organisation in industry (e.g. multiple superiors) could apply equally in the academic world.

A final word about structural arrangements is necessary. A number of organisations experiment with different types of structure, and at any one time a combination of individual groupings discussed in this section may be the most appropriate model.

It is still possible to find words of praise from an authoritative source for structural arrangements based on hierarchy. Elliott Jaques (1990) recognises that hierarchy as presently practised has drawbacks, and acknowledges that in business there is a widespread view that managerial hierarchy kills initiative, crushes creativity, and therefore has had its day. He goes on to say:

Yet 35 years of research have convinced me that managerial hierarchy is the most efficient, the hardiest, and in fact the most natural structure ever devised for large organisations. Properly structured, hierarchy can release energy and creativity, rationalise productivity, and actually improve morale. Moreover, I think most managers know this intuitively and have only lacked a workable structure and a decent intellectual justification for what they have always known could work and work well.

Mintzberg's Co-ordinating Mechanisms

According to Mintzberg (1979), structure of organisation amounts to the way tasks are divided initially, and then co-ordinated. He describes five major approaches by which tasks are co-ordinated:

TABLE 10.2

Matrix Organisation in a Business School

Subject Groups	Programmes			
	Undergrad. Programmes	Postgrad. Programmes	Postexp. Programmes Unit	Research & Consultancy Unit
Accounting/Finance				
Economics				
Marketing				
Law				
Organisational behaviour/HRM				
Business policy				
Quantitative methods and computing				
Operations management				

1. mutual adjustment;
2. direct supervision;
3. standardisation of employee skills (input);
4. standardisation of work processes; and
5. standardisation of outputs.

1. Mutual Adjustment. Co-ordination by mutual adjustment can be seen when employees use informal communication to bring about co-ordination of each other's efforts. This is perhaps more prevalent in very small organisations.

2. Direct Supervision. Co-ordination by direct supervision arises when the supervisor co-ordinates the efforts of subordinates. As more employees join the organisation, the co-ordination process becomes more com-plex, and direct supervision is necessary. In a small retail shop a few employees can co-ordinate the work by talking to each other about demand for product lines and the level of stock. But if the retail outlet grows sub-stantially in size, complexity increases, along with the number of full-time and part-time staff. As a result, direct supervision is required.

3. Standardisation of Employee Skills. The set of employee skills required in a particular work situation could be standardised as a result of training. In the hospital service doctors and nurses use skills developed through professional training, and these, together with communication skills, are relied on to co-ordinate the service to patients.

Although mutual adjustment as a co-ordinating device was mentioned earlier as applicable in less complex situations, it could be used also in complex situations to complement the standardisation of employee skills. For example, the doctors and nurses in the hospital setting may use it when faced with a difficult diagnostic and treatment procedure for patients; they use informal communication to co-ordinate each other's contributions.

4. Standardisation of Work Processes. The work processes refer to the methods used to transform inputs to the organisation into outputs. For example, franchised *Kentucky Fried Chicken* outlets standardise the preparation of its products, in accordance with a recipe originally devised by Colonel Sanders. Normally, one would expect the standardisation of work processes necessary to achieve the required level of co-ordination to be conspicuous when the organisation's tasks are fairly routine.

5. *Standardisation of Output.*   Co-ordination is achieved when the output (i.e. the product, service, or performance) of the employee meets the required standard or specification. The output could be achieved through the standardised work process described earlier, or alternatively the employee may be given some flexibility with regard to methods used (i.e. departure from the standardised process), provided the outcome meets the specification for the product or service. For example, the shoemaker or repairer has some flexibility in re-heeling a shoe to the required standard.

Standardisation (referred to in 3, 4, and 5) is usually set by staff specialists (e.g. production engineers or systems analysts) and overseen by line management so that predetermined standards with respect to skills, processes, and outputs can be achieved. In larger organisations, standardisation joins mutual adjustment and direct supervision in order to co-ordinate the work.

Forms of Organisation

Mintzberg maintains that the five approaches to co-ordination can be combined with dimensions of organisation structure to devise the following five forms of organisation:

- simple structure;
- machine bureaucracy;
- professional bureaucracy;
- divisional form; and
- adhocracy.

Simple Structure

This type of structure could be used by a small recently established organisation (e.g. a supplier of computer equipment) in a dynamic but not complex environment. There is not much specialisation; neither are there many formal policies, rules, and procedures. Also, there appears to be centralisation of authority and decision making, with the owner-manager at the apex of the organisation. He or she uses direct supervision as the primary co-ordinating mechanism. In order to survive in the market-place the organisation must adapt quickly to its environment.

Machine Bureaucracy

This could apply to a long-established, large organisation in a simple and stable environment. This organisation is characterised by a high level of specialised work activities and well-established formalised ways of executing work. The major co-ordinating mechanism is the standardisation of work processes. The organisation faces an environment that is simple and stable, and therefore problems of rapid adaptation to changes in the environment do not arise. An example of a machine bureaucracy could be a large insurance company, or a government department.

Professional Bureaucracy

This type of organisation operates in stable but complex environments. The major approach to co-ordination is the standardisation of skills. Bureaucratic practices are played down, and professional areas of expertise and a community of equals (horizontal specialisation) are given prominence. The relevant professional body acting for the profession has great significance in laying down rules and procedures to govern behaviour. Universities, colleges, hospitals, and professional firms could fall into this category.

Divisional Form

This type of structure could be found in large, well-established companies, with a number of different markets. Apart from the fact that the organisation is divided to serve different markets, it bears a similarity to the machine bureaucracy, and faces a relatively simple and stable environment. Standardisation of output is the major approach to co-ordination. The way company headquarters exercises control, with decision making split between head- quarters and divisions, encourages the adoption of machine bureaucracy in the divisions.

Adhocracy

This form of structure is applicable to organisations operating in highly technical areas where the environment is complex and dynamic. Experts wield much power, and decision making is dispersed throughout the organisation, with evidence of a strong organic climate. The experts or specialists are not located in their functional specialisms. Instead, they are attached to project groups with a strong market orientation. Co-ordination is by mutual adjustment, and this is achieved through frequent personal communication processes and various devices to encourage liaisons.

The adhocracy, unlike the other structures, is normally established to promote innovation. The organisation could be structured totally as an adhocracy, or alternatively a division could be set up as an adhocracy. *Johnson and Johnson*, a well-known, large US company, created a new products division nearly three decades ago to foster innovation, creativity, and risk taking. This has been a success, with over 200 products introduced in the USA over the past five years (Moorhead & Griffin, 1992).

Mintzberg (1981) stresses the need for the constituent elements of the organisation and its environment to fit together in order to facilitate effective functioning. For example, one combination of fit would be between organisation structure, factors influencing structure (for example, contingency variables—referred to in the next section—such as size, technology, and environment), and the strategy of the organisation. Another example of fit would be an appropriate interplay between the internal constituent elements of organisation structure, such as procedures, specialisation, and decision making.

CONTINGENCY FACTORS

Over the years, a great deal of attention has been paid to the study of contingency factors in organisational design. Two major contingency factors are the environment, and technology, and it is to these factors that our attention now turns. It will become clear that this approach to organisational analysis has a strong empirical tradition and has spawned many research studies. The major ones are reported in this section.

Environment

A recognition of the importance of the environment is understandable when one considers that a company must be organised in a way that accommodates internal and external factors in its environment if it is to achieve its objectives. Therefore, the design of an organisation should be contingent on forces in its internal and external environment.

Internal Environment

An example of the internal environment is the size of the organisation, and the calibre of the people employed. Size of the organisation has been singled out as a crucial contingency variable in organisation design and will be discussed in more detail later. As the number of people in a particular organisational situation increases, the company is likely to resort to more formalised ways of doing things. It becomes necessary to introduce policies, rules, procedures, and other manifestations of "formalisation", because one can no longer expect people to relate informally on a face-to-face basis in the efficient execution of tasks (Child, 1973). With a growth in the size of the organisation there is also the likelihood of an increase in specialised jobs, more standard operating procedures, and paperwork associated with the delegation of authority (Cullen & Anderson, 1986).

External Environment

An example of the external environment is the range of elements outside the boundaries of the organisation. Within this range are customers, shareholders, competitors, financial markets, manpower markets, government regulatory agencies, supply of physical resources, inland revenue, and cultural influences. Those who are responsible for the management of organisations ignore environmental forces at their peril. For example, a business organisation that focuses heavily on internal operations to the neglect of registering major shifts in its environment—such as changes in customer tastes, technological innovations, and new regulations—stands to lose out on opportunities. But it would be impracticable for an organisation to explore every minute aspect of its environment. The preferred course of action is for the organisation to monitor carefully those aspects of its environment that are salient, and respond accordingly. The response could include modification or change to organisation design.

In connection with the external environment, the following concepts will be examined:

- open systems;
- environmental uncertainty;
- differentiation and integration;
- resource dependency; and
- population ecology.

Open Systems. An integrated view of the organisation's environment has been postulated by Emery and Trist (1965). This is essentially an "open systems" view of organisations where the environment consists of a collection of interrelated parts that relate to the organisation. Four types of environment were identified:

1. placid randomised;
2. placid clustered;
3. disturbed reactive; and
4. turbulent fields.

These are shown in Table 10.3.

1. The placid randomised environment is characterised by organisational goals and problems that are relatively straightforward and unchanging. Nowadays it is difficult to find examples of this simple and almost static environment. The organisation system coping with this environment tends to be relatively small, and has little difficulty in adapting to it.
2. The placid clustered environment does not change much, but clusters of it interrelate. The type of organisation that relates to this environment tends to develop into a big, centralised, and co-ordinated grouping.
3. The disturbed reactive environment shows signs of moderate change, with interrelationships between environmental clusters. There is strong competition between organisations that are similar in nature. Companies inhabiting this environment possess large-scale bureaucratic structures.
4. The turbulent fields environment is both complex and dynamic, and features rapid change springing from parts of the environment interacting in a rather complex way. Coping with this type of environment presents difficulties for the organisation; as a consequence, the organisation may align itself with other organisations in the same turbulent field.

An extension of the open systems perspective can be found later in the chapter when socio-technical systems are discussed.

TABLE 10.3

Classification of the Environment by Emery and Trist (1965)

Type of Environment	Characteristics of Type of Environment	Examples
Placid randomised	Slow change, if any	Few in modern economy
	Few interrelationships between environmental components	Small job work-shop or family operated business in an isolated area
	Few new threats or opportunities	
	Changes are random and unpredictable	
Placid clustered	Slow change	Container industry
	Environmental components are interrelated	Some mass production manufacturing
	Change is relatively predictable	
	Some planning is possible	
Disturbed reactive	Moderate change	Automobile industry
	Few large firms dominate	Steel industry
	Heavy competition	Soft drinks industry
	Organisations are interrelated within an industry	
	Competitive actions produce reactions	
Turbulent fields	Very rapid change	Computer hardware and software industry
	Change is unpredictable	Communications industry
	Change may come from technological breakthrough government regulation, or customer preferences	
	Increasingly prevalent	

Source: Moorhead, G. & Griffin, R.W. (1989). *Organisational behaviour* (second edition). Boston: Houghton Mifflin. Used by permission.

Environmental Uncertainty   It is claimed that the characteristic of the environment having the most profound effect on organisation structure is uncertainty. Environmental uncertainty is said to emanate from complexity (the number of aspects of the environment that interact directly with the organisation's decision making) and dynamism (the degree to which the environmental aspects change) in the organisation's environment (Duncan, 1972), and it becomes apparent when managers have little information about the existence of environmental events and the way they affect the organisation (Daft, 1986).

In a low uncertainty environment there exists insignificant complexity and an almost static rate of change. A company in the cardboard box industry could fall into this category when demand for its product is steady, manufacturing processes are stable, and there is no appreciable change in regulations affecting the industry.

At the other extreme there is the high-uncertainty environment where there is a state of flux in aspects of the environment impinging on organisational decision making. The banking industry could fall into this category, particularly since deregulation in the financial services markets (Moorhead & Griffin, 1992). A diagrammatical representation of environmental uncertainty, postulated by Duncan, appears in Fig. 10.2.

Differentiation and Integration. The importance of the environment–organisation relationship is underlined in studies examining structural adaptation. A research study conducted by Lawrence and Lorsch (1969) focuses on the volatility of the environment and provides useful insights into the way in which departments within an organisation structure relate to their environment. The study was undertaken involving firms in the plastics, food, and container industries and addressed two critical features of organisation—differentiation and integration.

Differentiation means that within the organisation there are cells or sub-systems, each of which positions itself with respect to its own relevant external environment. For example, a manager near the apex of the structure may be relating to the external environment on matters connected with the impact of interest rates and inflation on the present and future position of the company. Further down the organisation, a manager is linked to the external environment whereby he or she is negotiating with management consultants exploring ways and means of improving production methods and processes. A danger with a highly differentiated organisation is that cells and sub-systems might go their own way to the detriment of the achievement of overall

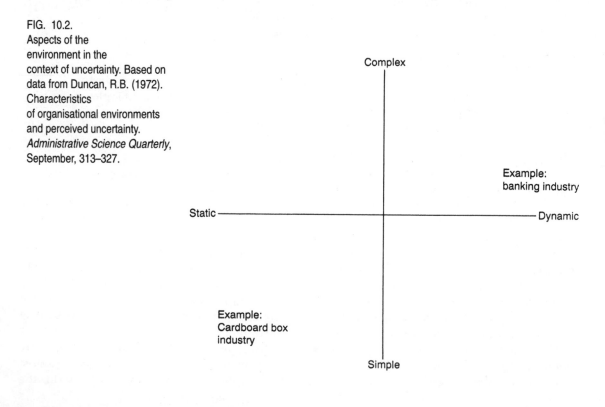

FIG. 10.2.
Aspects of the environment in the context of uncertainty. Based on data from Duncan, R.B. (1972). Characteristics of organisational environments and perceived uncertainty. *Administrative Science Quarterly*, September, 313–327.

objectives. Hence, there is a need for co-operation and collaboration.

It is in situations where there is insufficient co-operation that integration is a valuable process. In a bureaucratic structure integration could be achieved through policies, rules, and procedures governing employee behaviour, but in less bureaucratic structures integration is maintained by mutual co-operation and teamwork on the part of staff.

In the plastics industry the most effective structure adopted by firms seemed to have high levels of both differentiation and integration. For example, functions such as research, production, and sales had the facility to interact effectively with their own particular external environment, but at the same time it was also possible for employees to interact across functions to resolve conflict and achieve integration across the organisation. The research units experienced a lot of pressure to come forward with fresh ideas and product innovations. Their relevant sub-environment was the most dynamic. By contrast, the production units faced relevant sub-environments that were fairly stable and predictable at the technical and economic levels.

Firms in the container industry operated in the most stable environment, with a low level of differentiation, but surprisingly a high level of integration was considered necessary for effectiveness. The food industry firms were located in between the plastic and container industry firms with regard to the need for differentiation (Lawrence & Lorsch, 1969).

The important point to note about this research is that one has to look beyond the way the organisation as an entity interacts with its environment, important though that may be, and consider how individual functions or units interact with their own external sub-environments. Therefore, contingency factors of organisation design are valid when it comes to issues of structure at *all* hierarchical levels (Hodgetts, 1991).

Resource Dependency. Another matter to consider in viewing the relationship between the organisation and the environment is the importance of resources. In order to survive, organisations must maintain "resource exchanges" with their environments (Yuchtman & Seashore, 1967). Resources can be exchanged in two major ways: by developing links between organisations, and by changing the environment (Daft, 1986).

An organisation interested in developing links with other organisations having access to vital resources may develop relationships with these organisations in order to gain a resource advantage. These links may take the form of:

- joint ventures;
- mergers and acquisitions;
- contractual relationships; and
- co-opting to the board influential business leaders from other organisations as non-executive directors.

With regard to joint ventures or contractual relationships, refer to panel overleaf.

Instead of making structural adjustments to the organisation in response to changes in the environment, an organisation seeking to exchange resources may try to change its environment so that it is more compatible with the existing structure. A number of options are open to the organisation that is intent on changing its environment (Moorhead & Griffin, 1992):

- Diversify into other product lines as a means to counteract a decline in revenue from the original business (e.g. tobacco companies buying companies in food, leisure, etc, as a means to reduce their dependence on tobacco products).
- Take part in a trade association or similar body to advance the cause of the industry.
- Get involved in political activities, such as lobbying, to bring about changes in regulatory matters previously acting to the disadvantage of the organisation.

Strategic Alliances

In recent years the issue of "strategic alliances" has assumed importance in certain sectors of the economy—for example, the airline business. Recently there was a deal between *United Airlines,* USA and *Lufthansa,* the German carrier. A number of conditions are critical for effective alliances (Lorenz, 1993a):

1. Each company regards the other as its best partner.
2. Mutual need: Each partner must take what steps it can to ensure that the other continues to need it.
3. Shared objectives: There must be clear agreement on what the partners intend to maximise together.
4. Shared risk: Both personal and economic risks must be realistically shared by the partners.
5. Relationships and trust: These constitute the heart of a successful alliance, and it takes a lot of time to nurture and develop them. These extend beyond the formal legal contract, and the enthusiasm displayed by the initial deal makers should gradually penetrate various parts of the organisation.
6. Disputes: There must be a recognition that difficult matters must be placed on the table for serious discussion.
7. Exit strategy: This is something that ought to be considered at the outset. If case 1 or 2 above were to change, it could provide for a parting of ways without having to resort to court action.

For further information on the increasingly important topic of strategic alliances, the interested readers could profitably refer to Lorange and Roos (1992).

- Engage in activities likely to improve the strategic position of the organisation in its environment, and to lessen the standing of its competitors. It is conceivable that such behaviour could entail illegal activities.

Population Ecology. The fit between the organisation and the environment is also dealt with in an approach called the population ecology perspective. Unlike the resource dependence approach, the population ecology perspective is not concerned with managerial interventions in determining the optimal fit between the organisation and its environment. The basic tenet of this perspective is that the survival of the organisation depends on the fit between structural elements and environmental dimensions. This perspective, with its primary focus on the survival of the fittest, is akin to the biological theory of natural selection. When the environment is incapable of supporting all the organisations to which it relates, the companies enjoying the best fit with the environment will survive. Over a period of time it is said that environments select some organisations, or types of organisations, for survival and others for extinction (Aldrich & Pfeffer, 1976; Hannan & Freeman, 1977). In order to adapt, organisations need to match their environments to structure using appropriate mechanisms in order to survive. The analysis used in the population ecology perspective tends to be at a highly abstract level, and the perspective may be of little assistance to the manager because there is little explanation of why some organisations survive and others perish (Bedeian, 1984).

Technology

Scholars interested in the impact of contingency factors on organisational design point to technology—the application of mechanical and mental processes to work as having a major affect on the way activities are structured. This section is devoted to a discussion of the contribution of the technology theorists—Woodward, Burns and Stalker, Thompson, Perrow, and Hall—together with an analysis of just-in-time production systems and new technology. The Aston studies on size and technology are examined later in the chapter.

Woodward's Research

To test the applicability of the classical theory of organisation discussed earlier, Woodward (1965) conducted a research study into the relationship between technology and the organisational features of a number of industrial enterprises in Essex, England. The main theme of her findings is the influence of technology or production systems on shaping organisational characteristics, though the importance of the history of the firm and those who built it up cannot be discounted. The technology identified was manufacturing technology, and firms were classified as follows:

- *Unit and small batch production*. This amounted to one-off items, or a small number of units produced.
- *Large batch and mass production*. This is more complicated than unit and small batch production and involved producing standardised parts in very large batches. It is the type of technology used in car assembly plants.
- *Process production*. This was the most complex form of technology studied, where a continuous stream of the same product is manufactured, as in the production of liquids and gases.

This classification covers the oldest and simplest production system (unit and small batch) to, at that time, the most up to date and sophisticated (process production).

When firms were classified in accordance with the different systems of production technology, a strong relationship was found between organisation structure and success within each category. In other words, successful firms within a particular production system shared common organisational characteristics. The firms at the extreme ends of the production technology continuum (i.e. unit and small batch and process production), tended to have organic structures, whereas the firms in the middle of the continuum (i.e. large batch and mass production), tended to be mechanistically structured and accorded more closely with the recipe for the organisational form advanced by the classical theorists. Other features of organisation peculiar to firms differentiated by production technology are set out in the panel overleaf.

Hodgetts (1991) provides a comparison of some of the organisational characteristics that existed among the successful companies in each of the three production categories. This is shown in Table 10.4.

In a later study, Woodward (1970) concentrated her attention on the impact of variations in products, rather than production systems, on organisation design. She tentatively suggested that the nature of management control systems influences organisational structures and behaviour.

It is now over 30 years since the late Joan Woodward developed her classification scheme for production technology. There are those who feel that her classification scheme is still useful for analysing manufacturing organisations (Moorhead & Griffin, 1989), but some critics argue that her production categories are simplistic and fail to capture the true nature of technological complexity (Bedeian, 1984).

Burns and Stalker's Research

Around the same time as Woodward was publishing her findings, another study conducted by Burns and Stalker (1961) investigated 20 industrial companies in England and Scotland to establish how changes in the technological and market environment affected organisation structure and management processes. The companies ranged from a rayon manufacturer operating in a very stable environment to an electronics company operating in a very volatile and unpredictable environment.

Features of Firms Differentiated by Production Technology

- Decentralisation was more prominent in process production firms than in large batch and mass production firms.
- Management by committee or group decision making was more common in process production firms, where communication tended to be more in verbal form.
- Communication in large batch and mass production firms tended to be more in written form. Resorting to written communication in large batch and mass productions firms was said to be in some way influenced by the less congenial organisational circumstances associated with this production system.
- The executives working in the large batch and mass production firms displayed greater drive and ambition, but appeared to be subjected to greater stress.
- In the process production firms the quality of industrial relations was very much in evidence, probably due to people feeling less tension and pressure; also, there existed smaller working groups, and a narrower span of control.
- In the large batch and mass production firms the relationships between line managers and staff specialists left much to be desired. Line managers tended to produce memoranda to safeguard themselves in case of comeback on

a particular issue by staff specialists. This friction was exemplified in conflicts between accountants (staff specialists) and production managers (line managers). By contrast, there was no significant differences in attitudes or outlook between staff specialists and line managers in process production firms, allegedly because of the high level of interchangeability between line and staff roles. Neither were there problems in unit and small batch production firms, because there was no clear-cut distinction between these two organisational roles—i.e. technical expertise was embraced by the line manager.

- Production control procedures, with some exceptions, were well defined and rigid in large batch and mass production firms, and this had the effect of generating operating instructions, memoranda, and policy directives at a level of magnitude not found in unit and small batch and process production firms. In fact it was difficult to control production and make predictions about outcomes in unit and small batch production firms, and of course the in-built production control mechanisms made the task of control easier in process production firms (Woodward, 1965).

TABLE 10.4

Comparison of Organisational Characteristics Among the Successful Firms in Woodward's (1965) Research Study

Organisational Characteristics	Unit and Small Batch Production	Large Batch and Mass Production	Process Production
Number of employees controlled by first-line supervisors	Small	Large	Small
Relationship between work groups and supervisor	Informal	Formal	Informal
Basic type of workers employed	Skilled	Semi-skilled and unskilled	Skilled
Definition of duties	Often vague	Clear-cut	Often vague
Degree of delegation of authority	High	Low	High
Use of participative management	High	Low	High
Type of organisational structure	Flexible	Rigid	Flexible

Reprinted with the permission of Macmillan College Publishing Company from Hodgetts, R.M. (1991). *Organisational behaviour: Theory and practice.* Copyright © 1991 by Macmillan College Publishing Company, Inc.

Mechanistic and Organic Structures. The major outcome of the Burns and Stalker study is the categorisation of firms along a continuum, with mechanistic organisation at one end and organic organisation at the other. A mechanistic structure seemed appropriate to a company operating under relatively stable conditions, whereas an organic structure was more relevant to conditions of change, when technology and markets are likely to become unstable and less predictable. Definitions of organic and mechanistic systems are set out in Table 10.5.

In Table 10.6 the different types of companies in the Burns and Stalker study are placed on the mechanistic–organic continuum, with the highly structured bureaucratic organisations on the left, and the organisations with the in-built flexibility on the right (Hodgetts, 1991). The message coming across from this research is that if a company previously operating in a stable environment moves into a turbulent environment, this would necessitate a movement from a mechanistic to an organic form of organisation in order to ensure successful performance.

A prominent feature of the mechanistic system is the precise prescription of the duties involved in various jobs, whereas the lack of a precise prescription and the existence of a significant degree of discretion can be found in the organic system. However, the lack of a precise definition of what a role requires could have dysfunctional effects. Burns and Stalker recognised this when they maintained that

TABLE 10.5

Mechanistic and Organic Structures (Burns & Stalker, 1961)

Mechanistic System	Organic System
• Organisational tasks are broken down into specialised functions with each employee performing his or her individual jobs without much concern for the overall aims of the organisation.	• Structure has networks based on interests. There appears to be a greater sense of purpose when employees perform their job, with a commitment to the achievement of the goals of the organisation as a whole.
• The duties, rights, obligations and privileges associated with each job are defined clearly.	• There seems to be less emphasis on defining jobs clearly, and also less of a tendency to stress the status attached to jobs.
• Communication between superiors and subordinates takes place on a vertical basis on matters connected with work. The chain of command is very much in evidence with instructions and directives coming down and feedback going up.	• Employees communicate and relate to each other on a horizontal as well as a vertical basis.
• It is considered legitimate for control and direction to be exercised by senior management, the assumption being that all relevant knowledge is located at the apex of the organisation. The culture of the organisation is typified by an inward-looking perspective, with an emphasis on loyalty and obedience.	• The issuing of directives and instructions by supervisors is of lesser importance than a management process based on consultation and discussion.

Source: Adapted from Burns, T. & Stalker, G.M. (1961). *The management of innovation.* London: Tavistock Publications.

TABLE 10.6

The Position of Companies on the Burns and Stalker Mechanistic–Organic Continuum

Stable ⟵ Type of Environment ⟶ Least Predictable				
Rayon Mill	Electrical Engineering	Radio and TV Manufacturing	Other Electronics Firms	Electronics Development Manufacturer
Highly structured	Somewhat flexible structure	Relatively flexible structure	Flexible structure	Very flexible structure
Standing plans	Contingency plans for meeting	No organisational charts	No organisational charts	No organisational charts
Carefully defined roles and tasks	Special eventualities	No great degree of role definition or job specialisation	De-emphasis on job descriptions	No job descriptions
			Reliance on informal co-operation and team-work	Emphasis on team-work and interpersonal ineraction to ensure goal attainment

Source: Hodgetts, R.M. (1991). *Organisational behaviour: Theory and practice*. New York: Macmillan.

managers operating within the organic system were not always sure what they were responsible for because they did not realise the full extent of their authority. Neither did they feel sure of the status of their position within the hierarchy. As a result, they experienced personal anxiety and insecurity. The other extreme—a mechanistic system—is not without its drawbacks. After all, the precise prescription of work roles could be construed as rigid and inflexible which, for some people, could have an alienating effect.

More recent work dealing with this theme broadens the perspective. Apart from structure, the type of job and individual needs are also considered (Porter & Lawler, 1975; Vecchio & Keon, 1981). For example, individuals who seek challenge and

responsibility at work—i.e. they wish to satisfy higher-level human needs—are more likely to prefer relatively enriched jobs that are capable of stretching them. Such jobs fall more into line with an organic rather than a mechanistic system of organisation.

Thompson's Research

The classification of technology proposed by Thompson (1967) is:

- long-linked;
- mediating; and
- intensive.

Long-linked. This type of technology consists of operations that flow in sequence, with one operation feeding the other. A good example is the assembly line in a car manufacturing plant.

Mediating. This type of technology links different units of the organisation or different types of clients. For example, a building society draws its clientele from investors and borrowers. The building society resorts to various procedures and controls, within its formal rules, to bring together the two sides of the business. Nowadays, it relies heavily on information technology to assist with this task.

Intensive. This type of technology uses skills and resources in a focused and unique way to accomplish an organisational task. An organisation has its standard procedures, but clients of the organisation must be dealt with individually. For example, in a dental surgery the practitioner deals with the patient in a unique way, using skills and resources with reference to that patient's problem and the way he or she is responding to the course of treatment.

Thompson mentions that organisations design structures to protect their dominant technology. For example, a warehousing facility permits the build-up of manufacturing output and allows the production technology system to operate at a steady state at a time when demand for the product is seasonal or cyclical.

Perrow's Research

The classification used by Perrow (1970) is the routine–non-routine continuum. This categorisation process applies to all organisations, not just to manufacturing companies. Routine technology would be amenable to circumstances where, generally speaking, there exists familiar situations (e.g. a high level of predictability) lending themselves to rational analysis and solution. In these conditions a pronounced degree of formalisation and centralisation can be found, reinforced by low interdependency between work groups, with planning used as a

co-ordinating mechanism. Routine technology could be used, for example, by a company in the manufacture of toothpaste.

Where situations are unfamiliar, and there are no well-established procedures to solve the problems (i.e. situations that invite the use of discretion), the technology is non-routine. This type of technology could be used in the research and development function of a pharmaceutical company. The organisational climate in this setting is likely to be characterised by a flexible system, with much interdependency between work groups and co-ordination through mutual adjustment. (The latter was explained earlier in the chapter when discussing Mintzberg's work.) There are similarities between Perrow's model and that of Burns and Stalker.

Hall's Research

Whereas Woodward's research looked at the influence of technology among organisations (inter-organisational), Hall (1962) was only interested in the impact of technology within organisations (intra-organisational). The research was conducted among five commercial or industrial organisations and five government agencies. He found that departments dealing with situations which do not vary, such as assembly-line work or routine administrative tasks, tended to adopt features of Weber's bureaucratic model (e.g. a hierarchy of authority, division of labour, and procedures for processing work). A more flexible structure was compatible with non-routine events such as advertising and research.

Hall's study substantiates the research of Burns and Stalker, because he established that generally a mechanistic system of organisation (bureaucratic) is more appropriate for routine work, and organic structures more suited for the effective performance of non-routine work.

A theme running through the empirical work of the technology theorists is the flexibility of the technological system in response to various pressures. The technological systems could be placed on a continuum, ranging from flexibility at one end to inflexibility at the other end. This is shown in Table 10.7.

There may be a tendency to think of the relatively simple technologies (e.g. unit or small batch production systems) as not availing of developments in high technology. But this could be a misleading impression. For in the manufacture of, for example, custom made products, there are numerous situations where new technology capable of producing a computerised flow of information about the production process goes hand-in-hand with unit or small batch technology (Lengnick-Hall, 1986).

Just-in-Time
Nowadays, production technology is supplemented by production systems based on just-in-time (JIT). JIT was developed by Japanese car firms, and is currently fashionable in the UK, although one should recognise that not many companies are committed to the concept because they do not understand the practicalities of implementing it (Wickham, 1993). It is essentially a manufacturing and stock system in which, in order to improve the productivity of the plant, component parts arrive just in time to be used in the manufacturing process. This has the effect of reducing the costs of keeping stocks in a warehouse until they are required. Because of the reduction in buffer stocks,

employees are expected to be flexible and to solve problems on the spot, otherwise the next phase of the process would grind to a halt (Tailby & Turnbull, 1987). The flexibility required of employees is almost tantamount to the possession of multi-skills, so that the worker can move comfortably from one job to another. As a result, there could be the merging of tasks (such as maintenance and inspection) into the overall tasks of a production worker. Obviously, this requires greater knowledge on the part of the workers on issues such as quality control and information on a wide range of jobs, and would have a knock-on effect in terms of payment or reward systems. The advantage of combining skilled and unskilled activities in one person is underlined in a study of a West German car plant (Dankbaar, 1988).

JIT is not just an inventory system with flexible labour utilisation. It requires close managerial involvement in the production process, multi-purpose machinery and reductions in set up. The system frequently relies on a set of relations between companies and suppliers, reflected in tightly controlled, multiple sources of various inputs through layers of sub-contractors (see panel facing). The introduction of JIT appears to necessitate a shift in traditional attitudes to production work. According to Thompson and McHugh (1990): "Many companies are engaging in detailed and intensive selection and screening

TABLE 10.7

Technological Systems in Relation to Flexibility of Response

	Inflexibility ⟵		⟶ *Flexibility*
Woodward	Large batch/mass production	Unit or small batch products	Process production
Burns & Stalker	Mechanistic		Organic
Thompson	Long-linked	Mediating	Intensive
Perrow	Routine		Non-routine
Hall	Bureaucratic		Organic

JIT at *Nissan*, UK

At *Nissan*'s plant in Sunderland, England, raw materials arrive by the minute. For the *Micra*'s seats, data is read from barcodes on each vehicle as it passes along the assembly line and is transmitted to a mainframe at suppliers *Ikeda Hoover*, based less than two minutes away.

Ikeda then builds seats to order, from a range of 180 variations, in 45 minutes. There are similar arrangements with other local suppliers. Even material from more distant suppliers is collected on a JIT basis. A single haulier collects components four times a day from around the UK, instead of the supplier making its own delivery arrangements. This has cut the road miles needed for the delivery of *Micra* components by 2.3 million miles a year.

Information technology plays a leading role in running the JIT system at *Nissan*. *Nissan* relies to a reasonable extent on electronic data interchange (EDI)—the paperless communication process whereby orders, invoices and remittances are sent electronically between computers—to make JIT delivery work (Wickham, 1993).

---

processes for relatively routine jobs, often recruiting 'green' labour". Subsequently, a more exacting system of training is likely to ensue.

New Technology

When reflecting on the current impact of technology on the structure of organisations, one should acknowledge its broad influence, which contrasts with the narrower emphasis in terms of production technology in the past.

Back in the late 1950s it was forecast that computers would promote centralised decision making, because computers would make it possible to collect and transmit information quickly to enable decisions to be made centrally on a better-informed basis. There was also the prediction that considerable economies in staffing levels could be achieved at middle management level because computers would perform much of the information processing activities of middle managers (Leavitt & Whisler, 1958).

A decade later, the impact of the computer on management was considered in a study conducted in the services industry (insurance companies), and it was argued strongly that computers were likely to increase the centralisation of systems of control in organisations. This applied to clerical functions, and the computer was seen to have a number of capabilities (Whisler, 1970).

The computer ties together and integrates areas of decision making and control that were previously relatively independent of one another. Computers monitor, correct, and adjust actions over a much broader area than could be achieved by any human group. And because of the pyramidal structure of business organisations, the integrative function of computing contributes to the centralisation of control, with a wider span of control for senior managers.

This evidence, which relates to clerical functions in the service industry, is challenged by evidence from a study of the impact of the computer in a manufacturing industry context (Blau et al., 1976). The use of on-site computers was associated with the decentralisation of operational decisions, particularly in granting autonomy to plant managers. But it is pointed out that the physical location of the computer can influence the level of management at which decisions are made; a central location gives rise to centralisation, but where computer systems are distributed throughout the organisation a decentralisation process develops. This accords with the current trend to use more powerful individual micro- computers, which are relatively cheap, and can be easily placed on the executive's desk. The hardware is accompanied by more sophisticated software (e.g. financial modelling) and networking.

In recent years the centralisation versus decentralisation debate has been somewhat muted. There is a view that computer applications over a long period are confined to routine accounting and administrative activities, and that there have been no significant changes in the levels at which management decisions are made (Robey, 1977). However, other evidence would suggest that we have to be discriminating in the way we view the impact of the computer on the management process. This could mean that in certain circumstances centralisation is facilitated, but equally in other situations delegation may be assisted.

With new technology in the field of information processing, it is possible to communicate information quickly over a wide area. If that information is based on data input of an accurate and reliable nature, senior managers may not have to rely on middle management and lower-level employees for control information or its interpretation, provided the information can be transmitted from the local area of operations. For example: "The scanning of bar-coded or magnetically ticketed items in retailing establishments results in transmitting control data on the itemised sales—i.e. sales registered and outstanding stock—to the store manager and to the central buying department at the company's head office" (Child, 1984b).

Therefore, centralisation is encouraged, particularly when current and comprehensive information is transmitted directly to senior management who, according to Reed (1989), are now in a position to unify and co-ordinate previously fragmented control systems, thereby justifying a compressed and simplified organisational hierarchy because of the likely removal of layers of middle management. However, in these circumstances one should be aware of the need to use computer programs, if available, to integrate data and draw key analyses from them, otherwise the problem of information overload and complexity for senior managers will pose difficulties.

Other influences that account for centralisation are the managerial ethos of the organisation, particularly in those where entrepreneurial or family control is evident, and when production operations are fairly standardised and conditions in the organisation are not complex (Child 1984b; Robey, 1977).

Apart from the centralisation effect, information technology could be used to facilitate more effective delegation. This could be achieved in the following way:

1. Units of the organisation could be linked to form a common network, whereby each unit is made more aware of what other units are doing. This promotes awareness of the wider consequences of decisions taken by a particular unit. The local unit is able to inform other units and the central unit of its intentions and obtain rapid feedback. In this way consultation is facilitated, and the local unit is made aware of the intentions of the centre with regard to intervention. The end result could be a reduction in ambiguity and this is likely to encourage local initiatives and discourage intervention from the centre.

2. The improved analytical facilities offered by information technology—e.g. programs for sensitivity analysis and financial modelling—can enhance the capacity of local units to make sound judgements in the decision-making process. But, as mentioned earlier, the potential of information technology must be married with reliable information or data so that real benefits can be gained. Prior to the onset of the era of information technology, information processing capacity of a sophisticated nature normally resided at senior levels of the organisation where specialist staff could be called on to assist senior managers.

Huber (1990) has something to say about both centralisation and decentralisation when he maintains that new information technology will have an equalising effect on power distribution within organisations. People at the lower levels of the organisation will have more information than ever before, and therefore highly centralised structures become less prevalent because people are better able to question decisions. On the other hand, highly decentralised structures will be diluted as senior managers have better access to information that either did not exist previously, or alternatively was not easily accessible.

In what way is information technology likely to have an impact on the role of the manager? Child (1987) maintains that managers and similar employees will be subjected to pressures for simplification and standardisation of their tasks (something that was previously reserved for blue-collar workers), with a possible loss of autonomy. The introduction of computers could lead to a situation where the manager becomes less involved in the collection of information for the purposes of dissemination, simply because other members of the organisation may now have access to information previously denied to them. By reducing managerial tasks that are connected with the monitoring of information, interpersonal contacts between managers and others (an essential feature of the traditional managerial role) may become less important.

This could result in changes in the way people perceive the role of the manager (Eason, 1980). Likewise, it could lead to a diminution of management control when non-managerial staff have access to comprehensive and well-structured information (Oborne, 1985). However, there will always be a group of managers somewhere in the organisation, perhaps near the top, whose managerial control will not be undermined by the development of automated information systems; and, of course, there will be others who will experience an increase in their managerial or supervisory control simply because, with the aid of technology, they are better able to monitor the activities of employees—e.g. the

quality of work, costs, and revenue (Kling & Scacchi, 1980).

On this theme, Child (1984a) identifies three factors to consider when examining the impact of technological change on occupational groups:

1. White-collar workers are more likely to control the application of new technology to their own jobs, if they occupy a crucial role in decisions about its adoption.
2. The strength of white-collar groups in the labour market has a material influence on the strength of their position with respect to negotiations about proposals to introduce new technology. In this context, a factor to note is the strength of professional groups to counteract bureaucratic interference with their own concept of what constitutes good professional practice.
3. Where there is a strong tradition favouring the quality of service based on the personal touch, this could act as a powerful force against attempts to de-skill and automate jobs on grounds of cost. Branch bank managers and officials as a group do not seem to be strategically placed to resist a rationalisation process within the structure of the organisation that could lead to the de-skilling of jobs with the application of modern technology. By contrast, members of the medical profession (e.g. doctors in the hospital service), are better placed organisationally and institutionally to control the advent of technological innovation. This group in the UK has the advantage of having the backing of the influential British Medical Association.

Child and Loveridge (1990) conducted a major study which examined the introduction of information technology (IT) into three areas of service activity—domestic banking, hospital laboratories, and retailing. A particular aspect of the study was the focus on decision-making processes resulting in the choice of IT systems for the organisation, and how these systems would be applied to the work of employees. Among their findings was that employee participation in decisions related to the introduction of new technology had a bearing on the way it was used; the organisational politics surrounding the introduction of IT could lead to a certain resistance to learning to use the new technology in creative ways; and that this resistance was fuelled by the powers enjoyed by different groups within organisations.

A recent publication that explores the relationship between technology and organisations is a book by Scarborough and Corbett (1992). Although work-based issues are considered, there is a strong emphasis on theoretical frameworks using perspectives from power, meaning, and design.

Finally, though the computer may be viewed as a supportive tool, there have been circumstances where the implementation of computer systems fostered a negative view of the computer among managerial staff. This happened in eight organisations where managers experienced an increase in the work-load and variations in the pace of work following the implementation of computer systems (Eason, 1980).

Size and Technology

Research carried out at the University of Aston, Birmingham, examined a number of factors likely to influence the structure of organisation in 52 firms. Attention was directed at the transformation of organisational inputs into outputs, and the flow of work (workflow integration). Technology was divided into three categories:

- *Operations technology*: this type of technology refers to techniques used in the process of transforming inputs into outputs.
- *Materials technology*: the focus here is on the specific features of the materials used, such as availability, ease of machining, hardness, and so on.

- *Knowledge technology*: this refers to the soft side of technology, and is concerned with the specific nature, level of sophistication, and complexity of the knowledge required to do the job.

Size, Dependence, and Specialisation

In playing down the importance of technology as an influential factor determining the structure of the organisation, size, and dependence—i.e. the dependent relationship the organisation has with, for example, a holding company, suppliers, customers, etc—were mentioned in the research as factors truly influencing structural dimensions. Size was considered earlier in this chapter as an important internal environmental factor. In the Aston studies it was size, rather than technology, that bore the strongest relationship to the following dimensions:

- specialisation (number of specialised roles and activities);
- standardisation of procedures and roles;
- formalisation (the extent to which material appears in written form, such as policies, rules, and procedures); and
- centralisation.

However, technology was related to features of structure within its orbit—i.e. close to the shop floor (Pugh et al., 1969). A feature of bureaucratic organisation that seemed to influence other bureaucratic tendencies was role specialisation. This means that organisations with many specialists tended to have more standard routines, more documentation, and, as would be expected, a large hierarchy of staff specialists. The same degree of influence was not exerted by centralisation, leaving the researchers to conclude that centralisation cannot be considered an essential feature of bureaucracy (Pugh et al., 1968). The influence of size in shaping the hierarchy has also been endorsed by Blau and Schoenherr (1971). They found that more specialisation, more formalisation, more layers in the hierarchy, and larger spans of control are associated with increasing size.

Although economies of scale in manufacturing accrue to larger organisations, in recent years some large companies seemed to have challenged the notion that bigness is better in production units. The reasons stated (*Business Week*, 1984) are:

- a lower magnitude of investment is required for the smaller plant;
- a diminishing need to produce a variety of products;
- a resolve to reduce the number of layers in the hierarchy with fewer lines of communication; and
- in a number of situations the smaller plant was said to create improved teamwork, to increase productivity, and generate higher profits.

Over the years a practice has developed to increase the size of advisory or support staff to cope with complexity in the life of large organisations. More recently, large organisations faced with the possibility of becoming victims of corporate predators, or having to rationalise operations because of recessionary forces, have cut back significantly on numbers of employees, generally in order to create leaner but healthier entities. Particular targets in this pruning exercise have been headquarters or corporate staff, who have become victims of what is called "organisational downsizing"— i.e. reducing the size of corporate staff. For example, *Mobil* and *AT&T* (both large US corporations) have pruned headquarters and corporate staff drastically, with mixed results (Moore, 1987). Some claim this will emaciate the organisation in certain key functions, while others point to positive outcomes in terms of faster decision making due to the existence of fewer management levels through which decisions pass for approval.

Strategic Choice

The importance of contingency factors in organisational design was endorsed empirically earlier, where decisions to design the organisation were determined by the impact of environment, technology, and size. However, there is an influential view that decision makers at top management level make choices about the strategic direction of the company and, in the process, determine the structure of the organisation. As a consequence, managerial ideology and influence act as intervening variables in the relationship between structure and the major contingency factors of environment, technology, and size (Child, 1972; Montanari, 1978).

This proposition can be expanded to form a "strategic choice model" of organisational effectiveness, as shown in Fig. 10.3. In this model the strategic or managerial choices as far as organisation structure is concerned are influenced by the major contingency factors, both directly and indirectly through the purposes and goals of the organisation, and by certain characteristics of the manager (Bobbitt & Ford, 1980). The effectiveness of the organisation will then rest on the fit between the major contingency factors (contextual factors), strategies influenced by both organisational and managerial considerations, and structural features of organisation.

Once structure follows strategic considerations, there is always the potential for structure (e.g. centralisation, formalisation of rules and procedures) to reciprocate by influencing strategic decision making (Fredrickson, 1986).

The strategy–structure fit has been very much in evidence as UK corporations, such as *British Airways*, prepared themselves for privatisation in the 1980s. A likely course of action by top management in these circumstances is to simplify the organisational hierarchy, eliminate layers of management, dismiss a significant proportion of the

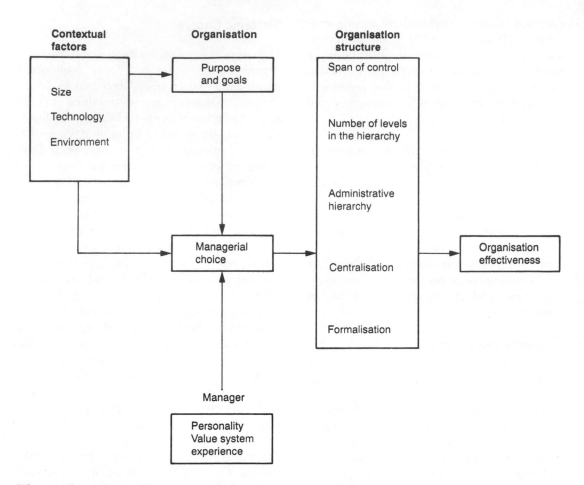

FIG. 10.3. The mediating effect of strategic choice. Source: Bobbitt, H.R. & Ford, J.D. (1980). Decision-maker choice as a determinant of organisational structure. *Academy of Management Review*, January, 13–23.

workforce, and bring about a cultural shift, such as rewarding management on the basis of merit rather than seniority.

Finally, the contingency approach to organisation structure has been criticised as being unrealistic because of the expectation that a manager modifies the structure in a rational manner after observing and registering a change in a contingency factor (Moorhead & Griffin, 1992). In practice this would be an exceedingly difficult, if not impossible task. However, Donaldson (1987) provides a defence of contingency theory, and argues that where there is a deficiency in the performance of the organisation due to a failure to respond adequately to changes in

one or more contingency factors, one can expect an appropriate organisational response.

SOCIO-TECHNICAL SYSTEMS

Earlier in the discussion of the impact of external environment on the organisation, an "open system" rather than a closed system perspective was adopted. An extension of the open system perspective is the concept of socio-technical systems. Any complex system consists of many sub-systems which, like the overall system, have elements such as those illustrated in Fig. 10.4.

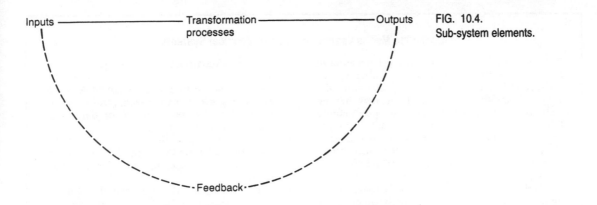

Inputs ———————— Transformation ———————— Outputs
processes

FIG. 10.4.
Sub-system elements.

Feedback

A socio-technical systems approach takes the organisation as an open system accommodating the technical (task) sub-system and the social sub-system. The technical sub-system receives the inputs and transforms them into outputs. For example, flour is an input to a bakery, and in the production process it is transformed into bread. In a service industry (e.g. a building society) loan applicants provides personal data about themselves that is used as input. When this information is processed and the application has been approved, a loan (output) may be forthcoming.

The social sub-system embraces interpersonal relationships within the organisation, and consists of personal preferences, mutual trust, insight into other peoples' behaviour, antagonisms, and so on. The task of management is to create socio-technical systems in which the two sub-systems reach optimum levels together, and are mutually supportive. The notion of socio-technical systems arose from research conducted by Trist and Bamforth in the early 1950s (see panel overleaf).

The notable contribution of the socio-technical approach is the emphasis on jointly harnessing the technical and social sub-systems with due regard to the relevant environment. However, Miller and Rice (1967), adopting a similar analysis, were less confident of the capacity of organisations to bring about a good fit between the "task" and "human" sub-systems. The latter sub-system has a leaning towards retaining routines and practices that could put a dampener on technological innovation and efforts to bring about greater profitability.

The socio-technical approach is also relevant to job redesign, considered in Chapter 2. For example, the car assembly methods adopted by *Volvo* were a departure from traditional methods, with a new emphasis on sensitivity to the interface of social and technological systems. Autonomous work groups represent one approach to meeting the human needs and technical demands within organisations, and this is likely to be acceptable to the modern proponents of socio-technical systems. In the final analysis, management can exercise choice when it comes to designing organisations and jobs around the technological system.

OVERVIEW AND FUTURE TRENDS

The diversity of perspectives on organisational analysis is apparent. However, it would appear that the development of contingency approaches is worth pursuing. One is aware that there are a number of scholars from the sociological tradition who draw our attention to the unsatisfactory state of organisation theory. Reed (1992), in the introductory chapter to an iconoclastic treatise on organisation studies, makes the point that "most of the crucial theoretical

Coal-mine Mechanisation and Socio-technical Systems

In this research, the process of mechanisation in the coal-mines of north-west Durham was observed. The researchers, who were from the Tavistock Institute, noted that the new mining techniques designed to increase productivity failed because they split up well-established work groups, with unfavourable consequences. Therefore, improvements in the technical system occurred, but at the expense of a deteriorating social sub-system.

Traditional methods of retrieving coal by hand involved limited technology, with small teams working their own part of the coal seam. This system created multi-skilled, self-selected, largely autonomous work groups that enjoyed a great deal of independence; in addition, workers obtained a relatively high degree of satisfaction from their work. The work groups did not compete with each other, and relationships were normally harmonious.

With the introduction of mechanical coal cutting (new technology) using the longwall method, workers belonged to shift groups that performed different functions. For example, one shift cut the coal with a mechanical coal cutter; the next shift loaded the coal on to a conveyor; and the third shift propped up the roof and moved the cutter and conveyor in readiness for the next shift. The longwall method was technically efficient, but it produced the following dysfunctional social consequences:

- Self-selected work groups were broken up, destroying some of the loyalty and cohesion required in the performance of dangerous tasks.
- As a result of specialisation by shift, greater co-ordination from the surface was needed to ensure that one cycle finished before the other started.
- Supervision became closer, and the workers reacted strongly to having to forego some of their traditional independence.

The researchers argued that a different organisational form could still maximise the technical and economic benefits, and minimise unrest and conflict. This organisational arrangement would still retain the three-shift cycle of the longwall method, but the following conditions would have to be imposed. First, there should be no sharp division of tasks between shifts. Second, the miners should be allowed to utilise their multiple skills. Third, there should be a restoration of some of the lost worker autonomy, with less supervision, whereby the work group would be given back responsibility for the allocation of workers to each shift (Trist & Bamforth, 1951).

---

questions and substantive issues which define organisational analysis as an identifiable and viable field of study seem to be matters of considerable dispute, not to say deep controversy". Having read the remaining chapters by various contributors, Reed asserts that "diversity, plurality, uncertainty, and fragmentation seem to be the epithets which most easily and readily spring to mind when attempting to provide a general characterisation of the current state of play, in, and future prospects for, organisational analysis".

Emerging Organisational Forms

Peter Drucker (1988) maintains that the typical business 20 years hence will have fewer than half the levels of its counterpart today, and no more than a third the number of managers. The typical future business will be:

... knowledge-based, an organisation composed largely of specialists who direct and discipline their own performance through organised feedback from colleagues, customers, and headquarters. For this reason, it will be what I call an information-based organisation ... We can perceive, though perhaps only dimly, what this organisation will look like, but the job of building the information-based organisation is the managerial challenge of the future.

According to Miles and Snow (1986), strong competitive pressures (e.g. globalisation, technical change, deregulation, and changing workforce demographics) will eventually create a new organisational form—a unique combination of strategy, structure, and management processes referred to as the dynamic network. Here there would be heavy reliance on self-managed groups and a greater willingness to view organisational boundaries and membership as highly flexible.

Taking stock of the current situation and looking into the future, Snow, Miles, and Coleman (1992) make the following observations:

Multi-level hierarchies are giving way to clusters of business units, co-ordinated by market mechanisms rather than by layers of middle management planners and schedulers. These market-guided entities are now commonly called "network organisations" .... Companies could focus on things they do especially well, "outsourcing" a growing collection of goods and services, and getting rid of assets that produce low returns. For example, one company in the network may research and design a product, another may engineer and manufacture it, a third may handle distribution, and so on. Competitive forces are brought to bear on each element of the product or service value chain.

Such "delayered" companies are not only less costly to operate, they are also more agile. By limiting operations to those functions for which the company has, or can develop, expert skill, and outsourcing functions that can be performed quicker, more effectively, or at lower cost by other companies, the organisation requires less planning and co-ordination. Also, the organisation can accelerate product and service innovations to keep pace with changes in the market-place.

In Chapter 2, empowerment was discussed as a motivational device. It basically means empowering employees to make their own decisions, with quality and service uppermost in their minds. Kanter (1992) maintains that empowerment can only come about in the context of new organisational forms. The organisational framework could possess the following features:

- Staff at headquarters are to act as support systems, rather than issuing instructions to people at the customer interface.
- Customers are treated as partners or allies.
- A "horizontal shift" takes place to counteract the fixation about upward progression and desire for titles denoting status. With horizontal shift, organisations consist of teams, project groups, and taskforces, rather than departmental empires, and people work to achieve a result as opposed to the traditional emphasis on working to acquire a title.
- Traditional pay structures are replaced by a new pattern of pay or reward (mentioned in Chapter 13), which, basically, targets individual and group achievements for reward purposes.

An alternative path to empowerment, called "employee self-management" has recently been suggested (Shipper & Manz, 1992). The idea behind self-management is that, to a large extent, workers become their own managers. It involves an increasing reliance on workers' creative and intellectual capabilities. Self-management will take root in organisations where formally designated and empowered work teams are established.

Apart from the organisational changes that are necessary in order to implement self-management, individuals must master certain basic skills. These are self-leadership skills (learning to lead oneself before attempting to lead others) and skills required to help other people to do the same.

In post-1992 Europe it has been suggested that there will be increasing competitive pressures for companies to operate in as many EC countries as possible. The organisations likely to be competitive will evolve new structures to take advantage of national markets as well as European economies of scale (Mitchell, 1989). A "Euro-network" organisation is predicted by Mitchell, with the following attributes:

- The company is divided into identifiable units, with clear business objectives.
- An organisational control system that maximises the need for referral of information across the structure is implemented.
- There is a recognition that duplication of support services in a devolved system is preferred over the greater level of complexity resulting from centralisation. If there is a central services function, its main purpose is to service the needs of various operating units.
- There is a firm commitment to the ideal of a single European market.
- The span of control is increased at all levels of the organisation to create greater scope for delegation, and fewer hierarchical levels.

The US multi-national corporation—3M—recently engaged in a radical re-shaping of the organisation's European operation. In the interests of improved cross-border effectiveness and quicker decision making,

3M has pushed most strategic and operational responsibility away from its national subsidiaries (geographical divisions), and centralised it in the form of 19 product divisions called European Business Centres, each with Europe-wide responsibility. As a consequence, the lives of numerous managers in the organisations have been transformed, having been given project responsibilities that cut across national boundaries (Lorenz, 1993).

From what has been said so far in connection with emerging forms of organisation, it is not surprising to read a newspaper headline proclaiming the following message: "Flat pyramids: the wave of the future". The journalist's opening comments are as follows (Oates, 1993):

If some management gurus are to be believed, we are in the middle of the most dramatic transformation in the way human beings organise themselves since the Chinese invented the pyramidal command structure 2000 years ago. The flattening of the pyramid, globalisation, networking, teleworking, a better educated work-force, and a leadership vacuum are all contributing to this fundamental shift.

SUMMARY: ORGANISATIONAL STRUCTURE AND DESIGN

- After defining what is meant by an organisation, principles of organisation were identified as hierarchy, communication, specialisation, chain of command, centralisation, and span of control. These principles have been derived from the classical principles of organisation. Although some of these principles have value as basic concepts, they have been subjected to criticism.
- Weber's ideal bureaucracy offered prescriptions with respect to positions, tasks, contracts, rewards, career structure,

control, records, impartiality, and ownership and control. The dysfunctional aspects of bureaucracy were discussed with reference to goal displacement, conflict, informal organisation, division of labour relevance, impersonality, and adaptation.
- Structural arrangements were defined as functional grouping, process grouping, product grouping, customer grouping, territorial grouping, and matrix organisation. There were reflections on the future of the hierarchy.

- Mintzberg's co-ordinating mechanisms within organisations were defined as mutual adjustment, direct supervision, standardisation of employee skills (input), standardisation of work processes, and standardisation of outputs. When these co-ordinating mechanisms are combined with dimensions of structure, we are in a position to specify different forms of organisation as follows: simple structure; machine bureaucracy; professional bureaucracy; divisional form; and adhocracy.

- Contingency factors of organisation were identified as the internal environment (including size), the external environment (comprising various external agencies), and technology. Size was discussed initially with reference to the internal environment of the organisation. The external environment was analysed with reference to types of environment, environmental uncertainty, differentiation and integration, resource dependency, and population ecology.

- A variety of theoretical perspectives (e.g. Woodward; Burns and Stalker; Thompson, and Perrow) formed a basis for examining the impact of technology on organisation. Size and technology as determinants of organisation (i.e. the Aston School) were also discussed.

- Production systems (e.g. just-in-time) were acknowledged as supplementing production technology. The impact of new technology was also discussed, and the role of strategic choice was mentioned. There were criticisms of the contingency approach, and a discussion of socio-technical systems. The final section was devoted to an overview and a discussion of future trends.

QUESTIONS

1. Examine the principles of organisation in the light of criticisms.
2. What do we mean by the dysfunctional aspects of bureaucracy?
3. Compare and contrast the structural arrangement referred to as the "functional grouping" with that of matrix organisation.
4. What is the outcome of combining Mintzberg's five co-ordinating mechanisms with dimensions of structure?
5. Examine the role of the external environment as a contingency factor.
6. Explain the following terms: (a) disturbed reactive environment; (b) differentiation; (c) resource dependency; (d) population ecology; and (e) just-in-time.
7. Assess ways in which technology, both old and new, influences organisation.
8. Examine the role of size as a determinant of organisation structure.
9. Explain the following terms: (a) formalisation; (b) mediating technology; (c) organic system of organisation; (d) strategic choice; and (e) downsizing,
10. Comment on an open system of organisation, with reference to socio-technical systems.
11. Explain the term "flat pyramid".
12. Examine the nature and significance of network organisations.

REFERENCES

Aldrich, H.E. & Pfeffer, J. (1976). Environment of organisations. *Annual Review of Sociology*, 80–83.

Baxter, A. (1993). Reorganisation into product divisions at JCB. *Financial Times*, 11 August, p. 8.

Bedeian, A.G. (1984). *Organisations: Theory and analysis* (second edition). Orlando, FL: Dryden Press.

Blau, P.M., Falbe, C.M., McKinley, W., & Tracey, P.K. (1976). Technology and organisation in manufacturing. *Administrative Science Quarterly, 21,* 20–40.

Blau, P.M. & Schoenherr, R.A. (1971). *The structure of organisations.* New York: Basic Books.

Bobbitt, H.R. & Ford, J.D. (1980). Decision-maker choice as a determinant of organisational structure. *Academy of Management Review,* January, 13–23.

Burns, T. & Stalker, G.M. (1961). *The management of innovation.* London: Tavistock Publications.

Business Week (1984). *Small is beautiful now, in manufacturing.* 22nd October, 65–76.

Child, J. (1972). Organisational structure, environment and performance: The role of strategic choice. *Sociology, 6,* 1–22.

Child, J. (1973). Predicting and understanding organisation structure. *Administrative Science Quarterly 18,* 2, June, 168–185.

Child, J. (1984a). *Organisation: A guide to problems and practice* (second edition). London: Harper & Row.

Child, J (1984b). New technology and developments in management organisation. *Omega, 12,* 211–223.

Child, J. (1987). New technologies in the service class. In K. Purcell, S. Wood, A. Watson, & S. Allen (Eds.), *The changing experience of employment.* London: Macmillan.

Child, J. & Loveridge, R. (1990). *Information Technology in European Services.* Oxford, UK: Basil Blackwell.

Cullen, J.H. & Anderson, K.S. (1986). Blau's theory of structural differentiation revisited: A theory of structural change or scale. *Academy of Management Journal,* June, 203–229.

Daft, R.L. (1986). *Organisation theory and design* (second edition). St. Paul, MN: West.

Dankbaar, B. (1988). New production concepts, management strategies, and the quality of work. *Work, Employment, and Society, 2, 1,* 25–50.

Davis, S.M. & Lawrence, P.R. (1977). *Matrix.* Reading, MA: Addison-Wesley.

Donaldson, L. (1987). Strategy and structural adjustment to regain fit and performance: In defence of contingency theory. *Journal of Management Studies,* January, 1–24.

Drucker, P.F. (1988). The coming of the new organisation. *Harvard Business Review,* January–February, 45–53.

Duncan, R.B. (1972). Characteristics of organisational environments and perceived uncertainty. *Administrative Science Quarterly.* September, 313–327.

Duncan, W.J. (1981). *Organisational behaviour.* Boston, MA: Houghton Mifflin.

Eason, K.D. (1980). Computer information systems and managerial tasks. In N. Bjorn-Anderson (Ed.), *The human side of information processing.* Amsterdam: North Holland.

Emery, F.E. & Trist, E.L. (1965). The causal textures of organisational environments. *Human Relations,* February, 21–32.

Fayol, H. (1949). *General and industrial management.* London: Pitman.

Fortune Magazine (1988). *Big blue wants to loosen its collar.* 29th February, 8.

Fredrickson, J.W. (1986). The strategic decision process and organisation structure. *Academy of Management Review,* April, 280–297.

Gerth, H.H. & Mills, C.W. (1948). *From Max Weber.* London: Routledge & Kegan Paul.

Hall, R.H. (1962). Intra-organisational structural variation: Application of the bureaucratic model. *Administrative Science Quarterly,* December, 295–308.

Hannan, M.T. & Freeman, J.H. (1977). The population ecology of organisations. *American Journal of Sociology, 2,* 929–964.

Hodgetts, R.M. (1991). *Organisational behaviour: Theory and practice.* New York: Macmillan.

Huber, G.P. (1990). A theory of the effects of advanced information technologies on organisation design, intelligence, and decision making. *Academy of Management Review, 15,* 47–71.

Jaques, E. (1990). In praise of hierarchy. *Harvard Business Review,* January–February, 127–133.

Joseph, M. (1989). *Sociology for business.* Cambridge: Polity Press.

Kanter, R.M. (1992). *Address to the National Conference of the Institute of Personnel Management,* Harrogate, UK.

Kling, R. & Scacchi, W. (1980). Computing as social action: The social dynamics of computing in complex organisations. *Advances in Computers, 19,* 249–327.

Larson, E.W. & Gobeli, D.H. (1987). Matrix management: Contradictions and insights. *California Management Review,* Summer, 126–138.

Lawrence, P.R. & Lorsch, J.W. (1969). *Organisations and environment: Managing differentiation and integration.* Homewood, IL: Irwin.

Leavitt, H. J. & Whisler, T. L. (1958). Management in the 1980s. *Harvard Business Review, 36,* 41–48.

Lengnick-Hall, C.A. (1986). Technology advances in batch production and improved competitive position. *Journal of Management,* Spring, 75–90.

Lorange, P., & Roos, J. (1992). *Strategic alliances formation, implementation, and evolution.* Oxford, UK: Basil Blackwell

Lorenz, C. (1993a). Strategic alliances (A meeting of minds). *Financial Times,* 25 October, p. 15.

Lorenz, C. (1993b). 3M's Europe-wide reorganisation (Here, there and everywhere). *Financial Times,* 10 November, p. 11.

Miles, R.E. & Snow, C.C. (1986). Organisations: New concepts for new forms. *California Management Review, 28,* 62–73.

Miller, E.J. & Rice, A.K. (1967). *Systems of organisation: The control of task and sentient boundaries.* London: Tavistock.

Mintzberg, H. (1979). *The structuring of organisations.* New York: Prentice-Hall.

Mintzberg, H. (1981). Organisation design: Fashion or fit. *Harvard Business Review*, January–February, 103–116.

Mitchell, D. (1989). 1992: The implications for management. *Long-range Planning, 22*, 32–40.

Montanari, J.R. (1978). Managerial discretion: An expanded model of organisational choice. *Academy of Management Review*, April, 231–241.

Moore, T. (1987). Goodbye corporate staff. *Fortune*, 21st December, 65–76.

Moorhead, G. & Griffin, R.W. (1989). *Organisational behaviour* (second edition). Boston, MA: Houghton Mifflin.

Moorhead, G. & Griffin, R.W. (1992). *Organisational behaviour* (third edition). Boston, MA: Houghton Mifflin.

Oates, D. (1993). Flat pyramids: The wave of the future. *The Sunday Times*, 28th March, 5.2.

Oborne, D.J. (1994). *Computers at work: A behavioural approach* (3rd ed.). Chichester: John Wiley & Sons.

Perrow, C.B. (1970). *Organisational analysis: A sociological view.* London: Tavistock Publications.

Porter, L.W. & Lawler, E.E. (1975). *Behaviour in organisations.* New York: McGraw-Hill.

Pugh, D.S., Hickson, D.T., Hinings, C.R., & Turner, C. (1968). Dimensions of organisation structure. *Administrative Science Quarterly, 13*, 65–105.

Pugh, D.S., Hickson, D.T., Hinings, C.R., & Turner, C. (1969). The context of organisation structures. *Administrative Science Quarterly, 14*, 91–114.

Reed, M. (1989). *The sociology of management.* Hemel Hempstead, UK: Harvester Wheatsheaf.

Reed, M. (1992). Introduction. In M. Reed & M. Hughes (Eds.), *Rethinking organisation: New directions in organisation theory and analysis.* London: Sage Publications.

Robey, D. (1977). Computers and management structures: Some empirical findings re-examined. *Human Relations, 30*, 963–976.

Scarborough, H., & Corbett, J.M. (1992). *Technology and organization: power, meaning and design.* London: Routledge.

Shipper, F. & Manz C.C. (1992). Employee self-management without formally designated teams: An alternative road to empowerment. *Organisational Dynamics*, Winter, 48–61.

Snow, C.C., Miles, R.E., & Coleman, H.J. (1992). Managing 21st century network organisations. *Organisational Dynamics*, Winter, 5–20.

Tailby, S. & Turnbull, P. (1987). Learning to manage just-in-time. *Personnel Management*, January.

Thompson, J.D. (1967). *Organisations in action.* New York: McGraw-Hill.

Thompson, P. & McHugh, D. (1990). *Work organisations: A critical introduction.* London: Macmillan Education.

Trist, E.L. & Bamforth, K.W. (1951). Some social and psychological consequences of the longwall method of coal-getting. *Human Relations, 4*, 3–38.

Van Fleet, D. (1983). Span of management research and issues. *Academy of Management Journal.* September, 546–552.

Vecchio, R.P. (1991). *Organisational behaviour* (second edition). Orlando, FL.: The Dryden Press.

Vecchio, R.P. & Keon, T.L. (1981). Predicting employee satisfaction from congruency among individual need, job design, and system structure. *Journal of Occupational Behaviour, 2*, 283–292.

Whisler, T.L. (1970). *The impact of computers on organisations.* New York: Praeger.

Wickham, T. (1993). Time is of the essence. Back to the Black. *The Sunday Times*, 17 October, p. 7.

Woodward, J. (1965). *Industrial organisations: Theory and practice.* London: Oxford University Press.

Woodward, J. (1970). *Industrial organisations: Behaviour and control.* London: Oxford University Press.

Worthy, J.C. (1950). Organisational structure and employee morale. *American Sociological Review, 15*, 169–179

Yuchtman, E. & Seashore, S. (1967). A system resource approach to organisational effectiveness. *American Sociological Review*, December, 891–903.

11

Organisational Culture

The chapter opens with various definitions and major dimensions of corporate culture. Next, three major ways of analysing organisational culture are discussed, followed by an examination of four major approaches (in addition to organisational socialisation) used in the development of organisational culture. The benefits derived from culture are then specified and, finally, national cultures and their impact on organisational characteristics are introduced.

This chapter draws widely on ideas developed in other chapters. For example, attitudes and commitment (Chapter 6), group norms (Chapter 7), socialisation (Chapters 1 and 4), management style (Chapter 8), creativity (Chapter 5), organisational forms, change, and development (Chapters 10 and 12), and human resource practices (Chapter 13).

DEFINITION

Before considering the impact of national cultures on organisational functioning, there will be an examination of corporate culture, which amounts to a consideration of organisational values and norms, with the focus on assumptions and beliefs. Organisational or corporate culture is still an important issue in the 1990s, but does not grab the headlines in the same way that it did in the last decade, when it was the subject of intensive study.

According to Pettigrew (1979), organisational culture consists of the behaviour, actions, and values that people in an enterprise are expected to follow. Alternatively, a definition by Moorhead and Griffin (1992) states that organisational culture is a set of values, often taken for granted, that help people in an organisation understand which actions are considered

acceptable and which are considered unacceptable. Often these values are communicated through stories and other symbolic means.

Schein (1990), in a penetrating analysis of organisational culture from an organisational psychological perspective, comes forward with the following definition of organisational culture:

- A pattern of basic assumptions,
- invented, discovered, or developed by a given group
- as it learns to cope with its problems of external adaptation and integral integration,
- that has worked well enough to be considered valid and, therefore,
- is to be taught to new members as the correct way to perceive, think, and feel in relation to those problems.

It is important to note that the values that make up an organisation's culture (e.g. never lose sight of the customer) are often taken for granted. In other words, they are basic assumptions made by employees, do not necessarily appear in a document, and are not necessarily transmitted in a training programme, although they can be expressed in written form. Organisational culture probably exerts the greatest influence on individual behaviour and actions when it is taken for granted. One of the major reasons why organisational culture is such a powerful influence on employees within an organisation is because it is not explicit. Instead it is an implicit part of the employees' values and beliefs (Moorhead & Griffin, 1992).

Although on many occasions we tend to speak of organisational culture as a uniform phenomenon, it is well to remember that organisations are made up of sub-cultures which are attached to different roles, functions, and levels (Hampden-Turner, 1990). Therefore, very few beliefs, attitudes, or values are shared by all organisational members. One could encounter a different sub-culture at, say, a factory of a company than at its head office in a different location. Also, organisations could have a management culture and a staff culture. According to Furnham and Gunter (1993):

> These sub-cultures can assume varying degrees of significance within the organisation, and can be beneficial if they adopt a common sense of purpose, but problems arise where they have different priorities and agendas. Then sub-cultures can clash with each other or with the overall corporate culture, impeding organisational functioning and performance.

Dimensions of Organisational Culture

The culture of the organisation is perceived by Trice and Beyer (1984) as consisting of four major dimensions:

- company practices
- company communications
- physical cultural forms, and
- common language.

Company Practices

These practices consist of rites and ceremonies designed to help employees identify with the organisation and its successes. For example, there could be a ceremonial launching of a new product at which employees are present, or an address by the chief executive at the "Salesperson of the Year" event. Likewise, there could be rituals when employees are given the opportunity to socialise and relax with each other at informal company social events.

Company Communications

This form of communication focuses primarily on vignettes and anecdotes about the dedication and commitment of corporate heroes and managers, or the devotion of ordinary employees. There are stories founded on events showing employees displaying heroism or, for example, adhering to high quality standards. Also, the great achievements of the leadership at the inception of the company could be highlighted. But there could also be myths, lacking foundation in fact, where older employees recall past happenings. These could be supplemented by legends—accounts of actual events fleshed out with fictional details—as well as by folk tales which amount to fictional stories with a message. To foster recognition there are symbols and slogans and logos or emblems (e.g. the *Mercedes Benz* symbol), and these represent an important identification sign.

Physical Cultural Forms

These forms are physical factors that convey something distinctive about the organisation, and range from the physical layout and decor of offices to computer hardware prominently displayed on office desks.

Common Language

The development of a common language is conspicuous. For example, the *Walt Disney* organisation refers to the work-force at its theme parks as the cast, the customers are guests, and when staff work with the public they are on the stage. *McDonald's* (hamburgers) refers to its workers as crew members.

Before examining frameworks used to analyse organisational culture, it must be acknowledged that certain companies (e.g. *IBM* and *Marks & Spencer*) possess corporate cultures of a highly distinctive nature. Also, creating a corporate culture that fits neatly with overall goals is relevant to any organisation, be it a commercial company, a trade union, a voluntary group, or a co-operative. One could argue that co-operative societies, for example, can fall short of their potential, and even decay, because they fail to develop appropriate mechanisms for transmitting the original ideals (cultural values) from the founders to new members and sustaining them through shared experience.

Manifestations of Corporate Culture in the UK

The following are examples of good management practices influenced by corporate culture. The first example looks at Japanese enterprises in Britain, and the second concentrates on a successful British company.

Japanese Companies in Britain

It is said that Japanese manufacturing enterprises in Britain perform well in terms of productivity and product quality, and the following factors exemplify the management style and practices they adopt (Eglin & Barber, 1981; Tighe, 1981):

1. Meticulous attention is given to the recruitment and training of employees, including special induction courses in the company philosophy. Managers are not encouraged to remain specialists; in fact they are trained to appreciate and understand the interrelationship and interdependencies between sales, finance, production, and research and development.

2. Discipline on the shopfloor includes no smoking, no eating, no chattering, and sometimes no tea breaks. A tough line is taken on absenteeism and poor time-keeping so as to ensure the continuity of production. Apparently the workers generally appreciate the reasons for this approach.

3. Performance charts, showing productivity for each section, are on display. As a means of keeping machine operators interested and sufficiently motivated to monitor quality, they participate in completing the charts. These charts can form a basis for the assessment of employees for promotion purposes. Employees do not receive output bonuses, because bonuses tend to be equated with hurried and low-quality production.

4. There appears to be a single-minded pursuit of product quality and, because of this, the production worker is an important member of the company. Managers are expected to identify with the quality of the product and the production process. The lack of distinction between skilled and unskilled operators means that the able and committed unskilled operator can eventually move easily to a supervisory or middle manager job. It is important that an operator can have a conversation about his or her machine on equal terms with a maintenance engineer.

5. Where shifts go round the clock, 10 minutes is set aside before each of the three shifts to discuss production targets, safety, and any other current topics. There are also monthly departmental meetings, as well as meetings of small working groups, to discuss matters such as safety.

6. Demarcation lines between jobs are less conspicuous. It is claimed that flexible

working agreements (whereby workers carry out a number of operations) generate greater commitment and pride in work.

7. Naturally, emphasis is placed on expertise and experience but, in addition, particular importance is attached to willingness and high standards of attendance, punctuality, and flexibility. As well as competitive remuneration, companies offer in return a sense of involvement and a virtual guarantee of no redundancy, the maxim being that the company surpluses in good trading conditions can compensate for excess capacity in bad times.

8. Workers wear company uniforms and peak caps emblazoned with the corporate logo. The classless canteen is very much in evidence. Company outings are looked on as social activities designed to foster team spirit and communication.

9. The company environment is friendly with an open style of management and frank disclosures to the work-force. Japanese managers take plenty of time to reach decisions, they listen a lot, they empathise with employees, they develop relationships of trust, and display managerial professionalism. The company tolerates the closed shop, and enters into lengthy negotiations with the trade union on manning levels and flexible working practices. British workers, who are not attached to the idea of working as a team, may react adversely to the frequent meetings.

Apparently, Japanese managers have few complaints about their British operations. Their nightmare appears to be the quality of the components bought in from British industry, which in the past were alleged to be 20% more expensive than those produced by companies in Japan.

A British Company
What management style and practices can we expect to find in a progressive British company in a service industry?

According to the then chief executive of *Marks & Spencer* (Sieff, 1981), a number of benefits, such as a stable work-force, ready acceptance of change, high productivity, high profits (for the benefit of shareholders, staff, and retired staff), and high staff morale are the consequence of inspired human relations practices. It is claimed that these practices are backed up by a strong commitment to the view that it is people who matter. Good human relations practices at *Marks & Spencer* apply not only to employees, but also to customers and suppliers (see panel facing).

FRAMEWORK OF ANALYSIS

These are a number of approaches to capturing the values embedded in organisational culture. The approaches of Ouchi, Peters and Waterman, Deal and Kennedy, and Harrison will be examined in this section. Taken together they produce useful insights into the dimensions of organisational culture.

Ouchi's Approach

Ouchi (1981) analysed the organisational cultures of three groups of companies, described as: typical American; typical Japanese; and type Z American.

A list of seven points was developed to facilitate the comparison of the three types of companies:

1. commitment to employees;
2. evaluation;
3. careers;
4. control;
5. decision making;
6. responsibility; and
7. concern for people.

From the analysis it emerged that the cultures of the typical Japanese companies and type Z American companies are quite different from the cultures of typical

---

Management Style and Practices at *Marks & Spencer*

- Top management must believe in and be committed to the implementation of human relations practices, and genuine respect for the individual is crucial.
- Personnel problems occupy much of the time of the senior board in the company. Advice and help should be delicately given where needed. Apart from mandatory staffing regulations, which are legally binding, regulations governing staff behaviour should be kept to a minimum.
- When delegated powers are given to local management, they are expected to act sensibly and generously in their dealings with people. By and large this is said to happen.
- Top management must know how good or bad the working conditions and amenities are. According to Lord Sieff: "They must eat in the employees' restaurants, see whether the food is decent and well cooked, visit the washroom and lavatories. If they are not good enough for those in charge, they are not good enough for anyone."
- Managers must not only be aware of the employees' problems, but also react to them. Topics of legitimate concern include the problems of the individual at work, his or her health, well-being and progress, the working environment and profit-sharing.
- The company must respect the individual's contribution and provide the necessary encouragement, backed by a full and frank two-way communication system.
- Managers must take subordinates into their confidence. There is very little need for secrecy. Managers must explain policies and developments clearly, and the views of their staff on proposed developments must be taken into account.
- People should be informed of their progress, or lack of it, and credit should be given where it is due. Poor work should be the subject of frank discussion, because this stimulates people to work better in the knowledge that they will eventually receive credit for work well done.
- A policy of good human relations costs time, effort, and money. The role of the personnel specialist in a store consists of identifying problems, seeking the views of staff, and responding to constructive suggestions and worthwhile criticisms. They also provide training and development programmes.
- Managers should play an active role in their communities, and are sometimes seconded for a specified time to community projects (Sieff, 1981).

American companies. These differences reflect the success of the former as opposed to the latter.

Commitment to Employees

The typical Japanese and type Z American company subscribes to the cultural value of endeavouring to offer long-term employment, and would lay off employees only as a last resort. This commitment would seem to have greater currency in Japan. In the USA an employee could be dismissed for unsatisfactory performance in a type Z company. By contrast, the typical American company would have a cultural expectation of short-term employment, whereby workers would be laid off when there is an adverse change in the company's fortunes.

In Japan today, the deep economic recession has posed a serious challenge to the system of lifetime employment. Many people have lost their jobs for the first time. Such happenings cause deep psychological distress because of people's close identification with the company, and because unemployment is considered such an embarrassment. In some cases, people join the ranks of the *shanai shitsugyo*, or in-house unemployed, where their salary is paid but they have nothing to do (Pollack, 1993). According to the Chairperson of *Mitsubishi*, a leading metals and ceramics supplier in Japan, the tradition of lifetime employment will change, but it will take a generation—so expect no revolutions (Dawkins, 1993).

Evaluation

Promotion is slow in the typical Japanese company and type Z American company because evaluation of an employee's performance, using both quantitative and qualitative measures, take place over an appreciable length of time. By contrast, in the typical American company the emphasis would be on a rapid process of evaluation, based primarily on quantitative measures, where short-term thinking is encouraged.

Careers

In the typical Japanese company, having a career steeped in experience of a number of different business functions is valued, although the career path in the type Z American company would not be as broad. The adoption of the values of specialisation—reflected in experience of only one or two business functions—leads to a narrow career path in the typical American company.

Control

Control is a normal feature of life within an organisation, and without it the co-ordination of activities would be almost impossible. Most of the typical Japanese companies and type Z American companies use organisational culture as a powerful control mechanism, from which can come guidance on how best to act. Stories convey what superiors expect subordinates to do.

By contrast, in the typical American company guidance is more likely to emanate from formal bureaucratic processes (e.g. explicit directions in job descriptions and procedures) and not from implicit cultural values. If stories exist, they are likely to highlight the benefits of sticking to the written guidelines.

Decision Making

The vehicle for decision making in the typical Japanese company and the type Z American company is the "group", based on sharing information and an attachment to consensus. By contrast, in the typical American company individual decision making occupies a prominent position, and a consultative process is not a prerequisite for the taking of decisions.

Responsibility

On the question of responsibility for decisions, there is a divergence in the practices of Japanese companies on the one hand and the two types of American companies on the other. In Japan, strong cultural values are supportive of the group bearing responsibility (collective responsibility), whereas in both the type Z and typical American companies there would be an attachment to the notion that a single person, rather than the group as a whole, ultimately bears responsibility for decisions made by the group.

You will notice that in the Japanese company, group decision making and collective responsibility go hand-in-hand, as does individual decision making and individual responsibility in the typical American company. However, the type Z American company is different in this respect, with group decision making coinciding with individual responsibility. This might be explained by attributing to certain American managers a skill in securing positive responses from the group in the decision-making process, but resorting to individual responsibility, because, by so doing, they reflect strong cultural norms of individuality and individual responsibility prominent in American society.

Concern for People

In the typical Japanese company and the type Z American company, the concern for people extends beyond the boundaries of the organisation, embracing their home-life and focusing on their outlook. In the typical American company there is a narrower concern for the worker, and the concern that exists is primarily geared to the workplace.

Ouchi maintains that the cultures of the typical Japanese company and the type Z American company assist them in producing better performances than the typical American company. It is interesting to note that successful Japanese car manufacturers located in the UK import the management style and culture that has proved so successful in Japan. They do not skimp on well-directed investment in employees and in operations over long periods of time. As a result, generally speaking, they experience sound improvements in long-term performance.

Peters and Waterman's Approach

In their popular book, *In Search of Excellence*, the authors emphasised the relationship between organisational culture and performance (Peters & Waterman, 1982). From a sample of highly successful American companies (e.g. *IBM*, *Boeing*, *Walt Disney*, and *McDonald's*) they tried to identify management practices associated with success, eventually analysing cultural factors leading to successful management practices. The cultural factors—attributes of excellence—were as follows:

- bias for action;
- closeness to the customer;
- autonomy and entrepreneurship;
- productivity through people;
- hands-on management;
- "stick to the knitting";
- simple form, lean staff; and
- simultaneous loose–tight organisation.

Bias for Action
Managers are expected to make decisions (even though all the necessary information may not be available) in conditions where delaying making a decision is tantamount to never making a decision. Delays would open the way for competitors to seize the opportunity.

Closeness to the Customer
The customer is a source of information about existing products, a source of ideas about new products in the future, and ultimately the rock on which the current and future financial performance of the company rests. Therefore, it is important to identify and meet customers' needs, and take the necessary action to retain customers' loyalty.

Autonomy and Entrepreneurship
To foster an innovative climate the organisation is divided into more manageable smaller business units. Then, independent, creative, and also risk-taking activity is encouraged.

Productivity Through People
Ingrained in the organisational culture is the belief that treating people with dignity and respect is essential. Also, the organisation provides opportunities for people to realise their potential.

Hands-on Management
It is important for senior managers to maintain close contact with business operations. Managers should leave their offices and wander around the plant and other parts of the workplace.

"Stick to the Knitting"
There is a reluctance on the part of management to enter business fields outside their area of expertise. The practice of operating businesses in unrelated industries is frowned on, and runs counter to a strong cultural norm.

Simple Form, Lean Staff
This type of structure is reflected in fewer management levels and relatively small groups of corporate staff. The main emphasis is on the performance of employees, not the size of the establishment.

Simultaneous Loose–Tight Organisation
On the one hand the adoption of the company's cultural values tends to create tightly organised organisations, wedded by common cultural bonds. On the other hand, the company is loosely organised, with lower administrative overhead costs, fewer rules and regulations, and a leaner establishment. The loose structure is said to be functional because it is supported by the common values accepted by employees in the organisation.

Criticisms

The research of Peters and Waterman has been subjected to criticism, with the lack of rigour in research methodology a prominent theme among critics. According to one critic, the samples of companies chosen were treated in a free and easy and uncontrolled manner (Silver, 1987). Some were deleted from the original list, and evidence from companies not included in the sample was used.

It is asserted that the tenuous link between cultures, excellence, and performance ended up as highly fragile. Included in the sample were companies with far from excellent performance, and a significant number of them subsequently encountered difficulties (Thompson & McHugh, 1990). A taste of the reality of the "people orientation" of one of the companies (*McDonald's*) is given by a critic. Behind the hoop-la and razzle-dazzle of competitive games and prizes lies the dull monotony of "speed-up", and de-skilled work based on the principle of the founder of scientific management (Taylor) at McFactory. The fuel of McFactory is cheap labour, teenage workers, part-time employment, minimum wage, and non-union workers (Silver, 1987).

Recognising the validity of the criticisms of the methodology used in Peters and Waterman's research, it is only fair to stress that this work has significance in promoting an attitude change in favour of the husbandry of human resources in organisations.

The message now projected by serious researchers on corporate culture is that cultures appropriate to today's business environment may be unsuitable, or even lethal, in tomorrow's. As was stated earlier, many of the companies praised by Peters and Waterman encountered difficulties soon afterwards. In a recent book, based on solid empirical data, Kotter and Heskett (1992) maintain that superior financial performance in most market conditions is significantly dependent on having a culture that helps the company anticipate and adapt to changes in its environment. A primary conclusion from the study is that there will only be appropriate adaptation by the company to its environment if all members care deeply about the company's competitive performance, and if the needs of key constituencies—customers, shareholders, and employees—are given serious attention. The company must anticipate and respond appropriately to changes in the preferences and priorities in any of these constituencies.

Deal and Kennedy's Approach

The research of Deal and Kennedy provides another way of comparing and contrasting organisational cultures. Their framework consists of four cultural profiles:

- tough-guy macho;
- work hard, play hard;
- bet your company; and
- process.

Two important factors shape the organisational culture; the first is the extent of the risk connected with the activities of the company, and the second is the speed of feedback on the outcome of employees' decisions (Deal & Kennedy, 1982). These factors are portrayed in Table 11.1, with risk on the vertical axis and feedback on the horizontal axis. The four cultural profiles also appear in the table. In the discussion that follows, an attempt is made (based on Deshpande & Parasuraman, 1986) to relate culture typology to strategic issues connected with marketing and the product life-cycle.

Tough-guy Macho

The heroes in this culture are tough, individualistic, superstitious, and risk takers. They keep up with fashion, and embrace trendy life-styles. They prefer sport that lends itself to solo performance (e.g. squash), and enjoy competitive verbal interactions. They turn a blind eye to co-operative assignments, stress the short-term nature of situations, and rarely learn from their mistakes. The entrepreneurial type in a company run by the

TABLE 11.1

Deal and Kennedy's (1982) Organisational Culture Profiles and Examples of Companies in Each Category

High	*Tough-guy Macho Culture—Examples*	*Bet Your Company Culture—Examples*
	Media	Aerospace
	Consultancy	Oil
	Construction	Capital goods
Risk	*Work Hard, Play Hard Culture*	*Process Culture*
	Computers	Banking
	Car distribution	Pharmaceuticals
	Retail Sales	Public utilities
Low		

Fast ←——————— **Feedback** ———————→ Slow

From Deal, T.E. & Kennedy, A.A. (1982). *Corporate cultures: The rites and rituals of corporate life.* Reading, MA: Addison-Wesley. Reprinted by permission

owner typifies this culture. Organisations associated with this culture can be found in construction, cosmetics, television, radio, venture-capital, and management consultancy.

The tough-guy macho culture has been associated with a situation involving the launch of a new product that does not yield much in the way of profits (Deshpande & Parasuraman, 1986).

Work Hard, Play Hard (Low Risk/Fast Feedback)
The heroes in this culture are super salespeople, friendly, not superstitious, fairly conventional in dress, prefer team sport and socialise in the company of others, and they have a high work rate with quick solutions to problems. They have a short-term perspective and are likely to be associated with companies in the following areas: computers, car distributors, estate agencies, mass-produced goods, and door-to-door selling.

Deshpande and Parasuraman (1986) suggest that a work hard, play hard culture relates to the situation when the product becomes a cash cow (as defined by the Boston Consulting Group), and the market share is large but not really growing.

Bet Your Company (High Risk/Slow Feedback)
The heroes of this culture are technically competent with respect for authority. They show a tendency to double check their decisions, are extremely slow, have a tolerance for ambiguity, and a capacity to make breakthroughs in a scientific sense. Their dress and life-style is fairly conventional and is compatible with their rank in the organisation. They like sport where one is not sure until the end what the outcome of the contest is going to be (e.g. golf), and they act as role models and mentors for younger members of the organisation. The organisations they are attached to (e.g. in oil, defence and aerospace, mining, and capital goods manufacture) are exposed to short-term changes in the economy and can face cash flow problems.

A bet your company culture is more suited to a situation of increasing market share and when the launched product becomes what the Boston Consulting Group call a "star" (Deshpande & Parasuraman, 1986).

Process (Low Risk/Slow Feedback)
The heroes in this culture are rather cautious and protective of their position which requires

the display of an eye for detail, order, and punctuality within the context of well-defined procedures. They put a lot of time into their work, but realise that initiative is not at a premium, while red tape is high on the agenda, as is a penchant for discussing memoranda. Their modest life-style reflects their rank, and they generally engage in low key sporting activities (e.g. jogging). The organisations they are attached to are located in banking, insurance, public utilities, governmental agencies, and pharmaceuticals.

Deshpande and Parasuraman (1986) associate a process culture with a small market share in a growing market, and when the product flops.

Hodgetts (1991) uses the Deal and Kennedy framework to categorise the culture of *AT&T* in the late 1980s. The company, prior to the break-up of the telephone industry in the USA, held a virtual monopoly in the telephone business, and was technology-driven, placing a lot of emphasis on research and development. Among its achievements were touch-dial and portable telephones. After the break-up, competition became severe; the company's culture could now be more accurately described as work hard, play hard, with a very heavy customer-driven momentum.

The cultural profiles shown in Table 11.1 could also be applied to particular functions within business. For example, a research chemist might be classified as the bet your company type and an accountant in a pharmaceutical company as a process type. When companies or individuals move from one type of culture to another, the problems of adjustment should be uppermost in the minds of management. For example, an executive used to functioning in a process culture could experience real culture shock and distress if abruptly moved to a work hard, play hard culture.

Harrison's Four Types

Harrison (1972) identified four types of culture found in organisations as power culture, role culture, support culture, and achievement culture:

1. Power culture is found where senior managers exert considerable influence and power within the organisation, and the managers are likely to manage in an autocratic way.
2. Role culture relates to situations where positions within bureaucratic organisations are the focal point of attention. The demands of bureaucracy (in terms of, for example, compliance with rules) are prominent.
3. Support culture applies where the organisation possesses values and mechanisms to integrate people within a community. The culture promotes a sense of community.
4. Achievement culture values success and personal growth. The climate encourages people to exercise initiative in conditions of high levels of autonomy.

Handy (1985) has been influenced by this typology, and proposes four types of culture related to the structure of organisation. These are power and role cultures (as in Harrison's definition), task cultures (e.g. successful completion of tasks by teams managing projects), and person cultures where the organisational setting is supportive of the individual in his or her pursuit of technical or creative accomplishments.

The evidence presented in this section supports two major conclusions. First, that organisational cultures vary between companies and, second, that organisational cultures influence performance.

DEVELOPMENT OF CULTURE

There are a number of ways to develop organisational culture. To begin with, the norms and desired behaviour must be made explicit, and then reinforced by top management. O'Reilly (1989) has recognised four approaches to the development of organisational culture:

- participation;
- information from others;
- symbolic action; and
- comprehensive reward systems.

Participation

The concept of participation has already been discussed in Chapter 8. It is essentially a process to facilitate the involvement of people in activities considered important by the organisation, and then to offer them recognition for their contributions. It is hoped that voluntary participation through appropriate mechanisms (e.g. quality circles, suggestion schemes, and advisory forums)

will activate responsibility for people's actions and develop commitment to the ideals and policies of the organisation. In this way participation helps to develop and reinforce culture.

Information From Others

A group situation is a powerful setting for the reinforcement of cultural values by colleagues or co-workers, as is apparent when looking at the influence exerted by work groups, discussed in Chapter 7. Where cultural values (e.g. ways of handling customers' complaints) have permeated the fabric of the group, one could expect older workers to provide hints and guidance to new employees on appropriate action and behaviour. If the culture is strong, this could give rise to uniformity of action with respect to certain practices in the organisation.

Symbolic Action

One form of symbolic action is a certain type of management behaviour considered important in the organisation. For example, if

"TEN YEARS AGO, OLD STAN HERE, FOILED ROBBERS BY QUAFFING ALL THE SECRET FORMULA...."

the chief executive of a supermarket chain were to make periodic visits to the company's stores to talk to staff about business and non-business related issues, this could reinforce the importance of this type of managerial style and behaviour.

As stated earlier, a common type of symbolic action is story-telling. For example, the experienced manager tells the new employee about a new recruit in the old days—now a senior manager—who went beyond the call of duty to rescue an awkward situation arising from the breakdown of the production system. The moral in the story is that those who put extra effort into the job will be rewarded with promotion. Story-telling is created as an exercise to reinforce attitudes and beliefs, the adoption of which is critical for corporate success. It is a process that helps to develop and sustain the culture of the company.

Research in social psychology indicates that people use stories or information about a single event more than they use multiple perspectives in arriving at judgements (Borgida & Nisbett, 1977). For example, it is conceivable that a neighbour's bad experience with a particular make of lawn-mower could influence your decision not to purchase that brand, despite favourable statistical evidence about the reliability of the product.

Another type of symbolic action is the mounting of ceremonies to reinforce organisational culture. Examples of these were given earlier when reference was made to recognising the performance of outstanding sales representatives. The rewards given at these ceremonies are meant not only to recognise past performance but also to encourage particular groups of employees to continue working even harder.

Finally, the importance of symbolism and symbolic acts in the management of strategic change is acknowledged by Johnson (1990). He argues that symbolic acts are a significant means by which leaders in organisations can bring about change, and gives the following example of how even symbolic artifacts can represent serious obstructions to change. In a large bank it became clear that the heavy emphasis on manual procedures which were consuming lots of paper, on stories of lending disasters, on the physical barriers of counters, and on job titles such as "tellers" were a severe constraint on developing the entrepreneurial business with a customer focus that the chief executive was seeking to encourage. The paperwork at branches was reduced, counters were removed, and products, systems, terminology, and stories were introduced that were more in line with a marketing-driven company.

Comprehensive Reward Systems

There is a discussion of monetary and non-monetary reward systems in Chapter 2 and in Chapter 13. Most organisations recognise and reinforce approved behaviour and, consequently, individual employees in such organisations feel a sense of satisfaction and accomplishment. Performance-related pay, for example, is often seen as a key factor in shaping employees' attitudes, and the end result is to create a performance-conscious culture (Fowler, 1988; Hendry et al., 1988). In Japan today the appeal of performance-related pay has put the spotlight on the issue of seniority *vs* merit (see panel facing).

Although it is acceptable to reward good performance, it would be unwise to punish those who fail to reach the desired standards because of a depressing effect this could have on others, perhaps eventually leading to risk-aversiveness (Hodgetts, 1991).

Organisational Socialisation

Closely related to these approaches to the development of organisational culture—particularly information from others and symbolic action—is organisational socialisation. The concept of socialisation was discussed in the context of a behavioural perspective on personality in Chapter 1, and

Seniority *vs* Merit in Japan

The Japanese system of paying employees according to seniority worked well for companies while the economy was growing. It fostered corporate loyalty and allowed companies to repay that loyalty in the form of increasing salaries. Seniority was also a method of assessing an employee's contribution to the company, and it complemented the Japanese belief in the value of experience and in the wisdom of old age. But it created a comfortable environment in which mediocre performance was condoned. As the employee's basic salary increased each additional year worked with the company, there was little incentive to improve job performance.

The maturing of the Japanese economy, and the ageing population, have undermined the seniority-based pay system in recent years. It was reported recently in Japan's national economic daily (*Nikkei*) that *Nissan*, Japan's second largest vehicle maker, is considering abolishing seniority-based pay for nearly 3,000 managers and putting them on a performance-related pay scheme. The news that one of Japan's most prominent industrial groups was planning to get rid of the cherished tradition of seniority conveyed to Japan's hard-working "salary man" that the secure life of ever-rising incomes could no longer be taken for granted.

A growing number of Japanese companies are experimenting with schemes that allow salaries to better reflect an employee's performance. *Fujitsu*, which owns *ICL*, is trying to do this with the bonuses its managers receive twice a year. *Honda* now uses a salary system that links pay to the previous year's performance. One lingering fear, even among companies that have embraced performance-related pay, is that greater emphasis on individual performance could destroy the group harmony that has served the Japanese companies so well in the past. However, the changing economic environment is dictating the need to consider merit in systems of pay (Nakamoto, 1993).

in connection with learning in Chapter 4. It is the process by which children learn, for example, to adopt various behavioural patterns, and to recognise what is both acceptable and unacceptable behaviour according to the norms of the society in which they live.

In a similar way to that in which people are socialised into society, they are also socialised into organisations. They perceive over a period of time notions of acceptable and unacceptable behaviour, modes of interaction with others, and ways of expressing their feelings. In the context of culture, organisational socialisation has been described as "the process through which employees learn about a company's culture, subsequently passing their knowledge and understanding on to others" (Moorhead & Griffin, 1992). It is recognised that the important factor in organisational socialisation is the behaviour of experienced people as perceived by newcomers to the organisation (Barney, 1986). This behaviour would include story-telling, and the contents of the stories could be used subsequently by new employees to guide theiractions.

Also, one must not ignore the part played in the socialisation process by formal training, as well as by pamphlets and statements prepared by the company on the culture of the organisation. But equally one should recognise that in some organisations the rhetoric used in pamphlets and training programmes bears little resemblance to the reality of the actual culture as reflected in people's behaviour. For example, a pronounced "people-centred" culture could be enshrined in the publicity literature, but the actual behaviour of managers may be the antithesis of these sentiments.

Having developed a culture appropriate to the company, the organisation cannot sit back and let things happen. The culture must be maintained by reinforcing beliefs, and making sure the cultural values are supported and sustained over time. Basically, this entails a first-rate process of communication of the beliefs and values to all employees, fostering commitment to the culture, and then rewarding people for their commitment (O'Reilly, 1989).

Before examining the benefits of culture in the next section, we shall acknowledge briefly the outcome of research into cultural change and development at *ICI, Jaguar*, and other companies in the UK (Pettigrew, 1990). In this context, a variety of factors could be viewed as important facilitators (see panel below).

Recently, Oglonna (1993) conducted a useful critique of the literature on managing culture, and suggested that there are clearly two ways in which culture is treated in relation to change. There are those who treat culture as behaviour, and those who treat it as

values and taken-for-granted assumptions. The consequence of this confusion is that there is no convincing conceptual model that demonstrates clearly how change of deeper level values should be attained. (There is a discussion of organisational change and development in Chapter 12.)

BENEFITS OF CULTURE

A number of benefits accrue to organisations from the development of an appropriate organisational culture. Hodgetts (1991) identifies the more important as:

Facilitators of Cultural Change and Development in Organisations

- In order to create a climate for change it is helpful to have a receptive external environment, together with managerial skills to take advantage of that environment.
- It is important to have a very clear and consistent drive for change from the apex of the organisation. This could emanate from the leadership displayed by senior or top managers brought into the organisation from outside, or from internal managers who have been pressing for change from a powerful internal position for some time.

  Pettigrew (1985) describes how Sir John Harvey-Jones and others at *ICI* had the licence and ability to think the unthinkable and to say the unsayable. In effect, they were a counter-culture force that changed culture and fostered corporate success, using a more open management style with pronounced decentralisation, together with simplification of the management structure. In addition, there was much emphasis on management and organisational development.
- Somewhat paradoxically, the agents of change at the top of the organisation have inarticulate and imprecise visions.
- Inconsistent action or behaviour is used by key figures in the new administration as a means to raise the level of tension within the organisation so as to promote change.
- Deviants and heretics, both internal and external to the organisation, are allowed to say the unsayable and think the unthinkable. Either internal or external consultants could be used in this context.
- As a means of releasing energy, people are moved about within the organisation and their jobs are changed.

- New forums are created where problems are aired and shared, and where energy is directed at the need for change.
- The nature of the management process at the apex of the organisation is changed. For example, there could be a move from management as a divisive force to it being more coherent and cohesive.
- When the desired cultural change is achieved, structural arrangements should be changed to complement the event. Then the changed culture and structural arrangements could be fortified by the use of the organisation's reward system.
- The key role models who, through their behaviour, project crucial aspects of the new culture, should be identified. These are the people who raise the level of awareness about the cultural change, and reinforce it continuously.
- The message that encapsulates cultural change is transmitted deep into the organisation with the help of training and development strategies. If necessary, the organisational communication processes should be revamped to transmit the message.
- The agents of change should persist with their strategy, but equally they have to be patient because breaking down the core beliefs of the old culture is quite a complex process. Sensing and articulating the new issues and convincing others that they are worthy of serious attention is no easy task, and this stage could be studded by very inarticulate and imprecise visions of the future (Pettigrew, 1990).

- effective control;
- normative order;
- promotion of innovation;
- strategy formulation and implementation; and
- strong commitment from employees.

Effective Control

A strong culture is reflected in shared beliefs and expectations that exact compliance. As such, organisational culture acts as a control mechanism in regulating behaviour. As culture seeps through the organisation, people register what they should do (e.g. perform efficiently and effectively and keep a firm grip on the quality of the product or service) and what they should not do (e.g. engage in poor team-work or be disrespectful to customers). When employees do not act in accordance with the beliefs and values of the culture, managers and colleagues are likely to intervene and initiate corrective action.

An example of measures taken to exert control in a cultural context involved the founders of a consultancy firm who established an open and charismatic managerial style capable of generating strong emotional ties among the consultants employed. The work undertaken by the consultants tended to be variable and flexible, and not amenable to conventional mechanisms of control. Obviously, this presented a problem for the management, more so because the work was carried out at the workplace of the client, with the potential for weakening the consultant's sense of identity with the firm. A corrective measure used in this situation was to develop a large number of social and leisure activities, underlining the value of fun, body contact, and support from colleagues. In addition, presentations were made about the firm's performance in order to promote favourable perceptions. The outcome of these processes was the building of social and emotional ties, and the adoption by the firm of a community culture (Alvesson, 1988).

Normative Order

The use of norms to guide behaviour (discussed in Chapter 7) is intimately connected with effective control. Norms reflect the culture, and in strong cultures they attract wide support and promote consensus. In weak cultures the consensus may still be there, but the support is weak. The problem with strong cultures that underpin strategies and behaviour is the great difficulty in changing them when business conditions dictate different directions with respect to markets and behaviour. When strong cultures support the right strategy for a company, the marriage of culture and strategy is a powerful mix in terms of company performance. But strong cultures that are the antithesis of efficiency and effectiveness, such as "quality is an expensive luxury", could be counter-productive.

Promotion of Innovation

The culture of an organisation can encourage creative thinking by the development of norms that support the promotion of innovation. O'Reilly (1989), having investigated norms supporting innovation across a wide range of industries, found a high degree of commonality between them in terms of their importance to managers, and that certain norms (listed in Table 11.2) were found to be useful in supporting and facilitating the process of innovation. Apart from the encouragement of creative thinking, subscribing to the norms was helpful to staff when faced with conflicts that emerge when ideas are proposed and implemented. (Creativity was also discussed in Chapter 5.)

Strategy Formulation and Implementation

There are occasions when organisational culture informs the adoption of a particular strategy for the company. For example, an important feature in the financial and market success of the US corporation, *Motorola*, is its

TABLE 11.2

Norms That Promote Innovation

Norms to Promote Creativity	*Norms to Promote Implementation*
1. Risk Taking	**1. Common Goals**
• Freedom to try things and fail • Acceptance of mistakes • Allow discussion of "dumb" ideas • No punishments for failure • Challenge the status quo • Forget the past • Willingness not to focus on the short term • Expectation that innovation is part of job • Positive attitudes about change • Drive to improve	• Sense of pride in the organisation • Teamwork • Willingness to share the credit • Flexibility in jobs, budgets, functional areas • Sense of ownership • Eliminate mixed messages • Manage interdependencies • Shared visions and a common direction • Build consensus • Mutual respect and trust • Concern for the whole organisation
2. Rewards for Change	**2. Autonomy**

• Respect for new ideas
• Build into the structure:
  • budgets • opportunities • time
  • tools • resources • promotions
• Top management attention and support
• Celebration of accomplishments
• Suggestions are implemented
• Encouragement
	• Decision-making responsibility at lower levels
	• Decentralised procedures
	• Freedom to act
	• Expectation of action
	• Belief that you can have an impact
	• Delegation
	• Quick, flexible decision making
	• Minimise the bureaucracy

3. Openness	**3. Belief in Action**
• Open communication and share information • Listen better • Open access • Bright people, strong egos • Scanning, broad thinking • Force exposure outside the company • Move people around • Encourage lateral thinking • Adopt the customer's perspective • Accept criticism • Don't be too sensitive • Continuous training • Intellectual honesty • Expect and accept conflict • Willingness to consult others	• Don't be obsessed with precision • Emphasis on results • Meet your commitments • Anxiety about timeliness • Value getting things done • Hard work is expected and appreciated • Empower people • Emphasis on quality • Eagerness to get things done • Cut through the bureaucracy

Source: O'Reilly, C. (1989). Corporations, culture, and commitment: Motivation and social control in organisations. *California Management Review*, Summer, *31*, 19–23.

strong commitment to substantial investment in research and development, and to the commercial exploitation of the ensuing inventions. The culture of the company has been created around significant research and development, high quality, and active enthusiasm for customer service (Thierren, 1989). What is interesting to note is that this culture has bolstered the strategy of the company, providing the impetus for the development of new products—e.g. light-weight cellular telephones and wrist-watch pagers, which have been hailed as major technological breakthroughs.

Currently there is an interest in corporate creativity associated with "reinventing strategy". Gary Hamel recently addressed the Annual Conference of the Strategic Management Society (September, 1993), and maintained that companies are pressurised by investors to improve the efficiency of their current operations and resources, but are not sufficiently stimulated to create new markets, products, or even industries. Downsizing seems to rule, with an epidemic of corporate anorexia (Lorenz, 1993a). Observations attributable to Hamel on reinventing strategy appear in the panel below.

Employee Commitment

The interaction of people and culture has reinforcing qualities, frequently resulting in committed employees. As employees develop their skills on the job, including interactive skills, there is a favourable impact on the level of morale which, in turn, enhances commitment to the organisation. The commitment is said to go through three phases, as identified in relation to the three sources of attitude change introduced in Chapter 6—i.e. compliance, identification, and internalisation.

With regard to compliance, people conform in order to obtain some material benefit. When they reach the identification stage, the demands of culture are accepted in order to maintain good relationships with colleagues. In the final phase—internalisation—people find that the adoption of the cultural values of the organisation produces intrinsic satisfaction because these values are in line with their own personal values. In many ways this is an ideal state as far as the acceptance of organisational values is concerned (because of the identification with the company), and if widespread is indicative of a strong culture.

The benefits of culture could be short-lived when unwelcome mergers or hostile takeover bids undermine the stability of corporate culture. It may not be easy to sustain loyalty

---

Reinventing Strategy

Restructuring (downsizing and delayering) was necessary because it made companies smaller, and so was process engineering because it made them better. But without the reinvention of strategy they would not become different and better. The only way a company can get ahead is to foresee the next round of competitive advantage and evolution in its industry and to create it. The biggest rewards will ultimately go to companies that transform their industries, change the rules of the game, redraw industry boundaries, and establish fundamentally new competitive parameters. The primary goal must be to become the architect of an industry's transformation.

One should note the barriers to reinventing strategy. These are:

- There are too many senior people in the organisation from the same industry, discipline, or cultural background who are blind to new opportunities.
- There are powerful figures in organisations with out-of-date knowledge.
- There are obvious difficulties because the industry is still emerging and its boundaries are ill-defined. In which case it would be probably better to concentrate on and exploit the organisation's core competencies (Lorenz, 1993a).

and identification with the company when possible threats to job security, or the removal of benefits are perceived. In other circumstances, the expected benefits of a merger of companies or a joint venture fail to materialise. For example, harmonisation of outlook does not occur because employees accustomed to performing their duties in a particular way are unable to subscribe to a different set of values brought about by the change in strategic direction of the enlarged enterprise. (There is a section on organisational commitment in Chapter 6.)

As a final comment on commitment, Peters (1992) advises employers to look for passion and commitment towards the work itself rather than loyalty to the company. However, this could be problematic for those who have very mundane jobs.

INTERNATIONAL COMPARISONS

Earlier (in reporting Ouchi's work) there was reference to comparisons between American and Japanese companies. In this section there will be an examination of cultural differences at the societal level likely to impinge on the way organisations operate. Those whose work takes them across cultural and national boundaries face different legal and political systems, as well as different primary values and practices that characterise particular countries.

Increasingly, managers in organisations are thinking internationally, and this is prompted by the creation of the single market in the European community, developments within the former Soviet bloc, and the growing importance of the Pacific Rim countries (e.g. China, Japan, South Korea, Taiwan, Hong Kong, and Singapore). The means at the disposal of managers to assist them in understanding and coping with cultural barriers that exist between countries are, basically, training programmes and direct experience of interacting and doing business with international clients and customers.

Cross-cultural Study

Hofestede (1980) conducted a cross-cultural study of a large number of employees of a multinational company in many locations throughout the world in order to identify similarities and differences between national cultures. The research data was analysed in such a way as to eliminate any differences that might be due to varying practices and policies in different companies. As a result, any variations found between countries were attributed to national culture. Four dimensions (listed here and in Table 11.3) which show differences between national cultures were discovered, and a culture could be rated high or low on these dimensions.

- power distance;
- uncertainty avoidance;
- individualism–collectivism; and
- masculine–femininity.

Power Distance

This dimension evaluates the extent to which a culture encourages superiors to exercise power. A culture ranked high in power distance encouraged the expectation that superiors wielded much power, with the recognition of a power imbalance between superiors and subordinates. Although subordinates showed a preference for a directive management style, this culture exemplified low trust between superiors and subordinates. Also, subordinates tended to be passive, organisation structure tended to be tall, and decision making centralised. Examples of countries falling into this category are Panama, Korea, Hong Kong, and Singapore.

By contrast, in a culture ranked low in power distance there was a closer relationship between superiors and subordinates, with greater mutual trust, and a firm expectation by subordinates to be involved in decision making. Apart from the tendency towards decentralisation, organisation structures would tend to be flatter. The UK, USA, The

TABLE 11.3

Four Dimensions on Which National Cultures Vary

The Power Distance Dimension (POW)

Low	*High*
(Australia, Israel, Denmark, Sweden)	(Philippines, Mexico, Venezuela, India, Brazil)
* Less centralisation	* Greater centralisation
* Flatter organisation pyramids	* Tall organisation pyramids
* Smaller wage differentials	* More supervisory personnel
* Structure in which manual and clerical work are equal jobs	* Structure in which white-collar jobs are valued more than blue-collar jobs

The Masculinity–Femininity Dimension (MAS)

Low	*High*
(Sweden, Denmark, Thailand, Finland, Yugoslavia)	(Japan, Australia, Venezuela, Italy, Mexico)
* Sex roles are minimised	* Sex roles are clearly differentiated
* Organisations do not interfere with people's private lives	* Organisations may interfere to protect their interests
* More women in more qualified jobs	* Fewer women are in qualified jobs
* Soft, yielding, intuitive skills are rewarded	* Aggression, competition, and justice are rewarded
* Social rewards are valued	* Work is valued as a central life interest

The Individualism–Collectivism Dimension (IND)

Low	*High*
(Venezuela, Columbia, Taiwan, Mexico, Greece)	(United States, Australia, Great Britain, Canada, The Netherlands)
* Organisation as "family"	* Organisation is more impersonal
* Organisation defends employee interests	* Employees defend their own self-interests
* Practices are based on loyalty, a sense of duty and group participation	* Practices encourage individual initiative

The Uncertainty Avoidance Dimension (UNC)

Low	*High*
(Denmark, Sweden, Great Britain, United States, India)	(Greece, Portugal, Japan, Peru, France)
* Less structuring of activities	* More structuring activities
* Fewer written rules	* More written rules
* More generalists	* More specialists
* Variability	* Standardisation
* Greater willingness to take risks	* Less willingness to take risks
* Less ritualistic behaviour	* More realistic behaviour

Source: Furnham, A. & Gunter, B. (1993). *Corporate culture: Diagnosis and change.* In C.L. Cooper & I.T. Robertson (Eds.), *International Review of Industrial and Organisational Psychology.* Chichester: Wiley.

Netherlands, Australia, and Canada would fall into this category.

Uncertainty Avoidance

This dimension is concerned with the extent to which a culture encourages or discourages risk taking. In certain cultures—e.g. Japan, Iran, and Turkey—there tended to be strict laws with stiff penalties for deviants. Need for security was high, and those with expert knowledge were respected. Managers tended to be low risk takers. Cultures rated high on uncertainty avoidance adopted particular strategies to counteract the high levels of anxiety and stress stemming from uncertain situations. These strategies included working hard, not changing jobs, and being unsympathetic to those not obeying the rules.

In the opposite situation, where cultures are rated low on uncertainty avoidance—e.g. Hong Kong and Taiwan—people tended to experience less stress from ambiguous situations, and attached less importance to adhering to the rules. Generally, people had strong feelings of personal competence and managers seemed more prepared to take risks.

Individualism–Collectivism

This dimension evaluates the extent to which a culture possesses individualistic features rather than group or societal features. The individualistic orientation, prevalent in the UK, Canada, and the USA, puts the spotlight on such characteristics as achievement and the use of personal initiative, with more inward concerns based on the self and the family.

By contrast, in a collectivist culture—e.g. Singapore, Philippines, and Mexico—the individual receives help and support from the extended family and tribal group, and is expected to reciprocate with loyalty. The emphasis could be on belonging, having a sense of duty, and a strong belief in the power of group decision making.

Masculinity–Femininity

This dimension portrays the type of accomplishments valued by the culture. In societies where masculinity prevailed—e.g. the UK, Germany, Japan, South Africa, and Italy—emphasis was placed on money, material possessions, and ambition, with clear lines drawn between male and female roles. A lot of emphasis could be placed on challenge and advancement and people are encouraged to be individual decision makers.

By contrast, where femininity prevailed—e.g. The Netherlands and Scandinavia—emphasis was placed on co-operation, friendly atmosphere, job security, caring, quality of life, and the environment, with blurred lines drawn between sex roles, and greater sexual equality. Group decision making is encouraged, and managers find it easy to subscribe to the value of giving autonomy to subordinates.

Hofestede located 40 cultures on a global cultural map, with each of these dimensions representing a continuum along which each culture is placed. There have been criticisms of Hofestede's work. For example, Tyson and Jackson (1992) maintain that:

> Hofestede's work deals in generalisations. There may indeed be national characteristics, but it is likely that there are major variations within societies. The notion that all managers have the same vision of power distance or uncertainty avoidance in the US or UK, for example, is absurd. The diversity at the organisational level means we must only use this research with caution, and not seek to perpetuate stereotypes.

Similarly, Furnham and Gunter (1993) state that "there appears to be very little evidence demonstrating the veracity, as opposed to the simplificatory appeal, of the different systems". They offer little in the way of process (e.g. their origin, maintenance, and impact); instead they are descriptive.

Though Hofestede's research and findings may have weaknesses, it would be unwise to relegate to insignificance the need to understand values underpinning culture, and the impact of culture on organisations. Other researchers have adopted Hofestede's approach to cultural clustering (i.e. the grouping of similar cultures). For example, Ronen and Shenkar (1985) concluded that most countries could be classified using eight basic cultural clusters— Nordic, Germanic, Anglo, Latin, European, Far Eastern, Arab, and Near Eastern.

In recent years, the conclusion from a survey of cross-cultural differences in management practices conducted by two management consultants (Grey & Thöne, 1990) states that:

> Our international research highlights cross-cultural differences in organisational readiness to meet the strategic challenges posed by Europe 1992. It reveals a European corporate culture which embodies greater vision, responsiveness, innovation, and employee involvement than the North American culture. The research further depicts a hard-driving, achievement-orientated North American culture which stresses individual performance and extrinsic rewards.

International Manager

Attempts have been made to differentiate between the effective and less effective international manager. In a survey of participants attending programmes at two major European business schools (Ratiu, 1983), it was concluded that the most effective international managers were those who were perceptive in a social sense, relied on intuition, monitored situations carefully, and adapted well. Their less effective counterparts were prone to evaluating situations in a rational way, were on the look out for patterns of behaviour that could then be used to put forward overall explanations, and tended to be withdrawn socially.

To operate in the international sphere it is said that possessing the right mental attitude ("mindset") and viewing the organisation as international in orientation is important. To arrive at this position requires adjustments along the following lines (Bolt, 1988):

- Communication systems need to be developed so that the organisation is aware of political developments likely to affect its trade.

- The structure of the organisation should be capable of coping with the distinctive international challenges.
- Management teams should be created with an international outlook and an ability to respond to the demands of world markets.
- The composition of the top management team should be international.
- Management development should be geared to creating a pool of senior managers who can operate with ease on the international scene.

The notion of the Euromanager, who will have experience of operating in a number of European countries, is now emerging. This will entail consideration of qualifications, conditions of service, rewards, and the development of managers across cultures in Europe. The *3M* company is spawning Euromanagers at a significant rate, and this is in line with the internationalism of its top management. International experience is a key to top careers (Lorenz, 1993b). The nature of the development of the Euromanager will be dependent on companies' strategies to meet the demands of Europe in the mid-1990s and beyond (Bournois & Chauchat, 1990).

Convergence or Divergence?

In comparative studies of different countries, a combination of culture and other factors (e.g. laws, state institutions, and mechanisms of economic control) influence various organisational processes. For example, in Chapter 8 when discussing macro participation, we witnessed differences between the UK and Germany. Likewise in Chapter 9, we noticed the influence of culture when looking at styles of handling conflict in different national settings, and, in Chapter 13, cultural differences are highlighted with regard to the use of management selection methods. Therefore, distinctive national circumstances should be considered when examining the application of concepts from organisational behaviour—e.g. leadership and motivation—to the organisational world.

An alternative view is that instead of the divergence acknowledged here, we could expect a form of convergence to arise where similarities between organisations in different countries will be more significant than differences, particularly for the multinational company. The latter allows staff from different countries to rub shoulders, and the combination of similar experiences and exposure to common organisational socialisation processes facilitates the transmission of ideas and the absorption of common values. Certain organisational

cultures (e.g. the old *IBM* culture) can be so potent as to hold in check national culture as determinants of behaviour. However, generally one has to acknowledge a fair amount of diversity between countries.

Postscript
The following observations have been made on the current status of culture. Oglonna (1993) points out that "the concept of culture has lost much of its value as a tool for analysing and interpreting the behaviour of people within organisations, and has reached the decline stage in its life-cycle. It may never be exterminated, but is unlikely to be as hot a topic in the 1990s as it was in the 1980s."

In similar vein, Furnham and Gunter (1993) conclude that "the corporate culture concept issue debate is here with us for some time to come. While it will no doubt lose its popular appeal as it gets replaced by yet another popular 'solution' to all management problems, it has uncovered enough of a hornet's nest among academics from different disciplines and epistemological perspectives to provide arguments and research for many years to come."

SUMMARY: ORGANISATIONAL CULTURE

- Culture is a complex phenomenon and not easy to define. One definition of corporate or organisational culture suggests that it "consists of the expected behaviour, actions, and values that people in an enterprise are expected to follow". It is reflected in company practices, company communications, physical cultural forms, and common language. The notion of sub-cultures was noted briefly.

- Researchers and practitioners have come forward with different approaches to capture the values embedded in organisational culture. For example, Ouchi's approach consists of a list of seven points used in comparing three types of companies—the typical

American, the typical Japanese and the type Z American. The cultures of the typical Japanese companies and type Z American companies are different from the cultures of typical American companies.

- Another approach is that of Peters and Waterman, who identified management practices associated with success. They pinpointed cultural factors—attributes of excellence—which led to successful management practices. This work has had a good reception, primarily among practitioners, but the research has been criticised by academics.

- Deal and Kennedy's approach compares and contrasts organisational cultures using four cultural profiles. These profiles are considered in the context of risk and feedback, and are applicable at both the organisational and departmental levels.

- The final approach—of Harrison—relates culture to organisation.
- There are a number of ways to develop organisational cultures, such as participation, information from others, symbolic action, comprehensive reward systems, and organisational socialisation. The development of culture at *ICI* and other UK companies was mentioned.
- Certain benefits, such as effective control, normative order, promotion of innovation, strategy formulation and implementation, and strong commitment from employees are said to accrue to the organisation from

the development of an appropriate organisational culture.

- A section on international comparisons was devoted to how national cultures influence organisation structure and processes. Hofestede is a major contributor to this debate. He differentiated between national cultures on the basis of power distance, uncertainty avoidance, individualism–collectivism, and masculinity–femininity.
- The Euromanager or international manager was noted, and the issue of convergence in the application of behavioural theories across cultures was addressed.
- Finally, the current status of culture was briefly noted.

QUESTIONS

1. What is meant by corporate or organisational culture?
2. Comment on the significance of sub-cultures.
3. Identify ways in which culture manifests itself within organisations.
4. Examine the frameworks for analysing organisational culture, and state which one you feel is the more credible.
5. What criticisms have been levelled at the Peters and Waterman approach?
6. Comment on the role of symbolic action in the development of culture.
7. Comment on the nature of research into cultural change and development in the UK.

8. What do we mean by organisational socialisation?
9. List the benefits associated with an appropriate corporate culture, ranking them in order of importance from your particular point of view.
10. What conclusions can we draw from Hofestede's cross-cultural study?
11. Examine the criticism levelled at Hofestede's research.
12. "To operate in the international sphere it is said that possessing the right attitude (or mindset) and viewing the organisation as international in orientation is important." Discuss.

REFERENCES

Alvesson, M. (1988). *Management, corporate culture, and labour process in a professional service company.* Unpublished paper presented at The Conference on the Labour Process. Aston/UMIST.

Barney, J.B. (1986). Organisational culture: Can it be a source of sustained competitive advantage? *Academy of Management Review*, July, 656–665.

Bolt, J.F. (1988). Global competitors: Some criteria for success. *Business Horizons*, January/February, 34–41.

Borgida, E. & Nisbett, R.E. (1977). The differential impact of abstract vs. concrete information on decisions *Journal of Applied Social Psychology*, July–September, 258–271.

Bournois, F. & Chauchat, J.H. (1990). Managing managers in Europe. *European Management Journal,* 8, 3–18.

Dawkins, W. (1993). Costly burden of tradition. *Financial Times,* 1 December, p. 10.

Deal, T.E. & Kennedy, A.A. (1982). *Corporate cultures: The rites and rituals of corporate life.* Reading, MA: Addison-Wesley.

Deshpande, R. & Parasuraman, A. (1986). Linking corporate culture to strategic planning. *Business Horizons,* 3, 28–37.

Eglin, R. & Barber, L. (1981). Japan's rising sun in Britain. *The Sunday Times,* 6th December, 56–57.

Fowler, A. (1988). New directions in performance-related pay. *Personnel Management,* November, 30–34.

Furnham, A. & Gunter, B. (1993). Corporate culture: Diagnosis and change. In C.L. Cooper & I.T. Robertson (Eds.), *International Review of Industrial and Organisational Psychology.* Chichester: Wiley.

Grey, R.J. & Thöne, T.J.F. (1990). Differences between North American and European corporate cultures. *Canadian Business Review,* Autumn, 26–30.

Hampden-Turner, C. (1990). *Corporate cultures: From vicious to virtuous circles.* London: Random Century.

Handy, C.B. (1985). *Understanding organisations* (third edition). London: Penguin.

Harrison, R. (1972). Understanding your organisation's character. *Harvard Business Review,* May–June, 119–128.

Hendry, C., Pettigrew, A., & Sparrow, P. (1988). Changing patterns of human resource management. *Personnel Management,* November, 37–41

Hodgetts, R.M. (1991). *Organisational behaviour: Theory and practice.* New York: Macmillan.

Hofestede, G. (1980). *Culture's consequences.* Beverley Hills, CA: Sage Publications.

Johnson, G. (1990). Managing strategic change: The role of symbolic action. *British Journal of Management,* 1, 183–200.

Kotter, J.P. & Heskett, J.L.. (1992). *Corporate culture and performance.* New York: Free Press/Macmillan.

Lorenz, C. (1993a). Corporate creativity. No less than rebirth. *Financial Times,* 4 October, p. 10.

Lorenz, C. (1993b). Here, there and everywhere (the lives of 3M's managers). *Financial Times,* 10 November, p. 11.

Moorhead, G. & Griffin, R.W. (1992). *Organisational behaviour* (third edition). Boston: Houghton Mifflin.

Nakamoto, M. (1993). When seniority is replaced by merit. *Financial Times,* 1 December, p. 10.

Oglonna, E. (1993). Managing organisational culture: Fantasy or reality. *Human Resource Management Journal,* Winter 1992–93, 42–54.

O'Reilly, C. (1989). Corporations, culture, and commitment: Motivation and social control in organisations. *California Management Review,* Summer, 31, 19–23.

Ouchi, W.G. (1981). *Theory Z: How American business can meet the Japanese challenge.* Reading, MA: Addison-Wesley.

Peters, T. (1992). *Liberation management: Necessary disorganisation for the nanosecond nineties.* Macmillan.

Peters, T.J. & Waterman, R.H. (1982). *In search of excellence: Lessons from America's best-run companies.* New York: Harper & Row.

Pettigrew, A.M. (1979). On studying organisational culture. *Administrative Science Quarterly,* December, 570–581.

Pettigrew, A.M. (1985). *The awakening giant: Continuity and change in ICI.* Oxford: Blackwell.

Pettigrew, A.M. (1990). Is corporate culture manageable? In D.C. Wilson & R.H. Rosenfeld (Eds.), *Managing organisations: Text, readings, and cases.* Maidenhead, UK: McGraw-Hill.

Pollack, A. (1993). New skill in Japan: Learning to cope when lifetime contract is broken. *International Herald Tribune,* 22nd/23rd May, 5.

Ratiu, I. (1983). Thinking internationally. *International Studies in Management and Organisation,* Spring/Summer, 139–150.

Ronen, S. & Shenkar O. (1985). Clustering countries on attitudinal dimensions: A review and synthesis. *Academy of Management Journal,* September, 435–454.

Schein, E.H. (1990). Organisational culture. *American Psychologist,* 45, 109–119.

Sieff, Lord (1981). It's people who matter. *The Sunday Times,* 13th December.

Silver, J. (1987). The ideology of excellence: Management and neo-conservatism. *Studies in Political Economy,* 24, Autumn, 1, 5–29.

Thierren, L. (1989). The rival Japan respects. *Business Week,* 13th November, 108–120.

Thompson, P. & McHugh, D. (1990). *Work organisation: A critical introduction.* London: Macmillan Education.

Tighe, C. (1981). A test-bed for togetherness. *The Sunday Times,* 6 December.

Trice, H.M. & Beyer, J.M. (1984). Studying organisational cultures through rites and rituals. *Academy of Management Review,* 9, 653–669.

Tyson, S. & Jackson, T. (1992). *The essence of organisational behaviour.* Hemel Hempstead, UK: Prentice-Hall.

12

Organisational Change and Development

After a description of the nature of change, resistance to change is examined. Next there is an analysis of sources of resistance to change, and an examination of approaches to controlling resistance to change. Ways of planning organisational change are then discussed. The final part of the chapter concentrates on organisational development through the application of behavioural science-based techniques and their evaluation.

This chapter deals with a number of issues that are relevant to material discussed in other chapters. For example: team-building (Chapter 7); power, politics, and conflict (Chapter 9); culture (Chapter 11); training (Chapter 4); attitude change (Chapter 6); managerial leadership (Chapter 8); personality (Chapter 1); motivation and job design (Chapter 2); and organisation design (Chapter 10).

ORGANISATIONAL CHANGE

Change is omnipresent in society, and is reflected in many forms. We find changes in values and tastes in society generally having an impact on markets, and ultimately they affect the way companies are organised and managed. Likewise, there are changes within organisations brought about by the application of new technology to work processes and products. All these are examples of organisations responding to events in their environment. Organisations can also influence their environments by internally generated changes, such as innovations that command wide acceptance in the external world.

It is safe to say that a number of organisations find it difficult to accommodate the many forces for change impinging on their structure. However, one must accept that change is not a recent phenomenon: change has always been with us, but now it is more intense and occurs more frequently and rapidly than in the past (Gottlieb, 1988). The main focus in this part of the chapter will be:

- sources of resistance to change;
- controlling that resistance, and;
- planning organisational change.

RESISTANCE TO ORGANISATIONAL CHANGE

Change creates uncertainty as to what the future holds, and as a consequence can lead to personal insecurity. Therefore, it is not surprising to encounter resistance to change within organisations.

An organisational change, such as a move to a better office, can be warmly accepted, simply because it is seen to have obvious advantages. But not all changes fit into this category. Where changes create ambiguity and uncertainty, then resistance to change is likely to emerge. In essence, the resistance is not to change as such—rather it is to the personal loss (or possibility of personal loss) that people believe will accompany the change (Burke, 1982).

There are occasions when employees (both superiors and subordinates) fear the introduction of new technology to their work (e.g. the automation of office systems) because of a feeling that they may be unable to cope with the job in the changed circumstances. Also, certain employees, particularly the older ones, fear that they may lose the personal investment (in terms of skill and experience) in the current system. For example, print workers in the newspaper industry vehemently resisted proposals to computerise their work in the early 1980s because of the perceived ramifications of the proposed change in terms of job loss, status, benefits, and conditions generally.

Sources of Resistance

Katz and Kahn (1978) identified six sources of resistance to change operating at the level of the organisation. Most of these sources are people-centred and are connected with people being fearful of loss in one form or another—e.g. loss of power, or resources, or the loss of the security of a predictable routine. The six sources, which do not necessarily reside in all situations of organisational change, are detailed in the panel below.

Moving away from the organisational level, a number of specific individual factors

---

Sources of Resistance to Change at the Level of the Organisation

- *Over-determination*: The structure of the organisation is designed to maintain stability by resorting to an elaborate process regulating such activities as recruitment, selection, training, rewards, and performance appraisal. The organisational system is over-determined in the sense that lesser control or safeguards could achieve the same outcome. As a result, the elaborate structure could become an impediment to change.
- *Narrow focus of change*: On many occasions efforts to introduce change in organisations take a rather narrow focus, instead of considering the likely knock-on effects arising from the existence of normal interdependencies between tasks, structure, and people found in organisations.
- *Group inertia*: The norms of the group constrain attempts by individuals to change their behaviour. In fact the group is obstructive. This could arise when the group refuses to engage in complementary behaviour in order to reinforce the position of the individual.
- *Threatened expertise*: A change to a job may result in an alteration to, for example, the skills requirement of that job. Such an eventuality may pose a threat to people's expertise developed over many years, with the inevitable consequence of resistance to change.
- *Threatened power*: A reorganisation may lead to changing the existing pattern of decision making. For individuals who benefited in the past from exercising the power to make decisions, but now stand to lose a significant part of their power base, the reorganisation may trigger resistance to change.
- *Resource allocation*: Individuals could be quite content with the way resources are currently allocated to them. A change that heralds less than satisfactory arrangements for individuals previously satisfied with the status quo, is likely to be resisted (Katz & Kahn , 1978).

have been identified as sources of resistance to change (Bedeian, 1980; Nadler, 1983; Zaltman & Duncan, 1977):

- *Habit*: A change to well-established procedures and practices could create discomfort and resistance on the part of a person who is very familiar with the current system. Inevitably this person is expected to make an extra effort (without necessarily receiving extra remuneration) to learn the new mode of operation. It is therefore understandable that this situation could give rise to resistance to the proposed change.
- *Security*: Doing things in a familiar way brings comfort and security, and people are likely to resist change if they perceive their security to be threatened.
- *Economic considerations*: People may fear that change could threaten the very existence of their jobs as presently constituted, and eventually lead to the loss of a salary or wage. As a result, they resist change.
- *Fear of the unknown*: Some people fear anything unfamiliar. Any disruption of familiar patterns within the organisation, such as changes in reporting relationships, may create fear. This might arise with people thinking that their flow of work will not be as smooth and as fast as previously because they believe it will take time to get to grips with the changed arrangements.
- *Lack of awareness*: Due to selectivity in perception, a person may overlook a critical facet in a change process. It could be that the facet ignored—e.g. requiring a double signature on travel expense claims— is something the person is opposed to, and somehow it is conveniently overlooked. As a result, there is no change in the person's behaviour (at least initially) as far as the changed practice is concerned.
- *Social considerations*: The motivation to resist change may spring from a group. If a change to rules and regulations was unilaterally imposed by management, but

resisted by a work group, a member of that group may oppose the change simply because acceptance of the change could amount to disapproval and perhaps be subjected to the application of sanctions operated by the group. (Group inertia was mentioned earlier as a source of resistance to change at the organisational level.)

An alternative perspective on the main sources of resistance to change, with some similarity to issues discussed earlier, follows.

Parochial Self-interest   People are anxious to maintain the status quo because of the benefits associated with it. Change could pose a threat to present advantages in terms of power, status, and security, and could undermine valued relationships developed over time, lead to unwanted geographic moves, and deny opportunities for social intercourse. Also, people may have invested heavily in knowledge and skills related to current jobs and systems, and see change as a threat to this investment. For these reasons people resist change.

Misunderstandings and Lack of Trust   If people do not understand what the change entails, why it is necessary, and what it is likely to lead to, then resistance can be expected. Where there is a climate of mistrust between managers and subordinates, management may be reluctant to disseminate information about proposed changes. Where information is given it may be incomplete or distorted. If this is the case, then one can expect to find conditions conducive to the creation of uncertainty and the spreading of rumours. Such a situation creates a climate in which people feel threatened. As a consequence, they become defensive and erect barriers to further flows of information about the proposed changes.

Contradictory Assessments   Not everybody shares the same view of the impact change is going to have. People will see different advantages and disadvantages to change. This situation is more prevalent when information about change is inadequate, and where certain key people are not well briefed. However, it is alleged that certain beneficial happenings spring from what appears to be an unsatisfactory situation. These are the airing of constructive criticisms, hopefully leading to an improvement in the proposals for change.

Low Tolerance of Change   People tend to have different abilities and skills to handle the ambiguity and uncertainty heralded by change. If the proposed changes require people to think and behave in a manner that they are not accustomed to, then one can expect a challenge to the concept the individuals have of themselves. If people have low tolerance for the ambiguity and uncertainty associated with change, this could be expressed in fundamental reservations about their competency to cope. Their apprehension and anxiety could motivate them to oppose or resist changes which at the cognitive level they acknowledge as beneficial (Bedeian, 1980).

A rich analysis of the dynamics of personality, including coping strategies, is provided by Leonard (1984) in the context of the individual's resistance to systems of control within the organisation. This places personality, discussed in Chapter 1, in a firm interface position with sources of resistance to change.

Controlling Resistance to Change

Encountering resistance to change should be used as an opportunity to re-examine the proposal for change. Resistance can be constructive if it forces managers to interact more frequently with subordinates, to review the decision to introduce change, and perhaps to explore alternative ways to meet the desired objective. It is possible that the alternative means to the desired end may be an improvement on those originally proposed, and equally could involve less resistance (Moorhead & Griffin, 1992). Also, the action taken by management to review the proposed change that is the cause of resistance may be perceived by employees as a desirable symbolic gesture, conveying the impression that management cares about them and has respect for their viewpoint (Pfeffer, 1981).

Six approaches have been put forward as ways of controlling resistance to change (Kotter & Schlesinger, 1979):

- education and communication;
- participation;
- facilitation and support;
- negotiation and agreement;
- manipulation and co-option; and
- coercion.

Education and communication

The reason for resorting to education and communication is to convey to employees the logic of the change, for by doing so it is assumed that resistance can be reduced. Education and communication can take place through the use of memoranda, reports, one-to-one discussions, and group presentations.

An important consideration for the use of communication and education as an approach is the belief that the source of resistance lies in misinformation or poor communication.

Therefore, it is assumed that misunderstandings will disappear and resistance becomes less of a problem if the full facts are placed at the disposal of employees. However, in a climate of mistrust an approach of this nature may not result in bringing about change successfully. Also, it could be a time-consuming exercise.

Participation

This approach, discussed in Chapter 8, is adopted in the belief that if people capable of making a valid contribution are involved in the decision process leading up to the sanctioning of change, they are unlikely to resist the outcome of a decision to which they have contributed. This type of involvement gives people the opportunity to utilise their knowledge and skills and allay their fears about the impact of change on them. Also, it is likely that they are going to be committed to the change. However, the potential for compromise on decisions relating to change in a participative forum is always present. This could be considered a drawback of the participative approach, and so could the time consumed in this process.

Facilitation and Support

Various supportive mechanisms to reduce resistance, such as counselling and training, could be used. These could eventually facilitate the process of adapting to change, particularly in conditions where fear and anxiety are high among employees. Again, this approach can be time consuming and expensive, with no guarantee of success arising from the adoption of these mechanisms.

Negotiation and Agreement

A negotiation process could be used in cases where it is believed that resistance to change is coming from a powerful group. This group may stand to lose a substantial advantage as a consequence of the change. As a result, management negotiates with those resisting change to pave the way for the satisfactory implementation of the proposed change. Inevitably, the resistors will exact something of value in exchange for their co-operation. However, caution should be exercised in the use of this approach, because if such a practice was widespread it could prove a costly exercise.

Manipulation and Co-optation

These two approaches may be used if, for some reason, it is not possible to employ the methods already discussed. Manipulation is a covert measure to influence events, where situations are depicted in a favourable light to the point of distortion, and perhaps critical information is withheld, in order to force people to accept change. For example, there may be a threat by management (which happens to be untrue) to axe a section unless employees climb down in their opposition to some fundamental proposals for rationalisation of that section.

By contrast, co-optation is a mixture of manipulation and participation. Prominent figures, perhaps the leaders in the group resisting the change, are involved strategically in the decision to promote change. Their advice is sought not as a means to enrich the decision but as a way of implicating them in the process so that eventually their approval is forthcoming. An extreme example of such an eventuality is where a recalcitrant shop steward of the old school is co-opted onto a committee contemplating a change that is resisted in his or her part of the organisation.

Both manipulation and co-optation do not require a heavy investment in time, and it is possible that the tactics involved are initially effective in neutralising the influence of opponents. But equally one has to acknowledge that the tactics could become ineffective if the recipients of undue influence feel they are being exploited or deceived. The end result would be a total undermining of the credibility of those engineering change.

Coercion

Obviously this would be a measure of last resort. Management is prepared to take action, such as a threat to close down a plant or make people redundant, if resistance to proposed changes in work practices continues. It is conceivable that this is an expeditious approach to dilute resistance to change. Nevertheless, the consequences of using such tactics could be disadvantageous in terms of morale and commitment in the future.

A summary of the main points relating to the situations where the different approaches to controlling resistance to change are used, with the advantages and disadvantages of each approach, appears in Table 12.1.

TABLE 12.1

Approaches for Controlling Resistance to Change

Approach	Commonly Used in These Situations	Advantages	Drawbacks
Education & Communication	Where there is a lack of information or inaccurate information and analysis	Once persuaded, people will often help with the implementation of the change	Can be very time-consuming if lots of people are involved
Participation & involvement	Where the initiators do not have all the information they need to design the change, and where others have considerable power to resist	People who participate will be committed to implementing change, and any relevant information they have will be integrated into the change plan	Can be very time-consuming if participators design an inappropriate change
Facilitation & support	Where people are resisting because of adjustment problems	No other approach works as well with adjustment problems	Can be time-consuming, expensive, and still fail
Negotiation & agreement	Where someone or some group will clearly lose out in a change, and where that group has considerable power to resist	Sometimes it is a relatively easy way to avoid major resistance	Can be too expensive in many cases if it alerts others to negotiate for compliance
Manipulation & co-optation	Where other tactics will not work, or are too expensive	It can be a relatively quick and inexpensive solution to resistance problems	Can lead to future problems if people feel manipulated
Explicit & implicit coercion	Where speed is essential, and the change initiators possess considerable power	It is speedy, and can overcome any kind of resistance	Can be risky if it leaves people mad at the initiators

Source: Kotter, J.P. & Schlesinger, L.A. (1979). Choosing strategies for change. *Harvard Business Review,* March/April, 106–114.

Planning Organisational Change

It is not good enough for an organisation to respond to change; it must try to anticipate it as well. This would necessitate the planning of organisational change as part of the organisation's strategy. The following are approaches that adopt a movement from a current position to a future desired state:

- process model;
- extended model; and
- action research.

Process Model
Lewin (1951) has described a three-step change process (still often cited in the literature) as involving unfreezing, changing, and refreezing.

Unfreezing. This is a process by which employees recognise the need for change. A key consideration in the unfreezing process is informing people about the importance of change and how it will affect their jobs. It is important for people to see that the current organisational activities to which they may be attached are not effective enough and that the proposed change is called for (e.g. restructuring the organisation, or the introduction of a new procedure) in order to transform the situation.

Change. This is the actual movement from the old situation to the new situation, and involves a process that alters existing relationships or activities.

Refreezing. This amounts to making the changed behaviour of people relatively solid and not easily reversed. Without refreezing, the old ways of doing things may dislodge the newly acquired behaviours. With regard to newly learned skills, it is obviously important that these are repeated in training sessions and that the organisational environment is conducive to the practise of those skills. In addition, rewards for trying to change the status quo are matters to consider. The application of learning theory, particularly reinforcement (examined in Chapter 4), is relevant during the refreezing stage, and so is group decision making (considered in Chapter 7) when people are faced with accepting change.

Extended Model

An alternative model, incorporating facets of the Lewin model, has been proposed by Moorhead and Griffin (1992). It is considered more realistic because it examines organisational change from the perspective of top management (see Fig. 12.1). Top management will be active in specifying the likely outcome of the changes proposed, having in the first instance indicated that certain changes are necessary. Also, alternatives for bringing about change are

discussed and evaluated, and acceptable alternative is adopted.

In the extended model you will role of a change agent. He or she is th charged with managing the efforts di....ed at change. The change agent could assist management with the line of activity suggested earlier. A change agent could be an internal or external consultant. As an internal consultant, he or she could operate with the advantage of having a deep insight into many aspects of organisational functioning, but of course there is the danger of a lack of objectivity because of proximity to the situation. By contrast, an external consultant may be viewed by organisational members as more impartial and detached and, as a consequence, more acceptable.

Generally, change agents must have the backing and support of top management and it is suggested (Beer, 1980) that they should possess a number of attributes, including status, credibility, and expertise in the eyes of those who relate to them. Also of importance is the trust people have in change agents because of the sensitive way in which they must handle information. Kanter (1989) would endorse a substantial part of this profile, and would include satisfaction in personal accomplishments, self-confidence, independence, ability to foster co-operation, ability to engage in dialogue with people across business functions and respect for the proposals of change. The arrival of the change agent may be greeted with satisfaction because his or her work offers an opportunity to change the organisation for the better in the eyes of employees dissatisfied with the status quo.

The processes of unfreezing, changing, and refreezing are used by the change agent during the implementation stage (step 4 in Fig. 12.1). In step 5, the change agent and top management evaluate the extent to which the change is producing the desired outcome. The actual outcome is measured against the objectives set for change earlier in the model, and deviations are handled appropriately. The

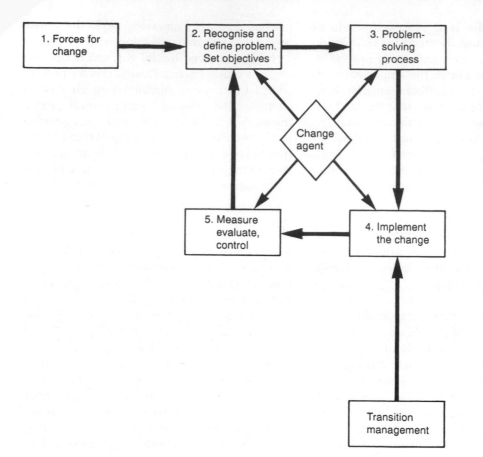

FIG. 12.1.
Extended model of organisational change. Source: Adapted from Moorhead, G. & Griffin, R.W. (1992). *Organisational behaviour* (third edition). Boston: Houghton Mifflin.

change agent will naturally be involved in all phases of the change process and, if capable, should be of immense help to the various parties by injecting into the discussion new ideas and opinions that challenge existing practices. This could be painful for some, but is likely to be beneficial in facilitating the change process.

There are many occasions when change is a major and complex task, taking a considerable amount of time to implement fully. In such circumstances it has to be managed carefully. The process of planning, organising, and implementing change in a systematic way from the inception of the change to the future desired state is called transition management, and this is shown in Fig. 12.1. One must realise that once the change process begins, the organisation is in a

transitional phase, probably somewhere between the old status quo and the planned future state, but normal business has still to continue (Ackerman, 1982).

It is necessary for managers within the organisation to become transition managers and liaise effectively with the change agent. If necessary, a transition management may be required to exercise overall control of the business during the transitional stage. Also, it is suggested that the natural constituency of the organisation—i.e. employees, suppliers, and customers—should be kept fully informed of the changes. This is an important aspect of transition management (Tichy & Ulrich, 1984).

In the extended model you will notice that top management are influential in setting the agenda for change. However, this approach has been challenged in a recent study of organisational change in six large corporations in the United States (Beer, Eisenstat, & Spector, 1990). The researchers found that the most effective senior managers recognised their limited power to prescribe corporate renewal from the top. Instead, they defined their role as creating a climate for change by specifying the direction in which the company should move, without insisting on specific solutions during the early phases of the company-wide change process. It would appear unrealistic to expect a chief executive to appreciate the necessary level of detail required to effect change in areas of the organisation far removed from the centre. Eventually, top management will be active in aligning structure and systems with changes at the periphery of the organisation to achieve enduring organisational change.

Beer and his colleagues do not rule out the instigation of change from the top, but they are keen to point out that many senior executives—who developed in an era when top-down hierarchical influence was the primary means for organising and managing—must learn from the younger unit managers closer to the scene of action.

Action Research
This is another mechanism for bringing about change in organisations. Action research could be defined as the application of the scientific method of fact finding and experimentation to practical problems awaiting solutions. It requires co-operation and collaboration between the action researcher and practitioners within the organisation. The preferred outcomes of action research are solutions to immediate problems and a contribution to scientific knowledge and theory (French & Bell, 1978).

Action researchers are normally outsiders and, unlike change agents who are charged with bringing about specific change, they carry out organisational research. The research process involves meticulous fact finding using interviews and the perusal of documentation that could result in the identification of problems and their causes. The information collected will be analysed and synthesised, and action plans to improve the situation will be produced. Using appropriate data at their disposal, action researchers are well placed to evaluate the effects on the organisation of the implementation of the action plans. Both researchers and the organisation benefit from the insight and understanding gained of the effects of organisational change.

ORGANISATIONAL DEVELOPMENT

Organisational development (OD) has been defined as "the process of planned change and improvement of organisations through the application of knowledge of the behavioural sciences" (Moorhead & Griffin, 1992). To supplement this definition one can use other definitions to reflect the broad coverage of this process. Organisational development has been described as an involved network of events that increases the ability of members of the organisation to solve problems in a creative fashion, to assist the organisation in adapting to the external environment, and to manage organisational culture. It embraces a broad range of interventionist processes from changes in organisational structure and systems to psychotherapeutic counselling sessions with individuals and groups in response to changes in the external environment. According to Beer and Walton (1987), the interventions seek to improve the effectiveness of the organisation and contribute to employee well-being.

From the various definitions it is clear that OD emphasises human processes and modes of interaction within an organisation, and is not concerned with factors in organisations, such as technology (though of course the latter could trigger the need for OD).

Of the three general strategies for bringing about change in human systems in organisations and society, postulated by Chin and Benne (1976), the "normative re-educative" strategy seems to be closest to OD. The major belief of this strategy is that behaviour is influenced largely by the social and cultural norms of the group or society to which individuals belong. Given that individuals have a pronounced commitment to conform to these norms, successful change is accomplished by changing the norms. The other two strategies identified by Chin and Benne are "empirical-rational" and "power-coercive".

The empirical-rational strategy makes the assumption that people are basically rational, and change can be introduced if it is shown that it is in the individual's own best interest to accept the change. The use of data and rational persuasion is conspicuous in this approach. The power-coercive strategy entails the use of, for example, the power vested in the manager's position, or power springing from the use of resources, to coerce individuals into accepting change.

In the past decade OD has broadened its perspective and has become linked more closely with strategic planning in organisations. It is concerned with reviewing desired future states for the organisation, and specifying the necessary steps open to the organisation to move from the present to the future (Pritchard, 1984).

DEVELOPMENT TECHNIQUES AND INTERVENTIONS

OD can be focused at different levels. For example, techniques could be used (individually or collectively) for the following purposes:

- to alter the structure of the organisation;
- to redesign tasks within the organisation; and/or
- to change the outlook of individuals and groups.

Structure

A structural change could entail a move from a functional group to a matrix organisation (described in Chapter 10). It could also involve the removal of layers of management, with wider spans of control, to create a flatter and less bureaucratic organisation. Likewise, authority and reporting relationships could be changed, as could the size of units or departments. Many of these changes could have a knock-on effect. For example, the decentralisation of authority could give rise to greater individual autonomy at the lower levels of the organisation, and accelerate the decision-making process. The role of technology in structural change has to be acknowledged: in Chapter 10, there is a discussion of technology and organisation.

To adapt the formal organisation in order to increase flexibility and responsiveness, a "collateral organisation" can be planned (Zand, 1974). A collateral organisation, which exists alongside the formal organisation, is set up by the management of the formal organisation. The purpose of the collateral organisation is to tackle problems with which the formal organisation—with its pronounced hierarchy of authority and established rules and procedures—cannot cope. The problems could include unexpected but dramatic changes in the product market or major new technological developments. A comparison between the typical formal organisation and the collateral organisation appears in Table 12.2.

Features of a collateral organisation that are worthy of note include the existence of a communication network in which inter-personal communication takes place without recourse to status or position power, and information that cuts across hierarchical lines. For example, a lower-ranked employee could gain access quickly to a senior manager to discuss ideas and decisions with respect to major events, such as matters critical to the competitive position of the company. The collateral organisation is relatively permanent and can be viewed as a non-hierarchical,

TABLE 12.2

A Comparison of Formal and Collateral Organisations

Characteristic	Formal Organisation	Collateral Organisation
Nature	Bureaucratic	Knowledge / Problem-based
Primary Purpose	Maximise output	Analyse or invent knowledge to solve problems
Task uncertainty	Routine operations, low uncertainty	Problem solving, high uncertainty
Levels of authority	Many	Few
Source of influence and power	Position in hierarchy	Ability to identify and solve problems
Use of rules	High	Low
Leadership	Function of level	Drawn from any level
Links to others in the organisation	Few	Many
Division of labour	High	Low
Job assignments	Fixed	Rotational, flexible
Depiction (in charts)	Functiona.lly specialised	Diagonal slices, mixed functions
Rewards	Pay and benefits	Learning, recognition, visibility, new contacts, bonus possibility

Source: Rubinstein, D. & Woodman, R.W. (1984). Spiderman and the Burma raiders: Collateral organisation theory in action. *The Journal of Applied Behavioural Science*, January / March, 4

problem-solving grouping attached to a larger, formal organisation.

The collateral organisation can serve as a permanent OD process to facilitate communication and problem solving (Moorhead & Griffin, 1989). However, it can suffer from difficulties that beset all problem-solving groups, such as negative consequences of groupthink (e.g. intolerance of dissent, scepticism of outside advice) and rigidity both of outlook and attention to important issues (Rubinstein & Woodman, 1984).

Task Redesign

The redesign of tasks was considered in Chapter 2. Here it is examined as a factor in organisational development. When changes

to a job are contemplated it is critical to evaluate the organisational structure, especially the work rules and authority for decision making within the department (Moorhead, 1981), quite apart from specific changes to the jobs concerned. The process adopted is what one would expect when faced with any major change. For example, there is initially a recognition of the need for change, followed by selecting the appropriate intervention (e.g. job redesign to give employees more freedom in the choice of work methods or the scheduling of work), and an evaluation of the change, bearing in mind a variety of influences (e.g. technology, leadership, group dynamics, costs, implementation) connected with the context of the proposed change (Griffin, 1982). (The relationship between technology and task design was discussed in Chapter 2.)

Individual and Group Emphasis

The OD intervention strategies falling into this category are aimed at changing the attitudes and behaviour of members of the organisation by resorting to processes of communication, decision making and problem solving. Among the well-known people-centred change techniques are:

- sensitivity training;
- survey feedback;
- process consultation;
- team-building;
- managerial grid;
- management by objectives;
- conflict management;
- management development; and
- career planning.

Sensitivity Training

This is a method used for changing behaviour through interaction of an unstructured nature in a group setting. The group can consist of 10–15 members supported by a professional trainer, and is referred to as a T-group (training group) or encounter group. Groups can remain in existence for up to two weeks in a secluded location, though they could function in a company or college setting.

A feature of the atmosphere within the group is the openness with which people discuss their ideas, attitudes, outlook, and the way they interact with others. The professional trainer plays the role of a facilitator rather than a leader, and group members learn from participating and observing rather than from being told what is correct or incorrect.

The main purpose of the T-group is to give members the opportunity to enhance awareness of their own behaviour and the behaviour of others, as well as to increase sensitivity concerning how others perceive them (Campbell & Dunnette, 1968).

Proponents of this technique would expect certain desirable consequences to flow from the exposure of participants to the group processes. These would include a greater capacity to empathise with others, to be a better listener, to be more tolerant of other people's ideas, to be more open, and to be better able to resolve interpersonal conflict.

Evidence has been cited that T-groups can generate negative psychological effects for a significant minority of participants (Lieberman, Yalom, & Miles, 1973). The process of exposing their personality exacts costs in terms of traumatic experiences for certain people. In general, it is maintained that sensitivity training changes the behaviour of those who participate in it, but there is considerable debate about whether the changed behaviour is incorporated into the normal work behaviour of the person on his or her return to the job (Robbins, 1991).

In some ways it is not surprising that the T-group never made the impact its supporters expected. It could be argued that the values exemplified in a strong belief in the importance of openness and trust for effective co-operative effort, which was prevalent in the 1960s, were in conflict with the norms of most organisations. Makin, Cooper, and Cox (1989) point out that sensitivity training was never widely accepted, and has now fallen into disuse mainly because of the differences between the values of T-groups and those of most organisations. Because of this clash of values, there was a poor transfer of learning from the training situation to the real organisational world, with its intricate political processes.

Survey Feedback

This technique is designed to collect data that is subsequently analysed, summarised, and returned to those who took part in the survey. The outcome of this exercise is used in identifying problems connected with change, and to provide an informed input to the solutions proposed.

The use of survey feedback techniques in organisational development is different from their use in normal attitude surveys. As part of an organisational development process, data are distributed to groups of employees at all levels of the organisation and used by them in their natural groupings to assist in the identification and solution of problems. Data would not be handled in this way with a normal attitude survey where senior management would receive the findings and then decide on the most appropriate course of action to take.

The change agent interviews selected employees from various organisational levels to determine the important issues to be examined during the data-collection stage of survey feedback. This would be invaluable if a questionnaire is to be designed specifically for data collection. Of course it would not be necessary to prepare a questionnaire if it is proposed to use a standardised instrument (i.e. a questionnaire already prepared externally) of a reliable nature. The latter may offer the facility to use comparative data from other organisations.

To ensure the anonymous nature of individual responses, the questionnaire results are analysed and summarised by unit or department (Franklin, 1978). A summary of the results for use in the group feedback sessions is prepared by the change agent. The feedback meetings are best handled when run by a "family group", which could be the manager and subordinates in a particular unit. Family groups are held down to small numbers in order to promote interaction and discussion among members.

Meetings are run by the managers rather than by the change agent in order to emphasise that ownership of the exercise resides in those involved in day-to-day activities. It is important to ensure that the role of the change agent is confined to that of an expert and a resource at the disposal of the group. In essence the change agent assists the manager in preparing for the meeting by reviewing the data, devising ways of identifying and solving problems, and stimulating discussion at the meetings.

The actual feedback that the groups receive is principally a series of profiles on such matters as the effectiveness of communication, the level of job satisfaction, the nature of decision making, and the quality of managerial leadership. During the actual feedback sessions the group members discuss the profiles and the problems that the data bring to light. The next step is for the group, with the assistance of the change agent, to concentrate on the lessons to be learned from the information presented at the feedback session, and to devise action plans aimed at bringing about the organisational improvements. Several sessions may be required to consider the plans and the best way to implement them. Also, follow-up action is crucial to establish to what extent the processes concerned have improved.

The survey feedback technique is a popular organisational change and development intervention. In comparing socio-technical systems, job redesign, and survey feedback interventions, Passmore (1978) suggested that the survey feedback approach was of value: not only did it help management to understand feelings of employees about an issue, but it also formed the basis for building trust between the management and work-force. However, the effectiveness of feedback meetings could be undermined if the findings are perceived as threatening. In such circumstances it is suggested that a group of managerial colleagues be created to review and discuss the findings before the meetings are arranged with subordinates in the family groups (Alderfer & Ferriss, 1972).

Process Consultation

There is some similarity between this technique and sensitivity training, in that it is concerned with improving organisational effectiveness through involving people in the resolution of interpersonal problems. However, it is more task-oriented than sensitivity training. An important feature of process consultation is using an outside consultant to help the client, usually a manager, to perceive, understand, and take action with respect to processes within his or her sphere of influence (Schein, 1969). These processes could include communication patterns, interpersonal relationships, the flow of work, roles, group norms, group problem solving and decision making, leadership styles, exercise of authority and power, and inter-group activities.

There are three stages in process consultation, described in the following sections.

Stage 1.   This is the initial contact with the client organisation. At this stage an assessment is made of whether or not the consultancy is likely to be successful. The assessment is based on the initial impressions of the client's intentions and suitability to embark on a project of this nature.

Stage 2.   This consists of setting up an exploratory meeting between the contact person (the client), the consultant, and a group of employees who are likely to have status and influence, but at the same time can appreciate the true nature of process consultation and have the ability to identify problems. At this particular juncture it would be advisable to include people who are not basically hostile to the process. The consultant will seek to establish the nature of the problem, and whether he or she is sufficiently interested in it and can be of assistance. If the consultant accepts the assignment, future plans can be devised.

There are two aspects to the contract that exists between the consultant and the client—one relates to the provision of a consultancy service, including the fee, and the other is called the psychological contract that deals with the expectations the consultant and client have of each other. For example, the client's expectation of the consultant could include the acceptance of expert opinion on how people problems should be managed as well as an evaluation of staff. The consultant's expectation of his or her own role and that of the client could include a personal expectation to put effort into the diagnosis and exploration of issues, to be supported by the organisation in collecting data, and to receive the commitment of staff to the project.

At preliminary meetings there is clarification of what is necessary in order to engage in process consultation. For example:

- there is a need for trust;
- the total organisation is to be seen as the client;
- the consultant must not be viewed simply as the "expert"; and
- any misunderstandings should be cleared up.

Also, it must be emphasised that the role of the consultant is that of a listener who may appear relatively inactive and certainly does not want to get involved in discussions of the content of subject matter addressed by the group. However, he or she may be asked by the group to comment on interpersonal processes, in which case feedback is given, as well as encouragement to come up with solutions to group problems.

Stage 3.   This involves the establishment of systems of working. A good starting point would be the apex of the organisation, where the greatest impact and influence for change can be achieved. The focal point for observation must be interpersonal and group processes aimed specifically at staff working on real jobs. Consultants should think clearly of the likely implications of what they say, because every question they ask is seen as an intervention.

When the consultant is engaged in information gathering it is felt that the interview is preferable to the survey questionnaire in data collection, because the questionnaire would tend to distance the consultant from the client due to its impersonality. It is so important for the consultant's questions to be relevant and not obscure. Good questioning could provide the client with an enlarged perspective of behavioural processes within the organisation.

It is now apparent that the consultant adopts two approaches—one is the gathering of information and the other is an intervention—although the two can be closely related. Schein (1969; 1987) has classified interventions as follows:

- *Agenda setting*. Here the group may put the spotlight on issues connected with "process" or rearrange the agenda for action.
- *Feedback*. When feedback is given to individuals or groups it should be done in a sensitive way, bearing in mind people's feelings.
- *Coaching or counselling*. From the feedback process it materialises that a manager registers an inappropriate piece of behaviour, and he or she wants advice on ways of changing it.
- *Structural suggestions*. This could mean creating awareness of the advantages and disadvantages of various structural attributes of the organisation. Because the consultant's role is connected with enabling clients to solve their own problems and not to solve problems for them, suggesting how work should be structured and executed is a rare occurrence. He or she is not really in a position to undertake such a role in normal circumstances.

The final stages are taken up with trying to obtain appropriate measures to evaluate the effectiveness of process consultation, and for the consultant to disengage from the exercise. A gradual rather than abrupt disengagement is advisable.

Schein makes the point that process consultation is fundamentally different from other types of consultancy, such as the "purchase" model and the doctor-patient model. The purchase model is applicable when the organisation identifies its problems without outside help and then appoints a consultant to solve them. In the doctor-patient model, the consultant conducts a diagnostic examination of the organisation and suggests remedies.

With the purchase model the difficulty could be that the organisation has defined its problems incorrectly, or the consultant chosen may not be the most suitable. With the doctor-patient model, the difficulty could be that the diagnosis is resisted, or the remedies are not implemented. In the case of process consultation, it should be reiterated that the consultant's role is not to suggest solutions to problems, but to help management understand organisational problems as clearly as possible, so that appropriate solutions are likely to be found. In an assessment of a number of interventions based on process consultation, the majority of them were considered positive (Golembiewski, Proehl, & Sink, 1982). However, a major limitation of the process consultation technique would be a skill deficiency on the part of the consultant.

Team-building

In circumstances where interaction between members of a group is crucial for effective performance, developing or building teams may be useful. A detailed discussion of team-building appeared in Chapter 7, and it is useful to refer back to the issues raised there. The main purpose of team-building is to assist people with related or interdependent jobs to examine ways in which their "team" works together, at the same time identifying strengths and weaknesses, and developing plans to improve team functioning.

In essence, team-building is a task-oriented activity with an emphasis on interpersonal interaction. Processes taken into account in team-building are setting goals, developing interpersonal relations, role analysis to clarify team members' jobs, and an overall analysis of the team process. There is also an endeavour to use substantial contact among members to foster trust and openness, and there is a pronounced emphasis on changes that will lead to improvements in specific aspects of team performance.

Team-building starts with a diagnostic meeting at which members of the team, in the company of the change agent, discuss in an open, unstructured way the current position on the functioning of the team. Each member is given ample opportunity to state the goals and priorities of the team together with its strengths and weaknesses, and what action is necessary to improve its effectiveness. The viewpoints expressed serve as a basis for discussion, which can lead to an agreed position within the team on desirable changes. At subsequent meetings, plans can be developed to implement the changes. Finally, the effectiveness of team-building has received some empirical endorsement (Golembiewski et al., 1982), but one can also find evidence showing that the effects are not substantial (Buller & Bell, 1986).

Inter-group Development
Team-building on an inter-group basis can be referred to as inter-group development. It has become an issue in OD because of the damaging effects inter-group conflict (discussed in Chapter 9) can create. Inter-group development sets out to change the attitudes, stereotypes, and perceptions that groups have of each other in order to foster co-operation and communication between them. The intervention is either initiated by a consultant using groups from the same department or, alternatively, groups from different departments, whose co-operation is necessary for successful organisational performance, can be used. The steps involved are as follows (Hodgetts, 1991; Liebowitz & De Meuse, 1982):

• The inter-group intervention starts with the leaders (or all members) of the two

groups meeting together when it is established that the relationships between them can be improved.
• Working in separate rooms the two groups prepare two lists—one contains the groups' perceptions, attitudes and feelings about the other group, and the other consists of what the group thinks the other group is saying about them.
• The two groups meet to share the information that they have listed, with each group stating how the other is perceived. At this stage the consultant invites questions on clarification of meaning, but not discussion of the listed items.
• The two groups return to their rooms to discuss the insights they have formed concerning themselves and the other group. It is conceivable that a fair amount of friction or differences of opinion between the two groups is based on faulty perceptions and communication difficulties. If this is recognised, the gulf between the two groups may be less than originally thought.
• The two groups resume their meeting, and again compare their lists. They co-operate in preparing an overall list of issues or difficulties that still need to be resolved. Items are listed on the basis of priority and action strategies are created, specifying what has to be done, when, and by whom. At this stage the intervention by the consultant ceases.
• In some situations there could be a review to establish whether the action plans have been implemented in order to see if the purpose of the exercise has been achieved.

In reviews of the effectiveness of intervention based on inter-group development it is suggested that, although attitudes can improve among members, the positive effects in terms of behavioural change and organisational performance are more elusive (Friedlander & Brown, 1974).

Grid Development

This is based on the managerial grid postulated by Blake and Mouton (1969), which was discussed in Chapter 8. The grid accommodates a "concern for production" and a "concern for people", as a means of analysing and improving the individual leadership styles of managers. The programme based on the grid is formulated with the express purpose of helping managers to identify their current as well as their ideal leadership style, and then to take action to move towards the latter. The six phases in the programme are set out in the panel below.

Although Blake and Mouton cite evidence to support their approach to organisational development, there have been criticisms of the methodology used. Also, there is a recognition that although people may show changes in attitudes towards styles of management, changes in actual behaviour have been more difficult to prove (Gray & Starke, 1984). The most fundamental criticism relates to leadership style in the form of a 9.9 team manager (high on production, high on people). Blake and Mouton make the assertion that this type of manager will always be the most effective regardless of the situation, but evidence from situational leadership would challenge that assertion (Bernardin & Alvares, 1976).

Management by Objectives (MBO)

MBO can be used as an organisation-wide OD intervention, but unlike the managerial grid it has assumed a variety of forms over the years.

Managerial Grid Technique For Inter-group Development

1. Managers attend a seminar, which is held outside the organisation and goes on for roughly a week. They concentrate on reading relevant material, diagnosing their leadership styles, engaging in problem-solving exercises, developing skills to take action in teams, offering critiques, and enhancing communication processes.

2. Team-work is improved by giving managers and their subordinates the opportunity to apply the knowledge and skills acquired in the first phase of the programme to their specific situation. There is also a determination to locate and understand the impediments to group effectiveness, to identify members' preferences for the way to operate, to foster a climate where the work of individuals is examined in a critical but constructive manner, leading to the creation of a timetable and set of objectives for improving the performance of the group.

3. The emphasis now swings from a preoccupation with events within a work group (intra-group) to attempts to develop closer integration between work groups (inter-group). Each group specifies what it considers to be ideal inter-group relationships, and shares these views with other groups. Representatives from groups that interact are asked to set in motion discussions about developing and implementing these ideal types of relationships.

4. This phase could last for one year and concentrates on the development of an ideal strategic plan for the organisation. The formulation of the strategic plan is put in the hands of the top management group. In this exercise there is a commitment to excellence, and the planning process is studded with much discussion and evaluation of ideas and suggestions. Attention is also given to matters connected with implementation.

5. This phase can consume a considerable amount of time (frequently two to three years) as the organisation tries to bridge the gap between the status quo and the future desired state for the organisation. Planning teams, supplemented by top management, will be busy establishing what has to be done in order to move in the desired direction.

6. The final phase places the emphasis on stabilisation. This means that every effort is made to ensure that changes made following earlier phases are not undermined by a reversion to old behaviours. The new methods and practices that have been introduced are reinforced, and when progress is reviewed any deviations are earmarked for future corrective action (Blake & Mouton, 1969).

The key elements of MBO are identifying the goals of the organisation, setting specific goals for employees—the achievement of which will bring about the attainment of organisational goals—and evaluating the progress of employees in trying to attain their individual goals. The following are features common to most MBO programmes (Szilagi & Wallace, 1983):

- *Diagnosis*: this will lead to developing an understanding of the needs of employees and aspects of their relevant environment at work.
- *Planning*: this entails various activities connected with learning to handle the MBO approach, getting management's commitment to it, and considering the overall goals and strategies of the organisation.
- *Defining the employee's job*: the nature of the job and the duties and responsibilities must be defined before individual goals can be set.
- *Goal setting:* the goals for a specified period of time, usually a year, are set by the subordinate. Attention is given to identifying goals, setting priorities, target dates, and the modes of measurement to be used.
- *Superior's review*: the superior reviews the subordinate's initial goals, provides feedback, and offers suggestions for improvement. Then the subordinate and superior arrive at an agreed set of goals for the subordinate for the specified period.
- *Interim review*: periodically throughout the specified period the subordinate and superior meet to discuss the progress made, as well as to adjust the agreed goals to reflect new information or changing environmental circumstances.
- *Final review*: at the end of the period for which the goals are set, the subordinate and superior meet to review the results. The emphasis is on analysis, discussion, feedback, and input to the next MBO cycle. The cycle repeats itself for the next period.

The effectiveness of MBO, in terms of better communication, improved planning, and positive attitudes towards systems of evaluation has been endorsed (Carroll & Tosi, 1970). However, there has been criticism, such as that MBO programmes generated too much paperwork, over-emphasised production, and failed to involve all levels of management (Gray & Starke, 1984). In an exhaustive study of the effectiveness of MBO programmes, it was concluded that positive results were lost after a lapse of about two years (Kondrasuk, 1981).

Conflict Management

A consequence of engaging in initiatives to bring about organisational change and development is the creation of conflict. To handle conflict of an interpersonal nature one could make use of expert intervention by a third party, who may be internal or external to the organisation. If one were to invoke an intervention based on Walton's (1969) interpersonal peacemaking, it would involve the adoption of a well-managed confrontation. For the confrontation to be successful the following conditions have to be met:

- both parties must have an interest in resolving the conflict;
- a relationship manifest in equality of power should exist between the two parties;
- the time chosen for the parties to confront each other should be just right;
- each party should have adequate time to air his or her views and to resolve differences of opinion, before moving on to explore common ground;
- the social conditions should be characterised by a climate of openness, and mutual understanding should be fostered by effective communication; and
- the stress and tension in the encounter should be controlled and maintained at a moderate level.

Normally one would expect the third party or consultant to carry out preliminary meetings (interviews with the two parties on neutral ground). Questions such as how formal the first meetings should be, how long the meetings should last, and whether people other than the two parties should be invited, will have to be addressed.

In the actual confrontation meeting, the role of the third party or consultant demands considerable skill in managing the process and guiding the confrontation towards an encouraging outcome. The consultant should set the agenda for the dialogue, prescribing what should be discussed at different stages of the confrontation. He or she should:

- ensure that the two parties have equal time to air their views;
- encourage the parties to give due weight to a diagnosis of the problems confronting them;
- summarise and restate the issues in question;
- deal delicately with interactions that are potentially damaging in the context of the continuation of the dialogue;
- provide feedback and comment on the proceedings as they occur; and
- settle the agenda for further meetings.

This type of interpersonal peacemaking intervention could be difficult to operationalise because of the exacting conditions necessary for its use and the high qualities required of the consultant. However, Walton's model appears intuitively plausible, and is supported by his own anecdotal case histories. He believes it worked for him.

Management Development

Programmes aimed at developing managers are similar in some ways to general training programmes because they attempt to improve certain abilities, skills, and perspectives. Management development was defined by a UK governmental agency (the then Training Services Agency) over a decade ago as "an attempt to improve managerial effectiveness through a planned and deliberate learning process". This definition could still be considered valid. The main objective of management development is to ensure that executives are developed to meet the organisation's short- and long-term requirements for specialist managers and general managers (Mumford, 1987).

In recent years there has been a plethora of reports (e.g. Handy et al.; Constable & McCormick) pointing out the inadequacy of provision in management education and training (see Sisson & Storey, 1988, and the reports cited there). Invariably, an expansion in the provision of programmes was advocated, with a stricture that they should be geared more towards the needs of organisations for managerial talent at all levels.

The fashionable approach currently is competency-based education, with a heavy reliance on skills development, and an emphasis on the importance of a partnership between educational and training establishments and the organisations in which managers or potential managers work. Sisson and Storey, who conducted research in management development in a UK context, point out that prior to embarking on management development as a strategy to increase managerial effectiveness, a number of key organisational issues should be considered:

- *Job definition*: exactitude in defining what is expected of managers.
- *Selection*: thoroughness in screening new entrants to the organisation with managerial potential to ensure the acquisition of the appropriate "raw material".
- *Identification of development needs*: an enlightened appraisal process in order to assess the precise nature of managerial needs.
- *Training or development*: complementary balance between off-the-job training (e.g. management education) and on-the-job development to meet identified needs.

- *Reward systems*: recognition of the significance of compensation packages linked to performance, as opposed to the traditional promotion system.

Increasingly companies are using assessment centres (described in Chapter 13), particularly in connection with two of the issues referred to earlier—selection and identification of development needs. It is suggested that assessment centres, or development centres when used in this context, are an efficient way of helping individuals get a clearer and better picture of their strengths and weaknesses, and of specifying the action required to facilitate their future development (Griffiths & Bell, 1985). The specified action entails a variety of planned educational and training programmes as well as experiences on the job.

Management training takes many forms. Apart from programmes that emphasise the dissemination of relevant knowledge in areas such as strategic planning, marketing, finance, operations management, and human resource management, participants can get involved in indoor exercises such as leading a discussion in a group, or acting as a leader in a complex task such as a difficult project. Alternatively, there are outdoor tasks that normally consist of some degree of physical deprivation (e.g. getting cold and wet). Exercises of this nature are designed to simulate real-life situations because they involve an element of stress, the need to inspire team-work, problem solving, resolution of conflict, the exercise of interpersonal skills, and the maintenance of morale.

When one reflects on the indoor exercises it is easy to conclude that the problems encountered lack realism, and that they are unlikely to generate stress in the way that real-life situations do. On the other hand, the outdoor exercises are for real, in the sense that bad decisions could result in groups losing their way, experiencing acute discomfort, or even real danger. Although risks to the person are closely controlled, they are still present to a sufficient extent to generate stress.

However, one should acknowledge the weaknesses of the outdoor exercises (Sadler,

"NOW THEN P.J.,...ABOUT MY CHANCES OF PROMOTION...."

1988). The circumstances relating to canoeing, abseiling, and mountaineering are radically different from those related to organisational problems connected with mergers, technological change, and international competition. The stress experienced by the more athletic members of the management training group is much less than for those who are not that way inclined. In particular, those who are experienced and skilled in the types of outdoor activities undertaken enjoy a significant advantage. The outward-bound type of activity is obviously more appropriate for younger managers in junior positions than those already in senior positions.

In an assessment of the value of rigorous outdoor training courses for the development of executives, Furnham (1993) has this to say:

> Outdoor training is neither a panacea, nor a total waste of time. Where there is a match between what a company wants and what a course can offer there is the likelihood of course participants enjoying an enriching and invaluable experience. A bad course with no planned outcomes may result in increased employee cynicism, on top of colds, scratches, and occasionally very bruised egos.
>
> Outdoor training courses should not be dismissed as nonsense nor embraced as the only solution. Chosen judiciously, and run well, outdoor training can provide a unique learning experience.

Are there ways in which managers can be developed by being exposed to real-life situations that generate an element of stress, but do not expose participants to physical dangers and discomfort associated with outward-bound exercises? The answer is "yes", and the following ways have been suggested (Sadler, 1988):

- Plan and provide a day's outing for mentally handicapped children.
- Plan and execute a presentation to senior pupils in a secondary school to persuade them of the desirability of pursuing a career in industry.
- Plan and conduct a survey of the attitudes of young people in ethnic minorities towards job opportunities and discrimination in employment practices.

An alternative to these approaches, particularly in the context of developing top managers, is the use of the managers' own work situation, and the problems encountered therein, as the main vehicle for learning. Invariably, learning from experience in this way could be productive if the process is structured with the support of skill coaching, counselling, and the provision of feedback. This brings us into the realm of action learning discussed in Chapter 7.

In addition, factors that contribute to success and failure in the way managers exercise their role could be noted, as well as receiving normal feedback from others about a particular manager's behaviour. All these could be examined, and would no doubt contribute to the overall learning experience.

Developing the unique qualities and skills required of chief executives and directors has captured the attention of some management educators in recent years (e.g. Mumford, 1987; Sadler, 1988). These qualities and skills are said to be elusive and difficult to define, and not quite the same as the attributes of effective managers and supervisors further down the organisational hierarchy.

Sponsored by the Manpower Services Commission, in the mid 1980s Mumford and colleagues conducted a survey designed to establish the nature of management development undertaken by directors of companies. Although there were examples of successful management development programmes meeting the needs of business, it was concluded that most directors in the survey acquired their skills through a mixture of accidental and unstructured experiences. Therefore, systems of management development for this category of management had not been influential.

Mumford's preferred option appears to be an integrated approach to management development where learning by experience is brought into line with clear development objectives set for the manager after a discussion with his or her superior. In addition, there would be regular reviews of progress and the emphasis would be on allowing the manager to "own" his or her development. In essence, this approach is akin to action learning, and is tantamount to planned learning in association with ongoing managerial experience, lending itself to self-development with the assistance of a coach or mentor.

Burgoyne (1988), reflecting on many years of research at the University of Lancaster's Centre for the Study of Management Learning, maintains that organisations become mature in terms of management development when there is a dynamic interplay between corporate strategy and strategies for the development of managers. He feels that there is too much emphasis on the individual and the way he or she could be developed, and too little emphasis on management development for the organisation as a whole. There is a need for the process of management development to inform decision makers engaged in corporate planning about the quantity and quality of managerial assets, together with their strengths, weaknesses, and potential.

Here the emphasis is on establishing what can be done to achieve corporate policy with the managerial resources at the disposal of the organisation. An enriched pool of managers, cultivated by a quality management development programme, could eventually lead to a profound influence in a positive sense on the formulation of corporate policy, and consequently on the direction in which the organisation plans to move, as well as leading to the actual implementation of policy. The latter requires having suitable systems in place, the right culture or ethos, and sensitivity to the development needs, career prospects, and aspirations of individual managers.

Factors contributing to both success and failure in management development schemes are listed in Table 12.3.

Career Planning

When attention focuses on career prospects we are entering the domain of career planning. In a management development context, it could be viewed as a managed process of dialogue between each manager and the organisation about career prospects, aspirations, skills, and development needs (Burgoyne & Germain, 1984). This process could be related to a cycle of events, usually on an annual basis, consisting of performance reviews for each person, together with an exploration of career potential and a clarification of learning needs.

The events described previously would be linked to organisational planning, and the two together would be phased to inform the formation of corporate policy, as well as its implementation. In this way individual managerial careers are reviewed in the light of changing corporate directions, and corporate directions are considered in the light of available information on the skills, aspirations, potential, and the agreed future vision of the management team in the organisation.

The purpose of career planning is to ensure there is an enhancement of individual and organisational performance, and it is said that career planning in organisations can help companies identify qualified personnel and future managers, improve job satisfaction and other attitudes, increase the involvement of key employees, and improve the vital match between individual and organisational wants and needs (Granrose & Portwood, 1987).

A word of caution comes from Williams (1984) who feels we should broaden our view of the notion of career planning. He maintains that careers are not the exclusive property of managers and professionals—they should be applicable generally to, for example, clerical staff and part-time employees. Also, he states

TABLE 12.3
Effectiveness of Management Development Schemes

Failure Factors	*Success Factors*
• Purpose of scheme is unclear	• Clear job objectives
• Scheme lacks the support of managers	• Effective job selection
• Actual process of management development has little appeal to the managers concerned	• Business opportunities and organisational problems determined the chosen scheme
• There tends to be an over-emphasis on one-off experiences, and an over-emphasis on formal, general off-the-job courses and succession planning for the future	• Match between the needs of individuals and the chosen scheme
	• Diagnosis of individual and group needs is a shared activity
• Commitment to "flavour of the month" programmes	Ownership of schemes is shared between interested parties, including the personnel function
• Ownership of schemes resides predominantly in the personnel function	• Links between various processes of management development
	• Learning process is identified and improved
	• Output of management development is identified and measured

Source: Adapted from Mumford, A. (1987). Myths and reality in developing directors. *Personnel Management*, February, 29–33.

that the upward and onward view of a career does not always fall into line with current conditions whereby organisations that survive are leaner and fitter with fewer promotion opportunities (see panel overleaf).

The continuance of these conditions would necessitate a shift away from a career with in-built advancement to an increased emphasis on career development at the same organisational level, or within the present job. With fewer promotions available, lateral moves—for instance, job rotation—provide opportunities for continual career development. Also, temporary secondments or exchanges with other organisations might be considered, provided the eventual re-entry of the employee is carefully planned.

However, employees with the most marketable skills, faced with limited advancement opportunities within their own organisation, will probably explore external openings despite a highly competitive labour market.

Career Planning Categories
The following are some of the ways of categorising career planning (Morgan, Hall, & Martier, 1979):

- career pathing;
- career counselling;
- human resource planning;
- career information systems; and
- special programmes.

Career Plateau

As organisations engage in restructuring with the inevitable consequence of fewer layers, the effect on the number of promotions will be pronounced. With a decreasing number of rungs on the career ladder, a career structure plateau will be a fact of life for many people. The results of a study conducted by a research group at Sundridge Park Management Centre suggest that managers are adapting to the changing circumstances because they believe that there are career development alternatives to "promotion" as an organisational reward. The research focused on 1646 managers from eight organisations in the UK finance sector, and many of these organisations had been restructured in the last five years.

Respondents (managers) were asked how likely they were to accept a variety of career alternatives if faced with them now. Four career types emerged, although they are not completely mutually exclusive.

1. Career Flexers: These managers are likely to accept a wide variety of jobs, and although they may not strive for upward hierarchical moves they would like their jobs to have attractive features. They tend to be younger and more ambitious than the average manager, and tend to have spent less time in their present or immediately previous job.
2. Ambitious Careerists: These managers are especially eager to be promoted and groomed for higher level positions. They have a particularly firm belief that promotion will come their way; this belief is more potent the younger they are, and the less time they have spent in their present and previous jobs. They are particularly hostile to any downward move, and they are confident that they will not be made redundant.

3. Career Disengagers: These managers are interested in retirement, redundancy, and part-time working. What they would like to do is stop working full-time, either immediately or gradually. The longer they are in the job the more bored they feel, and generally they could belong to any age group. But there is some evidence to indicate that this age group consists of older people who are no longer ambitious, and who hold an expectation of being made redundant or of being offered early retirement.
4. Career Lifers: These managers would like to be told that they can remain in their present job until they retire, and would welcome a loyalty bonus. They tend to be older, and are convinced that promotions are a thing of the past

The research shows that there is considerable variety in the career aspirations of managers in mid- or late-career. The challenge facing organisations is to cope adequately with these different career needs. If the challenge is accepted, a natural course of action would be to recast the traditional career structure, and remove the stigma attached to the plateau, because managers nowadays are reaching the plateau much earlier— between the ages of 30 and 40—as opposed to between 45 and 50 in the mid 1980s.

Finally, one has to consider the importance of "job mobility" as a predictor of beliefs, feelings, and career types, the extent to which organisations differ with respect to job mobility practices, and the differences between the genders.

Career Pathing. Ideally career paths extend over an appreciable period of time (i.e. a 5- or 10-year period), and are updated periodically, with a series of experiences that lead to a particular destination—e.g. a higher level position within the organisation. Some career paths may include assignments overseas to help the individual gain an understanding of the international operations of the organisation. However, overseas assignments should be carefully considered, ensuring the suitability of applicants for such assignments.

Di Prete (1987) suggests that most organisations are unlikely to adhere too rigidly to specific career paths; instead they are likely to provide opportunities for both lateral and vertical movement to enable individuals to develop their skills and breadth of experience.

A live issue in recent years has been the development of career structures for technical staff, such as engineers and scientists (see panel facing).

Career Structures for Technical Staff

There is a growing recognition in some European high-technology companies that scientists and engineers are a prime resource and that the management structure should be altered so that employees can be rewarded for the quality of their research, rather than how many staff they control, or their skill at managing a budget. According to the Technical Director of *ICL* (UK), part of *Fujitsu* of Japan, there were instances of quite good technical staff trying to turn themselves into managers so that they could advance their careers, even though the main benefit they brought to the company was their technical contribution.

In 1990, after 10 years of informal arrangements, *ICL* introduced its technical career structure to show junior staff how they can develop their technical skills. As one recent entrant at a reasonably senior level at *ICL* said: "I could see there were people very high up in the company who were doing purely research, free of line management responsibilities but with a good salary." However, the Technical Director expects a "strategic" contribution from the senior engineer, such as taking responsibilty for the design on which their team is working, or demonstrating their ability to work with, for example, the marketing department.

Titular rewards are given to engineers who reach the top. To date 10 employees are *ICL* Fellows, and 25 have received the title of Distinguished Engineers, wuth more to follow. Distinguished Engineers are expected to meet regularly to discuss developments and exchange ideas. According to the Chief Engineer at *ICL*, the technical career scheme has been successful in acknowledging the value of the technical staff, and retaining skilled staff.

Another company, *British Telecommunications*, has recently unveiled its professional career-path scheme. The aim of the scheme is to support the career development needs of technical and specialist staff. According to the Management Development Manager, the scheme should prove useful in maintaining the specialist's enthusiasm and innovative thinking within the growing demands posed by the "flatter" organisations, in which sideways rather than upwards moves become commonplace (Bradshaw, 1993).

Career Counselling.   The emphasis with the counselling approach is to make sure the employee recognises and understands the opportunities and constraints in career development. The counsellor acts as a sympathetic listener who makes some suggestions for resolving issues. Counselling can be conducted on both a formal and informal basis, and can be used in a variety of situations. It can be provided in performance appraisal sessions, and can be placed at the disposal of those moving up, down, or out of the organisation.

The following issues could be raised with employees during an effective career counselling programme (Maanen & Schein, 1977):

- Career goals, aspirations, and expectations of employees for five years or longer.
- Opportunities that exist within the organisation, and the extent to which the employees' aspirations are realistic and coincide with the available opportunities.
- Identification of what would have to be done by employees in the way of additional self-development in order to benefit from the new opportunities.
- Identification of new job assignments that are necessary in order to prepare employees for further career growth.

Human Resource Planning.   This involves forecasting an organisation's human resource needs, creating charts that show planned succession, and producing a record of the skills and abilities needed by individuals in order to progress within the organisation. The complex aspect of human resource planning is implementing the plans based on the assessment of individual and organisational needs.

Career Information Systems.   There are many ways in which the organisation can provide career information to help employees make their own choices about available opportunities. Vacancies can be advertised

internally on notice boards, or through an internal newsletter or job vacancy bulletin. Career information can be conveyed by senior managers to staff using leaflets, videotapes, talks, and discussions. This type of activity could be beneficial for the organisation and increase the motivation of employees.

Special Programmes.   There are a variety of ways of facilitating disengagement from the organisation or progression within it. Pre-retirement programmes, for example, could assist with adjusting to a different life-style after leaving the organisation. Likewise, outplacement programmes are designed to help people who are leaving the organisation, either voluntarily or involuntarily. They help people preserve their dignity and self-worth when they are made redundant or dismissed, and can reduce negative feelings about the organisation.

There are programmes to help people change career direction from technical posts to managerial ones, and programmes developed for minorities and women to help solve their special problems (Bowen & Hisrich, 1986).

Career Management

This is the process by which career planning is implemented. To create the right climate the support of top management is necessary. In addition, all human resource activity throughout the organisation must be co-ordinated, all employees should be involved, and realistic feedback should be provided (Moorhead & Griffin, 1992). The importance of the role of the supervisor in the process is heavily endorsed (Leibowitz & Schlossberg, 1981). The supervisor's role would embrace the following:

- communicating information about careers;
- counselling subordinates to help them identify their skills and the options open to them;
- evaluating subordinates' strengths and weaknesses;
- offering subordinates coaching, or teaching skills and behaviour;
- advising subordinates on the realities of organisational life;
- serving as a mentor or role model for subordinates; and

- attracting subordinates' attention to opportunities.

Outcome of Career Planning

A number of beneficial outcomes have been attributed to career planning (Leibowitz & Schlossberg, 1981; Williams, 1984):

- Employees develop more realistic expectations of what is expected of them at work, and what sort of a future they are likely to have in the organisation.
- Increased awareness of available opportunities and of organisational constraints.
- Supervisory roles in career counselling are clarified, and there are better quality discussions between superior and subordinate.
- Greater sense of personal responsibility for career planning and development.
- Clearer understanding of values, interests, abilities, and personal characteristics.
- Better ability to resolve job–career–family concerns.
- More effective use of personnel systems within the organisation.

The overall benefits are reflected as a strengthening of commitment to careers when individuals develop plans to take responsibility for their careers. Ultimately it is claimed that the organisation is well placed to make better use of employees' talents, turnover is reduced, and there is an increase in the performance of individuals and the organisation.

Certain dysfunctional consequences can occur if the career planning system raises people's expectations unrealistically (Moorhead & Griffin, 1992). These are an increase in anxiety, supervisors spending too much time counselling their subordinates, and personnel systems becoming overloaded. The end result could be frustration, disappointment, and reduced commitment, with the under-utilisation of talent, an increase in employee turnover, and a deterioration in both individual and organisational performance.

Nicholson and Arnold (1989) identified four defects in career development systems in organisations that are likely to undermine their effectiveness:

- Career moves are determined by rules and procedures that are unresponsive to changing conditions and do not accommodate exceptions.
- Career opportunities are created by managers intent on advancing their own interests to the detriment of the organisation or the individual whose career is under review.
- People are in the dark as to where they are going because possible career pathways and ways of using them are not stated.
- Unnecessary restrictions are placed on certain career moves, particularly sideways transfers between functions.

Finally, Herriot (1992) has come forward with some very interesting ideas about careers in organisations. He maintains that the idea of "career" is central to the 1990s, despite the fact that the notion of a career for life in an organisation is fast disappearing. He maintains that only those organisations that "negotiate" careers will retain the people they need to face the future with confidence.

Overall Evaluation of OD

In the earlier discussion of OD interventions, particularly those that focus on changing the outlook of the individual and group, assessments were made after an examination of each intervention. Now it is time to reflect generally on their effectiveness.

The OD interventions focusing on the individual and group are by and large based on humanistic and democratic values, such as respect for people, trust and support, participation, open confrontation of issues, participation, and power equalisation. Factors such as political systems, organisational conflict, and so on, do not feature prominently in the change agent's agenda, though one has to admit that OD has, in recent years, broadened its perspective. Apart from humanistic considerations, matters connected with job redesign and organisational structure are now taken on board, as well as strategic factors related to the overall direction of the organisation. It is interesting to note an observation by Thompson and McHugh (1990):

> Companies were finding that they could achieve change and secure corporate goals through technical and economic restructuring, with unemployment as an external discipline over the work-force. There simply wasn't a great deal of negotiation and consultation over major organisational changes such as those associated with new technology.

There are some issues that need to be emphasised when it comes to the implementation of behaviourally oriented OD interventions. First, there are the political forces prevalent during times of change (Shein, 1985). It would be unwise to ignore the political dimension and the impact that change interventions can have on the balance of power within the organisation. (Power and politics are discussed in Chapter 9.)

Second, there are individuals who feel uncomfortable engaging in a process that demands a frank disclosure of their feelings and attitudes, even if participation is voluntary. Such a process could be seen as invading a person's privacy and reducing personal freedom. There is also the fear that, though the climate surrounding the intervention is benevolent and supportive, sensitive information may be used vindictively at some later stage against the person who has divulged his or her fears or concerns.

Third, the values ingrained in OD interventions are likely to be out of step with organisational cultures that are characterised as strong on bureaucratic control, risk aversive, intolerant of conflict, and insignificant in supportive management. Of course, OD values could also be incompatible with particular national cultures, in which case negative outcomes can be expected. Therefore, the greater the match between OD values and a country's cultural dimensions, the greater the likelihood that OD intervention will succeed (Jaeger, 1986). (There is a discussion of culture in Chapter 11.)

Despite the widespread use and acceptance of OD, there has been little systematic evaluation of its effects. Where research studies on the effectiveness of OD have been undertaken, it is suggested that one should turn one's attention in the first instance to the methodology used. Terpstra (1981) argues that the more rigorous the evaluation research (i.e. whether or not particular interventions had the desired effect), the more difficult it is to find evidence supportive of OD. That means that with well-designed research, using a random selection of subjects, control groups, and sophisticated analysis, one is less likely to find evidence of the effectiveness of OD.

Terpstra makes the point that because the results of less rigorous research are often ambiguous, there is an unconscious bias on the part of researchers evaluating the effectiveness of OD to interpret the results as supportive, and that high expectations on the part of top management and pressure from the latter might also contribute to this bias. On the theme of expectations, Evden (1986) asserts that where gains stem from OD interventions, they can be attributable to managers being convinced by consultants that an intervention would succeed. This is communicated down the organisation through supervisors to workers, and any productivity improvements are due more to raised expectations about the effectiveness of OD than to the intervention chosen.

SUMMARY: ORGANISATIONAL CHANGE AND DEVELOPMENT

- Having defined what we mean by change, there was a discussion of resistance to change.
- The sources of resistance to change at the organisational level were listed as over-determination, narrow focus of change, group inertia, threatened expertise, threatened power, and resource allocation. At the individual level they were identified as habit, security, economic considerations, fear of the unknown, lack of awareness, and social considerations.
- An alternative explanation of sources of change suggested that key considerations are parochial self-interest, misunderstanding/lack of trust, contradictory assessments, and low tolerance of change.
- Approaches to controlling resistance to change were identified as education and communication, participation, facilitation and support, negotiation and agreement, manipulation and co-optation, and coercion.
- The need to plan organisational change was stressed, and the process model, the extended model, and action research were suggested as approaches.
- Organisational development (OD) was identified as the process of planned change and improvement of organisations through the application of knowledge derived from the behavioural sciences.
- General strategies to bring about organisational development were specified, and various techniques and interventions were stated. These interventions operate at three different levels—i.e. the levels of organisation structure, task redesign, and the individual/group.
- With respect to interventions at the individual/group level, a number of people-centred techniques were discussed. These are sensitivity training, survey feedback, process consultation, team-building, managerial grid, management by objectives, conflict management, management development, and career planning.
- The final section reflected on the effectiveness of OD interventions.

QUESTIONS

1. Define organisational change.
2. Describe the approach adopted by Katz and Kahn to the sources of resistance to change, and state how it differs from that of Bedeian.
3. How would you go about controlling resistance to change?
4. "It is not good enough for an organisation to respond to change; it must try to anticipate it as well." Discuss.
5. What is the difference between the process model and the extended model in the context of planning organisational change.
6. Define the following terms: (a) action research; (b) group inertia; and (c) co-optation.
7. Define organisational development.
8. What do we mean by people-centred change techniques in organisational development?
9. Discuss the significance of career planning in the 1990s.
10. Identify the main objectives of management development.
11. Comment on issues related to an evaluation of organisational development.

Transition management: An ... nanaging complex change. ...ics, Summer, 46–66.

...s, R. (1972). Understanding ... feedback. In W.W. Burke & ...ls.), *The social technology of organisational development* (pp. 234–243). Fairfax, VA:NTL Learning Resource Corporation.

Bedeian, A.G. (1980). *Organisations: Theory and analysis*. Orlando, FL.: Dryden Press.

Beer, M. (1980). *Organisational change and development: A systems view*. Santa Monica, CA: Goodyear.

Beer, M., Eisenstat, R.A., & Spector, B. (1990). Why change programs don't produce change. *Harvard Business Review*, November–December, 158–166.

Beer, M. & Walton, A.E. (1987). Organisational change and development. In M.R. Rosenzweig & L.W. Porter (Eds.), *Annual Review of Psychology*. Palo Alto, CA: Annual Reviews.

Bernardin, H.J. & Alvares, K. (1976). The managerial grid as a predictor of conflict resolution method and managerial effectiveness. *Administrative Science Quarterly*, 21, March, p. 84.

Blake, R.R. & Mouton, J.S. (1969). *Building a dynamic corporation through grid organisation development*. Reading, MA: Addison-Wesley.

Bowen, D.D. & Hisrich, R.D. (1986). The female entrepreneur: A career development perspective. *Academy of Management Review*, April, 393–407.

Bradshaw, D. (1993). Rewards for the scientists. *Financial Times*, 29 October.

Buller, P.F. & Bell, C.H. (1986). Effects of team-building and goal setting on productivity: A field experiment. *Academy of Management Journal*, June, 305–328.

Burke, W.W. (1982). *Organisational development: Principles and practice*. Boston: Little, Brown.

Burgoyne, J. (1988). Management development for the individual and the organisation. *Personnel Management*, June, 40–44.

Burgoyne, J. & Germain, C. (1984). Self-development and career planning: An exercise in mutual benefit. *Personnel Management*, April, 21–23.

Campbell, J.P. & Dunnette, M.D. (1968). Effectiveness of T-groups: Experience in managerial training and development. *Psychological Bulletin*, 70, August, 73–104.

Carroll, S.J. & Tosi, H.L. (1970). Goal characteristics and personality factors in a management by objectives programme. *Administrative Science Quarterly*, 15, September, 295–305.

Chin, R. & Benne, K.D. (1976). General strategies for effecting changes in human systems. In W.G. Bennis, K.D. Benne, R. Chin & K.E. Carey (Eds.), *The planning of change* (third edition). New York: Holt, Rinehart & Winston.

Di Prete, T.A. (1987). Horizontal and vertical mobility in organisations. *Administrative Science Quarterly*, December, 422–444.

Evden, D. (1986). OD and self-fulfilling prophecy: Boosting productivity by raising expectations. *Journal of Applied Behavioural Science*, 22, 1–13.

Franklin, J.L. (1978). Improving the effectiveness of survey feedback. *Personnel*, May–June, 11–17.

French, W.L. & Bell, C.H. (1978). *Organisational development* (second edition). New York: Prentice-Hall.

Friedlander, F. & Brown, L.D. (1974). Organisational development. In M.R. Rosensweig & L.W. Porter (Eds.), *Annual Review of Psychology*. Palo Alto, CA: Annual Reviews.

Furnham, A. (1993). Short cut to the top. *Financial Times*, 13 January.

Golembiewski, R.T., Proehl Jr., C.W., & Sink, D. (1982). Estimating the success of OD applications. *Training and Development Journal*, April, 90–93.

Gottlieb, C. (1988). And you thought you had it tough. *Fortune*, 25th April, 83–84.

Granrose, C.S. & Portwood, J.D. (1987). Matching individual career plans and organisational careers management. *Academy of Management Journal*, December, 699–720.

Gray, J.L. & Starke, F.A. (1984). *Organisational behaviour: Concepts and applications* (third edition). Columbus, Ohio: Charles E. Merrill.

Griffin, R.W. (1982). *Task design: An integrative approach*. Glenview, IL: Scott, Foresman.

Griffiths, P. & Bell, E. (1985). Using assessment centres. *Training Officer*, October, 300–302.

Herriot, P. (1992). *The career management challenge: Balancing individual and organisational needs*. London: Sage.

Hodgetts, R.M. (1991). *Organisational behaviour: Theory and practice*. New York: Macmillan.

Jaeger, A.M. (1986). Organisation development and national culture: Where's the fit? *Academy of Management Review*, January, 178–190.

Kanter, R.M. (1989). *When giants learn to dance: Mastering the challenge of strategy, management, and careers in the 1990s*. New York: Simon & Schuster.

Katz, D. & Kahn, R.L. (1978). *The social psychology of organisations* (second edition). New York: John Wiley.

Kondrasuk, J.N. (1981). Studies in MBO effectiveness. *Academy of Management Review*, 6, 419–430.

Kotter, J.P. & Schlesinger, L.A. (1979). Choosing strategies for change. *Harvard Business Review*, March–April, 106–114.

Leibowitz, Z.B. & Schlossberg, N.K. (1981). Training managers for their role in a career development system. *Training and Development Journal*, July, 72–79.

Leonard, P. (1984). *Personality and ideology: Toward a materialist understanding of the individual.* London: Macmillan.

Lewin, K. (1951). *Field theory in social science.* New York: Harper & Row.

Lieberman, M.A., Yalom, I.D., & Miles, M.B. (1973). Encounter: The leader makes a difference. *Psychology Today,* March, 69–76.

Liebowitz, S.J. & De Meuse, K.P. (1982). The application of team-building. *Human Relations,* January, 1–18.

Maanen, J. Van, & Schein, E.H. (1977). Career development. In J.R. Hackman & J.L. Suttle (Eds.), *Improving life at work.* Santa Monica, CA: Goodyear.

Makin, P., Cooper, C., & Cox, C. (1989). *Managing people at work.* London: Routledge and The British Psychological Society.

Morgan, M.A., Hall, D.T., & Martier, A. (1979). Career development strategies in industry: Where are we and where should we be? *Personnel,* March / April, 13–30.

Moorhead, G. (1981). Organisational analysis: An integration of the macro and micro approaches. *Journal of Management Studies,* April, 191–218.

Moorhead, G. & Griffin, R.W. (1989). *Organisational behaviour* (second edition). Boston: Houghton Mifflin.

Moorhead, G. & Griffin, R.W. (1992). *Organisational behaviour* (third edition). Boston: Houghton Mifflin.

Mumford, A. (1987). Myths and reality in developing directors. *Personnel Management,* February, 29–33.

Nadler, D.A. (1983). Concepts for the management of organisational change. In J.R. Hackman, E.E. Lawler III, & L.W. Porter (Eds.), *Perspectives on behaviour in organisations* (second edition). New York: McGraw-Hill.

Nicholson, N. & Arnold, J. (1989). Graduate early experience in a multinational corporation. *Personnel Review, 18,* 3–14.

Passmore, W.A. (1978). The comparative impacts of socio-technical system, job redesign and survey feedback intervention. In W.A. Passmore & J.J. Sherwood (Eds.), *Socio-technical systems: A sourcebook.* La Jolla, CA: University Associates.

Pfeffer, J. (1981). Management as symbolic action: The creation and maintenance of organisational paradigms. In L.L. Cummings & B.M. Straw (Eds.), *Research in organisational behaviour* (Vol. 3). Greenwich, CT: JAI Press.

Pritchard, W. (1984). What's new in organisation development. *Personnel Management,* July, 30–33.

Robbins, S.P. (1991). *Organisational behaviour: Concepts, controversies and application* (fifth edition). New York: Prentice-Hall.

Rubinstein, D. & Woodman, R.W. (1984). Spiderman and the Burma raiders: Collateral organisation theory in action. *The Journal of Applied Behavioural Science,* January / March, 1–21.

Sadler, P. (1988). *Managerial leadership in the post-industrial society.* Aldershot, UK: Gower Publishing.

Schein, E.H. (1969). *Process consultation: Its role in organisational development.* Reading, MA: Addison-Wesley.

Schein, E.H. (1987). *Process consultation, Volume II: Lessons for managers and consultants.* Reading, MA: Addison-Wesley.

Shein, V.E. (1985). Organisational realities: The politics of change. *Training and Development Journal,* February, 37–41.

Sisson, K. & Storey, J. (1988). Developing effective managers: A review of the issues and an agenda for research. *Personnel Review, 17,* 3–8.

Szilagi, A.D. & Wallace, M.J. (1983). *Organisational behaviour and performance* (third edition). Glenview, IL: Scott, Foresman.

Terpstra, D.E. (1981). Relationship between methodological rigour and reported outcomes in organisation development evaluation research. *Journal of Applied Psychology, 66,* 541–543.

Thompson, P. & McHugh, D. (1990). *Work organisations: A critical introduction.* Basingstoke, UK: Macmillan Education.

Tichy, N.M. & Ulrich, D.O. (1984). The leadership challenge: A call for the transformational leader. *Sloan Management Review,* Fall, 59–68.

Walton, R.E. (1969). *Interpersonal peacemaking: Confrontations and third party consultation.* Reading, MA: Addison-Wesley.

Williams, R. (1984). What's new in career development. *Personnel Management,* March, 31–33.

Zaltman, G. & Duncan, R. (1977). *Strategies for planned change.* New York: John Wiley.

Zand, D.E. (1974). Collateral organisation: A new change strategy. *Journal of Applied Behavioural Science,* January / March, 63–89.

13

Human Resource Practices

After a brief explanation of human resource management, this chapter examines human resource practices with respect to performance appraisal, reward systems, and personnel selection processes. The performance appraisal section begins with a perspective on the goals of performance appraisal and the evaluative criteria and techniques used. Next, the focus is on points to note in administering the appraisal process, followed by the use of appraisal information and the problems encountered. The purpose and philosophy of reward systems, and types of rewards are stated. Most attention is devoted to pay as a reward system, and to performance-related pay. The final section concentrates on personnel selection, with particular emphasis on selection methods, their fairness, validity, reliability, and utility.

This chapter is related to other chapters in Part III of this book, and issues covered in the first two parts of the book having particular relevance are personality and intelligence testing (Chapter 1), motivation (Chapter 2), interpersonal perception (Chapter 3), and learning and training (Chapter 4).

HUMAN RESOURCE MANAGEMENT

Nowadays, human resource practices can operate within a framework provided by human resource management, and a brief explanation of this is appropriate before we move on to look at human resource practices, which are the primary concern of this chapter.

A major theme running through human resource management is the acknowledgement that employees are valued assets of the organisation, that there should be an active interplay between a strategy for the human resource and the main strategy for the business, that corporate culture should be managed so as to make it compatible with the requirements of corporate strategy, and that

seeking the commitment of employees to the organisation has far greater value than mere forced compliance. To elicit commitment, reference is often made to mutuality. This represents human resource management policies that promote mutual goals, mutual influence, mutual rewards, and mutual responsibility. In a climate of mutuality the cause of commitment is advanced, with alleged benefits in terms of productivity and employee development, although it is recognised that mutuality is a fragile phenomenon (Armstrong, 1992).

Another feature of human resource management which is often mentioned is the existence of the "common interests" of management and employees in the profitability of the enterprise. This is said to lead to the tapping of a substantial reservoir of initiative within the work-force. There is also a concern within human resource management for the organisation to respond appropriately to forces in the company's environment by becoming flexible, adaptive, and competitive. For example, an organisation could respond to environmental forces by increased decentralisation in order to facilitate a better reaction to market forces. In line with delegation, there could be greater employee autonomy and accountability for the efficient use of resources. Flexibility may be injected into the roles employees play in teams (e.g. autonomous groups), and is manifest in a wider range of skills (multi-skilling).

Human resource management, as a strategic approach to acquire, develop, manage, and motivate people, became popular in the 1980s, and in some cases it absorbed and extended the personnel management function in business. It draws on a number of the behavioural ideas discussed in this book, but at the same time it adopts a hard-nosed business orientation.

The human resource or personnel management practices of primary interest to the occupational psychologist are training, performance appraisal, reward systems, and personnel selection. Training has been discussed at length in Chapter 4, so the human resource practices that will be discussed in this chapter are performance appraisal, reward systems, and personnel selection.

PERFORMANCE APPRAISAL

It is a common event in many spheres of work for the performance of subordinates to be evaluated by superiors and others as a means of developing human resources, with productivity firmly in mind. The normal practice is for the results of the appraisal process to be shared with the subordinate in a positive way so that the individual concerned is given the support to put right deficiencies or maintain good practice. Nowadays performance appraisal is often referred to as performance management when placed in a Human Resource Management context.

Goals of Performance Appraisal

Apart from the justification for using performance appraisal, mentioned earlier, there are other reasons why performance of employees is evaluated, such as the following:

- To assist with decisions about levels of compensation or reward. This would apply, in particular, to circumstances where a system of performance-related pay is in use.
- To assist superiors to evaluate the suitability of the subordinate for training and development. This could include the identification of employees with high potential, and the spotting of obstacles or barriers to performance. Generally, the emphasis is on identifying skills and competencies that are currently inadequate but for which remedial programmes exist.
- To assist managers to make informed decisions about matters such as promotions, demotions, transfers, and dismissals.
- To create a dialogue between the superior and subordinate on performance-related matters in order to clarify misunderstandings, provide relevant information, and establish agreement on expectations on both sides.
- To provide a forum at which superiors meet with subordinates and provide them with feedback on their strengths and weaknesses.
- To validate the effectiveness of past employee selection decisions, and the adequacy of previous training.

Criteria for Performance Appraisal

The importance of specifying the criterion or criteria to be used in performance evaluation must not be understated. Criteria used could embrace task outcomes, behaviours, and traits.

Task Outcomes
This could be the actual quantity of goods produced or, for instance, the number of invoices processed by a sales clerk over a certain time period.

Behaviours
Performance, though complex and multi-faceted at times, can be expressed as the actual behaviours expected of an employee at work. A starting point is job analysis, which amounts to a precise statement of the activities that constitute a job. An observer collects all available information on a particular job and normally interviews the current job holder and the immediate supervisor. From this exercise a job description will be prepared which consists of a list of descriptive statements defining the responsibilities of the job holder.

Sometimes it is not possible to identify task outcomes that can be directly related to the efforts of the individual. For example, it may be difficult to identify individual performance when the person is a member of a group with highly interdependent activities. In such circumstances it is possible to evaluate group performance. Also, employees, who act as advisers or internal consultants, may fall into the category of individuals whose specific task outcome it is difficult to identify.

To overcome these difficulties, the organisation may specify behaviours that would form the basis for evaluation. These behaviours could include the speed with which tasks are accomplished, and the style of behaviour used (e.g. management style) during interactions with other people.

Traits
This is beyond doubt the poorest set of criteria, but one still finds heavy reliance placed on it in organisations. Traits refer to projections of the personality, discussed in Chapter 1, and labels such as "displays confidence", "is co-operative and friendly", "is bright", and "has the right attitude", are not necessarily related in a positive sense to performance on the job. However, management in organisations seems to have an attachment to traits as criteria for assessing an employee's performance.

Performance Appraisal Techniques

When the emphasis shifts from the criteria (the things we evaluate) to techniques (how the appraisal is done) we enter the domain of methods used to evaluate performance. The major performance appraisal techniques used in the evaluation of individual performance, or the evaluation of individual performance when compared with other people's performance, are as follows:

1. Individual evaluation
   - Graphic rating scales
   - Essays
   - Behaviourally anchored rating scales
   - Behavioural observation scales
2.. Comparative evaluation
   - Ranking
   - Paired comparison
   - Forced distribution
3.. Multi-rater comparative evaluation
   - Objective judgement quotient (OJQ)
   - Assessment centres.

1. Individual Evaluation

Graphic Rating Scales
This is a basic method of rating the performance of the individual. Where a global measure is used, the rater places a circle on the point of the scale that appears to be a good reflection of the level of performance of the employee. This is illustrated in Table 13.1.

TABLE 13.1

Global Measure of Performance on a Graphic Rating Scale

Name of Employee	Rating				
	Poor	Below average	Average	Above average	Excellent
John Smith					

Where multiple measures of performance are used, the rater circles the point on each scale that is indicative of the performance of the employee (see Table 13.2).

Graphic rating scales are easy to develop and administer, and lend themselves to quantitative analysis and comparison between employees, although they do not provide the richness of data which some of the other techniques produce. They have, however, been in existence for a long time and are popular for the evaluation of employees who are entitled to receive overtime payments (Fombrun & Laud, 1983).

Essays
The rater writes a narrative describing an employee's strengths, weaknesses, potential, performance to date, and suggestions for improvement. This record could be based on the memory of the rater or drawn from his or her diary entries, and could provide much more insightful information on an employee's performance than can be derived from a graphic rating scale. However, one has to bear in mind that a rater's memory may not be the most reliable, and diary entries may fall short of what could be considered a good record. In such circumstances the essay method of rating is less than satisfactory.

Other matters to consider in connection with essays are that comparisons between employees whose performance is evaluated are not possible because of an absence of comparable points in narratives on various individuals. Also present is the danger of describing personality traits, rather than describing incidents of good or poor performance, particularly when the method is used by an inadequately trained evaluator.

TABLE 13.2

Multiple Measures of Performance on a Graphic Rating Scale

Name of Employee	Rating				
John Smith	Poor	Below average	Average	Above average	Excellent
1. Quantity					
2. Quality					
3. Expertise					
4. Initiative					
5. Co-operative					
6. Commitment					

Finally, essays are not as easy to develop or use as approaches relying on numerical analysis. Nor does the essay technique lend itself to computer applications (Bernardin & Beatty, 1984).

Behaviourally Anchored Rating Scales

These scales integrate graphic rating scales with descriptions of workers' behaviour that characterise or "anchor" various points on the scales. Under this method, the framework used to evaluate performance consists of a number of scales with each scale representing an important aspect of job behaviour (Smith & Kendall, 1963). An example of rating factors in behaviourally anchored rating scales appears in Fig. 13.1 (McBriarty, 1988).

The rater places the individual on an anchor along the continuum of each scale. The behaviourally anchored rating scales are developed by people, called experts, who are familiar with the jobs under review. They verify that the statements are clearly written and accurately describe actual behaviour of job occupants (i.e. critical incidents). Then the scales are developed whereby the statements of job behaviour are positioned on the scale and given a numerical value.

Although it is claimed to be a reliable measure, it has potential disadvantages (Moorhead & Griffin, 1992). These relate to the expense of developing and maintaining the system, because scales may need updating as jobs change with the progressive application of new technology. Also, the raters experience difficulties when the anchors do not coincide with the actual behaviours observed.

Behavioural Observation Scales

Yet another attempt to develop performance rating scales linked to actual behaviour was made by Latham and Wexley (1981). They used behavioural observation scales that were developed from a critical incident technique, similar to that used to compile the behaviourally anchored rating scales, in which job occupants and supervisors generate performance behaviours inherent in the job.

The evaluator is required to indicate the frequency with which an employee displays a specific behaviour. This differs from behaviourally anchored rating scales where the evaluator is asked to define superior versus inferior performance, and the employee is assessed on having displayed a particular behaviour during a specific rating period.

2. Comparative Evaluation

When one person's performance is evaluated against another or others' performance, we enter the realm of multi-person comparisons. Comparative evaluation is a relative rather than an absolute appraisal device.

Ranking

This involves taking all employees doing a particular type of job and then, using a global criterion, ranking them by performance after reflecting on the various individual contributions.

This method compensates for the weakness of the individual methods discussed earlier by stressing the relative performance of employees. Invariably it is easier to rank the top and bottom performers before consideration of those in the middle. Ranking based on a global criterion of performance has its shortcomings because of the tendency to reduce a very complex set of behaviours to a single value. Also it is difficult to use ranking with a large number of employees, and rankings do not disclose degrees of difference in the levels of performance. When critical decisions are made—e.g. transfers, terminating employment, promotions—it is inevitable that rankings would have to be supplemented by additional information on employees.

Paired Comparison

This is a variation of the ranking method, and requires the evaluator to appraise each employee in conjunction with all others employees in the set before making a judgement. The evaluator usually compares two people at a time on one global

1. Job Capability					
☐ Not observed	☐ Has gaps in fundamental knowledge and skills of job.	☐ Has satisfactory knowledge and skill for the routine phases of job.	☐ Has excellent knowledge and is well skilled on all phases of job.	☐ Has exceptional understanding and skill on all phases of job.	☐ Has far-reaching grasp of entire broad job area. Authority in the field.

2. Planning Ability					
☐ Not observed	☐ Relies on others to bring problems to attention. Often fails to see ahead.	☐ Plans ahead just enough to get by in present job.	☐ Is a careful effective planner. Anticipates and takes action to solve problems.	☐ Capable of planning beyond requirements of the present job. Sees the big picture.	☐ Capable of top level planning. A high calibre thinker and planner.

3. Executive Management					
☐ Not observed	☐ Is a poor organiser. Does not really make effective use of material or personnel.	☐ Maintains ordinary efficiency of operation. Control could be improved.	☐ Gives economy of operation careful attention. Makes wise use of personnel and materials.	☐ Maintains effective economy. Carefully weighs cost against expected results.	☐ Highly skilled in balancing cost against results to obtain optimum effectiveness

4. Leadership					
☐ Not observed	☐ Often weak in command situations. At times unable to exert control.	☐ Normally develops fairly adequate control and team-work.	☐ Consistently a good leader. Commands respect of subordinates	☐ Exceptional skill in directing others to great effort.	☐ Leadership qualities reflect potential to highest level

FIG. 13.1. A behaviourally anchored rating scale. Source: McBriarty, M.A. (1988). Performance appraisal: Some unintended consequences. *Public Personnel Management*, Winter, p.423, used by permission.

performance criterion. The better and weaker performer in each pair is identified, and eventually a list is prepared where people are placed in rank order based on the number of good scores achieved. Because ranking is by pairs the evaluator is not overwhelmed and confused by having to cope with too many employees at one time, but, with increases in the size of the pool of individuals to be appraised, this method shows potential weaknesses associated with handling more and more comparisons.

Forced Distribution

With this method the evaluator is required to place employees into particular categories according to their performance. For example, one system would be to create three categories with an equal distribution of people, as shown in Table 13.3. Alternatively, there could be a larger number of categories with variable distributions, as in Table 13.4.

In the case illustrated in Table 13.4, the evaluator must assign specified percentages of employees to each of the five categories. You will notice that an imposed normal distribution applies in the illustration, which suggests that 40% of performance falls into the average category. This could create difficulties if, for example, employees in a particular department were predominantly either superior or inferior performers, in which case a skewed distribution would be more appropriate. By placing all employees into a few groups, the forced distribution method produces less information than the straight ranking method.

3. Multi-rater Comparative Evaluation

Objective Judgement Quotient

The objective judgement quotient (OJQ) method (Edwards, 1983) operates on the principle of using more than one rater, with

TABLE 13.3

Distribution Among Categories—Equal

	Categories		
	Below average	Average	Above average
Distribution	33%	33%	33%

TABLE 13.4

Distribution Among Categories—Variable

	Categories				
	Unacceptable	Poor	Average	Above average	Excellent
Distribution	10%	20%	40%	20%	10%

different evaluation methods. The performance of individuals is compared with that of others using a number of raters, including the supervisor. The outcome of this exercise is the creation of a "performance profile" showing the position of each appraisee on the performance criteria in comparison with all other employees who have been appraised.

Assessment Centres

An assessment centre is also an example of a technique using multiple raters where comparative evaluation can be used. When used as a development centre it is a method of appraising managerial ability with the future firmly in focus, under which the appraisal of managerial abilities and skills takes place over a few days. The overall appraisal normally consists of interviews, psychometric testing, simulations (such as an in-basket exercise whereby the participant copes with a collection of correspondence from a manager's incoming mail), peer appraisals, and appraisal by experts in attendance. The aim of an assessment centre is to appraise current ability as a basis for making judgements about the suitability of the participant for promotion to a more senior position. A more detailed discussion of assessment centres takes place later in the chapter.

Administering the Appraisal System

Formal performance evaluation is normally conducted on an annual basis, but employees receive informal feedback on their performance from superiors on a frequent basis. The formal review does not have to take place at the same time of the year for all employees, but it normally does, and precedes the annual process for the determination of rewards. Where the performance review in the organisation takes place on the anniversary of the employee joining the company, evaluations can be dispersed throughout the year, and this could help

supervisors by spreading the burden of conducting appraisals over a longer period.

For employees serving a probationary period, the end of that period normally signals the need to conduct an appraisal, even if the time does not coincide with the organisation's annual review or alternative arrangements. After the evaluation of the employee at the end of the probationary period, a decision will be made as to whether or not the person's employment will continue.

Whether an organisation should stick rigidly to annual or semi-annual performance reviews is open to question. A number of influences could be considered. For example, it may be more important to conduct an appraisal when a distinct unit of work or assignment has been completed, or when the organisation needs information on employees' performance on completion of a particular project. A number of ways of evaluating performance outside the traditional annual process have been suggested (see Fedor & Buckley, 1988).

Apart from the frequency of performance appraisal in a formal sense, another matter to consider in connection with the administration of the system is who is charged with carrying out the appraisals? The simple answer is that there can be more people involved than the obvious person—i.e. the supervisor. Those charged with carrying out appraisals can be listed as:

- supervisors;
- self;
- peers;
- subordinates; and
- others.

Supervisor

The immediate supervisor is often considered to be the most logical choice of candidate for the role of evaluator of a subordinate's performance. Naturally it is felt that the immediate supervisor is well placed to observe the subordinate's behaviour and to judge his or her relative contribution to the effectiveness of the department. However, it is sometimes conceded that supervisors are not sufficiently close to their subordinates to enable them to pass judgement that is likely to be useful. The reasons given include the fact that supervisors may be geographically distant from certain types of subordinate (e.g. sales representatives in the field), preventing them from observing their behaviour. Also, supervisors are generally too absorbed in roles other than monitoring the performance of subordinates—such as representing their section or department, or handling budgets and report writing (Vecchio, 1991).

Self-appraisal

This approach to performance evaluation may be suitable when appraising and comparing an individual's performance on certain dimensions, such as the quality of performance, interpersonal skills, and leadership. It is claimed that employees have the capacity to evaluate themselves in an unbiased manner (Mabe & West, 1982). Self-appraisal is particularly appropriate in the context of employee development or management development, but there is a danger that sometimes self-ratings may amount to a distortion of reality and be out of line with supervisor ratings. When it comes to interpersonal comparisons it is said that self-appraisals have little value for the comparison of the performance of different individuals (Fletcher, 1984).

One way of improving the effectiveness of self-ratings is to combine them with supervisor ratings (Teel, 1978). Here the supervisor and subordinate complete the evaluation separately, using identical forms, and subsequently meet to compare the responses. In a supportive environment this approach has value in allowing both parties to exchange perceptions of the subordinate's behaviour and performance at work.

Self-ratings could be used where participative management processes exist, such as management by objectives (examined in Chapter 12). As stated earlier, self-ratings are particularly useful in training and development situations where subordinates obtain insight into the progress they have made to date. However, Vecchio (1991) suggests that self-ratings rarely have much influence on decisions about promotions, salary increases, transfers, etc.

Peers

Appraisals conducted by peers or co-workers are a rare event, but as a mode of evaluation this type of appraisal has some strengths. Peers are in a good position to observe a colleague's performance in a variety of situations over long periods of time. According to Korman (1968), one outcome of being in contact with co-workers for an appreciable length of time is the creation of more accurate assessments and predictions of each other's performance. Although peer ratings are likely to be more reliable than self-ratings, they are vulnerable to a number of potential biases. For example, one major limitation is that people are likely to rate their friends more favourably (De Nisi & Mitchell, 1978). Also, better performers may receive tougher evaluations at the hands of less able performers intent on protecting their own image.

Subordinates

Subordinates of supervisors or managers could be asked to evaluate their boss's performance. This exercise, which is not in widespread use, should be subject to anonymity, though the latter may be difficult to preserve where a group is small. The appraisal is likely to generate a number of impressions of the boss's performance, which could signal a weakness. Many subordinates may feel unhappy about participating in this type of appraisal because they feel that it is not their responsibility to evaluate their superior, or that they are not well placed to undertake an upward appraisal, or that they may fear reprisal.

It would be unwise to completely ignore subordinates' appraisal of their superiors, because the process could be valuable in providing feedback for the recipient to consider when reflecting on personal performance. In the field of training, and some branches of education, trainees or students are asked to complete evaluation forms at the end of a course. The data, when analysed, could be used to isolate deficiencies which should be addressed, or to form a basis for providing extra material rewards or career advancement when the overall evaluation is consistently very favourable.

Although subordinate appraisals have been conducted successfully in certain well-managed companies (e.g. *IBM* and *Pepsico*), nevertheless the resistance of superiors is probably the greatest barrier to implementation of the process. Some managers feel that their power will be usurped. Others object emotionally, if not intellectually, to the idea of a subordinate evaluating their performance. They are often also concerned that an over-emphasis will be placed upon being popular as opposed to being respected (Nevels, 1989).

According to Furnham (1993) enthusiasm for subordinate appraisals (the bottom-up system) has to some extent "gone off the boil", as in the case of *British Airways*, but he feels that if the system is working well it is both efficient and equitable. However, the conditions for a successful system should be noted—i.e. trust in staff to be honest, fair, and constructive; real commitment to the notion that communication is a two-way process; and finally the ratings of subordinates are taken seriously and acted on.

Other Appraisers
People outside the immediate work environment of the person to be appraised may be invited to participate in the process of performance appraisal. They could be clients or customers who are asked to give their considered judgement of the person concerned, and managers or supervisors from other sections and departments who are one hierarchical step above the person to be appraised. Other people likely to be involved

as appraisers are consultants who would normally be commissioned to undertake appraisal of the performance of the more senior managers. They would tap a variety of sources (e.g. superiors, peers, clients) before making a judgement.

A listing of the advantages and disadvantages of the different agencies for conducting performance appraisals appears in Table 13.5. An important point to bear in mind in connection with performance appraisal is that whoever performs the evaluation must be properly trained. Due attention should be given to reducing rating errors by sharpening the observation and behavioural categorisation skills of the rater at training sessions. Apparently employees usually consider appraisals of performance fair if raters receive the appropriate training and use some form of diary to record actual events (Greenberg, 1986).

Use of Appraisal Information

The information produced by the performance appraisal system can convey, for example, that an employee should be considered seriously for extra rewards, or is ready for promotion, or is in need of additional training, or is so seriously deficient in the necessary skills to do the job that he or she should be replaced. Also, the appraisal information can be used to prepare forecasts of staffing needs and inform decision making in areas such as succession planning, recruitment, training, and management development.

The outcomes described can be of benefit to both the employee and organisation if the appraisal system works well. An important process for providing information to those whose performance is appraised is the feedback interview.

Feedback Interview
The feedback of information to those appraised is said to have a beneficial effect on performance (Erez, 1977). Employees

TABLE 13.5

Advantages and Disadvantages of Using Different Appraisers.

Source of Appraisal	Advantages	Disadvantages
Immediate supervisor	Makes decisions on rewards Has perspectives on all subordinates	Personal bias possible Supervisor may be removed from subordinates
Self	Unique perspective A useful basis for comparison Useful for self-insight	Likely to be too lenient
Peers	Greater exposure to appraisee More accurate assessment	Competitive atmosphere confounds usage
Subordinates	Can give diagnostic-type feedback	Can subvert the leader's authority
Superiors of other units	Can be less subjective	Too removed from the individual
Customers or clients	Gives input from immediate client group	Only sees limited facet of appraisee
Consultants	Complete, thorough appraisal	Too expensive for use with all employees

Source: Vecchio, R.P. (1991). *Organisational behaviour*. Orlando, FL: The Dryden Press, p.243. Used by permission

normally like to know how well they are doing, and a mechanism for providing such information is the feedback interview. The purpose of this interview is normally to provide a supportive climate in which positive suggestions to improve performance would be discussed. It should be borne in mind that the impression the subordinate receives about his or her appraisal has a material effect on both self-esteem and future motivational disposition.

In practice, there is evidence to indicate that the outcome of the interaction of superior and subordinate in sharing appraisal information in the feedback interview is emotional tension and defensiveness (Vecchio, 1991). For example, superiors could feel very uncomfortable when relaying to subordinates the message that their performance has been below expectations. This situation could be made worse if the superior accumulates negative performance-related information over time and unloads it during the feedback interview. For these and other reasons, superiors may be tempted to cancel or delay the reviews, or avoid raising issues likely to be contentious. Of course reporting good news should present little difficulty for the supervisor.

Turning the spotlight on to the subordinate, how does the process affect his or her disposition? Because subordinates generally tend to view their performance as better than it really is, they are likely to feel discomfort when they disagree with the superior's assessments (Heneman, 1974).

The credibility and power of the appraiser are said to be important variables in the feedback interview (Ilgen, Fisher, & Taylor, 1979).

The appraiser must be perceived as credible before an appraisee is prepared to accept and respect the feedback. Acceptance of the feedback will be reinforced when the appraiser is viewed as not only credible but also able to wield power (in terms of authority to dispense rewards and sanctions). Where the appraiser is seen as lacking in credibility or power, the appraisee is likely to seek feedback from other sources—for example peers, self, or subordinates—and where there is a divergence between the views of these sources and the formal evaluator, the judgements of the alternative sources may be accepted as a means of shielding self-esteem.

According to Burke et al. (1978), to enhance the effectiveness of the process, a number of steps should be considered with respect to the feedback interview (see panel facing).

Problems with Appraisal

The quality of measurement systems is very important in performance appraisal. The measurement method produces the information used in a variety of decisions connected with promotions, transfers, training, salary increases, and so on. As was seen earlier, the focus of the approaches to measurement varies. In some cases the emphasis is on outcomes, whereas in other cases it is on behaviours and personality traits.

In a good performance appraisal system the measurement methods must be valid, reliable, and free of bias, producing ratings that are not too lenient, or severe, or bunched in the middle (central tendency), and that are free of halo and timing errors. But there are situations where imperfections creep into the performance appraisal process, and these will now be discussed.

Validity
The validity of a performance appraisal method rests on the extent to which it reflects the actual performance of the employee. The validity of a measure would be called into question in a situation where, for example, it is acknowledged that in a particular group John is the best performer, but formal indicators of performance evaluation show him as average. There are different types of validity:

"SEE? NOW THAT EVERYTHING'S OUT IN THE OPEN,... YOUR FUTURE WITH THE COMPANY IS ASSURED..."

Effective Feedback Interviews

- The appraiser should prepare carefully for the interview, and this involves collecting and reviewing available records on the appraisee's performance, such as quantity and quality of output, attendance record, commitment, etc. An outline of the points to be dealt with at the interview should be prepared in advance in order to sharpen the focus of the interview.
- In the notice of the interview, the appraisee should be told of its primary purpose—e.g. personal development or pay linked to performance—so as to be in a state of readiness.
- At the beginning of the interview the appraisee could be given the opportunity to comment on his or her performance. This could create a participative tone to the interaction right from the start, with alleged beneficial side effects.
- In providing crucial feedback data to the appraisee, the focus should be on issues rather than aspects of personality. An example of a comment hinging on personality traits is "You don't come across as somebody who has a need to achieve". Where personal characteristics—e.g. the way a person speaks or dresses—are relevant to the position occupied by the appraisee, it would appear to be acceptable to have these matters discussed at the interview. Otherwise it is sensible not to make an issue of the distinctive ways in which individuals express their personality.
- Where it is necessary to voice criticism, the appraiser should do it without adopting a hostile stance. Also, it should be clearly articulated why past behaviour is unacceptable. If it was a matter of poor performance, or shoddy work, the consequences for people inside and outside the organisation could be emphasised.
- Having made the criticism, the appraiser should listen attentively to explanations proffered by the appraisee and, after a discussion, the two parties should formulate an approach to resolving the difficulties with an intention to monitor the implementation of the solution. As people generally have a low tolerance for criticism, in circumstances where numerous criticisms could have been levelled at the appraisee it would appear wise to limit the criticism to a couple of problems.
- The identification of good performance is as necessary as suggestions for the improvement of poor performance. There is a belief that early in the interview the appraiser should emphasise the positive aspects of the appraisee's performance, then move on to the negative aspects, finally terminating the dialogue with more positive comments. This is known as the sandwich approach to the provision of feedback. It is claimed that by stressing favourable aspects of performance early in the interview the appraisee is likely to be less defensive. Equally, closing the interview with similar comments help to maintain good working relationships. However, there are those who feel that the sandwich approach may emasculate the aspect of the process given to critical evaluation.
- Towards the end of the interview it is useful to summarise the action required of the appraisee in order to improve performance. In addition, the appraiser could offer assistance in removing obstacles to achievement, and by doing so could be perceived less as a judge and more as a coach or counsellor by the appraisee.
- The provision of feedback is not something that should only take place in the formal appraisal session. Frequent feedback on an informal basis about a person's positive and negative performance shows that the supervisor is interested in his or her work, and provides a solid base for the formal feedback interview (Burke et al., 1978).

1. Content validity is the extent to which the measuring device adequately addresses all important features of performance in a job. If the measurement method does not assess the full content of job performance, one can question its validity. For example, a test of a trainee driver's ability to drive a car would not have content validity if it did not have a hill start and an emergency stop.

2. Convergent validity rests on the extent to which different measures of performance agree in their assessment of the same performance. If John's performance was rated as high by one measure, and as low by another, obviously the ratings of the same performance do not agree. Therefore, one questions convergent validity in this situation.

3. Discriminant validity rests on the extent to which ratings on a sub-set of performance (e.g. quantity of output) are in agreement with, and differ from, agreed ratings on another sub-set of performance (e.g. quality of output). This could be seen when two raters agree and rate John high on quality of output but low on quantity of output.

Reliability

The reliability of a measuring instrument rests on the extent to which the results obtained are consistent. Where the same performance is measured on a number of occasions (using the same methods) and the results are very similar, the measuring instrument can be considered reliable. But if the results are very different, one could question the reliability of the method of measurement. Another matter to consider in connection with reliability is *inter-rater reliability*. If an employee's performance is evaluated by more than one evaluator, and the ratings are consistent, inter-rater reliability is high. On the other hand, if the ratings differ, one can question the reliability of the measure. (There is further comment on reliability and validity later in the chapter in connection with the employee selection process.)

Bias

Apart from validity and reliability, bias is another issue to consider. It can undermine impartial judgement in assessments of performance. Bias is not only reflected in assessments made with reference to specific criterion, but also stems from applying different criteria to different appraisees. The information acquired from a biased assessment is less meaningful, undermines the purpose of the appraisal process, and contributes to career dissatisfaction among employees (Greenhaus, Parasuraman, & Wormley, 1990).

In the UK, and other countries as well, steps are taken to tackle discrimination in employment. Legislation has been introduced to safeguard groups of employees (e.g. women and minorities) who are very likely to be victimised by bias in employment practices, such as performance appraisal. There still appears to be a lot of scope for improvements in confronting discriminatory practices.

Leniency, Severity, and Central Tendency

These materialise when evaluators show a tendency to rate performance at a consistently high level amounting to overstatement (leniency), or a low level amounting to understatement (severity), or at about the mid-point, restricting the range (central tendency). In each situation the rater is incapable of distinguishing between different levels of performance. This is akin to the notion of low differentiation identified by Pizam (1975). Low differentiators tend to ignore or suppress differences and use a limited range on the rating scale.

The purpose of the appraisal is said to be a factor affecting leniency, particularly in self-rating exercises. Employees who rated themselves, tended to exercise leniency when the results were used for the dispensing of rewards or sanctions. But when they knew that their ratings would be checked by others, more accurate ratings were evident (Farh & Werbel, 1986).

Halo Error

This was discussed in relation to the halo effect in interpersonal perception in Chapter 3. Basically it is the tendency of the evaluator to allow an assessment of an individual on one trait to influence his or her evaluation of that person across the board. For example, an appraisee may come across as articulate, for which a favourable assessment is given, and this favourable impression is then generalised to other individual characteristics, without regard to actual performance.

Similarity Error

This arises when evaluators place special emphasis on the qualities of the person appraised which resemble those seen in themselves. For example, where an evaluator perceives himself or herself as assertive and sees this quality in others during the appraisal process, then those candidates who are perceived as assertive benefit, whereas those without this characteristic are penalised.

Timing Errors

The moment in time when appraisals take place can be critical. It is said that evaluations made after the performance has taken place are more accurate (Heneman & Wexley, 1983). Rating errors can occur when there is an appreciable amount of time between performance and the rating exercise. But the evaluator can reduce rating errors due to the lapse of time by relying on numerous observations of performance over time, and by recording observations soon after the appearance of the relevant bouts of behaviour.

Another type of error—recency error—comes about when the evaluator recalls only the most recent behaviours of the person appraised. This could be problematic because most employees are vigilant and likely to perform well in the period close to the performance review. Should the evaluator place heavy reliance on this bout of behaviour, bias in the appraisal could materialise.

Other Factors

Two further factors likely to distort the performance evaluation process are the single criterion, and using an appraisal process to justify a prior judgement on the performance of the employee (Robbins, 1991).

The use of the single criterion is evident when a single dimension of performance—e.g. the receptionist skills of a secretary—gains prominence in the evaluation process, whereas other dimensions—e.g. keyboard skills—are excluded. In such circumstances the secretary would be expected to pay most attention to the single dimension of performance to the neglect of the other job-related dimensions.

In the case of formal evaluation following the prior judgement of the employee's performance, the appraisal decision is made before the objective information to support the decision is sought. This may appear irrational, but in practice there could be other non-performance criteria—e.g. seniority—based on preferences or values in operation which are not part of the formal appraisal process.

To address some of the problems connected with performance appraisal, Fox (1987) has suggested that:

- multiple job criteria should be identified and evaluated;
- the importance of personality traits alone as predictors of performance should be de-emphasised;
- multiple evaluators should be used as a means to increase the accuracy of appraisal information; and
- there should be a move to evaluate selectively, whereby valuators assess only in areas in which they are qualified to pass judgement.

It seems appropriate to reflect on performance appraisal through the eyes of researchers who studied this process at the *General Electric* company in the USA (Lawler, Mohrman, & Resnick, 1984):

Performance appraisal in an organisation is only as good as its overall human resources climate, strategy, and policies, and especially the processes of fitting it to these. It is unrealistic to expect to have an effective performance appraisal system where jobs are poorly designed, the culture is negative, and subordinates are asked to be passive and do what they are told....

At best, it's two people sharing their perceptions of each other, their relationships, their work, and their organisation—sharing that results in better performance, better feelings, and a more effective organisation. At its worst, it is one person in the name of the organisation trying to force his or her will on another with the result of miscommunication, misperception, disappointment, and alienation. The best is achievable, but only with considerable effort, careful design, constant attention to process, and support by top management.

Finally, recent perspectives originating in the UK would tend to suggest that the following conditions are compatible with a successful performance appraisal or management system (Fletcher & Williams, 1992; Income Data Services, 1992):

- A proactive rather than reactive strategy for performance management.
- A climate within which people feel secure.
- Line managers are involved to an acceptable extent in deliberations and action connected with the system.
- The financial considerations (e.g. bottom line results) and the bureaucratic infrastructure supporting the system are not overstated.
- The introduction of the system is not justified entirely by the need to operationalise a performance-related pay scheme.

REWARDS

Reward systems in organisations are at the disposal of managers in order to motivate people in the desired direction. Therefore, motivation theory, discussed in Chapter 2, is relevant to rewards, as is the concept of reinforcement as part of learning theory, discussed in Chapter 4. The reward system comprises the various organisational activities aimed at the allocation of compensation and benefits to employees in return for the effort and contributions they make to the achievement of organisational objectives. It interacts with the performance appraisal process when judgements are made about the adequacy of employee performance and how it should be rewarded.

Rewards can be divided into intrinsic and extrinsic components. Extrinsic rewards—e.g.

money and other material benefits—emanate from sources that are outside, or external to the individual. By contrast, intrinsic rewards may be described as feelings of achievement, responsibility, or personal growth (which were discussed in connection with motivation theory in Chapter 2). The visibility of extrinsic rewards is pronounced when managers use compensation packages in influencing subordinates to improve performance. Though less visible, intrinsic rewards come to the fore when the redesign of jobs leads to a situation whereby opportunities are created for the enjoyment of intrinsic rewards.

Purpose and Philosophy

The purpose of the reward system is to attract, retain, and motivate qualified employees. An overall philosophy governing compensation or reward systems is as follows (Moorhead & Griffin, 1992):

- fair and equitable rewards;
- a recognition of the importance of each employee's contribution to the organisation, although in practice it is difficult to measure these contributions in an objective way; and
- the compensation package on offer must be competitive in the external employment market in order to attract and retain competent staff.

Although these statements can be taken as a guiding philosophy, an organisation must develop a philosophy of compensation based on its own needs and the conditions prevailing in the organisation. With an eye on more operational issues, a well-developed philosophical statement is likely to include the purpose of the system, offer a framework for making compensation decisions, and endeavour to accommodate relevant variables, such as labour market conditions, general economic conditions, changing technology and equal opportunities (see panel facing). In addition, there should be some indication of the

Equal Opportunities and Rewards

Pay parity between male and female workers was raised as an issue recently when the Equal Opportunities Commission said that the UK Government was failing to implement European Community Law on equal pay. Government ministers deny that Britain is dragging its feet over implementing equal pay legislation, and are likely to point out that the equal pay issue should be placed in a wider perspective. For example, they say that the UK's flexible deregulated labour market has helped create the biggest female job market in Europe, and women in the UK are less likely to be unemployed than men in a recession. Also, the costs of pay parity should be considered in the context of job creation.

The equal pay concept was widened by a 1975 European Community directive which stated that it was no longer the aim to ensure that men and women received the same pay for doing the same or similar jobs; there was also to be equal pay for work of equal value. To operationalise the latter could be difficult. This is not helped by the UK law on equal pay, the wording of which is considered imprecise.

The Equal Opportunities Commission (EOC) is concerned at the lack of progress towards equal pay, and points out that women in all sectors in the UK earn on average 71% of a man's weekly pay. In the manufacturing industry the figure falls to 59% of the weekly pay of male non-manual workers. There has been no significant narrowing of the gap since the early 1970s. The Department of Employment earnings survey for 1992 shows that women's average earnings were £241 a week against £340 for men. The EOC believes that legal complexities are hindering moves to close the pay gap, adding that complaints procedures for cases of "equal value" made through the industrial

tribunals are tortuous. Equal value claims take on average 32 months to process, and a number have taken more than seven years. Only 23 claims in "equal value" cases have succeeded in nearly 10 years. A further concern for the EOC is that an equal pay award made to one person cannot be extended to cover others doing the same jobs. At present the EOC is funding an equal value case brought by a senior grade speech therapist who is trying to compare her job with that of a senior grade pharmacist.

The EOC is proposing several changes to existing equal pay legislation to improve the process. The government's response was to concede that certain changes to speed up procedures in equal value cases were necessary, but other proposals were unlikely to be acceptable (Taylor, 1993).

Despite the low success rate of equal pay claims over the past decade, a recent victory is worth noting. In January 1994 the largest group of women to win an equal pay case in Britain were awarded pay rises of between 37% and 74%. This group consisted of 1500 female welfare assistants in West Sussex schools, who were awarded pay parity with council van drivers by a Southampton Industrial Tribunal. This case, submitted four years ago, focused on equal pay for work of equal value, and most of the female welfare assistants will see their hourly rate increase from £2.94 to £4.04, but that could rise to £5.13 with seniority. The local representative of *Unison* (the public service union) said that the basic increase on the annual pay bill of West Sussex County Council would be £1.2 million, but that could rise to £2.3 million as women move up seniority scales (Goodhart, 1994).

---

type of behaviour or performance—e.g. effective contributions, attendance, loyalty, and conformity—to be encouraged by the reward system. Rewards convey meanings, and apart from their objective significance in terms of size or relative importance, they also posses symbolic value.

Types of Rewards

A compensation package could incorporate the following types of reward:

1. Pay (i.e. wages and salaries).
2. Commission, normally based on sales revenue.
3. Piecework, based on the number of units produced.
4. Bonus, based on the performance of a unit or organisation.
5. Profit sharing, which could amount to a distribution of a proportion of profits at a predetermined rate to all employees.
6. Gain sharing, which could amount to passing on to employees income or

benefits as a result of reductions in costs, or arising from ideas related to improvements.

7. Long-term compensation, which could amount to management receiving substantial additional income from share price performance, return on capital, earnings per share, or a combination of these. This method of compensation could be a source of controversy because of the large sums involved and the basis for the payments.

8. Stock option plans, which could amount to setting aside a block of shares in the company for employees to purchase at a reduced rate, in the belief that employee shareholding at preferential rates leads to extra commitment and more effort, which in turn can be reflected in an increase in the value of the shares.

The incentive schemes numbered 2–8 are normally designed to provide extra income for certain types of performance. Apart from direct incentives, there are other benefits—on-the-job and off-the-job benefits—which are found in indirect compensation systems. On-the-job benefits could refer to payment for time associated with lunch breaks, rest periods, and tea breaks, while off-the-job benefits refer to vacations, sick leave, holidays, and so on. Other indirect benefits include contributions to life and health insurance cover, and occupational pension schemes. In addition, there could be special privileges—e.g. use of the company's accommodation or transport—or rewards for certain types of accomplishments.

Pay

Because of the importance of pay in compensation packages the greater part of the discussion that follows will focus on both pay and performance-related pay. For many people pay is the most important organisational reward, and its importance is reflected in the attention the salaries of senior

executives received during the boom conditions of the 1980s. It indicates comparative worth, and adjustments to pay can be viewed as a source of satisfaction or dissatisfaction.

The determination of a pay structure can begin with job analysis in which the information acquired can be used to develop a point system under which each job is assigned a value based on its relative worth. Jobs can be compared on the basis of skill, responsibility, and working conditions, and the higher the score given the higher the pay. Point systems and other means of comparing jobs are used to ensure internal fairness. This is the domain of "job evaluation".

To establish whether an organisation's pay scales are competitive, an organisation could undertake a survey of pay at other organisations in the same industry, or use appropriate incomes data prepared by various agencies. In the design of pay systems, attention will have to given to the number of grades, the number of increments within each grade and the minimum and maximum points, the amount of overlap between each grade, the procedure for progression within a grade, movement from one grade to the next, and finally the impact of changes in external conditions relating to the demand for and supply of labour (Henderson, 1984).

On the question of openness, most pay systems rest somewhere between complete secrecy and complete openness. An open system may clarify the relationship between pay and performance, but of course it is important for managers (because of the motivational implications) to defend the system to those who are paid less. In a secret system, employees tend to overestimate co-workers' pay, and this can cause motivational problems (Lawler, 1981).

The applicability of participation has been raised in connection with pay systems. A group of appropriate people, including human resource experts and employees, might discuss and vote on the pay of other employees; a manager's pay might be determined by a group of peers; and employees might set their own pay based on their perceptions of their performance (Lawler, 1981). Allowing individuals and work groups to set their own wages or salaries may not be appropriate for all organisations, but according to Moorhead and Griffin (1992) it can be successful in organisations characterised by a climate of trust, joint problem solving, and a participative leadership style. However, in today's economic climate, pay is likely to be centrally determined by those who hold the purse strings. A recent survey conducted by the Industrial Relations Research Unit at the University of Warwick, of 176 companies in the UK, each employing more than 1000 people, found that payroll budgets are still centrally controlled by the finance departments of most large companies, despite the trend towards decentralised bargaining. Generally, the personnel department has a greater role in policing than in setting pay objectives. In only 7% of the companies surveyed did the personnel staff play a leading role in setting pay budgets (Goodhart, 1993b).

It is said that pay is used frequently as an organisational reward because it possesses certain optimal characteristics, such as the following (Lawler, 1981):

1. *Importance.* A good reward should be valued by its recipients. There is no doubt that pay is important to most people.
2. *Flexibility.* The size of a reward should be flexible. For example, it is easy to adjust the size of an increase in salary, but taking a proportionate part of a reward would not apply to, for example, promotions.
3. *Frequency.* Pay can be used as a reward relatively frequently without losing its worth, but some rewards, such as verbal praise, can lose their value if used repeatedly.
4. *Visibility.* The relationship between a reward and performance must be obvious to ensure that a reward is effective. Because

of the visibility of pay, employees can easily see the relationship between pay and their own performance.

There is a general perception that performance and pay are closely related. However, in one survey this view was challenged when it was found that only 22% of US workers had faith in the link between hard work and the payment received (Lawler, 1984). But one has to acknowledge that hard work may not always lead to accomplishments of a high order, and anyway reality is studded with forces likely to undermine the employee's best intentions. These include uncooperative colleagues, unanticipated interruptions, and faulty equipment.

Performance-related Pay. This phenomenon is concerned with the explicit link of financial reward to individual, group, or company performance. It amounts to a broad interpretation of financial rewards ranging from pay incentives and bonuses to profit sharing and equity share schemes. According to a 1990 factsheet produced by the Institute of Personnel Management (Brading & Wright, 1990):

Performance-related pay is one of the most dynamic issues of human resources management and arguably the most topical component of reward policy today. Like many other innovations in pay, the impetus for change started at the top with the widespread introduction of bonus schemes and more discriminating approaches to the determination of base salaries for executives. Now performance-related pay is spreading throughout the workforce in one form or another.

However, in more recent times there has been some disquiet expressed by shareholders who have witnessed over-generous compensation packages for senior executives who have presided over operations where success is conspicuously absent. They would almost certainly concur with the following sentiments expressed in a recent *Financial Times* (1993) editorial:

> One of the yardsticks against which top people's remuneration packages should be judged is whether the directors feel the pinch when the company underperforms. Yet a study this week from Income Data Services confirms once again that the balance between risk and reward in the typical executive contract is all too often weighted in favour of the director against the company and its shareholders.

The single most important objective of performance-related pay is to improve performance by re-targeting the remuneration system so that it is more sensitive and responsive to a company's and employee's needs. The achievement of this objective would necessitate the nurturing of a performance-oriented culture which stresses pay for results, not effort, and rewarding the right people (whereby the high rewards go to those who merit them). Due consideration has to be given to group performance where team-work is necessary, as well as to individual performance. It is obvious that the setting of performance standards and the quality of the appraisal process are critical for the success of performance-related pay systems.

There is some evidence to suggest that individually based bonus schemes, relying on objective measures of performance, promote business success, efficiency, and gratification of some individual needs (Brading & Wright, 1990; Lawler, 1977). But we are advised by Lawler (1977) to dwell on some of the negative effects generated by such schemes. These are likely to include the danger of individuals with superior performance being ostracised, and performance reports being falsified.

By contrast, exponents of group and organisation-wide pay schemes refer to the greater sense of co-operation, rather than competition, among employees that such schemes produce, though Lawler is emphatic in stressing that there is no single best pay incentive plan, that each situation must be examined in terms of its unique characteristics, and that it is possible to have multiple or overlapping plans. In a later publication, Lawler (1984) seems to favour profit sharing, share ownership, and gain sharing as rewards having good motivational implications for both managerial and non-managerial staff.

The following are characteristics associated with a successful performance-related pay scheme (Brading & Wright, 1990):

- Business objectives have to be translated into meaningful performance criteria for individuals and groups, and it must be possible to be able to appraise performance in an objective way.
- Individual performance plans, or specific targets related to group or company performance, must be clearly stated and communicated at the outset. This can prove difficult where qualitative contributions are assessed.
- Jobs must be defined in ways that convey clear meaning to individuals and the company.
- For the scheme to be taken seriously and produce the desired motivational impact, significant rewards must be on offer.
- There must be sufficient differentials between levels of performance rating, otherwise high performers are inadequately rewarded and average performers are insufficiently motivated to improve.
- It is important that the scheme is well communicated to individuals, with the reasons for its introduction being stated clearly. Training is required to ensure that the total process of setting performance standards, appraising performance, and allocating rewards is handled properly.

In reflecting on future trends with regard to performance-related pay, Fowler (1988) makes the point that "paying for how well work is done, rather than for highly subjective assessments of personal qualities, seems likely to set the scene for most future performance pay policies, but the involvement of line managers in operating the process is of crucial importance. The lack of effective research into the impact of performance-related pay is unlikely to deter personnel practitioners from continually advocating its use". Additional recent observations on performance-related pay (PRP) appear in the panel overleaf.

At a conference for personnel practitioners, Kanter (1992) drew a distinction between traditional pay structures and what she termed a new pattern of pay or rewards. In the traditional pay structure there was often the tendency to overperform in early career, which resulted in underpayment, and to underperform in later career resulting in overpayment. A new pattern of pay or reward would place the emphasis on more bonuses and awards for individual and team achievements, with more bosses circulating at the place of work with cheque books in hand, ready to reward good deeds on the spot. According to Kanter, this puts the spotlight firmly on rewarding people for their actual contributions and takes pressure off them to strive for promotion as a method of obtaining more money.

As a postscript, consider the views expressed by Kohn (1993) in a provocative article which challenges the value of incentives. He maintains that the rationale for performance-related pay rests on a mistaken view of what motivates people:

- Pay occupies a dubious position as a motivator, and generally there is too much emphasis on financial rewards;
- Financial rewards secure at best only short-term compliance;
- Financial rewards do not change attitudes that underlie behaviour or commitment to any task, they merely alter them temporarily;
- The link between top managers' pay and company performance is not proven, and this still applies when qualitative as opposed to quantitative measures of performance are used;
- The more complicated the task in cognitive terms the more ineffective are financial rewards as a motivating force;
- Incentive schemes undermine cooperation between employees, and encourage subordinates to engage in obsequious behaviour. They can also undermine intrinsic motivation;
- Reliance on the use of financial rewards to solve a problem masks reality. Money is thrown at a problem as opposed to striving for people-centred solutions, such as trusting people, and offering them autonomy and support;
- Incentive schemes discourage people from using their imagination and cause them to display less enthusiasm about their work. They also minimise challenge, encouraging employees to refrain from taking risks; hence, the first casualty of financial reward is creativity.
- The dispensing of financial rewards encourages a narrow focus that highlights the relationship between the rewards and job performance, and this can lead to the falsification of records to secure rewards;
- Even when incentive schemes are group rather than individual based, active employee involvement in the organisation is thin on the ground;
- When incentive schemes are well established there is an inclination for managers and supervisors to exercise relatively less leadership.

Kohn's preferred strategy is for companies to enhance the quality of job content for employees, allow them to share in decision making, and to create a climate of support. Though this appears to be a firm endorsement of the value of intrinsic motivation, he believes

PRP in Action

Recent research from the Institute of Manpower Studies in England found that two-thirds of all UK organisations now have individual-based PRP for at least some of their staff. Little work has been done on evaluating the effectiveness of PRP schemes, but there is evidence from the Institute's case studies that PRP does more to demotivate than motivate staff, and does little to retain high performers or get rid of poor performers. Other studies have found that the motivational effects of PRP are at best neutral.

Nevertheless, the popularity of PRP is recognised, and the following factors could be responsible for this:

- PRP emits a powerful signal for a broad change of business culture.
- It symbolises moves towards individualising employer/employee relations.
- The scope to reward people through promotions becomes more difficult as organisations become flatter (after removing layers of management). PRP, and a widening of payscales, is one solution to their problem.
- A number of companies make savings in salaries when automatic increments on pay scales are abolished following the introduction of PRP.
- People making a substantial contribution in their job get a better deal than poor performers.
- People making an excellent contribution at a particular level do not have to be promoted to a level where they may not be equally effective in order to secure greater financial benefits.
- PRP, unlike a piece-rate system, takes into account factors that are not easily quantifiable, such as commitment and initiative.
- There is less opportunity for workers to get together to relate their output to pay, in the way they were able to do with piece-work schemes—the latter was the basis of shop steward strengths in industries such as vehicle manufacturing.
- The appeal of PRP is that it is determined by subjective managerial judgement following employee appraisal rather than by market forces.

The following illustrates the approach to PRP at the Civil Aviation Authority (CAA), a UK government body that regulates air traffic. A number of the observations are attributable to the Director of Remuneration and Staff Relations at CAA.

1. PRP is not meant to be a substitute for management action aimed at encouraging and motivating subordinates.
2. PRP is more appropriate in areas where the company can recognise a better than expected performance more easily. But where the prime concern of a particular job is safety (e.g. air traffic controllers and aircraft inspectors) the organisation does not feel it necessary to encourage exceptional behaviour. Instead, employees are expected to follow set procedures and routines.
3. PRP should be integrated into well-developed schemes that involve regular assessments of employees' job performances, as well as offering them the means to improve their performances.
4. The recent PRP scheme at CAA is separated from the annual appraisal scheme by about six months, so that a discussion of strengths and weaknesses can take place when pay is not directly an issue. Although PRP is influenced by the annual appraisal, it is not determined by it.
5. The company's pay system consists of three components:

   - An annual negotiated increase for everybody;
   - Movement through the pay scales, which is determined by performance; and
   - Performance-related non-consolidated lump sum bonuses, not normally exceeding 5% of the rate for the job. This amount may be awarded to those whose overall performance is much better than the standard performance level. The average award was £300.

The amount of money devoted to PRP is considered to be important. If the budget for this purpose were too big, the managers would not have to think too hard about who should receive awards. Large sums could be spread wider and deeper, and as a result the idea of what constitutes better than expected performance would diminish in importance. The current amount available at CAA is not large; it is less than 1% of the salary bill. An award under the PRP scheme is viewed as a bonus, not necessarily to be repeated. The position of those who do not receive awards is considered, and this is done by keeping awards at such a level of magnitude that non-recipients do not become disgruntled. It is felt that the object of the scheme would be undermined if rivalry were to be created, because the organisation relies heavily on teamwork and cooperation to ensure effectiveness (Goodhart, 1993a; Rowlinson, 1993; Wood, 1993).

that extrinsic motivation also has a part to play, in the sense that monetary rewards should be provided at an adequate level.

PERSONNEL SELECTION

The selection process is concerned with choosing from a sample of job applicants the individuals best suited to the jobs available. It is normally used to decide who shall enter the organisation, and it can be contrasted with the placement process which involves matching people already in the organisation to the available jobs. The principles associated with selection could equally apply to placement. Before selection techniques are used, it is necessary to analyse the appropriate jobs.

Job Analysis

Job analysis procedures are designed to produce systematic information about jobs, including the nature of the work performed, the equipment used, the working conditions, and the position of the job within the organisation (Arnold, Robertson, & Cooper, 1991). The techniques and procedures used in job analysis are wide ranging (Spector, Brannick, & Coovert, 1989), but the sources of job analysis data can be categorised as follows:

* written material;
* job holder's reports;
* colleagues' reports; and
* direct observation.

Written Material

For jobs already in existence, there are likely to be written job descriptions within the organisation. A job description is a written statement of what a job holder does, how it is done, and why it is done. If this is comprehensive and up to date, it can provide the analyst with useful information. A job description can be supplemented by other written material, such as organisation charts and training manuals.

Job holder's Reports

The job holder is asked by the interviewer to state the main tasks applicable to the job and the manner in which they are executed. Although the interviewer is expected to be thorough in his or her questioning, all relevant questions may not be asked. This could be a problem made worse by subjective and biased reports by the job holder. To counteract these difficulties, it may be helpful if workers complete diaries or activity records. Though time-consuming, this approach avoids the problem of placing total reliance on the worker's memory in an interview situation.

Another technique deals with critical incidents (Flanagan, 1954). Here the job holder is asked to recall specific incidents related to either very good or very poor job performance.

There are other approaches to job analysis relying on the perceptions of the job holder obtained by structured questionnaires. These can be very comprehensive, covering areas such as information input to the job, orientation of the job (data, people, or things), traits and skills required to do the job, and the output of the work process (Arnold, et al., 1991).

Colleagues' Reports

As a means to provide comparative data, one could rely on the perceptions held by superiors, peers, and (where appropriate) subordinates, of the job holder's activities.

Direct Observation

This amounts to direct observation of the way a particular job is done. Of course it is possible that the observer fails to detect some interesting features of the job, thereby undermining the credibility of the exercise, and the job holder may behave unnaturally because of being observed. However, direct observation offers potential in generating useful insights, more so perhaps if the analyst is a participant observer, engaged totally or partially in the job.

Having analysed the job, the data can be used for a number of different purposes. For a start, a job description can be produced and this could be useful to job applicants—it could provide the raw material from which job advertisements can be prepared. In addition, a job specification can be produced, stating the minimum acceptable qualifications in terms of knowledge, skills, and abilities that an employee must possess to perform a given job successfully. It should now be apparent that the job description and job specification are critical documents at the disposal of selectors.

Selection Methods

Those concerned with selecting applicants for jobs have at their disposal a number of selection methods. Although not all the methods are equally useful, by far the most widely used method is the selection interview.

The Selection Interview
The selection interview entails interaction between people, and has been referred to as a "conversation with a purpose". Achieving the purpose of the interview involves complex transactions of obtaining and giving information. Both the interviewer and interviewee bring hopes, fears, expectations, misconceptions, and many other cognitions to the interview process. By using appropriate behavioural strategies, the interviewer and interviewee hope to realise their objectives, and roles are adopted to further the aim of a successful outcome. If the parties to the interview process act skilfully, this should improve the quality of the interactive episode (Wicks, 1984). Skilful performance in this context is a function of skills connected with self-awareness, awareness of social interaction processes, and self-presentation based on an appropriate foundation of knowledge or information.

However, a satisfactory outcome to the interview process also requires adequate preparation for the actual event. The interviewer should be well briefed, rehearse the interview, and anticipate the actions required. In a job interview it is important to put across information about the organisation and an adequate description of the advertised job.

It is suggested that research on interviewing, as a device to select people for jobs, is fragmented and produces findings of little value to selectors (Harris, 1989; Lewis, 1984). However, on the basis of a comprehensive review of evidence about selection interviews, it was concluded that the following features were present:

- The selection interview offers some insight into a person's sociability and verbal fluency from a sample of his or her total behaviour.
- Though the selection interview may not be a valid process, it is easy to arrange and interviewers have faith and confidence in their judgement in interview situations.
- Though the selection interview may not be a valid process, it presents an opportunity to sell the job to the candidates being interviewed. It is difficult to identify an equally efficient alternative (Arvey & Campion, 1982).

Apart from these modest claims to success, the interview process has been subjected to some fundamental criticisms. Many of these criticisms are levelled at the interviewer. In panel interviews a proper role for each interviewer is sometimes not adequately specified. This is compounded by poor interviewing skills of individual panel members. Generally, there are too many occasions when interviewers spend time on irrelevant matters, missing the opportunity to explore a significant point in detail. Also, the public relations aspect of interviewing is ignored (Wicks, 1984). Other criticisms hinge on the following observations (Phillips & Dipboye, 1989; Robbins, 1991).

1. Interviewers make perceptual judgements that are often inaccurate.
2. Interviewers are poor at reaching agreement when rating interviewees.

3. Different interviewers see different things in the same interviewee, and thus arrive at different conclusions.

4. Interviewers arrive at early impressions that quickly become entrenched in their perceptual judgement. Negative impressions arising from negative information received early in the interview can become more heavily weighted than the same information given later.

5. Many decisions are arrived at by interviewers early in the interview and change very little after the first five minutes of the interview. So the absence of unfavourable characteristics early on in the interview could act to the advantage of the interviewee.

6. Prior knowledge about an applicant has the effect of biasing the interviewer's evaluation.

7. Interviewers tend to favour applicants who share their attitudes.

8. The order in which applicants are interviewed influences evaluations.

9. Negative information is given an unduly high weighting.

10. An applicant's ability to do well in an interview is irrelevant in most jobs.

In recent years the superiority of the structured interview over the unstructured interview has been endorsed. In particular, the benefits of requiring interviewers to ask only job-related questions is stressed as a means to reduce the incidence of irrelevant information, prejudice, and bias in selection decision making. The structured job-related interview is akin to the situational interview proposed by Latham and Saari (1984).

The approach to situational interviewing starts with a comprehensive analysis of the job. Key situations within a job are produced, with the support of job experts. Then benchmarks are devised for interviewers to use when scoring the responses of the interviewees. The interviewers should be well trained and experienced. The interview questions are based on, for example, a mini case study related to incidents and circumstances associated with the job in question (Robertson, Gratton, & Rout, 1990).

"OK, YOU TAKE IT FROM HERE, IF YOU HIT ANY SNAGS LET ME KNOW, I'LL DROP BY IN A BIT, TO SEE HOW YOU'RE GETTING ON . . ."

Psychometric Tests

Psychometric tests used in personnel selection can be divided into two categories. These are personality tests (e.g. the 16PF or OPQ) and cognitive tests (e.g. general intelligence, numerical ability), which were discussed in Chapter 1. The usefulness of personality tests as predictors of performance in a job has been questioned (see Chapter 1), but there have been suggestions that profiling personality for the purpose of making judgements about performance at work has some value (Day & Silverman, 1989). By contrast, cognitive ability testing across different occupational groups seems to have greater success (Arnold, et al., 1991).

The use of psychometric tests in selection and employee development (see Chapter 12) is perfectly acceptable to many. However, what is disturbing to many people, including Professor Ivan Robertson at UMIST, is the growing practice of the use of such tests to determine which long-serving employees to discard. Dixon (1994) reports on a situation where this has recently occurred. At the finance section of the London Borough of Southwark, constituting about 120 employees, a long and complex test was administered. This was believed to be a personality test and staff were assured that there were no correct answers to any question. After the results were analysed, 19 staff were told to stop working immediately and were escorted from the office. A further 10 staff were told they were considered unsuitable for employment.

Work-sample Tests

These tests require the applicant to perform a task or set of tasks that are considered, following job analysis, to have direct relevance to the job in question. Thus the applicant is requested to demonstrate his or her ability by performing part of the job. The activities involved can be wide ranging (Robertson & Kandola, 1982). For example, the applicant may be asked to type a letter, or operate a machine, or take decisions similar to those taken in the job in question. This is done through the use of in-tray exercises where the applicant is presented with a collection of letters, memos, etc., and is asked to deal with them. A more abstract version of the last approach would be to present applicants with a series of hypothetical situations and then ask them how they would respond. This is sometimes referred to as situational interviewing.

Other approaches are the testing of the applicant's knowledge of areas considered to be directly relevant to performance on the job, and group discussion or decision making. The latter is evident when two or more applicants come together to discuss a particular topic, and their performance in the discussion is evaluated. This approach is suitable for testing applicants for a job where an individual's performance in a group situation is crucial for job success.

When work-sample tests are administered to experienced applicants, the psycho-motor tests (e.g. typing) and the in-tray tests seem to command a superior position. Work-sample tests can also be administered to applicants who are not trained in the relevant job. In fact the main purpose of these tests, which can overlap with tests of cognitive ability, is to assess whether or not an applicant is suitable for training. Trainability tests have been developed for many occupational groups with reasonable results (Robertson & Downs, 1989).

Assessment Centres

Assessment centres make use of many different methods, including interviews, psychological tests, in-tray exercises, written tasks, and group discussions. They can last for a few days or a week, or alternatively they can be as short as a day. Assessment centres (development centres) are also used to evaluate people who already work in the organisation, as was described earlier in this chapter in connection with performance appraisal.

In the latter context the information derived from the assessment centre is used to facilitate decision making in connection with promotions and career development. Assessment centres, first used in selection on a small scale, now appear to be an increasingly popular method of personnel selection. Applicants for a job are usually assessed by trained assessors who normally hold fairly responsible positions in the organisation. These assessors observe applicants' performance on the various exercises and arrive at a consensus of opinion about the suitability of each applicant.

There is no doubt that assessment centres are viewed favourably as a selection method. The belief is that a combination of selection methods found in an assessment centre can significantly improve the probability of selecting appropriate applicants. Proponents of assessment centres would argue that the data obtained from applicants is comprehensive and comparable, and the methods used give applicants the opportunity to demonstrate capabilities unlikely to find expression in an interview alone. In addition, the total experience of the assessment centre is said to be invaluable for the applicant, while for the assessor it is an opportunity to develop skills in the objective assessment of people and in presenting personnel data in a professional way. The latter was borne out in study of the developmental effects of assessorship (Lorenzo, 1984).

Among the issues addressed by critics of assessment centres are that there is a need for substantial investment in resources to create and operate these centres, including the need to select and train suitable people as assessors. Also, the lack of commitment from top management (if that proves to be the case) may have a dampening effect on both assessors and applicants; and putting the spotlight on behaviour that can be observed and measured has its shortcomings when less visible and less easily assessed skills are ignored.

A survey conducted in 1989 points to results showing an impressive increase in the use of assessment centres by larger companies over a 16-year period. In 1989 37% of companies in Britain with over 1000 employees used assessment centres, and this can be compared with 21% in 1986 and 7% in 1973. The expectation is that assessment centres will increasingly be used for groups other than managers in both career development and selection (Bawtree & Hogg, 1989). As a postscript, it is worth reflecting for a moment on the following judgement made by Arnold, et al. (1991): "Clearly, assessment centres measure something of importance, but there is considerable uncertainty about what they do measure".

Biographical Information

Applicants for a job within an organisation are likely to complete an application form and other documents in which they are expected to provide certain biographical information about matters such as age, previous employment, education, training, and personal history. When such information is used in a systematic way, this method of personnel selection is often referred to as the biodata approach. Its fundamental characteristic is the identification (with an appropriately large sample of candidates) of correlations between items of biographical information and outcome measures on the job, such as performance or absenteeism. Items of biographical information shown to have a significant relationship with work outcome factors (e.g. performance) are accommodated in a questionnaire which may be administered to applicants.

The more important questionnaire items used in predicting success in the job are given the higher points-weighting. For example, for the job of senior economist in a bank, graduate status and a specified number of years experience doing similar work could command a higher points allocation than a period of employment as a professional footballer. The weighted items are added together to produce a total score, which is then used to accept or reject applicants. Prior to the preparation of the questionnaire it is advisable to use more than one sample in compiling the data and to keep the relationship between the biodata items and work outcomes under statistical review over time.

Studies have demonstrated the usefulness of biodata in selection (Asher, 1972). However, it is said that a number of problems arising from the use of biodata come about as a result of not being sufficiently critical in considering why there is a relationship between an item of biographical information (e.g. membership of clubs) and a particular beneficial outcome at work (e.g. capability as a team player). To confront problems of this nature it is suggested that one should engage in theoretical rationalisation of the nature of the relationship, and only retain biodata items that can be seen to be rationally connected to the appropriate work outcomes (Arnold et al., 1991; Owens & Schoenfeldt, 1979).

Other Methods

There are a number of other methods used in personnel selection, including references, peer assessment, self-assessment, graphology, and polygraphy.

References. Along with interviews, references are widely used as a selection method. The results of a survey of the techniques used for managerial selection revealed that although large organisations are increasingly using assessment centre type exercises and biodata, most organisations still select managers on the basis of interviews and references (Robertson & Makin, 1986). Normally, employing organisations take up references only when a job offer is imminent, but there are occasions when references are used as a screening device prior to the preparation of the final shortlist of candidates. Generally, the available research evidence does not support the popularity of references as a means of obtaining a third party's opinion of an applicant's credentials and achievements. It is said that bias is almost built into this method because the candidate is likely to nominate a referee who is capable of

conveying favourable information and impressions, and a positive recommendation. Practical suggestions to optimise the usefulness of references as a selection method are available (see Dobson, 1989).

Peer Assessment. When colleagues or peers are favourably placed to make an assessment of a candidate, peer assessment can be productive. It is probably more suited to particular work environments, such as a college or university, than to others, and for certain purposes, like career counselling, rather than selection (Arnold et al., 1991). Support for peer assessment has come from a study of non-unionised, hourly paid employees working in a food processing plant. This group were on relatively short tenure, had good experiences with previous peer assessment exercises, and did not hold the view that peer assessment contains a friendship bias (McEvoy & Buller, 1987). Most of the research studies in this area have used samples drawn from the military.

Self-assessment. This method is rarely used in selection. It is said to suffer from leniency errors (Fox & Dinur, 1988) among other shortcomings.

Graphology. An alternative label for this method is handwriting analysis, and it is based on the assumption that applicants reveal their personality characteristics through their handwriting. A description of this method appears in Chapter 1. Handwriting analysis is a frequently used selection method in France.

In a study comparing the methods used to select managers in 73 British and 52 French organisations, more than 77% of French firms used handwriting analysis to select managers, as opposed to 2.6% of British firms (Shackleton & Newell, 1991). Among the French firms it is interesting to note that the greater use of this method is found outside the larger organisations. Naturally the question is asked whether the larger organisations are better informed about the lack of scientific respectability of this method (see panel below).

Polygraphy. The lie detector test or polygraph might be considered by some to be particularly appropriate for selecting people for jobs involving the handling of cash. The polygraph is used to measure emotional stress shown by variations in blood pressure, pulse rate, perspiration, and respiration as applicants answer questions. The reasoning is that telling a lie is stressful, and the stress will be reflected in physiological reactions. But it should be kept firmly in mind that the polygraph measures emotional stress and is not a measure of lying. Many causes of emotional stress not related to lying may cause a person to fail a lie detector test. Also, many people can lie without being detected by a polygraph (Hall & Goodale, 1986). In a penetrating critique of the typical lie detection technique, Lykken (1974) concluded that empirical reports of high success rates are open to serious question, and a theoretical analysis of the customary procedures indicates that the expected probability of valid judgement is very low. There is no doubt that this method has severe limitations as a selection device, and its legal status is questionable in the US.

Fairness

Ideally, any selection method must be judged by the standard of fairness, which is the tendency to treat all applicants alike and to provide them with an equal opportunity to gain employment. In reality many organisations, whether intentionally or not, have a history of systematically eliminating a portion of applicants from the selection process on the basis of such personal characteristics as race, colour, sex, disability, etc. The lack of fairness might be due to the weaknesses of the selection methods used, thereby providing selectors with the opportunity to introduce their prejudices and biases. As a result, some people may be treated unfairly.

However, there is reason to believe that personnel methods and practices may often operate in a way that is systematically unfair to particular groups, such as women or ethnic minorities. For example, there is a view that some racial and ethnic minorities do not perform as well as other applicants in many tests of intelligence and aptitude, and therefore are not selected at the same rate. The difference in selection rate is usually referred to as "adverse impact" (Robertson & Cooper, 1983) (see panel overleaf), (but equally it should be recognised that a good test is not unfair or biased just because members of different sub-groups in society obtain different scores).

The Practice of Graphology

Graphology is used by *Warburg's*, the UK merchant bank, who require job applicants to submit handwriting samples for analysis. The handwriting test comes towards the end of a long selection process, and although the results of the test are taken seriously, an applicant would not be rejected on the outcome of this test alone. *Rhône-Poulenc*, the French chemicals company, used handwriting analysis to sift application forms at one time. Now it only uses graphology where there is doubt about a candidate's suitability, and even then the candidate would be called for a second interview. A decision is never made on the sole basis of a graphologist's comments. The handwriting analysis is one of a number of techniques designed to create an overall picture of a candidate (McGookin, 1993).

A recent report—*Graphology in Personnel Assessment*—published by the British Psychological Society concludes that graphology is not a viable means of assessing a person's character or abilities. There is no scientific evidence to support the claims of graphologists, and there is no relationship at all between what graphology predicts and subsequent performance in the workplace (The Psychologist, 1994).

Adverse Impact: the case of the Paddington Guards

In 1990 eight guards at London's Paddington Station, with the support of the Commission for Racial Equality (CRE), took British Rail to Court over alleged racial discrimination after failing the train driver assessment process. The assessment process included published psychometric aptitude tests, a personality questionnaire, an interview, and tests of vigilance and attention taken from a European railway administration test.

Following a review of the test performances of white and ethnic minority applicants, it became clear that the aptitude tests, particularly the test of verbal comprehension, were a source of "adverse impact". The CRE had already identified a similar problem with the published aptitude tests which were used as part of an assessment process by London Underground for management appointments. Like London Underground, British Rail reached an out of court settlement before the tribunal, and as part of the settlement the British Railways Board agreed to review the assessment process and implement an improved one (Kellett, Fletcher, Callen, & Geary, 1994).

Considerations such as those listed above, have given rise to legislation and other practices to offer protection to certain types of applicants. Even though legislation is on the statute book—e.g. the UK Race Relations Act, 1976—unfair discrimination still exists. Brown and Gay (1985) found that a disproportionate number of black applicants in the UK were not invited to attend various job interviews, even though they had similar qualifications to white applicants. Fletcher (1994) considers the question of equal opportunities and fair testing to be an issue of growing importance, but he also considers as essential the acknowledgement of an ethical framework for assessment practice. Finally, Kellet et al. (1994) rightly call for closer collaborative relationship is between interested parties, including employers, test publishers, professional bodies such as the British Psychological Society and the Institute of Personnel Management, statutory bodies such as the Commission for Racial Equality and the Equal Opportunities Commission, and the academic world, if standards of professional test practice are to be developed and modified.

Validity and Reliability

The critical phase of the selection process arises when a decision is made to hire or reject a candidate. In arriving at the decision, various strands of evidence relating to the present or past performance of candidates—e.g. references, psychometric test scores, interview performance—are considered. This evidence, which is used to decide on the suitability of candidates for the job in question, is referred to as a predictor. Prediction here means predicting future job-related behaviour on the basis of current or past performance with the help of selection methods.

Criterion-related Validity

Before we can test the validity of selection methods—i.e. whether high or low scores on the selection methods are associated with good or bad performance in the job—information has to be collected on the job-related performance of the person who was selected for the job. This type of performance, which can be gauged by measures such as output data, supervisor's ratings, etc, is referred to as the criterion. (Output data is referred to as objective criteria, whereas supervisors' ratings are referred to as subjective criteria. Cook (1994) mentions that there are relatively few types of work in which performance can be measured adequately by objective criteria alone. Therefore, in at least 60% of cases and possibly more than 75%, one has to settle for more subjective criteria, and the problem here is that it is subject to a range of biases.)

Criterion-related validity refers to the strength of the relationship between the predictor and the criterion, usually referred to as a validity coefficient. A perfect correlation between the two variables is represented by 1.0, whereas zero denotes no correlation.

When criterion-related validity is high, applicants who have high predictor scores also have high criterion scores, and applicants who have low predictor scores also have low criterion scores. Where the predictor–criterion relationship is perfect (a validity coefficient of 1.0), we should be able to predict a criterion score from a predictor score. In reality this idealised state is not achievable. It is very unusual to obtain validity coefficients much in excess of +0.5 (Robertson & Smith, 1989), but it should be noted that validity coefficients significantly less than +1.0 still offer a foundation for improved personnel selection. It is now apparent that criterion-related validity requires at least two measures for each applicant: a selection test score and a job performance score. There are two different ways to obtain these scores: predictive validity analysis and concurrent validity analysis.

Predictive validity analysis. The selection method—e.g. a psychometric test—is administered to job applicants, but decisions to recruit are made without reference to the test scores. In other words, the organisation will rely on whatever selection methods are currently in use while the criterion-related validity of the new selection method is being studied. After a number of months the job performance of those employed is measured and is correlated with the test scores to establish validity. If valid, the selection method will be used as an assessment device. As this type of validation process permits the selection of some candidates who will fail to perform adequately, it is suitable only for organisations that select numerous applicants, and that are seeking strong evidence that their selection methods are valid.

Concurrent validity analysis. The selection method (e.g. psychometric test) is administered to a group of current employees, rather than job applicants, and their test scores are correlated simultaneously with data on the measurement of job performance obtained from their personnel files or from their supervisors. In other words, the two exercises are carried out concurrently. This is a much more practical procedure, but it does not necessarily yield a good estimate of predictive validity.

An advantage of the predictive validity analysis approach is that data are examined under conditions that are very similar to those under which the selection test will actually be used. For instance, the selection test scores are obtained from actual job applicants who have indicated a real interest in gaining employment. The scores of the successful candidates are then examined at a later time to determine how well they predict performances on the job.

However, predictive validity analysis has two major drawbacks. First, there cannot be many employers who are prepared to administer a selection test to job applicants and then ignore the applicants' scores when making selection decisions. Second, the predictive validity analysis approach takes time. The successful applicants must be given enough time to learn their jobs and demonstrate their abilities. Because of these drawbacks, many employers and psychologists rely on the concurrent validity analysis approach.

With concurrent validity analysis there is no lengthy time interval between taking the test and gauging subsequent job performance because job holders complete the selection test that the organisation is experimenting with at the same time they have measures of their job performance taken or extracted from their personnel files. Another reason why concurrent validity is acceptable to employers is that they do not have to ignore anybody's test score.

Finally, a drawback of the concurrent validity analysis approach is that people who score on the selection test that is being tried out, and whose job performance is concurrently evaluated, may not be very representative of the population from which actual job applicants will emerge (Saal & Knight, 1988).

An important consideration with respect to validity studies, regardless of whether the approach is predictive or concurrent analysis, is that the initial validity study dealing with a fair number of predictors should always be followed by a cross-validation study on a second sample of people in order to cross-check the results obtained (Arnold et al., 1991).

With respect to selection, criterion-related validity is the most important type of validity, but face, content, and construct validity are also significant.

Face Validity
A selection method or test that portrays face validity gives the appearance of measuring whatever is intended to be measured. For example, a typing test looks as if it measures typing skills.

Content Validity
Like face validity, content validity is usually a judgemental rather than a statistical procedure. A predictor displays content validity when it incorporates a representative sample of the behaviour in the job being measured. For example, a content validity test of a car mechanic's ability would be expected to cover the key activities undertaken by a competent mechanic. A feature of this approach is that the skills can be observed and understood without appealing to abstract and unobservable traits or constructs.

Construct Validity
This type of validity is appropriate when it is the intention to assess the abstract traits or psychological constructs that are felt to underline more concrete, observable forms of behaviour. For example, intelligence, job satisfaction, and motivation are examples of constructs that help explain a wide variety of job-related behaviours. Construct validity involves drawing hypotheses about the likely connection between the concept of interest (e.g. intelligence) and other events. For instance, in order to demonstrate the construct validity of a measure of intelligence, one might hypothesise that high scorers on this variable would do better than low scorers in a particular type of task. The next step would be to find evidence to support or reject the hypothesis. An important factor in understanding what a psychological test measures is the exploration of the construct validity of that test.

Reliability
An important feature of any measuring instrument, be it a predictor or criterion, is reliability—i.e. the consistency with which it produces results. An example of an unreliable measure is when a candidate produces different scores when he or she takes a test on two different occasions (see the earlier discussion, p. 538).

In the final analysis, a measuring instrument used in personnel selection—i.e. a predictor or criterion—must be both valid and reliable. But this may not always be the case. According to Brotherton (1980) the issues and technicalities involved in validation are often not understood, except where occupational psychologists are associated with the shaping, review, and evaluation of selection procedures (For a recent critical review of resarch findings in this area, see Robertson, 1994.)

Utility

The use of personnel selection methods can be expensive, and having predictors with good predictive validity is no guarantee that selection tests will be cost-effective in use. When more jobs are available than applicants to fill them, the use of any selection test is likely to be of little benefit. In such circumstances the "selection ratio":

$$\frac{\text{number of jobs}}{\text{number of candidates}}$$

is greater than 1.0. Nevertheless, it would be wise to use selection methods in conditions where a selection ratio is in excess of 1.0, and if necessary leave jobs unfilled rather than offer employment to unsuitable candidates.

When the selection ratio is less than 1.0 (i.e. there are more applicants than jobs) obvious advantages can be gained from the use of selection methods. Finally, the cost of personnel selection should be offset against the benefits, and it should be borne in mind that bad selection can have a damaging effect on the organisation over a long period as sub-standard job holders who were poorly selected continue to serve the organisation.

SUMMARY: HUMAN RESOURCE PRACTICES

- Human resource management provides a framework within which human resource practices operate.
- Human resource practices examined in this chapter were performance appraisal, reward systems, and personnel selection.
- The goals of performance appraisal were stated. The criteria used in performance appraisal or evaluation embrace task outcomes, behaviours, and traits. The major appraisal techniques discussed were graphic rating scales, essays, behaviourally anchored rating scales, behavioural observation scales, ranking, paired comparison, forced distribution, OJQ, and assessment centres.
- In the administration of an appraisal system, questions addressed were the frequency of appraisal, and who is charged with carrying it out—i.e. the supervisor, self-appraisal, peers, subordinates, and others such as clients or customers, or consultants. The importance of training in this context was emphasised. Appraisal information can be used for a variety of purposes, and the nature and effectiveness of the feedback interview was considered.
- The measurement methods in appraisal were discussed with reference to validity (convergent and discriminant), reliability, bias (leniency, severity, and central tendency), halo error, similarity error, timing errors, and other considerations.
- Rewards were viewed in both intrinsic and extrinsic terms. After stating the purpose and philosophy of reward systems, examples of compensation packages were given. Because of the importance of pay in compensation packages, most of the discussion was devoted to pay. The characteristics of a reward system based on pay were noted, and there was specific comment on performance-related pay.
- Job analysis as the first step in the selection process was noted. Sources of job analysis data are written material, job holders' reports, colleagues' reports, and direct observation.
- Selectors have a number of methods at their disposal. These include the selection interview, psychometric tests, work-sample tests, assessment centres, bio-graphical information, and other methods such as references, peer assessment, self-assessment, graphology, and polygraphy. The notion of fairness was introduced.
- Validity and reliability were raised as important issues. Validity includes criterion-related validity, face validity, content validity, and construct validity. The utility of the selection process was noted.

QUESTIONS

1. What do we mean by criteria in the context of performance appraisal?
2. Having reviewed the major appraisal techniques, rank them in order of importance from your point of view.
3. Comment on self-appraisal, and appraisal of superiors by subordinates.
4. Define the following terms: (a) convergent validity; (b) central tendency; (c) construct validity; (d) feedback interview and (e) adverse impact.
5. Describe the sources of job analysis data.
6. Comment on the importance of performance-related pay in the 1990s.
7. Discuss the usefulness of psychometric testing.
8. What is meant by an assessment centre?
9. Why do you think the French are more attached to graphology as a selection method than the British?
10. Explain the terms criterion and predictor with respect to the validity of selection methods.

REFERENCES

Armstrong, M. (1992). *Human resource management: Strategy and action*. London: Kogan Page.

Arnold, J., Robertson, I.T., & Cooper, C.L. (1991). *Work psychology: Understanding human behaviour in the workplace*. London: Pitman Publishing.

Arvey, R.D. & Campion, J.E. (1982). The employment interviews: A summary and review of recent research. *Personnel Psychology, 35*, 281–322.

Asher, J.J. (1972). The biographical item: Can it be improved? *Personnel Psychology, 25*, 251–269.

Bawtree, S. & Hogg, C. (1989). Assessment centres. *Personnel Management*, Factsheet 22, October.

Bernardin, H.J. & Beatty, R.W. (1984). *Performance appraisal: Assessing human behaviour at work*. Boston, Mass.: Kent.

Brading, L. & Wright, V. (1990). Performance-related pay. *Personnel Management*, Factsheet 30.

Brotherton, C. (1980). Paradigms of selection validation: Some comments in the light of British equal opportunities legislation. *Journal of Occupational Psychology, 53*, 73–79.

Brown, E. & Gay, P. (1985). *Racial discrimination 17 years after the Act*. Report No. 646. London: Policy Studies Institute.

Burke, R.J., Weitzel, W., & Weir, T. (1978). Characteristics of effective employee performance at review and development interviews: Replication and extension. *Personnel Psychology, 31*, 903–919.

Cook, M. (1994, January). *Stature, credibility, and true performance*. Paper presented to the Occupational Psychology Conference, Birmingham, UK.

Day, D.V. & Silverman, S.B. (1989). Personality and job performance: Evidence of incremental validity. *Personnel Psychology, 41*, 25–36.

De Nisi, A.S. & Mitchell, J.L. (1978). An analysis of peer ratings as predictors and criterion measures and a proposed new application. *Academy of Management Review, 3*, 369–374.

Dixon, M. (1994). Bringing in, raising up, throwing out. *Financial Times*, 12 January, p.15.

Dobson, P. (1989). Reference reports. In P. Herriot (Ed.), *Assessment and selection in organisations*. Chichester: Wiley.

Edwards, M.R. (1983). OJQ offers an alternative to assessment centres. *Public Personnel Management Journal, 12*, 146–155.

Erez, M. (1977). Feedback: A necessary condition for the goal-setting performance relationship. *Journal of Applied Psychology, 62*, 624–627.

Farh J.L. & Werbel, J.D. (1986). Effects of purpose of the appraisal and expectations on self-appraisal leniency. *Journal of Applied Psychology, 62*, 527–529.

Fedor, D.B. & Buckley, M.R. (1988). Issues surrounding the need for more frequent monitoring of individual performance in organisations. *Public Personnel Management*, Winter, 435–442.

Financial Times (1993). *Failure pays*. Editorial comment, 13th August, 13.

Flanagan, J.C. (1954). The critical incident technique. *Psychological Bulletin, 51*, 327–358.

Fletcher, C. (1984). What's new in performance appraisal. *Personnel Management*, February, 20–22.

Fletcher, C. (1994). Validity, test use and professional responsibility. *The Psychologist*, January, 30–31.

Fletcher, C. & Williams, R. (1992). The route to performance management. *Personnel Management*, October, 42–47.

Fombrun, C.J. & Laud, R.L. (1983). Strategic issues in performance appraisal: Theory and practice. *Personnel*, November–December, 23–31.

Fowler, A. (1988). New directions in performance pay. *Personnel Management*, November, 30–34.

Fox, W.M. (1987). Improving performance appraisal systems. *National Productivity Review*, Winter, 20–27.

Fox, G. & Dinur, Y. (1988). Validity of self-assessment: A field evaluation. *Personnel Psychology, 41*, 581–592.

Furnham, A. (1993). When employees rate their supervisors. *Financial Times*, 1 March.

Goodhart, D. (1993a). Rewards for the top performers. (Curious appeal of UK performance-related pay schemes.) *Financial Times*, 3 November, p.16.

Goodhart, D. (1993b) Companies still set pay centrally. *Financial Times*, 22 December, p.5.

Goodhart, D. (1994). Equal pay victory for 1,500 women. *Financial Times*, 8 January, p.7.

Greenberg, J. (1986). Determinants of perceived fairness of performance evaluations. *Journal of Applied Psychology*, May, 340–342.

Greenhaus, J.H., Parasuraman, S., & Wormley, W.M. (1990). Effects of race on organisational experiences, job performance evaluation, and career outcomes. *Academy of Management Journal*, March, 64–86.

Hall, D.T. & Goodale, J.G. (1986). *Human resource management: Strategy, design, and implementation*. Glenview, IL: Scott, Foresman.

Harris, M.M. (1989). Reconsidering the employment interview: A review of recent literature and suggestions for future research. *Personnel Psychology*, Winter, 691–726.

Henderson, R.L. (1984). *Performance appraisal*. Reston, VA: Reston.

Heneman II, H.G. (1974). Comparisons of self and superior ratings of managerial performance. *Journal of Applied Psychology, 59*, 638–642.

Heneman, R.L. & Wexley, K.N. (1983). The effects of time delay in rating and amount observed on performance rating accuracy. *Academy of Management Journal*, December, 677–686.

Ilgen, D.R., Fisher, C.D., & Taylor, M.S. (1979). Consequences of individual feedback on behaviour in organisations. *Journal of Applied Psychology, 64*, 349–371.

Income Data Services (1992). *Performance management*. Study 518, November.

Kanter, R.M. (1992). *Address to the Institute of Personnel Management national conference*. Unpublished. London: Institute of Personnel Management.

Kellett, D., Fletcher, S., Callen, A., & Geary, B. (1994). Fair testing: The case of British Rail. *The Psychologist*, January, 26–29.

Klimoski, R.J. & Rafaeli, A. (1983). Inferring personal qualities through handwriting analysis. *Journal of Occupational Psychology, 56*, 191–202.

Kohn, A. (1993). Why incentive plans cannot work. *Harvard Business Review*, September/October, 54–63.

Korman, A.K. (1968). The prediction of managerial performance: A review. *Personnel Psychology, 21*, 295–322.

Latham, G.P. & Saari, L.M. (1984). Do people do what they say? Further studies on the situational interview. *Journal of Applied Psychology, 69*, 309–314.

Latham, G.P. & Wexley, K.N. (1981). *Increasing productivity through performance appraisal*. Reading, MA: Addison-Wesley.

Lawler, E.E. (1977). Reward systems. In J.R. Hackman & J.L. Suttle (Eds.), *Improving life at work*. Glenview, IL: Scott, Foresman.

Lawler, E.E. (1981). *Pay and organisation development*. Reading, Mass.: Addison-Wesley.

Lawler, E.E. (1984). Whatever happened to incentive pay? *New Management, 1*, 37–41.

Lawler, E.E., Mohrman, A.M., & Resnick, S.M. (1984). Performance appraisal revisited. *Organisational Dynamics*, Summer, *13*, 20–35.

Lewis, C. (1984). What's new in selection. *Personnel Management*, January, 14–16.

Lorenzo, R.V. (1984). Effects of assessorship on managers' proficiency in acquiring, evaluating, and communicating information about people. *Personnel Psychology, 37*, 617–634.

Lykken, D.T. (1974). Psychology and the lie detection industry. *American Psychologist, 29*, 725–739.

Mabe, P.A. & West, S.G. (1982). Validity of self-evaluation of ability: A review and meta-analysis. *Journal of Applied Psychology*, June, 280–296.

McBriarty, M.A. (1988). Performance appraisal: Some unintended consequences. *Public Personnel Management*, Winter, 423.

McEvoy, G.M. & Buller, P.F. (1987). User acceptance of peer appraisals in an industrial setting. *Personnel Psychology, 40*, 785–797.

McGookin, S. (1993). Graphology: a waste of money. *Financial Times*, 19 November, p.12.

Moorhead, G. & Griffin, R.W. (1992). *Organisational behaviour* (third edition). Boston: Houghton Mifflin.

Nevels, P. (1989). Why employees are being asked to rate their supervisors. *Supervisory Management*, December, 5–11.

Owens, W.A. & Schoenfeldt, L.F. (1979). Towards a classification of persons. *Journal of Applied Psychology, 64*, 569–607.

Phillips, A.P. & Dipboye, R.L. (1989). Correlational tests of predictions from a process model of the interview. *Journal of Applied Psychology*, February, 41–52.

Pizam, A. (1975). Social differentiation: A new psychological barrier to performance appraisal. *Public Personnel Management*, July/August, 244–247.

Psychologist, The. (1994). *New Report on Graphology*, January, p.2.

Robbins, S.P. (1991). *Organisational behaviour: Concepts, controversies, and applications* (fifth edition). New York: Prentice-Hall.

Robertson, I.T. (1994). Personnel Selection Research: Where are we now? *The Psychologist*, January, 1721.

Robertson, I.T. & Cooper, C.L. (1983). *Human behaviour in organisations*. Plymouth: Macdonald & Evans.

Robertson, I.T. & Downs, S. (1989). Work-sample tests of trainability: A meta-analysis. *Journal of Applied Psychology, 74*, 402–410.

Robertson, I.T., Gratton, L., & Rout, U. (1990). The validity of situational interviews for administrative jobs. *Journal of Organisational Behaviour, 11*, 69–76.

Robertson, I.T. & Kandola, R.S. (1982). Work-sample tests: Validity, adverse impact, and applicant reaction. *Journal of Occupational Psychology, 55*, 171–183.

Robertson, I.T. & Makin, P.J. (1986). Management selection in Britain: A survey and critique. *Journal of Occupational Psychology, 59*, 45–57.

Robertson, I.T. & Smith, M. (1989). Personnel selection methods. In M. Smith & I.T. Robertson (Eds.), *Advances in selection and assessment*. Chichester: Wiley.

Rowlinson, M. (1993). Pay is not dertermined by the market [Letter to the editor]. *Financial Times*, 5 November, p.18.

Saal, F.E. & Knight, P.A. (1988). *Industrial/ organisational psychology: Science and practice*. Belmont, CA: Wandsworth.

Shackleton, V. & Newell, S. (1991). Management selection: A comparative survey of methods used in top British and French companies. *Journal of Occupational Psychology, 64*, 23–36.

Smith, P.C. & Kendall, L.M. (1963). Retranslations of expectations: An approach to the construction of unambiguous anchors for rating scales. *Journal of Applied Psychology, 48*, 149–155.

Spector, P.E., Brannick, M.T., & Coovert, M.D. (1989). Job analysis. In C.L. Cooper & I.T. Robertson (Eds.), *International review of industrial and organisational psychology*. Chichester: Wiley.

Taylor, R. (1993). Not a penny more, not a penny less. *Financial Times*, 1 September.

Teel, K.S. (1978). Self-appraisal revisited. *Personnel Journal, 57*, 364–367.

Vecchio, R.P. (1991). *Organisational behaviour* (second edition). Orlando, FL: The Dryden Press.

Wicks, R.P. (1984). Interviewing: Practical aspects. In C.L. Cooper & P. Makin (Eds.), *Psychology for Managers*. Basingstoke, UK: B.P.S. and Macmillan Publishers.

Wood, L. (1993). Take care when rewarding high flyers. *Financial Times*, 17 November, p.22.

14

Health and Work: Hazards

The main focus in this chapter and the next is the relationship between conditions at work and the health and welfare of the employee. This chapter draws heavily on applied ergonomics, and supplements the discussion of the senses in Chapter 3. There is comment on problems connected with visual perception, hearing, exposure to chemicals, temperature changes, and body posture and movement.

INTRODUCTION

Modern industrial society creates conditions in which it is all too easy for people to become victims of hazardous events at work. A number of environmental hazards impinge upon our senses—for example, an intolerable level of noise could be the cause of acute discomfort and eventually lead to industrial deafness. Likewise, workers who operate typesetting machines can suffer some physical discomfort from closely watching visual display units for long periods.

The environmental hazards referred to in this chapter impinge in one way or another on the senses of both blue-collar and white-collar workers. (The senses were explained in Chapter 3 in connection with perception.) Environmental hazards examined here are associated with the factors listed in Table 14.1, and can be studied within the realm of ergonomics. Ergonomics is concerned with studying people at work and examining how they cope with the equipment they use and their working environment.

VISUAL DEFECTS

To begin with, the focus will be on colour perception, followed by an examination of age and visual performance, lighting and glare, and visual fatigue.

Colour Perception

Colour vision defects are seldom treated with the seriousness they deserve. Those affected are often unaware of their abnormality until an obvious error of judgement brings it to light. It is said that 6% of males and 0.5% of females have a deficiency when it comes to discriminating between colours (Oborne, 1994), but very few people are colour blind.

The most common form of deficiency in discriminating between colours is not being able to discriminate between the colours red, green, and blue. The most common type of colour blind person is the individual who might confuse red with green, or yellow with blue. The relatively rare individual who is really colour blind (about 0.003% of the population) sees only white, black, and

TABLE 14.1

Environmental Hazards

1. Visual perception
   - Colour perception
   - Age and Visual performance
   - Lighting and glare
   - Visual fatigue

2. Noise and vibration
   - Impact of noise
   - Music
   - Hearing loss
   - Vibration

3. Exposure to chemicals
   - Inhalation of vapour and dust
   - Skin irritants

4. Temperature changes
   - Responses to heat and cold

5. Body movement and posture
   - Walking
   - Lifting
   - Climbing
   - Seating
   - Body size

shades of grey. Such a person is described as *monochromat* (Oborne, 1994). However, it should be noted that certain colours placed on certain backgrounds can be a significant problem for those with normal vision and may lead to difficulties in focusing on a range of colours simultaneously, causing headaches or fatigue. Mistaking colours can be traced to a genetic factor, and there are a number of diseases associated with colour vision defects. These are shown in Table 14.2.

Apparently tests to diagnose colour abnormalities, indicating the type and severity of both inherited and acquired defects, are now available at a modest price, but it is said that industry continues to use outdated and inferior procedures (Voke, 1982). It is important to be realistic in the choice of diagnostic tests. Those chosen should place the pass/fail mark at a level appropriate to the job in question. The recognition of signal colours in the form of colour vision lanterns plays an important role in examining personnel from the railways, civil aviation, and the armed services for colour vision defects.

The human eye experiences difficulty accommodating a variety of colours shown simultaneously on a display, and this can result in fatigue. This is more common when one colour is distanced from another. For example, a wiring operator may have to manipulate a small coloured cable, while at the same time attending to a colour-coded wiring diagram, perhaps several centimetres away from the cable itself. After a time, the operator may find that he or she is confusing the colours of the cables and the colours on the diagram and making errors, actually mistaking one colour for another.

Because our eyes tire very quickly if forced to focus in one place for any length of time, there should be a large quantity of restful

TABLE 14.2

Diseases Causing Colour Vision Disturbances

Disease	Colour Vision Change
Diabetes mellitus	Blue defects
Multiple sclerosis	Red-yellow defects
Pernicious anaemia	Green defect
Addison's disease	Blue-yellow defect
Vitamin A deficiency	Most colours
Congenital jaundice	Blue and green defects
Malnutrition	All colours
Spinal cerebellar ataxia Friedrich's ataxia	Red-green defect first, then mostly green defect
Brain tumour, trauma, concussion	Red-green or blue-yellow defects
Vascular accidents (stroke)	Various
Cerebral cortex disease	Blue defect
Cortical lesions	Blue defect
Syphilis	Red-green defect, blue defect
Alcoholism and cirrhosis of the liver	Blue defect

Source: Voke, J., (1982) Colour vision problems at work. *Health and Safety at Work, January,* 27–28. Reproduced by the permission of the publisher.

scenes in the periphery of the field of vision. This environment should consist of muted colours, restful pictures, plants, and other suitable objects.

Age and Visual Performance

Age can effect visual performance. In one study it was found that subjects aged 50–60 years required illumination in the range 100–400 lux to perform as well as younger subjects (aged 20–30) who functioned with illumination in the range 2–5 lux (Bodman, 1962). It follows that the age of a worker is an important consideration when faced with the design of visual tasks. Another problem with increasing age is the reduced ability to focus on objects at different distances.

For example, the eyes of the ageing operator typing text at a computer keyboard move between the written material on the manuscripts and the VDU screen. If the positions of the VDU screen and the manuscript are at different distances from the eye, the eye needs to accommodate them rapidly to avoid blurred images. To counteract the effects of ageing we naturally resort to the use of appropriate spectacles. With increasing age the ciliary muscles in the eyes deteriorate, creating a long-sighted effect, whereby the nearest point at which the eye can be sharply focused moves further away.

Lighting and Glare

Lighting is also of critical importance. The aims of a good system of lighting are to facilitate performance on the job, to promote safety, and to assist in the creation of a pleasing environment. When computerised systems are introduced, they are often installed in an office environment with many of the characteristics of the conventional office. Frequently there are big windows to admit as much sunshine as possible, light and bright walls, and direct overhead lighting (i.e. useful for the conditions prevailing in the pre-computerised era). So we have light streaming through the windows and bouncing off the gloss-painted walls, creating mirror images and reflections on operators' visual display units (VDUs). Similar problems are created by direct overhead lighting.

How could an office environment such as that described be improved? Blinds or curtains could be put up at the windows, and walls could be covered in a more sombre coloured matt finish. The brightness of the typical VDU display supplemented by a low level of overhead lighting (100 lux or less), is just acceptable for reading the source documents used by operators. However, it may be necessary to supplement this lighting with brighter, local, fully adjustable lighting. One could ensure that a VDU is not sited in such a way that the operator is seated facing an unshielded window or other source of light (Anderson, 1980).

Glare is something one must consider in relation to lighting and illumination provision, because it is as troublesome as inadequate lighting. It manifests itself in many different forms. For example, reflections from a VDU screen, from a bright metal trim, from decorations on the units, and from the keys and the keyboard can all cause glare. Badly positioned signal lamps can be a source of glare, and it can also arise because of the positioning and intensity of artificial light.

Glare is apparent when one part of our field of vision is brighter than the level of light to which the eye has adapted. An example of the brighter field of vision is a car headlight at night. Direct glare occurs when the light comes directly from a particular source. On the other hand, reflected glare is caused by very bright reflections from polished or glossy surfaces. When glare interferes with visual performance it is known as *disability glare*; where it causes discomfort, annoyance, irritation, or distraction, it is referred to as "discomfort glare". It may not be easy to distinguish between the two in practice, but what is not in dispute are the effects, such as reduced performance through increased arousal and distraction, and the consumption of valuable mental power to avoid the glare.

Whatever the source of glare, the visual comfort of the VDU operator is at stake. Glare can be compounded by the quality of characters displayed on the screen. Significant luminance contrasts between the VDU screen and its surroundings, where reflections exist and where characters on display vary in brightness, can lead to annoyance and irritation and redness of the eyes of the operator (Laubli, Hunting, & Grandjean, 1981).

Steps have to be taken to control glare. One obvious way to control reflected glare from a VDU screen is to do something about the source of glare. Where appropriate, blinds can be pulled down, the position of the screen can be changed so that the window light does not shine on it, and lights can be arranged so that they are not reflected. However, it may not always be possible to take such action. Sometimes the sun makes its presence felt only for a brief period. Of course, screen filters might be used to combat the problem of reflections from the screen, but a problem with screen filters is that although they can be effective in reducing screen reflections, they could also reduce character brightness and screen resolution.

If blinds cannot be used, other measures are available. Tinted glass can be used; also, vertical fins on the window, and translucent blinds, to reduce the area of sky visible from any position in the room, can be fitted. In addition, an overhang above the window can be built, or the angle of the source of glare can be increased by having windows placed higher up the wall (Hopkinson, 1972). To reduce glare and reflection at VDU work stations, matt surfaces are preferred, and if signal lamps are provided on the unit they should be of low intensity, glare-free, and preferably out of the immediate line of sight.

If glare problems originating from windows continue to be a serious issue, then the removal of the windows, and the installation of light directly under the control of the operators, may have to be considered. But that begs the question, how would people react to windowless offices? In one study of windowless offices in the United States (Ruys, 1970), there were few complaints about the quality of the artificial lighting, but 90% of the office workers (who worked on their own) expressed dissatisfaction with the absence of windows. To them the lack of windows amounted to a lack of daylight, poor ventilation, lack of awareness about the state of the weather, or the lack of a view. Also, the potential for depressive feelings and tension was found to exist. Apparently windowless factories do not appear to create the same effect.

As well as glare, another issue to consider is visual flicker. Instead of our eyes coming into contact with a stimulus in the form of a stable light or illumination, we encounter a light that flickers. Warning lights that flash, or indicator lights, are examples of visual flickering. Excessive flicker from whatever source—e.g. deteriorating fluorescent lights—can have a detrimental effect on both health and working conditions.

Visual Fatigue

Poor lighting, due either to inadequate illumination or glare, can give rise to visual fatigue which, in turn, can contribute to general fatigue. Keyboard operators may also experience visual fatigue when reading poor quality source documents, such as those with illegible handwriting. Other considerations to bear in mind hinge on the VDU screen itself. It is beneficial to have an image on the screen that is clear and stable, and it is important to refresh the screen image to an acceptable level because too low a refresh rate can result in a flickering image that itself could lead to eye strain. Attention has also been given to the spacing and colours of characters on the screen, the adjustable nature of the screen, and the extent of operator control over brightness, contrast, and positioning.

According to Murray-Bruce (1982), a medical practitioner in occupational health, typical symptoms of temporary eye strain or visual fatigue (resulting in strain on the small ciliary muscles of the eye that are used to focus on small objects) in their severest form include:

- eyes that are sore and dry, with an itchiness that rubbing makes worse;
- eyesight that temporarily blurs, making focusing difficult;
- photophobia, which is an acute sensitivity to light and takes the form of a fear of bright lights; and
- a general headache that spreads to the neck and shoulders.

These conditions can be aggravated by an overheated, overdry and smoky environment, and the overall effect is a general deterioration in a person's ability to focus and concentrate on a visual task. This could lead to increased error rates and increased accident potential in certain circumstances. In explaining the connection between complaints of eye strain and performance of a task using a VDU, Oborne (1994) makes the following observation:

This is probably a function of the amount of work the eye is called upon to do, particularly the volume of work undertaken by the ciliary muscles that control the lens shape. In order to perceive objects that are near and far away, the shape of the lens has to be altered so as to focus the visual image on the retina. The process is known as "accommodation". In a practical sense all objects further than six metres from the normal eye are sharply in focus, but the nearer an object is to the eye the greater is the amount of muscular effort that is required to maintain the correct lens curvature. The document the operator works from and the screen he or she uses are placed close to each other and, as a consequence, the ciliary muscles in the operator's eyes are subjected to a heavy load. On a positive note, the correct prescription of glasses has been known to reduce the incidence of complaints by VDU operators.

IMPACT OF NOISE AND VIBRATION

Noise

Noise is frequently described as unwanted sound—it can be unpleasant and bothersome, can interfere with the perception of wanted sound, and can be harmful in a physiological sense. Unwanted sound of this type can be referred to as acoustic noise. Too much noise can create an arousal state not compatible with good performance.

Noise below 16Hz is normally described as *infrasound*, and can be produced by any pulsating or throbbing piece of equipment, as we would expect to hear from ventilation systems in offices. Commonly experienced noise levels are shown in Table 14.3.

What is called *continuous noise* can have a detrimental effect on both individual and group behaviour. With reference to social interaction within a group of school children, the effects of aircraft noise were studied (Crook & Langdon, 1974). The findings indicate that aircraft noise produces

TABLE 14.3

Noise Levels Related to Environmental Conditions

Decibels	Type of Noise
140	Pain threshold
130	Pneumatic chipper
120	Loud automobile horn
110	
100	Inside underground train
90	
80	Average traffic on street corner
70	Conversational speech
60	Typical business office
50	Living room
40	Library
30	Bedroom at night
20	Broadcasting studio
10	
0	Threshold of hearing

Source: adapted from Oborne, D.J. (1994). *Ergonomics at work* (third edition). Chichester: Wiley.

distraction which has an impact on social interaction as follows:

There was a change in the style of teaching on the noisier days—i.e. lessons were cancelled, or there were more pauses in the flow of speech of the teacher; there was increased fidgeting on the part of the pupils; there was reduced teacher satisfaction with the class as a whole; and both teachers and pupils became irritable and tired, whereby pupils developed headaches, with the more vocal ones being less inclined to work.

An example of noise that we invariably find irritating is the hum or whine of a cooling fan. The hum from a poor ventilation system, if acute, can be fatiguing and hypnotic, as the writer found to his personal discomfort in a hotel bedroom some time ago.

Apart from continuous noise, we also encounter *intermittent noise* in the form of sudden large bangs or impulses coming from any percussion type of machine—e.g. a gun or road hammer.

It hardly needs stating that general architectural design should pay special attention to acoustics in places of work, for any spillover of ambient sound is irritating. Noise can be reduced at source by certain methods of noise absorption, such as placing padding around noisy machinery, using sound absorbing wall and floor materials, arranging equipment in an appropriate way, and creating screens to reduce the level of reflected sound.

Communication and Noise

Good verbal communication depends on both the ability of the communicator to produce the correct sounds in the form of speech, and on the listener's ability to receive and decode those sounds. A noisy environment is likely to interfere with the reception and decoding of sound because of an effect known as masking. The latter weakens the perception of a signal projected as speech or sound from an auditory system. One should try to be sensitive to the existence of masking, and be prepared to confront it and reduce its worst effects. People who operate in noisy environments can develop coping skills supplemented by social and non-verbal cues.

Annoyance generally arises when noise interferes with a person's ability to carry out some activity that he or she wishes to pursue. A significant source of noise in offices can be speech. In a study of noise in landscaped offices (Nemecek & Grandjean, 1973), it was concluded that 46% of employees who reported that they were disturbed by noise felt that noise produced by conversation was most annoying, the majority feeling that it was the content of the conversation, rather than its loudness, that was most disturbing; 25% of the said employees disliked office machinery noise; and 19% of them disliked the noise of telephones.

Another cause of annoyance is *overhearing* conversations. Where a person overhears other peoples's conversations, then that person could feel uncomfortable at the thought that others could be privy to his or her own private conversations. Also, if the intruding speech is understood, rather than merely registered as loud, this could destroy the feeling of office privacy (Waller, 1969).

Official Action to Control Noise

In the early 1980s, the European Commission's Advisory Committee on Health and Safety received a draft directive, subsequently revised, dealing with the protection of workers from harmful exposure to noise. A maximum noise level of 70dB(A) was proposed for simple administrative workplaces and 80dB(A) for other places of work, and it was suggested that a priority aim of employers should be to reduce noise levels at source. A similar stand was taken by the Health and Safety Commission in the UK when, in its discussion documents on proposed regulations on hearing protection, it encouraged employers to tackle noise problems by resorting to noise control engineering rather than the use of hearing protectors. The current legally accepted level for exposure to industrial noise in the UK is 90dB(A).

In the European Commission's draft directive, referred to earlier, ear protectors were looked upon as temporary measures for dealing with the problem of noise. More appropriate measures would include reducing the level of noise by installing noise absorbent material, or covering the source of noise with sound deadening hoods or screens, as well as reducing the exposure of workers to noise. The view of the Health and Safety Commission in the UK was that the use of ear protectors was only permissible if it could be demonstrated that the adoption of noise control engineering would be prohibitively expensive and not reasonably practicable.

Sometimes there is an aversion to the use of ear protectors by employees because they are considered unappealing aesthetically, and may prevent the worker from hearing audible warning alarm signals. Another likely explanation for not wearing ear protectors, particularly on construction sites, is based on perceived inconvenience. The canal plug cannot be easily handled once work has started because it can only be inserted safely with clean hands. Ear-muffs do not suffer from this disadvantage, but they may be considered too bulky to be carried about comfortably by a worker on an open-air construction site (Corfield, 1987).

According to a survey of 200 companies in British industry (British Labour Party, 1981) the control of noise is less than adequate (see panel below).

Music

We refer to noise as unwanted sound, whereas in suitable circumstances music could be considered wanted sound, often desired and enjoyed by many workers. Music at work can be classified as either background music or industrial music (Fox, 1983). Background music takes the form of an endless flow of light, quiet music, frequently found in supermarkets, hotels, and similar places, designed to put shoppers and customers at ease. By contrast, industrial music varies—it may not be continuous and can be played at certain times of the day. This was popular in British factories some years ago—"music while you work".

Although much has been written about the effects of noise on cognitive functioning and productivity, there is controversy surrounding the suggested relationship. However, the theoretical justification for suggesting that music can help worker performance might be explained as follows: the music alleviates the boredom and fatigue that often accompanies repetitive work, and it

---

Noise at Work in the UK

- In 90% of the companies sampled, ear-muffs and ear-plugs were the only method of noise protection offered consistently.
- There was a totally inadequate provision for the control of noise at source in 25% of the companies, and of all the employees in the companies sampled only 10% could be disciplined for not wearing hearing protection devices.
- The marking of areas where noisy machinery was located applied in only 50% of the companies.
- Consultation with the union on matters connected with hearing protection only occurred in 50% of the companies.
- Only 12% of employers gave safety representatives the noise levels of new equipment.
- In 57% of the companies a request by the safety representative to have a noise survey conducted was met, but only 66% of the safety representatives drawn from these companies could be present during the process of noise measurement.
- It was felt that the compensation received from either the state or employers as a result of industrial deafness was totally inadequate (British Labour Party, 1981).

produces a stimulating effect when there is an absence of such stimulation in the immediate environment.

One writer speculates that music influences not only the attention and vigilance we show at work, but our feelings of well-being and job satisfaction. The latter could be manifested in a reduction in absenteeism, improved timekeeping and a reduction in the turnover of staff. The end result is likely to be an increase in overall productivity (Fox, 1983). The suggested beneficial consequences stemming from music at work might be extended to include increased quality of the output, as well as a reduction in errors and accidents.

What would be the best times of the day to play industrial music? According to Oborne (1994), it would be early in the morning and after lunch when the individual's level of arousal may be low, but it would be necessary to assess the prevailing local circumstances. Also, worker involvement in the choice of music could be worth pursuing.

Hearing Loss

This can result from the combined effects of long-term exposure to normal noises and sounds that we encounter every day, such as those generated by loud vehicles and disco music. Hearing loss can also be the consequence of the normal process of ageing, with changes occurring in the structure of the auditory system due to the deposit of substances, such as cholesterol, and changes in the elasticity of parts of the inner ear. However, a certain type of deafness, having a detrimental effect on a person's social life and personal safety, is known as *conduction deafness*.

In this type of deafness, airborne vibration is unable to produce an adequate vibration in the ear-drum for reasons such as wax in the ear canal or infection of a scarred ear-drum. Another type of deafness, where there is reduced sensitivity of the nerve cells in the inner ear, results in the worker experiencing difficulty hearing normal environmental noise.

Deafness caused by noise is a real issue in modern industrial society. As a consequence, many countries have legislated for maximum noise levels to which workers are exposed. It is known that excessive noise can damage hearing permanently and, therefore, there is a need for audiometric testing to detect gradual hearing loss.

Vibration Problems

Sound at the low end of the sound range is felt as vibration. One has to be vigilant to the effects of vibration. It is known that the levels of vibration experienced by vehicle drivers who drive on rough ground for very short periods could cause some structural damage to the body over time. In a major survey (Rosegger & Rosegger, 1960) of the health complaints of 371 tractor drivers who frequently drove their tractors over rough ploughed ground, it was found that those who operated their tractors for long periods experienced stomach complaints and spinal disorders, particularly in the lumbar and thoracic regions of the body.

Prolonged exposure to frequent vibration in the high frequency range is likely to cause injuries. In the contemporary industrial world, frequent exposure to a vibrating stimulus is common for workers who handle equipment, such as road drills, stone-breakers and chain saws. Intense vibration from holding these hand tools can be transmitted to the operator's fingers, hands, and arms, producing effects such as intermittent numbness or clumsiness of the fingers, and perhaps damage to the bones, joints, or muscles.

Prolonged rest is the only cure for all or some of these symptoms, although they can reappear when the worker is exposed again to the vibrating stimulus. Though intense vibration affects the control exercised by the limbs, thereby having some effect on work performance, apparently no adverse effects apply to intellectual functioning (Oborne, 1994). But the professional, who is intent on preparing a talk or presentation while travelling on a London Transport tube train, could experience significant vibration that prevents him or her from reading and, particularly, writing a script, thereby affecting performance. Also, vibrating structures are capable of producing motion sickness, and possible headaches.

The message or signal coming from the source of vibration can provide useful information. For example, a particular noise and vibration from the engine of a motor car informs the driver that something is amiss.

EXPOSURE TO CHEMICALS

Under this heading inhalation of vapour and dust, and skin irritants will be considered.

Inhalation of Vapour and Dust

The inhaling of certain vapours, as well as asbestos and aluminium dust, is a problem under continuous review. For example, the Health and Safety Executive issued a warning to the engineering industry and allied trades as long ago as 1982, drawing attention to the dangers of cold degreasing solvents following reported deaths from their use. Unfortunately these solvents are used in such a way that the operator may be exposed to a high concentration of vapour which can prove fatal even if the exposure is for a very short period of time (see panel below).

Solvents with a pleasant odour, which give the effect of a drug-like "high" when inhaled, are also open to deliberate abuse, which can cause deaths either through poisoning by the solvent itself, or through accidents occurring because the individual is not alert and able to react quickly.

The Health and Safety Commission announced much tighter control limits for asbestos—though they are not absolutely safe levels—from January 1983. Where adequate engineering controls to meet the new limits cannot be instituted, then the workforce will be required to wear suitable protective equipment. There are likely to be a number of future measures for the control of exposure to asbestos dust, not to mention an enquiry into both the adequacy and problems of wearing suitable respiratory protective equipment and protective clothing. Other measures will include the licensing of asbestos insulation contractors, prohibiting the spraying of asbestos, prohibiting the use of asbestos in insulation, and prohibiting the import, use, and marketing of crocidolite and products containing it.

Pure aluminium dust can also pose a health hazard. Aluminium as a metal is widely used both on its own and in the form of an alloy in

---

The Dangers of Cold Degreasing Agents

Deaths have occurred to young people working at small degreasing tanks containing only a few inches of the solvent. Before work commences some of the solvent evaporates and forms a layer of heavy vapour. A typical piece of behaviour by the operator is to lean over the tank in order to scoop the solvent over the components, brushing the components with the solvent, or swishing the components through the solvent. In the process the vapour is disturbed and the operator is likely to inhale it. Matters are made worse if the tank is in a room with still air and little ventilation (although one such death occurred in the open air).

Commercial chlorinated solvents such as 1.1.1. trichloroethane, upon which degreasers are based, are potent anaesthetics. A fairly common cause of the reported deaths is loss of consciousness followed by unobserved collapse into the vapour concentration itself as a result of falling over the side of the degreasing tank, or collapse in a confined space where the solvent vapour has had the chance to build up in still air (Safety Representative, 1982).

the manufacture of utensils, laboratory equipment, cable, wire, and foil; or it can be used in powder form in paints. Exposure to pure aluminium dust may produce a form of pulmonary fibrosis, the main features of which are rapidly progressive dyspnoea (i.e. difficulty in breathing), coughing, and weight loss. Therefore the advent of new technology in the form of paint-spraying robots and the automation of work processes involving asbestos, lead-based products, and where an atmosphere of intensive dust exists, is welcome on health grounds.

Certain aspects of life in the modern office can be considered hazardous. For example, a discussion of carbonless copying paper is included in the panel below.

Skin Irritants

The skin is particularly vulnerable to substances in the work environment. Industrial dermatitis has tended to become more prevalent with the increase in the use of chemical-based products on construction sites, and many working days are lost through

this disease or disability. Substances such as brick and plaster stone dust, cement containing chromates, pitch, tar, bitumen, certain wood dusts, certain epoxy resins, paints, varnishes, stains, organic solvents, petrol, white spirit, thinners, acids, alkalis, and ionising radiations, harm the skin in one of several ways.

Oily contaminants can block the pores and hair follicles, abrasives can remove the protective horny layer of the epidermis, and chemicals can dry up the skin's natural moisture or dissolve and remove the protective oily secretion of the skin. The end result is that the outer layers of the skin are damaged and vulnerable to contamination by particles and bacteria. The skin's natural protection is reduced further by cuts, scratches, blisters, etc, acquired from work requiring rough handling. Even though injuries may appear trivial, workers should seek first aid in these circumstances.

Allergic dermatitis occurs through hypersensitivity to specific substances (e.g. certain hardwoods or synthetic resins) that may prove harmless to many people. Once the

---

Symptoms associated with Carbonless Copying Paper

The modern carbonless copying paper used in offices in the mid 1980s was identified as a cause of mysterious symptoms that reach a peak at busy working periods. The symptoms take the form of rashes, irritations to the eyes, nose, and throat, headaches, and drowsiness, and are caused by dust and chemical vapours created by the carbonless copying paper.

This paper is coated with chemicals and tiny micro capsules containing more chemicals. When the typewriter key hits the paper, the micro capsules are crushed at that particular spot and they release their chemicals. These chemicals react with the chemicals in the coating of the paper to form permanent dyes.

Handling the paper in small quantities would not be a problem but dealing with large quantities could create dry eyes and throat and, for staff working in a confined office, a feeling of abnormal tiredness. This condition is aggravated by overheating and badly ventilated

offices, causing what is referred to as "paper sickness".

In a reported case of a businessman who suffered from paper sickness after spending only a day in a small office leafing through records kept on carbonless paper, it was found that he developed a burning sensation on his face, throat, and tongue. The following day he woke up with aches in his legs. That was Saturday, but he felt much better on Sunday. On Monday, he experienced the same symptoms, having handled carbonless paper records for the morning only.

Symptoms similar to the common cold—runny eyes and nose—were detected in four women who handled the carbonless paper. This was most acute in the last week of the month when the office was very busy. The women would frequently place their hands between sheaves of carbonless paper to extract a particular sheet, and they all noticed that this caused a tingling sensation of the skin (Gillie, 1982).

person is sensitised to the substance he or she can never again safely handle it.

Irritant dermatitis usually only attacks the areas of the skin in direct contact with the harmful substance, and it will usually respond to proper medical treatment. The preventative measures for counteracting ordinary irritant dermatitis are as follows:

- Substitute a safer material in place of the harmful material.
- Sometimes in order to get rid of irritant substances, such as paint, tar, oil, and stains, people resort to using petrol or abrasives, or strong detergents, or solvents and thinners. These should be used carefully because they can be harsh on the skin and could themselves cause dermatitis, leaving the skin rough, sensitive, and liable to crack.
- The skin should be washed with soap and warm water and thoroughly dried, ideally applying some lanolin-based skin cream to the dried hands. The employee should avoid going to the toilet with dirty hands, so as to prevent contamination to the groin, which is a sensitive area susceptible to skin troubles.
- Use of no-touch techniques—e.g. gloves, footwear, mechanical aids, or remote control. There are obvious advantages to using gloves in rough handling jobs, but one has to consider what happens on the inside of a glove. Outside dirt may get in and the glove prevents perspiration evaporating into the air. As a result, the skin remains moist and soft and vulnerable to the entry of contaminants.

Gloves can also interfere with the operation of controls held in the hand. A glove that is too thick may result in grasping objects in an insecure manner. To counteract this effect, the operator may grip the control unnecessarily tightly, thereby increasing fatigue in the finger and other muscles. Ideally, gloves should be resistant to slip and be able to fit comfortably, but gloves worn for protection against injury may not possess these important features. Where controls have built-in coded differences in the texture of the mechanism (for example in the control lever or handle), the wearing of gloves could undermine the perception of the ingrained code.

As a means to protect the feet, special footwear is recommended for certain types of jobs. But heavy protective footwear may not permit the feet to be moved with the necessary precision, because the appropriate feedback may be either missing or of low quality. With shoes the question of the height of the heels arises, particularly when one is concerned about the distance between the foot pedal for braking and the floor in a vehicle. A mismatch in an ergonomic sense could affect stopping distances.

Apart from gloves and footwear, protective clothing is worn by workers when faced with certain hazards at work. Protection clothing includes garments such as outdoor welding suits, clean room garments for the pharmaceutical and electronic industries, toxic material protection of all types, flame-retardant clothing, weather protection suits for hostile environments, and chemical splash protective clothing. Ideally the aim in some occupations is to ensure that appropriate protection is afforded and at the same time that the clothing is comfortable to wear.

It is said that in a 24-hour period a person engaged in hard physical work can produce a half gallon of water through perspiration for every metre of skin area. That water has to evaporate off into the atmosphere, or the worker becomes hot, damp, very uncomfortable, and lacking in concentration. In practice, the twin aim of protection and comfort may be difficult to achieve in certain circumstances. Protective clothing that can withstand chemicals, acid, fine dust, water, or even fire, might well cause the wearer to suffer from fatigue and exhaustion through a build-up of condensation. The reality is that a worker will probably, if at all feasible, sacrifice his or her protective clothing for the sake of comfort.

Protective clothing is now available that can withstand various hazards (e.g. it acts as a barrier to water and other liquids and is completely windproof). At the same time it will permit perspiration vapour to pass freely through, so the worker can be fully protected and yet remain dry and comfortable at the job he or she is doing. As a result, one can expect more efficient job performance. Fabrics like the new membrane will make a significant impact in the field of protective clothing. This thin material has a microporous structure with nine billion pores to the square inch. Further applications for such fabrics could include outdoor welding suits, clean room garments for the pharmaceutical and electronics industries, toxic material protection of all types, flame-retardant clothing, weather protection suits for hostile environments, and chemical splash protective clothing (Safety Representative, 1982).

IMPACT OF TEMPERATURE CHANGES

As stated in Chapter 3, there are receptors in the skin for registering cold and warmth. The body's temperature is controlled by a complex self-regulating system located in the hypothalamus section of the brain. Under ordinary conditions of rest, the temperature deep in the body is maintained within the normal range of 97–99°F.

Hyperthermia (Heat Stroke)

If the body temperature reaches 108°F, for example, the individual could be prone to heat stroke known as hyperthermia, with likely loss of consciousness following a short period of general weakness or confusion and irrational behaviour. The eventual outcome is death unless a cooling process is used.

When conditions are hot the hypothalamus sets in motion the following processes for the body to lose heat—the blood vessels dilate, the sweat glands produce cooling sweat, the body's respiration rate increases, and the

body's metabolic rate is lowered. However, there are occasions when the body cannot get rid of excess heat, as we saw in the example of the individual suffering from hyperthermia. Why is it that the body's self-regulatory system does not work in the event of excess heat? Two related reasons have been put forward (in a work context) by Oborne (1994):

1. The worker operates in such humid environmental conditions that the body cannot reduce its heat through the evaporation of sweat. Between the inside of some protective clothing and the surface of the body a climate supersaturated with water develops, and this situation prevents or impairs adequate evaporation.
2. Some protective clothing has heat-retaining and perhaps impenetrable qualities that produce an insulation effect. These circumstances could contribute to heat stress. The heat stress can be related to the main body temperature, rather than the external conditions, which could be less than the critical 42°C. Strenuous physical exercise can cause heat stroke if the heat created by the expenditure of effort is greater than the body's ability to get rid of the excess heat.

A group vulnerable to heat stroke are likely to be motivated young individuals who are engaged in hard work, such as military training and sport. To prevent heat stroke requires adequate rest and consumption of liquid before physical exertion and during rest periods in order to compensate for the increased loss of liquid while sweating (Shibolet, Lancaster, & Danon, 1976).

Radiation

Conditions which are very hot due to heat being radiated from a hot source (e.g. a steel furnace) can have a material effect on the operator's personal comfort. Radiation is emitted by the heat source as electromagnetic waves. If the radiation is severe enough it can burn the skin tissue, as can happen to holiday-makers lying on the beach under a hot sun. In normal circumstances we get relief from air that moves over the body because it has a cooling effect in the sense that it helps to evaporate the sweat and dissipate the heat from the surface of the body, and thereby leads to increased body comfort. Air movement that is too fast can lead to people complaining of draughts at work.

Humidity

Closely related to our comfort is the level of humidity. It is measured by the amount of water vapour in the air. In conditions of relatively high humidity there is excessive water vapour in the air, and this will affect the efficiency with which the body can handle the evaporation of sweat from the skin for the purposes of cooling. We normally associate body discomfort with high levels of humidity, but equally we should be aware of the discomfort caused by a very low level of humidity—e.g. drying of the moist membranes in the nose and throat— particularly if the air temperature is rather high.

Hypothermia

When our attention shifts to a consideration of cold conditions the opposite effects to those discussed earlier occur. Now the body needs to conserve, and even generate, heat. The hypothalamus causes the blood vessels to constrict, and to route the blood in such a way as to cause a blue appearance. It also increases the metabolic rate by inducing the muscle activity known as shivering. In this way an optimum body temperature is achieved in the face of unfavourable external conditions. When exposed to the cold, the regulation system of the body tries to generate heat quickly by an increase in muscular activity—e.g. shivering increases, and reaches a maximum at body temperatures around 93–95°F. This was acknowledged in outline earlier. The cardiovascular system responds to the cold by constricting the peripheral blood vessels, and this leads to an increase in blood pressure. If the temperature falls below the range of 93–95°F the heart rate falls. In the range 86–91°F, shivering gradually stops and is replaced by muscular rigidity.

Clinically, a state of hypothermia is said to occur when the body's core internal temperature falls to the 95°F level, and below 86°F there is the likelihood of imminent death from cardiac arrest. Accidental hypothermia can occur from exposure to severe weather, or being immersed in very cold water for a short time. Likewise, the elderly are vulnerable in bad weather, particularly when their resistance is low following a bout of ill-health. However, susceptibility to hypothermia varies significantly between individuals, and the extent of body fat, weight, and size are critical factors in this respect.

Cold Conditions and Performance

The cold can affect the performance of manual tasks in two ways. First, where the cold affects the arms and legs, muscular control is interrupted, leading to a reduction in manual dexterity and strength. Obviously, this could be countered to some extent by warming the affected limbs using appropriate work wear or local heating. Second, where the cold affects the whole body, performance can be undermined as a result of shivering. But equally if the conditions giving rise to shivering are improved, then there could be a return to previous levels of manual performance.

Does a low temperature affect the performance of tasks requiring mental or cognitive skill, such as thinking, reasoning, and judging? One answer to this question can be provided with reference to the findings of a research study of divers whose safety depends on clear, efficient thinking. When they were asked to perform different cognitive tasks (using reasoning ability and memory, as well as being vigilant) in water with a temperature of 40°F for 50 minutes, they did so without any significant impairment to their cognitive efficiency, particularly when conditions were good and the divers were all motivated (Baddeley et al., 1975). However, the reverse position is likely to apply when less well-motivated workers carry out complex tasks in cold conditions (Oborne, 1994).

BODY MOVEMENT AND POSTURE

The two proprioceptive senses (kinaesthetic and vestibular), described briefly in Chapter 3, are concerned with perceiving the body's own movement.

Kinaesthetic

The kinaesthetic system is concerned with the feeling of motion and consists of sensors in the muscles, tendons, and joints. The sensors inform us of the relative positions and movements of our limbs and of different parts of our body. A proprioceptive sense (e.g. kinaesthetic), unlike other senses (e.g. vision), does not have a visible organ. But one must not ignore the fact that kinaesthesis underpins a visible sensory organ (e.g. the eyes); the position of the eyes is maintained by muscles that attach the eyes to the socket. The kinaesthetic receptors in these muscles provide information about the degree and direction of the eye's movement.

The worker, relying on kinaesthetic receptors, is kept informed unconsciously of what the body is doing without every part of it having to be monitored. For example, people who do not suffer from a physical disability can climb stairs efficiently because of kinaesthetic feedback emanating from the muscles, tendons, and joints, when in motion. When walking or climbing we do not always have to look down in the direction of our feet in order to know where to place the next step. The kinaesthetic sensory receptors, located in the hand, arm, and shoulder muscles, allow the worker to use the hands efficiently above the head or out of sight.

Receptors located in the muscles convey information about the extent to which a muscle is being stretched, as well as the rate of stretching. Receptors in the tendons provide information about the degree of movement of the joints (i.e. the speed and the direction of movement). Another kinaesthetic receptor is sensitive to deep pressure and to any deformity in the tissue in which it is located. It is now apparent that the kinaesthetic system is made up of a number of sub-systems, all giving the worker information about where the limbs and body generally are positioned in space.

The kinaesthetic system is of critical importance in the field of training and the utilisation of motor skills (e.g. manual dexterity, finger dexterity, wrist and finger movement and reaction time). Typing is a motor skill, and feedback from the kinaesthetic receptors located in the fingers, arms, shoulder muscles, and joints is valuable information for the typist, because it allows him or her to be able to sense where the fingers ought to be placed without engaging in a conscious act.

All muscular activity should ideally take place on an intermittent basis to allow blood to flow through the muscle. For example, a typist may develop back and shoulder pain unless there is adequate opportunity to relax and contract the muscles, perhaps by walking about or doing other work. However, working practices are changing for keyboard operators as a result of the application of new technology. Work can now be done more quickly and efficiently on word-processors than on the manual or electric typewriter. But muscular fatigue often occurs more quickly, affecting different muscles, because the new technology does not demand the natural breaks and movements required by the old technology (e.g. changing paper, and anticipating auditory signals such as bells). Therefore, it is recommended that there should be relatively frequent posture changes between sitting and standing during prolonged VDU work (Oborne, 1994).

Most muscular actions generally require the use of a number of muscles in an integrated manner. For example, pushing a cycle pedal requires turning the ankle as well as extending the knee and the hip, and, of course, positioning the pelvis and the trunk in a stable position on the seat. The maximum force applied in such circumstances will depend on the weakest link in the muscular chain.

When a skill has been fully developed through a good training programme, we can be reasonably confident that the kinaesthetic system is being used efficiently. For example, the motorist has learned that the right foot controls the accelerator and brake, and the left foot the clutch in a manually operated transmission car. Therefore, it would take a conscious decision to operate the brake with the left foot. Even if the motorist did so, he or she would feel discomfort in the lower leg and ankle.

The timing of a response can be crucial in the exercise of skills in, for example, physical exercise, such as participation in certain competitive sport. Before a player in gaelic hurling (an Irish game resembling hockey) hits a ball in flight, he has to be able to anticipate the arrival of the ball, and be able to time a response using a hurley so that the ball is struck at a specific spot. In this example, the kinaesthetic receptors provide information about the location of the hand and arm so that both can be placed in the correct position. Likewise, the receptors inform the player about the speed and direction of the arm movement so that the appropriate part of the body is in the correct place at the correct time.

This example underlines the fact that in the performance of certain skilled behaviour the kinaesthetic system cannot function without the help of another sensory organ. In such cases, vision is crucially important for accurate motor skill timing (Smith & Marriott, 1982).

Lifting

A sphere of human activity in which the muscles feature prominently is that of lifting. People suffer from backaches, ruptures, hernias, and strained muscles from working in the home, garden, and in do-it-yourself building activity. Lifting heavy loads at work may then aggravate an already weakened condition. The Chartered Society of Physiotherapy offers guidance on maximum weights for safe lifting. For example, the maximum safe weight capable of being lifted repeatedly by an adult male is 54.4kg (120lb). When walking with a load, the maximum weights that can be lifted vertically, then carried over a distance, are shown in Table 14.4 for a range of distances.

Maximum safe weights vary depending on the height and physique of the person. Injury to the small of the back and hernia damage as a result of lifting heavy loads are not uncommon. The expending of muscular force

TABLE 14.4

Lifting and Carrying Loads Safely

	Carrying Distances (Range)		
	Short		Long
Max. safe weight	0–61 cm (2 ft) 54.4 kg (120 lb)		1.8 m (6 ft) 9.0 kg (20 lb)

in the face of resistance, or supporting a heavy load without moving, consumes energy and can be painful and unacceptable. For example, the repeated grasping and lifting of smooth-surfaced heavy cartons of awkward dimensions onto high stacks in a warehouse can be uncomfortable. If employees feel a strain when lifting a load, but persist, they may hurt themselves.

The Chartered Society of Physiotherapy has come forward with some tips (listed in the panel below) to reduce the number of gardeners, estimated at 250,000, requiring hospital treatment for their back each year in the UK (The *Guardian*, 1990).

The Chartered Society of Physiotherapy (1966) has also issued guidelines on lifting, specifically aimed at the industrial worker:

- The feet should be far enough apart so that there is a balanced distribution of the person's weight.
- The knees and hips should be bent and the back kept as straight as possible with the chin tucked in.
- The arms should be held as near to the body as possible.
- The whole of the hand should be used to grasp the object wherever possible.

- Lifting should be done smoothly without jerks or snatches.

To these guidelines could be added the following (Hammond, 1978):

- Avoid lifting and carrying above the level of the eyes.
- Avoid lifting or supporting a load in a vertical axis when the load is located any distance from the vertical axis of the body.
- Provide an intermediate platform where loads are lifted on to the shoulder or lowered from the shoulder.
- Look out for and eliminate features of job design that impose awkward postures.

There appears to be a connection between back injuries and handling over a range of occupations (Oborne, 1994). In some industries—e.g. construction—apprentices infrequently receive instruction in the prevention of accidents due to back injury. It is often the younger male worker in the construction industry, who takes pride in his physical strength, that is often willing to lift heavy materials without giving sufficient thought to the risk involved. Nurses are also a high risk group, in particular student and

---

Safer Gardening

- Whenever you venture into the garden, always begin with a simple warm-up exercise. Bend and stretch your back a few times to limber up.
- When using a machine such as a hover mower, never swing your body from the waist as this could strain your back. Turn the whole body in line with the mower.
- As digging and shovelling are the most notorious causes of back trouble, stop frequently and change chores or take a stroll. Shovel small amounts each time you move rubble or earth and use a long-handled spade to avoid bending so far.
- As the leg muscles are stronger than those in the back, keep your back straight and slightly arched, and avoid stooping.

- When lifting, keep your back straight, bend your knees, keep your feet about 18 inches apart for balance, and push up with your leg muscles. Do not reach for the load or try to pull it towards you—instead move it closer to you.
- Do not stoop down when weeding or planting. Instead kneel on a mat or use special knee-pads. Alternatively, use a long-handled fork or hoe.
- When pulling plants, take the strain on your leg and arm muscles rather than your back. Crouch, bend your knees, and lean away from the object with feet apart. Pull the plant by straightening your legs. Keep your back straight and bend your knees slightly, allowing your legs to take the strain (Adapted from *The Guardian*, 1990).

auxiliary nurses (Stubbs et al., 1983). They were most at risk of back pain from handling patients, though other factors (e.g. type of ward) had a part to play as well.

The proficiency with which an object can be handled depends on the arm and hand postures and the way it is grasped. Grips and handles can be useful, though few boxes have handles. It is suggested that a symmetrical diagonal handle position for most movements of box-like objects is best, with the left hand being higher than the right hand for right-handed lifters (Drury, 1985).

Strength and endurance are two important aspects of muscular activity. The endurance factor is dependent on how much oxygen our cardiovascular system pumps to working muscles. Muscular training, of benefit to those engaged in sport or doing a great deal of lifting, pulling, or pushing in heavy industries, can influence the cardiovascular supply system by making it carry more oxygen to peripheral parts of the body in need. This helps to lower the load on the heart, and produce a higher output per heart beat. Other techniques to increase muscular endurance are as follows (Muller, 1965):

1. Use a massage during rest pauses, though this technique would have a greater potential in sport than in industrial work.
2. Restrict temporarily the blood supply to the appropriate muscles prior to work. For example, place a cuff around the thigh for up to 10 minutes.
3. Immerse the limbs in cold water at 60°F during rest phases.

Vestibular

The vestibular system is located in the ear and is primarily concerned with maintaining the body's posture and equilibrium. The vestibular receptors enable the person to maintain an upright posture, and to control the body's position in space. These receptors also provide information about the speed and direction of the body, the head's rotation, and its position when static—is it upright, upside down, or leaning over?

In conditions of substantial motion found on board ship in rough seas, certain people can be prone to motion sickness (e.g. nausea, leading to vomiting), though it is possible to adapt to these conditions over time. It is the vestibular system in the ear that triggers the sensation of motion sickness. In another situation, a person suffers from a severe head injury following a road accident or an accident on a construction site; as a result, the balance organs are affected, producing symptoms of dizziness, nausea, disorientation, and so on.

Seating and Posture

The spine, the pelvis, the legs and the feet (a mechanical lever system) are the main body structures used by the sitter during sitting in order to stabilise the body. The ideal seat allows the sitter to lose all awareness of the seat and sitting posture and creates minimum discomfort of any part of the body's supporting structure. Therefore, the person can give his or her undivided attention to whatever activities need to be performed. Much work has gone into the ergonomics of chair design in order to ensure the comfort and efficiency of the operator. The points listed in the panel below encapsulate some of the important considerations (Oborne, 1994). A suggested ideal sitting position for a VDU operator is shown in Figure 14.1.

Are You Sitting Comfortably?

Height

An optimum position is when the thighs of the sitter are horizontal, the lower legs are vertical, and the feet are flat on the floor (with appropriate adjustments for the short-legged person). The height of an easy chair (e.g. 38 to 45cm) should permit the legs to be stretched forward because this is a preferred relaxing posture and helps to stabilise the body. The height of a working chair (e.g. 43 to 50cm) should permit the sitter to be in a more upright position with the feet flat on the floor. If a chair has to be higher to cater for a situation where a worker has to service a tall machine or sit at a high workbench, an adjustable foot rest is suggested.

Depth

The sitter should be able to find support in the lumbar area from the backrest, and the seat should be able to accommodate even the shortest person. The suggested depth for an easy chair is 43 to 45cm and 35 to 40cm for a work chair. A backward sloping seat pan helps relax the sitter in an easy chair, and a forward sloping seat is generally more functional for a working chair. According to one authority, most work is carried out in a forward bent posture. Therefore, a forward sloping seat is more appropriate. Having a backward sloping work chair of even 5° would cause discomfort (Mandal, 1976).

Backrest

The suggested height is up to 48 to 63cm (i.e. the distance from the shoulder to the underside of the buttocks) and 35 to 48cm wide (i.e. shoulder width). The shape and angle of the backrest are extremely important in preventing fatigue of the spinal posture. It is often suggested that the backrest should have an "open" area, or alternatively be designed in such a way that the lumbar area of the body fits into the backrest in order to accommodate the buttocks. Too high a backrest might prevent full mobility of the arms and shoulders in certain tasks (e.g. typing) where a small backrest supporting the lumbar region only is functional. The angle of the backrest (103 to 112°) serves two purposes: it prevents the sitter from slipping forwards; and it helps the body to lean against the backrest with the lumbar part of the back and sacrum supported.

Armrest

The armrest's main function is to rest the arm and lock the body in a stable position. The support provided can be of assistance when one wants to rise from the chair or to change the sitting position. The disadvantage, particularly in a working chair, is the restriction of free movement of arms and shoulder.

Cushioning

Two important functions of cushioning are evident. First, it allows the pressure on the ischial tuberosities, caused by the weight of the sitter, to be distributed. This is important because this pressure will cause discomfort and fatigue if not relieved. Second, a stable body posture is maintained when the body is allowed to sink into the cushioning where it is supported. However, cushioning that is too soft should not be used because the buttocks and thighs sink deeply into the cushioning with little chance for the sitter to be able to adjust his or her position (Oborne, 1994).

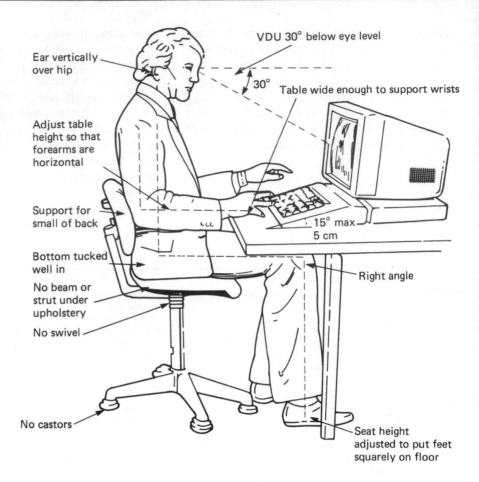

FIG. 14.1.
The ideal sitting
position for a
computer operator.
Source: Lately, P.
(1982). Computing
can damage your
health. *Practical
Computing*, 5,
126–127.

Movement

Human movement in the workplace involves a different set of considerations to sitting, with the emphasis on forces in our physical environment. When workers walk down passageways, or between machines, the available space should be at least fractionally greater than the shoulder breadth, with allowances for the arms and the thickness of the operator's clothing. Where movement is between two machines, one should be aware of any protruding controls that could come into contact with the body of the operator, resulting in either injury or unintentional operation of the machine.

While walking, slips can take place when turning, and matters can be made worse if the worker is carrying a load. Slipping is a common cause of accidents on the job, and it is estimated that injuries resulting from slipping, tripping, and falling can account for up to 40% of time lost due to accidents (Davies, 1983). There are occasions when the worker encounters slippery surfaces—e.g. icy conditions in a builder merchant's yard—and adapts to the conditions by, for example, shortening the stride. However, if the muscles are used too often to overcome the tendency to slip they will quickly become fatigued. In normal conditions one should become aware of the relationship between different combinations of floor material and shoe material when devising ways to prevent slipping.

Stairs, ladders, or ramps are considered when the operator moves between different levels. Accidents on stairs could be reduced if the user is provided with handrails to facilitate stability of movement. The factors normally considered in this context are the shape, diameter, and height of the rail. An optimum height is said to be 90cm (Maki, Bartlett, & Fernie, 1985).

Ladders are a practical means by which workers move from one level to another. Falls from a height resulting in a fracture were 17% of approximately 46,000 industrial accidents in 1982 (Buck & Coleman, 1985). In an analysis of 248 ladder accident reports, it was suggested that 66% of accidents happened when the ladder slipped while the person was climbing or when working on the ladder; and 34% of accidents happened when the climber stumbled while climbing or misplaced the feet (Dewar, 1977). On climbing a ladder both the hands and feet are used, with the hands helping to propel and stabilise the body. Particular attention should be paid to the question of restraints at the lower end of ladders and to the angle of the ladder, which has an impact on the ease with which the climbing action takes place.

Body Size
The physical size of the body (anthropometry) is related to its ability to function in its environment. For example, the dimensions of the pelvis and buttocks determine the size of hatch openings or seats, and the size of the hand determines the physical dimensions of control mechanisms and supportive bars (Oborne, 1994). In order to position control panels at the appropriate distance from the controller, it is necessary to be in possession of details of arm reach. A joystick would not be useful if placed outside the reach of the user. Therefore, it should be placed within the reach of the smallest member of the population who will use it.

By contrast, the design of an escape hatch in a nuclear submarine would need to accommodate all fully-clothed military personnel, because all users could be expected to go through it in an emergency. At the other extreme, the height of an office desk does not have to conform to the physical requirements of all users if adjustable chairs are available.

Sex differentiation has to be considered in the design process. Although men have generally longer, thicker, and deeper hands, women are consistently larger than men in the four dimensions of depth of chest, breadth of hip, and circumference of hip and thigh.

Differences between people in an ethnic or international context are matters to consider in the design process, because a mismatch between the job requirements and anthropometric considerations could be a risk factor as far as accidents are concerned. This could manifest itself in over-strain and inadequate protection from personal protective equipment and machine guards. In one study, significant differences in limb dimensions were found between the ethnic groups tested in the context of openings in machinery guarding. For example, "the West Indian worker had larger diameter fingers and hands than either the European or Asian workers, and therefore will be automatically protected by any standard dimension which prevents the other two races from putting the whole length of the fingers of the hand through the aperture" (Booth & Thompson, 1981).

Compensatory Behaviour

In an ideal world the sensory and physical characteristics of the person would match the requirements of the job. But sometimes the person's sensory and physical characteristics are deficient in some respect, and some extra time or precautions are taken to ensure that the job is performed safely. This is referred to as compensatory behaviour.

This conclusion is borne out by a study of disabled people where it was found that disabled workers generally had a lower accident rate than able bodied workers. The researcher makes the important point that "given an environment that takes note of the limitations, if any, imposed by a disability, disabled workers are generally less likely than other workers to sustain accidents at work; and the idea that *a disabled worker* represents a safety hazard receives no support from the findings of the study" (Kettle, 1984).

"OK THEN, 'PEE-WEE'....CARE TO SHOW US WHAT IT IS YOU GOT THAT MAKES YOU BOUNCER MATERIAL...?"

However, individuals endowed with certain abnormal perceptual experiences involving sensory distortions and sensory deceptions may experience difficulty in holding down certain jobs. Sensory distortions amount to seeing stimuli in an altered state (e.g. colour might appear more vivid, and sounds are louder), whereas sensory deceptions involve illusions or hallucinations (Cohen & Hart, 1988).

With regard to disability, the preferable course of action is to match the physical and sensory characteristics of the disabled person with the requirements of the job. An organisation, such as *Remploy Ltd.*, does good work in this respect, but it is unique in the sense that most of its shop floor workers are severely disabled. As a consequence, the organisational system seeks to accommodate the needs of disabled people.

It is said that compensatory behaviour is likely to disappear in a crisis situation when there may not be time to trigger it off. However, this observation should not be used as justification for not offering a job to a person whose disability does not come in the way of performing a job safely (Hale & Glendon, 1987).

SUMMARY: HEALTH AND WORK—HAZARDS

- Both blue-collar and white-collar workers are vulnerable to hazardous conditions at work.
- A selection of hazards in the work environment were examined. These are related to colour perception, lighting and glare, visual deterioration and fatigue, noise, vibration, inhalation of vapour and dust, skin irritants, temperature changes, and mechanical processes connected with the proprioceptive senses (movement, lifting, and posture).
- As well as purposeful action to counteract hazardous conditions, people can also engage in compensatory behaviour.

QUESTIONS

1. Comment on the way an understanding of ergonomics can be of value when examining the reaction of people who are confronted by occupational hazards.

2. Identify the problems people are likely to encounter with respect to vision at places of work.

3. Examination the justification for the official action to control noise at work.

4. What do you think is the value of music at work?

5. Identify some of the measures taken by workers to protect themselves from chemical hazards.

6. How does cold effect the performance of manual tasks on a building site or in a factory?

7. Briefly consider the significance of the two proprioceptive senses (kinaesthetic and vestibular) in an industrial setting.

REFERENCES

Anderson, D. (1980). Eyestrain or eyewash. *Health and Safety at Work*, August, 36–39.

Baddeley, A.D., Cuccaro, W.J., Egstrom, G.H., Wetman, G., & Willis, M.A. (1975). Cognitive efficiency of divers working in cold water. *Human Factors, 17*, 446–454.

Bodman, H.W. (1962). Illumination levels and visual performance. *International Lighting Review, 13*, 41–47.

Booth, R.T. & Thompson, D. (1981). Anthropometry and machinery guarding: An investigation into forced reach over barriers and through openings. Part II: Research through openings. *Journal of Occupational Accidents, 3*, 87–99.

British Labour Party (1981). *Noise at work*. Research Department Bargaining Report No. 17. London: Labour Party Headquarters.

Buck, P.C. & Coleman, V.P. (1985). Slipping, tripping, and falling accidents at work: A national picture. *Ergonomics, 28*, 949–958.

Chartered Society of Physiotherapy (1966). *Lifting*. Pamphlet. London: Chartered Society of Physiotherapy.

Cohen, R.I. & Hart J.J. (1988). *Student psychiatry today*. London: Heinemann Medical Books.

Corfield, T. (1987). *Safety management*. Lichfield, UK: The Institute of Supervisory Management.

Crook, M.A. & Langdon, F.J. (1974). The effects of aircraft noise in schools around London airport. *Journal of Sound and Vibration, 12*, 221–232.

Davies, P.R. (1983). Human factors contributing to slips, trips, and falls. *Ergonomics, 26*, 51–60.

Dewar, M.E. (1977). Body movements in climbing a ladder. *Ergonomics, 20*, 67–86.

Drury, C.G. (1985). The role of the hand in manual materials handling. *Ergonomics, 28*, 213–227.

Fox, J.G. (1983). Industrial music. In D.J. Oborne & M.M. Gruneberg (Eds.), *The physical environment at work*. Chichester: Wiley.

Gillie, O. (1982). Feeling tired at the office? Blame it on the copy paper. *The Sunday Times*, 19th December.

The Guardian (1990). *Tips to avoid injury to gardeners' backs*. 25 May, p.29.

Hale, A. & Glendon, I. (1987). *Individual behaviour and the control of danger*. Amsterdam: Elsevier.

Hammond, J. (1978). *Understanding human engineering. An introduction to ergonomics*. Newton Abbot, UK: David & Charles.

Hopkinson, R.G. (1972). Glare from daylight in buildings. *Applied Ergonomics, 3*, 206–215.

Kettle, M. (1984). Disabled people and accidents at work. *Journal of Occupational Accidents, 6*, 277–293.

Lately, P. (1982). Computing can damage your health. *Practical Computing*, July, 126–127.

Laubli, T., Hunting, W., & Grandjean, E. (1981). Postural and visual loads of VDT workplaces II: Lighting conditions and visual impairment. *Ergonomics, 24*, 933–944.

Maki, B.E.E., Bartlett, S.A., & Fernie, G.R. (1985). Effect of stairway pitch on optimal handrail height. *Human Factors, 27*, 355–359.

Mandal, A.C. (1976). Work chair with tilting seat. *Ergonomics, 19*, 157–164.

Muller, E.A. (1965). Physiological methods of increasing human physical work capacity. *Ergonomics, 8*, 409–424.

Murray-Bruce, D. (1982). Promoting the healthy banker. *Journal of the Institute of Bankers*, December, 199–200.

Nemecek, J. & Grandjean, E. (1973). Noise in landscaped offices. *Applied Ergonomics, 4*, 19–22.

Oborne, D.J. (1994) *Ergonomics at work* (third edition). Chichester: Wiley.

Rosegger, R. & Rosegger, S. (1960). Health effects of tractor driving. *Journal of Agricultural Engineering Research, 5*, 241–275.

Ruys, T. (1970). Windowless offices. MA thesis, University of Washington, cited in D.J. Oborne (1987) *Ergonomics at work* (second edition). Chichester: Wiley.

Shibolet, S., Lancaster, M.C., & Danon, Y. (1976). Heat stroke: A review. *Aviation, Space, and Environmental Medicine, 47,* 280–301.

Smith, M.M. & Marriott, A.M. (1982). Vision and proprioception in simple catching. *Journal of Motor Behaviour, 14,* 143–152.

Stubbs, D.A., Buckle, P.W., Hudson, M.P., Rivers, R.M., & Worrington, R.M. (1983). Back pain in the nursing profession, part I: Epidemiology and pilot methodology. *Ergonomics, 26,* 755–765.

Voke, J. (1982). Colour vision problems at work. *Health and Safety at Work,* January, 27–28.

Waller, R.A. (1969). Office acoustics: Effects of background noise. *Applied Acoustics, 2,* 121–130.

15

Health and Work: Stress

This chapter begins with a definition of stress which includes burnout and post-traumatic stress disorders, and then looks at stress in different occupational groups. Next there is an examination of stressors attributable to the self, the organisation, and outside influences. Remedies for the alleviation or elimination of stress are then examined, and there is a commentary on health promotion programmes.

This chapter has particular relevance to personality (Chapter 1), role analysis (Chapter 7), and new technology and job design (Chapter 2), and is complementary to Chapter 14.

DEFINITION

Stressful conditions have been acknowledged in the discussion of environmental hazards in the previous chapter. Before looking at various facets of organisational life that can generate stress, it is appropriate to be more precise in specifying what is meant by a stressful condition.

To use an analogy from physics, stress arises because of the impact of an environmental force on a physical object; the object undergoes strain and this reaction may result in temporary distortion, but equally it could lead to permanent distortion.

In human terms any situation that is seen as burdensome, threatening, ambiguous, or boring is likely to induce stress. This is the type of situation that would normally strike the individual as deserving immediate attention or concern and is viewed as unfortunate and annoying. There tends to be the feeling that the situation should not exist, but because of it the person feels disappointed

or annoyed and eventually is prone to anxiety, depression, anger, hostility, inadequacy, and low frustration tolerance.

In other circumstances, pressure arises when the individual is expected to perform in a particular manner and finds it a source of discomfort and anxiety, but at the same time finds the experience a source of excitement, challenge, and personal growth. It could be said that when under some pressure—mild levels of stimulation—we function better because we are more aware, more attentive, clearer in our thinking, and physically alert. Some see this as a healthy form of stress. For example, the pressure of accountability for one's own work or the meeting of a deadline could produce a positive effect leading to a feeling of pride and accomplishment. Of course excessive pressure can be detrimental, contributing to poor performance.

It is suggested that no objective criteria is good enough to describe a situation as stressful; only the person experiencing the internal or external threat can do this

(Lazarus, 1966). Therefore, the potential for stress exists when an environmental pressure is of such a magnitude as to threaten the individual's ability to cope with it in conditions where successful coping is a rewarding experience (McGrath, 1976). In practice this means that one could find an individual flourishing in a setting which, for another, creates suffering and stress-related illness.

In everyday life we rarely encounter severe stressful situations, such as prolonged lack of sleep or physical torture. Instead, weaker but important generators of stress such as the death of a spouse, divorce, impairment of one's faculties, loss of a job, rejection by a colleague, unrequited love, failure in examinations, all play a crucial part.

But people respond differently to stressors. For example, on retirement one group of executives may feel severely depressed, another group may feel moderately sad and frustrated, and a third group may feel content and happy. For others, travelling in a train is less likely to be stressful than travelling by car or by air. Many of us would find it less stressful to work in difficult or dangerous conditions with people we trust than in similar conditions where we distrust others or lack confidence in ourselves.

Physiological Reactions

When a person perceives a situation as frightening or threatening, a pattern of physical changes in the body is activated resulting in the "flight or fight" response. These changes are regulated by the autonomic nervous system which consists of many nerves that connect the brain and spinal cord to the various organs of the body. The autonomic nervous system is divided into two parts—the sympathetic and parasympathetic systems.

The sympathetic system—which is dominant for a very stressed person—increases the heart rate and blood pressure and directs blood to the peripheral muscles. It tends to be active when we are preparing for action. It discharges the hormones known as adrenalin and nor-adrenalin from the adrenal glands. These hormones affect many organs when they enter the blood stream. The liver is activated to dispense glucose, the heart beats faster, and increased arousal is triggered by the flow of adrenalin to the brain. If the person experiences only mild stress, the flow of adrenalin to the brain can produce excitement and pleasure as well as improved performance.

What we should be concerned with, of course, is the frequency of the temporary physical changes in the body (as just described) in the face of acute stress, because the end result could be the onset of permanent physical changes causing illness. The critical factor to note with regard to acute stress is that frequently the fight or flight action mentioned earlier is inappropriate or not possible, and problems arise from the continuous pressures on our system from which there is no escape. Our bodies continue to react, with the result that the build-up of tension develops. If the threatening stimuli continue, we are faced with exhaustion and eventually reach the stage of collapsing under the strain (psychological breakdown).

The opposite to the sympathetic system is the parasympathetic nervous system. It decreases the heart rate and blood pressure, and diverts blood to the gut; it tends to function when we are calm and relaxed.

A specialist in occupational medicine (Murray-Bruce, 1983) described the body's reaction to stress in the following terms:

> The heart and breathing rates increase, blood pressure goes up, sweating increases, muscles get tense, the eyes widen, and there is heightened alertness. Tense muscles cause headaches, backaches, shoulder and back pains. Clenched hands, clenched jaws, and hunched shoulders are tell-tale signs of stress, along with frowning and fidgeting, finger tremor, and the mopping of a sweaty

brow. An anxious person has "butterflies" or churning in the stomach, a dry mouth, weak legs, nausea, a thumping heart, breathlessness and a feeling of light-headedness.

Course participants at a management college reported on symptoms of stress that they had previously experienced. These included dim or fuzzy vision, some chest pains, unusual heart beats, occasional sleep difficulties, frequent episodes of irritability, tiredness, or depression (this was by far the most frequent), and periods in which their work performance was impaired for a few days (Melhuish, 1977). As we shall see later, the effects of stress can be fatal.

Cost of Stress

We are becoming increasingly aware of the true costs of stress at work. In financial terms occupational stress is said to cost 10% of gross national product each year in the USA. The CBI in the UK put the annual cost of stress-related absenteeism and staff turnover alone at £1.3 billion (Summers, 1990b). To these costs could be added rising medical costs and the cost of a reduction in the quality of work. On the emotional side, one has to recognise the existence of negative feelings. By impairing the psychological and physical well-being of an employee, stress also affects the employee's family. At the level of society, the effects of stress are reflected in an increase in welfare costs, an increase in socially disruptive behaviour (such as alcoholism and drug abuse), and less involvement in the community.

With regard to UK developments, it is interesting to note the views of Professor Cary Cooper. He maintains that the UK is swiftly moving towards the US occupational stress levels. He is beginning to receive letters from solicitors who have clients pursuing stress claims, and attributes increased occupational stress in the UK to the drive by industry for increased competitiveness, technological

change, and the growth of dual-career families. It is the poor handling of these factors that causes problems (Summers, 1990b).

Burnout

Burnout, though not the same as stress, is a related concept. It has been defined as consisting of the development of negativity in a person's response to others, a lowering of one's estimation of personal achievements, and total exhaustion on all fronts (Lee & Ashforth, 1990). Those suffering from burnout lack energy, are fatigued, feel nothing they do is rewarded or encouraged, lack adequate control of their work life, feel helpless, and harbour pessimistic views about life generally.

Factors causing burnout are many and varied, including stressors in organisations (which will be discussed later), and unrealistic expectations or ambitions. The consequences of burnout bear some similarity to the consequences of stress (e.g. absences from work, low commitment, and problems with relating to colleagues and others). Those affected by burnout are often competent and able executives and, in particular, they can be found in the helping professions, such as counselling, teaching, childcare, policing, and nursing (Cook, 1988). Apparently burnout, or the premature retirement from one's career due to stress, is prevalent among nurses who are coming forward for treatment for mental disorders to a greater extent than in the past (Arnold, Robertson, & Cooper, 1991).

Finally, some argue that burnout could be viewed as a coping mechanism, because it forces the person to disengage from perhaps a pressurised existence.

Post-traumatic Stress Disorder (PTSD)

The concept of psychological trauma was accepted by the judiciary in the UK in recent years when two booking clerks and a fireman were awarded damages of £65,000 and £34,000 respectively for trauma following the King's Cross London Underground fire disaster which claimed 31 lives (Frost, 1990). This type of trauma is related to accidents at the workplace, fire, crashes, or similar disasters. By contrast, cumulative trauma could arise from, for example, prolonged exposure to organisational stress. This will be discussed later.

Psychological disorders stemming from traumas are called PTSD. Physicians frequently consider PTSD in connection with Vietnam or other war veterans. These veterans suffer the classic symptoms of PTSD. They cannot stop thinking about, dreaming about, or having nightmares about traumatic wartime experiences. They might react to any sudden loud noise, such as a car backfiring, by trying to gun down the enemy—they have a flashback and relive the war experience. They also display an inability to maintain previously close relationships, and often suffer from drug and alcohol abuse. People who suffer from this disorder often try to blank out the experience. When this fails, they display symptoms including sleeplessness, anger, and extreme jumpiness. According to Dr Curran, a Consultant Psychiatrist at the Mater Infirmary, Belfast, and a specialist in PTSD, these symptoms can often be emotionally crippling (Frost, 1990).

Though not generally recognised, the PTSD syndrome could also apply to occupational injuries. From the case-loads of medical practitioners in an occupational medicine clinic, it has been recognised that some patients with medially unexplained symptoms were suffering from PTSD (Schottenfeld & Cullen, 1986). A typical PTSD case in an occupational setting appears in the panel below.

A combination of drug therapy and psychotherapy are used in the clinical management of patients with PTSD. Re-experiencing the trauma is often blocked by some tricyclic anti-depressant medications, and depressive symptoms may be ameliorated by anti-depressant medications. This would be complemented by psychotherapy where the patient is helped to explore the psychological and emotional reactions experienced (Schottenfeld & Cullen, 1986).

Recently, Britain's first in-patient facility for post-traumatic stress sufferers was opened, based at Ticehurst Hospital, Kent. The director, Dr Turnbull, a former airforce psychiatrist, hopes that by addressing the problems of PTSD, people can avoid long-term problems such as chronic heart disease, abnormal blood pressure, and

---

PTSD at Work

Mr. Jones, a 55 year old married man, had a perfect work record as a labourer until he suffered a severe crush injury to his legs while he was at work. After more than a year of a series of orthopaedic operations and a painful rehabilitation, he returned to work.

About six months later, he began to experience recurrent episodes of apprehension, lightheadedness, dizziness, and nausea. Eventually, during one of these episodes, he was rushed to a nearby hospital emergency room. He was subsequently classified as disabled because of the repeated episodes, although no abnormalities were identified during medical evaluations.

He was then referred to the occupational medicine clinic. Prior to the clinic's evaluation of his condition, the possibility of PTSD was not considered because there was no recognised connection between his occupational trauma and the subsequent delayed appearance of his symptoms.

In the clinic he reported that his recurrent episodes were triggered by reminders of the accident. He first experienced the episodes at work when the man responsible for his accident returned to the worksite. The symptoms would also appear whenever he walked past the plant. He was plagued by nightmares about the accident, and even while awake, he would suddenly see the load of steel that had crushed his legs rolling towards him. He desperately attempted to avoid any reminders of his workplace, and had to make sure that he never walked by the plant. He became severely depressed (Schottenfeld & Cullen, 1986).

diabetes, which research has shown are connected with stressful incidents (Rogers, 1993).

STRESS IN DIFFERENT OCCUPATIONS

There is a belief that some occupations are sources of greater stress than others. An analysis of mortality due to arteriosclerotic heart disease among US males by occupational classification in the age range 20–64, shows that teachers fare better than lawyers, medical practitioners, estate agents, and insurance agents (Guralnick, 1963). However, general practitioners are more vulnerable to heart disease than are other physicians (Morris, Heady, & Barley, 1952).

As to suicide rates, those connected with law enforcement had higher mortality rates than those administering the law, though (surprisingly) individuals who are exposed to life-threatening situations suffer less stress than those who are not. Among medical and related personnel, practitioners with above average suicide rates are dentists and psychiatrists (Daubs, 1973).

Dentists are said to experience significant pressure from the demands of developing their practice. The dentist prone to stress tends to be anxiety prone and more easily upset when confronted with excessive administrative duties and when faced with too little work because of a preoccupation with building and sustaining the practice. Dentists with raised blood pressure perceived, to some extent, their image as inflictors of pain. They also experienced stress from their job interfering with their personal life (Cooper, Mallinger, & Kahn, 1978).

It would be unwise to attribute stress, and its fatal consequences, only to professional and executive groups. There is a view that occupational stress is more likely to be found among blue-collar and routine white-collar workers (Fletcher, Gowler, & Payne, 1979). This is a view shared by the chief medical officer of an insurance company who addressed a conference on managing stress

(Reynolds, 1981). She maintained that the highest mortality rate from all causes was more likely to be found in socio-economic groups 3, 4, and 5.

In certain occupations,—e.g. the police and fire service—the normal retirement age is 55. This might suggest that such occupations are stressful, and that it would be unfair to expect an employee to continue working until he or she has reached the customary retirement age for most occupations (60 or 65). Of course it could also suggest that age and fitness are more critical factors for the successful operation of these services. Another occupational group in the emergency services—ambulance personnel—are said to be using the stress factor to secure a similar advantage to that enjoyed by the police and fire service. An ambulanceman in Liverpool, who was fitted with an electrocardiogram, experienced a significant increase in heart beat when he responded to an emergency call. The highest heart beat was recorded during two spells of stressful driving through heavy suburban and city traffic (Brooks, 1980).

The fire brigade trade union has carried out a number of health studies jointly with the British Home Office, one of which included the taking of electrocardiogram readings from a number of fire service employees to establish whether their duties made them vulnerable to cardiovascular stress likely to result in excessive heart strain and related health hazards.

In the US there is research evidence suggesting that a number of factors cause stress among the police. These include low penalties imposed by the courts; distorted media publicity; an increasing number of complaints and criticisms by minority groups; lack of adequate resources; lack of public appreciation; fear and danger in the work undertaken; the fragmented nature of the work; and shiftwork. Some of these factors may very well apply to the police force in the UK. The effects of police stress are said to be an increased incidence of alcoholism, infidelity, wife beating, child abuse, divorce, isolation, heart disease, and nervous disorders (Brooks, 1980).

The National Conference of Roman Catholic Priests held in Birmingham, England in 1984 considered the results of a survey of the clergy. Though it is recognised that many clergy lead fulfilled and happy lives, there are strong indications that a number of priests are demoralised and overburdened by pressures from both inside and outside the church. They experienced a certain amount of role ambiguity (particularly the middle-aged priests). The survey identified two major sources of stress—loneliness and difficulty in handling personal relationships. At one time the status of the priest was that of father figure to his parish—a man set apart from his parishioners who in their eyes had no problems or feelings. Now the priest wants his parishioners to treat him as a person, and younger priests particularly are impatient for change (Longley, 1984).

A survey of senior managers in 112 financial organisations conducted by MORI and reported in the *Financial Times* in October 1986, shortly before the Big Bang (the shake up of the financial markets) in the City of London, showed that 64% identified stress as their main health concern. The worst affected were accountants and building society managers. Presumably, the latter are feeling the effects of the cold winds of competition in the financial services market.

Those who worked in the City identified "too much work" as the biggest single factor in causing stress. Other causes mentioned were long hours, competition, pressure to perform, over-promotion, conflict between work and private life, and job insecurity. The most frequently mentioned symptom of stress was a deterioration in the employee's performance. Other symptoms stated were irritability, absenteeism, problems with making decisions, difficulties with drinking, and depression.

Recently, Professor Tom Cox prepared a report on stress at work for the UK's Health and Safety Executive (HSE). The HSE plan to publish guidelines in 1994 to help employers manage stress at work (Donkin, 1993). The report calls for further research into the problem of stress at work, as well as advocating training for employers. It identifies excessive periods of repetitive work, lack of management support, and over-demanding work schedules as contributory causes of stress. Additional factors were low pay, poor relationships with management, lack of variety, job insecurity, and conflicting demands of work and home.

STRESSORS

Among the typical stressful conditions facing people at work (Kay, 1974; Kearns, 1973; Sofer, 1979) are the following:

- too much or too little work;
- time pressures and deadlines to meet;
- having to make too many decisions;
- endeavouring to cope with changes that affect the job;
- concern about the costs in monetary and career terms of making mistakes;
- excessive and inconvenient working hours;
- highly repetitive work;
- the necessity to work fast;
- erosion of salary differentials;
- the prospect of redundancy or being forced into premature retirement;
- disparity between real authority and authority vested in the job;
- the feeling of being trapped in a job without much chance of getting a similar or better job elsewhere;
- a perceived mismatch between performance on the job and the financial benefits secured; and
- reservations about the value of the job in contributing to the output or welfare of the organisation.

In practice one may find certain organisationally devised ways of alleviating pressure at work: for example, deadlines could be set at an unrealistically early date to permit a margin of error so that mistakes or shortcomings could be rectified before it is too late; decisions could be made in groups so as to share the burden of responsibility for a decision; and duties could be reallocated in a department when an individual is very busy and is forced to shelve certain duties. However, in practice there may be occasions when these devices are not directly at the disposal of the manager.

It is now time to examine in some detail the factors that have potential to cause stress at work. These factors, which reside inside and outside the organisation, are divided into categories as follows:

- factors within the organisation;
- factors within the individual, plus outside influences.

An expanded version of these factors is included in Table 15.1.

STRESS FROM WITHIN THE ORGANISATION

The discussion of stress within the organisation will begin with an analysis of roles, a topic examined earlier in Chapter 7.

Role Overload

Frequently it is said that executives put in more hours at the office than employees at a lower level in the organisational hierarchy, and that they bring more work home at night. Evidence from a survey conducted by Executive Life in the USA suggests that one group of employees—presidents, vice-presidents, and high potential middle managers—worked between 57 and 60 hours a week. They spent 45 to 48 hours a week in the office during the day, entertained once a week, and worked three nights a week (one night at the office and two at home). This was the work pattern during normal times, but when on a business trip, attending a

TABLE 15.1

Factors Causing Stress to the Individual at Work

Stressors	
From within the Organisation	*From within the Individual, plus Outside Influences*
<ul><li>Role overload</li><li>Role complexity</li><li>Role ambiguity</li><li>Role conflict</li><li>Boundary roles</li><li>Responsibility for people</li><li>Machine-paced and repetitive work</li><li>Decision latitude and job control</li><li>Shift work</li><li>New technology: VDU work</li><li>Hierarchical level</li></ul>	<ul><li>Personality</li><li>Work relationships</li><li>Career development</li><li>Redundancy and early retirement</li><li>Domestic considerations</li></ul>

conference, or dealing with an emergency, they might put in 70 or 80 hours per week (Schoonmaker, 1969).

A relationship exists between too heavy a work-load—i.e. taking and making more telephone calls, more office visits to and from other people, and more meetings for a given unit of work—and heavy cigarette smoking; the latter is an important risk factor as far as coronary heart disease is concerned (French & Caplan, 1970). Too much work can also give rise to a number of symptoms of stress, such as escapist drinking, absenteeism from work, low motivation to work, lower estimation of oneself, and unwillingness to suggest improvements to work procedures and practices (Margolis, Kroes, & Quinn, 1974). Working at more than two jobs that required an excessive number of work hours (60 plus per week) was found to be a critical contributory factor to coronary heart disease (Russek & Zohman, 1958). It is worth noting that the working married woman has a heavy overall work-load and is frequently denied the opportunity to recuperate from her remunerative work; this could result in chronic fatigue.

In today's economic climate, managers have responsibility for keeping costs and staffing levels in check. In their role of pruning expenditure they will inevitably encounter resistance at the subordinate level, with consequences in terms of damaging relationships of trust and impairing good communications. They also have to contend with pressures from top management who are naturally concerned that policy is implemented in accordance with agreed guidelines. If there are redundancies at shopfloor level and among their colleagues in management, there is a likelihood that their work-load will increase. They may also feel that they ought to be seen to be working harder.

In recent years there are indications that certain employees, who have suffered stress due to role overload, are contemplating legal action. For example, a former junior hospital doctor sued his employers—Bloomsbury Health Authority in London—for stress arising from an 88-hour week. His claim was that the stress was caused by unreasonable working hours. These conditions left him exhausted and depressed, and endangered the health of his patients. The case was backed by the British Medical Association (Summers, 1990b). Suing for stress may be new to the UK, but it has been a feature of the US scene for nearly 30 years. In a recent report prepared by employment lawyers in the UK, it is suggested that stress cases will follow the path of other injuries at work, and that laws which were drafted to prevent accidents can easily be directed to include the mental effects of stress. Employers who have taken no steps to identify and reduce stress at work may experience financial sanctions (Kellaway, 1993).

Although some people put great pressures on themselves and others, the overload situation may be brought about by poor delegation and poor management of time.

Role Complexity

Apart from too much to do, too difficult a job can also create problems. In one study, changes in the cholesterol levels of tax accountants at different times in the fiscal year were observed (Friedman, Roseman, & Carol, 1957). During the experimental period of approximately five months each accountant was closely questioned about any job-related stress he or she had experienced during the two preceding weeks. After each interview a blood sample was obtained. Serum cholesterol levels of the accountants remained fairly low during the early months of the year, but a significant increase in cholesterol was observed for approximately six weeks before the April tax deadline.

Following the tax deadline, the cholesterol levels of the accountants fell to the levels observed during January and February. It is interesting to note that there was no change in diet, which might account for the changes described, and members of a control group (company accountants) showed no such effect.

In another study, blood samples were taken from medical students at times when they were under no examination pressure, and then on the day or near the day of an important examination when the work-load was arguably more exacting. An increase in serum cholesterol was observed in the latter situation (Dreyfus & Czaczkes, 1959).

In a more elaborate study, 100 coronary patients were compared with a control group consisting of the same number. In 91% of the coronary patients it was noted that before the attack there was prolonged emotional strain which was associated with job responsibility. Only 20% of the control group, who were normal, suffered similar emotional strain. There was not much difference between the two groups in heredity factors, high fat diets, obesity, smoking, or lack of exercise. In most respects, the young coronary patient had a history of overwork because of a strong urge to gain recognition or not to disappoint an employer, family, or others. He or she tended to be aggressive, ambitious, and operated beyond his or her normal capacity and tempo (Russek, 1965). A lengthy questionnaire and interview schedule was administered to 46 coronary patients and 49 members of a control group. It was found that 50% of the patients, as opposed to 12% of the control group, reported that they worked long hours with few holidays under considerable stress and strain before falling victim to heart disease (Miles et al., 1954). One might therefore conclude, as French and Caplan (1973) did, that too difficult a job can contribute to increased heart rate, tension, embarrassment, and lower self-esteem.

Role Ambiguity

Sometimes we overlook the importance of clearly specifying what the job requires of the individual. There are a number of circumstances in an organisation when the requirements of a job are unclear as to the objectives laid down and the scope of responsibilities; as a result, colleagues are not altogether clear about what the job entails. In such circumstances a number of undesirable consequences are likely to ensue (Kahn et al., 1964). These consequences consist of a lowering of job satisfaction, self-confidence, and self-esteem, a general dissatisfaction with life and a feeling that the whole thing is futile, leading to a depressed mood, low motivation to work, an intention to quit the job, and increased blood pressure and pulse rate (French & Caplan, 1970; Margolis et al., 1974).

Role Conflict

If a job is arranged in such a way that the individual performing the tasks connected with the job is confused by conflicting demands—e.g. the person is sandwiched between two groups of people who expect a different kind of service, or expect a service different from the one that is presently rendered—or if the person is doing things he or she does not want to do or does not think are part of his or her job description, then the seeds of conflict are sown. As conflict develops, a lowering of job satisfaction is experienced—more so if the conflicting demands originate from the desks of powerful figures in the organisation. In addition, an increase in heart rate and feelings of tension about the job is likely to materialise (French & Caplan, 1970; Kahn et al., 1964). A significant relationship was found between role conflict and coronary heart disease among managerial employees in the kibbutz system in Israel; however, occupations requiring excessive physical activity (e.g. agricultural work) were associated with a lower incidence of coronary heart disease (Shirom et al., 1973).

Boundary Roles

It is often suggested that one of the more stressful types of job is that performed by people occupying a boundary role—that is, when the job takes them into contact with people in other departments and outside the organisation (Kahn et al., 1964). It is in this capacity, as representatives of their own department, that strain arises. The supervisor (the "man in the middle"), who performs a boundary-spanning role that is vulnerable to a high degree of conflict, was found to be particularly at risk in the sense that he or she was seven times more likely to develop ulcers than shopfloor workers (Margolis & Kroes, 1974).

Chief executives in Israeli state business enterprises, who perform a boundary-spanning role between the organisation and government bureaucracy, were said to experience conflict over objectives, decisions, and government relationships, and these were a source of stress (Dornstein, 1977). Sometimes one finds a certain rigidity in management and worker roles where the potential for better understanding and communication is not fully realised due to a concern with outmanoeuvreing one's opponent and the absence of a serious attempt to solve long-term problems. This is likely to be reflected in management and trade union relations. Managers, or for that matter industrial relations specialists, playing this type of role in a harsh economic climate could experience severe stress.

Responsibility for People

Bearing responsibility for people, rather than for things (i.e. where one has to spend more time interacting with others, having to attend more meetings, and having to meet deadlines often working alone) is associated with coronary heart disease in the form of diastolic blood pressure and serum cholesterol levels (Wardwell, Hyman, & Bahnson, 1964). This appears to be the predicament of the older executive who has assumed greater responsibility (Pincherle, 1972). But one must concede that as one gets older, considerations other than increased responsibility may become a potent force as generators of stress. For example, there may be the realisation that further career advancement is not possible,

that the prospect of approaching retirement is unwelcome (particularly for the individual with narrow or insignificant interests outside work), and a feeling that one is isolated within the organisation (Eaton, 1969). Just as we identify greater responsibility as a source of stress, the same could be said of too little responsibility.

Machine-paced and Repetitive Work

The nature of repetitive work varies from company to company, as does the individual's susceptibility to stressful experiences. Nevertheless, repetitive work is said to be potentially stressful, and for certain individuals can threaten the quality of their life and health. Repetition could be compounded by other factors such as the worker's posture, and also shift work. With regard to the latter, night work is critical. The most obvious manifestation of nightwork is sleep disturbance.

According to Cox (1985), repetitive work amounts to a discrete set of activities, repeated over and over again in the same order without planned interruptions by other activities or tasks. The discrete set of activities are simple and unskilled, with perhaps a short time cycle. Features of repetitive work are "switching off" and "letting your mind go blank"; these are strategies used by car assembly workers to cope with repetitive and monotonous tasks.

A source of dissatisfaction could be lack of control over the task, whereby workers enjoy little autonomy and experience little responsibility. Under-utilisation of skill is frequently associated with repetitive work, as are relatively high levels of machine pacing (often in a relatively isolated work station with reduced social contacts) and a conspicuous lack of job complexity and participation.

There is a view that workers engaged in repetitive work practices suffer poorer health than most other occupational groups, and this would be particularly so for those engaged in shift work that involves night working (Cox,

1985). From a starting point that there is no clear evidence to support the suggestion that repetition, pacing, and short cycle time (so-called evils of assembly line work) harm workers' health, a group of researchers undertook a government-backed research study at a large car factory (Broadbent & Gath, 1981). The index of health used in the study consisted of:

- anxiety (feelings of tension and worry);
- depression (lethargy and inability to make an effort);
- somatic symptoms (stomach upsets, giddiness, and similar sensations when mental health is poor); and
- obsessional problems, manifest as obsessional personality (reflected in, for example, perfectionism) and an obsessional stance (reflected in recent failures in the exercise of control due to, for example, unwanted thoughts).

The results to emerge from the study were:

1. Workers doing repetitive work disliked the job, but were not necessarily unhealthy.
2. Workers who were machine paced to a marked extent in their work showed a higher level of anxiety.
3. Workers with a pronounced obsessional personality (i.e. meticulous, conscientious, and precise) were no less satisfied than other people, but they suffered more anxiety when they worked in machine-paced jobs. Therefore, a particular personality type—the obsessional personality—is unsuited to jobs that are machine paced. It certainly seems reasonable to assume that workers are likely to become anxious if they have no control over the speed of their operations.
4. Short work cycle (under one minute) was not connected with either job dissatisfaction or ill health, when compared with work cycles of up to half an hour in repetitive jobs.

5. A slightly higher proportion of workers in machine-paced jobs may need psychiatric help than other people.

From the research evidence it is clear that machine pacing, rather than short cycle times, is a hazard, and that people can become stressed without being dissatisfied with the job. The message for practitioners is that they should be cautious in applying the results of the study, and be aware of the hazardous nature of machine pacing.

Decision Latitude and Job Control

Decision latitude relates to the opportunity for the significant use of judgement and discretion in the job. When this factor was high and combined with a demanding job, people experienced job satisfaction and reduced depression. The opposite appeared to be the case, particularly with respect to satisfaction, when jobs were rated low in terms of decision latitude and demands posed by the task (Karasek, 1979). To relieve job strain it is suggested that the employee should be given greater scope for decision making and use of discretion at work but, at the same time, that this should not be overdone in the quest to obtain more substantial job responsibilities.

In a later study, the positive health implications (i.e. a reduction in illness among full-time workers, including heart disease among males) of greater control in one's job, together with greater opportunities for democratic participation at work, are endorsed (Karasek, 1990). The researcher points out that one of the most disturbing conclusions of his study is that current changes to white-collar jobs often involved less opportunity to exercise control at work, especially for older workers and women. Added to this is the stressful experience of lack of employee involvement in processes leading up to job reorganisation and change.

It should be noted that change is potentially stressful because people move from predictable environments where they feel secure. They may take one or two changes in their stride, but if too many things are changed at the same time they may become stressed and defensive.

On the question of job control, Fisher (1985) maintains that when blue-collar workers are compared with white-collar workers, the former fare worse in the sense that they experience less control. The alleged disadvantages accruing to blue-collar workers, which could result in more distress at work, are as follows:

- Blue-collar workers, who operate directly on the line handling a product or process, are more likely to feel helpless in that they are less able to avoid unpleasant conditions, and have less control over how their time is spent at work. By contrast, those in certain managerial posts may have the opportunity to avoid circumstances they do not like, but they have to be careful in case they are penalised for such behaviour.
- Blue-collar workers have less scope to modify the task, because their work is a well-defined process and integrated in an overall production process in a systematic way. Should there be unpleasant conditions in the job—often expressed as a greater range of industrial hazards and uncomfortable working conditions than that experienced by white-collar workers—they are generally lumbered with them, and the only option open to them is to put up with the conditions or leave the job.
- In the sense of marketability, it is not easy for blue-collar workers to change jobs, because of lower income (with consequent lower savings) and reduced options.
- Opportunities for social activity at work are greater if the worker enjoys greater discretion. In this sense the blue-collar worker is at a disadvantage. It is said that the blue-collar worker cannot easily counteract the unfavourable conditions at work by exercising control outside mainstream work activity.

Shift Work

A number of studies have found shift work to be a stress factor at work. It can affect neurophysical rhythms—such as blood temperature, metabolic rate, blood sugar levels, mental efficiency, and work motivation—which may ultimately result in stress-related disease (Monk & Tepas, 1985). In a study of offshore oil workers it was concluded that the longer the shift the greater the stress (Sutherland & Cooper, 1987).

Recently, Sigman (1993), drawing on empirical studies, addressed the issue of shift work, and concluded that the following consequences are associated with it:

- It leaves peoples' body clocks in a perpetual state of disarray;
- Workers on night shift are more irritable than day workers; they are also less alert, are quicker to make mistakes at work, and are also more lethargic at home. In a North American study, it was found that working night shifts had a modestly negative effect on the quality of a marriage, with issues of jealousy and concerns about infidelity featuring prominently;
- Rotating night shifts can be even worse. Having one's working hours changed every few days or weeks causes not only sleep deprivation, but also has an effect described as having permanent jet lag. This is a fate that affects workers in a range of jobs, including the investment and electronic media, as well as factory production. In one study "over 80% of rotating shiftworkers experienced serious sleep disruption, including insomnia at home and drowsiness at work, which lowered their productivity as well as the quality of their lives. There was also a higher risk of cardiovascular and digestive tract disorders" (Sigman, 1993);
- Shift work can create a sense of isolation by making it much more difficult to see friends, or even ring someone up for a chat.

New Technology: VDU Work

A feature of recent years has been the development of computer technology and its application in a wide variety of industrial and commercial processes. Part of this development is the growth in the use of visual display units (VDUs) and in the use of business machines and equipment, such as word-processors. Concern has been expressed over the direct health effects of VDU operation, particularly the effects of exposure to radiation.

Apparently there is no need to fear any threat from radiation emitted by VDUs. Significant improvements in the design of the cathode ray tube (CRT) and associated equipment in recent years have resulted in ionising radiation emission from VDU terminals becoming almost negligible (only fractionally above the level of natural background radiation). A report prepared by the National Radiological Protection Board concluded that radiation from VDUs cannot cause physical injury to either the skin or the eyes of people working with them (Anderson, 1980). A similar conclusion was arrived at in a Health and Safe Executive report (Mackay, 1980).

The majority of problems connected with VDU operation stem from indirect factors of a visual and postural nature, and possibly anxiety related to fatigue (Mackay & Cox, 1984). In recent years there has been much comment on physical disorders—referred to as repetitive strain injury or RSI. This arises when the operator maintains the same posture at a keyboard over time, placing the muscles in the arms and back under constant strain (i.e. static loading), which results in pain.

RSI became an issue in recent years in the UK newspaper industry when nine journalists suffering from RSI, as a result of working on computer keyboards, were informed by their employer—the *Financial Times*—that they should take early retirement on health grounds. The company was served with six writs from RSI sufferers (The *Independent*, 1991). In a court ruling in October, 1993, a British judge rejected a claim for damages by an RSI sufferer—a journalist employed by *Reuters*—and said that the term RSI had no place in the medical books. However, in January 1994 a former typist, and now an RSI sufferer, received an out of court settlement (see panel below).

Williams (1985) feels that RSI emanates from a combination of new technology and the relentless repetition of many traditional office jobs. The design of equipment and furniture has obviously a part to play in solving this problem. However, Williams maintains that job enlargement, rest pauses, and exercise programmes have a greater part to play to counteract the monotony of the keyboard.

The frequency with which a computer terminal is used can have a material influence on the outcome. Johansson and Aronsson

---

Compensation Award for RSI Sufferer

A former Inland Revenue typist in Britain was awarded a record £79,000 compensation for the loss of her job because of RSI in an out of court settlement on 18 January 1994. The typist was forced to leave her job after suffering for two years from tennis elbow, which she claimed was caused by using an electronic typewriter. Her condition was related to posture, lack of breaks from typing between 13,000 and 16,000 strokes an hour, the general inadequacy of the office furniture she used, and a putative management environment that emphasised greater effort to achieve higher output.

The former typist is now registered as disabled, cannot pick up a 1lb bag of sugar, and is unable to do housework such as ironing, vacuuming and cleaning. It is reported that management in the Inland Revenue are planning to pay greater attention to ergonomic aspects of work in the future (Donkin, 1994).

(1984) found that those who occasionally used a computer terminal felt that the experience helped them to do their job quicker and better. However, frequent users of the computer suffered stress, eyestrain, headaches, and pains in the arms and shoulders. A primary source of stress resulted from the breakdown of the computer and from phone calls interrupting work. A particular irritation was not knowing how long the interruptions would last and seeing the work pile up. This seemed to influence people's work behaviour because there was a tendency to work harder in the morning in anticipation of a computer breakdown. This resulted in frequently spending more time on the computer than prescribed by the company regulations. A suggested way forward is that work should be planned to allow for computer breakdowns, with the attendant prescription that rest pauses should be scheduled.

Mackay and Cox (1984), based on the outcome of their research, have summarised the impact of VDUs on work under three headings:

- underload;
- de-skilling; and
- control.

Underload. This amounts to being under-stretched and it is a principal characteristic of many repetitive work practices, particularly machine-paced assembly lines. It is now associated with VDU operation where simple clerical tasks are computerised. Following computerisation, these tasks retain their monotonous and repetitive features, such as short cycle and repetition. In the earlier section on machine-paced and repetitive work, the dissatisfying features of repetitive work were described.

De-skilling. When a job is changed to accommodate new technology, an element of de-skilling can occur. Should this happen, it amounts to the loss of some of the past investment in skills development. Therefore, the existing patterns of skills are not fully utilised, with the likely absence of challenge and job interest.

Control. An important factor determining stress-related symptoms among VDU operators is the lack of control. It can increase substantially the number of considerations the operator has to confront, and inevitably leads to fatigue. In some computerised systems the machine is able to monitor the performance of the operator in keying-in data. The resultant control information could, in many instances, be used to determine levels of remuneration through piece-rate payment systems. Understandably, this type of machine control is often resented and regarded with suspicion by computer operators. Consequently it is associated with feelings of fatigue and stress.

The response of the computer itself following the keying-in of information is also a factor to consider. Where response times are very long, or variable in length, uncertainty and frustration can be created. These problems can be exacerbated by technical disturbances and breakdowns, if they occur frequently.

Some ideas about how to tackle the factors identified here as negative outcomes arising from VDU operations are set out in the panel facing. (Other aspects of VDU operation are discussed in Chapters 2, 10, and 14.)

Hierarchical Level

The incidence of stress can vary depending upon the organisational level at which the manager operates. Partners in accounting firms experienced less stress and strain than other staff, with junior staff experiencing most stress (Gaertner & Ruthe, 1981). Lower and middle managers are said to experience more symptoms of emotional and physical ill health than senior managers (Cooper, 1979). This is not far removed from a view that suggests that the most likely candidate for a heart attack is

Counteracting VDU Problems

Minimise Repetition

The repetitive elements in the operator's task should be minimised by introducing a variable work-load during the day, instead of long periods of concentrated work. It is also helpful for operators to know what is in store for them.

Discretion on Work Allocation

With regard to the allocation of tasks over a set period of time, allow the individual some discretion on how work is allocated. This offers some potential for the use of individual skills.

Introduce Challenge

Endeavour to avoid treating the VDU operator as essentially a machine-minder. Where possible, jobs should be designed to be mentally challenging, but at the same time to be within the realm of the operator's abilities.

Screen Quality

If the VDU equipment is used intensely and continuously, then there is a need for optimum screen features (considered in Chapter 14) and good workplace conditions. But if the VDU operator's task consists of a variety of work activities, some of which may include VDU operation, then less than satisfactory screen features could be tolerated.

Design Procedures

Improvements in the ergonomic aspects of the VDU equipment will have little overall effect if staff are demotivated and suffer from low morale. Any process leading to the enrichment of the jobs of VDU operators should involve both the designers and users of the system during the various phases of design and implementation.

Rest Breaks

In many jobs we take natural breaks or pauses. For VDU operators this would mean time spent not viewing the VDU screen because they are doing other things, and this distraction would help to prevent the onset of fatigue, which in turn affects performance. But informal breaks are less frequent in certain types of VDU work—for example, data entry tasks requiring continuous and sustained attention, concentration, and high rates of data entry. In work of this nature the introduction of formal rest pauses should help the maintenance of attention and concentration.

Issuing guidance about the duration of rest pauses can prove difficult. Some people complain that they are too short to prevent fatigue occurring, whereas others view them as unnecessarily prolonged and frustrating. In the final analysis the length of a rest pause can only be determined by a consideration of the individual operator's job. However, some general statements can be made (Mackay & Cooper, 1987):

- As adverse symptoms often arise when people try to maintain their performance in the face of accumulated fatigue, rest pauses should be arranged prior to the onset of fatigue, and should not be provided as a means to recuperate from it. The rest pause should be introduced when performance is at a maximum, just before a decrease in productivity sets in.
- Short, frequently occurring, rest pauses appear to be more satisfactory than longer pauses taken occasionally.
- Ideally, the break from work should be taken away from the location of the VDU.
- The nature of the work should be considered. Rest pauses are more effective for work that requires concentration than for work that is more or less automatic. The latter leaves the employee free to day-dream, converse with others, or to follow similar monotony-reducing strategies.
- Rest pauses are likely to be more useful for relatively ineffective workers.

not the senior executive, but the junior executive, probably striving for the top, or the white-collar worker surrounded by frustration (Packard, 1962).

Life at different levels of the organisation is viewed as both a source of satisfaction and stress (Cooper, 1979). Top managers showed a tendency to be more outgoing and derived more satisfaction from managing people and putting aside time for problems connected with the development of people. They appear to feel pressure from a substantial amount of communication and consultation, and are satisfied when they are free from decision-making processes based on consultation. They feel prone to pressure from bureaucratic rules and regulations that tend to constrain their behaviour unduly, and they feel that their present jobs, as opposed to their previous jobs, make greater demands on their leisure and family time; the latter is a source of pressure because of the time spent and the conflict with home demands. They are not very interested in opportunities outside the company, and the fact that they have reached their career ceiling and may have to retire early poses little problem.

For middle managers, dealing with personnel problems was a source of pressure, as was using new systems or methods on a frequent basis. Like the top manager, they also felt prone to pressure from bureaucratic rules and regulations and the intrusion of business into leisure and family time. Middle managers did not like to feel pushed for time. They are more likely to feel pressure as a result of perceiving a lack of opportunity within the company at a time when new jobs are more demanding and competition for them is severe.

In recent years the "plight of the female manager" has been acknowledged (Davidson & Cooper, 1981). It is suggested that as more women are entering managerial positions they are subjected to a greater number of work-related pressures compared with their male counterparts. In addition, married women in management are often subjected to additional pressures of trying to maintain a family or a home, which is more prominent in the west that it is in Asia. Female managers in Asia, with or without children, normally avail themselves of good domestic help from maids, parents, or relatives (Zoher, 1993). Differences between the sexes in sources and levels of occupational stress is poorly supported by the evidence at our disposal (McKenna & Ellis, 1981; Reynolds, 1981).

It appears that making important decisions is a source of pressure for middle managers, unlike top managers who are more likely to share important decisions. This calls to mind a classic study which showed that making a

decision can cause ulcers in conditions when all other factors are kept constant (Schoonmaker, 1969). Two monkeys were strapped in seats facing a light and a lever, with an electrified rod at their feet. One monkey had access to a dummy lever and the other was able to control the flow of electric current by using an operational lever (executive control). A light flashed every 20 seconds and both monkeys would get a mild electric shock unless the monkey with executive control pressed the lever. The monkey with access to the dummy lever soon ignored it because it was totally ineffective, and therefore had to rely on the other monkey to press the lever every time the light flashed. This required the monkey with executive control to act fairly quickly.

The monkey with the dummy lever remained in excellent health, but the decision-making monkey who exercised executive control died on the 23rd day, the apparent victim of an ulcer. However, contradictory evidence comes from a group of researchers at the University of Wisconsin, who exposed monkeys to a loud, irritating noise, but allowed half of them to interrupt the sound by pulling a chain (Wallis, 1983). Although both groups of monkeys were exposed to the same noise, those with access to the chain showed lower levels of stress-related hormones in their blood. Being in control seemed to be an advantage in these circumstances, unlike the previous situation. Perhaps the difference in stimuli—an electric shock as opposed to a loud noise—may have contributed to the eventual outcome.

STRESS FROM WITHIN THE INDIVIDUAL, PLUS OUTSIDE INFLUENCES

As shown in Table 15.1, this topic will be discussed with reference to personality, work relationships, career development, redundancy and unemployment, early retirement, and domestic considerations.

Personality

A number of perspectives on personality were discussed in Chapter 1. When considering the effects of stress on executives, it is wise to take into account the individual's personality, and their ability to withstand stressful conditions. As the following studies show, personality appears to be a key factor in this respect. Patients in one study with coronary heart disease or related diseases were considered to be emotionally unstable and introverted (Lebovits, Shekelle, & Ostfeld 1967). Employees with rigid personalities were more prone to rushing jobs assigned to them from above and to be dependent on other people, while those with flexible personalities were more likely to be influenced by others and to suffer from work overload. Introverts are said to withdraw from interpersonal relationships that produce stress and, in doing so, complicate matters by preventing communication and making interaction and problem solving more difficult (Kahn et al., 1964).

Friedman and Rosenman's research identifies a relationship between certain behavioural traits and a proneness to heart disease (Rosenman, Friedman, & Strauss, 1964). The individuals in their studies were rated on personality factors prior to the actual medical diagnosis, and this was conducted without awareness of the behavioural traits. Those classified as Type A in behaviour were people who exhibited coronary-prone behaviour, which can be expressed as follows:

- extreme competitiveness;
- striving for achievement;
- aggressiveness;
- haste;
- impatience;
- restlessness;
- hyperalertness;
- explosive speech;
- tenseness of facial muscles;
- feelings of being under pressure of time; and

- keenness to assume the challenge of responsibility.

Type A people tend to set deadlines or quotas for themselves at work or at home at least once per week, whereas the opposite—type B—will do so only occasionally. Type A people tend to bring work home frequently, whereas type B will rarely do so. Also, Type A people are in general substantially involved and committed to their work, and other aspects of their lives are relatively neglected. They tend to possess the following risk factors: high serum cholesterol levels, elevated beta lipoproteins, decreased blood clotting and elevated daytime excretion of norepinephrine, more incidence of acute myocardial infarction, and angina pectoris. They are also less likely to give up smoking.

It is also suggested that individuals susceptible to Type A behaviour tend to be professional or managerial staff between the ages of 36 and 55 years, living in urban environments. They show a tendency to suppress stress symptoms and fatigue because they believe that illness might interfere with the completion of various important tasks.

The relationship between Type A behaviour and symptoms of stress is supported in a study of 236 managers in 12 different companies (Howard, Cunningham, & Rechnitzer, 1976). This showed that Type A behaviour was associated in a significant way with high blood pressure and higher cholesterol and triglyceride levels. A high percentage of the managers in each of the age groups studied were cigarette smokers, and Type A managers were less interested in exercise.

However, in a more recent study of 384 male salaried employees in the USA (based on questionnaires, interviews, and physical examinations), it was found that there was no direct association between Type A behavioural patterns and risk factors connected with coronary heart disease (Chesney et al., 1981), a view that would be challenged by Friedman and Booth-Kewley (1987).

Other evidence from the USA, where most of the research on this subject originates, shows an absence of data on the association between Type A behaviour and coronary heart disease in women, blacks, Hispanics, and young adults. Also, sufficient data has not been accumulated to show conclusively what aspects of Type A behaviour are coronary-prone, and what aspects are not (Matthews & Haynes, 1986). It is difficult to identify research evidence tracing subjects from the point of selection for a job through their careers in order to discover how changes and influences over time affect their behaviour.

Locus of Control

The concept of locus of control has been discussed already as a dimension of personality in Chapter 1. A prevailing view of the relationship between locus of control and life stress holds that people who define events in their lives as being outside their control (i.e. external locus of control) will be less able to cope effectively with stress, and are therefore more likely to experience physical and psychological distress than people with internal locus of control beliefs. Externals see themselves as powerless to influence day-to-day events.

On the other hand, if people define stressful situations as amenable to their own control (i.e. internal locus of control) it is possible that they have sufficient confidence in themselves to deal with stressful situations in a way that minimises the negative impact (Krause & Stryker, 1984). This was confirmed in a study of female student nurses. The internals were more adaptive at modifying their coping strategies after having appraised the particular stressful situation. This flexibility was not evident in the case of the externals who appeared hardly to alter their mode of coping (Parkes, 1984).

Apparently, internal locus of control dispositions in a group of undergraduates can be traced back to health habits as a child. Health habits included regular visits by children to medical practitioners for check-ups and vaccinations. Apart from the promotion of good health, these habits—more likely to be found in the higher socio-economic groups—are important in that they contribute to the development of beliefs that underpin sound preventative health behaviour (Lau, 1982). Paradoxically, early experience of illness was not positively related to internal locus of control beliefs in this study. Specific behaviour, where locus of control is related to health, includes seeking information on health hazards and remedies, taking medication, keeping appointments with physicians, maintaining a diet, and giving up smoking. With regard to these types of behaviour, internals fared well, though in some cases externals showed positive interest and action (Wallston & Wallston, 1978).

It is suggested that one should look to the extreme positions on a continuum ranging from "internal" to "external". According to Phares (1976), both the extremely internal and extremely external person may be especially vulnerable to the effects of life stress. In particular, the extremely internal types who confront stressful conditions may be so overcome with a sense of personal responsibility for the occurrence of the stressful event that they may suffer from anxiety and depressive reactions.

The plight of the extreme internal is substantial at both the theoretical and empirical levels. At the theoretical level it is suggested that extreme internals possess an hysterical rigidity that produces an incapacity to live with uncontrollable events in life, and prevents them from taking effective coping action (Antonovsky, 1979). In an empirical study (Krause & Stryker, 1984) of men aged 45 to 54, extreme internals (who were gripped by guilt feelings on account of feeling personally responsible for the initial event) were coupled with moderate externals as people who are less likely to initiate constructive efforts to deal with stressful events, because they feel their best attempts cannot influence life events. (The stressful events included financial loss, unemployment, increased job pressure, and retirement.) But the results showed that moderate externals were the most vulnerable to the effects of job and economic stress, whereas the group that came out best in ability to cope effectively with stressful events were the moderate internals.

Work Relationships

A number of desirable and undesirable consequences stem from the relationship between superiors, subordinates, and colleagues. When the relationship is good it leads to the advancement of individual and organisational health. When the relationship is deficient or bad, as one finds in circumstances where distrust among staff is rampant, it can give rise to poor or inadequate interpersonal communication, leading to reduced job satisfaction and a feeling of being threatened by one's colleagues and superiors (French & Caplan, 1970; Kahn et al., 1964).

Jealousy, humiliation, arguments, and reprimands all contribute to feelings of stress, and may lead to negative emotions that can be exhausting and debilitating. John Hunter, the 18th century physician, who was prone to angina pectoris, once remarked that his life was in the hands of any rascal who chose to annoy or tease him. He got into an argument with a colleague who contradicted him and became very involved in a verbal encounter; he then stopped talking, left the room, and immediately dropped dead (Barnard, 1981). Where rivalry and office politics occur in relationships between colleagues, support from one's peers in difficult situations may be lacking, with obvious repercussions (Lazarus, 1966).

If a highly competitive atmosphere exists, sharing of problems may cease as an activity because people fear that they may not be able to stand their ground and perform adequately. In today's conditions of proposed cuts in expenditure and programmes of rationalisa-

tion, quite understandably people feel anxious in the face of uncertainty as to what is going to happen next. In such conditions there is a real danger of losing a sense of belonging and identification with the organisation or part of it, with clear repercussions in terms of anxiety and stress.

The dampening influence emanating from an incompetent superior cannot be overstated. This may be reflected in a number of ways. The superior may be bankrupt technically in conditions where a deficiency in this respect is serious. He or she may be unable to focus seriously on key issues, be prone to digress frequently and listen inattentively, fail to act on sensible ideas or suggestions put forward for serious consideration, and may lack the confidence to take initiatives backed up by a reasonable amount of preparation. In addition, a failure to empathise with others and the lack of a modicum of charisma are limiting factors. The subordinate who expects a better calibre superior, but is encumbered with the type of manager just described, may suffer from some of the classical symptoms of stress.

In comparatively recent times the desirability of encouraging managers to adopt a participative leadership style has been advocated. It is believed that the superior who extends the hand of friendship to subordinates, who develops mutual trust, respect, and warmth with subordinates, and who is constructive in his or her criticisms, without playing favourites or taking advantage of subordinates, is likely to go a long way in neutralising pressure that originates from the job (Buck, 1972). It is claimed that more involvement in the decision-making process by subordinates, where they get feedback on their performance and are duly recognised for their contribution, leads to higher productivity, better relationships between superiors and subordinates, more individual control and autonomy, and less staff turnover, all of which are conducive to good mental health (Coch & French, 1948).

On the other hand, lack of participation in decision making is said to promote strain and stress at work because the freedom of thought and movement enjoyed by subordinates is restricted as a result of close supervision and low autonomy (Buck, 1972). One group of researchers claims that failure to allow participation to take root was related in a significant way to a number of risks to personal health. These are poor overall physical health, escapist drinking, depressed mood, low self-esteem, low job satisfaction and satisfaction with life, low levels of motivation to work, an intention to quit, and absenteeism (Margolis et al., 1974).

A word of caution is called for before unequivocally endorsing the participative approach as a panacea for problems connected with management style. To use this approach successfully in managing subordinates, managers must be adept at delegating responsibilities and be able to manage effectively through an open process (Donaldson & Gowler, 1975). Otherwise, a certain level of anxiety, stress, and resentment may arise because managers recognise that their actual power falls short of their formal power and, as a consequence, their formal role and status is eroded. It is also conceivable that the participative approach is seen as "soft" and a waste of time, partly because of the view that subordinates do not wish to get involved or participate in decision making. This eventually places a barrier in the way of doing a good job and achieving a high level of productivity. A full discussion of the participative leadership style appeared in Chapter 8.

Career Development

Progression in a career is of prime importance to many executives and managers. But with fairly rapid technological, economic, and social change and development in society, uncertainty arises because of the real possibility of having to change career during one's working life. As a consequence, career development stress is likely to occur much more frequently later in life, unless executives and managers adapt their expectations to coincide with these developments. Middle age is a particularly vulnerable stage because it is then that career opportunities can decrease significantly and career progress can grind to a near halt.

In the case of men, various manifestations of the "male menopause"—considered by some to be a myth—are likely to occur (Constandse, 1972). These include:

- a proneness to dwell on fears and disappointments;
- a feeling of being isolated;
- doubting one's ability to get on top of a new assignment or job;
- a belief that the old knowledge and skills are no longer as relevant as they once were;
- a realisation that energy is becoming more scarce or is being channelled into family activities; and
- coping with competition from younger colleagues.

In the case of women, apparently, blockages to career development are pronounced among female managers (Davidson & Cooper, 1983). The most damaging health and job satisfaction factors were associated with career development and related issues—e.g. sex discrimination in promotion, inadequate training, insufficient delegation of assignments to women, and male colleagues being treated more favourably.

At the present time, pruning of expenditure and cutting back on staffing levels is tending to lead to a situation of more competition for the limited number of promotions within organisations. Also, with restricted career opportunities outside the organisation, a number of managers are likely to feel trapped because a barrier is placed in the path to the realisation of their ambition and potential. In circumstances such as these, frustrations develop and can be directed negatively against the organisation, or the system of authority within it, or, where that is not possible, against colleagues and the family (Culbert, 1974).

The situation can even be worse if the manager is passed over in the promotion stakes: psychosomatic illness has been attributed to such an event (Morris, 1956). Equally sensitive might be a situation in which a previous subordinate now becomes a person's boss.

In one sense, occupational mobility has a positive aspect to it, but in another sense it may produce negative consequences. Those who were occupationally mobile (four or more job changes) and geographically mobile (two or more cross-country moves) were said to be more vulnerable to heart disease than those who belonged to stable occupational groups (Syme, Hyman, & Enterline, 1964). Some people may feel uneasy about being over-promoted, just as others would feel uneasy about being under-promoted or having reached the end of their career path.

The over-promoted manager may be grossly overworked in order to hold down the job and, at the same time, may engage in behaviour designed to mask inner insecurities (McMurray, 1973). People who were fully stretched, having been given responsibility exceeding their ability, were found to progress from minor psychological symptoms to marked psychosomatic complaints and, finally, to mental illness (Brook, 1973). Apparently, under-promoted people, given responsibility below the corresponding level of their ability, suffered similar complaints.

Redundancy and Unemployment

Before examining the adverse effects of being without a job, it seems appropriate to dwell for a moment on the significance of work (see panel below).

Feelings of insecurity arise because of the fear of redundancy or demotion, the fear that one's skills are becoming obsolete, or when there is talk of early retirement. Redundancies among all staff, and executives in particular,

---

The Nature of Work

A job offers us a recognised place in a community, confers self-respect and status, and provides a standard by which others judge us. In social introductions, questions are often asked such as "What do you do?". However, job titles can be misleading because some groups use grandiose titles. Also, where a job title is not considered to be particularly significant, some workers may mention the organisation for which they work. A good fit between the employee's characteristics and the requirements of the job could lead to a satisfied outlook and a balanced disposition. A poor fit, on the other hand, may produce the opposite effect.

Work is generally a highly organised activity and as such provides many people with a number of benefits apart from income. It offers the opportunity to structure a significant part of our waking hours, and forces us to engage in purposeful activities; it provides us with the opportunity to associate with people outside our immediate circle of family and friends; it allows us to test and clarify our own personal impressions about our status and identity; and it can permit the attainment of personal goals while contributing to the achievement of organisational goals.

The work ethic is deeply ingrained in Western industrialised society, and in the UK in the past we tolerated waste and overmanning in order to preserve employment, presumably to ensure that people felt socially useful. Political ideologies focus narrowly on work as the creator of wealth. Though one can draw a distinction between work and leisure, there are certain types of leisure activity that have a number of attributes in common with work. For some people, however, enforced leisure is not a welcome experience because it is an inadequate substitute for work. It is interesting to note that being a lady or gentleman of leisure used to be held in high social esteem, and this was at a time when work was morally justified. The work ethic is unlikely to be dislodged by unacceptably high levels of unemployment, but it could be subjected to a significant overhaul in these circumstances (Shimmin, 1966).

have been increasingly common in recent years (Cooper, 1979). Prior to the announcement of any redundancies, rumours circulate and anxiety springs from job insecurity. If redundancy is to be selective, trust and openness suffer, leading to suspicion and perhaps severe competition. Uncertainty about the future develops and, ironically, the actual announcement of the redundancy programme may initially be considered a relief because people know where they stand.

But this will soon wear off and the process of instituting the redundancy programme may be equated with an exercise in removing "dead wood". Feelings of guilt and shame arise as a consequence, even though the redundant person obtains the sympathy of colleagues. Events may not take the course outlined in the case of mass redundancies or voluntary redundancies, but it seems plausible that the process in such an eventuality would contain certain similarities.

Having been made redundant, individuals suffer the loss of status that accompanied the job and, for some people, there is the danger of withdrawal due to a sense of failure. Loneliness and a feeling of isolation is not uncommon at this stage, but redundant employees may regard their loss as only temporary and tend to look at the new situation as if it were a long-deserved holiday. They are cushioned by a redundancy settlement and can get on with jobs needed to be done about the house (Fagin, 1979). In the search for another job, extreme competition is encountered and perhaps there is a feeling that a prospective employer may be unfavourably disposed to somebody who has been made redundant. With continual lack of success in securing another job comes an increasingly long period of unemployment. Even for the most optimistic of people, this is something that erodes self-confidence and contributes to depression.

If the main wage earner in a family—traditionally the man—suffers prolonged bouts of unemployment, these create problems of structuring time and organising daily life, and contribute to pessimism, distress, fatalism, and apathy. A spill-over to family life is likely as the individual's influence becomes less in the home (Jahoda, 1979). This is due to his own negative view of himself as well as a negative evaluation by the family and, quite naturally, this becomes a source of domestic anxiety. At a time when the wife is suffering strain from the burden of financial worries, and perhaps planning a change in life-style, she has also to contend with her husband's need for encouragement and emotional support. This places added strain on her. Eventually the roles may have to be reversed when the wife goes out to work and the former breadwinner stays at home, much to the relief of the wife. The children may suffer a loss of prestige among their friends, and homework may suffer. The waning of the father's authority may encourage disobedience, emotional upset, and antisocial behaviour.

From preliminary studies of redundancies it was shown that, when employees expected plant closures, blood pressure rose, and for those who became unemployed it continued to do so. Feelings of depression, irritation, and low self-esteem were associated with the high blood pressure. Those who found employment experienced rapid reduction in blood pressure levels towards normal. Levels of serum uric acid behaved in a similar fashion to blood pressure as a consequence of unemployment (Kasl & Cobb, 1970). Emotional instability was associated with increasing unemployment among unemployed engineers (Shanthamani, 1973).

Eventually, the job aspirations of the unemployed could be lowered, and a lower-status job with a lower salary accepted. Where the unemployed person cannot secure another job, the individual settles for new standards and a different way of life. Social activities of all sorts are curtailed for emotional and financial reasons, and roles within the family could suffer a dramatic change (Fagin, 1979).

In a survey of a small group of unemployed male managerial staff in the UK it was concluded that, though the men passed through the shock phase on losing their jobs, none had reached the pessimism or acceptance of unemployment stage, whether they had been unemployed for six months or over a year (Swinburne, 1981). Though aware of the negative and pessimistic feelings associated with unemployment, they used conscious strategies to delay these feelings—for example, it is to be expected that it will take longer to secure a managerial or professional job; the contemporary unemployment scene makes one realise that the job situation is highly competitive, and failure to land a job is not a personal deficiency. Savings and redundancy payments act as a buffer against the financial hardships of unemployment, and the reduction in the stigma attached to it helps. But "bitchy" neighbours can rub salt in the wound. There is still a reluctance to discuss unemployment.

In more recent times, Fryer and Payne (1986), having examined a number of studies, concluded that "the unemployed as a group have higher mean levels of experienced strain and negative feelings, lower mean levels of happiness and present life satisfaction, with lower mean levels of experience of pleasure and positive feeling than comparable employed people". In addition, it was asserted that there tends to be a view among physicians that the physical health consequences of unemployment were real and possessed serious implications for the health of the community.

Three areas of health concern have been identified as worthy of note:

1. Studies of depression have consistently shown the unemployed to be more affected by depression than the employed (Fryer & Payne, 1986).
2. The bulk of studies of suicides report higher rates of suicides for the unemployed than for the employed (Fryer & Payne, 1986). But it is pertinent to ask, were the unemployed group more vulnerable to suicide independent of their state of being without work?
3. Certain cognitive difficulties could arise. For example, in a study of 954 working class men, stratified by age and length of unemployment, it was found that 31% of the sample reported taking longer over doing things, had difficulties in concentrating, and got rusty. However, only about 10% reported an increase in making mistakes in shopping or understanding written material (Fryer & Warr, 1984).

Certain intervening variables have to be considered when examining the relationship between the person and the unemployed state—namely:

- length of unemployment;
- social class; and
- role of the family.

Length of Unemployment. It is suggested that the negative mental health consequences of being unemployed occur within the first three months after the loss of the job, and remain fairly stable thereafter (Warr & Jackson, 1984). However, one should maintain a flexible position when interpreting the significance of the length of unemployment as an intervening variable in the relationship between ill-health and unemployment.

Social Class. With regard to social class, it is said that there is not much difference between professional/white-collar workers and semi-skilled/blue-collar workers in terms of reactions to unemployment, except that the working class group reported greater anxiety over financial difficulties, and greater problems in occupying their time (Fryer & Payne, 1986).

Role of the Family. On the role of the family, it is suggested that unemployment is associated with increased family stress, particularly among the long-term unemployed and those in the lower occupational groups (Fagan & Little, 1984). However, other evidence emphasises the resilience of the family. For example, it is said that unemployment actually reactivates dormant family ties, and for a majority of families, including white and blue-collar workers, a family crisis does not accompany the husband's unemployment (Fryer & Payne, 1986). It is understandable to underline the supportive role of the family in conditions of unemployment, but equally one must acknowledge the potential for power struggles and highly charged emotional exchanges brought about by stringent financial circumstances and changed status.

Inevitably, there is going to be a reduction in activities where expenditure is involved and this could create certain strains. The plight of the children has to be considered. The continuation of unemployment for some months led to economic deprivation which increased pressure on the social relationships of children, leading to poorer performance at school and a deterioration in emotional and physical health. In some cases matters deteriorated to a point where children were physically abused (Madge, 1983).

Turning Unemployment to Advantage
Though the negative aspects of unemployment have been highlighted at length, it could be said that unemployment may be construed as an opportunity (where possible) for somebody to change direction. However, in the chronic unemployment conditions of the early 1990s, such an opportunity could be rather elusive. Nevertheless, unemployed people have the option of being active, relying on their talents, interests, and so on, in order to counteract the malaise of unemployment (Fryer & Payne, 1986).

This could entail engaging in meaningful activities, such as pursuing hobbies, seeing friends, attending to an allotment, do-it-yourself work in the home, etc, as a way of instilling a vestige of non-material meaning in their lives. This could be a welcome change in some respects for the unskilled factory worker, now unemployed, who is no longer subjected to the dehumanising effects of the assembly line. However, a fundamental constraint on the unemployed person's freedom to act, particularly where expense is involved, has to be considered. Due to lack of resources, the unemployed person may not be able to engage in certain types of activities, such as decorating the house or repairing furniture. Where it is possible to purchase inferior materials or tools to do the job, the quality of the outcome may be less than satisfactory. This could engender a sense of failure and lowered self-esteem. Some unemployed people, who take an active stand to cope with their predicament, may break the social security laws in order to maintain their standard of living.

Early Retirement

For some managers nearing retirement the call of a job with lighter responsibilities and more flexible hours is attractive, and they decide to move on (Sleeper, 1975). Those who are compelled to retire early and those who are ill-prepared for retirement may feel dissatisfied, as would perhaps those who retire for health reasons, at least initially. There are those who retire early and find it difficult to adjust emotionally to the life of a retired person, and they can feel bored, depressed, and lonely (Cooper, 1979). There are others who miss the social contacts at work, and will be ill-equipped to cope with a situation in which a lot of time is spent with the spouse.

However, one must not lose sight of a number of advantages attached to early retirement. These include more personal freedom, more leisure time, more time with the family and friends, and opportunities to pursue hobbies, to travel, and to engage in educational pursuits. These advantages would be even more attractive if the person is provided with an adequate pension and feels financially secure.

Domestic Considerations

There are a number of circumstances that originate outside the organisation which can create stress. These include family problems, life crises, financial difficulties, conflict of personal beliefs with those of the organisation, and family commitments competing with commitments to the organisation.

A topic that has attracted a fair amount of analysis and comment is the relationship between the male manager and his wife and family (Handy, 1975; Pahl & Pahl, 1971). The work and home situation are interrelated because the manager has to rely on support from the home to alleviate stress originating at work, and to keep him in touch with certain realities. In this way the wife's role may be seen as supportive and caring while the "thruster" husband pursues a demanding job in the knowledge that, provided the marital relationship is not in jeopardy, the home environment is a refuge.

The husband may run the risk of strain and ineffectiveness if he tries to execute both the work and home roles to an adequate level. The young executive may find himself in the situation where he has to maintain a distance between his wife and the organisation as he is building up his career and putting a lot of effort into the job, just at the very time his young housebound wife is also making demands on his time. By maintaining the distance between the wife and the organisation he is not forced to choose between the two, at a time when he ought to involve his wife because of the need for her sympathy and understanding (Beattie, Darlington, & Cripps, 1974).

It would be an over-simplification to view the relationship between the husband and his family as being strictly of the nature described here. Some wives, though, acting in a supportive role, are bored and lonely at home and may be jealous of the husband because of his career. Others are very adept at acting as a buffer between problems arising in the home and their husband. In other situations a wife may take an outside interest and step up entertaining on behalf of her husband when the children are grown up, and may find this life absorbing and satisfying. Or, instead of acting in a supportive capacity, a wife may be envious of the fact that the husband has insufficient time to consider her problems or achievements, and as a retaliatory measure objects to him bringing work home or moving house because of the job. This could create a situation of overload during office hours, and frustrated ambitions for the husband which he is likely to resent.

There are of course relationships where the wife pursues a career, because to do so is satisfying or financially rewarding, and both husband and wife share the housework. It is when the husband expects his home comforts and does not receive them, that problems are likely to arise. Many husbands do not fully appreciate the implications for the wife of moving house as a result of changing jobs. This is even more important when the move is to a foreign country. It is almost inevitable that the mobile family is prone to developing temporary relationships, with a capacity to live for the present and to turn on instant sociability, as well as an ability to display indifference to the local community (Packard, 1975).

From the husband's viewpoint, this may be due to a shortage of time and the realisation that they are short-stay inhabitants. The wife may bear the brunt of the move; she has to attend to a number of matters connected with the house move; she has to create a new life in the new neighbourhood and does not have the advantage of her husband whose job status is transferred; and she is expected to provide a stable environment for the children and her husband and to be in a state of readiness for the next move. In the process she may have had to sever contact with a close circle of friends or family, and this loss is very prevalent soon after the move (Marshall & Cooper, 1976).

Increasing divorce rates in the United States are said to be a consequence of the continuous success of the aspiring senior manager who leaves his socially unskilled wife at home (Immundo, 1974). Alcoholism may be a problem for some corporate wives. It is said that the ratio of female to male alcoholics in the USA rose from 1:5 in 1962 to 1:2 in 1973 (Seidenberg, 1973). Perhaps this may be due to frustration and loneliness. Generally the plight of the wife may not be as bad as it seems because she may not encounter too many difficulties getting involved in the community, even if it is a transient one, and this involvement could act as compensation for being somewhat isolated because of her husband's ambitions and career involvement. It is in the husband's interest to see that his wife has made a successful adjustment following the move.

In today's world, the position of the working wife of executive rank is considered by some companies (e.g. *J. Sainsbury* and *ICI* in the UK) when a career move is contemplated for her spouse. According to Professor Peter Herriott, the organisations likely to survive in the 1990s will have to accept "couple careers" as well as individual careers (Thomas, 1993). This could be prompted by the growth in the number of female managers. It may be unrealistic to expect wives with established jobs to uproot in order to relocate with career-minded spouses. Career planning is discussed in Chapter 12.

SUGGESTED REMEDIES FOR STRESS

Stress does not have to be viewed as a bad thing, for there is only one kind of person without conflicts—a dead one. However, too much stress is harmful and measures should be taken to tackle it with the hope of eventually reducing it.

To cope with tension or stress, drugs or tranquillisers can be used, but this remedy helps the person to deal with the immediate condition or symptoms without equipping him or her to confront future stressful situations. It is suggested that allowing greater individual autonomy and participation by employees in matters that concern them is a useful approach. Where there is evidence of deficiencies in personal and interpersonal skills, techniques are available, such as sensitivity training and team building, which are designed to analyse and perfect behavioural skills, but it is by no means conclusive that results following the adoption of these techniques (discussed in Chapter 12) match the expectations of those committed to their use.

One could also create an organisational environment in which people feel free and confident to say they cannot cope, where they can air their basic fears, and invite help if necessary. This would require a significant shift in attitudes because, to many people, an admission of being a victim of stress is tantamount to acknowledging that one is unstable and incompetent. Understandably, people prefer to brush it under the carpet and remain secretive about it.

However, in this context the technique of rational emotive therapy (RET) might be useful (Ellis, 1974). RET emphasises the rebuilding of one's thinking process about particular issues, and is designed to help people who over-react to stressful situations by giving them almost complete responsibility to examine their own faulty reactions. The assumption is that they will be able to change their emotional reactions if they modify their ideas, philosophies, and attitudes about various kinds of stressors that impinge on their lives. The technique consists of a multi-pronged attack at the emotional and intellectual levels on dysfunctional ways of thinking and behaving. It tries to teach people how to treat themselves—that is, how to cope with present and future stressful conditions by recognising that because these conditions exist they should attempt to cope with them as sensibly as possible, frequently trying to change them for the better by continually confronting them. A clinical psychologist (Suinn, 1976) has indicated a number of steps that the Type A person might take to change his or her habits (see panel below).

It would appear sensible to recognise personality differences between people (and people's medical condition) when specifying the most appropriate stress-relieving techniques to use. For example, meditation may be effective for hypertension, but inappropriate for dealing with a peptic ulcer. In another situation, psychotherapy may be suitable for treating one Type A personality, whereas regular exercise and vacations would suit another.

Apart from remedies based on psychotherapy and meditation, regularity of meals and their nutritional balance are of major importance in keeping fit and in raising resistance to stress. Adequate sleep and moderation in the consumption of food, drink, and drugs are also worth pursuing. Regular exercise, which can be pleasurable, at the end of the day, in the lunch break, and at the weekends, can help to get rid of anger, irritation, and frustration. See the funny side of life; enthuse about things generally; put

---

Breaking the Cycle of Stress

1. (a) Select a quiet place in your home; then sit down or lie comfortably and close your eyes. Listen to soothing instrumental music and let yourself float along with the melody. Imagine yourself in a soothing environment and allow the music to relax your muscles.

   (b) In an alternate fashion, tighten and relax the muscles of your hands, biceps, face, shoulders, chest, stomach, legs, and feet. Concentrate on the feeling of relaxation that follows the tightening of the muscles.

   (c) As you breathe out repeat the word "one" and maintain this pattern of breathing for 10 minutes. Feel the release of tension with each breath. If you find that you are able to relax by any one of the above methods, then use it at times when you feel stress. Take a break from the activity causing the stress and make your way to a private place and relax. Allow your mind to float away from the pressures of daily activities and remember how you felt when you relaxed at home; relive those feelings.

2. If you have mastered the technique of relaxing quickly, use imagery to neutralise the emotional reactions that arise as a consequence of the pressures you frequently encounter. First relax, and then imagine yourself facing a situation that normally makes you tense—e.g. the pressure that comes about when you face a deadline. You continue to imagine this situation but at the same time you retain an awareness of relaxation. Repeat this several times, and each time imagine that you are handling the situation calmly. Should the visualisation of the stress scene make you feel more tense than relaxed, terminate the exercise temporarily; then repeat it until you work your way through the entire scene without feeling any tension.

3. Take active steps to control and manage your environment. For example, arrange your appointments realistically and allow enough time in between meetings so that you are not always rushing from one meeting to another. Set your priorities, if you can, in the morning of each day, and adhere to that order. Only undertake a new task when you are finished with the priority items. Learn how to cope with what others expect of you. Be frank and let them know how much effort and time you are prepared to give them, and be forthcoming when you feel you cannot accept their requests. If somebody wants you to take on another task, and you feel your present work-load is more than sufficient, get that person to assist you in evaluating the urgency of his or her request and then decide whether it fits among your priority items.

4. Try to avoid acting in a rushed manner, otherwise you will feel pressure. Take it easy and practise eating with slower movements, putting down your knife and fork between bites. Slow down your steps when you walk and slow down your speech when you talk. Repeat briefly what you hear others say as you are listening to them. This will help you to understand them better and will contribute towards minimising your impatience (Suinn, 1976).

aside time for little things; encourage, pay compliments to, and praise other people when it is appropriate and proper to do so. Nurture friendships, and build a mutual support system so as to be able to discuss stresses with a trusted friend, a relative, or professional helpers. Talking through problems and putting stresses in perspective can be productive and may point in the direction of a solution. Take on hobbies which can be a source of relaxation (Murray-Bruce, 1983). Finally, a healthy interaction between work and the home should be promoted.

Social Support

The support of people (social support) has been referred to briefly earlier. The study of social support with its group emphasis emerged from almost nowhere in the 1970s, but "support" as a concept has occupied a central position in the social sciences for quite a while. In distant studies of participative management, the principle of supportive relations was recognised as a core element in effective supervision, when supervisors related to subordinates in such a way that the individual's sense of personal worth and importance was enhanced. Supportive behaviour assumes a central position in certain branches of psychotherapy and counselling (House & Kahn, 1985).

Although there is not complete agreement as to what constitutes social support, it refers generally to the existence or quality of social relationships, and in a specific sense could refer to a marriage, friendship, or membership of an organisation. It is highlighted in the give and take in interpersonal relationships—i.e. giving and receiving at the emotional level—and also giving and receiving when help and assistance are at stake, but with emotional concern as the central plank. It is suggested that the popularity of social support has been promoted by the recognition of the part it can play in reducing the prevalence and impact of one of the major health hazards of the modern

industrial world—i.e. stress inside and outside work.

The manner in which supportive social relationships alleviate the problem of stress at work can be viewed as follows (Williams & House, 1985):

1. Support can enhance health directly by creating the setting in which needs for affection, approval, social interaction, and security are met.
2. Support can reduce levels of stress directly, and improve health indirectly, by reducing interpersonal tensions as well as having a positive effect generally in the work environment.
3. Support acts as a buffer between the person and health hazards. As the level of social support increases, health risks decline for individuals exposed to stressful conditions. Conversely, with the decline in social support, the adverse impact of stress on health becomes increasingly apparent.

We must be careful not to be overwhelmed by the alleged beneficial effects of social support, because there are occasions when, for example, social interaction can have a detrimental effect on a person's health. This could arise where conflict and strife is inherent in social relationships.

The process of social support is said to vary from one group to another. It was concluded in one study that female managers were more likely to use social support to deal with job-related problems than their male counterparts (Burke & Belcourt, 1974). Apparently, women are more likely to be the providers of support (Belle, 1982), and can become more emotionally affected by the problems of others and, as a consequence, incur higher psychological costs.

The concept of social support has also been considered in a racial context. The relationship between occupational stress, health, and social support among 90 black and 93 white clerical employees in nine government agencies in South Africa was examined. Cognisant of earlier evidence that blacks place greater value on the support available in an occupational context than their white counterparts, racial differences within a framework of social support were analysed. The study found that social support reduces the negative effects of job stress among blacks, but not among whites (Opren, 1982).

Enhancers of Social Support

Three important measures to enhance social support and improve the flow of supportive behaviour among blue-collar workers have been identified as:

- structural arrangements;
- other organisational change processes; and
- facilitation of supportive supervisory behaviour.

However, it should be stated that these measures have relevance to other occupational groups as well (Williams & House, 1985).

Structural Arrangements. Work is organised in such a way as to facilitate stable interaction between employees in the performance of various tasks, as well as maintaining social ties. Here the importance of social interaction is emphasised as a means to reduce stress in the working environment (Alcalay & Pasick, 1983). It is suggested that people who had a constant set of co-workers (colleagues) had lower cholesterol levels than those whose co-workers changed frequently (Cassel, 1963).

This finding is interesting in the light of evidence from the functioning of Japanese organisational systems, where a high level of job security results in membership of a group throughout a person's entire career. The cohort of workers who enter the organisation together develop strong feelings of group solidarity over time. As a consequence, individual interests are said to be absorbed into the work group interests, and the work group offers satisfying emotional support and

social ties in a friendly atmosphere (Matsumoto, 1970).

The importance of emotional support is recognised elsewhere. Emotional support among a sample of social workers—in this case the provision of empathy, caring, trust, and concern by co-workers and supervisors—was beneficial in helping them to cope better with stress and strain in the workplace. However, it was not viewed as a total stress-reduction process (Jayaratne & Chess, 1984).

Other Organisational Change Processes. Another process which has been discussed in Chapter 8 is participative management and quality circles. Participative management schemes, broadly conceived, have potential not only to improve the quantity and quality of production, but also to increase social support, reduce stress and, as a consequence, to enhance health and well-being (Cobb, 1976). Involvement in the participative management process is said to enhance employees' psychological and social functioning in ways that make them more effective as spouses, parents, and members of the community. This experience teaches employees new skills and attitudes which are capable of improving the giving and receiving of social support (Crouter, 1984).

Central features of the quality circle are the emphasis given to the group process and effective team-work, with scope for the provision of social support. It is suggested that social needs are met in quality circles where an outlet is provided for grievances and irritations, and immediate recognition is provided for members' abilities and achievements. It is, therefore, not surprising that quality circles provide workers with a new sense of dignity and a higher level of morale. In addition, the group cohesiveness developed at work spreads to non-work activities as circle members engage in social activities outside the workplace.

A word of caution about participative management is echoed, because it can have unanticipated negative effects. We are told that employees may feel more responsible for problems on the job, and they worry about these problems. Then they take this new stress into their non-work life. There is also evidence to suggest that marriage relationships can suffer when employees who are wives transfer the new independence and competence learned at work to the home environment (Crouter, 1984).

Another avenue for delivering social support is through health promotion programmes discussed later. They could be concerned with the management of stress, and are often group-based rather than person-based. Therefore, they could act as social support interventions and serve as powerful stress reducing strategies.

The following is an example of a formal social support scheme developed by a large chemical company in the UK. An employee counselling service, with a full-time counsellor having a psychiatric social work background, was set up. The objectives of this service were to provide a confidential counselling service to all employees and their families; to work with outside care agencies for the welfare of employees; and to provide other activities that are likely to improve the quality of working life. About half the employees who availed themselves of the service came for advice on education, family matters, work-related housing problems, separation, divorce, children, ageing parents, and consumer issues. The other half received longer-term counselling on fundamental personal and interpersonal problems. Over a four-year period roughly 10% of total employees per annum took advantage of the service. This is the type of programme some would argue should be encouraged to deal with the pressures of modern industrial society (Cooper, 1981).

In the absence of a formal social support system, an informal approach for individuals suffering from stress is suggested as follows (Cooper, 1981):

- Pick somebody at work that you feel you can talk to—someone you don't feel threatened by and to whom you can trustfully reveal your feelings. Don't pick someone who, on reflection, you may be using on an unconscious level as a pawn in a game of organisational politics!

- Approach the person you can trust and explain to him or her that you have a particular problem at or outside work that you would like to discuss. Admit that you need help and that you are consulting the person because you trust their opinion, like them as a person, feel that they can usefully identify with your circumstances, and so forth.

- Try to maintain and build on this relationship, even at times of no crisis or problems.

- Review, from time to time, the nature of the relationship, to see if it is still providing you with the emotional support you need to cope with the difficulties that arise. If the relationship is no longer constructive or the nature of your problems has changed (requiring a different peer counsellor), then seek another person for support.

Facilitation of Supportive Supervisory Behaviour. Supportive behaviour is generally endorsed by a number of empirical studies. Proponents would argue it should be encouraged and expanded, and be adopted at the different layers of the organisation, and that managers and supervisors who use it should receive appropriate recognition and rewards for doing so. Those supervisors and managers who are rewarded solely on the basis of non-social criteria, such as a single-minded approach to productivity, are likely to have little motivation to be supportive to subordinates.

Finally, for a discussion of worksite stress management interventions, refer to Ivancevich et al. (1990).

"THANKS FOR LISTENING, IT'S SUCH A RELIEF TO TALK TO SOMEONE WHO'S COOL, CALM AND CONFIDENT...."

Health Promotion Programmes

Health promotion programmes are broader in scope than the preventative strategies outlined earlier. They range from purely educational schemes to promote health, to learning to take one's own blood pressure, using stress management techniques, or altering one's life-style.

There has been a steady growth in employee health programmes in recent years. Employers take greater responsibility for paying the health insurance costs of workers in the United States, principally because of the absence of a national health service. However, it is the larger companies that offer the more comprehensive programmes. There are signs that this trend is increasing in the UK, partly because of the increasing provision of private medical insurance by employers. Perhaps paternalism and philanthropy may have a part to play in this development in some large and long-established companies. However, an increasing number of employees adopt the position that investing in the health of employees produces dividends. The dividends could include increased productivity, lower medical and disability costs, reduced absenteeism and turnover of staff, and improved satisfaction and morale among employees (Murphy, 1984).

It is the substantial increase in medical care expenditure in the United States that has generated interest in health preventative programmes. Also, US employers are most vulnerable to legal action in connection with occupational stress when they have not taken preventative measures. Hence, they are motivated to take such measures. A particular development is the "wellness" movement, which is proactive rather than reactive in the field of preventative health management.

The promotion of wellness can be viewed as a four-step process (Reed, 1984):

1. Employees are educated about health-risk factors such as poor nutrition, lack of exercise, smoking, drinking and drug abuse, and being overweight.
2. Employees receive information about their health-risk factors through life-style assessments and physical examinations.

3. Plans are developed for employees to reduce risks through healthier life-styles.
4. Employees receive assistance from the organisation to continue with the changes in their life-style. This necessitates a process of monitoring and evaluation.

Wellness programmes vary in their degree of comprehensiveness. Some companies merely distribute educational material on desirable life-styles, whereas others can go as far as providing an indoor track, weightlifting equipment, bicycles, and workout clothes to their employees, and claim consequential benefits such as reductions in absenteeism, smoking, and excess weight.

An example of a wellness programme is the "Staywell" programme introduced in 1979 by *Control Data Corporation* of the USA (see panel below).

Beneficial outcomes of wellness programmes include 50% reductions in sickness rates and absenteeism, increases in job performance, improved attitudes towards

---

The Staywell Programme

The programme consisted of creating profiles of health risk, medical screening, health education, and activities to change life-styles. It was offered to the company's employees in San Diego and New York, and, subsequently, other sites were included (McCann, 1981). The programme was offered without charge to all the company's employees and their spouses. Participation was on a voluntary basis and all activities were provided at the place of work. Employees were allowed time off to attend an orientation session and to participate in other activities such as the health-risk profile and a group interpretation meeting.

Those who signed on for the Staywell programme were weighed and measured, had their blood pressure taken, and gave a blood sample. Also, they completed a questionnaire on their medical outlook. The results of the physical examination and the questionnaire responses were used to provide a computerised health-risk profile on each person. The profile compared the individual's chronological age with his or her "risk age", and it showed how the risk could be improved if the individual changed certain behaviour.

Next, those who participated in the programme were encouraged to select courses from a group of one-hour health awareness courses. These ranged from how to utilise the health care system to breast self-examination and substance abuse. However, the multi-session behaviour and life-style change programmes were the most popular. These covered specific high-risk areas such as smoking, fitness, nutrition and weight control, hypertension, and stress. Specific activities to change life-style and improve health were planned for each individual.

An important feature of Staywell was the introduction of a follow-up programme and the use of support systems. One characteristic of the follow-up programme was the formation of employee groups consisting of individuals interested in or troubled by similar problems. Changing the culture at work and people's attitudes would be necessary for the success of the programme.

The group sessions took place at the end of each of the education and life-style change courses, and for a certain period had an instructor at their disposal. Eventually, group members learned to help one another to sustain the change in their behaviour, and they practised various techniques and strategies to avoid failure. Support from one's peers in the group, whether it was an exercise in reducing weight or stopping smoking, helped to persuade people to persevere with the modified behaviour. In the mid 1980s it was said that approximately 22,000 people, either employees of *Control Data* or their spouses, participated in the Staywell programme in 14 American cities.

The Staywell programme at *Control Data* was based on the following premises (Hall & Goodale, 1986):

- life-style has a major effect on illness and life spans;
- people can change their habits, with appropriate help;
- the work place is the most effective place to help people change their behaviour, because people spend so much of their time there; and companies have a major stake in promoting a healthier life-style for their employees, because of the potential benefits in terms of reduced insurance costs, decreased absenteeism, improved productivity, and better morale.

work, improved stamina, sounder sleep, and loss of weight (Hall & Goodale, 1986). At *Control Data*, significant reductions in health care costs were associated with a decline in cigarette smoking, a lack of hypertension, and an increase in regular exercise. A decrease in absenteeism and lost time due to illness went hand-in-hand with an increase in the number of good health habits developed in the Staywell programme. It is probably too early to establish whether or not "wellness" programmes are successful generally, because only a limited amount of evaluation of these programmes has so far taken place. However, there are signs of some promising results for the future.

In the UK it is not surprising that health promotion programmes at the workplace are viewed by many employers as one of the most promising strategies to cope with rapidly increasing health care costs. For many employers this could be the primary justification for embracing preventative measures (Ashton, 1990).

It is interesting to note that in recent years the two major insurance companies in the UK specialising in health care (*BUPA* and *PPP*) have promoted preventative measures—medical screening, stress management programmes, and occupational health advice—no doubt believing that a healthier work-force will mean fewer claims. This could also mean lower premiums in the future. However, the predicted fall in premiums may not happen, particularly in the short term, because the introduction of medical screening could lead to the diagnosis of illness or disease requiring medical attention. Obviously, this would lead to an acceleration in claims.

What are British companies doing in connection with preventative health measures? There are some interesting developments (Summers, 1990a). For example, at the headquarters of the *Marks & Spencer* organisation in London there are facilities such as a gym, dentists, doctors, nurses, osteopaths, physiotherapists, and health administrators. According to the company's deputy head of health services, there is no doubt that the service reduces absenteeism, increases the efficiency of the work-force and is an example of the commitment of the organisation to its staff.

The Post Office takes its mobile clinics and health education roadshows to its widely dispersed work-force numbering 200,000. Also, in the early-1990s Professor Cary Cooper spearheaded a stress audit among the 24,000 blue-collar workers of the *Scottish & Newcastle Breweries* company. According to the chief medical officer of the company, the results might indicate the need for a number of improvements in organisational practices ranging from encouraging managers to improve the way they work with people to the overhaul of production methods (Summers, 1990b). These are examples of what some large and successful companies are doing in this area.

Du Pont, a US corporation with operations in the UK, has a scheme called "Health Horizons". There is a belief that employees can learn to extend their life expectancy by adopting improved life-styles. Employees complete a life-style questionnaire which is analysed by computer. The analysis aims to show employees where to concentrate their efforts to improve their health. Also, self-help kits are available, and incentives (e.g. free track suits) are provided to encourage appropriate behaviour.

Little scientifically valid assessment of health promotion programmes in the UK has been undertaken, but in the US the Staywell Programme, discussed earlier, appears to be well researched (Cooper, 1986).

SUMMARY: HEALTH AND WORK—STRESS

- Following a definition of stress, which included burnout and PTSD, it was suggested that occupations differ in terms of stress and risks to health.
- Certain stresses and strains were associated with different facets of organisational life. These covered role overload, role complexity, role ambiguity, boundary roles, responsibility for people, machine-paced and repetitive work, decision latitude and job control, shift work, new technology in the form of VDU work, hierarchical level, work relationships, career development,

redundancy and unemployment, early retirement, and personality factors, including locus of control.
- A number of remedies to counteract a stressful state were suggested. These ranged from psychotherapy and meditation to nutritional balance in intake of food, regular exercise, a balanced personal and social existence, and social support.
- Finally, the importance of preventative health management was emphasised, and health promotion programmes, including workplace wellness programmes, were mentioned.

QUESTIONS

1. Distinguish between pressure and stress in an organisational context.
2. Define PTSD and burnout.
3. Identify the costs associated with stress at work.
4. Comment on the suggestion that certain occupations are more stressful than others.
5. What is the difference between role complexity and role ambiguity?
6. Discuss the relevance of the following factors in the context of stress originating from within the organisation: (a) machine-paced/repetitive work; (b) decision

latitude/job control; and (c) new technology.
7. How important is personality in the relationship between stressful conditions and the individual's response to them?
8. Examine the human costs of unemployment, and the coping strategies used by the unemployed.
9. Discuss the significance of social support as a technique to cope with stress.
10. What are the likely benefits to the organisation and to individuals from health promotion programmes, including "wellness" schemes?

REFERENCES

Alcalay, R. & Pasick, R.J. (1983). Psychosocial factors and the technologies of work. *Social Science and Medicine, 17*, 1075–1084.

Antonovsky, A. (1979). *Health, stress and coping.* San Francisco: Josey-Bass

Arnold, J., Robertson, I.T., & Cooper C.L. (1991). *Work psychology: Understanding human behaviour in the workplace.* London: Pitman Publishing.

Ashton, D. (1990). *The corporate health care revolution.* London: Kogan Page and Institute of Personnel Management.

Barnard, J.M. (1981). Stress: Its effects on people at work. *Occupational Health,* 7th July, 353–361.

Beattie, R.T., Darlington, T.G., & Cripps, D.M. (1974). *The management threshold.* B.I.M. Paper OPN II. London: British Institute of Management.

Belle, D. (1982). The stress of caring: Women as providers of social support. In L. Golberger & S. Breznitz (Eds.), *Handbook of stress.* New York: Free Press.

Broadbent, D. & Gath D. (1981). Ill-health on the line: Sorting out myth from fact. *Employment Gazette,* March, 157–160.

Brook, A. (1973). Mental stress at work. *The Practitioner, 210,* 500–506.

Brooks, P. (1980). The tension of the bells. *Health and Safety at Work*, October, 47–48.

Buck, V. (1972). *Working under pressure*. London: Staples Press.

Burke, R.J. & Belcourt, M.L. (1974). Managerial role stress and coping responses. *Journal of Business Administration, 5*, 55–68.

Cassel, J. (1963). The use of medical records: Opportunity for epidemiological studies. *Journal of Occupational Medicine, 5*, 185–190.

Chesney, M.A., Sevelius, G., Black, G.W., Ward, M.M., Swan, G.E., & Rosenman, R.H. (1981). Work environment, Type A behaviour, and coronary heart disease risk factors. *Journal of Occupational Medicine, 23*, 531–555.

Cobb, S. (1976). Social support as a moderator of life stress. *Psychosomatic Medicine, 38*, 300–314.

Coch, L. & French, J.R.P. (1948). Overcoming resistance to change. *Human Relations, 11*, 512–532.

Constandse, W.J. (1972). A neglected personnel problem. *Personnel Journal, 51*, 129–133.

Cook, M. (1988). Stress management. *Management Services*, November, 18–21.

Cooper, C.L. (1979). *The executive gypsy: The quality of managerial life*. London: The Macmilliam Press.

Cooper, C.L. (1981). Social support at work and stress management. *Small Group Behaviour, 12*, August, 285–297.

Cooper C.L. (1986). Job distress: Recent research and the emerging role of the clinical psychologist. *Bulletin of the British Psychological Society, 39*, 325–331.

Cooper C.L., Mallinger, M., & Kahn, R. (1978). Identifying sources of occupational stress among dentists. *Journal of Occupational Psychology, 51*, 227–234.

Cox, T. (1985). Repetitive work: Occupational stress and health. In C.L. Cooper & M.J. Smith (Eds.), *Job stress and blue-collar work*. Chichester: Wiley.

Crouter, A.C. (1984). Participative work as an influence on human development. *Journal of Applied Developmental Psychology, 5*, 71–90.

Culbert, S. (1974). *The organisation trap*. New York: Basic Books.

Daubs, J. (1973). The mental health crisis in ophthalmology. *American Journal of Optometry and Archives of American Academy of Optometry, 50*, 816–822.

Davidson, M.J. & Cooper, C.L. (1981). Occupational stress in female managers: A review of the literature. *Journal of Enterprise Management, 3*, 115–138.

Davidson, M.J. & Cooper, C.L. (1983). *Stress and the woman manager*. Oxford: Martin Robertson.

Donaldson, J. & Gowler, D. (1975). Prerogatives, participation, and managerial stress. In D. Gowler & K. Legge (Eds.), *Managerial stress*. Epping: Gower Press.

Donkin, R. (1993). Workplace stress increasing sharply. *Financial Times*, 8 December, p.9.

Donkin, R. (1994). Record payout for RSI injury. *Financial Times*, 19 January, p.7.

Dornstein, M. (1977). Organisational conflict and role stress among chief executives in state business enterprises. *Journal of Occupational Psychology, 50*, 4, 253–263.

Dreyfus, F. & Czaczkes, J.W. (1959). Blood cholesterol and uric acid of healthy medical students under the stress of an examination. *Archives of Internal Medicine, 103*, 708–711.

Eaton, M.T. (1969). The mental health of the older executive. *Geriatric, 24*, 126–134.

Ellis, A.A. (1974). *Humanistic psychotherapy: The rational emotive approach*. New York: McGraw-Hill.

Fagan, L. & Little, M. (1984). *The forsaken families*. Harmondsworth: Penguin.

Fagin, L.H. (1979). The experience of unemployment (1): The impact of unemployment. *New Universities Quarterly*, Winter, 48–64.

Fisher, S. (1985). Control and blue-collar work. In C.L. Cooper & M.J. Smith (Eds.), *Job stress and blue-collar work*. Chichester: Wiley.

Fletcher, B., Gowler, D., & Payne, R. (1979). Exploring the myth of executive stress. *Personnel Management*, May, 30–34.

French, J.R.P. & Caplan, R.D. (1970). Psychosocial factors in coronary heart disease. *Industrial Medicine, 39*, 383–397.

French J.R.P. & Caplan, R.D. (1973). Organisational stress and individual strain. In A.J. Marrow (Ed.), *The failure of success*. New York: AMACOM.

Friedman, H.S. & Booth-Kewley, S. (1987). The disease-prone personality: A meta-analytic view of the construct. *American Psychologist*, June, 539–555.

Friedman, M., Roseman, R.H., & Caroll, V. (1957). Changes in the serum cholesterol and blood clotting time of men subject to cyclic variation of occupational stress. *Circulation, 17*, 852–861.

Frost, B. (1990). Firemen awarded £34,000 for trauma after King's Cross. *The Times*, 19 December, p.3.

Fryer, D. & Payne, R. (1986). Being unemployed: A review of the literature on the psychological experience of unemployment. In C.L. Cooper & I.T. Robertson (Eds.), *International review of industrial and organisational psychology*. Chichester: Wiley.

Fryer, D.M. & Warr, P. (1984). Unemployment and cognitive difficulties. *British Journal of Clinical Psychology, 23*, 67–68.

Gaertner, J.F. & Ruthe, J.A. (1981). Job-related stress in public accounting. *Journal of Accountancy*, June, 68–74.

The Guardian (1990). *Tips to avoid 'injury to gardeners' backs*. 25 May, p.29.

Guralnick, L. (1963). Mortality: By occupation and cause of death (Report No. 3); By industry and cause of death (Report No. 4); By occupational level and cause of death (Report No. 5). *Vital statistics: Special reports*, Vol. 53. Washington DC: US Public Health Service.

Hall, D.T. & Goodale, J.G. (1986). *Human resource management: Strategy, design, and implementation*. Glenview, IL: Scott Foresman.

Handy, C. (1975). Difficulties of combining family and career. *The Times*, 22nd September, 16.

House, J.S. & Kahn, R.L. (1985). Measures and concepts of social support. In S. Cohen & L. Syme (Eds.), *Social support and health*. Orlando, FL: Academic Press.

Howard, J.H., Cunningham, D.A., & Rechnitzer, P.A. (1976). Health patterns associated with Type A behaviour: A managerial population. *Journal of Human Stress*, March, 24–31.

Immundo, L.V. (1974). Problems associated with managerial mobility. *Personnel Journal*, 53, 910.

Independent, The. (1991). *Staff at 'FT' angry over retirements*. 11 December.

Ivancevich, J.M., Matteson, M.T., Freedman, S.M., & Phillips, J.S. (1990). Worksite stress management interventions. *American Psychologist*, February, 252–261.

Jahoda, M. (1979). The impact of unemployment in the 1930s and the 1970s. *Bulletin of The British Psychological Society*, 32, 309–314.

Jayaratne, S. & Chess, W.A. (1984). The effects of emotional support on perceived job stress and strain. *Journal of Applied Behavioural Science*, 20, 141–153.

Johansson, G. & Aronsson, G. (1984). Stress reactions in computerised administrative work. *Journal of Occupational Behaviour*, 5, 159–81.

Kahn, R.L., Wolfe, D.M., Quinn, R.P., Snoek, J.D., & Rosenthal, R.A. (1964). *Organisational stress*. New York: Wiley.

Karasek, R.A. (1979). Job demands, job decision latitude, and mental strain: Implications for job design. *Administrative Science Quarterly*, 24, June, 285–309.

Karasek, R.A. (1990). Lower heath risk with increased job control among white-collar workers. *Journal of Organisational Behaviour*, 11, 171–185.

Kasl, S.V. & Cobb, S. (1970). Blood pressure in men undergoing job loss. *Psychosomatic Medicine*, 32, 19–38.

Kay, E. (1974). Middle management. In J. O'Toole (Ed.), *Work and the quality of life*. Cambridge, MA: MIT Press.

Kearns, J.L. (1973). *Stress in Industry*. London: Priory Press.

Kellaway, L. (1993). Legal dangers of stress. *Financial Times*, 20 August, p.8.

Krause, N. & Stryker, S. (1984). Stress and well-being: The buffering role of locus of control beliefs. *Social Science and Medicine*, 18, 783–790.

Lau, R.R. (1982). Origins of health locus of control beliefs. *Journal of Personality and Social Psychology*, 42, 322–334.

Lazarus, R.S. (1966). *Psychological stress and the coping process*. New York: McGraw-Hill.

Lebovits, B.Z., Shekelle, R.B., & Ostfeld, A.M. (1967). Prospective and retrospective studies of CHD. *Psychosomatic Medicine*, 29, 265–272.

Lee, R.T. & Ashforth, B.E. (1990). On the meaning of Maslach's three dimensions of burnout. *Journal of Applied Psychology*, December, 743–747.

Longley, C. (1984). Loneliness: Main cause of stress for priests. *The Times*, 5 September.

Mackay, C. (1980). *Human factor aspects of visual display unit operation*. London: HMSO.

Mackay, C.J. & Cooper, C.L. (1987). Occupational stress and health: Some current issues. In C.L. Cooper & I.T. Robertson (Eds.), *International Review of Industrial and Organisational Psychology*. Chichester: Wiley.

Mackay, C. & Cox, T. (1984). Occupational stress associated with visual display unit operation. In B.G. Pearce (Ed.), *Health hazards of VDUs*. Chichester: Wiley.

Madge, N. (1983). Unemployment and its effects on children. *Journal of Child Psychology and Psychiatry*, 24, 311–319.

Margolis, B.L. & Kroes, W.H. (1974). Work and the health of man. In J. O'Toole (Ed.), *Work and the quality of life*. Cambridge, MA: MIT Press.

Margolis, B.L., Kroes, W.H., & Quinn, R.P. (1974). Job stress: An unlisted occupational hazard. *Journal of Occupational Medicine*, 16, 654–661.

Marshall, J. & Cooper C.L. (1976). *The mobile manager and his wife*. Bradford: MCB Publications.

Matsumoto, Y.S. (1970). Social stress and coronary heart disease in Japan: An hypothesis. *Millbank Memorial Fund Quarterly*, 48, 9–36.

Matthews, K.A. & Haynes, S.G. (1986). Type A behaviour pattern and coronary disease risk: Update and critical evaluation. *American Journal of Epidemiology*, 123, 923–959.

McCann, J.F. (1981). Control Data's Staywell programme. *Training and Development Journal*, October, 39–43.

McGrath, J.E. (1976). Stress and behaviour in organisations. In M.D. Dunnett (Ed.), *Handbook of industrial and organisational psychology*. Chicago: Rand McNally.

McKenna, E.F. & Ellis, A. (1981). Counterpoint to Davidson and Cooper (occupational stress in female managers). *Journal of Enterprise Management*, 3, 139–142.

McMurray, R.N. (1973). The executive neurosis. In R.L. Noland (Ed.), *Industrial mental health and employee counselling*. New York: Behavioural Publications.

Melhuish, A.H. (1977). Causes and prevention of executive stress. *Occupational Health, 29*, 193–197.

Miles, H.H.W., Waldfogel, S., Barrabee, E.L., & Cobb, S. (1954). Psychosomatic study of 46 young men with coronary artery disease. *Psychosomatic Medicine, 16*, 455–477.

Monk, T. & Tepas, D. (1985). Shift work. In C.L. Cooper & M.J. Smith (Eds.), *Job stress and blue-collar work*. Chichester: Wiley.

Morris, J.N. (1956). Job rotation. *Journal of Business*, October, 268–273.

Morris, J.N., Heady, J.A., & Barley, R.G. (1952). Coronary heart disease in medical practitioners. *British Journal of Medicine, 1*, 503–520.

Murphy, L.R. (1984). Occupational stress management: A review and appraisal. *Journal of Occupational Psychology, 57*, 1–15.

Murray-Bruce, D. (1983). Promoting the healthy banker: Stress. *Journal of the Institute of Bankers*, April, 62–63.

Opren, C. (1982). The effect of social support on reactions to role ambiguity and conflict: A study of black and white clerks in South Africa. *Journal of Cross Cultural Psychology, 13*, 375–384.

Packard, V. (1962). *The pyramid climbers*. New York: McGraw-Hill.

Packard, V. (1975). *A nation of strangers*. New York: McKay.

Pahl, J.M. & Pahl, R.E. (1971). *Managers and their wives*. London: Allen Lane.

Parkes, K.R. (1984). Locus of control, cognitive appraisal, and coping in stressful episodes. *Journal of Personality and Social Psychology, 46*, 655–668.

Phares, E. (1976). *Locus of control in personality*. Morristown, NJ: General Learning Press.

Pincherle, G. (1972). Fitness for work. *Proceedings of the Royal Society of Medicine, 65*, 321–324.

Reed, R.W. (1984). Is education the key to lower health care costs? *Personnel Journal, 63*, 40–46.

Reynolds, M. (1981). Counterpoint to Davidson and Cooper (occupational stress in female managers). *Journal of Enterprise Management, 3*, 145–147.

Rogers, L. (1993). Absorbing the shock waves. *The Sunday Times* [Style and Travel Section]. 5 September, p.23.

Rosenman, R.H., Friedman, M., & Strauss, R. (1964). A predictive study of CHD. *Journal of the American Medical Association, 189*, 15–22.

Russek, H.I. (1965). Stress, tobacco, and coronary heart disease in North American professional groups. *Journal of the American Medical Association, 192*, 189–194.

Russek, H.I. & Zohman, B.L. (1958). Relative significance of hereditary and occupational stress in CHD of young adults. *American Journal of Medical Science, 235*, 266–275.

Schoonmaker, A.N. (1969). *Anxiety and the executive*. New York: American Management Association.

Schottenfeld, R.S., & Cullen, M.R. (1986). Recognition of occupation induced post-traumatic stress disorders. *Journal of Occupational Medicine, 28*, 365–369.

Seidenberg, R. (1973). *Corporate wives—corporate casualties*. New York: American Management Association.

Shanthamani, V.S. (1973). Unemployment and neuroticism. *Indian Journal of Social Work, 34*, 83–102.

Shimmin, S. (1986). Concepts of Work. *Occupational Psychology, 40*, 195–201.

Shirom, A., Eden, D., Silberwasser, S., & Kellerman, J.J. (1973). Job stress and the risk factors in coronary heart disease among occupational categories in Kibbutzim. *Social Science and Medicine, 7*, 875–892.

Sigman, A. (1993). Working shifts on the 'red eye'. *Personal Management Plus*, October, p.19.

Sleeper, R.D. (1975). Labour mobility over the life cycle. *British Journal of Industrial Relations, XIII*, 2.

Sofer, V. (1970). *Men in mid-career*. Cambridge: Cambridge University Press.

Suinn, R.M. (1976). How to break the vicious cycle of stress. *Psychology Today*, December, 59–60.

Summers, D. (1990a). An act of faith that can reap rewards. *Financial Times*, 23 November.

Summers, D. (1990b). Testing for stress in the workplace. *Financial Times*, 7 December.

Sutherland, V. & Cooper, C.L. (1987). *Man and accidents offshore*. London: Lloyds.

Swinburne, P. (1981). The psychological impact of unemployment on managers and professional staff. *Journal of Occupational Psychology, 54*, 47–64.

Syme, S.L., Hyman, M.M., & Enterline, P.E. (1964). Cultural mobility and the occurrence of coronary heart disease. *Journal of Health and Human Behaviour, 6*, 178–189.

Thomas, T. (1993). Move me, move my spouse. *The Sunday Times*, 14 February, 4.2.

Wallis, C. (1983). Stress: Can we cope? *Time*, 6 June, 44–52.

Wallston, B.S. & Wallston, K.A. (1978). Locus of control and health. *Health Education Monographs*, Spring, 107–115.

Wardwell, W.I., Hyman, M., & Bahnson, C.B. (1964). Stress and coronary disease in three field studies. *Journal of Chronic Diseases, 17*, 73–84.

Warr, P.B. & Jackson, P.R. (1984). Men without jobs: Some correlates of age and length of unemployment. *Journal of Occupational Psychology, 57*, 77–85.

Williams, D.R. & House, J.S. (1985). Social support and stress reduction. In C.L. Cooper & M.J. Smith (Eds.), *Job stress and blue-collar work*. Chichester: Wiley.

Williams, T. (1985). Visual display technology, worker disablement, and work organisation. *Human Relations, 38,* 1065–1084.

Zoher, A. (1993). How women are winning at work. *Asia Business*, November 24–29.

Author Index

Subject Index